The Emergence of a National Economy

1775–1815

THE ECONOMIC HISTORY OF THE UNITED STATES
Edited by Henry David, Harold U. Faulkner, Louis M. Hacker,
Curtis P. Nettels, and Fred A. Shannon

THE EMERGENCE OF A NATIONAL ECONOMY

1775–1815

By CURTIS P. NETTELS

VOLUME II
The Economic History of
the United States

M. E. SHARPE, INC.
Armonk, New York   London, England

This book was originally published as volume II of The Economic History of the United States series by Holt, Rinehart and Winston in 1962. This edition is published by arrangement with Holt, Rinehart and Winston, Inc.

Library of Congress Cataloging-in-Publication Data

Nettels, Curtis P. (Curtis Putnam)
      The emergence of a national economy, 1775-1815.
      (The Economic history of the United States series ; 2)
      Reprint. Originally published: New York : Harper & Row, 1969, c1962.
      Includes bibliographical references.
      1. United States—Economic conditions—To 1865. I. Title.
II. Series.
HC105.N48   1989   330.973   89-10649
ISBN 0-87332-096-4

Printed in the United States of America

ED   10   9   8   7   6   5   4   3   2   1

Contents

Illustrations

Tables

Foreword

WHEN this series of ten volumes on the economic history of the United States was first conceived, the nation's economy had reached a critical stage in its development. Although the shock of the depression of 1929 had been partially absorbed, the sense of bewilderment which it produced had not yet vanished, and the suffering and the bitterness of its first years were being transformed into less substantial, though still anguished, memories. Reform measures, either in operation or proposed, were being actively debated, but with less sense of urgency than earlier.

To the Editors of this series a fresh consideration of America's economic history was justified by more than the experiences of the recent past or the obscurity of the future. Rich contributions to the literature of American history had been made through cooperative series dealing with the political, social, and cultural aspects of American life. Numerous single-volume surveys of the country's economic development have been written. But, as late as the end of the fourth decade of the twentieth century, the world's foremost economic power had not yet produced an integrated, full-length, and authoritative treatment of its own economic history.

Scholarly concern with American economic history has been constantly growing during the past half century, and chairs of economic history have been established in leading universities. A more profound understanding of the role of economic forces in the nation's history has not only been developed by historians and economists, but has also won some measure of popular acceptance. The earlier thin trickle of monographs has broadened in recent years into a flood of publications. At present, such specialized studies, the many collections of documentary materials, and the mountains of government reports on different facets of American economic life, are staggering in their richness and scope.

This series has been planned to utilize these available sources in the preparation of a full-scale, balanced, cooperative, and readable survey of the growth of American economy and of its transformation from one of primitive character to world pre-eminence in industry, trade, and finance. Clearly, in ten volumes all aspects of the nation's economic life cannot be treated fully. But such a series can point the way to new fields of study and treat authoritatively, if not definitively, the main lines of economic development. Further, the series is intended to fill a present need of those professionally concerned with American economic history, to supplement the economic materials now available in general school and college histories of the United States, and finally to provide the lay reader with the fruits of American scholarship. If these objectives are attained, then the efforts which have gone into the creation of this economic history of the United States will have been amply repaid.

Contributors to the series have been chosen who have already established their competence in the particular periods they are to survey here; and they are, of course, solely responsible for the points of view or points of departure they employ. It is not intended that the series represent a school of thought or any one philosophical or theoretical position.

In this, the second volume of the series, Professor Nettels—with a clarity and an easy command of the materials—tells an exciting story: nothing less than the conversion of the American colonial economy into a national economy as a result of the Revolution. The political narrative of independence and its aftermath has been told repeatedly and well; it remained for Professor Nettels to recite, step by step, the processes by which independence and the formation of a national Union released all those creative forces that were ultimately to make the American economic record of growth and improving standards of living one of the truly great accomplishments of modern times.

By 1815—in the forty years since 1775—America had been transformed. In this brief interval, Americans had endowed themselves with a vast domain, made easy entrance into it on a freehold basis, dedicated it to internal free trade, and decreed that contracts and debts should be uniformly protected by federal law. The country had its own money of account and a national coinage; the large fund of federal securities provided capital for business, substitutes for currency, and a safe medium for long-term investments. Modern commercial banks—in considerable part directed by the central banking of the First Bank of the United States—expanded credit for industry and trade. Thus stimulated, innovation flourished—in transportation, manufactures, insurance; at the same time, Americans, freed from the restraints of the British colonial system, pushed their commerce into many remote or once forbidden areas. The national commitment to private accumulation and enterprise—within a vast domestic and free market—inevitably encouraged innovation in agriculture, transportation, and manufactures: Oliver Evans originated automation with his integrated milling machine; Eli Whitney, in addition to the cotton gin, devised the process of making standard, identical parts. The Industrial Revolution had taken firm root in the United States by 1815, as had the cultivation of cotton—two developments that were to shape the character and destiny of the United States in the following half-century.

THE EDITORS

Preface

WHEN treating a period of political stability, one may often take for granted the influence of government on economic pursuits. However, in a time of revolution, war, and reconstruction, such factors as money, credit, prices, taxation, land tenure, commercial policy, foreign trade, and even production may be so affected by changes in government that the historian must consider political innovations and emerging institutions. During the years 1775–1795 the American people rejected an established government, formed another one, modified it considerably, and devised a new system of national policy. Such political acts so impinged upon economic life that the student of the times must give special attention to the role of government. This is especially necessary because the achieving of independence, the making of the Constitution, and the establishing of the federal government provided the legal foundations on which the structure of the economy of the United States has rested since 1789. For this reason the present volume may differ somewhat from many economic histories in its emphasis on political factors.

I wish to take this occasion to express my gratitude to the staff of the Library of Cornell University.

Curtis P. Nettels

Ithaca, New York

The Emergence of a National Economy

1775–1815

THE UNITED

BRITISH

OREGON

Astoria

COUNTRY

Natural   boundary

Mandan

Natural

boundary

MISSOURI

TERRITORY

1812

M E X I C O

PACIFIC

OCEAN

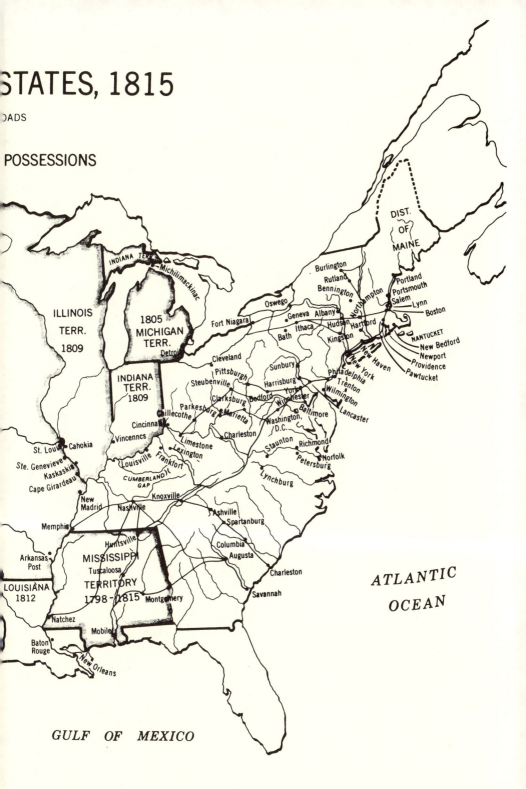

STATES, 1815

OADS

POSSESSIONS

DIST. OF MAINE

INDIANA TERR.

Michilimackinac

ILLINOIS TERR. 1809

1805 MICHIGAN TERR.

Detroit

Fort Niagara

Oswego

Burlington
Rutland
Bennington
Northampton

Portland
Portsmouth
Salem
Lynn
Boston

Geneva Albany
Bath Ithaca Hudson Hartford
Kingston

NANTUCKET
New Bedford
Newport
Providence
Pawtucket

New Haven
New York

INDIANA TERR. 1809

Cleveland

Pittsburgh
Steubenville

Sunbury
Harrisburg

Philadelphia
Trenton
Wilmington

Chillecothe
Cincinnati
Vincennes

Clarksburg Bedford
Parkersburg Marietta

York Winchester
Baltimore
Lancaster

St. Louis Cahokia
Ste. Genevieve
Kaskaskia
Cape Girardeau

Limestone
Lexington
Louisville Frankfort

Washington, D.C.

Charleston

Staunton
Richmond
Petersburg
Norfolk

CUMBERLAND GAP

New Madrid

Knoxville

Nashville

Lynchburg

Memphis

Ashville
Spartanburg

Arkansas Post

Huntsville

MISSISSIPPI
Tuscaloosa
TERRITORY
1798 - 1815 Montgomery

Columbia
Augusta

Charleston

Savannah

ATLANTIC
OCEAN

LOUISIANA 1812

Natchez
Mobile
Baton Rouge
New Orleans

GULF OF MEXICO

Lilli Mautner

CHAPTER I

The Disruption of the Colonial Economy

DURING the forty years after 1775 the American people brought forth, not only a new nation, but also a national economy. The Revolution began a process of change that modified nearly every phase of American life.

Foreign trade first felt the shock of new forces. After October, 1774, the Continental Congress moved steadily toward the goal of freeing the people of the Union from their former dependence on British vessels, merchants, markets, and goods. Congress did this both to weaken Britain and to supply American troops with the sinews of war. In June, 1775, Congress established the Continental Army; thereafter the business of supplying it had a pronounced effect on the internal trade of the states. In order to pay the troops and to obtain army supplies, both Congress and the states issued paper currencies that soon permeated all business dealings. As the war went on, Americans undertook to build up manufacturing industries, largely to meet the need for war goods, in view of the uncertainties of foreign trade. Within the states, changes in landholding freed most of the people from survivals of English feudalism and extended the principle of free land tenure throughout the country.

AN AMERICAN COMMERCIAL POLICY

During the war the foreign trade of the Union was of highest importance. Americans had previously imported from Britain many scarce or high-grade products, such as woolen cloth, blankets, cannon, gunpowder, edged tools, paper, scientific apparatus, and instruments of navigation. The war both reduced the importation of such articles and intensified the need for them. Forced to get supplies from other sources, the Union had to wage war while devising a new commercial order.

1

The acts of the Continental Congress quickly transformed the external trade of the country. Before 1774, British laws had prohibited foreign vessels from trading with British-America, had required that the thirteen colonies should import goods of European or East Indian origin only from Britain, and had decreed that many native American products, including tobacco, rice, indigo, furs, and naval stores, should be exported from a British-American colony only to a British port.[1] American actions after 1775 swept away all these restraints. By January, 1776, both Congress and Britain had prohibited all direct trade between the British Empire and the area of the thirteen states. The closing of the old channels of commerce forced Congress to act as an independent power and to open American ports to friendly and neutral nations.

The antecedents of an American commercial policy are to be found in the work of the First Continental Congress. On October 20, 1774, its members signed the Continental Association, seeking thereby to put pressure on the British government, with the aim of inducing it to repeal twelve obnoxious laws. In so doing, Congress adopted a *de facto* code of law and declared it to be binding on all the thirteen colonies except Georgia. In effect, the association prohibited the importation into twelve colonies, after December 1, 1774, of any goods exported from Britain or Ireland, any East Indian tea, any slaves, any British sugar, molasses or coffee, any Madeira wine, or foreign indigo. The association also imposed a ban, to become effective September 10, 1775, on all American exports to Britain, Ireland, or the British West Indies.[2]

By attempting to stop the American trade of Britain, the Continental Association violated the spirit of the British laws which decreed that most of the trade of Britain's colonies should be carried on with Britain. However, the First Congress in 1774 resorted only to the weapons of embargo and boycott; it did not then strike at Britain by opening American ports to foreign vessels, traders, and goods. But once the fighting had started, in April, 1775, Congress quickly adopted more positive measures. On July 15 it authorized foreign vessels to import essential war materials during the following nine months and to export American produce in payment.[3] Congress next undertook to engage, in an official capacity, in a limited trade with foreign islands of the West Indies. On September 19, 1775, it appointed a "Secret Committee" and empowered it to make contracts for the purchase of foreign war supplies. Soon afterward, on November 8, the committee received the authority to export to the foreign West Indies, on the account of and at the risk of the United Colonies, such

---

[1] S[amuel] E. Morison, *Sources and Documents Illustrating the American Revolution, 1764–1788, and the Formation of the Federal Constitution* (2d ed.; Oxford: The Clarendon Press, 1929), pp. 75, 76, 78.

[2] Worthington C. Ford and others, eds., *Journals of the Continental Congress, 1774–1789* (34 vols.; Washington: Government Printing Office, 1904–1937), I, 76–77.

[3] *Ibid.*, II, 184–185.

American products as it might "deem necessary for the importation of arms, ammunition, and saltpetre."[4]

About four months later Congress made a guarded move toward establishing a direct trade with France. In December, 1775, two French merchants, Messrs. Penet and Pliarne, arrived in Philadelphia, sent thither from Cambridge by Washington with a plan for supplying the colonies with arms and ammunition. At that time the army faced a shortage of firearms so acute as to cause Washington to hint that he would resign if Congress could not fill the need.[5] The Penet-Pliarne plan, "to establish between America and France a branch of trade sufficient to supply all the wants of the new Empire," met a favorable response in Philadelphia; and on January 27, 1776, Congress authorized its Secret Committee to contract with "proper persons" for the importation of goods to the value of £40,000 and for the delivery of American produce "to some European market." In the following November, Penet, Pliarne and their associates reported from Nantes to the Secret Committee that, in conformity with their contract with it, they had purchased goods to the amount of £30,000 or £40,000 and had recently dispatched the vessel *Sally* with a cargo of lead, powder, muskets, bayonets, ramrods, gunlocks, needles, and linen.[6]

Having moved to open a trade with France, to be conducted by French merchants, Congress next prepared to establish commercial contacts with the French government. The impulse for this decisive step came from a drastic action on the part of Britain. At the end of February, 1776, Congress received full information concerning a British statute, the Prohibitory Act of December 22, 1775. It declared the armed resistance in America to be treason and rebellion, prohibited all vessels, with minor exceptions, from trading with any port or place in the thirteen colonies, and ordered the confiscation of all vessels, with their cargoes, which should be seized when trading in violation of the act.[7] In answer to this threat, the Secret Committee of Congress authorized Silas Deane to go to Paris, there to supervise contracts which it had made for importing goods from France, to be paid for with shipments of American products, the proceeds of which were to be deposited with three firms—one at Bordeaux and two at Amsterdam. Deane was instructed to draw on such deposits. He also received letters of introduction to several houses in France.[8]

[4] *Ibid.*, III, 336.

[5] Curtis P. Nettels, *George Washington and American Independence* (Boston: Little, Brown and Company, 1951), pp. 229–230.

[6] *Journals of the Continental Congress,* IV, 96–98; Samuel Flagg Bemis, *The Diplomacy of the American Revolution* (New York: D. Appleton-Century Company, 1935), p. 34.

[7] Peter Force, ed., *American Archives: Fourth Series* (6 vols.; Washington: M. St. Clair Clarke and Peter Force, 1837–1846), V, 1666–1676.

[8] Edmund C. Burnett, ed., *Letters of Members of the Continental Congress* (8 vols.; Washington: Carnegie Institution of Washington, 1921–1936), I, 372.

At this time another agency of Congress—the Secret Committee of Correspondence—instructed Deane to get in touch with the French foreign minister, Vergennes, and to inform him that the colonies needed ammunition, clothing, and arms for 25,000 men, 100 fieldpieces, goods for the Indian trade, and great quantities of linens and woolens. Noting that "there is a great appearance that we shall come to a total separation from Great Britain," the committee told Deane to say that the commerce of the colonies might go to France if her aid should win their friendship and that they would pay for supplies as soon as their shipping could be protected —presumably by French convoys.[9]

In order to give force and authority to Deane's mission, Congress on April 6, 1776, adopted a historic resolve which opened American ports to all traders except subjects of Great Britain. Of the terms and the purpose of this act John Adams wrote: "Foreign nations, all the world I hope, will be invited to come here, and our people permitted to go to all the world except the dominion of him [George III] who is adjudged to be *Nerone Neronior* [more Nero than Nero]. I think the utmost encouragement must be given to trade, and therefore we must levy no duties at present upon exports and imports, nor attempt to confine our trade to our own bottoms or our own seamen." [10]

In France, a zealous friend of the American cause, Caron de Beaumarchais, persistently urged the government to supply the Americans with military stores. When Deane arrived in Paris, he dealt with Vergennes through Beaumarchais, to whom the French court granted 1,000,000 livres, with which he bought the needed goods. To this end he used a firm which he founded, Hortalez and Company. By October, 1776, Deane had obtained 30,000 muskets, 200 cannon, 27 mortars, 100,000 balls, 13,000 bombs, clothing for 30,000 men, and a large quantity of gunpowder. These supplies, shipped clandestinely to America, contributed decisively to the great victory at Saratoga in October, 1777.[11] That, in turn, inspired the French court to make two treaties with the United States, one of commerce and one of alliance—both signed on February 6, 1778.

Thanks to the generosity of France, the United States entered the circle of trading nations as the equal of a great European power, for the French-American treaty of commerce was such as France might have made with Britain or Spain. It contained no suggestion of a patronizing attitude toward a weak dependent. Each country accorded to its ally the status of a most favored nation in regard to commercial concessions, port charges, and imposts. Each pledged to protect the vessels of the other within its jurisdiction and to use its warships to guard the other's mer-

[9] *Ibid.*, pp. 375–377.

[10] *Ibid.*, pp. 402–403.

[11] Claude H. Van Tyne, "French Aid Before the Alliance of 1778," *American Historical Review*, XXXI, No. 1 (October, 1925), 39–40.

chantmen at sea. The two parties agreed to an exchange of consuls, to rules regarding contraband, to procedures concerning maritime searches, and to a common form of passports. The inhabitants of each country were guaranteed the right to dispose of their property within the territory of the other; shipwrecked or damaged vessels and ships seeking shelter were assured of friendly treatment in each country; goods and ships recovered from pirates were to be returned to their owners. France offered to the United States the use, in both Europe and the French West Indies, of free ports where American products could be imported and disposed of. Each party accorded to the other the right to bring prizes of privateers into its ports.[12]

It was the good fortune of the American states to plunge into international trade while they were warring with Britain at a time when she was cordially feared and disliked by the major powers of Europe. France, Spain, the Netherlands, and Prussia all nursed feelings of enmity toward the island kingdom that had profited abundantly at their expense in wars recent or remote. The Seven Years' War had inflated British power to the point that it threatened to dominate the European states and to reduce them to a secondary rank. Consequently, they were disposed to help the American Union—not because they loved it but because it offered an opportunity to strike at a potent rival. Even though reluctant to go to war against Britain by recognizing the independence of the United States, a European power could give much aid short of war. It could harbor American vessels in disguise, without asking questions. Frictions and rivalries that were intensified by the American conflict eventually brought Spain into the war as an ally of France in April, 1779.

In 1780–1783, Russia, Denmark, Sweden, the Netherlands, Prussia, Austria, Portugal, and the two Sicilies joined together in a league of armed neutrality, seeking thereby to protect their shipping from attacks of belligerents. Aimed mainly at Britain, the league insisted that neutrals possessed the right to trade with nations at war, that goods owned by citizens of a belligerent state should be immune from seizure if carried on neutral ships, with the exception of contraband, and that a blockade, in order to be legal, must be enforced by vessels stationed at blockaded ports. The favoritism of the Dutch toward the American cause moved Britain to declare war against them in December, 1780. A treaty between the United States and the Netherlands of October 8, 1782, and another with Sweden of April, 1783, reaffirmed the principles of the French-American Treaty of Commerce of 1778. All these treaties were based on "a plan of treaties to

[12] Richard Peters, ed., *The Public Statutes at Large of the United States from . . . 1789 to March 3, 1845* (8 vols.; Boston: Charles C. Little and James Brown, 1848–1850), VIII, 14, 16, 18, 20, 22, 25, 26, 28; Vernon G. Setser, "Did Americans Originate the Conditional Most-Favored-Nation Clause?" *Journal of Modern History*, V, No. 3 (September, 1933), 320, 322.

be entered into with foreign states" which Congress had adopted on September 24, 1776. Throughout the war the United States adhered to a consistent commercial policy—one that aimed to bring friendly nations into a concert of commercial freedom—one that called for ports open alike to the goods and vessels of all nations, for freedom of travel and security of residence for all merchants, and for laws guaranteeing equal treatment to all countries. Such was the American answer to Britain's restrictive commercial system from which the colonists had suffered for more than a hundred years.[13]

ECONOMIC ASPECTS OF NAVAL WARFARE

Sea-borne trade during the Revolution, carried on largely by armed vessels, was almost as warlike as military operations on land. American ships had to contend with a naval power that menaced them wherever they went. The sea lanes and ports of British-American trade were the scenes of a boundless maritime war.

In 1763, Britain's overseas trade, soon to become the target of its enemies, consisted of many branches. That reaching to Ireland was highly valuable, ranking third in importance and accounting for nearly 9 percent of the whole. The lands adjacent to the Baltic Sea supplied Britain with timber and naval stores. Germany held second place among Britain's outlets, and—together with the Netherlands—sustained more than 19 percent of all its overseas commerce. France was still a good customer. Another area included Spain, Portugal, and the Mediterranean. British trade with Africa supplied slaves to the Spanish colonies in America, thereby enabling the British to obtain large quantities of silver for re-exportation to India. Thus the slave trade supported the India trade, which ranked fifth among the branches of Britain's maritime traffic. In the Caribbean, six sugar islands—Jamaica, St. Kitts, Barbados, Montserrat, Nevis, and Antigua—contributed more than 9 percent to all Britain's external commerce.[14]

All such trades took on an added importance after 1775, by reason of Britain's loss of most of its business with the thirteen colonies—a loss that amounted to about 10 percent of all its commerce overseas. To protect the remaining trades was a task to tax the resources of any navy. To defend the homeland, to blockade the coasts of the United States, to guard

[13] Sir Francis Piggott and G. W. T. Omond, eds., *Documentary History of the Allied Neutralities, 1780 and 1800* (London: University of London Press, 1919), pp. 16, 233, 239, 247, 252, 270, 276, 278; Knute Emil Carlson, *Relations of the United States with Sweden* (Allentown, Penn.: H. Ray Haas & Co., 1921), pp. 23–24, 43; Edmund C. Burnett, "Note on American Negotiations for Commercial Treaties, 1776–1786," *American Historical Review*, XVI, No. 3 (April, 1911), 579, 581–582.

[14] Arthur Pierce Middleton, *Tobacco Coast* (Newport News, Va.: The Mariners' Museum, 1953), pp. 176–177.

transports and supply ships serving the British Army, to convoy merchant-men, and to seize American vessels—such were the duties of the British Navy. Its effectiveness in America depended largely on its bases there. In the north, its most important base was at Halifax in Nova Scotia—an outpost that guarded the trade of Britain's possessions nearby and that sent out cruisers to harass the shipping of New England. Forced to evacuate Boston on March 17, 1776, the British never regained that important base. The evacuation proved that, without a very large army, the British Navy could not hold a base in opposition to strong local land forces. The loss of Boston weakened the hold of the British on the eastern New England coast. However, they retained Newport, Rhode Island, until December, 1779. It served as a center of operations in southern New England and as a point for controlling the entrance to the port of New York through Long Island Sound—the route of ships engaged in the coastal trade.

After the British occupied New York in the summer of 1776, they used it as their principal American base during the remainder of the war. The extensive deep waters of the harbor gave the Royal Navy ample room for its movements. The two separated approaches to the port—one from the south through the Narrows and one from the east through Hell Gate—could not easily be closed simultaneously by an enemy fleet, so that British ships ran little risk of being bottled up from the outside. Britain occupied Philadelphia between September 26, 1777, and June 18, 1778, but it proved to be inferior to New York as a naval base. After France entered the war its fleet might have gained control of Delaware Bay and thus have caught a British fleet at Philadelphia in a trap. The geography of the Chesapeake Bay area would have favored the Royal Navy if the British had had an army large enough to hold Norfolk, from which the entrance to the bay might have been controlled. Lacking such a force, the British fleet was not often effective there, since it had to operate from remote bases. Nor could the Royal Navy control the coastal waters of North Carolina; too shallow for a large ship, they favored small American boats that could hug the shore and thus avoid capture by large vessels, while the British could not use many small ones so far from their bases. British sea power did not become effective off Georgia and South Carolina until the occupation of Savannah on December 29, 1778, followed by the taking of Charleston on May 12, 1780. Those successes extended the sway of British sea power northward to Chesapeake Bay, but at the cost of abandoning Newport and of neglecting the New England coast, thereby letting loose a swarm of New England privateers that battened on British shipping.[15]

Britain's failure to suppress American trade arose in good measure from its shortage of troops. In view of the slow-moving vessels of that time, an effective blockade required that Britain occupy Halifax, Boston, Newport, New York, Philadelphia, Norfolk, and Charleston. In November, 1777, when Britain held only Halifax, Newport, Philadelphia, and New York, the head of the Royal Navy, Lord Sandwich said: "It must not . . . be imagined that any force will be sufficient entirely to execute the purpose of blocking up all the rebels' ports and putting a total stop to their privateering; for along so extensive a coast, full of harbors and inlets, many ships will, in spite of all our efforts, get in and out by taking advantage of their knowledge of the coast, of dark and long nights, and events of wind and weather favorable to their purpose." [16] In the face of the hostility of a people in arms, British bases needed the protection of strong land forces. Norfolk was burned on New Year's Day, 1776. In order to occupy New York, the British had to evacuate Boston and to neglect the South. Philadelphia proved to be untenable, and a belated effort to control the South entailed the loss of Newport. Britain did not hold, at any one time, more than four of the seven ports that were needed for blockading the North American coast.

In addition to the handicaps that hampered the British Navy, the Americans benefited from some positive advantages on the sea. For one thing, they had a large fleet of merchant vessels that were well suited to all branches of maritime commerce—particularly the coastal trade from state to state and the highly important traffic with the West Indies. The mariners who manned such ships knew the principal routes of trade and had learned, during the Seven Years' War, the tricks of privateering and of eluding enemy vessels. In Europe and in the West Indian colonies of France, the Netherlands, and Spain, the states had the benefit of contacts with traders and officials who were either hostile or indifferent toward Britain. In New England a well-developed shipbuilding industry was equipped to build vessels suited to every trade of the time.

PRIVATEERING

Of economic pursuits during the war, privateering—the operating of privately owned commerce raiders—was the most exciting, dramatic,

---

Annual Report . . . 1915; Washington: Government Printing Office, 1916), pp. 173–175; Charles Christopher Crittenden, *The Commerce of North Carolina, 1763–1789* (Vol. XXIX of *Yale Historical Publications;* New Haven, Conn.: Yale University Press, 1936), pp. 122–123; John Richard Alden, *The American Revolution, 1775–1783* (The New American Nation Series, H. S. Commager and R. B. Morris, eds.; New York: Harper & Brothers, 1954), pp. 41, 94–95, 207, 228, 231; Robert Greenhalgh Albion, *The Rise of the Port of New York* [1815–1860] (New York: Charles Scribner's Sons, 1939), pp. 20–21.

[16] Quoted in Albion and Pope, *Sea Lanes in Wartime,* p. 37.

and colorful. It started in 1775 in efforts to seize British ships bringing supplies to Boston. In September and October, Washington acquired for the Continental Army a fleet of six small vessels which soon captured several prizes. Although Washington's ships were not privateers, they engaged in something akin to privateering in that he granted to the men on board a third or a half of the proceeds from the vessels they brought in.[17] On November 25, Congress endorsed his actions, which he had taken independently on his authority as commander in chief.[18]

In November, 1775, Massachusetts enacted a law which authorized the issuance of commissions to privateers and provided for the establishment of prize courts.[19] Other colonies soon took similar action. In March, 1776, Congress empowered the inhabitants of the Union to fit out privateers under its authority and approved the issuing of Continental commissions. However, Congress at that time did not establish prize courts; it merely provided that appeals from provincial prize courts might be heard by one of its own committees.[20] Later, in January, 1780, Congress established a court of appeals for prize cases. Under the dual system for privateers both the states and Congress commissioned vessels. The states provided the prize courts, with right of appeal to an agency of the Union.[21]

American merchants managed the business of privateering. Usually they acted as a group when fitting out a vessel, each purchasing a share or shares, thereby spreading the risk. One participant might own as many as half of the shares or only one fiftieth. Shares were sold freely and became articles of speculation.[22] The owners paid all expenses and gave bond to a Continental or state agent to assure that they would abide by regulations framed by Congress to assure that only enemy vessels were captured. The privateers varied in size from 15 to 320 tons and were well supplied with guns. On large vessels the ship's company consisted of captain, prize masters, lieutenants, sailing master, surgeon, petty officers, gunners, and seamen. Prize money was divided into halves or thirds: one half or one third went to the officers and crew; one half or two thirds to the owners. The portion for the ship's company was distributed by shares: five to the captain, five to the prize master, one to each seaman, and two,

[17] Octavius T. Howe, "Beverly Privateers in the Revolution" (Colonial Society of Massachusetts, *Publications*, Vol. XXIV; Boston: The Society, 1924), pp. 324–327.

[18] *Journals of the Continental Congress*, III, 375.

[19] Gardner Weld Allen, *Massachusetts Privateers of the Revolution* (Massachusetts Historical Society, *Collections*, Vol., LXXVII; Cambridge, Mass.: Harvard University Press, 1927), pp. 25–31.

[20] *Journals of the Continental Congress*, IV, 229–232.

[21] Claude Halstead Van Tyne, *The American Revolution, 1776–1783* (Vol. IX of *The American Nation*, A. B. Hart, ed.; New York: Harper & Brothers, 1905), pp. 191–192; Sidney G. Morse, "State or Continental Privateers?" *American Historical Review*, LII, No. 1 (October, 1946), 68–73.

[22] Howe, "Beverly Privateers in the Revolution," p. 421.

three, or four to each of the others.[23] The vessels usually set out alone, but occasionally as many as ten or twelve went out together.

Massachusetts and Pennsylvania accounted for about two thirds of the privateers that gave bonds to the United States. Maryland ranked third, with about 14 percent; Connecticut was fourth with 11 percent; Virginia and New Hampshire each contributed about 3 percent; Rhode Island and New Jersey each less than 1 percent. The principal bases were Baltimore, Philadelphia, the Connecticut River towns, Boston, Newburyport, Salem, Beverly, and Portsmouth, New Hampshire. Prominent among the owners in Baltimore were Daniel Bowley, Hugh Young, and Robert and Samuel Purviance. The leaders in Philadelphia were Robert Morris, Blair McClenachan, Alexander Stewart, John MacPherson, James and Andrew Caldwell, Thomas Leaming, Isaac Moses, and George Ord. Among the most active owners in Boston were John Codman, William Smith, John Coffin Jones, Stephen Higginson, Isaac Sears, Daniel Sargent, and Samuel Broome, while Elias Hasket Derby, Nathaniel Silsbee, William Gray, Benjamin Goodhue, John Norris, and the Cabots—John, Andrew, and George—represented the Salem-Beverly area. John Langdon was first at Portsmouth.[24] Three Massachusetts vessels—the *Pilgrim*, the *Essex*, and the *Grand Turk*—proved to be especially profitable to their owners.

Almost at will the privateers scoured the seas, haunting the principal routes of British trade. They swept up and down the coastal waters of North America, combed the Caribbean Sea, and seized enemy ships sailing between Britain and the West Indies. They skirted the Irish coast, traversed the English Channel, and cruised in the North Sea and along the Atlantic shores of France and Spain.[25]

In the sea fighting in which the privateers engaged the Americans made a good showing. They developed a long, low, swift, narrow schooner of about 90 tons.[26] The men were adept in handling their well-armed ships, which carried a gun to every four to eight men. Success depended in good measure upon the skill and aggressiveness of the captain. The share plan of rewards gave all the men a personal stake in victory. The privateer sought to compel its victim to surrender, either by a superior show of force and speed, by disabling it, or by boarding it and overpowering its crew by hand-to-hand fighting. A British captain could justify

[23] Kenneth Wiggins Porter, ed., *The Jacksons and the Lees* (Vol. III of *Harvard Studies in Business History*, 2 vols.; Cambridge, Mass.: Harvard University Press, 1937), I, 20.

[24] Charles H. Lincoln, ed., *Naval Records of the American Revolution, 1775–1788* (Washington: Government Printing Office, 1906), prints data relating to Continental bonds of letters of marque vessels. See pp. 217–495.

[25] Edward Channing, *A History of the United States* (6 vols.; New York: The Macmillan Company, 1905–1925), III, 311.

[26] John C. Miller, *Triumph of Freedom, 1775–1783* (Boston: Little, Brown and Company, 1948), p. 110.

a surrender, in order to save his ship, with the hope that it might soon be retaken by a British warship or privateer—an event that often happened. Once a vessel had surrendered, the privateer put on board a prize master and a small party of armed men to take it into port. This practice explains why the privateers set out with a relatively large body of men and why one vessel was able to take several prizes. Sometimes the privateer escorted the prize into port; sometimes a prize master took it in alone. When homeward bound a large vessel piloted the prizes it had seized en route and often docked with several to its credit. American ports not in the hands of the British were havens sought by incoming raiders. There a prize court made its award, whereupon the ship and its cargo were sold at auction. In Europe, the Spanish port Bilbao and the coastal towns of France—Brest, Le Havre, Nantes, Bordeaux—received many American privateers and their prizes. While in France, Benjamin Franklin commissioned three raiders: the *Black Prince*, the *Black Princess*, and the *Fearnot*. Manned largely by English and Irish smugglers, they preyed upon British shipping in the English Channel and in the waters between Britain and Ireland. On twelve cruises in 1779 and 1780 they took 114 prizes. In the West Indies, French Martinique served the Americans well. When France and Spain were neutral their port officials often connived in the American operations by judging privateers to be merchantmen or by treating prizes as American ships, thereby permitting them to be sold.[27]

During the war, owners gave bonds to agents of the Union for 1,697 privateers. In Massachusetts, 1,554 commissions were obtained for 958 vessels.[28] It is estimated that 10,000 men served on American privateers in 1778. The fleet of the Salem-Beverly area ranged from 30 vessels in 1777 to 100 in 1782.[29] Salem alone sent out more than 200 ships during the war, a third of which were captured or destroyed.[30]

The outbreak of the war caught the Royal Navy in a state of inefficiency and neglect, with the result that it did not provide adequate protection to British shipping. Later, in 1778, when Britain had developed a system of convoys, France's entry into the war compelled the Admiralty to divert much of its naval force to the defense of Britain's coastal towns,

[27] James Duncan Phillips, *Salem in the Eighteenth Century* (Boston: Houghton Mifflin Company, 1937), pp. 392–442; James B. Hedges, *The Browns of Providence Plantations* (Cambridge, Mass.: Harvard University Press, 1952), pp. 279–285; William Bell Clark, *Ben Franklin's Privateers* (Baton Rouge: Louisiana State University Press, 1956), p. 177; Helen Augur, *The Secret War of Independence* (New York: Duell, Sloan & Pearce, 1955), p. 330.

[28] Phillips, *Salem in the Eighteenth Century*, p. 396; Allen, *Massachusetts Privateers of the Revolution*, p. 38.

[29] Alden, *The American Revolution*, p. 205; Phillips, *Salem in the Eighteenth Century*, pp. 401, 432.

[30] Robert A. East, *Business Enterprise in the American Revolutionary Era* (New York: Columbia University Press, 1938), pp. 159–161.

so that American enterprise flourished in the period 1778–1782. The privateering fleet grew larger year after year, reaching its peak in 1781, when 550 vessels with Continental commissions were busy. At the end of the war the Americans had acquired many large ships and were profiting by a wealth of experience.[31] "Not only were the new vessels ships and brigs, but they were larger and faster and the guns, though perhaps not more numerous, were nine- and twelve-pounders instead of fours and sixes. The masters were no longer amateurs; they were veterans of a dozen well-fought fights and knew how to train and drill their crews." [32]

By supplying the country with all sorts of goods, privateering compensated for the decline of normal peacetime trade. Captured cargoes contained English goods, rum, flour, lumber, military stores, logwood, beef, furs, West Indian products, and many other needed commodities. Privateers also brought imports from France, as well as passengers and dispatches. Franklin said in 1777 that the United States was "enriching itself by prizes upon British commerce, more than it ever did by any commerce of its own, under the restraints of a British monopoly." [33] According to an informed observer, Stephen Higginson obtained $70,000 from privateering, and a reliable informant said that Providence, Rhode Island, gained £300,000 from privateering and shipbuilding in about twelve months—a sum that was double the property of the whole town in 1774.[34] Britain's total wartime losses of £18,000,000 signify that privateering supplied the states with an immense quantity of goods.[35]

The heavy losses inflicted by American raiders on Britain severely crippled its war effort. Altogether, Britain lost 2,000 vessels and 12,000 sailors, including a Quebec fleet worth $500,000 and half of a rich Jamaica fleet, taken in 1776. New England privateers, by seizing supply ships en route to Boston, weakened Britain's hold on the port and hastened the evacuation. By virtue of British losses many British mercantile houses failed, the prices of American products in Britain soared, and marine insurance rates rose to 28 percent—higher than during the Seven Years' War. Franklin cited reports that Britain's West Indian trade had suffered losses amounting to £1,800,000.[36] The Earl of Sandwich said in August,

---

[31] William M. James, *The British Navy in Adversity* (London: Longmans, Green and Company, 1926), pp. 415, 424–425; Evarts Boutell Greene, *The Revolutionary Generation, 1763–1790* (Vol. IV of *A History of American Life*, A. M. Schlesinger and D. R. Fox, eds.; New York: The Macmillan Company, 1943), p. 266.

[32] Phillips, *Salem in the Eighteenth Century*, p. 427.

[33] Quoted in Miller, *Triumph of Freedom*, p. 111.

[34] Thomas Wentworth Higginson, *Life and Times of Stephen Higginson* (Boston: Houghton Mifflin and Company, 1907), p. 34; East, *Business Enterprise*, p. 78.

[35] Alden, *The American Revolution*, p. 206; Miller, *Triumph of Freedom*, p. 111.

[36] Letter of February 6, 1777, Francis Wharton, ed., *The Revolutionary Diplomatic Correspondence of the United States* (6 vols.; Washington: Government Printing Office, 1889), II, 262–263.

1777: "The sea is overspread with privateers . . . and the demands for convoys and cruisers so great that we know not how to supply them."[37]

By employing vessels that otherwise would have lain idle, by taking ships from the enemy, and by stimulating shipbuilding at home, privateering enabled the United States to maintain a merchant fleet. Undoubtedly, the Americans captured many more vessels than they lost. The prizes of 1776 numbered at least 342; those of 1777 came to 464. Many of the 12,000 captured British sailors later served on American ships.[38] Franklin observed in 1777: "America has the whole harvest of prizes made upon British commerce, a kind of monopoly that has its advantages, as by affording greater encouragement to our cruisers, it increases the number of our seamen and thereby augments our naval power."[39]

FOREIGN TRADE

In addition to goods obtained through privateering, the states imported many products from Europe. Before 1775, the thirteen colonies had secured most of their manufactures from Britain, paying with native commodities or with returns obtained in the West Indies or in Spain, such as sugar, coffee, logwood and foreign coins, especially Spanish pieces of eight. The products of the thirteen colonies which were exported directly to Britain included rice, indigo, and deerskins from Georgia and South Carolina, tobacco from the Chesapeake Bay area, and furs, pig iron, whale oil, masts, ship timber, pitch, tar, potash, and American-built ships from New England and the middle colonies. The wartime disruption of commerce with Britain forced the states to develop direct trades with France, Spain, and the Netherlands. To retain and to increase long-established trades with foreign islands in the Caribbean was another urgent need.

The records of wartime commerce tell a fairly coherent story, of four chapters. First, before April, 1776, restraining acts of both Britain and Congress so stifled the foreign trade of the colonies as to afflict them with acute shortages of imported goods.[40] In July and November, 1775, Con-

---

[37] Quoted in Miller, *Triumph of Freedom*, p. 293.

[38] Porter, *The Jacksons and the Lees*, I, 23; Phillips, *Salem in the Eighteenth Century*, pp. 409, 411, 413; Susie M. Ames, "A Typical Virginia Business Man of the Revolutionary Era: Nathaniel Littleton Savage . . . ," *Journal of Economic and Business History*, III, No. 3 (May, 1931), 410–411.

[39] Alden, *The American Revolution*, p. 205; Samuel Eliot Morison, *The Maritime History of Massachusetts* (Boston: Houghton Mifflin Company, 1921), p. 29; Wharton, *Revolutionary Diplomatic Correspondence*, II, 311.

[40] East, *Business Enterprise*, pp. 133, 139; Margaret E. Martin, *Merchants and Trade of the Connecticut River Valley, 1750–1820* (Smith College *Studies in History*, Vol. XXIV, Nos. 1–4; Northampton, Mass.: 1938–1939), p. 34; Oscar Handlin and Mary F. Handlin, "Revolutionary Economic Policy in Massachusetts," *William and Mary Quarterly*, Third Series, IV, No. 1 (January, 1947), 10–11.

gress authorized a limited trade with the foreign West Indies, for the procuring of arms and ammunition. American vessels were soon importing small shipments. Thus John Brown in November brought to Providence from Surinam 45 hundredweight of powder which he sold to the Continental Army at 6s. a pound—a price which Washington regarded as "most exorbitant." [41]

The second stage, beginning in April, 1776, when Congress authorized unrestricted foreign trade, lasted until about the middle of 1778. During this period, France supplied large quantities of goods by way of New England or the West Indies. France was then a neutral, and Britain shrank from seizing French vessels trading with the West Indies. Consequently, the United States had to keep open only the trade routes that linked its ports with the French islands.[42] Small American vessels could elude British cruisers by sailing close to the continent and by darting into the numerous ports and inlets that dotted the coast from Savannah to Maine.[43]

The foreign trade of the states reached its high point in the period from the middle of 1778 until 1782. At that time Americans had ample buying power in France, the benefit of the French Navy, and easy access to French ports, plus the aid of its later cobelligerents, Spain and the Netherlands. Britain's military and naval tasks multiplied to the point where she could not maintain a tight blockade of the American coast. The trade of the Union with Europe and the non-British West Indies flourished, supplying an abundance of European goods and West Indian products.[44] However, during the last full year of the war, 1782, the states suffered heavy losses. By that time Britain had abandoned important military operations in America and had concentrated on attacks on American shipping. Entrenched at Savannah, Charleston, and New York, the Royal Navy sent out cruisers that seized American vessels trading with the West Indies. Boston merchants reported in May, 1782, that "the risk of capture off Philadelphia was greater than at any time." [45]

The merchant who best illustrates the wartime commerce of the states was Robert Morris of the Philidelphia firm of Willing and Morris. Well established in foreign trade by 1774, Morris in December, 1775, became a member of the Secret Committee of Congress, which he soon

[41] Hedges, *The Browns of Providence*, p. 219.

[42] Albion and Pope, *Sea Lanes in Wartime*, pp. 51–52; East, *Business Enterprise*, p. 169.

[43] Albion and Pope, *Sea Lanes in Wartime*, p. 39.

[44] Hedges, *The Browns of Providence*, pp. 239, 251; Handlin, "Revolutionary Economic Policy in Massachusetts," p. 18; William G. Sumner, *The Financier and Finances of the American Revolution* (2 vols.; New York: Dodd, Mead and Company, 1891), II, 137–140.

[45] East, *Business Enterprise*, p. 60.

dominated. The Secret Committee made contracts with firms and individuals who undertook to supply it with military stores. Such a contractor received a commission of $2\frac{1}{2}$ to 5 percent on the goods he delivered to the committee, which forwarded them to the army. Morris exposed himself to criticism because—while he was a member—the committee entered into contracts with his firm and because he enlisted agents of Congress overseas to participate in his private ventures. Such affiliations greatly increased his reputation and prestige abroad. His principal associates were Silas Deane at Paris and William Bingham at Martinique, a Philadelphia merchant who went there on government business in 1776.[46] Willing and Morris sent flour, tobacco, and rice to Bingham, who exchanged them in Martinique for French goods, rum, sugar, molasses, and coffee that were shipped to the partners in Philadelphia. Bingham forwarded the tobacco and rice to Silas Deane in Paris in payment for French goods that he had dispatched to Martinique. Willing and Morris disposed of the French products they received from Bingham either by general sales or by fulfilling contracts with Congress. It appears that an ambitious trading group was formed in 1776 that centered in Morris and Deane and that included merchants and bankers of France, the Netherlands, and Britain. Operating with a reputed capital of £400,000, this concern made large profits by purchasing prize ships and by importing clothing and dry goods into the states. Morris wrote to Deane in 1776: "You may depend that the pursuit of this plan deserves your utmost exertion and attention, so far as your mind is engaged in making money, for there never has been so fair an opportunity for making a large fortune since I have been conversant in the world." [47]

France, Spain, and the Netherlands served as the Union's principal suppliers of foreign goods. The records of trade list such exports from Europe as powder, muskets, flints, gunlocks, sulfur, saltpeter, knives, steel, window glass, pottery, medicines, liquors, tea, salt, raisins, lemons, cordage, Russian duck or sailcloth, shoes, blankets, woolens, sheeting, ribbons, silks, velvets, handkerchiefs, broadcloth, and two kinds of coarse linens known as Osnaburgs and ticklenburgs. By the spring of 1777, Portsmouth, New Hampshire, had received 9 vessels from France that had been fitted out by Beaumarchais. One of the cargoes contained 1,000 barrels of powder, about 12,000 muskets, and 24 cases of cloth. Foreign trade supplied the Union with 90 percent of its pre-1778 stock of gunpowder.

[46] Clarence L. Ver Steeg, *Robert Morris, Revolutionary Financier* (Philadelphia: University of Pennsylvania Press, 1954), pp. 10–20.

[47] Margaret L. Brown, "William Bingham, Agent of the Continental Congress in Martinique," *Pennsylvania Magazine of History and Biography*, LXI, No. 1 (January, 1937), 55, 58, 60, 64–65; Thomas P. Abernethy, "Commercial Activities of Silas Deane in France," *American Historical Review*, XXXIX, No. 3 (April, 1934), 478–479.

Before October, 1777, the states imported 478,000 pounds of saltpeter, and 1,454,000 pounds of powder brought in by more than 100 ships.[48] Bordeaux sent out 95 vessels in the American trade between January, 1777, and March, 1778. At Philadelphia, Stephen Girard asked his father in France to send a shipload of goods, saying that one could not lose on such a venture and adding that he believed "there ought to be a big profit in view of the high prices of every kind of merchandise in this market."[49] A vessel arriving in Virginia in 1778 had on board goods worth about £50,000. Statements of merchants indicate plentiful supplies in the port towns during the years 1778–1781. The wealth derived from the import trade evoked complaints that its beneficiaries indulged in luxurious living. Allusions to "sudden riches," "extravagant dress," "Holland gin," "French claret," "dissipation," "Rome," and "Tyre" bewailed the gains of the merchants of Boston and Philadelphia.[50]

Soon after the war began American merchants and Dutch traders mutually solicited business. Among the Dutch houses engaged in American trade the leader appears to have been John de Neufville and Son of Amsterdam, who made overtures to all the leading American merchants. In 1780 and 1781 that firm dispatched sixteen vessels to the United States, supplying clothing to the Continental Army and engaging in the tobacco trade at Alexandria, Virginia. Many Americans imported goods from Holland, among whom were Robert Harrison and R. T. Hooe of Alexandria; Aaron Lopez of Newport; Nicholas Brown of Providence; Robert Morris, Charles Biddle, and Blair McClenachan of Philadelphia; Caleb Davis, W. D. Cheever, John Cameron, William Smith, and Jonathan Amory of Boston; and Daniel Parker of Watertown, Massachusetts.[51] Dutch-American commerce produced one of the striking features of the war—a lively trade carried on at St. Eustatius. Located about 180 miles southeast of Puerto Rico, that little island was so convenient a link between North America and Europe that the Dutch made it an open port where all nations might trade freely. Americans sought out the Dutch there at the start of the war. Trade grew steadily until, midway in the conflict, 3,182 vessels left the island during a period of thirteen months. Baltimore's ships sailing to the Dutch West Indies in 1780 totaled 4,900 tons.[52] As an arsenal of the Revolution, St. Eustatius figured in Britain's

[48] Orlando W. Stephenson, "The Supply of Gunpowder in 1776," *American Historical Review*, XXX, No. 2 (January, 1925), 277–279.

[49] John Bach McMaster, *The Life and Times of Stephen Girard* (2 vols.; Philadelphia: J. B. Lippincott Company, 1918), I, 17.

[50] East, *Business Enterprise*, pp. 35–36, 38, 51, 60, 75, 138, 176; Hedges, *The Browns of Providence*, p. 252.

[51] East, *Business Enterprise*, pp. 39, 40, 59, 61 note, 119, 136, 159, 161, 174, 175; Hedges, *The Browns of Providence*, pp. 254–257.

[52] J. Franklin Jameson, "St. Eustatius in the American Revolution," *American Historical Review*, VIII, No. 4 (July, 1903), 683–708.

decision of December 20, 1780, to go to war against the Netherlands. The first important fruit of that decision was the conquest of the island, February 3, 1781, by a British fleet under Sir George Rodney. He found in the harbor a swarm of American privateers, captured British vessels, and American merchantmen, along with 2,000 American merchants and sailors. The British conquest, which netted between £2 million and £3 million in goods and vessels, ended the glory of this mecca of American commerce.[53]

Trade with the Dutch had yet another angle. It opened a channel by which Americans could import British goods when that importation was forbidden both by Britain and by Congress. A British publicist, Lord Sheffield, asserted that during the war large quantities of British goods reached the states via the West Indies and Nova Scotia. At Amsterdam, the leading export center of this trade, British products were given non-British markings and were mixed with Dutch goods. Some American merchants made payment directly to London firms.[54] Carter Braxton in Virginia said in 1777 that America then winked at every importation of British merchandise, so much was it preferred. When Rodney occupied St. Eustatius he seized from British merchants there a large stock of goods on the assumption that they had come from or were bound to the states. Bermuda and the Bahamas were also intermediaries in a British-American trade.[55]

In colonial times, the seacoast towns of Massachusetts, as headquarters of the New England fishery, had carried on a fairly extensive trade with Spain, whither they had sent the best grades of codfish. When the Revolutionary War broke out, merchants of Boston, Salem, Newburyport, and Beverly had contacts with Spanish houses and an intimate knowledge of Spanish markets. Cadiz was one of the chief ports involved. At Bilbao, the firm of Joseph Gardoqui and Sons was outstanding for its New England connections. After 1775 merchants of the Salem area continued to send cargoes to Spain, despite the hazards of the war. However, the trade was soon transformed. The disruption of the New England fishery deprived Yankee merchants of their principal export. Privateering helped to take up the slack as Bilbao became a haven for American prizes. Spain also served as a receiving point for American produce bound for other European countries, particularly Holland. Early in the war Spain contributed a small subsidy to the United States which privided money for the payment of Spanish goods for the American Army. In 1780, Spain permitted the states to trade with her colonies in the West Indies. During

---

[53] Channing, *History of the United States*, III, 323, 325.

[54] East, *Business Enterprise*, p. 32; Ames, "A Typical Virginia Business Man," p. 416.

[55] Hedges, *The Browns of Providence*, pp. 257–258; East, *Business Enterprise*, pp. 31, 63, 177.

the next two years, Philadelphia and the Chesapeake area exported large quantities of flour to Havana, the focal point in the traffic. Sugar, military stores, and coin came back in return. Baltimore merchants, it was said, got rich by selling flour at Havana for nine times as much as it had cost them. In 1780 they sent to Havana vessels aggregating only 100 tons; in 1782, the figure was 6,800 tons.[56]

PAYING FOR IMPORTS

The question now arises, How did the states find the means for paying for a large inflow of imports during the war? Before 1775, the thirteen colonies had always imported goods and services of a money value in excess of the value of their exports. Their difficulty of finding adequate means of payment for imports had long been at the root of their most acute problem of foreign trade. The Revolution intensified this problem, for the states experienced more difficulty in carrying on an export trade than in obtaining imports.

For one thing, the shipping available for bulky exports shrank drastically. The states lost the services of British vessels that had previously transported most of their produce to Britain. In addition, privateering absorbed shipping that otherwise might have been devoted to an export trade. In the second place, the war deprived the states of certain kinds of exports that had once helped them to pay for imports. In this category were indigo, pitch, and tar—products that in late colonial times had had the benefit of British bounties, which made it profitable for Americans to produce them for sale to Britain. The war stopped such bounty payments and in so doing lessened the importance of such products as returns. After 1775, New England no longer supplied the Royal Navy and British shipping with masts. The states also lost their onetime highly important market in Britain for American-built ships. Thus vanished a principal source of New England's buying power abroad. Warfare on the frontiers killed off the Indian trade of the states, depriving them of the sorts of furs that had once been a valued export. In addition, the war prostrated the New England fishery, long a leading supplier of export products —fish for Spain, whale oil and whalebone for Britain, and fish for the West Indies, where the colonists had obtained money and produce that could be used for purchases in Europe.[57]

    [56] Albion and Pope, *Sea Lanes in Wartime,* p. 55; Porter, *The Jacksons and the Lees,* I, 22, 333, 336; East, *Business Enterprise,* pp. 39, 59–63.
    [57] Robert Greenhalgh Albion, *Forests and Sea Power* (Vol. XXIX of *Harvard Economic Studies;* Cambridge, Mass.: Harvard University Press, 1926), p. 282; Raymond McFarland, *A History of the New England Fisheries* (New York: University of Pennsylvania, D. Appleton and Company, 1911), pp. 124–125; Elmo Paul Hohman, *The American Whaleman* (New York: Longmans, Green and Company, 1928), p. 34; Emory R. Johnson, T. W. Van Metre, G. G. Huebner, and D. S. Hanchett,

By reason of such losses, the exports of the states could not possibly pay for all their imports of European goods. In 1777, Robert Morris described the wartime plight of New England, noting that its exports to Europe had shrunk to masts and spars from New Hampshire and a little beeswax and flaxseed from Connecticut and Rhode Island.[58] In 1780, a Boston firm sent flaxseed, white-oak pipes, headings, and spars to Europe. Silas Deane, William Duer, and James Wilson undertook in 1779 to secure contracts for supplying European navies with masts.[59] Another product of colonial times, rice, continued to be exported, but the rice trade of the patriots dwindled after the British occupied Savannah at the end of 1778 and all but ceased with the British conquest of Charleston in May, 1780. At the end of the war there was evident a demand in France for American wheat.[60]

One American export—tobacco—towered above all others. Prewar shipments to Britain had amounted annually to about 100,000,000 pounds, four fifths of which was re-exported, mainly to Europe.[61] To wrest this lucrative trade from Britain was an impelling commercial ambition of France: its conduct in foreign affairs might be called "King Tobacco Diplomacy." The price of tobacco in France, high in 1776, rose steadily until the end of the war. The First Continental Congress did not ban tobacco exports to Britain until September 10, 1775; hence the American industry did not undergo an initial dislocation. North Carolina's tobacco exports in 1775 exceeded those of 1772 by 40 percent.[62] Soon the tobacco planters were free to export directly to Europe; and their plantations did not suffer severely from the ravages of war until Cornwallis's invasion of North Carolina and Virginia in 1781. Even then Maryland escaped.

Northern merchants obtained tobacco by supplying the planters with European goods and West Indian products. The state governments of both Virginia and Maryland exported the staple in order to buy arms and powder. At St. Eustatius in 1777, tobacco alone would bring cash. Rodney seized much of it there in February, 1781. Direct exports to Spain, Holland, and France increased after 1779, particularly to Nantes, the matrix of the French munitions trade. On the whole, however, such exports did not realize the hopes of France.[63]

History of the Domestic and Foreign Commerce of the United States (2 vols.; Washington: Carnegie Institution of Washington, 1915), I, 124–125.

[58] Martin, *Trade of the Connecticut Valley*, p. 34.

[59] East, *Business Enterprise*, p. 135.

[60] *Ibid.*, pp. 39, 63, 169; Lewis Cecil Gray, *History of Agriculture in the Southern United States to 1860* (2 vols.; Washington: Carnegie Institution of Washington, 1933), II, 581.

[61] Albion and Pope, *Sea Lanes in Wartime*, p. 44.

[62] Crittenden, *The Commerce of North Carolina*, pp. 119–120.

[63] East, *Business Enterprise*, pp. 169, 174, 176–177; Hedges, *The Browns of Providence*, pp. 252–257.

In the face of inadequate exports, the United States had to seek other sources of income in Europe. Relief came in three forms: subsidies, loans, and expenditures of the French forces in America. In the case of subsidies, the money tendered was generally used in France or Spain to buy goods to be donated to the Union, which thus obtained imports without having to send returns. In the case of public loans, the foreign lender kept the money in Europe and placed it at the disposal of Congress in a form akin to a bank deposit, thereby enabling Congress to use it by drawing bills of exchange that were comparable to bank checks. Congress drew such bills to purchase supplies and to pay its debts.[64] They were soon acquired by American merchants, used to buy imports, and sent to the lending country, where the money was paid to the possessor of the bill from the loan fund or deposit. The states obtained buying power from the French armed forces in two ways. French purchasing agents bought provisions in America with bills of exchange drawn on the French government and payable in France. Such bills were acquired by American merchants, remitted to France, and used there to pay for exports to America. Thus they served the same purpose in trade as bills drawn by Congress on foreign funds. In addition, the French forces brought sizable amounts of gold and silver coin in order to meet expenses incurred in the states.

Thus the funds advanced by European countries helped to finance their exports to the Union and brought them its trade, at Britain's expense.

Wartime subsidies from France and Spain amounted to $1,996,500. The loans from France, 1777–1783, came to $6,352,500; from Spain, 1781–1782, to $174,017; from Dutch investors, to $1,304,000—a total of $7,830,-517. Loans and subsidies together totaled $9,827,017.[65] Expenditures by the French armed forces added appreciably to the whole, in view of the stay of d'Estaing's fleet off Boston between August 28 and November 4, 1778, and the presence of Rochambeau's army of 5,000 men in the states between July 10, 1780, and the spring of 1782. France's total expenditures for its armed forces in America have been estimated as $6,000,000. Many merchants engaged in the business of supplying the French forces. Among them were Thomas FitzSimons of Philadelphia, John Brown and Thomas Lloyd Halsey of Providence, and Samuel Breck and John Welsh of Boston. The most important of the contractors were Jeremiah Wadsworth of Hartford and his partner, John Barker Church, alias "Mr. Carter." They purchased hay, oats, rye, beans, flour, and cattle in interior New Eng-

[64] Sumner, *The Financier of the Revolution*, I, 247; Rafael A. Bayley, *The National Loans of the United States, from July 4, 1776, to June 30, 1880* (Washington: Government Printing Office, 1881), pp. 5–14.

[65] Charles J. Bullock, *The Finances of the United States from 1775 to 1789* (University of Wisconsin *Economics, Political Science and History Series, Bulletin*, Vol. I, No. 2; Madison: 1895), p. 147; Davis Rich Dewey, *Financial History of the United States* (8th ed.; New York: Longmans, Green and Company, 1922), p. 47.

land and delivered them to the French, receiving payment largely in bills of exchange, plus a commission of 5 percent. Through agents at Providence and Philadelphia the partners sold bills to other American merchants.[66]

Some records of 1781 indicate the extent of the French business. One report of July noted the recent arrival at Boston of French frigates bringing 9,000,000 livres. Samuel Breck sold French bills there to the sum of over £30,000 specie value. At Philadelphia, the agent of Wadsworth and Carter disposed of 73 sets of bills amounting to 484,260 livres. Congress received $300,000 from bills drawn on France—enough to pay half the expenses of the Yorktown campaign—in addition to $450,000 in specie.[67]

All told, Congress in 1781–1783 obtained $2,713,000 from French bills and $574,521 in specie imported. Wadsworth and Carter received £129,570 for French bills they sold in Philadelphia during their partnership. Wadsworth's success as a contractor explains his rapid rise as a merchant, as illustrated by the fact that late in 1782 he owned bank stock worth $41,600 specie value.[68]

It appears that in furnishing supplies to the French the American contractors charged higher prices than those current in local markets. This practice protected the contractor against possible loss in disposing of the French bills, for they had to be sold to merchants at varying discounts. The sum in coin which a bill of exchange yielded depended largely upon the supply of them in relation to the existing supply of goods or coin. When bills were superabundant, without a matching increase in the stock of goods or coin, they fell sharply in price. Robert Morris asserted in August, 1781, that French bills ought to yield 80 percent of their face values and complained that they were then netting only between two thirds and one half.[69] Some of the rates at which French bills were discounted, when sold for coin, were as follows: May, 1780—5 per cent; August, 1780—15 percent; September, 1780—25 percent; April 1781—25 percent; July, 1781—30 to 33 percent; August, 1781—33 to 50 percent; December, 1782—10 to 25 percent.[70] When bills depreciated sharply, merchants deferred purchasing them in anticipation of a further decline, or bought them with an eye to a future rise in price.

CONCLUSION

Maritime activity during the war invigorated the commercial life of the states. Many towns made notable progress. Portsmouth, New Hampshire, added materially to its wealth. Boston increased its trade with in-

[66] East, *Business Enterprise*, pp. 57–58, 61, 68, 77–78, 88–95, 145, 162–163.
[67] *Ibid.*, pp. 67, 68, 162–163; Ver Steeg, *Robert Morris*, p. 77.
[68] East, *Business Enterprise*, pp. 162–163.
[69] *Ibid.*, pp. 161–162.
[70] *Ibid.*, pp. 67, 68, 69, 162–163.

terior New England and drew to itself, near the war's end, a number of well-to-do merchants from the Salem area. Salem itself went forward at the expense of its smaller neighbors. Providence came out of the war with a greatly expanded coastal trade and a group of merchants whose operations were international in scope. In Connecticut, Norwich and Hartford registered substantial gains. Lafayette described Hartford in 1784 as a "rising city," blessed with advantages "which were the reward of virtuous efforts in the noblest cause." Albany also fared well.[71] Philadelphia enjoyed a boom during the latter part of the war, when it was the financial capital of the Union. The city attracted newcomers from France, Ireland, and Scotland, foremost of whom was Stephen Girard. Many resident merchants, such as William Bingham, Charles Biddle, Blair McClenachan, and Haym Solomon, acquired modest fortunes. An observer said of Lancaster in 1777: "The shops are full of goods, and everybody busy, so that you would think yourself in a seaport town whose trade was open." In the Chesapeake country, both Baltimore and Alexandria profited from the wheat and flour trade of a farming area that escaped serious wartime damage. Baltimore's shipping to the foreign West Indies jumped from 5,400 tons in 1780 to 15,900 tons in 1782. The war aggrandized the chief commercial towns and strengthened their grip on American business. So potent were the merchants who prospered during the war that they were able to exert a powerful influence in national politics between 1785 and 1800.[72]

The war also extended the commercial contacts of Americans in Europe and freed them, for a time, from dependence on British firms. American merchants made numerous trips abroad, conducted trade through foreign correspondents, set up branch houses in France, and undertook projects with European partners. New contacts fostered a spirit of independence; the rigorous activities of war had a toughening effect, inuring shippers to a way of life in which hazard, struggle, and danger were ever-present. Experience and skill gained in the hard school of conflict, an increased knowledge of the intricacies of foreign business and finance, and a quickened spirit of adventure equipped American merchants, after the war, to engage in a world-wide trade, in the face of uncertainty, hardship, and peril.

[71] *Ibid.*, pp. 79, 232, 233.
[72] *Ibid.*, pp. 149–150, 164, 175–176, 233–235.

CHAPTER II

The Genesis of a National Economy

MONEY FOR WAR

PAPER money, or bills of credit, exerted a more pervasive influence on the economic life of the states than any other factor of the Revolutionary War. In June, 1775, Congress decided to form a Continental Army of 15,-000 men and to provide the currency both for paying the officers and troops and for purchasing needed supplies.[1] Soon afterward, Congress undertook to acquire and support a navy, to maintain special forces in individual states, and to send agents abroad. Almost unbounded was its need for funds.

At the same time, Congress had only the most meager financial resources. It lacked the authority to tax, since its members agreed that only the provincial governments should exercise that power. The Union as a whole suffered from an acute shortage of hard money; all the coin in circulation in 1775 would not have paid a year's expenses of the Continental Army.[2] Nor did the colonies have a single, uniform paper currency. Each had its special issues that differed from one another—a source of confusion and perplexity in trade. Colonial paper currency was not money; under British law the colonies could not make it legal tender. Since banks did not exist anywhere in the Union, Congress did not have the help of agencies that could lend it money and provide the country quickly with an adequate supply of bank notes. In 1775, Congress could not borrow money from citizens through long-term loans. Many of the richest men, as partisans of Britain, would not aid the Union. Others

[1] E. James Ferguson, *The Power of the Purse* (Chapel Hill: The University of North Carolina Press, 1961), p. 26.

[2] Albert S. Bolles, *Financial History of the United States, from 1774 . . . to 1885* (3 vols.; New York: D. Appleton and Company, 1879–1886), I, 7–8.

feared to lend to an infant government that lacked the normal means of paying its debts—debts that certainly would be repudiated if its cause should fail.

In these circumstances, Congress had but one recourse: printing bills of credit and using them to buy army supplies and to pay the soldiers. It was the most natural thing in the world for Congress to turn to this expedient. Most of the colonies had used it in financing wars during the past eighty-five years. Congress authorized the first issue of such bills, $2,000,000 worth, in June, 1775.[3] Technically they were promissory notes. They resembled present-day paper currency in that they circulated from person to person without individual endorsements. They did not become lawful money until a state made them legal tender. Congress did not provide any fund or reserve of coin or other assets from which the bills might be redeemed on demand in specie or its equivalent. Congress merely called upon the states to levy and collect taxes, payable presumably in the bills, so that they might then be destroyed. In choosing the dollar as the unit of value, instead of the British pound, Congress added another element to a new American economy. The coin Congress used as its standard was the Spanish milled dollar or piece of eight. It contained 17½ pennyweight of silver and was worth 4s. 6d. in English coin.[4]

During the war, Congress issued Continental bills to a total of $191,-552,380. The sums for each year were as follows: 1775—$6,000,000; 1776—$19,000,000; 1777—$13,000,000; 1778—$63,500,300; 1779—$90,052,380.[5] The increases over a period of five years occurred because the states failed to collect taxes that were supposed to take the bills out of circulation. Soon after Congress issued them, they were acquired by individuals; hence when the states did not scoop them up by taxation they remained in private hands. Before 1780, most of the states shrank from collecting taxes for any purpose. Massachusetts did not vote any levy in 1776, and in 1778 resorted to a lottery to raise $2,000,000. Virginia waited until 1781 before making a serious attempt to obtain revenues from taxes. The performances of the other states were not much better.[6]

Initially, the state governments were novices, deficient in authority over citizens who had a strong aversion to paying taxes. Like Congress, the states took the easiest means of getting money—printing bills of credit. When the money from one issue had been spent, great was the temptation to spare the taxpayer by printing a new supply. Only two states, Georgia and Delaware, provided security for their bills other than the pledging of future tax revenues. So large were the issues of 1775–1777

[3] Burnett, *Letters*, I, 140.

[4] Sumner, *The Financier of the Revolution*, I, 36–37.

[5] Ralph Volney Harlow, "Aspects of Revolutionary Finance, 1775–1783," *American Historical Review*, XXXV, No. 1 (October, 1929), chart.

[6] *Ibid.*, pp. 66–67; Handlin, "Revolutionary Economic Policy in Massachusetts," p. 9.

that redemption at par in coin became impossible. The states endeavored to keep up the buying power of their bills by making them legal tender and by imposing penalties for refusal to accept them. The states also issued treasury notes, different from the ordinary bill of credit in that they bore interest, payable annually, and were not made legal tender. The emissions of all the states exceeded $200,000,000. Virginia led the way, followed by North Carolina; then came South Carolina. Georgia, Delaware, and New Jersey exercised the most restraint.[7]

It is ironical that state governments that avoided taxation by issuing bills of credit were called upon to collect taxes in order to redeem similar bills put out by Congress. Without a revenue from taxes, Congress repeatedly found itself in the same situation that had existed in June, 1775. The need for funds grew apace, and only by printing bills could it be met. Since earlier issues remained in circulation, each new emission enlarged the volume of bills in use. Inevitably the quantity increased much faster than did the supply of coin and goods, with the result that the buying power of the bills steadily declined. Prices of commodities, as measured in the bills, soared. Wartime shortages of goods also contributed to this result.[8] So likewise did the ever-growing streams of state paper. The depreciation of the Continental bills, which set in soon after they appeared, corresponded closely with the increase in the quantity of them in use. In December, 1776, $1.00 in coin equaled $1.50 in bills; in October, 1777, the ratio was 1 to 3; in December, 1778, 1 to 6.84; in December, 1779, 1 to 42.2; in December, 1780, 1 to 99.54; and in April, 1781, 1 to 146.67.[9]

As soon as depreciation became serious it provoked bitter criticism and opposition. Many persons suffered. Only a few people then lived wholly on fixed incomes; hence such victims of inflation exerted little influence. More important was a group of creditors whose returns from investments supplemented earnings from their occupations. A Philadelphia merchant, Pelatiah Webster, pointed out that depreciation menaced everyone who had money invested in bonds, mortgages, and book debts. He thought that the doubling of the supply of money would cut buying power of the dollar in two, thereby depriving investors of half their property. Depreciation incensed him because, as he said, it "brings the burden beyond due proportion, on the most virtuous and useful of our people, such as by prudence and economy have made money and got a good command of cash. . . ."[10]

[7] Harlow, "Aspects of Revolutionary Finance," pp. 49, 51–52; Dewey, *Financial History of the United States*, pp. 36–37.

[8] Anne Bezanson and others, *Prices and Inflation During the American Revolution: Pennsylvania, 1770–1790* (Philadelphia: University of Pennsylvania Press, 1951), pp. 61, 81, 117, 127, 191, 225.

[9] *Ibid.*, p. 65.

[10] Pelatiah Webster, *Political Essays on the Nature and Operation of Money, Public Finance, and Other Subjects* (Philadelphia: 1791), p. 31.

Wealthy merchants, then the most influential segment of the creditor class, found that a fast-depreciating currency injured them in their local business dealings. The merchant supplied goods to the farmer, who paid for them when he sold his produce. In normal times the farmer, in order to pay taxes, interest, and debts, had to sell all his surplus products when they were ready for the market; hence the merchant could buy them at favorable prices. Acute inflation, however, rapidly increased the prices of farm products. Because the farmer's tax, interest, and debt payments did not go up so much as did the price of produce, he needed to sell only a part of his surplus in order to meet his fixed obligations. Consequently, he could hold back a part of his produce from the merchant, in anticipation of still higher prices in the future. On the merchant's side, it did not pay him to keep his wares on his shelves. He made his profit by quick sales and by turning over his capital frequently. Moreover, he did not dare to retain the rapidly depreciating currency he received, lest it waste away "in the desk." Nor did he dare invest it in securities that might be made worthless by depreciation. The merchant, then, was forced to sell his goods quickly; hence he could not demand the most favorable prices. He must immediately get rid of the paper he received, with a resulting loss of his bargaining power as a buyer. And when he bought from the farmers, he found that they could hold back produce, thereby exacting a high price for it.[11]

Undoubtedly, the most severe opposition to depreciating paper came from General Washington and the officers and soldiers of the army. Soaring prices exhausted its purchasing funds before anticipated needs had been met.[12] It became increasingly difficult for the army to use paper to buy supplies. Farmers would not take it in exchange for their produce. By 1778 the army found it necessary to seize supplies, giving receipts to dispossessed farmers, who grew bitter when they saw their property driven or hauled away. Even more damaging was the injury inflicted by depreciation on the morale of the soldiers. Men who had enlisted for three years' service grumbled when their pay dwindled. Later recruits had to be offered higher compensation, to the anger of veterans who received less. Shrinking pay retarded enlistments and bred desertions. "What officer or soldier," asked an observer, "will enter into the service in future, if the common and immediate necessaries of life are denied because they have it not in their power to lay down any other than Congress money?"[13] Washington wrote in October, 1778: "Can we carry on the war much

[11] Curtis P. Nettels, "The American Merchant and the Constitution" (Colonial Society of Massachusetts, *Publications,* Vol. XXXIV; Boston: The Society, 1943), p. 31.

[12] Douglas Southall Freeman, John Alexander Carroll, and Mary Wells Ashworth, *George Washington* (7 vols.; New York: Charles Scribner's Sons, 1948–1957), V, 133, 142, 278, 307.

[13] Kenneth R. Rossman, *Thomas Mifflin and the Politics of the American Revolution* (Chapel Hill: The University of North Carolina Press, 1952), p. 75.

longer? Certainly no, unless some measure can be devised and speedily to restore the credit of our currency . . . ." Later he described the currency as "the great impediment to all vigorous measures." He believed that the financial weakness of the Union had prolonged the war. "More than half the perplexities I have experienced . . . ," he said, "and almost the whole of the difficulties and distress of the Army have their origins here." [14]

Depreciation of the paper currency occurred in spite of widespread and persistent efforts to stop it. The most popular remedy was price fixing by state law. This panacea appealed particularly to the people of the middle states and New England. State governments or local authorities adopted codes that fixed wages, transportation rates, charges of innkeepers, and prices of imported goods and domestic products. Such codes made it an offense to refuse to accept paper money, to discriminate against it in favor of coin, or to charge more than the legal prices. Penalties for violations included fines, public denunciations of offenders as enemies of the community, and the sale of seized goods at "fair" prices. The sponsors of the codes often attributed high prices to wicked persons— profiteers, speculators, and monopolizers—who, having acquired large stocks of goods, mulcted the public. Hence the codes prohibited such practices as "regrating" or speculative buying, "forestalling" or the buying of all supplies coming into a town, and "engrossing," or obtaining a monopoly. Toward the enforcement of such codes the state governments did little or nothing. Punishments were inflicted mainly by authorities of towns and counties. Occasionally, indignant citizens seized goods, drove profiteers from their midst, or applied coats of tar and feathers. [15]

When in October, 1774, the First Continental Congress banned the importation of English goods, it advised also that profiteers in stocks on hand should be boycotted and urged that "all manufactures of this country should be sold at reasonable prices." During the winter of 1774–1775, many communities set up committees to enforce these proposals. Congress next fixed prices for imported goods and called upon Pennsylvania to suppress profiteering in clothing and other goods needed by the army. [16] Among the states, Connecticut first adopted a comprehensive price code, in October, 1776.

Depreciation of the paper currency uncovered many practices that tended to defeat price fixing. Some farmers refused to sell at the legal prices and even threatened to raise only enough produce to support

[14] John C. Fitzpatrick, ed., *The Writings of George Washington* (39 vols.; Washington: Government Printing Office, 1931–1944), XIII, 21; XIV, 7; XXVI, 277.

[15] Richard B. Morris, *Government and Labor in Early America* (New York: Columbia University Press, 1946), pp. 92–125; Anne Bezanson, "Inflation and Controls in Pennsylvania, 1774–1779," *Tasks of Economic History*, VIII (1948), 16–17.

[16] *Journals of the Continental Congress*, I, 78, 79; VI, 980–981.

their families. Merchants would not part with their goods unless at prices they deemed high enough to compensate for increased risks or a lessened volume of trade. Master artisans, asserting that legal prices did not yield them a living, avowed that they would close their shops and discharge their hands. There were people who hoarded goods or resorted to barter. Others adulterated products or gave short weight. Sellers sent goods where they would bring the most. This practice revealed that, if price controls were to succeed, they must be reasonably uniform throughout a large area. That in turn led to efforts to fix prices on a regional basis.[17]

In December, 1776, delegates from the four New England states met at Providence and approved a detailed schedule of wages and prices. With minor changes it was enacted into law by the four state governments.[18] Its sponsors submitted it to Congress, requesting that it be approved. Congress, however, merely called upon the other states to send delegates to two conventions for the purpose of drafting similar codes. The meeting proposed for Georgia and the Carolinas did not materialize. Six states sent delegates to York, Pennsylvania. Their efforts failed when Maryland, Pennsylvania, and Delaware rejected a plan approved by New Jersey, Virginia, and New York. Nonenforcement of codes in New England soon led to another demand for action by the Union. In November, 1777, Congress advised the states to send delegates to three regional conventions. The southern states did not respond, but delegates from New England, New York, New Jersey, Pennsylvania, and Delaware met at New Haven in January, 1778, and endorsed a new code which four states enacted into law. Nine states having failed to act, Congress in June, 1778, advised the removal of all controls.[19] Thereupon the states that had adopted the New Haven code repealed their enacting laws. With the collapse of state programs, towns of the middle states and New England tried to keep the cause alive by working through local authorities. Their labors again revealed the inadequacy of action by isolated communities. In 1779 another trend toward cooperation appeared, as the towns sent delegates to state conventions that drafted new codes. This movement led to a meeting in October, 1779, at Hartford, where delegates from New England and New York approved yet another plan. Congress in January, 1780, reversed itself, endorsed the Hartford proposals, and recommended them to the states. By this time, however, the depreciation of paper money had gone so far that price controls were futile. The states soon gave up the effort to enforce them.[20]

[17] Morris, *Government and Labor*, pp. 102, 115, 116.
[18] James Truslow Adams, *New England in the Republic, 1776–1850* (Boston: Little, Brown and Company, 1926), pp. 35–36.
[19] *Journals of the Continental Congress*, XI, 569.
[20] Morris, *Government and Labor*, pp. 103–116.

No state south of Maryland enacted a price-fixing code. In New England the demand for the remedy seems to have had its greatest strength among town dwellers, who strove to keep down the price of food. Although local authorities may have succeeded in some cases in forcing compliance with the codes, such success could have been only temporary. All the bodies that adopted codes frequently revised them upward. It is probable that in Massachusetts the program checked wage increases and reduced the specie income of employees.[21]

ATTEMPTS AT FINANCIAL REFORM

As soon as the evils of depreciation became serious, Congress sought another source of income, in order to avoid additional issues of bills of credit. On October 3, 1776, it arranged to borrow $5,000,000 on a long-term basis. To this end it authorized the sale of certificates that were to yield 4 percent interest, to be paid after three years, to be issued in denominations ranging from $300 to $1,000, and to be sold at loan offices throughout the states.[22] The sponsors of this plan assumed that wealthy men would buy the certificates with paper currency and lay them away, and that Congress, by thus obtaining cash, would not be forced to print more bills of credit. When the certificates failed to attract buyers, Congress on February 26, 1777, raised the interest rate to 6 percent.[23] Even then only $3,787,000 was subscribed by September. After France made its first loan to the United States, Congress voted to use some of the proceeds to pay the interest on its long-term debt. This decision increased the demand for the certificates, with the result that they brought in $63,289,000 after September, 1777. Since the certificates could be bought with depreciated paper currency, Congress promised to pay only their specie value as of the time they were issued. To carry out this plan Congress prepared a schedule showing the depreciation of the Continental bills. However, the table underestimated the extent of depreciation and therefore gave buyers of certificates unduly large claims for future payments.[24]

The loan policy hastened the depreciation of the Continental bills. They were not taken out of circulation; they were merely transferred from private persons to the government, which immediately paid them out again. Since Congress never received enough money from the loans to finance the war, it had to issue additional bills of credit. Meanwhile, the loan certificates often served as a substitute for money, thereby in-

---

[21] *Ibid.*, p. 228; Handlin, "Revolutionary Economic Policy in Massachusetts," pp. 17, 21.

[22] *Journals of the Continental Congress*, V, 845.

[23] Burnett, *Letters*, II, 282.

[24] Bullock, *Finances of the United States*, pp. 133, 143.

creasing the quantity of paper currency in use. Depreciation of the bills of credit therefore went on most rapidly when large amounts of the certificates were being issued.[25]

Congress finally adopted drastic measures to end the paper-money troubles. On March 18, 1780, it called upon the states to retire the Continental bills by means of thirteen monthly tax collections, each of $15,-000,000. Forty dollars of such taxes could be paid with forty dollars in the bills or with one dollar in coin. At this time Congress asked the states to issue new bills to the sum of one twentieth of the face value of the old bills that were retired. The new bills were to yield interest, were to be redeemed by the states in coin after five years, to be taken in tax payments at par with coin, and to be apportioned among Congress and the states, four tenths to the former and six tenths to the latter.[26] The states collected taxes sufficient to retire only $119,400,000 of the old bills, thus leaving about $78,000,000 in circulation. After July 1, 1781, Congress did not recognize them as currency; hence they lost all value as money. The new bills issued under the 1780 plan totaled only $4,468,625. They, too, depreciated sharply.[27]

The policy of 1780, uniting Congress and the states in a new plan, had a bearing on the bills and notes that had been issued by the states. Since the states had made both the Continental bills and their own bills legal tender, the two types of paper formed a single currency and depreciated in unison. Rates of depreciation varied from state to state, since the supply of bills was not uniform in all parts of the country. Some states issued much greater quantities of bills than did others. In any case, a reform of the currency required that the state bills should be taken out of circulation, or greatly reduced in quantity. The states, therefore, in 1780–1782 provided for the retirement of their bills through tax payments, for which the bills were valued in relation to coin. Virginia and Georgia set their rates at $1,000 in bills to $1 in coin. North Carolina's rate was 800 to 1; New York's 128 to 1; Maryland's 40 to 1. The other states retired their bills by receiving them in tax payments at the rate of depreciation which existed when the bills were issued. By such methods the wartime paper currency was withdrawn from circulation by the end of 1783. In keeping with the retiring of the bills, the states repealed their legal tender acts. Twelve states had done that by 1781; South Carolina followed in 1782.[28]

For six years the Union put up with a depreciating currency. That happened largely because nine lengths of the people were farmers who

---

[25] Benzanson, *Prices and Inflation During the Revolution: Pennsylvania*, p. 321.
[26] *Journals of the Continental Congress*, XVI, 264.
[27] Bullock, *Finances of the United States*, pp. 136–138.
[28] Harlow, "Aspects of Revolutionary Finance," pp. 62, 64–65.

had some measure of protection against the worst effects of deprecia-tions: prices of farm produce shot upward; the burdens of old debts and interest payments were reduced; most farmers could refuse to sell produce if they were not offered enough for it. Depreciation acted as a tax on money and therefore penalized most severely those persons who received the largest quantities of the bills.[29] Wealthy merchants acquired an in-tense aversion to such paper. But perhaps the distresses of the army counted for more, politically, than did the complaints of the merchants. In any event, Americans got such a bitter lesson in the evils of runaway inflation that—except for the Confederates of the Civil War—they have ever since succeeded in avoiding a repetition of the experience of 1776–1782.

By July 1, 1781, Congress had sought, by means of long-term loans, to stop the issuing of paper currency, had undertaken to get rid of the Continental bills of credit, and had moved to deprive all bills remaining in circulation, whether state or Continental, of their status as money. Such measures, however, did not provide the Union with either an ade-quate source of revenue or a satisfactory currency. Yet the war remained to be won and the needs of the army were great. All these factors worked together to give birth to a new financial program. On February 20, 1781, Congress had elected Robert Morris to a newly created office, that of Superintendent of Finance, which he held until December, 1784. Then the foremost merchant of America, Morris had a reputation and con-nections that enabled him to dominate the financial policies of the Union during his term of office.

In his work as "financier of the Revolution," Morris endeavored to achieve two primary purposes: to provide the Union with a stable paper currency redeemable in specie, and to make provision for paying, in coin, the interest on the debts that Congress had contracted, except the Continental bills of credit. Morris reasoned that if public creditors were assured of having their claims against the government paid in good dol-lars, they would readily lend to it either coin or its equivalent. The Union could thereby borrow sound money in emergencies and avoid the issu-ance of bills of credit. To realize these aims Morris had one indispensable asset at his disposal: large quantities of coin and bills of exchange that the United States was then obtaining from France and Holland. Such specie assets could be used to redeem, or pay the interest on, government or quasi-government notes and certificates of debt, thereby keeping them at or near par in coin and giving them the quality of sound money. Since foreign loans were not likely to continue after the war, Morris realized that the Union must have a permanent source of specie income. Hence

[29] Albert Henry Smyth, ed., *The Writings of Benjamin Franklin* (10 vols.; New York: The Macmillan Company, 1905–1907), VII, 294; IX, 234.

he urged that Congress should be vested with the power to levy and collect taxes payable in coin.[30]

Morris first undertook to create a new paper currency redeemable in specie. Immediately after he took his new position he devised a plan for the "Bank of North America." Congress gave its approval on May 26, 1781. The plan called for subscriptions to a total capital stock of $400,000, in shares of $400 each, to be purchased with gold or silver. The bank would then issue notes, redeemable in coin on demand, which it might lend to the government in anticipation of receipts from taxes or foreign loans. Private purchases of stock netted only $70,000 at the start, but the arrival of $450,000 in specie from France enabled Morris to pay in about $254,000 on behalf of the Union, which became the chief stockholder. The president of the bank was Thomas Willing, a close friend and former partner of Morris. It was largely a Philadelphia concern. Congress granted it a charter on December 31, 1781. It officially opened its doors January 7, 1782, in the presence of General Washington. From time to time it made substantial loans to the Union. Its note issues permitted Morris to borrow $400,000, less discounts, during the first six months of its existence. Such notes, used for government payments, served the purpose of paper currency. Total loans from the bank to the Union, 1782–1784, came to $1,272,842.[31]

In order to supplement the bank's notes, which did not exceed $400,-000 in 1782, Morris issued two other kinds of paper known as Morris Notes and Morris Warrants. These were orders signed by him as Superintendent of Finance, directing the Treasurer of the United States to pay designated sums. The notes were payable to the bearer on demand; the warrants, to a specified person at a stated time. Morris used them to buy supplies for the army. Since they were issued in anticipation of taxes and receipts from foreign loans, he expected that they would be redeemed in coin or other cash when presented to the Treasury. He hoped also that they would be used for tax payments and otherwise circulate as currency. In 1782, the bank's loans and the Morris Notes and Warrants totaled about $1,000,000, or between 35 and 40 percent of the year's expenditures of the government. Morris expanded the issues to $1,000,000 in 1783, partly to pay the soldiers. Specie resources then available made the notes and warrants as good as coin in the area around Philadelphia. Together with the notes of the bank, they took the place of the old Continental bills

[30] Ver Steeg, *Robert Morris*, pp. 194–197.

[31] Joseph Stancliffe Davis, *Essays in the Earlier History of American Corporations* (Vol. XVI of *Harvard Economic Studies*, 2 vols.; Cambridge, Mass.: Harvard University Press, 1917), II, 36–39; Burton Alva Konkle, *Thomas Willing and the First American Financial System* (Philadelphia: University of Pennsylvania Press, 1937), pp. 98–103; Lawrence Lewis, *A History of the Bank of North America* (Philadelphia: J. B. Lippincott and Company, 1882), pp. 24–36.

of credit.[32] They brought supplies to the army, as indicated by Washington's statement in February, 1783, that the troops were then "better covered, better clothed, and better fed than they have ever been in any winter quarters." [33]

The Morris Notes and Warrants provided a fairly satisfactory currency. However, they could not survive because they were based on foreign loans that would not outlast the war. The coming of peace promised to reduce the expenditures of the government, but, even so, Morris thought that it would continue to need a large revenue to pay the interest on the Union's debts. Such debts in 1782 consisted mainly of those due France, Spain, and the Dutch, plus claims in the form of loan-office certificates that had been issued to obtain long-term loans, and a bewildering variety of other certificates which agents of the Union had given to citizens when buying or impressing supplies. Morris also proposed that the Union should pay war debts incurred by any state in excess of its share of the cost of the war. "Provision for our debts," he wrote, "is the first object and therefore must take place of every other demand . . . ." [34]

In a report on the public credit, dated July 29, 1782, Morris outlined his policy in full. He thought that the principal of the debts of the Union, which would amount to $30,000,000 in 1783, need not be paid in the near future. Provision should be made only for payment of the interest, which he estimated as $2,000,000 a year. He proposed that the owners of certificates should exchange them, at par, for new long-term securities on which interest in coin would be guaranteed by the Union. For revenue he proposed four kinds of federal taxes, each to yield about $500,000: duties on imports, a land tax, a poll tax, and an excise tax on distilled liquors. "A public debt," he observed, "supported by public revenue, will prove the strongest cement to keep our confederacy together. Sound policy would also dictate that we should do justice to those who have trusted us, in order that we may have . . . credit in the future. We might, then, tax the present race of citizens at six pounds instead of a hundred, and leave posterity to pay the principal . . . ." [35]

Most of Morris's program broke down because, with the drying up of foreign loans, the Union lacked revenues from taxes that were needed to service its debts and to support a specie currency. The states still failed to provide Congress with an income adequate to such needs. Congress rejected Morris's proposal for land, poll, and excise taxes. However, in 1781 it had endorsed the principle of a federal tax of 5 percent on imports, but that required the unanimous consent of the states. By the fall of

---

[32] Ver Steeg, *Robert Morris*, pp. 87–88, 117–120, 141, 152, 179–181.

[33] *Writings of Washington* (Fitzpatrick), XXVI, 97.

[34] Ver Steeg, *Robert Morris*, p. 89.

[35] *Ibid.*, pp. 124–128.

1782 all had agreed except Rhode Island.[36] Earlier, Morris, Washington, and Gouverneur Morris had engaged Thomas Paine, at a salary of $800 a year, to write in favor of the proposed import tax. Paine published six supporting letters in *The Providence Gazette and Country Journal* during the winter of 1782–1783.[37] Rhode Island, however, did not yield, and Congress did not then get the power to tax.

In order to put paper currency on a secure footing, Morris deemed it necessary that the Union should have an ample supply of uniform coins. In January, 1782, he proposed to establish a national mint that would issue American coins in order to free the country from its dependence on numerous foreign coins that were often mutilated or debased and difficult to evaluate. The Morris plan was highly intricate because he tried to base a new coinage on the conflicting monetary standards of the individual states. A national mint was not established at this time, although Congress authorized one, and some sample coins were struck.[38]

FOOD FOR THE ARMY

The American armies had to rely on domestic production for many necessities, especially food. The primitive economy of the states did not yield large surpluses of products; hence it could spare only a limited number of men for the armed forces without seriously curtailing production at home. Farmers tilled their fields with crude plows, harvested crops with scythe or sickle, and threshed grain by hand. Artisans worked with hand tools. Goods moved over dirt roads in wagons and carts drawn by horses and oxen. On the streams small boats, bateaux, and canoes had to suffice. The main sources of power were human energy, horses, oxen, water wheels, streams, and wind and sails.

In 1775, the total population of the Union was between 2,500,000 3,000,000 souls. Of these perhaps 700,000 were males of sixteen and over, including about 125,000 Negroes, most of whom were slaves. Such were the resources of manpower available for the armed forces, privateering, foreign trade, and heavy work in mills and shops and on the farms, plantations, rivers, and roads.[39]

It is estimated that during the eight years of the war 395,858 men

[36] Merrill M. Jensen, *The New Nation* (New York: Alfred A. Knopf, Inc., 1950), pp. 63–66.

[37] Harry H. Clark, ed., *Six New Letters of Thomas Paine* (Madison: University of Wisconsin Press, 1939), p. xiv and *passim*.

[38] Sumner, *Financier of the Revolution*, II, 42–45.

[39] Channing, *History of the United States*, II, 221; Greene, *The Revolutionary Generation*, p. 67; Robert E. Brown, *Middle-Class Democracy and the Revolution in Massachusetts, 1691–1780* (Ithaca, N. Y.: Cornell University Press, 1955), p. 52; Herbert Moller, "Sex Composition and Correlated Culture Patterns of Colonial America," *William and Mary Quarterly*, Third Series, II, No. 2 (April, 1945), 126.

were enlisted in the American forces, of whom 164,087 were militia. One generous estimate states the total number in service in 1776 as 89,651. It is impossible to calculate the full extent of military service, since most enlistments were for short terms of a few weeks or months. The maximum paper strength of the main army under Washington appears to have been attained in September, 1776, when 27,273 names were on the rolls. Washington had his largest force of effective troops—16,782—in June, 1778. He estimated a year's supply for 15,000 men as at least 100,000 barrels of flour and 20,000,000 pounds of meat. Whatever may have been the drain of the armed forces on the civilian population, it is certain that it was large enough to tax severely the simple economy of the time.[40]

The story of the army as a consumer of food is, alas, a tale of shrinking supplies. When the troops were at Boston, the New Englanders provided them with reasonably good meals. Soldiers from poor families in Connecticut fared better than they had at home, receiving pork or beef, bread, rice, corn meal, butter, peas, and beans as staples, with rum, milk, molasses, coffee, chocolate, sugar, and fresh vegetables as extras. Such profusion prompted Congress on November 4, 1775, to authorize a standard ration consisting of one pound of beef, or three quarters of a pound of pork, or one pound of fish a day, along with one pound of bread or flour and one point of milk a day, together with three pints of beans, peas, or like vegetables a week, in addition to a weekly offering of a pint of corn meal or a half pint of rice, plus either a quart of spruce beer or cider a day or nine gallons of molasses a week for one hundred men. The army traveled on a well-filled stomach until its withdrawal from Manhattan Island in October, 1776. After that there was a tightening of belts, as the regular fare dwindled to ill-cooked meat and hard bread. The low point came at Valley Forge in mid-February, 1778, when the men had only three ounces of meat and three pounds of bread in seven days. Spring brought relief, and thereafter supplies held up fairly well until the winter of 1779–1780, when the troops with Washington at Morristown, New Jersey, suffered dire want. Then another improvement occurred that continued until the end of the war.[41]

Every part of the Union contributed to the army's food supply. Eastern and southern New England produced cattle, hogs, sheep, rye, a variety of fruits and vegetables, copious quantities of cider, and an

[40] Willard M. Wallace, *Appeal to Arms* (New York: Harper & Brothers, 1951), p. 271; Christopher Ward, *The War of the Revolution* (John Richard Alden, ed., 2 vols.; New York: The Macmillan Company, 1952), I, 246; II, 594; Charles Knowles Bolton, *The Private Soldier under Washington* (New York: Charles Scribner's Sons, 1902), pp. 46–47, 88.

[41] Victor Leroy Johnson, *The Administration of the American Commissariat During the Revolutionary War* (Philadelphia: University of Pennsylvania, 1941), pp. 11, 41, 58–59, 105, 153, 159, 185–187, 193–194; Bolton, *The Private Soldier under Washington*, pp. 84, 87.

abundance of Indian corn, the staple crop. Good roads linked the area with Boston, its market town. The area from the Connecticut River Valley extending southwesterly to the Potomac was the granary of America —the chief producer of wheat, flour, and bread, the cattle country of 1776, a land of diversified farms raising pork, Indian corn, oats, vegetables, and fruits. Connecticut was a main source of beef; the Connecticut Valley yielded wheat for export; astride the Hudson, the New York counties of Westchester, Dutchess, Orange, and Ulster sent wheat, flour, beef, and pork to the port of New York, then the second town of the Union. In the Mohawk and Schoharie valleys west of Albany a surplus of grain and cattle was available for the northern armies. The main supply area extended across New Jersey, where Middlesex and Essex counties shared in the provision trade of the port of New York. In Bucks, Chester, and Philadelphia counties in eastern Pennsylvania were the finest farms in the Union, tilled by thrifty Germans whose bulging barns and well-fed livestock contrasted with the lean cattle and poorly kept fields of the western parts of the state. Between Lancaster and York flowed the Susquehanna, carrying wheat and flour to the rising town of Baltimore, the trading center of eastern Maryland. Through western Maryland and the piedmont of the South and the mountain valleys of Virginia and North Carolina extended chains of small farms and pioneer clearings devoted to diversified agriculture, yet inferior as sources of supply by reason of meager surpluses, the dispersion of settlement, poor roads, and long hauls necessary to get products to the principal scenes of action, so that cattle on the hoof were the chief asset to the American cause.[42]

Before midsummer, 1775, the New England governments provisioned the minutemen outside Boston. Soon after Washington took command, Congress in July appointed Joseph Trumbull of Connecticut commissary general of the new army. Trumbull had succeeded conspicuously in feeding the troops of that colony. He soon formed a supply network that covered New England and reached to New York and Philadelphia. His deputies directed purchases; hired drivers, wagons, and teams; engaged butchers, coopers, bakers, and superintendents of warehouses; and forwarded products to the camps. Trumbull got only a modest salary, whereas his deputies received commissions on their purchases. He kept the army

[42] Albert Laverne Olson, *Agricultural Economy and Population in Eighteenth-Century Connecticut* (Tercentenary Commission of the State of Connecticut, *Publications*, No. XL; New Haven, Conn.: Yale University Press, 1935), pp. 4–5; Richard H. Shryock, "British Versus German Traditions in Colonial Agriculture," *Mississippi Valley Historical Review*, XXVI, No. 1 (June, 1939), 46–54; Paul H. Giddens, "Trade and Industry in Colonial Maryland, 1753–1769," *Journal of Economic and Business History*, IV, No. 3 (May, 1932), 515, 531–532; Frederick Jackson Turner, *The Frontier in American History* (New York: Henry Holt and Company, 1920), pp. 107–108; Johnson, *The American Commissariat*, pp. 8–10, 43, 57, 84, 90, 160, 177–178.

reasonably well supplied until July 19, 1777, when he resigned because Congress then insisted on naming his deputies. His successors were William Buchanan of Baltimore, 1777–1778, Jeremiah Wadsworth of Hartford, 1778–1779, and Ephraim Blaine, 1779–1781. All experienced many troubles in the era when the paper currency was rapidly going downhill. In February, 1780, Congress in desperation called upon the states to collect and deliver quotas of supplies in kind, seeking thereby to operate through thirteen detached agencies—an experiment that bred much confusion, uncertainty, and dismay. In June, 1780, ninety-two Philadelphians, headed by Robert Morris, organized a purchasing agency, the Pennsylvania Bank, and pledged themselves for £300,000 in Pennsylvania currency. This bank, the precursor of the Bank of North America, issued notes, used them to buy supplies for the army, and redeemed them with cash received from Congress, which gave its blessing to the enterprise. When Robert Morris was Superintendent of Finance he introduced a method of purchasing supplies through contractors rather than by commissary agents of the government. Prospects of victory after 1781, private initiative, and a better currency derived from foreign loans combined to sustain the soldiers during the last stage of the war.[43]

Supply depots or magazines linked the army with the countryside. So vital were they to its movements that Washington received the power to designate their locations on the routes by which he planned to advance. During the siege of Boston, the main magazine was at Watertown, a nexus between Cambridge and the interior, with smaller magazines located twenty miles inland. When the army moved to New York in April, 1776, Joseph Trumbull established a chain of magazines across Connecticut. Happily, the provincial authorities of New York had collected a three months' supply of flour, pork, and beef for five thousand men. Additional provisions came in from Philadelphia and Connecticut. After the army left Manhattan Island late in August, 1776, it retreated without benefit of magazines established in advance; since its supplies followed fitfully, it fared badly in New York and New Jersey during the rest of the year. Disease from poor food took a heavy toll. The production area between the lower Hudson and the Susquehanna now became the main theater of the war, and so remained until 1780. Fortunately, the army succeeded in keeping a supply line open to New England across the Hudson above Peekskill. Beef, pork, cattle, and flour moved westward along a string of magazines in Connecticut. In northern New Jersey, the route from New England led to Morristown, twice the winter headquarters of the army and a base that drew supplies from its own hinterland as

[43] Ver Steeg, *Robert Morris*, pp. 106–107, 147–149; Lewis, *The Bank of North America*, pp. 16–22; Johnson, *The American Commissariat, passim;* Louis Clinton Hatch, *The Administration of the American Revolutionary Army* (Vol. X of *Harvard Historical Studies;* New York: Longmans, Green and Company, 1904), pp. 113–117.

well as from Connecticut and Pennsylvania. South of Morristown a magazine at Trenton obtained supplies from eastern Pennsylvania and central New Jersey. Sixty miles west of Trenton was Reading, Pennsylvania, market town for the fertile farms of Berks County. To the southwest, magazines at Lancaster and York received supplies from two other rich counties and from wagon roads leading to Baltimore and the back country of Maryland, Virginia, and the Carolinas. South of Reading was Head of Elk (Elkton), in Maryland, terminus for ships bringing produce up Chesapeake Bay from the eastern parts of the southern states.[44]

Superiority in supply facilities contributed decisively to the great American victory at Saratoga in October, 1777. The British forces nearly ran out of supplies in the northern wilderness when isolated from their main base in Canada, whereas the Americans had an adequate network of magazines to the rear. In the northern theater Albany served as the principal American base. It received supplies from magazines down the Hudson at West Point and Fishkill. In western Connecticut, magazines at Derby on the lower Housatonic River and at Sharon, Salisbury, and Canaan near the headwater of that stream sent supplies northward to Albany. The importance of Bennington, Vermont, as a supply base occasioned one of the decisive engagements of the campaign. The road westward from Bennington met the northern road from Albany near Fort Edward, a southern point in a chain of magazines northward through Fort Ann and Skenesboro to Ticonderoga. Eventually Burgoyne at Saratoga was cut off entirely from supplies, while American magazines, close at hand, supported a growing army that surrounded its enemies.[45]

The labor of getting foodstuffs to the army matched its task of moving them while on the march. Transportation by land proved to be more important than by water. In New England and the middle states—the main areas of military movements and supply shipments—the routes of travel crossed rather than followed the rivers; hence they hindered more than they helped. Bridges and ferries were more useful than boats going up and down the streams. Occasionally American leaders contemplated sending goods by sea between Philadelphia and New England, but the risk of capture by the enemy dictated a land route. Chesapeake Bay provided the best water passage, but even so Congress in 1778 designated a route from Albemarle Sound to Head of Elk that for the most part went along the shore rather than across the bay.[46]

[44] Johnson, The American Commissariat, see index, p. 236, "magazines"; Edmund C. Burnett, "The Continental Congress and Agricultural Supplies," Agricultural History, II, No. 3 (July, 1928), 118–119.

[45] Johnson, The American Commissariat, passim; Alden, The American Revolution, pp. 135–149; New York State Division of Archives and History, The American Revolution in New York (Albany: The University of the State of New York, 1926), pp. 195–196.

[46] Burnett, Letters, I, 196; Journals of the Continental Congress, X, 82, note 2; Johnson, The American Commissariat, p. 147.

Wagons, horses, and oxen were the mainstays of the transportation system. The quartermaster general, who had the duty of obtaining them for the commissary department, commonly hired them from farmers, since there was no organized transportation service. At harvest time the farmers were loath to part with their teams, so that supplying the army in winter quarters called for energetic action before the roads became impassable except for pack horses. Many troubles arose when currency depreciation caused farmers and teamsters to demand more pay than Congress had stipulated. On one occasion farmers shrank from renting horses, fearing that they would not come back. The army's hardships at Valley Forge arose partly from a shortage of wagons and teams. Washington reported that the British had seized most of the horses near Philadelphia, charged that the quartermaster's department had failed miserably, ordered the impressment of horses and wagons, and proposed to employ free Negroes as wagoners.[47] To supply the teams with hay, corn, and oats created problems akin to those that plagued the commissary agents in their work of provisioning the army.

The supply of salt affected the transporting of meat. A shortage of salt made it necessary to drive cattle and hogs to the camps and to have them slaughtered there. In preparing for the northern campaign of 1777, Congress ordered that a thousand head of cattle should be purchased and driven to Ulster County, New York, there to be "dispersed" among farmers who would feed them hay and corn.[48] At Valley Forge, the arrival of a herd from Connecticut inspirited the hungry soldiers for a time, but soon afterward came the depressing news that the British had captured nearby another herd of 133 head. Remote outposts, such as Albany and Fort Pitt, usually got their beef on the hoof, by reason of the scarcity of salt in adjacent settlements.

Although a network of roads existed in 1775, the conditions of travel were still crude and laborious. Horses, oxen, and teamsters strained to get wagons over fords, up hills, and out of mudholes. Repairs often had to be made en route without benefit of shops. Ten miles a day was good progress. Heavy snows brought winter travel to a standstill and imperiled the army's food supply. During the Canadian campaign of 1775–1776, fall rains obliterated roads, demolished bridges, and carried off forage. Teamsters spoiled salt pork by taking off the brine in order to reduce their loads. Others left their jobs when soldiers riled them with rough treatment.[49] In North Carolina, rainy seasons in 1780–1781 turned the poor roads into quagmires. What pulling and tugging, pushing and shoving, shouting and cursing attended the battles with the mud! The eight years of the war, however, served to develop the inland transportation network. Wagons that could carry only small quanities of forage depended upon

---

[47] Writings of Washington (Fitzpatrick), X, 179, 194, 217, 390, 401.
[48] Journals of the Continental Congress, VII, 316.
[49] Johnson, The American Commissariat, pp. 113–114, 120.

stores, farms, magazines, and taverns at intervals along the roads. In 1783, Robert Morris knew of men at key points on the overland route from Boston to Philadelphia and enlisted them to help in moving specie. New roads were opened; trails became highways; the main arteries were widened and improved. Certainly the people knew much more about inland travel in 1783 than in 1775. The lines of Washington's wartime journeys suggest a modern railroad network of New England and the middle states. In October, 1783, enterprising promoters opened a stage line between Boston and New York via Hartford, when before the war travel between the two ports had been mainly by sea.[50]

American officials and purchasing agents incessantly complained that profiteers bought up large quantities of produce which they sold to the government at exorbitant prices. Such "forestallers" and "monopolizers" were the established merchants and traders. They justified themselves on the ground that they had to pay high prices to the farmers, that the risks and costs of handling goods increased, and that since the paper money they received would soon depreciate, they had to protect themselves by charging high prices. At least they served the army by collecting and delivering supplies in quantity. In a time of inflation nearly everyone found it hard to draw a sharp line between profiteering and prudence. Without adequate taxation and a restricted currency, price controls and lamentations about profiteering were futile. Shortages of goods, an expanding paper currency, intensified hazards of trade, and the necessity felt by all citizens to increase charges for goods and services created a situation in which the merchants, as the most conspicuous links between the army and the public, became symbols of greed and targets of blame. Many merchants were devoted patriots who risked their estates to supply the forces when funds could not otherwise be obtained.[51]

GOODS FOR WAR

A survey of 1787 shows that Philadelphia then manufactured about sixty types of products. Nearly all had been made there before the war. Two clues to such industrial success are evident: the neighboring farmers provided the market, and the raw materials were close at hand. Only a few commodities, such as loaf sugar, cotton cloth, and silverware, were made of raw materials that came from afar. Nearby forests and groves

[50] Ver Steeg, *Robert Morris*, pp. 84–85; Oliver W. Holmes, "Levi Pease, The Father of New England Stage-Coaching," *Journal of Economic and Business History,* III, No. 2 (February, 1931), 241–243.

[51] Benzanson, *Prices and Inflation During the Revolution: Pennsylvania*, pp. 311–317, 320, 323–324. Examples of assisting merchants are Robert Morris, Jeremiah Wadsworth, James Price at Montreal, and Oliver Pollock at New Orleans. For Pollock's service see James G. Randall, "George Rogers Clark's Service of Supply," *Mississippi Valley Historical Review,* VIII, No. 3 (December, 1921), 259–262.

provided wood for potash, timber for ships and boats, and lumber for tool handles, wagons, carriages, gunstocks, trunks, chairs, and cabinet work. From surrounding farms came hides for harness, saddlery, boots, shoes, gloves, and other leather goods; grain for liquors, meal, and starch; flax for linens, paper, and linseed oil; wool for woolen cloth, stockings, and clothing; hemp for cordage; fats for candles and soap; and tobacco for snuff. Neighboring mines of iron, zinc, and copper supplied the makers of cannon, muskets, anchors, plowshares, edged tools, card teeth, nails, printer's type, clocks, brassware, and copperware. The earth and the quarries furnished the manufacturers of bricks, tiles, pottery, stoneware, glassware, and millstones; the sea gave up its fish for oil.[52]

The special industrial needs of the Union in 1775 are revealed by acts of assemblies and committees that urged the people either to initiate or to speed up the production of certain articles. Generally, the authorities called for an increased output of linens and woolens. North of Maryland the farmers were asked not to slaughter sheep; south of Pennsylvania the plea was for breeding them. Especially acute was the need for cards or wire combs used for straightening the fibers of wool, cotton, and flax. Other articles emphasized were salt, saltpeter, gunpowder, hemp, and ironware. The southern colonies showed a special interest in paper and cotton cloth. Among other products mentioned one finds tin plate, glass, dyes, blankets, stockings, malt liquors, and grindstones.[53]

The Revolution wrought some material changes in the making of cloth and clothing. In 1774, Britain sent woolen cloth worth £645,900 to twelve of the colonies, exports to New York being excluded from this total. In three years after Christmas, 1776, similar exports from Britain to these twelve were valued at only £7,620—an average of £2,540 a year. This drastic change forced the Americans to increase their output of woolens, linens, cottons, and leather articles. Fortunately, the farmers of New England and the middle states had learned the art of making linen and woolen cloth in their homes. Thanks to the exertions of the womenfolk, the supply of homespun, when augmented by goods brought in by privateers and trading ships, increased sufficiently after 1775 to keep the people properly clothed. In the back country and on the frontiers the settlers had relied on linen and deerskins. They got along as before. In the South, a large increase in the production of homespun linens, cottons, and linsey-woolsey met the needs of the generality of the people. In October, 1776, Congress provided that each soldier who enlisted for the war should receive four shirts, two pairs each of overalls, stockings,

[52] Allan Nevins, *The American States During and After the Revolution, 1775–1789* (New York: The Macmillan Company, 1924), p. 573; Carl Bridenbaugh, *Cities in Revolt* (New York: Alfred A. Knopf, Inc., 1955), pp. 268–269.

[53] J[ohn] Leander Bishop, *A History of American Manufactures from 1608 to 1860* (2 vols.; Philadelphia: Edward Young and Company, 1864), I, 381–383.

and shoes, and one pair of breeches, one leather or woolen coat, and one hat or leather cap. The supply of linen was adequate in the summers, but chilling shortages of woolens and shoes sent shivers through the army when in winter quarters. A Philadelphia manufacturer, Samuel Wetherill, Jr., notified Congress in 1777 that, in the face of soaring costs, he could not meet a contract for woolen cloth. Farmers did not increase their flocks and the output of their looms fast enough both to make good the loss of English woolens and to meet the large and rapid demands of the war.[54]

The Revolution could hardly have succeeded if the states had not possessed a vigorous iron industry. In 1775 the Union produced 30,000 tons of crude iron—one seventh of the world's total output. Charcoal-burning furnaces smelted native ores into pig iron, and forges hammered it into wrought iron. The industry flourished in hills and mountains where sites afforded deposits of iron ore and limestone, timber for charcoal, power for water wheels that drove tilt hammers, and streams giving access to nearby towns and settlements. To such advantages Pennsylvania owed its pre-eminence. Before 1776, industrial pioneers there had erected 73 forges and furnaces—all in the southeastern part of the province in the valleys of the Delaware, Schuylkill, Cumberland, and Susquehanna rivers. Berks County, north of the Schuylkill, had more than a third of the plants, some of which, notably the Reading Iron Works and the Warwick Iron Works, equaled in size and equipment the best in England. There also was the now-famed site of Valley Forge. In New Jersey the principal forges and furnaces stood in the northwestern part of the state about twenty miles above Morristown, in a triangle marked by Andover, Hamburg, and Rockaway. During the war Washington located his winter camps so as to guard the mines, furnaces, and forges that were most essential to the army. In Maryland, which had many profitable mines, the Principio Company owned extensive properties in Baltimore and Cecil counties. After 1775, Virginians operated forges and furnaces at or near Fredericksburg and Richmond, in New Kent and Prince William counties in the tidewater, and in the central part of the state near the Blue Ridge Mountains. The small forges of eastern New England, depending on bog iron, were of declining importance, but in the Berkshire Mountains rich deposits supplied furnaces and forges that turned out high-grade products, especially at Salisbury in northwestern Connecticut.[55]

[54] Rolla M. Tryon, *Household Manufactures in the United States, 1640–1860* (Chicago: The University of Chicago Press, 1917), pp. 57, 59–60, 112, 117–118, 121–122; Arthur Harrison Cole, *The American Wool Manufacture* (2 vols.; Cambridge, Mass.: Harvard University Press, 1926), I, 63–64; Bolton, *The Private Soldier under Washington*, p. 94.

[55] Arthur Cecil Bining, *Pennsylvania Iron Manufacture in the Eighteenth Century* (Pennsylvania Historical Commission, *Publications*, Vol. IV; Harrisburg: The Commission, 1938), pp. 50–51, 53, 55, 75, 92, 179–180, 187–189; Kathleen Bruce, *Virginia Iron Manufacture in the Slave Era* (New York: The Century Company,

The states also had the benefit of mines that served the makers of copperware and articles of brass. The richest zinc deposits then available were located in the Andover-Hamburg-Rockaway triangle in northwestern New Jersey. Several places yielded copper: Cumberland in Rhode Island, Somerville and Bound Brook in New Jersey, Berks County in Pennsylvania, and Cotocktin Mountain in Maryland.[56]

In addition to an abundance of crude iron, the states benefited from the labor of a large number of village blacksmiths and other metal workers who were skilled in precision work and competent to train apprentices and to supervise helpers. Such craftsmen succeeded in furnishing the army with its essential needs. Shortages of cannon, cannon balls, shot, muskets, and camp kettles, pots, and pans do not figure in reports of the army's troubles. The ironmakers also succeeded in satisfying the wants of civilians and in providing many products essential to other wartime industries. Largely under the stimulus of government aid and contracts, promoters built foundries at Springfield, East Bridgewater, and Easton in Massachusetts, at Principio in Maryland and at Lancaster and Trenton. Such war babies grew so fast that before long they equipped the army with artillery, rifles, shot, and shells that the enemy could respect. The mines also supplied sulfur or saltpeter in amounts sufficient to quicken the production of gunpowder. By the fall of 1777, domestic saltpeter had yielded 115,000 pounds of gunpowder, in contrast with the Union's total supply of 80,000 pounds in 1775. Powder mills arose at Andover, Stoughton, and Bradford in Massachusetts and at Morristown in New Jersey. In 1786 Pennsylvania's twenty-one mills could turn out 651 tons a year.[57]

Owing to a relative shortage of tin, the foundries used iron in the casting of kettles, pots, pans, and other hollow ware. In so doing the ironmakers helped to overcome a scarcity of salt. The decrease in the quantity of imported salt prompted enterprising coast dwellers to obtain supplies by evaporating salt water at Cape Cod and along the New Jersey shore. To this end they used large shallow iron vats or pans that were cast especially for the emergency.[58]

By the close of the Revolution, new or improved tools used in fashioning nails, tacks, and card teeth enabled the Union to supply itself with those useful articles. So also the manufacture of steel forged ahead during

---

1931), pp. 32–33, 46, 63–64; William B. Weeden, *Economic and Social History of New England, 1620–1789* (2 vols.; Boston: Houghton Mifflin Company, 1891), II, 497, 500, 685, 734; Victor S. Clark, *History of Manufactures in the United States, 1607–1860* (Washington: Carnegie Institution of Washington, 1916), pp. 496–497.

[56] Bishop, *History of American Manufactures*, I, 545–546, 548, 503, 553, 588.

[57] Bining, *Pennsylvania Iron Manufacture in the Eighteenth Century*, p. 182; Stephenson, "The Supply of Gunpowder in 1776," p. 277; Clark, *History of Manufactures in the United States*, p. 222.

[58] J[ohn] Franklin Jameson, *The American Revolution Considered As a Social Movement* (Princeton, N. J.: Princeton University Press, 1940), pp. 58–59.

the war. An improved process of making steel, "in the German way," was utilized in 1776 by William Hawxhurst at Sterling, Pennsylvania, and was extended to Rhode Island and possibly to New Jersey and New York. During the war twice as many steel plants were built as existed in 1750. By 1783 the states were nearly self-sufficient with respect to leather goods and hats. The manufacturers of pottery and paper had also made good progress. In 1787 Delaware and New Jersey together had fifteen paper mills and Pennsylvania had forty-eight.[59] The Americans of '76 undoubtedly did more paper work than any other revolutionists in history. The wartime writings of Washington alone fill more than twenty-two large volumes.

Although the war stimulated manufactures, it did not have revolutionary effects. The process of making salt by the evaporation of sea water proved to be inefficient and ceased to be important when cheaper sources of supply again became available. Among the enduring results of the war were increases in the output of nails, tacks, wool cards, firearms, linens, cottons, paper, gunpowder, and steel. All such branches of manufacture continued to thrive and to that extent freed the country from its earlier dependence on foreign goods. After 1783 the once large export trade in crude iron did not revive. Since the production of crude iron in the states was greater in 1783 than in 1775, it follows that domestic forges, foundries, mills, and shops had increased their output to a large extent. In the years 1775–1783 Pennsylvania erected at least eleven new forges and furnaces. The growth of the iron industry enhanced the importance of the middle states. Since iron was essential to the tools used by the great mass of the farmers and artisans, it became the basis of the national economy. With respect to clothmaking, the outstanding change occurred in the South. There the farmers exerted themselves to extend household and plantation manufactures of cottons and linens, with the result that those fabrics kept the common people in decent attire. The growth of inland transportation and the success of the Pennsylvanians in manufactures enabled them to enlarge their markets in the interior of the South and to replace the English as the principal suppliers of finished goods in that area.

[59] Clark, *History of Manufactures in the United States*, pp. 221–223; Bishop, *History of American Manufactures*, I, 207; Tryon, *Household Manufactures in the United States*, pp. 137–139.

CHAPTER III

Postwar Trade and Depression

THE REVIVAL OF TRADE WITH BRITAIN

IN spite of the wartime progress of industry, the states in 1783 found themselves in urgent need of manufactured goods. The new country normally had an insatiable craving for such products, since they were indispensable to the higher standard of living to which the people aspired. During the war large quantities of goods, both imported and homemade, had been destroyed or had worn out. The British had burned many towns and villages—Falmouth in Maine, Norfolk in Virginia, Cherry Valley and German Flats in New York, New London and Groton in Connecticut, and frontier outposts in the Wyoming Valley in Pennsylvania.[1] The southern states had experienced the most systematic destruction. After the British occupied Savannah at the end of 1778 they overran all Georgia except remote frontier settlements, whereupon the state suffered severe property losses occasioned by raids and guerrilla warfare. From Georgia the British in the autumn of 1779 made a devastating march through lower South Carolina to Charleston. After occupying that city in May, 1780, and confiscating a large amount of property, they moved into the interior of South Carolina, which then felt the scourge of foraging parties, raids, and the battles fought between August, 1780, and February, 1781, at Camden, Kings Mountain, and Cowpens. The British took possession of Wilmington, North Carolina, in 1780 and inflicted much damage on the Cape Fear region. In the spring of 1781 the central part of North Carolina was the battleground. The British invaders of Virginia in 1781 ravaged the tidewater area of the York and James river valleys. Britain's hold on the seacoast towns and her incitement of the southern loyalists so prolonged irregular warfare that the South did not get a chance to recover until after Congress proclaimed peace in April, 1783.[2]

[1] Ward, *The War of the Revolution*, I, 134; II, 628, 631, 633, 635, 848.

[2] Gray, *History of Agriculture in the Southern United States*, II, 595–597; Robert C. Pugh, "The Revolutionary Militia in the Southern Campaign, 1780–1781," *William and Mary Quarterly*, Third Series, XIV, No. 2 (April, 1957), 154–174.

War-born shortages of goods quickly brought about a revival of the import trade. Lists of goods ordered by American importers in 1783 reveal the postwar demand. First of all, the merchants sought many kinds of cloth and fabrics—linens and silks, velvets and gauze, flannels and denim, corduroy and crepe, serge and canvas. Ready-made clothing was represented by a dozen varieties of small articles, such as gloves, stockings, children's shoes, muffs, aprons, and women's hats. Americans then wanted many things for the table: china, glass, knives, forks, and spoons. The list of household aids included candlesticks, basins, warming pans, hourglasses, locks, latches, and looking glasses. Religion, study, and writing called for Bibles, Testaments, other books, paper, quills, ink, pencils, sealing wax, and slates. Some people would divert themselves with playing cards, fiddle strings, or tobacco pipes. Housewives needed kettles, crockery, pins, and thread; working folk could use gimlets, fishing lines, screws, bellows, spades, spurs, gunpowder, and shot. A market existed for such raw materials as copper, brimstone, and lead.[3]

For practical purposes the war ended on November 30, 1782, when representatives of Britain and the United States signed a preliminary treaty of peace. American and British merchants were then at liberty to make arrangements for the resumption of legal trade between the two countries. At once it appeared that France would not realize its aim of dominating the postwar foreign commerce of the Union in the way that Britain had commanded the trade of the thirteen colonies. France's disappointment did not arise from any official acts of the American governments. Congress in 1783 lacked the legal powers necessary to an effective promotion of trade abroad, and the states individually did not engage in diplomacy or make treaties with foreign powers.[4]

This political vacuum meant that American merchants determined the course of postwar trade. On the whole they manifested a preference for Britain over France. Their customers in the states, long habituated to English goods, liked them better than French products. For more than 150 years English manufacturers had been adapting their merchandise to the American market; hence they knew its requirements and could best supply them. American merchants felt more at home in England than in France, knowing as they did the English language, the customs of the country, and the English money of account.[5] Writing in London in April, 1783, Silas Deane said: "Our countrymen are collecting here, from every quarter of their late dispersions, . . . and they go as far as their money and credit will carry them in the purchase of goods . . . ."[6] England also

---

[3] Hedges, *The Browns of Providence*, pp. 291, 362 note.

[4] Articles of Confederation in Morison, *Documents Illustrating the American Revolution*, Article IX, p. 181.

[5] Johnson, *History of Commerce*, I, 126.

[6] *The Deane Papers: Correspondence between Silas Deane and His Brothers . . . ,*

benefited from its location between America and Europe and from its world-wide trading contacts that made it a great emporium where goods of every description could be purchased in small lots, so that American traders did not need to visit several countries in order to make up cargoes consisting of the manifold products that were exported to the United States.[7]

After the war, British merchants bestirred themselves to recapture the American trade. Their commercial wisdom dictated a policy toward the Americans of holding them, as they held the rest of mankind, enemies in war, in peace friends. British firms therefore courted American merchants and energetically solicited their business. To this end they offered what the American merchant then needed urgently—the privilege of buying goods on credit. Intimate knowledge of American houses enabled British exporters to act quickly in rating their customers and in extending credit, whereas the French, less informed, hesitated or refused to take risks. Counting on an almost unlimited demand in the Union for foreign goods, American merchants utilized such credit to the utmost.[8]

In some respects the mercantile interests received aid from the British government. For one thing, it accorded to British goods exported to the states the same sort of drawbacks, exemptions, and bounties that had been granted formerly on exports to the colonies. The government also allowed potash, pearlash, and bar iron from the United States to enter Britain duty-free. American ships received the privilege of importing tobacco, indigo, pitch, tar, turpentine, masts, yards, and bowsprits into Britain, where such American products were subject to the same duties that applied to similar imports from the British dominions. In December, 1783, the crown ordered that imports of American tobacco intended for reexportation might enter Britain duty-free.[9]

During the first three years after the war, the United States purchased large quantities of British goods. Such imports in 1784 and 1785 were valued at £5,987,490.[10] American importers paid dearly for such imports, since an abnormal demand in England, combined with limited supplies, forced prices upward. An English firm wrote in March, 1784,

---

1771–1795 (Connecticut Historical Society, *Collections,* Vol. XXIII; Hartford: The Society, 1930), pp. 172–173.

[7] This point is emphasized in Lord Sheffield, *Observations on the Commerce of the American States* (London: 1783), reprinted in part in Guy Stevens Callender, ed., *Selections from the Economic History of the United States, 1765–1860* (Boston: Ginn and Company, 1909), pp. 210–214. See p. 213.

[8] Gray, *History of Agriculture in the Southern United States,* II, 597–600; Hedges, *The Browns of Providence,* pp. 288–289.

[9] Clark, *History of Manufactures in the United States,* p. 228; Gray, *History of Agriculture in the Southern United States,* II, 600.

[10] Timothy Pitkin, *A Statistical View of the Commerce of the United States of America* (New Haven, Conn.: Durrie and Peck, 1835), p. 30.

that "tradesmen and manufacturers are so glutted with orders that they must at this present moment be courted instead of commanded to obtain anything out of their hands." [11] American merchants bought on credit between three fourths and four fifths of the goods they purchased in England. As early as the spring of 1783 one English firm had extended credits of £150,000 to Boston merchants. American prices of foreign goods were fairly high early in 1783, partly because importers sold at advances raging from 50 to 100 percent above the costs of importation. Since the importers commonly supplied American dealers, retailers, and consumers on credit, a network of debt soon covered the country. In October, 1783, Providence merchants agreed to charge 6 percent interest on accounts that were four months over-due. The extent to which the British re-established themselves in the foreign trade of the United States is suggested by shipping records pertaining to Virginia, Maryland, South Carolina, and Georgia for twelve months of 1789–1790. The tonnage of British vessels engaged in their trade was 49 percent of the total; that of other foreign countries, 8 percent; that of American vessels, 43 percent.[12] Even so, Britain's annual exports to the United States, 1783–1788, averaged £1,300,000 less than comparable exports during the years 1770–1775.[13]

PAYMENTS FOR IMPORTS: EXPORTS TO BRITAIN

Inasmuch as the bulk of the imports from Britain after 1781 had been procured there on credit, American merchants again had to grapple with the perennial problem of finding remittances or returns for the payment of debts that was essential to future purchases. Of all such returns or exports, gold and silver coin and bullion best served the needs of trade. The war had enlarged the supply of the precious metals in the states to an abnormal extent, thanks to large exportations by Britain and France for the purchase of supplies for their armed forces. Privateering had tended to conserve the Union's stock of coin, in that American merchants obtained foreign goods without bothering to export specie. In December, 1781, purchasers of stock in the Bank of North America laid out $85,000 in gold and silver, in addition to about $254,000 in specie paid in by Robert Morris from a shipment of $470,000 recently arrived from France. A prominent North Carolinian, Samuel Johnston, observed in 1788 that "for thirty years, I have not known so much specie in circulation as we had . . . in 1783." In 1784, the founders of the Massachusetts Bank of Boston purchased 551 shares of its stock with $225,500 in specie. When forming a partnership in Providence in 1783, Nicholas Brown agreed to

[11] Quoted in Hedges, *The Browns of Providence*, pp. 292–293.

[12] *Ibid.*, pp. 289, 291; Gray, *History of Agriculture in the Southern United States*, II, 597–598, 601.

[13] Clark, *History of Manufactures in the United States*, p. 229.

contribute "the full and complete sum of ten thousand Spanish silver milled dollars in solid coin." [14]

This wanted but unwonted abundance of specie did not last long. In three years, 1784–1786, the United States imported from Britain goods valued at £7,591,935. And this figure does not include such items as interest charges on debts due British creditors, the profits of British merchants who sold directly to planters in the South, and the cost of slaves purchased from British firms. During these three years, products exported from the United States to Britain amounted to only £2,486,058. An unfavorable balance of trade, considerably in excess of £5,000,000, acted like a magnet to draw gold and silver from America to Britain. One estimate puts such exportations for the three years at £1,260,000.[15] From all this it is clear that, although the states lost much of their specie, large debts remained that would continue to drain them of coin. The difficulty arose in large measure from an inadequacy of commodity exports in American trade.

In colonial times the area of the Union had sent two types of products to Britain as returns: those produced within the area itself (direct exports), and those obtained in various branches of external commerce (indirect returns). It was the misfortune of Americans in the 1780's that a variety of factors affected adversely both types of returns and that in consequence the country suffered a severe drain of its specie and a continuing burden of debt.

A dozen commodities or groups of commodities produced within the area of the Union had previously provided returns to Britain. Of these, tobacco was by far the most important. In 1763, the Chesapeake area, with tobacco as its staple, accounted for about 44 percent of Britain's trade with the thirteen colonies. Jefferson said in 1787 that one third of the exports of the United States consisted of tobacco.[16] The end of the war found Virginia and Maryland in a depleted state. It was estimated that Virginia had lost 30,000 slaves during the war, most of whom had been taken away by the British invaders. The state's tobacco production in 1783–1784 was about 18 percent less than in 1774 and about 7 percent less in 1784–1785, and although it regained its prewar volume in 1786, it declined again in 1787–1789. During six years, 1785–1790, Britain's annual tobacco imports averaged 44,774,000 pounds less than during

---

[14] Lewis, *The Bank of North America*, pp. 27, 33, 35; Crittenden, *Commerce of North Carolina*, p. 163; N[orman] S. B. Gras, *The Massachusetts First National Bank of Boston* (Vol. IV of *Harvard Studies in Business History;* Cambridge, Mass.: Harvard University Press, 1937), pp. 25, 222; Hedges, *The Browns of Providence*, p. 289.

[15] Roy A. Foulke, *The Sinews of American Commerce* (New York: Dun and Bradstreet, Inc., 1941), p. 102.

[16] Middleton, *Tobacco Coast*, p. 177; Julian P. Boyd and others, eds., *The Papers of Thomas Jefferson* (15 vols., in progress; Princeton, N. J.: Princeton University Press, 1950–1958), XI, 617.

the six years before the war, with an average yearly loss in value of
£843,506.[17]

In addition, tobacco as a return to Britain declined in effectiveness
by reason of relatively low prices in 1783, 1785, and 1786. Observers
attributed such price declines to two main causes. Britain imposed taxes
of 15d. sterling a pound on foreign tobacco consumed there—duties
which, by constricting the home market, decreased the demand. Second,
France granted to a single purchasing agency, the Farmers-General, the
privilege of buying all tobacco imported into that country. This monopoly
tended to keep down the price. In 1785, the Farmers-General made a
contract with Robert Morris which provided that he was to supply them
with all the American tobacco imported into France during three years
1785–1787. This dual monopoly moved Jefferson to charge that it reduced
the price of tobacco in America from 40s. to 22s. 6d. a hundredweight and
cost Virginia and Maryland £400,000 in one year.[18]

The drastic decline of tobacco exports to Britain marked the most
sweeping change in American commerce that occurred immediately after
the war.

In prewar times a second major export, rice, was produced in South
Carolina and Georgia. The losses suffered by the planters there during
the war are suggested by a report that the British carried away 25,000
slaves from South Carolina. So acute was the shortage of labor in the rice
fields in 1783 that slaves brought between £75 and £105 and even then
could be obtained only with difficulty. Since slaves were indispensable
to rice culture, the labor shortage was reflected in low production. In the
four years 1770–1773 the area of the United States exported 277,124,000
pounds of rice; in the four years 1783–1786, the exports amounted to only
128,371,000 pounds, or but 46 percent of the earlier total. Even in colonial
times the market for rice in Britain had been so inadequate that the
government had permitted direct exportation of American rice to the
foreign West Indies and to points in Europe south of Cape Finisterre.
After the war Britain discouraged the use of rice as a food by imposing
high duties on imports consumed there. In consequence the southern
planters had to depend largely upon markets in the West Indies, the
Madeiras, Portugal, Spain, France, Germany, and the Baltic lands. Prices
of South Carolina produce collapsed in 1783 and although they recovered
in 1784, "the revival was for a few months only and was followed by a
drastic downward movement which continued for nearly two years." As

[17] Gray, *History of Agriculture in the Southern United States*, II, 596, 603–605;
Jensen, *The New Nation*, p. 196.

[18] Dumas Malone, *Jefferson and His Time* (2 vols.; Boston: Little, Brown and
Company, 1948–1951), II, *Jefferson and the Rights of Man*, 39–44, 46–48; Gray,
History of Agriculture in the Southern United States, II, 603–604; Frederick L. Nussbaum, "American Tobacco and French Politics, 1783–1789," *Political Science Quarterly*, XL, No. 4 (December, 1925), 501–503.

a means of paying for imports, rice was probably only half as efficacious in 1783–1786 as it had been before the war. Exports to Britain in 1784–1789 averaged £196,526 a year less than in 1769–1774.[19]

Before 1775, the British government had so esteemed American naval stores—pitch and tar—that it had paid bounties to colonial producers of those products. Under the stimulus of such aids the industry developed steadily in America, particularly in the pinelands of North Carolina. That colony exported 130,000 barrels of pitch, tar, and turpentine in 1775, most of it going to Britain. The war had a decisive effect on the industry. Exports to Britain declined sharply in the 1780's by reason of the discontinuance of the bounty payments, with the result that increased shipments went to the northern states. It appears that naval stores as returns to Britain were not a third as valuable in 1788 as before the war.[20]

Another product of South Carolina, indigo, had also been favored by a British bounty in colonial times. Exports to Britain in 1765–1775 averaged 700,000 pounds a year. In 1785, Jefferson sought to interest the French in buying the American product but was told that they made plenty of it in their colonies and "that they thought it better than ours." Although no longer enjoying the British bounty, American indigo received some favors in Britain and continued to go there after the war. Since the production of indigo depended wholly on slave labor and was linked with the cultivation of rice, it is likely that in the years 1782–1785 it lost much of its prewar importance as an export. Probably its yearly value did not then exceed £50,000.[21]

The southern states clearly suffered from a severe deficiency of returns after the war, by reason of the difficulties that beset the production or marketing of tobacco, rice, indigo, and naval stores. Gloomy indeed was their prospect of selling produce to Britain in the mid-1780's on favorable terms as a means of paying debts and of buying adequate supplies of European goods at reasonable prices.

Equally depressing was the plight of the states north of Maryland. That area had habitually bought British goods greatly in excess of the value of its direct returns to Britain. For instance, in 1770, Pennsylvania, New Jersey, New York, and New England imported from Britain products

[19] Gray, History of Agriculture in the Southern United States, II, 593, 610, 1030; George Rogers Taylor, "Wholesale Commodity Prices at Charleston, South Carolina, 1732–1791," Journal of Economic and Business History, IV, No. 2 (February, 1932), 367.

[20] Justin Williams, "English Mercantilism and Carolina Naval Stores, 1705–1776," Journal of Southern History, I, No. 2 (May, 1935), 8; Crittenden, Commerce of North Carolina, p. 160; Benzanson, Prices and Inflation During the Revolution: Pennsylvania, p. 179.

[21] Jefferson Papers (Boyd), IX, 141. Ernest Ludlow Bogart, Economic History of the American People (2d ed.; New York: Longmans, Green and Company, 1939), p. 58; Commerce of Rhode Island, 1726–1800 (Massachusetts Historical Society, Collections, Vols. LXIX, LXX; Boston: The Society, 1914–1915), LXX, 242.

valued at £1,410,000 and exported thither commodities valued at only £178,000, thereby incurring a deficit of £1,232,000. After the war, the scanty direct exports of the area to Britain were more meager than before.

One colonial export of the northern area which disappeared after 1775 had not figured in the statistics of British-American trade: ships built there and sold to British merchants. In colonial times, British law defined vessels built in the British colonies as British vessels, entitled to engage fully and freely in all British commerce, from most of which foreign-built vessels were excluded. After 1782, ships newly built in the states became foreign vessels in the eyes of British law and therefore disqualified from nearly all trade with British ports. A vigorous shipbuilding industry had taken root in the colonies during the seventeenth century, largely because English shipowners found it cheaper to have vessels built in New England than in England. By 1720, more than half the tonnage of American-built ships was contracted for by British merchants, who paid for them with British goods exported to the colonies. In the 1770's, New Hampshire and Massachusetts produced at least half of the tonnage of American shipyards. Massachusetts then built on the average about 125 vessels a year.[22]

Shipbuilding survived in New England during the war, as merchants replaced small craft with larger and faster vessels, largely under the stimulus of privateering. Thus Elias Hasket Derby in 1783 had seven new ships, four of 300 to 350 tons, as contrasted with seven small sloops and schooners in 1775. Thanks to such wartime construction and to prizes captured by privateers, the merchant fleet of American shipowners in 1783 was adequate to the needs of postwar trade. The shipbuilding industry then felt the loss of the onetime British market for American vessels. The output of Massachusetts dwindled to fifteen or twenty ships in 1785; in 1789 New England yards laid only eleven keels. The war had deprived the Union of another means of paying for British goods—a loss amounting, perhaps, to as much as £100,000 a year.[23]

Misfortune struck another American industry, the whale fishery of Massachusetts, which had yielded exports to Britain in colonial days. In 1775, Nantucket employed more than 150 vessels of 15,000 tons that brought in spermaceti, a waxy substance used in making candles, sperm or whale oil used for lighting, and whalebone used in making corsets and fans. The industry all but vanished during the war. Among the fishing villages Nantucket alone tried to carry on, with the result that it lost 151 vessels and 1,200 seamen to the British and the elements. Only 24 of its

[22] Clark, *History of Manufactures in the United States*, p. 95; Weeden, *Economic and Social History of New England*, II, 764–765; Adams, *New England in the Republic*, p. 119.

[23] Weeden, *Economic and Social History of New England*, II, 776–777, 806; Clark, *History of Manufactures in the United States*, p. 147; Adams, *New England in the Republic*, p. 201.

whalers remained in 1784. Massachusetts then tried to reinvigorate the industry with bounties, but the resulting revival coincided with low prices and a declining demand. During the war, Americans had grown accustomed to tallow candles and continued to use them afterward. More important, Britain in December, 1783, closed completely its once lucrative market by subjecting American whale oil to a prohibitive import duty of £18 3s. a ton. In 1784, the Providence firm of Brown and Benson sent 160 tons of oil to Boston, only to lose £2,000 on the shipment. In 1785 the *Massachusetts Centinel* asserted that the British duty had ruined the whale fishery and had deprived the state of half its total exports to Britain. The whaling fleet of the state dwindled from 300 vessels in 1775 to 100 vessels in 1789.[24]

Another export product that decreased in importance after the war was iron. In five years, 1770–1774, colonial pig iron sent to Britain averaged 3,929 tons a year; exports of bar iron averaged 1,276 tons.[25] Parliament had attempted to foster this trade by admitting American crude iron into Britain duty-free and by forbidding the colonies to erect mills, forges, and furnaces in which their ores would be converted into nails, sheet iron, or steel.[26] The war stopped the iron trade with Britain and increased the consumption of crude iron in the states to the extent that exports were negligible thereafter. In twelve months of 1791–1792, the United States sent to Britain only 797 tons of pig iron and 21 tons of bar iron—or about 16 percent of the annual exports before the war, when the total probably had a value of about £62,000 a year.[27]

In the colonial era, furs derived from the Indian trade of the Northwest were valuable exports to Europe. Pennsylvania and New York had shared this resource with the French. The war shut the states out of the traffic and enabled British merchants in Canada to monopolize it. They had the superior route to the interior by way of the St. Lawrence River and the Great Lakes. After 1783, the British, in order to retain their monopoly, refused to evacuate seven posts they held within the United States along the Canadian border. These included Niagara, Detroit, and Michilimackinac. The furs obtained by the British in the 1780's had a yearly value

[24] Hohman, *The American Whaleman*, pp. 35, 36; Weeden, *Economic and Social History of New England*, II, 748, 749; Hedges, *The Browns of Providence*, pp. 295–296; Adams, *New England in the Republic*, pp. 117, 121; Johnson, *History of Commerce*, I, 161; J[ohn] Franklin Jameson, ed., "Letters of Stephen Higginson, 1783–1804" (American Historical Association, *Annual Report . . . 1896*, 2 vols.; Washington: Government Printing Office, 1897), I, 723.

[25] Arthur Cecil Bining, *British Regulation of the Colonial Iron Industry* (Philadelphia: University of Pennsylvania Press, 1933), p. 133.

[26] *Ibid.*, pp. 71–72.

[27] Bining, *Pennsylvania Iron Manufacture in the Eighteenth Century*, pp. 159, 177–178, 182–183; Arthur Harrison Cole, *Wholesale Commodity Prices in the United States* (Cambridge, Mass.: Harvard University Press, 1938, with *Statistical Supplement*), Supplement, pp. 62, 64, 65, 69.

of £200,000, at least half of which represented the losses of the states arising from their exclusion from the traffic in the vast area now comprising Ohio, Indiana, Illinois, Michigan, Wisconsin, and eastern Minnesota.[28] When Jefferson in 1785 summarized the condition and prospects of trade between the United States and France he alluded to furs and peltries, observing: "Our posts being in the hands of the English, we are cut off from that article. I am not sure even, whether we are not obliged to buy of them, for our own use. When these posts are given up, if ever they are, we shall be able to furnish France with skins and furs, to the amount of two million livres, in exchange for her merchandise; but at present, these articles are to be counted as nothing." [29]

Of minor consequence were other exports which the colonies had sent to Britain. Charleston was the entrepôt of a trade in deerskins obtained from the Creeks, Choctaws, and Chickasaws, who occupied the back country of South Carolina and Georgia. This trade fell on evil days after the war by reason of conflicts between the southern frontiersmen and the Spaniards in Florida. In May–July, 1784, the Creeks, Choctaws, and Chickasaws made treaties with Spain by which they pledged to admit into their nations only such traders as had been licensed by the Spaniards. Spain then granted a monopoly of the southern fur trade to a British loyalist firm, Panton, Leslie and Company. Such actions antagonized the southern Americans, then at war with the Creeks. In the 1780's South Carolina's trade in deerskins appeared to be at best only a precarious source of exports to Britain.[30]

The unimportance of all other returns to Europe—potash, pearlash, flaxseed, masts, yards, bowsprits, and spars—is illustrated by the trade of Connecticut, a producer of all those products. In 1774, its direct exports to Britain mounted to only £10,000. In 1784, a merchant proposed to build ships there, saying that otherwise it would be "utterly impossible for us to make remittances to the amount of the goods we import." Stephen Higginson wrote in 1785 that Boston's exports of pot and pearl ashes were "far short of what it was before the War." [31]

---

[28] Wayne E. Stevens, "The Organization of the British Fur Trade, 1760–1800," *Mississippi Valley Historical Review*, III, No. 2 (September, 1916), 182; Louise Phelps Kellogg, *The British Régime in Wisconsin and the Northwest* (State Historical Society of Wisconsin, *Publications*; Madison: The Society, 1935), pp. 47–48, 198, 202; James Alton James, "Some Phases of the History of the Northwest, 1783–1786," Mississippi Valley Historical Association, *Proceedings* (1913–1914), VII, 180–181.

[29] *Jefferson Papers* (Boyd), IX, 118.

[30] Lawrence W. Kinnaird, ed., *Spain in the Mississippi Valley, 1765–1794* (American Historical Association, *Annual Report* . . . *1945*, Vols. II–IV; Washington: Government Printing Office, 1946, 1949), III, xv–xvi.

[31] Weeden, *Economic and Social History of New England*, II, 758; Martin, *Trade of the Connecticut Valley*, p. 41; Jameson, "Letters of Stephen Higginson," p. 719.

PAYMENTS FOR IMPORTS: INDIRECT RETURNS

The postwar inadequacy of American exports to Britain was matched by similar deficiencies of those kinds of products, which in colonial times had been secured in foreign trades and sent to Britain as returns. In all such trades the states met conditions which hampered their efforts to obtain ample buying power abroad.

Before the Revolution the British West Indies had ranked high among the sources of remittances to Britain. In July, 1783, the British government, in order to promote its imperial interests, excluded American shipping from its West Indian islands and prohibited them from importing salted fish and salted meats from the United States. The exact effects of the new British policy cannot be known, in view of the oft-repeated assertions that American merchants found ways of evading the restraints. Many bits of evidence, however, indicate that American trade suffered severe losses.

Channing, who minimizes the decline of the West Indian trade, cites records which show the following reductions of ship entries at American ports in 1788 as compared with 1766: a decline of 23 percent for ships arriving from all the West Indies; of 46 percent for ships coming from the British islands. New England's fishery did not fare so well in the 1780's as before the war. Comparing the years 1765–1775 with the period 1786–1790, one finds that the proceeds from New England fish shipped to all the West Indian islands dropped from $448,000 to $284,000 a year. The almost ruinous decline of the New England shipbuilding industry reflected the shrinkage of the West Indian trade. In 1770, the northern colonies exported 6,692 horses to the West Indies; in the years 1790–1794, such exports to all places averaged only 5,540.[32] At Philadelphia, the price of Indian corn, a leading export to the islands, fell from 6s. 3d. a bushel in mid-July, 1783, to 3s. 6d. in February, 1785, and the price of flour—another important West Indian supply commodity—went down from 28s. a barrel in 1784 to 17s. 6d. in December, 1787. A merchant firm at Philadelphia complained in August, 1787, that "the late restrictions of the British have stopped every avenue to these islands. They have so deranged us that we are quite at a loss what to do with our brig. We have laid her up for the present in hopes that we may sell her." [33] The price of pork also declined at this time. "Pork is not likely to be wanted"; "Beef a perfect glut, both New England and . . . our own . . ."; "The sales of New York and Connecticut beef will be very small"—such are comments of Philadelphia

[32] Weeden, *Economic and Social History of New England*, II, 832; Percy Wells Bidwell and John I. Falconer, *History of Agriculture in the Northern United States* (Washington: Carnegie Institution of Washington, 1925), pp. 136, 137.

[33] Bezanson, *Prices and Inflation During the Revolution: Pennsylvania*, pp. 120, 103.

merchants in 1787–1788. A merchant at New York found the price of beef so low in November, 1788 that he advised against selling, and a Philadelphia merchant said about this time: "Neither can any kind of salted provisions [be sent to the British West Indies] . . . , so tight is the English Government on the people of their own plantations." Reporting from Connecticut, a merchant wrote in 1786: "Our West India business is ten times worse than it was before the War. Trade is almost at a stand." "The Revolution," wrote Madison in July, 1785, "has robbed ‿ᴗ ᴜf our trade with the West Indies, the only one which yielded us a favorable balance, without reopening any other channels to compensate for it." [34]

The exclusion of American shipping from the British West Indies deprived the states of another source of returns—freights once earned by ships that carried sugar, logwood, and other products from the islands to Britain. It had been common before the war for New Englanders to freight a vessel in the Caribbean and sell it on arrival in London. Such business was lost to them after 1783.[35]

Supplementing the British West Indies were the Caribbean islands of France: Martinique, Guadeloupe, and Haiti or Saint Dominque, the western part of Hispaniola. The United States carried on an extensive trade with them after the war. In August, 1784, the French government decreed that American vessels up to sixty tons might import into the islands American produce except wheat and flour. Salt fish and salt beef were subjected to duties of 3 livres a quintal or barrel. Only by special permission, in times of scarcity, could American flour be imported. The United States received the privilege of exporting the products of the islands, except sugar. Such regulations—designed to foster the French fishery and to confine sugar exports to France—permitted the states to supply the islands with most of their provisions.[36]

Undoubtedly, the new French policy reduced the market for American flour. The French islands, however, took nearly one half the output of the American fisheries. With the closing of the British West Indies to American fish, that commodity became so plentiful in the French islands that in 1786 American merchants "suffered great losses upon all they shipped thither, and the fishery exhibited . . . [extreme] symptoms of decline. . . ." [37]

At the close of the war, Spain withdrew the temporary privilege of trading with its West Indian islands, Cuba, Puerto Rico, and Hispaniola,

---

[34] *Ibid.*, pp. 138–140. Martin, *Trade of the Connecticut Valley*, p. 38; *Letters and Other Writings of James Madison* (4 vols.; Philadelphia: J. B. Lippincott and Company, 1867), I, 158.

[35] Jameson, "Letters of Stephen Higginson," p. 719.

[36] Pitkin, *Statistical View of the Commerce of the United States*, pp. 216–217.

[37] Arthur Harrison Cole, ed., *Industrial and Commercial Correspondence of Alexander Hamilton* (Chicago: A. W. Shaw Company, 1928), p. 169.

which it had granted to the United States in 1780, and reinstated its traditional policy of excluding foreign merchants and vessels from direct trade with its colonies and of requiring that they import goods only from Spain. "Spain and Portugal," wrote Jefferson in 1793, "refuse to those parts of America which they govern all direct intercourse with any people but themselves." [38] For a short time after 1780 trade with the Spanish islands had been a valuable asset to the Union. The extent to which the Spaniards succeeded in shutting out American traders after 1780 is uncertain. But one thing is certain: established merchants disliked to rely indefinitely on illegal methods of trade that exposed them to sudden seizures and the uncertain demands of alien officials.

Before 1774, the commerce of the colonies with southern Europe had produced returns to Britain in that the proceeds had been used there for purchasing British goods. Jefferson, who was well informed on the point, estimated that in prewar times the countries adjacent to the Mediterranean Sea had absorbed annually one sixth of American wheat exported and one fourth in value of the fish, thereby employing eighty to one hundred ships. The colonial trade had been sheltered by the British flag, made effective, presumably, by protection money paid to the governments of Tripoli, Tunis, and Algeria, which, together with their subjects, engaged in a species of piracy or commercial racketeering. After the war the American trade vanished, a prey of the marauders. Jefferson described their vessels as "sharp built and swift" and "crowded with men, one-third Turks and the rest Moors, of determined bravery and resting their sole hopes on boarding." In 1785, the Algerines seized two American ships and held twenty-one captives as slaves. The pirates menaced the seamen with "the perils of the engagement preceding . . . surrender," "temporary deprivation of liberty, perhaps chains," "the danger of the pest," and "possible delays of the ransom." "Our navigation, then, into the Mediterranean," Jefferson proclaimed, "has not been resumed at all since the peace." [39]

The British fishery at Newfoundland also figured in the postwar losses of American commerce. The New England colonies had long traded with the island, supplying it with provisions, lumber, and rum in return for coin, bills of exchange, and fish suitable to the West Indian markets. After the war, Britain excluded American vessels from the island and so restricted its trade with the states as virtually to prohibit that trade. Although the

[38] "Report of the Secretary of State on the Privileges and Restrictions on the Commerce of the United States in Foreign Countries, December 16, 1793," in *State Papers of the United States* (10 vols.; Boston: T. B. Wait and Sons, 1817), I, 430.

[39] "Report of the Secretary of State Relative to the Mediterranean Trade, December 28, 1790," *ibid.*, X, 41–47; Louis B. Wright and Julia H. Macleod, *The First Americans in North Africa* (Princeton, N. J.: Princeton University Press, 1945), pp. 16–17.

values involved were not great, the loss was injurious to an area sorely deficient in exports to Britain.[40]

In the years before the Revolution the importation of slaves into the colonies of the European powers had provided American merchants with returns to England in the form of southern produce, coin, and bills of exchange. The tobacco colonies had not contributed much to the American traffic, for they purchased nine tenths of their slaves from British traders. In the lower South, where they were active, colonial mercha...s often bought slaves for local sale from the British traders, who maintained several exporting depots or castles on the coast of Africa. The British colonies in 1750 imported 10,050 slaves from Africa. Since the colonial traders then carried on about 13 percent of this trade, and also shared in the lucrative traffic with the Spanish colonies, their part of the proceeds amounted to a sizable sum. During the Revolution the participation of Americans in the traffic ceased altogether. The business revived soon after the end of the war, particularly in South Carolina, which imported 7,000 slaves in 1783–1785. But the trade was doomed. By 1779, all the states had banned importations except North Carolina, South Carolina, and Georgia. North Carolina levied a prohibitive duty in 1786, and South Carolina imposed a temporary prohibition in 1787. During the years 1787–1788 the New England states forbade their citizens to engage in the traffic. Despite the flurry of activity immediately after the war, it seemed in 1787 that the discredited traffic was drying up. As a source of returns in late colonial times it had yielded annually substantial returns to Britain, by reason of high profits necessary to offset its repulsive features.[41]

New trades as well as old suffered from difficulties arising from the war. West of the Allegheny Mountains pioneer outposts had barely taken root when they became involved in serious commercial troubles. By 1784, expanding settlements bordered numerous streams flowing toward the Mississippi. Such were the frontier farms in eastern Tennessee near the headwaters of the Tennessee River. Another cluster of settlements surrounded Nashville on the Cumberland. Pioneers were swarming into Kentucky, occupying the Kentucky and Green River valleys, and pushing northward toward the Ohio. The Union now held the old French villages

[40] Ralph Greenlee Lounsbury, *The British Fishery at Newfoundland, 1634–1763* (Vol. XXVII of *Yale Historical Publications;* New Haven, Conn.: Yale University Press, 1934), p. 325; Andrew Cunningham McLaughlin, *The Confederation and the Constitution, 1783–1789* (Vol. X of *The American Nation*, A. B. Hart, ed.; New York: Harper & Brothers, 1905), p. 73; Jameson, "Letters of Stephen Higginson," p. 719.

[41] Middleton, *Tobacco Coast,* pp. 136–138; Elizabeth Donnan, "The Slave Trade into South Carolina before the Revolution," *American Historical Review,* XXXIII, No. 4 (July, 1928), 806–828; East, *Business Enterprise,* p. 250; Crittenden, *Commerce of North Carolina,* p. 156; W[illiam] E. Burghardt Du Bois, *The Suppression of the African Slave-Trade to the United States of America, 1638–1870* (New York: The Social Science Press, 1954), pp. 51–52.

of Cahokia and Kaskaskia in the Illinois country and Vincennes on the Wabash. From Virginia, pioneers were moving into the valley of the Kanawha; in western Pennsylvania, farms and villages along the Monongahela, Allegheny, and Ohio rivers overspread the lands in the vicinity of Pittsburgh.

The spearheads of this advance were the settlements in Tennessee and Kentucky, inhabited by 109,000 people in 1790. "Do you think to prevent the emigration from a barren country loaded with taxes and impoverished with debts, to the most luxurious soil in the world?" asked a pioneer on the Ohio in 1787. "You may as well endeavor to prevent the fishes from gathering on a bank in the sea which affords them plenty of nourishment." [42] The frontier settlements were well suited to the kinds of products that then made up about 56 percent of the total exports of the Union. The staples included livestock, Indian corn, wheat, flour, beef, pork, whiskey, and lumber. Such products were floated down the streams on rafts or flatboats to Natchez or New Orleans, partly for the use of the Spaniards in western Florida and Louisiana and partly for exportation to the West Indies and southern Europe. In return the interior settlements obtained firearms, powder, cloth, notions, edged tools, and iron utensils from older communities. Whether such imports were transported across the mountains from the East or were brought up the Mississippi in keelboats, or were carried overland along the Natchez Trace from Natchez to Nashville, the interior settlements depended upon their exports down the rivers to provide them with the money for paying for the manufactures they needed. [43]

By the Independence Treaty of 1783, Britain recognized the right of the United States to navigate the Mississippi from its source to the Gulf, Britain having received that right from France in 1763. Entrenched at Natchez and New Orleans, and occupying both banks of the Mississippi between those towns, the Spaniards in 1784 refused to recognize or respect a British grant to which they had not consented. They feared that the American advance would soon force them out of Florida and Louisiana. Consequently, they decided to strike at the Mississippi trade of Kentucky and Tennessee, seeking thereby to force the settlers into a partnership that would either incorporate them into the Spanish empire or place them under a government that would be subordinate to Spain. To this end, the Spanish court in 1784 instructed the governor of Louisiana to announce that the United States did not have the right of free navigation of the Mississippi; whereupon the Spanish authorities in Louisiana tried

---

[42] Quoted in McLaughlin, *The Confederation and Constitution*, p. 45.
[43] Arthur Preston Whitaker, *The Spanish-American Frontier, 1783–1795* (Boston: Houghton Mifflin Company, 1927), pp. 95–96; Arthur P. Whitaker, "Reed and Forde: Merchant Adventurers of Philadelphia: Their Trade with Spanish New Orleans," *Pennsylvania Magazine of History and Biography*, LXI, No. 3 (July, 1937), 241.

to close the river altogether to American trade. They seized American boats at Natchez and confiscated their cargoes. Late in 1787 the Spanish court replaced the embargo with a tax of 25 percent on American products. The Spaniards did not succeed in closing the river completely, except during short periods, but even so American shipments down the river were negligible until 1790. In the meantime, the Spanish measures had involved Kentucky and Tennessee in a turmoil of intrigue and unrest.[44]

In 1793 Jefferson summarized the restrictions of European countries on American exports that shackled Americans in their efforts to obtain buying power in Britain. He pointed out that Britain collected heavy import duties on American tobacco and rice, prohibited the importation into Britain of American fish, whale oil, and salted meats, and ordinarily subjected American grain to prohibitive duties. Ships built in the United States could not be sold to British merchants. Vessels owned by Americans could not trade with Britain's colonies in America and could carry only the products of the United States to Britain. In the West Indies, Spain prohibited the states from trading with its colonies; Britain excluded American fish and salted meats from its islands; France subjected American fish to a heavy duty and received American salt pork and breadstuff (except Indian corn) under temporary laws. All these handicaps to American trade had existed in 1785.[45]

A COMMERCIAL DEPRESSION

The economic conditions existing in the Union in the 1780's proved to be extremely important. They formed an essential part of the background of the making of the federal Constitution. That event in turn has exerted an enormous influence on the economic development of the country since 1789.

Evidences of difficulties ahead became visible soon after the war. The immediate cause of distress was an excessive importation of European goods at a time when the states lacked adequate returns. In May, 1783, observers reported an oversupply of English goods in New York and Philadelphia. Speculation in imports reminded a Boston merchant in July of the South Sea Bubble: enough goods had come in recently to last for seven years. Prices dropped to the point that merchants had to sell at auction or at a profit barely above costs and charges.[46] Payments to Britain drained the country of coin, thereby lessening the people's capacity to pay. In April, 1784, a Charleston merchant affirmed that he had never

[44] Kinnaird, *Spain in the Mississippi Valley*, III, xv–xxiii; Frederic L. Paxson, *History of the American Frontier, 1763–1893* (Boston: Houghton Mifflin Company, 1924), pp. 82–84.

[45] *American State Papers* (Wait), I, 431–432.

[46] Jensen, *The New Nation*, p. 186; East, *Business Enterprise*, pp. 240, 245, 246.

known money to be so scarce. Of Hartford it was said in July that the "alarming scarcity of money creates an almost total stagnation of business." A writer in Maryland referred to a pervading shortage of specie and urged an issue of paper currency. Another report from Charleston in June, 1785, blamed the scarcity of money for ruining merchants. Describing Boston, Elbridge Gerry wrote in 1785: "The scarcity of money in consequence of our excessive and extravagant importations of British frippery has occasioned stagnation of trade." "The scarcity of money," said James Warren, also alluding to the Boston area, "is beyond your conception." [47]

The money shortage contributed to the distress of importers because they commonly sold their goods within the states on credit. They soon found that dealers and retailers could not pay their debts when due. At Providence, the firm of Brown and Benson suffered from this trouble. "The collecting of your debts goes on very slowly as does the sales of your goods in my hands," reported the agent of Jeremiah Wadsworth at Hartford in July, 1784, adding later: "as to trusting . . . , it never was nor ever will be so good as the goods themselves, however poor they may be. I had rather have them—and I would keep them till they were rotten before I would credit in these bad times." In the summer of 1785, "country buyers could not pay for what they had bought." [48] In the face of prospective losses, solvent merchants put pressure on their debtors. Ensuing legal actions forced many traders into bankruptcy. Some fairly substantial merchants failed—among them Clement Biddle of Baltimore and Samuel A. Otis of Boston. Other prominent merchants, including George Meade, Haym Solomon, and Robert Morris in Philadelphia, the Purviance brothers in Baltimore, and Jackson and Higginson in Boston found themselves hard pressed for funds. Ruin befell many small inexperienced traders who, unable to collect money from their debtors, lost their assets through forced sales for the benefit of their creditors. Hamilton later spoke of a "number of adventurers without capital and in many instances without information, who at that epoch rushed into trade, and were obliged to make sacrifices to support a transient credit." We read that in 1785 daily bankruptcies occurred in Baltimore and that many new merchants and shopkeepers "set up since the War" failed in New York.[49]

Banking operations both reflected and intensified the ills of the time. In the face of the exportation of coin to Britain, the Bank of North America

[47] Jensen, *The New Nation*, pp. 187, 189; Martin, *Trade of the Connecticut Valley*, p. 40; Philip A. Crowl, *Maryland During and After the Revolution* (Johns Hopkins University *Studies in Historical and Political Science*, Series LXI, No. 1; Baltimore: The Johns Hopkins Press, 1943), p. 89; Adams, *New England in the Republic*, p. 122; *Warren-Adams Letters* (Massachusetts Historical Society, *Collections*, Vols. LXXII–LXXIII; Boston: The Society, 1917, 1925), LXXIII, 264.

[48] Martin, *Trade of the Connecticut Valley*, pp. 40, 41; Weeden, *Economic and Social History of New England*, II, 819.

[49] East, *Business Enterprise*, p. 257; Jensen, *The New Nation*, p. 192.

—in order to protect its specie reserves—reduced its loans and insisted upon payment of debts when due. Its strict policies exposed it to a storm of criticism. In March, 1785, the Pennsylvania Assembly received a petition from inhabitants of Chester County who charged that "the best security" would not enable a person to borrow from the bank. The petitioners asserted that they had "repeatedly seen the stopping of discounts at the Bank operate on the trading part of the community with a degree of violence scarcely inferior to that of a stagnation of blood in the human body, hurrying the wretched merchant who hath debts to pay into the hands of griping usurers . . . ." [50]

At Boston, the Massachusetts Bank, founded in 1784, paid dividends of only 2½ per cent in the first half of 1785. That bank limited loans to thirty days and allowed one director to veto an application. When discounting, the bank paid out its notes to the borrower but required him to pay the interest in advance in coin. In its effort to reduce loans the bank made provision for reducing drastically its capital stock. Some of its stockholders had used their stock as collateral for loans. When such loans were not paid, the bank found it embarrassing not to extend them. Such favoritism to stockholders evoked criticism from would-be borrowers whose applications had been rejected. By retiring most of the stock, the bank sought to squeeze out a debtor element that was using the stock as a means of securing and renewing loans.[51]

Since a depression means, first of all, depressed prices, the hard times of the 1780's were indeed a depression, for prices became severely depressed. Beginning in mid-1784, wholesale commodity prices at Charleston, Philadelphia, and New York started to fall, and—with the exception of an upsurge at Charleston in 1786—followed a downward trend until 1788 or mid-1789. During these years prices dropped about 25 percent in Philadelphia and Charleston.[52] At Philadelphia, some declines were as follows: flour, from an index figure of 120 to 95; beef, from 130 to 98; pork, from 130 to 90; iron, from 155 to 100; naval stores from 120 to 65.[53] Speaking of Virginia, Madison said in July, 1785: "In every point of view, indeed, the trade of this country is in a deplorable condition. A comparison of current prices here with those in the northern States, either at this time or at any time since the peace, will show that the loss direct on our produce, and indeed on our imports, is not less than fifty per cent." [54]

Industries dependent upon foreign trade felt particularly the force of the depression. An English newspaper said in 1784 that Boston's fishery

[50] Bezanson, *Prices and Inflation During the Revolution: Pennsylvania*, p. 260; Lewis, *The Bank of North America*, pp. 56–57 note.

[51] Gras, *The Massachusetts First National Bank*, pp. 44–45, 52–53.

[52] Cole, *Wholesale Commodity Prices*, p. 106 (chart).

[53] Bezanson, *Prices and Inflation During the Revolution: Pennsylvania*, pp. 81, 127, 160, 179.

[54] *Writings of Madison* (1867), I, 158.

was "exceedingly trifling." Weeden estimates that in 1786–1790 New England's receipts from the cod fishery averaged $464,400 a year less than in the period 1765–1775—a loss amounting to 43 percent.[55] Boston's distilling business was reported in 1784 as "entirely at a stand" and its peltry and fur trade as "entirely over." Of the losses to American shipping in the postwar years, Jefferson said in 1793 that British restrictions had "already lost us in our commerce with that country and its possessions between eight and nine hundred vessels of near 40,000 tons burden, according to statements from official materials in which we have confidence. This involves a proportional loss of seamen, shipwrights, and shipbuilding . . . ." The decline of the fishery and the exclusion from practically all the trade of the British Empire of American-owned vessels, of ships newly built in the United States, and of privateers constructed during the war—such factors combined to put the shipbuilding industry in an acute state of depression.[56]

Nor did trade with Britain escape the shock. It soon appeared that the inadequacy of returns would prevent Americans from paying for the heavy postwar imports. An English newspaper in 1784 noted the arrival at London of two ships in ballast from America bringing only specie. At Philadelphia, merchant Thomas FitzSimons deplored in 1785 that markets for American produce were so restricted that "exportation is very unprofitable." Bad crops in South Carolina in 1784 aggravated its shortage of returns. The inability of British exporters to collect debts incurred by American importers caused five large London firms to fail in August, 1784. Exportations to the states declined sharply thereafter—so much so that the total for 1785 and 1786 combined amounted to £3,911,000, as compared with £3,679,000 for 1784 alone. By the summer of 1785 New England merchants were getting their English debts extended. The account of Brown and Benson on December 31, 1784, showed a sum of £26,144 owed to an English firm. The American company still owed £23,706 of this debt at the end of 1789, having succeeded in paying only £2,438 during five years.[57]

Writing in behalf of the Bank of North America, James Wilson presented a convincing analysis of the postwar depression.

. . . the disagreeable state of our commerce has been the effect of extravagant and injudicious importation. During the War, our ports were in a great measure

[55] Weeden, *Economic and Social History of New England*, II, 832.

[56] Jensen, *The New Nation*, p. 191; *American State Papers* (Wait), I, 436; J[ohn] Franklin Jameson, ed., "Letters of Phineas Bond, British Consul at Philadelphia to the Foreign Office of Great Britain, 1787, 1788, 1789" (American Historical Association, *Annual Report . . . 1896*, 2 vols.; Washington: Government Printing Office, 1897), I, 611.

[57] Jensen, *The New Nation*, pp. 187, 189–190; East, *Business Enterprise*, p. 245; Weeden, *Economic and Social History of New England*, II, 819; Hedges, *The Browns of Providence*, pp. 293, 300.

blocked up. Imported articles were scarce and dear; and we felt the disadvantages of a stagnation in business . . . . When hostilities ceased, the floodgates of commerce were opened; and an inundation of foreign manufactures overflowed the United States: we seemed to have forgot, that to pay was as necessary in trade as to purchase; and we observed no proportion between our imports, and our produce and other natural means of remittance. What was the consequence? Those who made any payments made them chiefly in specie; and in that way diminished our circulation. Others made no remittances at all, and thereby injured our credit. This account of what happened between the European merchants and our importers corresponds exactly with what happened between our importers and the retailers spread over the different parts of the United States. The retailers, if they paid at all, paid in specie: and thus every operation, foreign and domestic, had an injurious effect on our credit, our circulation, and our commerce.[58]

[58] Randolph G. Adams, ed., *Selected Political Essays of James Wilson* (New York: Alfred A. Knopf, Inc., 1930), pp. 145–146, quoted in Jensen, *The New Nation*, pp. 190–191.

CHAPTER IV

Depression Remedies

HARD is the lot of one who, burdened with taxes and debts and destitute of cash, is beset by falling prices of the things he makes and sells. The distressing conditions of the 1780's seemed especially deplorable because they resurrected old evils from which Americans had suffered repeatedly in colonial times and which they hoped would be done away with by the war and independence. Moreover, the depression threatened to get worse and to overwhelm its victims.

Deepening distress and dreary prospects impelled active men to think about remedies. A profusion of letters, essays, reports, and statutes, setting forth a variety of proposals for reform, exhibited substantial agreement as to the causes of the depression but differed widely with respect to measures that should be adopted. Nearly everyone who thought about such things believed that the country needed more money, but bitter disagreements arose over the ways and means of obtaining it. The remedy of promoting foreign trade—of enlarging the outside markets for American products—made a wide appeal. Many critics of the old order sought salvation in the fostering of home manufactures that would presumably reduce the importation of foreign goods, stop the outflow of specie, and end the domestic scarcity of coin. Many southern leaders saw in the West an opportunity for growth that would release energies then repressed by the restraints and burdens of the depression.[1]

EFFORTS TO ENLARGE FOREIGN MARKETS

In its diplomacy after the war Congress sought in the main to extend the markets abroad for American ships and products. Such were its principal objectives in its dealings with Britain, the Barbary States, and Spain. John Adams made the initial attempt to secure concessions from Britain. As the first American minister to Britain he negotiated with the ministry

[1] *Writings of Madison* (1867), I, 92–93, 136–139.

from June, 1785, to February, 1788, seeking to induce it to evacuate the northern posts it held within the United States, and to open the British West Indies, Canada, Nova Scotia, and Newfoundland fully to the vessels and products of the United States. To gain the latter objective he submitted a draft of a treaty which proposed that Britain and the United States should each receive into its ports the other's goods and vessels on the same terms and under the same duties that applied to its own vessels and goods. Adams argued that Britain's restraints on American trade, by preventing the United States from obtaining adequate remittances to Britain, would disable American merchants from paying debts due British creditors, would compel Americans to foster manufactures as a means of freeing the nation from British goods, and would force the states to enact navigation laws hostile to British shipping.[2]

Adams had not been in London a month before he realized that Britain would not enter into a commercial treaty favorable to the Union. He reported that the British believed that Americans would continue to buy British manufactures because they were cheaper or better than other goods. The ministry sought to promote British sea power by fostering the British fishery and the British merchant marine; this aim would not be abandoned. Neither the Union nor the individual state could put pressure on the British authorities. Congress lacked the power to enact retaliatory tariffs, embargoes, or navigation laws; the states would not cooperate in adopting uniform measures; one state acting alone would be impotent. Adams concluded that only by endowing Congress with full and exclusive power over foreign trade could the Union offer concessions and inflict penalties that would be effective in securing favors from foreign countries.[3]

So adamant was the British opposition to a commercial treaty that Adams was obliged to concentrate on the issue of the northern posts. This subject involved him in prolonged, complicated arguments over the fourth article of the Treaty of 1783, which provided that "creditors on either side, shall meet with no lawful impediments to the recovery of the full value in sterling money, of all bona fide debts heretofore contracted." In order to justify its continued occupation of the northern posts, in violation of the treaty, the ministry charged that the states had consistently violated this article.[4]

Adams admitted the futility of his mission in December, 1785, when he said: "I find myself at the end of my tether; no step that I can take, no language I can hold will do any good, or indeed much harm." [5]

[2] *The Diplomatic Correspondence of the United States of America from . . . 10th September, 1783 to . . . March 4, 1789* (7 vols.; Washington: Francis Preston Blair, 1833–1834), IV, 258, 216–217, 220.

[3] *Ibid.*, pp. 245, 277, 331–334, 447.

[4] *Ibid.*, V, 7–9, 132–134, 328.

[5] *Ibid.*, IV, 474.

A failure of the United States to secure protection for its trade in the Mediterranean paralleled the rebuffs suffered by John Adams in Britain. In 1784, Congress authorized Adams and Jefferson to negotiate commercial treaties with foreign powers and appropriated $80,000 for the purpose of placating the Barbary States of North Africa. Late in July, 1785, the Algerines went to war against the United States by seizing two American vessels and enslaving their crews. Jefferson, then minister to France, acting with John Adams in London, sent one John Lamb to Algiers in March, 1786, to ransom the captives, empowering him to pay $200 for each man. Lamb reported on March 29: "The people will cost, for their deliverance, at least twelve hundred dollars per head. The number is twenty-one." So exorbitant were the demands of the Algerian dey that Lamb advised Jefferson to abandon the rescue undertaking, "as it will be entirely vain to persevere." [6] About the same time, John Adams had an interview with the Tripolitan ambassador at London, who imparted the information that Tunis and Tripoli would each insist upon 30,000 guineas for a protection treaty, in addition to various gratuities and *douceurs*. The two states, he said, always demanded that much for a treaty, for in making one they surrendered a valuable asset: "Upon the arrival of a prize, the Dey and the other officers were entitled by law to large shares, by which they might make greater profits than these sums amounted to, and they never would give up this advantage for less." Adams estimated that to buy off the pirate states would cost £200,000, which sum he thought the United States might borrow in Holland. Such outlays, he believed, would be less expensive than a war.[7]

A report at this time from an American agent at Madrid informed Jefferson that a treaty then being negotiated with Algiers would cost Spain nearly $1,500,000.[8] Jefferson was quite willing to ransom the American captives, who, as slaves, were forced to carry timber and rocks on long hauls over rough mountainous roads, but he preferred war to a purchased treaty, believing that the Algerines would not abide by one unless the United States could enforce it with a navy. However, neither Jefferson's policy of war nor Adams's proposal for a Dutch loan came to anything. John Jay, then Secretary for Foreign Affairs of the United States, pointed out that the Union did not have money for a war and that it should not borrow abroad when it was not paying the interest on former loans. A treaty between the United States and Morocco, ratified by Congress in July, 1787, at a cost of $30,000, was only a minor victory, for it did not give immunity from attacks by Algiers, Tripoli, and Tunis, or secure the release of the Americans held by Algiers.[9]

---

[6] *Ibid.*, III, 33.
[7] *Ibid.*, IV, 496–498.
[8] *Ibid.*, III, 40.
[9] Malone, *Jefferson and His Time*, II, 28–31.

In its dealings with Spain, Congress endeavored in three ways to enlarge the foreign markets for products of the Union: first, by soliciting permission to export to the Spanish colonies; second, by seeking favorable access to markets in Spain; and third, by trying to get from Spain a recognition of the right of the western settlers to ship their produce down the Mississippi River.

In 1784, the Spanish government became fearful that Florida and Louisiana might soon be overrun by the rapidly growing American settlements in Kentucky and Tennessee. The Spaniards then decided that they could best protect their provinces by stifling the trade of the rival settlements, as a means of checking their growth. To achieve this end, the Spanish court on June 26, asserting that it possessed the sole right to the navigation of the lower Mississippi, closed the river to the trade of the settlers of the United States. The Spaniards next decided to send an agent to America for the purpose of obtaining from Congress a recognition of their exclusive control over the southern part of the Mississippi. The envoy chosen for this mission was Don Diego de Gardoqui. He arrived in Philadelphia late in May, 1785, to begin what proved to be a long and fruitless negotiation with John Jay.[10]

By 1785 the depression had intensified desires for benefits and advantages in two rival sections of the Union. The southern states, deeply involved in westward expansion, gave strong support to the frontiersmen, whereas leaders of the northern states, fearful of the growth of the Southwest, were willing to sacrifice its immediate interests to the commercial needs of the seaboard.[11] The Spaniards would not move an inch in the direction of opening their colonies to the exports or vessels of the United States, but they were prepared to offer concessions in regard to American exports to Spain. Apparently, the partisans of the West, mistrusting John Jay, a northern man, subjected him to extraordinary instructions which forbade him to make or to agree to any proposal until it had been submitted to Congress.[12] Jay was also directed to insist that the Union must retain all the territory it claimed down to the thirty-first parallel, and that it must not "relinquish or cede, in any case whatsoever, the right of the citizens of the United States to the free navigation of the river Mississippi, from its source to the Ocean." [13]

Since Jay alone could neither suggest nor agree to proposals, and because he was specifically directed to secure what Gardoqui was instructed most emphatically not to concede, a treaty could not be made. Jay could merely ascertain the demands and offers of the Spaniards. Finally, on August 3, 1786, he submitted a report to Congress in which he

[10] Whitaker, *The Spanish-American Frontier*, pp. 64–65, 68–72.
[11] *Ibid.*, p. 75; Jensen, *The New Nation*, p. 171.
[12] *Diplomatic Correspondence, 1783–1789*, VI, 89.
[13] *Ibid.*, pp. 65, 102–103.

advised that, in return for commercial concessions which Gardoqui promised to the United States in its trade with Spain, Congress should surrender for twenty-five or thirty years the right to the navigation of the Mississippi.[14] Although seven states endorsed Jay's plan, the opposition in the South was so vehement that both Jay and Gardoqui deemed it futile to draw up a treaty, inasmuch as the votes of nine states—the number necessary for ratification—could not be secured for any treaty that Spain would accept. Jay took the position that the United States could not make good its western claims without a war. In April, 1787, he described the diplomatic impasse, saying: ". . . a treaty disagreeable to one-half of the nation had better not be made, for it would be violated; . . . a war disliked by the other half would promise little success . . . ."[15] Jay used the failure of the Spanish negotiation to emphasize the weakness of the United States under the Articles of Confederation. In his report of August 3, he said that the Union, "unblessed with an efficient government, destitute of funds, and without public credit, either at home or abroad," must "be obliged to wait in patience for better days or plunge into an unpopular and dangerous war, with very little prospect of terminating it by a peace, either advantageous or glorious." He concluded by saying that the "seriously delicate" situation of the Union, "both at home and abroad," would persist until a "vigorous national government" could be formed.[16] Whatever may have been the intention of Jay, his proposal for the West—a surrender dictated by the feebleness of the Union—publicized that weakness and dramatized in the South and the West the need for a stronger central government.

DOMESTIC MANUFACTURES AND AMERICAN SHIPPING

Several of the states attempted to overcome the hardships of the 1780's by enacting defensive or remedial laws. The depression is important because, among other things, it gave birth to the American movement for protective tariffs. In 1785 manufacturers, artisans, and mechanics of New York, Philadelphia, and Boston held meetings at which they besought their state governments to impose duties for the purpose of curbing importations, stopping the outflow of specie, and aiding domestic producers.[17] In the mid-1780's New York, Massachusetts, Pennsylvania, Rhode Island, and New Hampshire enacted tariff laws that gave substantial protection to local industries, which were then being injured by the competition of low-priced foreign products. Such laws exhibited four fairly dis-

---

[14] *Ibid.*, pp. 169–170, 173.

[15] *Ibid.*, p. 207.

[16] *Ibid.*, p. 177.

[17] George Bancroft, *History of the Formation of the Constitution of the United States of America* (New York: D. Appleton and Company, 1896), pp. 138–139.

tinct features. In the first place, they taxed foreign luxuries, such as silverware, jewelry, carpets, and silks, with the aim of reducing the needless exportation of specie. Second, relatively high duties—15 percent or so— were imposed on goods that were produced so widely at home that local manufacturers could supply the need. In this category were boots, shoes, hats, saddles, harness, nails, iron tools and other hardware, candles, soap, and furniture. A third group of products included useful things that were not then produced in America in quantities sufficient to meet the people's needs. Such were glassware, china, stoneware, books, and coaches. Finally, the acts imposed duties on foreign liquors in order to raise revenue, to encourage the drinking of home brew, and to check the exportation of specie. In the states which adopted such tariff laws the policy took root and survived. Later laws both extended the lists of articles taxed and increased the rates—in some cases to 25 percent of the value of the imports. A New Hampshire act of 1786 was continued in 1788 because it proved to be "very beneficial." The code of Massachusetts was probably the most severe and comprehensive of those adopted at this time; a Pennsylvania act of 1785 stands out because in 1789 it served as the model for the first tariff law of the United States.[18]

At the outset of the campaign for protective tariffs its promoters realized that action by a single state would not be fully effective; hence they proposed that Congress should adopt a schedule of duties that would apply to the whole Union. This attitude had not changed in 1791, when a survey initiated by Alexander Hamilton revealed that leading manufacturers strongly favored federal tariff duties. The insufficiency of state action arose in part from the fact that in the 1780's some northern industries had advanced to the point that they were selling their products in several states.

In 1791, Fairfield County, Connecticut, contained nine recently erected iron works, most with two forges, which exported bar iron to New York.[19] Manufacturers in Providence said in 1790 that its nail makers could furnish the "whole country." Stamford and Norwalk, Connecticut, also turned out large quantities of nails.[20] In 1784 an American inventor devised a machine capable of finishing teeth for wool and cotton cards at the rate of 36,000 an hour, and by 1790 domestic production of cards met the needs of the Union. The two leading manufacturers of such articles were Westcott and Adgate of Philadelphia, and Giles Richards and Company of Boston. The latter made 63,000 pairs of cards in 1788.[21] An informed writer said in 1790 that American paper mills, chiefly in the

---

[18] Albert Anthony Giesecke, *American Commercial Legislation Before 1789* (University of Pennsylvania, *Publications;* New York: D. Appleton and Company, 1910), pp. 131–134; Johnson, *History of Commerce,* I, 135–138.

[19] Cole, *Hamilton's Industrial Correspondence,* p. 20.

[20] *Ibid.,* pp. 84, 36–37.

[21] *Ibid.,* p. 119; Weeden, *Economic and Social History of New England,* II, 852.

middle states, were on the point of supplying the national market. Hat-makers at Danbury and Stonington, Connecticut, who were exporting hats in 1791 "to different parts of the Union," complained that foreign importations "very much injure the business." [22] At Boston a large plant, reputed to be the most modern in the country, produced 2,000 yards of sailcloth a week.[23] Manufacturers at New Haven and Farmington, Connecticut, were turning out buttons so successfully that some of them were shipped to Europe. Providence then produced 40,000 pounds of candles and 10,000 of hard soap yearly, but labored "under embarrassment by reason of large quantities imported into the Southern States with very little profit to the federal Chest." [24] Boston exported 63,752 pounds of loaf sugar in 1787; Philadelphia's sugar refineries were so active in 1790 that the city imported 5,692,000 pounds of brown sugar. Pennsylvania then had 21 powder mills, capable of making 625 tons of powder yearly, worth $200,000 to the state. "It is said that the largest gunpowder works existing anywhere are those at Frankfort, near Philadelphia . . . ." [25]

By 1785 the most successful manufacturers in the states were intent upon utilizing machinery and the subdivision of labor in order to produce goods on a large scale and at a low cost. Such a mode of production required a market larger than that of a single state. On the whole, the northern manufacturer had to seek outside markets, not in other manufacturing states, but in the agricultural South. But there he had to compete with English goods, many of which were produced at such low cost that English importers could afford to sell them, for a time, at prices ruinous to his business. From all this it appeared that American manufacturers needed protection in a large, nation-wide market to which they would have free access. Now, state tariff laws did not provide such a large, free, assured, and sheltered market, for two reasons. Inherent in state tariff laws was the danger that some states might tax the exports of a neighbor, thereby limiting its market. Madison asserted that Connecticut taxed imports from Massachusetts.[26] More important, the legislatures of many states—Delaware, Maryland, Virginia, North Carolina, South Carolina, and Georgia—did not impose adequate protective duties for the benefit of the exports of the northern area. It followed, therefore, that only a federal tariff law could provide the kind of protection sought by many manufacturers. Since, under the Articles of Confederation, Congress lacked the power to enact tariff laws, the manufacturing interest looked with favor on proposals to deprive the states of that power and to lodge it solely in Congress.[27]

[22] Cole, *Hamilton's Industrial Correspondence*, pp. 117, 20, 30.

[23] *Ibid.*, p. 116; Weeden, *Economic and Social History of New England*, II, 851.

[24] Cole, *Hamilton's Industrial Correspondence*, pp. 39, 50.

[25] *Ibid.*, pp. 120–121.

[26] *Writings of Madison* (1867), I, 216.

[27] For statements of need for federal protection, see Cole, *Hamilton's Industrial Correspondence*, pp. 6, 10, 14, 30, 39, 50, 62, 68, 70, 75, 77, 83, 86, 88, 91, 97, 125.

Britain's exclusion of American ships from the British colonies and from most of the trade of Britain moved many of the states to enact retaliatory laws which were designed to penalize British shipping and to give preferential benefits to American shipowners. Laws of one type imposed discriminating tonnage duties on British vessels entering the ports of the legislating states. New York, Pennsylvania, Delaware, New Hampshire, Massachusetts, Maryland, Virginia, and North Carolina made use of this weapon. The five states last named each subjected British vessels to a special tax of 5s. a ton. Pennsylvania in 1785 fixed the special tax at 7s. 6d. a ton but reduced it to 1s. 2d. in 1788. In each case, the tax on British vessels was higher than a comparable tax on American vessels.[28]

Another kind of duty that found favor with state legislatures aimed to give protection, at one stroke, to both American producers and American shipowners. The lawmakers of six states tried to do this by putting special taxes on goods imported in British ships. In 1785 and 1786, such imports were subjected to the following impositions: in New Hampshire, Massachusetts, and New York, to duties twice as high as those on goods imported in American ships; in Rhode Island, to treble duties; in North Carolina, to a special duty of 20 percent ad valorem.[29]

In 1787, British merchants complained that the shipping taxes of the states gave advantage to American shipowners.[30] Yet it is clear that the system of state duties did not satisfy American shipowners, for on the whole they preferred to have Congress enact a single uniform code. From their point of view, several disadvantages arose from the state duties. In the first place, such duties offered no assurance that the states would not discriminate against each other, with a resulting danger that shipowners of one state would be hampered by taxes on their trade with other states. The acts of some states discriminated in favor of the vessels of the enacting state, to the detriment of shipowners of other parts of the Union.[31] Connecticut taxed foreign goods from Massachusetts, and New York in 1787 put special duties on foreign goods imported by American vessels from Connecticut and New Jersey.[32] Certainly, the states at this time were not above taking advantage of each other in imposing duties on trade. Had the state system continued, the temptation would have been strong for one state to favor its own merchant-shipowners at the expense of their competitors in other states.

[28] Giesecke, *American Commercial Legislation*, pp. 137–138; Thomas C. Cochran, *New York in the Confederation* (Philadelphia: University of Pennsylvania Press, 1932), p. 167; Jensen, *The New Nation*, pp. 292–293.

[29] Giesecke, *American Commercial Legislation*, pp. 128–129, 134; Jensen, *The New Nation*, p. 293.

[30] Jensen, *The New Nation*, p. 300.

[31] Giesecke, *American Commercial Legislation*, pp. 134, 139.

[32] *Ibid.*, p. 135; *Writings of Madison* (1867), I, 216; Jensen, *The New Nation*, p. 339.

In the second place, a number of states did not give adequate protection to American shipping as a whole. Connecticut, New Jersey, Delaware, South Carolina, and Georgia either did not discriminate against British shipping or taxed it only to a slight extent. Such states therefore not only withheld aid from shipowners of other states but also stood to attract British ships and possibly to gain at the expense of their neighbors as distributors of British goods and as exporters of American produce. In the third place, the system of state taxes exposed merchants to uncertainties in that state legislatures might suddenly alter duties after voyages had been undertaken on the assumption that other duties would be in force. Finally, state duties added considerably to the labor of carrying on interstate trade. They obliged merchants to keep informed about a multitude of vexing details—a task far more difficult than that of familiarizing themselves with a single code enacted by Congress. Discrimination, lack of full protection, uncertainty, and additional labor—such were the fruits of the state system of duties.

New Hampshire, Massachusetts, and Rhode Island resorted to the most extreme form of retaliation. Each of those states enacted a law which prohibited British vessels from loading American products in its ports. This device, like other retaliatory measures, proved to be defective when used by only a few states. Apparently, it encouraged British shippers to go to nearby states and to use them as bases for distributing European goods and for obtaining American produce. The readiness of Connecticut to receive British vessels without subjecting them to penalties forced Rhode Island virtually to suspend its act, lest it lose trade to its western neighbor. So also the assembly of New Hampshire moved to suspend its law until New York and Connecticut should adopt similar acts. Otherwise, much of New Hampshire's trade would be diverted from Portsmouth to the Connecticut River route. Massachusetts repealed its law in July, 1786, because, as Governor Bowdoin explained, other states, refusing to cooperate, had tried to use it for one sided advantage.[33]

A prohibitive navigation act, like a protective tariff, could not accomplish its intended purposes unless it applied uniformly to all the states. Many American leaders appreciated this fact. Jefferson, visiting Boston in July, 1784, found "the conviction growing strongly that nothing could preserve our confederacy unless the band of Union, their common council, be strengthened." By June, 1785, Jefferson's European experiences had convinced him that the "interests of the States ought to be made joint in every possible instance, in order to cultivate the idea of our being one nation, and to multiply the instances in which the people shall look up to Congress as their head." [34] In April, 1785, merchants and tradesmen of

[33] Jensen, *The New Nation*, p. 298; Giesecke, *American Commercial Legislation*, pp. 128, 137; Bancroft, *History of the Formation of the Constitution*, p. 141.

[34] *Jefferson Papers* (Boyd), VII, 356; VIII, 229.

Boston turned to Congress for measures to overcome the depression. The town of Boston complained in July that, because foreigners were monopolizing commerce and threatening to annihilate American shipping, Congress should be granted powers necessary to deal with the crisis, on the assumption that only joint action of all the states could be effective. Governor Bowdoin at this time proposed that Massachusetts take steps to call a convention for the sake of endowing Congress with enlarged powers. The Massachusetts legislature then resolved, on July 1, that the powers of Congress were inadequate "to the great purposes they were originally designed to effect." [35] Writing from England, John Adams asserted that the "means of preserving ourselves" could "never be secured entirely, until Congress shall be made supreme in foreign commerce, and shall have digested a plan for all the States." [36]

Similar opinions were voiced in other states. Early in 1785 the New York Chamber of Commerce advised Congress to give special attention to trade in order to offset the harmful actions of foreign powers; and the artisans and tradesmen of the city proposed to make the powers of Congress equal "to every exigency of the Union." Citizens of Philadelphia asserted in June, 1785, that relief from depressed trade could come "only from the grant to Congress of full constitutional powers over the commerce of the United States," whereupon the Council of Pennsylvania urged that "further authorities" ought to be vested in Congress. The legislatures of Virginia and Maryland in 1783 endorsed proposals to empower Congress to enact a law to counteract foreign restraints on American shipping.[37]

"Unless the United States in Congress assembled shall be vested with powers competent to the protection of commerce, they can never command reciprocal advantages in trade; and without these, our foreign commerce must decline, and eventually be annihilated." Thus spoke Congress on April 30, 1784, when it recommended to the states that it be granted the authority to adopt a navigation law. To give Congress such authority required an amendment to the Articles of Confederation, and that in turn required the unanimous approval of the thirteen states. Since, in 1784, many leaders—particularly in the South—feared that Congress might misuse the power in question, the recommendation of April 30 outlined the provisions of a specific law that Congress would be authorized to enact. The state legislatures, therefore, were asked to approve, at one stroke, both a grant of power to Congress and the provisions of a specific

[35] Bancroft, *History of the Formation of the Constitution*, pp. 139–140.

[36] *Diplomatic Correspondence, 1783–1789*, IV, 289.

[37] Bancroft, *History of the Formation of the Constitution*, pp. 138–139; Giesecke, *American Commercial Legislation*, p. 129 and note; Jensen, *The New Nation*, pp. 401–402.

act. Under the plan submitted by Congress, the suggested law would prohibit British vessels from engaging in the coastal trade of the Union. The plan also proposed to prohibit British merchants from importing into the states any goods except those produced in Britain. Such a law was to become effective only if approved in Congress by the delegations of at least nine states and was to continue in force not longer than fifteen years.[38] Most of the states endorsed the proposal in principle, but some insisted on modifications, with the result that ensuing conflicts delayed a final agreement. Rhode Island and North Carolina, for instance, were willing to prohibit British vessels from importing goods but refused to prohibit them from exporting American produce.[39] In October, 1786, Congress requested these two states to agree to the original plan, but they failed to comply.[40] Thus it happened that when the Constitutional Convention met in May, 1787, Congress had not gained the power to enact navigation laws or otherwise to put pressure on foreign states that adhered to policies injurious to American shipping and trade.

MERCHANTS' BANKS AND LAND BANKS

"Another unhappy effect of a continuance of the present anarchy of commerce," wrote Madison in March, 1786, "will be a continuance of the unfavorable balance on it, which, by draining us of our metals, furnishes pretexts for the pernicious substitution of paper money, for indulgences to debtors, for postponements of taxes. In fact, most of our political evils may be traced to our commercial ones . . . ." [41] In this statement Madison explained why many men of the propertied, creditor class were intent upon reducing imports, fostering American shipping and manufactures, and stopping the exportation of specie. Such reforms were necessary to assure that the Union would have an adequate stock of coin, without which there would arise an irresistible demand for paper money. In 1786, memories of the evils of runaway inflation were extremely vivid, for only five years had elapsed since the extravagant depreciation of the wartime paper currency had occurred. A repetition of such a disaster was to men of substance a calamity to be avoided at almost any cost.

Low prices of American products, a shortage of hard money, business stagnation, private debts, and relatively high taxes worked together in the 1780's to create a social and political ferment. Rarely has such an abrupt contraction of a nation's money supply taken place as happened after 1780, for the paper currency of the war years had scarcely been

---

[38] *Journals of the Continental Congress*, XXVI, 322.
[39] Giesecke, *American Commercial Legislation*, p. 143.
[40] McLaughlin, *The Confederation and the Constitution*, p. 85.
[41] *Writings of Madison* (1867), I, 226–227.

withdrawn from circulation when the drain of coin to Europe occurred. People of all shades of opinion attributed the price declines of the mid-1780's, in part at least, to the acute scarcity of money. Certainly the states did not have enough cash for the needs of business. The three private banks then in existence were not equipped, even in normal times, to meet the demands for currency in their communities, Boston, Philadelphia, and New York; and the depression lessened rather than increased the quantity of their notes in use. The notes and warrants which Robert Morris had issued near the end of the war had now been withdrawn. Mints, whether state or federal, did not exist. Such coin as remained in the country had gravitated to the commercial centers, leaving the rural districts denuded. Congress had failed completely to supply a uniform, dependable paper currency. Notes of individuals, bills of exchange, depreciating public certificates of debt, small quantities of paper issued by states in anticipation of tax collections, the scarce notes of the three merchants' banks, and a trifling amount of coin constituted in 1784 the Union's medium of exchange. Its utter inadequacy was responsible for a widespread use of barter. In such unhappy circumstances, debtors had to find some means of meeting their obligations and citizens had to seek money for paying taxes.

Private debts of the time cannot be fully known, for complete records of them do not exist. However, estimates of trade with Britain throw some light on the subject, since British goods were commonly sold on credit granted by importers to retailers and by retailers to consumers.[42] During the three years 1784–1786 the total imports from Britain had a value of about £3,845,000 in excess of the value of American exports to Britain.[43] That sum may be considered as representing some of the debts owed by Americans to British creditors—a figure that does not include pre-Revolutionary debts or debts incurred for the purchase of slaves from British traders.[44] The country's surpluses of wheat and corn in 1785 were probably worth less than half the sum of the trade deficit of 1784–1786.[45]

The end of the war found the governments of both the Union and the states deeply in debt. Most people then regarded a public debt much as they regarded a private one—something that should be paid in full within a reasonably short time. They did not as yet accept the idea that

[42] For a good statement of the chain of indebtedness, see Bray Hammond, *Banks and Politics in America, from the Revolution to the Civil War* (Princeton, N. J.: Princeton University Press, 1957), pp. 58–59, quoting Robert Morris.

[43] Pitkin, *A Statistical View of the Commerce of the United States*, p. 30; Foulke, *The Sinews of American Commerce*, p. 102.

[44] This estimate assumes a white population in 1783 of 2,500,000 (Greene, *The Revolutionary Generation*, pp. 306, 308, 67).

[45] Gray, *History of Agriculture in the Southern United States*, II, 581; Cole, *Wholesale Commodity Prices, Statistical Supplement*, p. 79.

the principal of a public debt might conveniently be permanent. Massachusetts, for instance, originally undertook to pay its war debt by 1785, and in 1783 Congress proposed to pay the federal debt in full within twenty-five years.[46]

In 1790–1791, the debts that all the states and Congress had incurred on account of the war amounted to $71,060,000.[47] One may get some notion of the burden of taxes in relation to public debts by considering an imaginary situation. Assume that the total debts, state and federal, amounted to $52,000,000 in 1785. Suppose that the governments had arranged to pay the principal of these debts in yearly installments over the next twenty years, plus interest on the unpaid balance. The tax bill for 1785 would thus have amounted to $2,600,000 for principal and about $3,000,000 for interest. Assume that the Union then produced a wheat surplus of 3,500,000 bushels, the wholesale price in Philadelphia averaging $1.06 a bushel during 1785—a total of $3,710,000. This sum would have amounted to 66 percent of the total tax payments of $5,600,000 on account of the public debts.

Some such estimate, rough as it must be, is necessary to give a conception of conditions in 1785. To state the debts of that time merely in terms of dollars is meaningless in the modern age, when dollars are plentiful and when the economy produces in abundance a bewildering variety of goods. Only by keeping in mind that the economy of 1785 yielded but a few important commodities for commercial sale and that the surpluses available for tax payments were meager can one get a proper sense of the then existing burden of debts and taxes.

There can be no doubt whatsoever that taxes and private debts, if collected when due, would have imposed a staggering burden on an economy of low productivity that suffered from a dire scarcity of money.

Hardly anyone denied the need of additional currency. But how should it be created and what should be its nature? Disagreements over that question divided men into sharply defined groups that fought each other with extreme bitterness. On one side stood men who feared that they would be crushed by a burden of debts and taxes intensified by the shortage of money. On the other side were men who saw ruin in a possible repetition of the frightful depreciation of the wartime paper money. The programs of the two parties differed most essentially with respect to the means of issuing paper currency.

One group, strongest among the merchants of the port towns, regarded privately owned and managed banks as the proper agency for enlarging the currency supply. Of the three such banks existing in 1784, the Bank of North America was the archetype of the Massachusetts Bank

[46] Jensen, *The New Nation*, p. 307.
[47] Bayley, *National Loans of the United States*, pp. 31, 33.

and the Bank of New York.[48] In each case private citizens, chiefly merchants, had purchased shares in the bank, thereby endowing it with a stock of gold and silver coin. The value of a share—$400 for the Bank of North America and $500 for each of the other two—tended to limit ownership to relatively wealthy men. Each bank issued notes which it lent to borrowers and which it undertook to redeem in coin on demand. Each made loans, usually by discounting notes and bills secured by commodities involved in the course of trade. Each bank received deposits that could be withdrawn in specie on demand. Each sought a state charter in order that stockholders would be liable for the bank's debts only to the amount of the stock they owned.[49]

Such a bank was first of all a source of profit to its owners.[50] It provided a means of multiplying the specie they paid in, so that in effect they had more money earning interest than before they had purchased shares. The bank multiplied its specie by issuing notes and by crediting borrowers with deposits that were usually drawn on by checks. The notes thus issued and the deposits thus created exceeded the amount of specie in the bank's possession. Since this excess was the bank's source of profit, a pressing concern of the bank's managers was to make sure that demands for note redemptions in coin and specie withdrawals of deposits did not exhaust the bank's specie reserves. The early bankers did not know exactly how much additional credit-currency, in the form of bank notes and deposits, could be based on a given quantity of coin. But it was certain that specie could be enhanced in this way to a considerable extent.[51]

The banks sought to inspire faith in notes and deposits, so that holders of them would not demand specie. It was a great boon to a bank if governments would accept its notes at par in tax payments, thereby giving such notes a general, continuing utility as a currency equal to coin. The Bank of North America resorted to ingenious services to publicize its specie treasure. Stockholders ostentatiously made large "deposits" of coin taken from its own stock. Porters were set to work moving boxes of specie to and fro within the bank to impress observers with the ample quantities on hand.[52] Large vaults and buildings with strong walls sug-

[48] Henry W. Domett, A History of the Bank of New York, 1784–1884 (3d ed.; Cambridge, Mass.: Riverside Press [Preface, 1884]), pp. 4, 15, 17; Gras, The Massachusetts First National Bank, pp. 11–13.

[49] Hammond, Banks and Politics in America, pp. 75, 81; Domett, A History of the Bank of New York, pp. 8, 14.

[50] Allan Nevins, History of the Bank of New York and Trust Company (New York: Privately printed, 1934), pp. 17, 29.

[51] Gras, The Massachusetts First National Bank, pp. 40–41; Hammond, Banks and Politics in America, pp. 69, 81, 85; Webster, Political Essays, p. 436; Harry E. Miller, Banking Theories in the United States Before 1860 (Vol. XXX of Harvard Economic Studies; Cambridge, Mass.: Harvard University Press, 1927), p. 30.

[52] Hammond, Banks and Politics in America, p. 70.

gested that the bank had abundant riches to protect, and participation of the officers in public ceremonies signified a high standing in the community. The president of the Bank of North America was once almost a public functionary in Pennsylvania, and the president of the Massachusetts Bank was entitled to sit on the platform at Harvard commencements. When the directors of the Bank of North America once feared that a would-be borrower wanted to obtain specie to export in a ship about to sail, they put him off until it had departed.[53]

Stockholders gained in many ways. Notes of a bank that were lost or destroyed without proof added to its profit, since it need not redeem them. Stockholders could obtain personal loans, and their stock was an ideal type of long-term investment. "It offers," said Pelatiah Webster, "a much better security than can be found in the hands of any private man . . . ." A bank also relieved the stockholder, as an investor, of the unpleasant necessity of refusing to make loans to individuals and of collecting money from embarrassed debtors.[54]

The benefits of a bank extended beyond the stockholders. It provided the community with additional currency but under restraints that guarded against overissue and depreciation: since a bank's notes were not legal tender, a person need not accept them if he doubted their value. The bank also stimulated business by granting credit to solvent merchants who were not stockholders. Deposits facilitated payments by checks, which also served as receipts, and a bank's vaults offered a safe depository for surplus coin.[55]

The three banks of the 1780's prospered. Each paid dividends ranging from 2½ to 14 percent. The managers limited loans to thirty or sixty days, refused renewals, and insisted on punctual payments. Each bank succeeded in maintaining specie payments continuously on all its notes and deposits. Loans and discounts were confined in the main to a limited number of local merchants with whom the officers were acquainted. None of the banks catered to the common people.

The nature of the merchants' banks accounts for the opposition they provoked. Their enemies complained that they benefited only a small group in one town. Short-term loans did not accommodate producers such as farmers, who had to finance work that extended over several months before it yielded the means of paying debts. The notes of a merchants' bank, which circulated mainly in or near the port towns, did not supply the state as a whole with an adequate currency. A limited, exclusive business, reinforced by monopoly and a formidable power, en-

[53] Domett, *A History of the Bank of New York,* p. 26; Hammond, *Banks and Politics in America,* pp. 57–58, 67 note; Konkle, *Thomas Willing,* pp. 101–102.

[54] Webster, *Political Essays,* pp. 435, 436.

[55] Miller, *Banking Theories in the United States,* p. 22; Gras, *The Massachusetts First National Bank,* p. 38.

abled a bank to favor its friends, to deny credit to outsiders, and to crush needy borrowers by refusing to extend loans.[56]

The principal opposition to the merchants' banks came from farmers, who, as taxpayers and debtors, needed some agency to supply them with currency. They could not readily form a private bank, since they lived apart from one another and did not frequently act together. There was, however, an organization with which they had contact—their state government—which was capable of issuing paper money. Colonial legislatures had repeatedly issued two kinds of bills of credit.[57] One type had been used by governments to buy supplies in wartime or to pay public debts. The bills then passed from hand to hand as currency until they returned to the public treasury in tax payments, whereupon they were destroyed. Under the second plan, the government set up a "land bank" and lent bills to citizens on the security of land. The borrower agreed to pay each year an installment on the principal and the interest on the unpaid balance. Land banks thus put the bills immediately into the hands of landowners throughout a colony.[58]

Borrowers favored such land banks because they commonly provided loans at 5 percent interest or less, whereas private lenders charged 6 percent or more. A sudden increase in the quantity of money raised the prices of produce, to the benefit of debtor-producers. A farmer who received a loan could use the money to pay his taxes and debts; hence he could withhold his surplus produce from sale until he could get favorable prices. Without such cash, he might have to sell his surplus at a sacrifice to meet his tax and debt payments.[59] If adversity prevented his paying interest or an installment when due, he might hope for indulgent treatment from an agrarian legislature. Above all, land banks had the merit of reducing taxes, for the government could support itself largely from revenues received from interest payments on the loans.

Before 1775, Pennsylvania, Delaware, New Jersey, New York, and Maryland managed land banks so prudently that they realized the benefits claimed for them.[60] However, in South Carolina, Rhode Island, and Massachusetts serious depreciation occurred which writers cited to condemn paper money as a whole. Undoubtedly it was the disastrous deprecia-

---

[56] Hammond, *Banks and Politics in America*, pp. 53–55, 59.

[57] Curtis P. Nettels, *The Money Supply of the American Colonies Before 1720* (University of Wisconsin *Studies in the Social Sciences and History*, No. 20; Madison: 1934), pp. 208–209, 255–277.

[58] *Ibid.*, pp. 268–273.

[59] Anne Bezanson, Robert D. Gray, and Miriam Hussey, *Prices in Colonial Pennsylvania* (Philadelphia: University of Pennsylvania Press, 1935), shows that in Philadelphia prices of farm products dropped after harvest and slaughtering time. See pp. 22–23, 26, 66, 106, 108–110, 338–339.

[60] Richard A. Lester, *Monetary Experiments: Early American and Recent Scandinavian* (Princeton, N. J.: Princeton University Press, 1939), pp. 56–151.

tion of the Revolutionary currency that evoked impassioned opposition to paper money in the 1780's. Creditors now feared that state legislatures would again open the floodgates, whereupon debts public and private would be swept away by a torrent of paper. Opponents of land banks apprehended that the legislatures would issue bills in excessive quantities because land, on which they were based, was so plentiful as to provide an unlimited security. The only barrier to extreme inflation was the self-restraint of legislators—a defense that seemed most precarious to prudent men in 1785.

CONFLICTS OVER PAPER MONEY

In the mid-1780's seven states issued paper currency. In four other states the advocates of the remedy were so potent that only with difficulty did their opponents defeat proposals for new issues. The popularity of land banks at this time signifies that private debts were oppressing many citizens. Had additional money been needed only for paying public debts, the legislatures might have issued ordinary bills of credit and have used them in the first instance to pay the public creditors, thereby reducing taxes. Since landowners received money directly from the land banks, the demand for them denoted that additional cash was needed, not only for tax payments for the benefit of public creditors but also for the payment of private debts.

Among the seven states that issued paper currency, Georgia managed to avoid a serious social conflict. After the war, pioneers swarmed into the state; the number of people who obtained land there in five years before 1789 was probably twice the total population in 1784. This almost incredible increase wrought a change in state politics that shifted political power from the seacoast planters and merchants to the yeomen of the up country. In consequence, the legislature in 1786 authorized an emission of £50,000 in paper money, for the dual purposes of paying the claims of the state's Revolutionary veterans and of financing a frontier war with the Creek Indians. However, only £30,000 in bills was issued, for the war did not occur. Based on the security of state lands, with a pledge of redemption within four years, the bills were made legal tender in all payments. Evidently Georgia's example did not cause alarm outside the state. Madison, at this time a well-informed foe of paper money, said in August, 1786: "Of the affairs of Georgia I know as little as of those of Kamskatska." [61]

[61] William W. Abbot, "The Structure of Politics in Georgia, 1782–1789," *William and Mary Quarterly*, Third Series, XIV, No. 1 (January, 1957), 60, 65; E[llis] Merton Coulter, *Georgia: A Short History* (Chapel Hill: The University of North Carolina Press, 1947), p. 170; *Writings of Madison* (1867), I, 245; Kenneth Coleman, *The American Revolution in Georgia* (Athens: University of Georgia Press, 1958), p. 214.

South Carolina held to a moderate course in its management of paper currency. At the end of the war the planters there incurred heavy debts for slaves purchased at high prices from British traders. Debtors soon sought relief. A proposal for an issue of £400,000 in bills of credit led to a compromise in October, 1785, when the legislature provided for an emission of £100,000 in bills, to be lent to citizens mainly on the security of land. Such loans, to be repaid within five years, bore 7 percent interest. Although the bills were not legal tender in private payments, the state received them for taxes, thereby obtaining money to pay the interest on its long-term debt. Merchants and planters agreed to accept the bills at par. They maintained their face values in specie until May, 1787; afterward they passed at about 10 percent discount. In the spring of 1788 a sharp drop in prices occurred, and Charleston merchants complained anew of an acute scarcity of money.[62]

In 1786, North Carolina struck legal-tender bills to the amount of £100,000. The state used £36,000 of the issue to buy tobacco and the remainder to satisfy one fourth of the claims of its Revolutionary soldiers. State agents purchased 1,000,000 pounds of tobacco with the bills, paying twice its current price in coin and later selling it for half the sum which they had paid for it. The money thus obtained, $60,000 in coin, went to the United States Treasury toward paying the Union's foreign debt. This arrangement enabled farmers to sell tobacco at a high price and thus to obtain cash for paying taxes and debts. Many irregularities attended the payment of the bills received by the soldiers. In 1787–1788 the specie value of the paper had shrunk by more than 50 percent. Coin vanished, and since the paper had practically no value outside the state, merchants could not use it to pay debts they owed abroad; hence they suffered severe losses when they had to accept it at inflated values in the settlement of local debts. North Carolina's performance warned merchants anew of the menace of depreciating paper money which they were forced to receive at par from their debtors but which they could not pass on to their creditors.[63]

The experience of New Jersey illustrates the workings of a land bank. A shortage of money, private indebtedness, and the inability of citizens to pay taxes provoked a heated conflict between the assembly, sympathetic to debtors, and the council, partial to creditors. In May, 1786, popular pressure forced the council to agree to an emission of £100,000 in legal-tender bills of credit, to be lent to citizens on the security of real estate. A borrower might obtain up to £100 at 6 percent,

[62] Jensen, *The New Nation*, pp. 318–319; Taylor, "Charleston Prices," pp. 368–369; *Writings of Madison* (1867), I, 244.

[63] Jensen, *The New Nation*, pp. 319–320; Crittenden, *Commerce of North Carolina*, p. 163; *Writings of Madison* (1867), I, 243–244.

the loan to be repaid within twelve years. The state used the interest payments for the ordinary expenses of government. Numerous applications for loans reduced the average amount to well below the £100 maximum. Only borrowers with unmortgaged estates could benefit. Of the New Jersey paper, Madison said in August, 1786, that the "terror of popular associations stifles, as yet, an overt discrimination between it and specie; but as this does not operate in Philadelphia and New York, where all the trade of New Jersey is carried on, its depreciation has already commenced in those places . . . ." Fears of a repetition of extreme depreciation, such as had afflicted the wartime paper money, animated the opponents of the issue of 1786.[64]

The conflict in New York paralleled that in New Jersey. The farming districts demanded additional paper currency; merchants and creditors, headed by the New York Chamber of Commerce, resisted. After the state senate had killed two paper bills in 1784 and 1785, the popular party triumphed in 1786, when the senate, re-formed by a recent election, consented to an issue of £200,000, three fourths to be lent at 5 percent on real estate or specie, and one fourth to be used to pay interest on public debts. The law put a maximum of £300 on loans and required the borrower to repay one tenth of his debt in 1791 and the balance in nine yearly installments thereafter. In lawsuits the paper had the force of legal tender. This rule helped to prevent depreciation and to make the issue a success. It eased the burdens of taxpayers and relieved public creditors by providing good money for paying part of the interest on the state debt. Depreciation never exceeded 12 percent, and the paper often passed at par.[65]

Rhode Island's adventures with paper money outraged creditors and embroiled its citizens in turbulent strife. In May, 1786, the legislature approved an emission of £100,000, made the bills a legal tender, apportioned them among the towns on the basis of assessed property values, and authorized loans in equal amounts to all landowners. Such loans, to be repaid after fourteen years, bore 4 percent interest during the first seven years and none thereafter.[66]

For several reasons Rhode Island became a symbol of iniquity in the eyes of creditors. Its record of unsound financial practice in colonial times

[64] Richard P. McCormick, *Experiment in Independence: New Jersey in the Critical Period, 1781–1789* (New Brunswick, N. J.: Rutgers University Press, 1950), pp. 186–206; *Writings of Madison* (1867), I, 244.

[65] E. Wilder Spaulding, *New York in the Critical Period, 1783–1789* (New York: Columbia University Press, 1932), pp. 143–149; Cochran, *New York in the Confederation*, p. 160; Jensen, *The New Nation*, pp. 320–322.

[66] Frank Greene Bates, *Rhode Island and the Formation of the Union* (Columbia University *Studies in History, Economics and Public Law*, Vol. X, No. 2; New York: The Macmillan Company, 1898), p. 124.

was especially glaring. Armed resistance to tax collections had preceded the enactment of the paper-money law. The quantity of bills printed in 1786 greatly exceeded on a per capita basis that of any other state: in relation to population, Rhode Island's issue was more than twice as large as New York's and three times more than North Carolina's. Creditors disliked the low interest rate with which the state favored borrowers. Equally offensive were certain measures adopted to give value to the bills. The original act provided that a person could pay a debt by depositing sufficient paper with a judge of a county court, thereby preventing a creditor from refusing to accept the bills. A supplementary law imposed a fine of £100 on anyone who refused to receive the paper at its face value in specie, and a third law provided that a person so accused might be tried in a special court of three judges, without benefit of jury trial or right of appeal.[67]

So determined was the opposition to the paper that merchants refused to take it, and when some of them closed their stores, would-be buyers resorted to force and rioting. Farmers pledged to withhold produce from townsmen who resisted the law. The state, wrote Madison, was thrown into a sort of convulsion. At Newport, a butcher, John Weeden, refused to sell meat to one John Trevett for paper money. Trevett's complaint led to a legal action against Weeden in the Superior Court. Four of its five judges dismissed the complaint, on the ground that they lacked jurisdiction in the case—a verdict which meant that a person could not be compelled by law to accept the paper. Thereupon the legislature summoned the judges to appear before it to answer for their conduct. Three of the five complied, stoutly defended their decision, and escaped without punishment. Eventually, both sides gained and lost, for the legislature in December, 1786, repealed the act which imposed a fine for non-acceptance of the paper, and in the following election only one of the judges was returned to the Superior Court. Rhode Island had previously defeated, singlehanded, a plan to enable Congress to levy taxes necessary for paying the federal debts. Its intransigence on that occasion incensed the creditors, who now vigorously advertised its malfeasance in issuing paper money.[68]

A violent collision between the partisans of state paper currency and patrons of merchants' banks occurred in Pennsylvania. In March, 1785, farmers and public creditors united to push through the legislature a bill for the emission of £150,000 in bills of credit—£100,000 to be used to pay interest on public debts and £50,000 to be lent to individuals on the se-

[67] *Ibid.*, pp. 116–117, 124, 125, 128–129.

[68] *Ibid.*, pp. 126–127, 131–138, 141; *Writings of Madison* (1867), I, 244; McLaughlin, *The Confederation and the Constitution*, pp. 151–153; Jensen, *The New Nation*, p. 325; Adams, *New England in the Republic*, pp. 127–128.

curity of land. Holders of the bills could use them in payments to the state but they were not legal tender in private transactions.[69]

Once the new bills were in circulation, the Bank of North America refused to give specie for them at par. When the bank accepted them for deposits, it stipulated that the depositor must take them when withdrawing cash. Since they were worth less than the notes of the bank, its enemies charged that the bank undermined the state's currency and that its power exceeded that of the state itself. The foes of the bank also asserted that it did not afford loans to farmers, that it was a monster destructive of democracy, and that it tended to "engross all the wealth, power, and influence of the State." The paper party, in an effort to crush the bank, moved to annul its charter, which had been granted by the state in 1782. This threat touched off a lengthy debate on the pros and cons of merchants' banks and state paper. The bank suffered a setback when, on September 13, 1785, the legislature annulled the charter. The bank immediately sought a new one and the war went on. In February, 1786, one of the bank's defenders, Pelatiah Webster, published an essay on credit in which he argued that the charter of 1782 had created a property right which the state constitution protected. The charter, he said, was a contract that could be legally annulled only by mutual consent of the two parties or by a court decision based on proof that the bank had violated its trust. In this manner Webster expounded the doctrines of vested property rights, the sanctity of contracts, the supremacy of the constitution over the legislature, judicial review of state laws, and due process of law. The immediate result of the currency war in Pennsylvania was to expose the weakness of a merchants' bank when it was opposed by a hostile state legislature.[70]

Three of the states that did not issue paper money managed to avoid serious domestic strife. Delaware, the least populous of the thirteen states, then inhabited by about 45,000 whites, was so bound to Philadelphia that it found relief from the money shortage in the notes of the Bank of North America and the state paper currency of Pennsylvania. Long noted for its prudence in financial affairs, Connecticut in the 1780's granted emergency tax reductions to distressed towns and individuals, and authorized deferred payments of taxes and debts, thereby lessening the pressure on citizens and avoiding an issue of bills of credit. In Virginia, many liberal leaders, such as George Mason, Madison, and Jefferson, looked

[69] Hammond, *Banks and Politics in America*, p. 53; Jensen, *The New Nation*, p. 317.

[70] Lewis, *The Bank of North America*, pp. 54–67; Webster, *Political Essays*, pp. 448–449, 451–454, 456–458; Robert L. Brunhouse, *The Counter-Revolution in Pennsylvania, 1776–1790* (Harrisburg: Pennsylvania Historical Commission, 1942), pp. 171–175; Charles Page Smith, *James Wilson* (Chapel Hill: The University of North Carolina Press, 1956), pp. 151–154.

askance at the paper remedy, and joined with conservatives in opposing it. The devastating depreciation of the wartime paper had sorely embarrassed Jefferson, for it had occurred when he was governor in 1780–1781 and had severely hampered his efforts to protect the state at the time of the British invasion.[71]

A strong paper party sprang up in Maryland, where armed attacks on creditors and tax collectors took place in 1786, after the state senate rejected a paper-money bill. Such outbreaks moved the legislature to suspend the forced sale of property of delinquent taxpayers and to extend the time limit on tax collections. The program of the paper party called for an issue of £350,000 in bills, of which £250,000 was to be lent to landowners at 6 percent. On December 15, 1786, the house of delegates endorsed this plan, 37 to 25, but on December 30 the senate unanimously turned it down. The weight of private debts, amounting to at least £2,291,000 in 1786, no doubt accounts for the proposal to lend such a large sum to citizens. The decisive defeat of the paper party in Maryland caused men of wealth to look upon an effective senate as a bulwark of property rights.[72]

In New Hampshire, the burden of taxes and the execution of court orders for the sale of property of delinquent taxpayers oppressed many farmers and embittered them toward the government. In September, 1786, a large band of armed men descended upon the town of Exeter, imprisoned an unsympathetic legislature, importuned it to relieve their distress by an issue of paper money, and threatened to keep it in session until it yielded. Defenders of the government raised a counterforce of citizens and militia, who drove off the remonstrants. The legislature then referred a paper-money plan to the towns. The voters rejected it by a decisive margin.[73]

The turmoil in New Hampshire echoed more menacing disturbances across the border in Massachusetts, where Shays' Rebellion of 1786 became the focus of a widespread interest in the dark deeds of debtors. The foremost cause of that upheaval appears to have been a heavy burden of taxes that proved to be unbearable to many a poor citizen. After 1783, the Massachusetts legislature undertook to pay state and federal debts amounting to about £3,000,000, in addition to meeting the current costs of the government. The levies of 1786 for all these purposes amounted to £300,000. A poll tax of about £1 6s. a person, imposed on each of 90,-

[71] Jensen, The New Nation, p. 311; Writings of Madison (1867), I, 233, 239, 245, 251, 252; Irving Brant, James Madison (5 vols.; Indianapolis: The Bobbs-Merrill Company, 1941–1955), II, 361–363; Malone, Jefferson and His Time, I, 343.

[72] Crowl, Maryland During and After the Revolution, pp. 86–87, 90–91, 93–96, 102.

[73] Jeremy Belknap, The History of New Hampshire (3 vols.; Philadelphia: The author, 1784–1792), II, 466–477.

000 males over sixteen, yielded between 33 and 40 percent of the state's revenues and bore with crushing weight on the poor. The leaders who manned the state government adhered to a harsh and rigorous course. After 1780 they refused to issue additional paper money, retained a law which recognized only gold and silver as legal tender, and favored private creditors by imposing strict rules for the forced sale of real and personal property of defaulting debtors. If the foreclosure process did not yield enough money to pay a claim, the debtor might be sent to jail, where the accommodations were not of the best. Creditors became so energetic that, in 1784, Worcester County, with fewer than 50,000 inhabitants, brought forth more than 2,000 civil suits for the collection of debts, and, in 1785, 94 of 104 of its residents who were sentenced to jail went thither for failing to meet their obligations.[74]

Unhappily, many victims of hard times sought relief in direct action instead of concentrating their efforts on the state legislature. They gathered in town meetings and at county conventions, where they urged such reforms as paper money, lower taxes on land and polls, a reduction of salaries of public officers, the removal of the legislature from Boston, the abolition of the state senate, and taxes on luxuries. Above all, the malcontents insisted upon stopping foreclosures, and to this end they demanded either the abolition or the adjournment of the intermediate courts that had dispossessed debtors or had sent them to jail. Not content with verbal pleas, insurgents marched to county towns, where they closed the courts, coerced judges into suspending business, and raided jails to release debtor inmates. In Berkshire, Hampshire, and Worcester counties and at Concord in Middlesex County the civil courts did not function during the last five months of 1786.[75]

In the early stages of the resistance the legislature neither granted relief nor acted firmly against the insurgents, with whom probably half the people of the state sympathized. Their resort to force and the training of armed bands thoroughly aroused their opponents, who singled out one of their leaders, Captain Daniel Shays, a respected officer of the Revolution, and made him a personalized symbol of the revolt. In October, 1786, the appearance of a treasonable letter, allegedly signed by Shays but which he later disavowed, instigated the legislature to pass

---

[74] George Richards Minot, *The History of the Insurrections in Massachusetts* (2d ed.; Boston: James W. Burditt and Company, 1810), pp. 5–6; Robert A. East, "The Massachusetts Conservatives in the Critical Period," *The Era of the American Revolution: Studies Inscribed to Evarts Boutell Greene* (Richard B. Morris, ed.; New York: Columbia University Press, 1939), pp. 354–356; Walter A. Dyer, "Embattled Farmers," *New England Quarterly*, IV, No. 3 (July, 1931), 463.

[75] "The Depression of 1785 and Daniel Shays' Rebellion" (by Jonathan Smith), *William and Mary Quarterly*, Third Series, V, No. 1 (January, 1948), 85–86; Richard B. Morris, "Insurrection in Massachusetts," *America in Crisis* (Daniel Aaron, ed.; New York: Alfred A. Knopf, Inc., 1952), pp. 38–39.

a riot act and to authorize Governor Bowdoin to suppress the revolt with state troops. A large force under General Benjamin Lincoln soon dispersed the poorly armed farmers, who fled without giving battle. The end coincided with an action of Congress on February 21, 1787, when it called upon the states to elect delegates to a national convention for the purpose of revising the Articles of Confederation. "Events," declared Rufus King at this time, "are hurrying us to a crisis. Prudent and sagacious men should be ready to seize the most favorable circumstance to establish a more perfect and vigorous government." "Among the ripening incidents," wrote Madison, "was the insurrection of Shays in Massachusetts . . . ."[76]

[76] Marion L. Starkey, *A Little Rebellion* (New York: Alfred A. Knopf, Inc., 1955), pp. 90–91; Adams, *New England in the Republic,* pp. 159–162; Bancroft, *History of the Formation of the Constitution,* p. 191; James Madison, *Journal of the Constitutional Convention* (E. H. Scott, ed., Chicago: Albert, Scott and Company, 1895), p. 45.

CHAPTER V

The Economics of the Constitution

DURING the Revolution a national economy took shape. However, it rested on a weak foundation, hastily built. The depression of the 1780's shook the edifice severely, with the result that men who appreciated its potentialities decided that it should be strengthened, reinforced, and set upon a new and solid base. To this end they devised the federal Constitution.[1] They did the work so well that ever since it has served as the legal foundation of the national economy. Its effects on the economic history of the Union can scarcely be exaggerated.

INTERESTS AND OBJECTIVES

In 1913, Charles A. Beard published an illuminating book, *An Economic Interpretation of the Constitution of the United States*. Its second chapter set forth for the first time an extended statement of many of the economic interests and purposes which animated the leaders who drafted the historic document. An able criticism of the volume shows that Beard erred in interpreting the Constitution as the embodiment of the interests of a relatively few men.[2] Certainly, his implication that it was repugnant to the farmers of that day is not justified. How is one to account for the fact that in such agricultural states as Delaware, Georgia, and New Jersey each of the conventions which ratified the Constitution voted for it unanimously, that the conventions of agricultural Connecticut and Maryland ratified it by votes of more than three to one, and that agricultural Pennsylvania and South Carolina favored it by two to one? Although Beard portrayed correctly most of the objectives of the framers,

[1] Henry Cabot Lodge, ed., *The Federalist: A Commentary on the Constitution of the United States* (New York: G. P. Putnam's Sons, 1888), p. 82.

[2] Charles A. Beard, *An Economic Interpretation of the Constitution of the United States* (New York: The Macmillan Company, 1913; reissue 1935), pp. 55–56, 63, 64, 71–72, 149–150.

he failed to realize that the Constitution had widespread popular support.[3]

The men who deplored the weaknesses of the postwar economy ascribed them to certain features of the central government under the Articles of Confederation. Congress lacked the power to tax and therefore suffered the inadequacies of poverty. Since the states alone could levy duties on imports and exports, Congress could not create a national free-trade area or put pressure on foreign powers by means of concessions or reprisals. The states possessed the decisive powers over money and credit and did not use them to provide the country with a uniform and stable currency. The Articles did not equip the Union with the money or the authority essential for sustaining a national army. Lack of military force and of diplomatic prowess enfeebled Congress in its efforts to deal with the formidable problems of the West.[4]

The men who wished to strengthen the central government and who took an active part in the movement for the Constitution were designated in 1787–1789 as both "nationalists" and "federalists." Neither word describes accurately the opinions of all the leaders who then supported the cause of "a more perfect union." If only one word is used, "nationalist" is preferred, for the majority of the unionists then sought to devise a government that would be national in scope and character. However, most of the "nationalists" did not advocate a central government of unlimited power.[5] Most of them preferred to leave extensive powers with the states. The kind of government which the "nationalists" wanted becomes evident when one reviews the purposes they sought to attain, since the essential nature of a thing is indicated by the objectives it is designed to realize.[6]

The original aim of the nationalists was to provide for the payment in specie of the wartime debts of the Union.[7] The depression of 1785–

[3] Robert E. Brown, *Charles Beard and the Constitution* (Princeton, N. J.: Princeton University Press, 1956), pp. 142–143, 197.

[4] Beard, *An Economic Interpretation of the Constitution,* pp. 56–57; *The Federalist* (Lodge), pp. 84, 122, 125–127, 176, 278; *Writings of Madison* (1867), I, 350; Joseph Story, *A Familiar Exposition of the Constitution of the United States* (New York: Harper & Brothers, 1879), pp. 30–32; *Writings of Washington* (Fitzpatrick), XXIX, 260.

[5] *The Federalist* (Lodge), pp. 79, 98–99, 186–187, 237–238, 290; *Writings of Madison* (1867), I, 344, 346.

[6] William Winslow Crosskey, *Politics and the Constitution in the History of the United States* (2 vols.; Chicago: The University of Chicago Press, 1953) argues that the framers intended to create an all-powerful, uninhibited national government. Irving Brant designates Madison in 1780–1787 as a "nationalist," although he was an author of *The Federalist.* Washington used both "national" and "federal" when speaking of the Constitution in 1787–1788. For a statement concerning "nationalists" see Jensen, *The New Nation,* pp. xiii–xiv, 425.

[7] *The Federalist* (Lodge), pp. 178–179, 274; Nettels, "The American Merchant and the Constitution," pp. 33–34.

1787 then emphasized other interests. These included the creation of a single, stable, national currency based on coin—a reform that called for the surrender by the states of their power to issue paper money.[8] The nationalists also wished to deprive state legislatures and state courts of their then uninhibited power of favoring debtors at the expense of creditors. In addition, the nationalists desired to make the central government equal to the task of enlarging foreign markets for the exports and the shipping of the Union. A comparable interest was that of enabling the central authority to foster domestic manufactures.[9] Also, many nationalists regarded a strengthened Union as essential to the defense of the West and to the effective development of its resources.[10] Finally, the social unrest of the 1780's convinced apprehensive men that a potent national government was needed for the suppression of domestic insurrections that might menace the owners of private property.[11]

To achieve these objectives the nationalists deemed it necessary to endow Congress with several additional powers, of which the most fundamental was the power of taxation.[12] The central government should also be vested with the supreme authority over money.[13] To the end that the diplomacy of the Union might be invigorated, the states should give up the right to levy duties on imports, and Congress should be granted the exclusive power to regulate both foreign and interstate trade.[14] Congress should also be empowered to maintain a national army that would function independently of the states. For efficient action in the West, the central government needed the authority to supervise the Indians and to regulate the territories of the Union.[15]

The nationalists anticipated that such powers might be used both to stimulate economic activity and to protect established interests. The grant to Congress of adequate powers over commerce and money would make possible the establishment of a single trading area to which every American merchant would have free access; the abolition of the confusing currencies, commercial codes, and tariffs of thirteen individual states

---

[8] Nettels, "The American Merchant and the Constitution," p. 30; *The Federalist* (Lodge), pp. 277–278; Story, *A Familiar Exposition of the Constitution*, pp. 115–116.

[9] *The Federalist* (Lodge), pp. 61–62; Story, *A Familiar Exposition of the Constitution*, p. 113.

[10] *The Federalist* (Lodge), pp. 16, 18, 33, 144–146, 231.

[11] *Ibid.*, pp. 97, 164, 174.

[12] Beard, *An Economic Interpretation of the Constitution*, p. 50; Story, *A Familiar Exposition of the Constitution*, p. 102; *The Federalist* (Lodge), pp. 174–175, 177, 182, 191, 202, 291.

[13] Story, *A Familiar Exposition of the Constitution*, pp. 115–116; *The Federalist* (Lodge), pp. 277–278.

[14] Story, *A Familiar Exposition of the Constitution*, p. 108; *The Federalist* (Lodge), pp. 262–263.

[15] Story, *A Familiar Exposition of the Constitution*, pp. 113–114, 122–124, 250; *The Federalist* (Lodge), pp. 19–20, 136–137, 263, 250, 270.

would so simplify and facilitate business as to give a vigorous spur to enterprise. Once the states had lost the right to impair commercial contracts, interstate commerce—dependent as it was upon credit—would receive a fresh impetus from an enhanced feeling of security among traders. If the Union should provide for the payment in specie of the interest on the national debt, public securities would acquire a durable value, and would, in effect, increase the supply of currency, thereby giving new life to production and exchange.[16]

The program of the nationalists also promised to stimulate many domestic industries. A national trading area, open to all American producers, would assure them of the large market they needed for large-scale production. Congress might impose tariff duties on imports for the benefit of American manufacturers, levy tonnage duties to help American shipbuilders and shipowners, and grant bounties to depressed industries such as the fisheries.[17] Sound public securities could either be used abroad to buy tools and machines sorely needed by American manufacturers, or be used at home as collateral for loans that would facilitate production. In the foreign sphere, a strong government might improve the markets for American exports, while American merchants could use new public securities, worth their face values in specie, to pay debts they owed abroad, thereby securing credit for future purchases.[18]

The program of the nationalists was defensive in several respects. It aimed to protect creditors and investors from hostile acts of state governments.[19] It also promised to safeguard maritime trade, as in the Mediterranean, by means of an adequate navy.[20] To the West, the program offered security from attacks by the Indians and from encroachments of foreign powers.[21] New bulwarks would guard property owners if imperiled by insurrections such as Shays' Rebellion. The underwriting of property would reinforce slavery and assure federal aid to slaveowners when threatened by revolts too formidable to be put down by local authorities.[22]

Twelve states elected delegates to attend the Constitutional Convention, which assembled at Philadelphia in May, 1787. Their legislatures thus manifested a widespread interest in the cause of a strength-

---

[16] Story, A Familiar Exposition of the Constitution, pp. 106, 115–116; The Federalist (Lodge), pp. 65–66, 85, 262–263, 278; Broadus Mitchell, Alexander Hamilton: Youth to Maturity, 1755–1788 (New York: The Macmillan Company, 1957), p. 274.

[17] Story, A Familiar Exposition of the Constitution, p. 113.

[18] Beard, An Economic Interpretation of the Constitution, pp. 40–46; Bancroft, History of the Formation of the Constitution, pp. 138–139.

[19] The Federalist (Lodge), pp. 278–279.

[20] Ibid., pp. 62–63.

[21] Ibid., pp. 16, 18, 64.

[22] Ibid., pp. 32, 49, 97, 164, 272; Beard, An Economic Interpretation of the Constitution, p. 30.

ened Union. By August, 1788, conventions of eleven states had ratified the Constitution, and seven had done so by votes of at least two to one. This record denotes that a considerable majority of the active men of the time approved of the work of the framers—a result that is understandable when one considers its bearings on the economic interests of various groups of citizens.

To farmers the Constitution offered substantial benefits. Its provision for a government that could act with vigor in foreign affairs promised to enlarge the export markets for farm produce, while the pledge to pay the debts of the Union gave assurance that a fund of new securities, equivalent to coin, would have an uplifting effect on prices.[23] In *The Federalist*, No. 12, Hamilton pointed out that, in the main, duties on trade would finance the central government, thereby exempting farmers from heavy taxes on land.[24] As property owners, solvent farmers shared in the guarantees which the Constitution conferred on that large group. Frontiersmen and promoters of settlement in the West could look to the new government for assistance in opening the Mississippi River to the pioneers, in making good the Union's claim to the then Southwest, and in effecting the withdrawal of Britain from the northern posts.[25] Advantages to slaveowners included a commitment of federal aid in capturing and returning fugitive slaves. In Georgia, the yeomen then needed the support of the Union in their struggle with the Creek Indians.[26] The farmers of New Jersey and Connecticut had a common interest in freeing themselves from taxes imposed by New York on their trade—levies that did not benefit the victims. Should New York surrender to the Union the power to collect taxes on trade, New Jersey and Connecticut might share in the benefits that would flow from the expenditure of federal revenues.[27]

The Constitution held out to merchants and manufacturers the advantages of a large free-trade area, a single national currency, the protection of commercial credits in all the states, and a stimulus to business that would come with the issuing of sound public securities. Merchants and shipowners also stood to profit from federal laws giving preference to American-owned ships and from the backing in foreign trade of a strong government endowed with effective bargaining power. Manufac-

[23] *The Federalist* (Lodge), p. 68.

[24] *Ibid.*, pp. 72–73, 124–125.

[25] Beard, *An Economic Interpretation of the Constitution*, p. 50.

[26] *The Federalist* (Lodge), pp. 80–81; *Writings of Madison* (1867), I, 357; Orin Grant Libby, *The Geographical Distribution of the Vote of the Thirteen States on the Federal Constitution, 1787–8* (University of Wisconsin *Economics, Political Science, and History Series, Bulletin*, Vol. I, No. 1; Madison: 1894), pp. 40, 45.

[27] *The Federalist* (Lodge), pp. 34–35, 262–263; Libby, *Geographical Distribution of the Vote on the Constitution*, p. 16; Forrest McDonald, *We the People: The Economic Origins of the Constitution* (Chicago: The University of Chicago Press, 1958), pp. 118–119, 124, 130, 138, 155, 157.

turers and artisans could now look to the Union for additional benefits in the shape of bounties and tariffs. Among the industries in need of such assistance were the fisheries, shipbuilding, and manufactures of iron-ware, soap, candles, cordage, leather goods, glassware, and refined sugar.[28]

In all the above groups were creditors and investors to whom the Constitution opened such pleasing prospects as the payment in specie of the national debt, protection from domestic insurrections, and the safe-guarding of investments from injurious state laws.[29]

TAXATION AND THE PUBLIC DEBT

The attainment of every objective of the nationalists depended upon a grant to Congress of an independent taxing power. From the economic point of view, the heart of the Constitution is the first clause of Section 8, Article I, as follows: "The Congress shall have the power to lay and collect taxes, duties, imposts, and excises, to pay the debts and provide for the common defense and general welfare of the United States . . . ." Among the uses of the taxing power, the payment of the debts of the Union ranks first. This feature points to the first clause of Article VI, which states: "All debts contracted and engagements entered into, before the adoption of this Constitution, shall be as valid against the United States under this Constitution, as under the Confederation." Thus the framers pledged the new government to pay all outstanding debts of the Union and vested it with the power essential to raising the necessary revenue.

In 1784 the total debts of the central government, foreign and do-mestic, principal and unpaid interest, amounted to approximately $39,-323,000. The yearly interest on this sum came to $1,875,000. The income of the Union from all sources totaled, in 1785 and 1786, about $1,110,000 —a yearly average of $555,000. Income thus fell short of the interest charges on the national debt by about $1,320,000 a year. Such deficiencies explain in large measure why the national debt grew until, on January 1, 1790, it reached an estimated total of $52,788,000—an increase of $13,465,000 over 1784. The financial plight of the country that confronted the Constitutional Convention is illustrated by the fact that in 1786 the total income of the central government was less than one third of the annual interest charges on the national debt.[30]

Nationalist leaders had deplored the financial inadequacies of the

[28] Beard, An Economic Interpretation of the Constitution, pp. 41–47.

[29] The Federalist (Lodge), pp. 32, 164, 272, 274; Story, A Familiar Exposition of the Constitution, pp. 146–156, 249; Beard, An Economic Interpretation of the Consti-tution, pp. 32–35.

[30] Dewey, Financial History of the United States, p. 56; Jensen, The New Nation, p. 387; Bayley, National Loans of the United States, p. 31.

Union during the Revolution, when they had urged that Congress be vested with an independent taxing power. To this end Congress on February 3, 1781, proposed an amendment to the Articles of Confederation which would empower it to levy duties of 5 percent on imports, for the purpose of paying the interest and principal on the public debt. Rhode Island vetoed the plan, objecting to a grant of power unlimited in time because it implied that the principal of the national debt might never be paid in full. Rhode Island also disliked the proposal that federal rather than state officials should collect the duties.[31] To meet such objections Congress on April 18, 1783, submitted a second plan which limited the proposed grant of power to twenty-five years and which provided that specified duties on imports should be collected by state officials under regulations framed by Congress. Every state except New York gave a satisfactory endorsement to the 1783 plan, which also required the unanimous approval of the thirteen states. New York at the time derived a large revenue from its own duties on imports. If it should concede to Congress the power to levy such duties, it might lose half the income of its state government and be forced to make up the loss by increased taxes on land. The group then in power in the state, an agrarian party headed by Governor George Clinton, objected to such an addition to the tax burden on farmers and refused to approve all the essential features of the 1783 plan. Hence, when the Constitutional Convention met, the likelihood that Congress would obtain an independent taxing power seemed rather dim and remote.[32]

The securities which represented the domestic debts of the Union in the 1780's consisted mainly of loan-office certificates, comparable to government bonds, and various kinds of paper that had been issued during or after the war to buy military supplies, to pay officers and soldiers, and to meet other obligations of the Union. After 1783, Congress paid the interest on the loan-office certificates by means of "indents"— paper which it did not redeem in coin and which was somewhat akin to paper currency. Nonpayment of interest in coin caused all this paper to depreciate drastically and to become an object of speculation, bought by purchasers who hoped that Congress would some day redeem it in specie.[33] Depreciation and fluctuating values deprived the paper of the advantages which businessmen looked for in sound public securities, and

[31] *Journals of the Continental Congress,* XIX, 112–113; Bates, *Rhode Island and the Union,* p. 78.

[32] *Journals of the Continental Congress,* XXIV, 257–258; Cochran, *New York in the Confederation,* pp. 172–176; E. Wilder Spaulding, *His Excellency, George Clinton* (New York: The Macmillan Company, 1938), p. 170; *Diplomatic Correspondence, 1783–1789,* IV, 409–413.

[33] Jensen, *The New Nation,* pp. 382–383, 388, 390; Beard, *An Economic Interpretation of the Constitution,* pp. 32, 34–35.

had effects that extended far beyond the disappointments of unpaid creditors.

Many nationalists of the 1780's were intent on the expansion of the country and were familiar with British public finance that had long stimulated British enterprise. One of its essential features was a fund of public securities that yielded interest in coin. Such securities offered to businessmen a safe and durable form of investment that enabled them either to conserve their capital or to obtain funds when needed by selling the securities or by using them as collateral for loans. Public securities also provided a means of buying goods and paying debts in foreign countries; and they served at home as a substitute for currency in large transactions, thereby invigorating business while avoiding the issuance of irredeemable paper money.[34]

The depreciating, fluctuating paper of the Union of the 1780's provided not one of these advantages. As long-term investments, the public securities were woefully defective, since the owner did not receive interest in coin. As currency, they resembled depreciating paper money. They were worthless as collateral for specie loans. Having no standing outside the Union, they could not be used to buy goods or to pay debts in foreign countries. Hence they could not expand the resources of businessmen or give them that confidence in investment which was deemed essential to the growth of enterprise. On the other hand, a guarantee by Congress to pay in coin the interest on the national debt would greatly increase the specie value of the securities, swell the credit resources and the currency supply of the Union, and give a potent impetus to business.[35]

A few rays of light penetrated the financial gloom of the 1780's. Investors in Holland were willing to lend money to the Union, partly from confidence in the future value of its public lands. When Holland was a partner of the United States during the Revolution, John Adams negotiated at Amsterdam a loan of $2,000,000. He dealt with three banking firms: Wilhelm and Jan Willink, Nicholas and Jacob van Staphorst, and De la Lande and Fynje. The contractors did not make available, at once and from their own funds, the entire sum of the loan. Rather, they undertook to obtain the money gradually from Dutch investors. They succeeded in raising $720,000 in 1782 and the remainder during the years 1783–1786. In 1784, a contract was made for a second loan, of $800,000, the money to be advanced to the United States in seven payments between 1785 and 1797—largely for paying the interest on the loan of 1782. Thus it appears that the Dutch had enough faith in the Union to underwrite interest payments due themselves. The loans of 1782 and 1784 yielded enough income to the United States to support its diplomatic agents in

[34] Webster, *Political Essays*, p. 243.
[35] Robert A. East, "The Business Entrepreneur in a Changing Economy, 1763–1795," *Tasks of Economic History* (1946), p. 26.

Europe during the 1780's, but not enough to engage in expensive adventures, such as a war with the Barbary pirates.[36]

The wartime debts of the states dovetailed with those of the Union. After 1783 the states owed sizable sums to their revolutionary soldiers and officers, to their citizens who had furnished military supplies, and to holders of state paper issued during the war. Perhaps the total of such war debts in 1787 was about $13,500,000. Most of the states did reasonably well in meeting the claims of their creditors. Records of the early 1790's show that the unpaid war debts of all the states then amounted to $18,271,-000. Eight states—New Hampshire, Rhode Island, New York, New Jersey, Pennsylvania, Maryland, Delaware, and Georgia—owed a total of only $4,000,000, or an average of $2.80 per white inhabitant. The debt of South Carolina equaled that of these eight states combined, with an average for each white resident of $28.50. Massachusetts (including Maine), Connecticut, Virginia, and North Carolina had per capita debts ranging from $8.50 to $6.20.[37]

The state war debts figured in the movement for the Constitution. A primary cause of the collapse of the national credit was the fact that several states preferred to use their slender resources to care for their own citizen creditors rather than to supply Congess with the money needed for the national debt. In Massachusetts, generous treatment of the state's creditors necessitated the heavy land and poll taxes that provoked Shays' Rebellion. The merchant-creditors of the state were then beset by conflicting interests. They favored the payment of the state debt, disliked taxes on trade, and preferred taxes on polls and land. Yet heavy land and poll taxes jeopardized the public peace. The merchants found a way out in the proposal that Congress should pay the state's war debt. In the Constitutional Convention Rufus King, a delegate of Massachusetts, said that "he would have no objection to throwing all the state debts into the federal debt, making one aggregate debt of about $70,000,000, and leaving it to be discharged by the General Government." Hamilton's argument in *The Federalist* in behalf of a national excise tax also pointed toward the assumption by Congress of the state debts.[38]

The breakdown of the national finances is illustrated by the fact that some states presumed to pay claims held by their citizens against the Union. Pennsylvania and New York in 1786 each arranged to give state securities to its citizens in exchange for national loan-office certificates. In this wise the two states became creditors of the Union. The advan-

[36] Jensen, *The New Nation*, p. 384; Bayley, *National Loans of the United States*, pp. 15–19.

[37] Jensen, *The New Nation*, pp. 303, 307–308; Bayley, *National Loans of the United States*, p. 33.

[38] East, "Massachusetts Conservatives in the Critical Period," pp. 375–377, 387–391; Madison, *Journal of the Constitutional Convention*, p. 350; *The Federalist* (Lodge), pp. 177, 202, 211.

tage to individuals lay in the fact that the states paid the interest on their securities in money, whereas the central government did not so honor its certificates. In 1783–1784, New Jersey, indignant that some of the states were not paying anything to the Union, refused to make additional contributions and undertook to pay directly to its citizens the interest on national loan-office certificates which they owned. Thereafter the state continued to by-pass the central government in this manner. Congress in 1786 implored New Jersey to withdraw its refusal to contribute to the Union, but the legislature remained adamant. Its defiant course put a severe burden on its taxpayers, which caused them to welcome the federal Constitution as a means of relieving the strain.[39]

In September, 1785, Congress asked the states for $3,000,000. A year later it had received less than $100,000. Such was the financial prostration of the Union on the eve of the Constitutional Convention.[40]

REINFORCING THE NATIONAL ECONOMY

In their efforts to overcome the postwar depression the states adopted measures which threatened to disrupt the national economy that had taken shape during the war. It was the function of the Constitution to halt this trend and to direct the development of the country along national lines. To accomplish this, the Constitution reduced sharply the importance of the states and conferred upon the central government many new powers in addition to the power of taxation.

The authority to define, create, and regulate the money of a country ranks with taxation as a highly prolific source of power. The monetary features of the Constitution were more nationalistic than the grant of a taxing power to Congress, for they abolished state power over money, whereas the states retained the right to levy many kinds of taxes. In giving Congress the sole power to coin money, the Constitution deprived the states of a power they had shared with Congress, on a concurrent basis, under the Articles of Confederation. The states also lost their former power of declaring currencies other than gold and silver coin to be a tender in payment of debt.[41]

The Constitution has provoked many controversies concerning its bearing on bills of credit. It clearly prohibited the states from emitting them. But did such a ban apply also to Congress? The framers definitely refused to specify in the Constitution, among the enumerated powers of

[39] Brunhouse, *The Counter-Revolution in Pennsylvania*, p. 185; McCormick, *Experiment in Independence*, pp. 235–243; Jensen, *The New Nation*, p. 396.

[40] *Journals of the Continental Congress*, XXIX, 745; McCormick, *Experiment in Independence*, p. 243.

[41] Article I, Sections 8, 10.

Congress, the authority to issue paper currency.[42] Yet the power is surely granted by implication. Congress received both the right to borrow money on the credit of the United States and the power to "make all laws which shall be necessary and proper for carrying into execution the foregoing powers, and all other powers vested by this Constitution in the government of the United States, or in any department or officer thereof." [43] Hence, if Congress should deem it necessary and proper to issue bills of credit, or to sell government bonds, in order to borrow money or to give effect to any other power vested in the federal government, such action would obviously be within the authority conferred by the Constitution. Congress is not specifically authorized to order the sale of government bonds, yet who can doubt that the framers intended that it should have that power? Such authority is not more valid than the power to issue paper currency.

The Constitution left to the states their power to charter private banks and to endow them with the privilege of issuing notes. By inference Congress received a similar power. The reasoning that justifies federal bills of credit also empowers Congress to charter banks and to authorize them to issue promissory notes that may serve as a medium of exchange.

With respect to credit, contracts, and investments, the Constitution prohibited the states from enacting any laws impairing the obligation of contracts, declared the Constitution itself to be the supreme law of the land, and authorized the establishment of federal courts to be vested with judicial power in all cases in law and equity arising under the Constitution. Thus a state law impairing the obligation of contracts would violate the Constitution, and the offended person might seek redress in a federal court. The Constitution therefore made the federal government the final arbiter in cases arising from state laws impairing contracts. Beyond this, the Constitution vested Congress with the power to enact a uniform national bankruptcy law; and its implied power to issue paper currency carried with it the authority to make such currency legal tender when used in fulfilling private contracts.[44]

The clauses of the Constitution pertaining to money and credit aggrandized Congress at the expense of the states. Congress received four specified powers: to coin money, to regulate the value of coin, to enact bankruptcy laws, and to establish courts authorized to set aside state laws impairing the obligation of contracts. Three implied powers could be claimed for Congress: to issue bills of credit, to charter banks,

[42] Madison, *Journal of the Constitutional Convention*, pp. 541–543.
[43] Article I, Section 8.
[44] Article I, Sections 8, 10; Article VI; Article III, Sections 1, 2; Charles Warren, *Bankruptcy in United States History* (Cambridge, Mass.: Harvard University Press, 1935), pp. 4–5.

and to determine legal tender. In the monetary sphere, the Constitution did not subject Congress to any positive restraints. The states retained only one positive power—that of chartering banks; and they were prohibited from coining money, emitting bills of credit, impairing contracts, and making anything except gold and silver coin a legal tender. As for money and credit, twelve features of the Constitution favored the Union; only one favored the states.

The nationalists intended to create a national currency based on coin. In depriving the states of their former powers over money and credit, the framers condemned the paper currencies, the legal-tender acts, and the debtor-relief laws to which state legislatures had resorted during the depression. Madison said that such "evils" had "contributed more to that uneasiness which produced the Convention, and prepared the public mind for a general reform, than those which accrued to our national character and interest from the inadequacy of the Confederation to its immediate objects." [45] Hamilton wrote in *The Federalist:* "The loss which America has sustained since the peace, from the pestilent effects of paper money on the necessary confidence between man and man, on the necessary confidence in the public councils, on the industry and morals of the people, and on the character of republican government, constitutes an enormous debt against the States chargeable with this unadvised measure, which must long remain unsatisfied; or rather an accumulation of guilt, which can be expiated no otherwise than by a voluntary sacrifice . . . of the power which has been the instrument of it." [46]

In providing for a single, national monetary system and in safeguarding commercial contracts from state laws, the Constitution moved far toward creating a large free-trading area so essential to merchants and manufacturers. Other features of the Constitution had a like effect. Businessmen gained assurance that they would have ready access to all the markets of the Union, would receive protection for their persons and property in all the states, and would enjoy immunity from discriminations and impositions of a local character. To these ends the Constitution provided that "the Citizens of each State shall be entitled to all privileges and immunities of Citizens in the several States," that no state, without the consent of Congress, should "lay any imposts or duties on imports or exports, except what may be absolutely necessary for executing its inspection laws," that no state, without the consent of Congress should "lay any duty of tonnage," and that Congress should not give any preference "by any regulation of commerce or revenue to the ports of one State over those of another" or require vessels bound to, or from, one state "to enter, clear, or pay duties in another." The exclusive power of Congress to regulate commerce among the states assured merchants that all shipments in

---

[45] *Writings of Madison* (1867), I, 350.
[46] *The Federalist* (Lodge), p. 278.

interstate trade would be subject to a single set of uniform rules, while the grant of taxing power required that all federal duties, imposts, and excises should be uniform throughout the United States.[47]

In order to facilitate business in the national trading area the Constitution provided for a single postal system and a common standard of weights and measures. Manufacturing stood to receive a strong stimulus from the power of Congress to grant patents to inventors, thereby safeguarding their rights throughout the Union while relieving them from the trouble of securing thirteen separate patents, without which their inventions might be pirated in some state or states.[48] National copyrights would serve authors and publishers in a similar way. In the 1780's Noah Webster labored for more than four years to obtain copyright laws in twelve states.[49] Another feature of the Constitution—the grant to Congress of the power to establish a "uniform rule of naturalization"—promised to aid promoters of industrial projects who wished to encourage foreign artisans to come to the United States. Such a uniform rule would give an immigrant residence credit toward citizenship in every state in which he lived, whereas under state naturalization laws he might lose such credit if he left a state before fulfilling its requirements.[50]

The advocates of a strengthened Union included five leaders who were pre-eminent in the field of foreign affairs: Franklin, Washington, John Adams, Jefferson, and John Jay. In their dealings with foreign powers all these men had suffered anxieties, failures, or disappointments traceable to the weaknesses of the Confederation. Hamilton spoke for all five when he wrote in *The Federalist:* "Let the Thirteen States, bound together in a strict indissoluble Union, concur in erecting one great American system superior to the control of all trans-Atlantic force or influence, and able to dictate the terms of the connection between the old and the new world!" Four elements of the Constitution gave new force to the Union as a power among the nations. The states lost their onetime power to levy duties on imports and exports; Congress received the sole power to regulate interstate and international trade; and the Constitution designated all treaties made under the authority of the United States as a part of the supreme law of the land, outranking state laws and state constitutions. These clauses strengthened the Union as a negotiator of commercial treaties by enabling it to grant effective favors and to retaliate. The taxing power per-

[47] Article I, Sections 9, 10; Article IV, Section 2.

[48] Article I, Section 8. ". . . a patent can be of no use unless it is from Congress, and not from them till they are vested with much more authority than they possess at this [time]." F. W. Geyer to Silas Deane, May 1, 1787 (?), *Deane Papers,* p. 244.

[49] Harry R. Warfel, ed., *Letters of Noah Webster* (New York: Library Publishers, 1953), pp. 1, 57.

[50] F. G. Franklin, "The Legislative History of Nationalization in the United States, 1776–1795" (American Historical Association, *Annual Report . . . 1901,* 2 vols.; Washington: Government Printing Office, 1902), I, 307, 310–311.

mitted Congress to establish and maintain military forces such as the recent poverty of the Union had forbidden. On this subject Hamilton wrote that an efficient navy would make the Union the deciding power in European conflicts in America.

This would be more particularly the case in relation to operations in the West Indies. A few ships of the line, sent opportunely to the reinforcement of either side, would often be sufficient to decide the fate of a campaign, on the event of which interests of the greatest magnitude were suspnded . . . . A situation so favorable would enable us to bargain with great advantage for commercial privileges. A price would be set not only upon our friendship, but upon our neutrality. By a steady adherence to the Union, we may hope, ere long, to become the arbiter of Europe in America, and to be able to incline the balance of European competitions in this part of the world as our interest may dictate.[51]

In 1787, pioneers and promoters of settlement needed a central government that could foster the development of the Southwest, for expansion thither was essential to the southern economy. The settled areas of New England, bursting at the seams, were ready to send forth a host of emigrants to the land north of the Ohio River. Congress had given little aid to western interests in the 1780's. The Spaniards and their Indian allies harassed the pioneers of the Southwest; the British and their Indians held sway in the Old Northwest and closed it to settlers. The Articles of Confederation, adopted before the Union had acquired title to any inland territories, did not endow Congress with power to act in the West. By 1787, however, the Union had secured title to most of the land north of the Ohio; and the territory of the southern states extended to the Mississippi. The control of the great inland rivers that bound together the western lands required some means of concerted action.

The Constitution equipped the central government for the tasks of settling, governing, and defending the West, by giving Congress both the power "to dispose of and make all needful rules and regulations respecting the territory . . . belonging to the United States," and the power to regulate trade with the Indian tribes. The Constitution also reaffirmed the title of the United States to land westward to the Mississippi. The Independence Treaty of 1783 defined the southwestern boundary of the Union, between the Mississippi and the Chattahoochee rivers, as the thirty-first parallel. On July 29, 1784, Spain asserted a claim to the land between the Mississippi on the west, the Ohio-Tennessee-Hiwassee rivers on the north, and the Flint River on the east. In consequence, both Spain and the United States claimed a large strip of present-day Georgia, practically all Alabama and Mississippi, the western fourth of Tennessee, and the western tip of Kentucky. In his negotiations with Gardoqui, John Jay had failed

[51] *The Federalist* (Lodge), pp. 62–63, 67; Beard, *An Economic Interpretation of the Constitution*, pp. 171–173.

to assert strongly the rights of the Union. The Constitution declared the Independence Treaty to be the supreme law of the land, thereby asserting emphatically the title of the United States to the territory southward to the thirty-first parallel.[52] Congress, now vested with the taxing power, could provide an effective national army to back up the land claims of the states and to defend the western settlements. Since the Constitution recognized the Indians as constituting separate nations, a national army could be employed against them within the limits of a state. Under the Articles of Confederation a political vacuum had existed in the West. In effect, the Articles authorized only Congress to deal with a foreign power, and yet they withheld from the Union the force necessary for opposing Britain and Spain.

To guard against social unrest the Constitution empowered Congress to use state militias to suppress insurrections and directed the United States to protect each state against domestic violence when requested to do so by state authorities. Commenting on these guarantees, Hamilton wrote: "The tempestuous situation from which Massachusetts has scarcely emerged, evinces that dangers of this kind are not merely speculative. Who can say what might have been the issue of her late convulsions, if the malcontents had been headed by a Caesar or by a Cromwell?" Madison, referring to possible slave revolts, said: "I take no notice of an unhappy species of population abounding in some of the States, who, during the calm of regular government, are sunk below the level of men; but who, in the tempestuous scenes of civil violence, may emerge into the human character, and give a superiority of strength to any party with which they may associate themselves." [53]

The power of Congress to regulate commerce included the power to enact navigation laws for the benefit of American shipbuilders and shipowners. Since the southern states did not own much shipping, some of their leaders feared that the commercial states, if unrestrained, might use the federal commerce power to monopolize the carrying trade, thereby exploiting the South. Such fears moved cautious Southerners to urge in the Convention that a vote of two thirds in each house should be necessary to the enactment of a law regulating foreign trade. This issue, becoming linked with a proposal to prohibit the slave trade, figured in one of the main compromises of the Constitution. The final decision granted to Congress the power to enact a navigation law by a majority vote and restrained Congress from prohibiting the slave trade before 1808—a decided victory for economic nationalism.[54]

[52] Article I, Section 8; Article IV, Section 3; Article VI; 8 *Statutes at Large*, p. 55; Whitaker, *The Spanish-American Frontier*, p. 69.

[53] *The Federalist* (Lodge), pp. 121, 273.

[54] Madison, *Journal of the Constitutional Convention*, pp. 608–609; Article I, Section 9; Max Farrand, *The Framing of the Constitution* (New Haven, Conn.: Yale University Press, 1913), pp. 147–151.

Washington's first term began officially on March 4, 1789, although he did not take the oath of office until April 30. Many writers have viewed his administration as a whole and in so doing have given emphasis to the influence on his policies of the war in Europe that arose from the French Revolution. That conflict, however, did not begin until April, 1792. By then Congress had enacted into law the principal policies favored by Washington—the Federalist program. In the years 1789–1791, when American leaders were fashioning those policies, no one foresaw the events in Europe that would cast shadows over Washington's second term. Not events in Europe after 1792 but the American experience during the years 1763–1789 shaped the thinking of Washington in 1789–1791. The forces that brought forth the Constitution also gave birth to the Federalist program.

As Washington had emerged as the pre-eminent leader of the Revolution and had taken the foremost part in the movement for the Constitution, so also he dominated his Presidency. By 1789 his leading ideas and objectives, the fruits of twenty-five years of experience, were deeply embedded in his mind. The first statements concerning public policy which he made after it became apparent that he would be elected President appear in letters he wrote to Lafayette and Jefferson early in 1789. These letters indicate that Washington's primary aim was to achieve an economic self-sufficiency for the Union by promoting manufactures and internal trade. He said: ". . . my endeavors shall be unremittingly exerted . . . to extricate my country from the embarrassments in which it is entangled, through the want of credit; and to establish a general system of policy which if pursued will insure permanent felicity to the commonwealth. I think I see a *path*, as clear and direct as a ray of light, which leads to the attainment of that object." To Jefferson he wrote that "the greatest and most important objects of internal concern, which at present occupy the public mind, are manufactures and inland navigation." He emphasized one recent "disadvantage" of the country—the decline of foreign trade, which he attributed to inadequate exports to Europe. However, as a result of this change, "the useful arts have been almost imperceptibly pushed to a considerable degree of perfection." More "substantial improvements in manufactures" had recently been made "than were ever before known in America." He noted the recent erection of a large glass factory in Maryland, the success of Pennsylvania in manufacturing cottons, hats, and leather goods, the production of an "incredible" number of nails and shoes in Massachusetts, and the establishment there of "factories of duck, cordage, glass, and several other branches." He reported that he had ordered Hartford domestic broadcloth, "to make a suit of clothes for myself," adding that he hoped that "it will not be a great while, before it will be unfashionable for a gentleman to appear in any other dress." "Many successful efforts in fabrics of different kinds are made every day. Those composed of cotton, I think, will be of the most immediate and extensive utility." "I use no porter or cheese in my family, but such as is made in America." [55]

Closely linked with Washington's interest in promoting manufactures was his aim of establishing a sound public credit. This required a monetary system based on coin. Hence he deemed it necessary to curtail the exportation of specie—an end that could be best attained by the development of manufactures and a reduction of unnecessary imports which drained the country of its precious metals.

The origins of Washington's economic ideas go back to the 1760's, when he discovered that it was unprofitable for him, as a tobacco planter, to depend upon British merchants for markets and manufactured goods. He therefore undertook to manufacture at Mount Vernon such articles as cloth, shoes, rope, and harness. He also developed a fishery in the Potomac, invested in western lands, produced more wheat and less tobacco on his farms, and engaged in the milling of flour.[56] His experiences during the Revolution confirmed him in his aversion for dependence upon European imports. Inadequate domestic industries could not supply the army with needed war materials, and the scarcity of coin—induced by excessive imports—led to the issuance of irredeemable paper money— an expedient that probably caused him more grief than any other evil.[57]

Seven acts of Congress, adopted in 1789–1792, made up the Federalist program: three revenue laws, a funding act, a bank act, a coinage act, and a patent law. Since these acts embodied proposals that were set forth in five historic reports which Hamilton submitted to Congress in 1790 and 1791, many writers have attributed the Federalist program to his influence and have called it the Hamiltonian system. Hamilton certainly worked out the details, fitted the parts together, provided a theoretical basis, and furnished cogent arguments. However, he did not originate the aims, policies, and underlying ideas. Viewed in its larger aspects, the program should be regarded as the work of many Federalist leaders—Washington above all. In most of its essential features it duplicated the financial system which Robert Morris had fashioned in 1781–1783 and which Washington had endorsed.[58] Hamilton, having served as Washington's aide during four years of the Revolution, had had the best possible opportunity to become familiar with Washington's ideas and the workings of his mind.

[55] Washington to Lafayette, January 29, 1789; to Jefferson, February 13, 1789, *Writings of Washington* (Fitzpatrick), XXX, 186–187, 199–200.

[56] Nettels, *George Washington and American Independence,* pp. 67–78.

[57] Rose Charlotte Engelman, "Washington and Hamilton" (Cornell University, Doctoral Thesis, 1948), pp. 50–52.

[58] Ver Steeg, *Robert Morris,* p. 199; Engelman, "Washington and Hamilton," pp. 53–57.

Hamilton had clearly recognized Washington as his chief, for when he resigned he said that he "always disliked the office of an aide-de-camp as having in it a kind of personal dependence." His most recent biographer says that he acquainted himself so thoroughly with Washington that he could express the General's wishes without specific instructions.[59] In writing his *Federalist* papers, Hamilton thrust aside his own ideas and preferences and expounded ideas which Washington strongly endorsed.[60] In 1789–1791 there was nothing in Washington's character to suggest a weakening of his habit of command. He wrote in January, 1789, that he intended to establish a general system of policy, "even at the hazard of former fame or present popularity," and that he saw a path to that goal "as clear and direct as a ray of light." [61]

The policies of Robert Morris differed from the Federalist program in that the latter asserted a purpose of promoting domestic manufactures. In December, 1791, Hamilton submitted to Congress his extraordinary *Report on Manufactures*—the charter of American industrialism. His genius as an analyst and organizer permeates this great state paper, but can one say that it presents ideas that were peculiar to him? Before 1788 he had not manifested any interest in manufacturing industries. His associates in New York were landed magnates and city merchants.[62] Washington, on the other hand, had exhibited, since 1765, a continuing interest in manufacturing. His father for many years had given much of his time to the iron industry as a shareholder in the famous Principio Company and as superintendent of its mining and smelting operations.[63]

In the *Report on Manufactures* Hamilton explained how each of the parts of the Federalist program served to promote industry and how they were all connected so as to form an engine capable of exerting a concentrated force. He also explained at some length the benefits that a country derived from manufacturing pursuits. A nation, he said, that produced only a few agricultural staples must depend upon foreign outlets for the disposal of its surplus. Yet conditions of foreign trade often dictated sales at a loss because of glutted markets and low prices. Ordinarily, a country producing a few farm products incurred an unfavorable balance of trade and suffered from a shortage of coin caused by payments abroad for manufactured goods. Hamilton asserted that "the uniform appearance of

[59] Mitchell, *Alexander Hamilton*, pp. 115, 229.

[60] *Writings of Washington* (Fitzpatrick), XXX, 66.

[61] *Ibid.*, p. 186.

[62] Mitchell, *Alexander Hamilton*, *passim*. For an analysis of the Report and a résumé of Hamilton's principal ideas see Louis M. Hacker, *Alexander Hamilton in the American Tradition* (New York: McGraw-Hill Book Company, 1957), pp. 171–183, 132–137, 147–154, 162–164.

[63] Nathaniel Wright Stephenson and Waldo Hilary Dunn, *George Washington* (2 vols.; New York: Oxford University Press, 1940), I, 25.

an abundance of specie, as the concomitant of a flourishing state of manufactures, and the reverse, where they do not prevail, afford a strong
presumption of their favorable operation upon the wealth of a country." [64]

Throughout the *Report* Hamilton spoke in terms of factories, machines, and large-scale production. He considered various handicaps in
the United States to industries so organized, dwelling particularly upon
the scarcity of labor, high wages, and the shortage of capital. On this
subject he observed:

> There are large districts which may be considered as pretty fully peopled;
> and which, notwithstanding a continual drain for distance settlement, are
> thickly interspersed with flourishing and increasing towns. If these districts have
> not already reached the point at which the complaint of scarcity of hands
> ceases, they are not far from it, and are approaching fast toward it; and having,
> perhaps, fewer attractions to agriculture than some other parts of the Union,
> they exhibit a proportionably stronger tendency toward other kinds of industry.
> In these districts may be discerned no inconsiderable maturity for manufactur-
> ing establishments. [65]

Hamilton concluded that the scarcity of skilled mechanics and a shortage
of capital in the form of machinery were the principal drawbacks to
industrial progress and he explained how the Federalist program would
overcome them. [66]

In surveying the Union in 1791, Hamilton dwelt upon twenty-eight
types of products or industries that had advanced so far as to justify public
support, in view of native conditions that favored expansion on a profitable
basis. [67] He insisted that the men best qualified to manage industries were
not rash speculators but persons of prudence and caution who valued
stability, regularity, and certainty. To induce such men to invest in manufactures it was necessary to give them government aid and protection.
He considered eleven types of governmental assistance and assigned
special value to protective tariffs, bounties, patents, and inland transportation facilities. [68]

At all points Hamilton asserted the importance of agriculture and
defended home manufactures as a boon to the farmer. They would enlarge
the demand for his produce and raw materials and provide him with a
home market that would be more steady, certain, and profitable than
foreign markets. Soon the native industries would supply goods more
cheaply than could foreign producers, since domestic merchandise would

[64] Henry Cabot Lodge, ed., *The Works of Alexander Hamilton* (9 vols.; New
York: G. P. Putnam's Sons, 1885–1886), III, 356.
[65] *Ibid.*, p. 330.
[66] *Ibid.*, pp. 335–348.
[67] *Ibid.*, pp. 348–349, 384–411.
[68] *Ibid.*, pp. 364–381.

not have to bear the costs of transportation across the ocean.[69] Hamilton repeatedly echoed the statement of Washington that he "would not force the introduction of manufactures by extravagant encouragements, . . . to the prejudice of agriculture." [70]

[69] *Ibid.*, pp. 318–321, 334.
[70] *Writings of Washington* (Fitzpatrick), XXX, 186.

CHAPTER VI

The Federalist Program

REVENUE AND PROTECTION

WASHINGTON sounded the note of national economic independence when he signed the first Federalist measure, the Tariff Act of 1789, on July 4. "Indeed we have already been too long subject to British prejudices," he had written earlier in the year.[1] Congress began its work on the tariff by designating dollars and cents rather than English pounds and shillings as the money of account of the new government.

Madison opened the tariff debate in the House by offering a simple proposal to levy imposts, mainly for the sake of revenue. He recommended special duties on eight kinds of imports and the taxing of all other articles at a single rate.[2] Immediately there arose a demand for protection which arrayed Southerners against sponsors of manufacturing in the North. Thomas Hartley of Pennsylvania, pleading for infant industries, asserted that nations had long considered it proper "to give great encouragement to the establishment of manufactures, by laying such partial duties on the importation of foreign goods, as to give the home manufacturers a considerable advantage in price when brought to market."[3]

The Act of 1789, proclaiming its objectives to be "the support of the government, the discharge of the debts of the United States, and the encouragement and protection of manufactures," levied duties on sixty-five types of articles, fifty-five of which were manufactures of the sort then made within the Union. All imports not named in the act were to pay at the rate of 5 percent ad valorem. Coaches and carriages drew the highest rate—15 percent. The products subject to a 10 percent duty in-

[1] *Writings of Washington* (Fitzpatrick), XXX, 87.
[2] *The Debates and Proceedings of the Congress of the United States* (42 vols.; Washington: Gales and Seaton, 1834–1856), 1 Cong., 1 Sess., I, 106–108; F[rank] W. Taussig, *The Tariff History of the United States* (8th ed.; New York: G. P. Putnam's Sons, 1931), p. 15.
[3] *Debates of Congress*, 1 Cong., 1 Sess., I, 114.

cluded paints, gunpowder, chinaware, stoneware, earthenware, and glass. The next category consisted of articles taxed at 7½ percent: tinware, pewterware, ready-made clothing, brushes, canes, whips, hats, saddles, buttons, cabinetwork, paper, anchors, slit iron, rolled iron, and iron castings. The act imposed specific duties on twenty-one kinds of products, as follows: wool and cotton cards, nails, unwrought steel, candles, soap, boots, shoes, cables, cordage, twine, beer, ale, porter, cider, malt, cheese, snuff, tobacco, loaf sugar, and salt.[4] The articles thus taxed applied to industries which, having taken root, were deemed most worthy of public aid. Madison consented to protectionism on the ground that the manufacturing states, having surrendered the power to tax imports, deserved assistance from Congress.[5]

The first tariff act levied specific duties on only six kinds of noncompetitive imports—tea, molasses, wine, brown sugar, coffee, and cocoa. The proposed duty on molasses evoked a spirited opposition from representatives of Massachusetts, who pointed out that their state imported more molasses than all the rest of the Union combined and that such imports provided both the raw material for their rum distilleries and the principal return for their exports of fish to the West Indies. Predicting ruin for their fishery and shipping if a proposed molasses duty of 8 cents a gallon were adopted, the Massachusetts representatives succeeded in beating down the rate to 2½ cents a gallon.[6]

Patrons of protection repeatedly professed an interest in aiding agriculture. Many of the articles taxed were made of raw materials that were produced on American farms—beer, ale, cider, cheese, malt, leather goods, manufactured tobacco, snuff, soap, candles, cordage, twine, oil paints, brushes, and articles of wood. The act also gave specific protection to American hemp, indigo, and cotton. With respect to hemp, a lively conflict broke out. Manufacturers and shipbuilders sought cheap raw material for rope and cordage, whereas spokesmen of the South wished to encourage the production of hemp in South Carolina, Georgia, and the West. In this case agriculture won, obtaining a duty of 60 cents per 112 pounds—approximately the same as the duty on steel.[7]

Manufacturing gained at other points in that the act encouraged the importation of scarce raw materials by admitting them duty-free. Such were saltpeter, tin, lead, copper, wool, dyes, hides, furs, and deerskins.[8]

The Federalists also acted promptly to provide protection to American shipbuilders and shipowners. The first tariff law imposed especially

[4] Ibid., II, 2183–2185.
[5] Ibid., I, 116; Orrin Leslie Elliott, The Tariff Controversy in the United States, 1789–1833 (Leland Stanford Junior University Monographs: History and Economics; No. 1; Palo Alto, Calif.: 1892), pp. 69–70.
[6] Debates of Congress, 1 Cong., 1 Sess., I, 134–144; II, 2183.
[7] Ibid., I, 2185, 155–162.
[8] Ibid., p. 2185.

high duties on Oriental products if imported into the United States in foreign vessels—a device that served to encourage American shipowners to increase a direct trade with China, which they were then developing. The tariff act also provided for a discount of 10 percent of all duties on goods that should be imported in vessels that were American-built and -owned.[9] The second major law of the Federalists, the Tonnage Act of July 29, 1789, sought both to raise a revenue and to give protection to American shipping interests. This measure required that vessels which were both foreign-built and foreign-owned should pay a duty of 50 cents a ton on every entry into a port of the Union. Vessels that should be built in the United States in the future and owned by foreigners should pay an entry duty of 30 cents a ton. American shipowners were required to pay an entry duty of only 6 cents a ton on vessels both built and owned in the United States, and if such vessels were employed in the fisheries or the coasting trade, they were required to pay the duty only once a year. This arrangement gave to American shipbuilders and shipowners a monopoly of the fisheries and the coastal trade of the country.[10]

The House debates on the tonnage act exposed a conflict of interests between the planters of South Carolina and the shipowners and shipbuilders of Pennsylvania, New England, and New York. Madison, acting as a harmonizer, urged that a vigorous American shipping industry would train the seamen needed for manning a national navy. He thought that an act discriminating against British shipping would serve as a weapon to force Britain to open its West Indian ports to American vessels. If the taxing of British ships should reduce imports from Britain, manufacturing in the United States would be stimulated. Madison implied that the adoption of the Constitution committed the Union to aid the shipping interests, since the commercial states had given up their own tonnage duties on the assumption that they would be replaced by a single national code. Northern spokesmen pictured the distress of the American shipbuilding industry and urged protective duties as a proper means of providing relief.[11]

On the other side, representatives of South Carolina and Georgia emphasized their dependence on foreign shipping, pictured the poverty of their states, and asserted that existing low prices of rice and indigo would not bear increased shipping charges. In the debates on both the tariff and the tonnage acts, South Carolinians and Georgians repeatedly complained that the proposed taxes, far from benefiting their states, would impose disproportionately large burdens upon them, for the benefit of manufacturers, shipbuilders, and shipowners of the North.[12]

---

[9] *Ibid.*, II, 2184.
[10] *Ibid.*, p. 2186.
[11] *Ibid.*, I, 246–248, 266, 284, 292, 295, 297.
[12] *Ibid.*, pp. 263, 266, 267, 270–272, 275, 296, 298–299.

INFLATION AND PUBLIC DEBTS

Having provided the new government with an abundant revenue, Congress in September, 1789, created the Treasury Department, and in the following January its first Secretary, Alexander Hamilton, submitted a *Report on the Public Credit*, in which he outlined a plan for paying the debts of the Union. He proposed to do this in such a way as to increase the currency supply of the country and to stimulate business by raising prices. He estimated the sum of the debts, federal and state, which were owed mainly to American citizens, as $65,414,085.[13] He proposed to satisfy the public creditors by giving them new federal securities in exchange for the old certificates that they held. Some of the new securities, on which interest of 6 percent was to be paid in coin from the now assured federal revenues, would gain and maintain a value in specie equal, or nearly equal, to their face values. Such securities would be worth far more than the old certificates, which had depreciated to the extent that they had passed for as little as fifteen cents specie on the dollar. The new securities, if kept at a high level in coin, would therefore make a great addition to the country's stock of paper wealth.[14]

Hamilton conceived of sound public securities as a substitute for, or an equivalent of, money. He thought that the public debts might be paid in such a way as both to create a large fund of paper currency and to avoid an emission of bills of credit by Congress. He believed that well-supported government securities would offer many of the advantages of a paper currency and guard against the sort of extreme depreciation that might occur if Congress, without legal restraint, should exercise the power of printing paper money. Hamilton's plan to create a large fund of new public securities promised to bring about a controlled inflation. The price depression of the 1780's had not ended when he offered his first *Report on the Public Credit*. Like most other informed men of the time, he recognized that the country needed more currency than was then in circulation. Of this need he said:

The effect which the funding of the public debt, on right principles, would have upon landed property, is one of the circumstances attending such an arrangement, which has been least adverted to, though it deserves the most particular attention. The present depreciated state of that species of property is a serious calamity. The value of cultivated lands, in most of the States, has fallen, since the Revolution, from twenty-five to fifty per cent. In those farther south, the decrease is still more considerable. Indeed, if the representations continually received from that quarter may be credited, lands there will command no price which may not be deemed an almost total sacrifice. This de-

[13] *Hamilton's Works* (Lodge), II, 73–74.

[14] Esther Rogoff Taus, *Central Banking Functions of the United States Treasury, 1789–1941* (New York: Columbia University Press, 1943), p. 12.

crease in the value of lands ought, in a great measure, to be attributed to the scarcity of money; consequently, whatever produces an augmentation of the moneyed capital of the country must have a proportional effect in raising that value. The beneficial tendency of a funded debt, in this respect, has been manifested by the most decisive experience in Great Britain.[15]

Hamilton further insisted that sound public securities would stimulate commerce, manufactures, and agriculture. Merchants and producers would have enlarged capitals which they could use in business and which, if not so employed, would yield them interest from the government.[16]

The conviction that public securities should serve as currency moved Hamilton to make two extremely important and controversial proposals. If public securities were to form a national paper currency, it was necessary that they should be uniform throughout the country, and that they should pass freely from person to person at substantial values in coin. To attain these ends Hamilton proposed that the federal government should assume and pay in coin the long-term debts of the states. It should do this by giving new federal securities to the present owners of the state certificates—new securities to be worth in specie the full face values of the old.[17] The assumption of the state debts would replace thirteen different kinds of securities with new types of paper based on a single authority. Such a change would go far toward giving the country a uniform paper currency, thereby helping to create a single, unified trading area which was indispensable to the growth of commerce and manufacturing on a nation-wide scale.

Hamilton reasoned that if public securities were to circulate as money, each citizen must have faith that they would always be as good as gold. The only guarantee of such value would be the readiness of the federal government to pay in full both interest and principal when they were due. Hamilton therefore insisted that the government should guarantee to pay to every present owner of old certificates their full face values in specie, thereby assuring all future owners of public securities that the government would always satisfy their claims at 100 cents in coin on the dollar.[18] Such an assurance would cause people to accept public securities at or near par and they would therefore circulate without depreciation and almost as freely as coin. If, on the other hand, the new government should begin its financial operations by failing to pay its creditors in full and in specie, then no one could feel confident of receiving full payment in the future, with the result that the public securities would be exchanged at varying rates of discount. Such depreciation would then deprive the securities of the character of a fluid and stable currency.

[15] *Hamilton's Works* (Lodge), II, 54–55.
[16] *Ibid.*, pp. 52–54, 77–78.
[17] *Ibid.*, pp. 103–106.
[18] *Ibid.*, pp. 48–52.

Hamilton's proposals offered to benefit both the creditors of the Union and the creditors of those states which had the largest long-term debts. The creditors of the Union were most numerous in the middle states and New England and least numerous in the South. However, South Carolina, North Carolina, and Virginia each had a large state debt.[19] For these reasons, the proposal to pay both the state debts and those of the Union promised to spread new federal securities, or paper currency, throughout the country. Hamilton noted that the states had surrendered to the Union the power of levying duties on imports, and he argued that other taxes levied by the states for paying their debts would hamper business with "interfering regulations" and lead to "collision and conflict." [20] He added: "If all the public creditors receive their dues from one source, distributed with an equal hand, their interest will be the same. And having the same interest, they will be united in the support of the fiscal arrangements [taxes] of the Federal Government. . . . Union and concert of views among creditors . . . in every government is of great importance to their security, and to that of the public credit . . . ." [21]

Critics of Hamilton's plan pointed out that some persons would reap an undeserved profit from the payment at par, in specie, of the debts of the Union. Speculators had bought up claims, paying for them in specie only a small part of their face values. Hamilton's plan appeared to offer a gain, say, of $80 in coin to a man who had bought, for $20 specie, a claim of $100. Persons who had lent money to the Union and who had later been forced to sell their claims at a large discount not only would fail to profit, but would be required to pay taxes for the benefit of speculators. To avoid such injustice, Madison proposed in the House of Representatives that the Treasury should pay a speculator a sum less than the face value of his claim and give the difference to the original lender. Hamilton strongly opposed this plan on the ground that the new government would begin its financial career by failing to pay in full the claims of its present creditors. Such a failure would cause the government's securities to be sold at uncertain, fluctuating prices and would therefore deprive them of the character of a stable, reliable currency.[22]

A second criticism of Hamilton's plan revolved around the proposed assumption of the state debts. Opponents objected that it would aggrandize a remote central government, weaken the states, and tend to enfeeble home rule among the people. In the end, Jefferson made a bargain with Hamilton which gained the votes needed in Congress for assumption, in return for an agreement to locate the national capital on the Potomac.

[19] Bayley, *National Loans of the United States*, p. 33.
[20] *Hamilton's Works* (Lodge), II, 64.
[21] *Ibid.*, pp. 65–66.
[22] Dewey, *Financial History of the United States*, pp. 91–92.

The outcome suited Washington, for he favored assumption, and the bargain resulted in placing the capital city near Mount Vernon.

Hamilton's proposals formed the basis of the Funding Act of August 4, 1790, by which Congress made provision for the payment of the public debts. According to Hamilton's estimates, the United States, in January, 1790, owed $11,710,378 to foreign creditors—$10,070,307 on account of principal and $1,640,071 on account of unpaid interest.[23] Since this indebtedness represented value received by the United States, nearly everyone agreed that it must be paid in full. Consequently, the funding act authorized the President to borrow $12,000,000 to be used for that purpose. A second part of the national debt, the domestic debt, consisted of claims held by citizens against the United States. In January, 1790, the principal of such debts, as estimated by Hamilton, amounted to $27,383,917 and arrears of interest to $13,030,168.[24] The funding act provided, in effect, that public creditors might exchange their certificates representing the principal of the domestic debt for new government stocks or bonds. Such a creditor would receive two kinds of securities. For two thirds of his claim he was to be given securities bearing 6 percent interest from the date of issue; for the other third, he was to receive securities that would not bear interest until 1801. Thus, during the 1790's, he would receive 4 percent interest on his claim. The funding act further authorized the government to borrow money at 3 percent for the purpose of paying the arrears of interest on the domestic debt.[25]

The arrangements made by the funding act for refinancing the debts of the states were somewhat complicated. Holders of such claims were to receive three kinds of securities: one—for four ninths of the debt— bore interest at 6 percent; the second—for three ninths of the debt—bore interest at 3 percent; the third—for two ninths of the debt—did not bear interest until 1801. In addition to such payments to private creditors the funding act made provision for payments to state governments which were creditors in their accounts with the federal government.[26] All the state debts which were assumed totaled $18,271,786.[27]

By the end of 1794, new securities amounting to $63,054,936 had replaced the old certificates that represented the debts of the states and the domestic debt of the Union. The Treasury made quarterly payments of interest at thirteen places throughout the country. On the whole, the new 6 percent securities were bought and sold at or near par in coin; hence they afforded a safe form of investment. Haste in executing Hamilton's

[23] *Hamilton's Works* (Lodge), II, 73.
[24] *Ibid.*
[25] *Debates of Congress,* 1 Cong., 3 Sess., II, 2005.
[26] *Ibid.,* 1 Cong., 2 Sess., II, 2309.
[27] Bayley, *National Loans of the United States,* p. 33.

plan caused the government to assume excessively large debts of the states. The variety of securities, with different interest rates and separate dates of maturity, made the Treasury's bookkeeping so complicated as to bewilder the ordinary citizen.[28]

When Congress had enacted the two revenue laws of 1789, it did not levy taxes for the purpose of paying the interest on the debts of the states. Assumption therefore forced the Treasury to seek an additional income— in the neighborhood of $825,000 a year. In his first *Report on the Public Credit,* Hamilton proposed to obtain such revenue by means of federal taxes on spirits.[29] Congress followed his advice closely when it adopted the Excise Act of March 3, 1791. This law imposed taxes on liquors distilled within the United States. Such spirits, if made from imported products, were to be taxed at rates varying from 11 to 30 cents a gallon. Spirits distilled from native products, chiefly whiskey from grain, were to be taxed at rates ranging from 9 to 25 cents a gallon. The amount of the tax depended on the alcoholic content of the article. Distillers were required to pay license taxes on the productive capacity of stills, at the rate of 60 cents a gallon.[30] This act, intensely unpopular, provoked the Whiskey Rebellion of 1794 in western Pennsylvania and met so much resistance elsewhere that the cost of collecting the taxes amounted to 16 percent of the proceeds.[31]

Hamilton never ceased to esteem government securities as a safe and convenient medium of investment and as a substitute for money in large transactions. Their usefulness in these respects depended upon their continuous exchangeability for coin, at par. To maintain their full market price was therefore a paramount aim of Hamilton's finance. It "ought to be the policy of the Government," he wrote, "to raise the value of its stock to its true standard as fast as possible." [32] To attain this end he proposed a federal sinking fund—a cash surplus in the Treasury which it could use to buy the government's securities in the open market. Such purchases would exert an upward push on security prices. The sinking-fund plan appealed to conservative men because it offered a means of paying the national debt. The funding act authorized the government to purchase its own securities with certain tax revenues and with proceeds from public land sales. A later act of May 8, 1792, established a regular sinking fund but provided it with only slight resources. A third act of March 3, 1795, pledged additional revenues to the fund.[33] However, during the era of Federalist finance the Treasury failed to reduce the

[28] Dewey, *Financial History of the United States*, p. 96.

[29] *Hamilton's Works* (Lodge), II, 96–97.

[30] *Debates of Congress*, 1 Cong., 3 Sess., II, 2390–2391.

[31] Dewey, *Financial History of the United States*, p. 106; Leland D. Baldwin, *Whiskey Rebels* (Pittsburgh: University of Pittsburgh Press, 1939).

[32] *Hamilton's Works* (Lodge), II, 103.

[33] Dewey, *Financial History of the United States*, pp. 113–114.

principal of the national debt. That result squared with Hamilton's opinion that sound public securities were a positive good.

THE BANK AND THE MINT

In response to an order of the House of Representatives calling for suggestions for establishing the public credit, Hamilton submitted a *Report on a National Bank,* bearing the date of December 13, 1790. In this paper he set forth proposals that looked toward the fostering of manufacturing. He noted two important circumstances affecting the country: "Vast tracts of waste land" and "the little advanced state of manufactures." He observed that the settlement of the West "diminishes or obstructs . . . the *active* wealth of the country . . . . In the early period of new settlements, the settlers not only furnish no surplus for exportation, but they consume a part of that which is produced by the labor of others." Emigration from older settlements was also a "cause that manufactures do not advance, or advance slowly." Such conditions, Hamilton thought, resulted in excessive importations of foreign goods that drained the country of its precious metals. The need of the time was to check the settlement of "waste land" and to promote manufacturing industries.[34] A great national bank might help to achieve such results, if properly constituted. In line with such ideas, Hamilton insisted that land should not be used as a basis for the capital stock of such a bank or as a security for its loans.[35]

If businessmen were to promote manufacturing, they would need an enlarged supply of money and the opportunity to obtain loans or bank credit.[36] Hamilton wished to increase the country's stock of paper currency, but he objected strongly to proposals that the government should issue it.[37] If paper currency was to serve a good end it must be readily convertible into coin, dollar for dollar. But how might a large fund of sound paper currency be based on a small supply of coin? That could be done, Hamilton thought, if the paper was issued by a single bank that would have the backing of the government. If the capital of such a bank should consist of coin and securities of the United States, then paper currency—or bank notes—might safely be issued to an amount of two or three times the quantity of such coin.[38] Hamilton believed that two conditions might enable a national bank to keep its notes at par with specie. First, if the government would accept such notes in tax payments, a widespread demand for them would keep them in circulation and thus deter the holders of them from asking the bank to redeem them. Second, a strong

---

[34] *Hamilton's Works* (Lodge), III, 147–148.
[35] *Ibid.,* p. 161.
[36] *Ibid.,* pp. 127–130, 137, 155.
[37] *Ibid.,* pp. 147, 149.
[38] *Ibid.,* p. 128.

bank, backed by the government, would receive, from private parties, deposits of coin which might be used by the bank to redeem its notes on demand.[39]

Hamilton advised that a national bank should be owned and managed, in the main, by private citizens. He feared that management by the government might result in abuses if its emergency needs for money should dictate banking policies. Private managers would adhere to sound business methods in order to safeguard a bank's credit.[40] However, Hamilton also insisted that a large bank should have the benefit of prestige, favor, and support of the government. He therefore emphasized the public services that such a bank might perform. It would lend money to the government, provide convenient depositories in the leading seaports, where most of the federal revenues were collected, serve the Treasury by transferring funds safely and cheaply from place to place, and facilitate the payment of taxes by increasing the supply of currency. The use of the government's securities as a part of the capital stock of a bank would create an added demand for them and thus tend to keep up their values. Finally, the government, as a stockholder of a bank, would share its profits.[41]

As authorized by an act of Congress of February 25, 1791, the Bank of the United States was so constituted as to enable it to perform the services for the government which Hamilton had anticipated. The bank received a charter for twenty years and a pledge that during that time Congress would not establish another bank. The capital stock of the bank was to be $10,000,000, of which sum the government was to subscribe $2,000,000. Private parties were permitted to invest $8,000,000—$2,000,000 in coin and $6,000,000 in United States securities. The bank received the right to accept deposits, to make loans, to discount bills, and, in effect, to issue notes or paper currency up to $10,000,000. The charter authorized the stockholders to elect a board of directors who were empowered to choose its officers, such as the president and the cashier, and to establish branches in cities other than Philadelphia, the home office.[42] Perhaps the most valuable asset of the bank was the government's pledge to receive its notes in all payments to the United States—the only national bank notes to be so favored.

Although the charter of the bank was granted in February, 1791, a special law provided that the stock—each share to have a face value of $400—should not be subscribed for until July, to enable people in all localities to participate. So great was the demand that all the stock was

---

[39] Ibid., pp. 170, 129.
[40] Ibid., pp. 162–163.
[41] Ibid., pp. 131, 132, 150, 166–167, 168, 171–172.
[42] Debates of Congress, 1 Cong., 3 Sess., II, 2375–2382.

spoken for within an hour after the subscription books were opened. A private subscriber was permitted to purchase shares in four installments, payable over eighteen months. The charter required that $400,000 in gold and silver must be paid into the capital fund of the bank before it could be organized. The election of a board of directors took place on October 21, 1791. Immediately they named Thomas Willing of Philadelphia president and John Kean of South Carolina cashier. Willing, then president of the Bank of North America and a coadjutor of Washington, was a sagacious merchant whose reputation inspired confidence in business circles. He served as president until 1807.[43]

From the outset the bank made a wide appeal. Businessmen in New York, Boston, and Charleston quickly sought to secure its benefits. Even before the parent office opened for business at Philadelphia on December 12, 1791, the stockholders had voted to establish branches in Boston, New York, Charleston, and Baltimore. The bank was operating in those cities by the spring of 1792.[44] Of this development Hamilton wrote that "the whole affair of the branches was *begun, continued,* and *ended,* not only without my participation, but *against* my judgment, . . . I was never consulted . . . ."[45] Four other branches were established later: at Norfolk, in May, 1800; at Washington, in January, 1802; at Savannah in August, 1802; and at New Orleans, in October, 1805.[46]

For each branch the directors of the main bank at Philadelphia elected the directors, appointed the cashier, provided the specie capital, set a maximum sum for loans, and prescribed general policies. Frequently, local businessmen who owned only a share or a few shares of stock obtained branch directorships in order to secure personal loans.[47] On the whole the Philadelphia office succeeded in limiting loans of the branches to less than three times their specie capital. The Charleston, Boston, and New York branches towered above the others. The specie capital of the Charleston branch rose from $75,000 in 1792 to $600,000 in 1810, while its discounts increased from $170,000 to $1,409,000.[48] Before 1797 the bank as a whole fared well in collecting debts; afterward it had to employ attorneys to recover sizable outlays by legal actions. The bank did not become closely connected with the state banks of the time, for law or

[43] Hammond, *Banks and Politics in America,* pp. 122–123; Konkle, *Thomas Willing,* pp. 141–143.

[44] James O. Wettereau, "The Branches of the First Bank of the United States," *Tasks of Economic History* (1942), pp. 73–75.

[45] *Hamilton's Works* (Lodge), VIII, 237.

[46] Wettereau, "Branches of the First Bank," pp. 79, 83, 88; Jonathan Elliot, *The Funding System of the United States and Great Britain* (Washington: Blair and Rives, 1845), p. 95.

[47] Wettereau, "Branches of the First Bank," pp. 75, 83–84, 89–92.

[48] *Ibid.,* pp. 92–94.

opinion then forbade a bank to own stock in another bank and disapproved of interlocking directorates.[49]

The financial success of the bank is indicated by its dealings with the government. Eventually the government made a profit of $671,860 when it sold the shares of stock it had acquired. While the government was a stockholder, between 1791 and 1802, it received dividends of $1,101,720 or about 8⅜ percent a year. Originally, the government had procured its shares without putting any capital into the bank. In effect, the Treasury obtained them by giving it a promise to pay.[50]

All the Federalist measures assumed that paper currencies and public securities should be payable in coin. However, the country as yet lacked coins of its own. Under the Articles of Confederation the states had the power to operate mints, but none of them had provided an adequate supply of coins. Of the coins then widely used—all issued by foreign mints—the most common was the Spanish silver dollar. In 1789 it was important because it provided the unit in which the debts and the face values of the paper currency of the Union were stated. In its initial revenue laws of 1789, Congress provided that federal duties should be paid in the gold coins of England, France, Spain, and Portugal. At the same time, the laws expressed the duties in terms of dollars and cents. The Spanish money of account divided the dollar—or piece of eight—into eighths; Congress divided it into tenths and hundredths. Later, American usage blended the Spanish and English monies of account. The American dollar and the quarter harked back to Spanish practices; the cent and the quarter suggested the English penny and shilling.[51]

The use of foreign coins in American finance caused much trouble. Each coin had to be evaluated in terms of dollars and cents, and the coins varied as to weight and fineness. The Constitution called for a uniform national coinage that would simplify tax collections, business dealings, and accounts. To meet this need, Hamilton in June, 1790, submitted a *Report on the Establishment of a Mint*. Congress wrote most of his suggestions into law when it adopted the Coinage Act of April 2, 1792. Although Hamilton preferred a single gold coinage, he took into account the scarcity of gold in the country and therefore recommended the minting of both gold and silver.[52] The coinage act defined the dollar as the numerical monetary unit, dividing it into hundredths and tenths. The gold coinage was to consist of eagles or ten-dollar pieces, half eagles, and quarter eagles. Contrary to Hamilton's advice, the act did not provide

[49] *Ibid.*, pp. 94–95, 74–75.
[50] Hammond, *Banks and Politics in America*, pp. 123–124; John Jay Knox, *A History of Banking in the United States* (New York: Bradford Rhodes & Co., 1900), p. 39.
[51] A. Barton Hepburn, *A History of the Currency of the United States* (New York: The Macmillan Company, 1915), pp. 33–40.
[52] *Hamilton's Works* (Lodge), III, 241–243.

for the minting of a dollar coin of gold. The silver dollar was to contain 371.25 grains of pure silver. Since the content of the gold coins amounted to 24.75 grains of pure gold per dollar, the act set a mint ratio of 15 to 1. Small coins authorized included half dollars, quarters, and dimes of silver, and pennies of copper. The act made the gold and silver coins legal tender in all payments, and gave to owners of either kind of bullion the privilege of having it coined at a national mint, in unlimited quantities and without cost to themselves.[53]

Located in Philadelphia, the mint began its work in 1794. It soon appeared that owners of gold bullion could get more money by selling it as a commodity than by having it minted into coin. Conversely, it proved to be profitable for owners of silver bullion to have it coined into dollars; hence a silver coinage was the result of the 15 to 1 ratio. Because the silver content of the American dollar was slightly less than that of the Spanish milled dollar, traders made a profit by exchanging the one for the other and by having the Spanish coins reminted into American dollars.[54] Coins in use in the country in 1800 probably averaged about $300 a person.

THE INCIDENCE OF THE FEDERALIST PROGRAM

The Federalist program of taxation, public credit, bank, and coinage broadened the foundations of the national economy. The immediate result was a vast increase in the paper wealth of the country—of credit resources, of currency available for business. By 1792 the funding of the national debt and the assumption of the state debts may have added $30,000,000 to the assets of the public creditors, while the Bank of the United States promised an increase of paper currency and bank credit of perhaps $20,000,000. It seems likely that the flood of new paper had an inflationary effect. Deflation after 1783 reached its low point in March, 1789. During the months when the Federalist tax laws and the Funding Act were being incubated, wholesale prices rose substantially. Charleston records show an upswing from an index figure of 78 in March, 1789, to 100 in mid-1790—a gain of 28 percent. One survey indicates that Philadelphia prices went up from 72 in March, 1789, to 88 in December, 1790—an increase of 22 percent; and another Philadelphia study reveals a rise from 90 in March, 1789, to 115 in December, 1790—an advance of 27.7 percent.[55] The force of the new paper wealth also caused an upsurge in business activity. Speculative buying and selling of government securities

[53] *Debates of Congress,* 2 Cong., 2 Sess., III, 1351–1356; David K. Watson, *History of American Coinage* (New York: G. P. Putnam's Sons, 1899), pp. 54–58.

[54] J[ames] Laurence Laughlin, *The History of Bimetallism in the United States* (New York: D. Appleton and Company, 1896), pp. 29–30.

[55] Taylor, "Charleston Prices," p. 370; Cole, *Wholesale Commodity Prices,* p. 106, chart; Bezanson, *Prices and Inflation During the Revolution: Pennsylvania,* p. 13.

became intense and a real-estate boom boosted property values in the financial centers. Seventeen new corporations, chartered within seven months after August, 1791, reflected an absorbing interest in toll bridges, banks, insurance, turnpikes, the improvement of inland waterways, and manufacturing. Prominent among the new ventures were banks of Providence, New London, Albany, South Carolina, and New Hampshire. The wave of speculation broke in March, 1792, with the failure of William Duer, prince of speculators and onetime assistant of Hamilton in the Treasury.[56]

Incomplete and baffling records leave in the dark the exact gains that individuals may have reaped from the Federalist measures. Yet they certainly augmented the wealth and influence of a group of men who owned public securities or who participated in the Bank of the United States. In Philadelphia this select company included Thomas Willing, William Bingham, Robert Morris, George Clymer, and Thomas Fitz-Simons. Among the Federalist elite of New England were George Cabot, Fisher Ames, and Stephen Higginson of Massachusetts, Jeremiah Wadsworth and Roger Sherman of Connecticut, Nicholas Brown and John Brown of Rhode Island, and John Langdon of New Hampshire. In the circle of wealth at New York one found Brockholst Livingston, Rufus King, Philip Livingston, Philip Schuyler, and Nicholas Low. Elias Boudinot was a pillar of Federalist finance in New Jersey; Charles Carroll best represented Maryland; Washington led in Virginia; Samuel Johnston was the most prominent North Carolinian, and Charles Coatesworth Pinckney and William Smith spoke for South Carolina.[57]

Pelatiah Webster once averred that "the influence of merchants is the safest of any that can affect a government."[58] Such in good measure was the theory of the Federalist program. It did not give birth to many large new fortunes; its principal beneficiaries were men of substance who had become affluent before 1789. Their enlarged wealth enhanced their influence in government and society and pointed to an age of big business in which captains of finance would occupy the seats of the mighty. The charter of the Bank of the United States permitted a subscriber to buy a thousand shares of stock, amounting to $400,000, and endowed a stockholder who owned a hundred shares with twenty votes. Successful men commonly regarded opulence as a mark of fitness and ability; who was better qualified to deploy great financial resources in such a way as to direct the energies of the people into productive channels?

On September 6, 1785, John Jay wrote to John Adams: "I wish most

[56] Davis, *Earlier History of American Corporations*, I, 278–279, 294–295.

[57] Beard, *An Economic Interpretation of the Constitution*, pp. 84, 92, 120, 124–126, 138; George Adams Boyd, *Elias Boudinot* (Princeton, N. J.: Princeton University Press, 1952), pp. 184–185; Higginson, *Stephen Higginson*, p. 234; Hedges, *The Browns of Providence*, pp. 321–323; Konkle, *Thomas Willing*, p. 142.

[58] *Political Essays*, p. 436.

sincerely that . . . we could purchase nothing abroad, but for ready money. Our . . . importations would be diminished, we should have less to pay—domestic manufactures would then be encouraged."[59] In his first annual message of January 8, 1790, Washington spoke in favor of promoting manufactures, of importing "new and useful inventions," and of stimulating "the exertions of skill and genius in producing them at home."[60] In response to this plea, the House on January 15 directed Hamilton to report a plan for the promotion of manufactures that would "tend to render the United States independent of other nations for essential . . . supplies." Such was the setting of Hamilton's *Report on Manufactures,* which he submitted to the House on December 5. He sought, first of all, to make certain that the country would have a paper currency redeemable at par in coin. This aim required that the outflow of specie should be checked, and that in turn called for an expansion of home industries in order that specie-draining imports might be reduced. Every Federalist measure served to foster home industries. The first tariff law was distinctly protectionist, and the funding policy and the bank offered credit facilities to manufacturers. The first federal Patent Law of April 10, 1790, granted to inventors a fourteen-year guarantee of the exclusive right to make, use, or sell their products.[61] A sound, uniform currency promised to facilitate the sale of manufactures in a large national market. On this point, two button makers described the need. The greatest handicap to their business, they said, "lies in not getting as good pay [money] as we could wish . . . . The retailer in general sells his goods for produce; therefore he will not give us our price in cash. We are obliged to . . . barter away our buttons for articles which we are obliged to . . . [sell at] a very great discount to get them into money again in order to purchase stock, for we cannot purchase one ounce of stock without money."[62]

Hamilton's inquiries convinced him that manufactures lagged because the country lacked machinery and scientific apparatus. Since such capital goods had to be imported, a severe obstacle to industrial progress was the inadequacy of American exports to, or buying power in, Europe and Britain. Hamilton saw in good public securities a remedy. Before 1789, the old public certificates of debt had had little value abroad. But once the new government had provided that its securities were to be based on and backed by coin, they would sell at good prices in Europe and thereby yield money for the purchase of capital goods needed by American manufacturers.

In 1791 several of Hamilton's associates devised a plan for a grand

[59] *Diplomatic Correspondence, 1783–1789,* IV, 229.

[60] James D. Richardson, ed., *A Compilation of the Messages and Papers of the Presidents, 1789–1897* (10 vols.; Washington: Government Printing Office, 1896–1899), I, 66.

[61] *Debates of Congress,* 1 Cong., 2 Sess., II, 2271.

[62] Cole, *Hamilton's Industrial Correspondence,* pp. 49–50.

corporation to be styled "The Society for establishing useful Manufactures." Promoters in New York secured the backing of the chief political leaders of New Jersey and of a few capitalists in Philadelphia. On November 22, 1791, the Society received a charter from New Jersey which authorized a capital stock of $1,000,000 in shares of $100, to be purchased with the securities of the United States. The promoters intended at the start to build a large cotton factory. They preferred New Jersey as a site because of its central location, the absence of strong competing interests there, and a likely supply of labor. The state aided by investing $10,000 in the stock of the Society, by giving it certain tax exemptions, along with the right to build canals and to raise money by lotteries, and by making its charter so liberal that it was free from political control. Investors bought shares in excess of $625,000. The promoters contemplated an enterprise vastly greater than any existing concern—one that would exert in manufacturing a power comparable to that intended for the Bank of the United States in finance. Three of the promoters were later directors of the Bank of the United States, but, unfortunately, none was an experienced manufacturer.[63]

A lively interest in manufacturing animated many northern communities between 1785 and 1792. Enterprising men organized state or town societies for the fostering of new industries. Philadelphia, Boston, New York, Baltimore, Burlington, Morristown, and Wilmington, Delaware, took part in the movement. The societies of New York and Pennsylvania collected modest sums, parts of which they used to erect and operate factories for making cottons and linens. The members of the Pennsylvania Society published literature extolling the cause, paid premiums for superior products, and pledged to buy only goods made in America. Several companies and entrepreneurs introduced new machines and experimented with the factory system. At Frederick, Maryland, J. F. Amelung reported a large investment in a glass factory. O. Burr and Company of Danbury, the leading hatters of Connecticut, made hats that competed in the export trade. The cotton factory of Almy and Brown at Providence, using up-to-date machinery, finished 7,800 yards of cloth in twenty-eight months after June, 1789. A Hartford woolen factory, organized in 1788, produced a good cloth that sold in New York. Its fabric adorned Washington at his inauguration. In Boston, a large factory turned out glass of high quality and another efficient plant fabricated sailcloth so successfully as to employ 300 persons in 1791. The Cabots of Beverly, Massachusetts, owned a large interest in a cotton factory which, in 1791, had a force of 40 hands who produced 800 yards of cloth.[64]

[63] Davis, *Earlier History of American Corporations*, I, 349, 367, 370–371, 375, 380–381, 384–395.

[64] *Ibid.*, I, 369; II, 256–258, 260–266, 272–273, 275; Henry Cabot Lodge, *Life and Letters of George Cabot* (Boston: Little, Brown and Company, 1878), pp. 43–45.

The progress of manufacturing on the principle of the factory system was seriously interrupted after 1792. One after another of the most promising concerns—the Boston Sail Cloth Manufactory, the Boston Glass House, the Hartford Woolen Factory, the New York Manufacturing Society, and the Beverly Cotton Manufactory—either failed or suspended operations.[65] The bellwether of the movement—The Society for establishing useful Manufactures—did not complete its plant until mid-1794 and thereafter it operated fitfully on a small, local scale. Its poor showing resulted from numerous causes. The panic of March, 1792 bankrupted some of the directors and sent its head manager, William Duer, to a debtors' prison. Other promoters, hard-pressed financially, refused to put more money into the venture. The Society's reputation suffered from its affiliation with deflated speculators whose prestige dwindled. Hamilton, the father of the project, lost interest after 1792 and withdrew his support.[66]

The trend toward factory production arose largely from conditions of the years 1786–1792, when inadequate foreign markets depressed the prices of American exports, put the country at a disadvantage in paying its debts and in purchasing goods from Europe, and intensified the scarcity of coin, thereby causing a demand for irredeemable paper money. Events abroad in 1793 brought an end to the era that gave birth to the Constitution and the Federalist program. At that time a new influence struck the country with a powerful force—the war arising from the French Revolution. On February 1, 1793, an initial struggle between France and Austria broadened when France declared war on Britain and Holland. The warring powers soon sought great quantities of American foodstuffs and raw materials.[67] A resulting trade boom stimulated anew the older industries of the Union—grain and cattle farming, shipbuilding, shipping, lumbering, and the fishery. The American experiments of 1787–1792 with the factory system had revealed some severe handicaps: lack of experience; a shortage of skilled managers, artisans, and mechanics; and a deficiency of good machinery. Had the conditions of foreign trade remained unfavorable to American exports, it is likely that in the 1790's Americans would have overcome such handicaps and have established factory production on a solid basis. However, after 1792, it proved to be most profitable for the country to produce and to export raw materials and shipping services, when the demand for them was strong and sustained.

The Federalist program could stimulate foreign trade as well as domestic manufactures. The new government securities furnished buying power to American importers which they could use for purchasing con-

---

[65] Davis, *Earlier History of American Corporations*, II, 262, 264, 267, 274, 275.
[66] *Ibid.*, I, 474, 495, 503–504.
[67] Harold Hutcheson, *Tench Coxe* (Johns Hopkins University *Studies in Historical and Political Science*, Extra Volumes, New Series, No. 26; Baltimore: The Johns Hopkins Press, 1938), pp. 113–114.

sumers' goods abroad. The Bank of the United States could provide credit for commercial operations. The trend of prices in South Carolina after 1789 suggests that merchants used the new government securities to pay debts in Europe and to buy new supplies of foreign goods, for prices of imports rose considerably more than prices of Carolina products.[68] By June 30, 1803, foreigners held United States securities to the amount of $32,119,000, of a total of $70,154,000.[69] The rapid increase of the export trade that accompanied the onrush of war in Europe entangled the Federalists more than ever in foreign affairs. They continued to insist that the securities of the Union must be kept at par in coin. The government obtained the needed money largely from taxes on imports. The growth of foreign trade therefore identified the interests of American merchants with the interests of security owners at home who looked to import duties to uphold the value of their property. Thus there occurred a shift in the emphasis of Federalist policy from domestic manufactures to foreign commerce.

THE REPUBLICAN OPPOSITION

For many years after 1789 the elements of the Federalist program figured decisively in the party politics of the Union. The men who consistently supported the tariff, the bank, and the funding act made up the nucleus of the Federalist party, while critics of those measures, or of some of them, united under the leadership of Madison and Jefferson in the Republican opposition. The strife between the two groups has been pictured as a conflict between capitalists and agrarians. Certain it is that leading merchants, bankers, public creditors, and manufacturers adhered to the Federalist cause. However, Congress adopted all the Federalist laws at a time when perhaps nine tenths of the people were farmers. Congressmen representing the then agricultural states of Massachusetts, Connecticut, New Jersey, Delaware, and South Carolina voted 19 to 1 in favor of the assumption of the state debts.[70] The Excise Act of 1791 passed the House by a large majority. Assumption and the excise tax relieved the farmers of Massachusetts of heavy taxes which the state government had levied in its attempt to pay the state's debt. The federal excise taxes did not press upon the Bay State farmers because they drank cider or rum instead of whiskey. Seaboard farmers, like city capitalists, could be owners of public securities, favor home manufactures as a means of increasing the demand for farm products, welcome inflation that would raise land values, and approve of a strong government that might enlarge

---

[68] Taylor, "Charleston Prices," p. 367.

[69] Bayley, *National Loans of the United States*, p. 34.

[70] Charles A. Beard, "Some Economic Origins of Jeffersonian Democracy," *American Historical Review*, XIX, No. 2 (January, 1914), 297.

foreign markets for American exports. Farmers living near cities stood to profit from their growth.

The Federalist financial policies made their primary appeal to residents of the coastal area whose interests centered there, or in a seaboard-European nexus. The Jeffersonian Republicans spoke for debtor farmers and planters, pioneers, men interested in the development of the West, and countrymen who cherished agriculture as a way of life. A French minister, M. Fauchet, observed in October, 1794: "The proprietors of an unfertile coast fear that their fields will be deserted, once the Mississippi is opened and its numerous streams are in active use." [71] The frontiersmen of western Pennsylvania forcibly resisted the excise act. Representatives of Virginia, North Carolina, and Georgia—the states then most deeply involved in westward expansion—opposed assumption almost to a man. The leading critics of Federalist policies were John Taylor, Madison, and Jefferson of Virginia, Albert Gallatin of western Pennsylvania, James Jackson of Georgia, and George Clinton, expansionist of New York.[72] In 1798 the link between southern East and West was revealed when the legislatures of Virginia and Kentucky protested against the alien and sedition acts, which tended to stifle criticism of the Federalist policies. Hamilton had explained those policies as designed to enrich the seaboard and to retard the growth of the West.

Jefferson preferred agrarianism to manufacturing because he thought that freeholds made men virtuous, vigorous, and independent, whereas "the mobs of great cities" were like sores on the human body. Approving of skilled craftsmen as necessary to husbandry, he hoped that Americans would spurn the factory system. When people "get piled upon one another in large cities, as in Europe, they shall become corrupt as in Europe." He concluded that vacant lands and an open, westward-moving frontier offered the best assurance that Americans would remain a virtuous people.[73]

The speculators who bought certificates of debt at low prices became the first targets of the critics of federalism. As early as November, 1789, Stephen Higginson warned Hamilton of the dangers inherent in the funding process.

There is nothing that would so much alarm and raise the feelings of the state governments and of their constituents, as a proposition . . . to pay the full interest on public securities in specie . . . . They cannot think it right for those who have bought them up at 2 shillings or 3 shillings in the pound to derive so great an income from them, and eventually to receive the full sum of the principal in specie. They would consider this, when done by any sort of

[71] Frederick J. Turner, ed., "Correspondence of the French Ministers to the United States, 1791–1797" (American Historical Association, *Annual Report* . . . *1903*, 2 vols.; Washington: Government Printing Office, 1904), II, 448.

[72] Spaulding, *George Clinton*, p. 148.

[73] *Jefferson Papers* (Boyd), VIII, 426; XIII, 442.

taxes upon the public, as stripping the poor to increase the wealth and influence of the rich . . . . Rich men are in all countries, and at all times, objects of envy with the common people; but they become much more so when it is believed that the poor are depressed to increase their wealth.[74]

In December, 1790, the Virginia legislature asserted that the funding act tended "to erect and concentrate and perpetuate a large moneyed interest" that would end in "the prostration of agriculture at the feet of commerce." [75] A Maryland Congressman, J. F. Mercer, said in 1792 that "the effect of stocks is to transfer the fruits of the labor of the many . . . into the hands of the few, who exchange them for foreign luxuries and consume in an hour the labor of industrious families for years." [76] In Virginia, John Taylor of Caroline County subjected the Federalists' measures to scathing attacks. In 1793 appeared his pamphlet, *An Examination of the Late Proceedings Respecting the Official Conduct of the Secretary of the Treasury*, to be followed the next year by his *Inquiry into the Principles and Tendencies of Certain Public Measures*. The funding of the public debt, Taylor charged, "imperceptibly created a financial class which threatens to become the aristocratic order of the state." "Money in a state of civilization is power." "An aristocracy . . . have good reason to exclaim 'a national debt is a national blessing,' and in pursuance of their maxim, to create one that is fictitious, payable to themselves out of the hard-earned fruits of labor. To them it is a mine, yielding gold without work." [77] Later, a Republican penman, James T. Callender, asserted that the funding act had converted the whole continent "into an immense gaming table." [78] Samuel E. Morison has brought to light a homely essay, "The Key of Libberty," in which the author complains that "what we have already paid and have now to pay comes to a hundred million of dollars that the public never received . . . and seposing that their is 4 million persons belonging to the United States, it is 25 dollars apeas for each man woman and child to pay . . . which according as taxes are leaveled in Masachusets it would come to near two hundred dollars apeace for common or midling farmers to pay." [79]

Foes of the Bank of the United States objected that its affiliation with the government converted it into an engine of monopoly. It was the only bank to be blessed with a federal charter, to draw strength from

[74] James O. Wettereau, ed., "Letters from Two Business Men to Alexander Hamilton on Federal Fiscal Policy, November 1789," *Journal of Economic and Business History*, III, No. 4 (August, 1931), 685.

[75] Charles A. Beard, *Economic Origins of Jeffersonian Democracy* (New York: The Macmillan Company, 1956), p. 216.

[76] *Ibid.*, p. 208 note.

[77] *Ibid.*, pp. 197, 208, 209.

[78] *Ibid.*, p. 213.

[79] Samuel Eliot Morison, ed., "William Manning's *The Key of Libberty*," *William and Mary Quarterly*, Third Series, XIII, No. 2 (April, 1956), 244.

the Treasury, and to enjoy the privilege of having its notes used uniformly in tax payments throughout the Union.[80] The act of chartering it served to crystallize the incipient discontents of the opposition. Writing in New York to Jefferson on July 10, 1791, Madison reported: "The Bank shares have risen as much in the market here as at Philadelphia. It seems admitted on all hands now that the plan of the institution gives a moral certainty of gain to the subscribers, with scarce a physical possibility of loss. The subscriptions are consequently a mere scramble for so much public plunder, which will be engrossed by those already loaded with the spoils of individuals . . . . It pretty clearly appears, also, in what proportion the public debt lies in the country, what sort of hands hold it, and by whom the people of the United States are to be governed."[81] "Banking," said John Taylor, "in its *best* view is only a fraud whereby labor suffers the imposition of paying an interest upon the circulating medium."[82]

The whiskey tax of 1791, said James Jackson of Georgia, would "deprive the people of almost the only luxury they enjoy, that of distilled spirits . . . ."[83] According to Representative John Steele of North Carolina, the tax had the effect of taking from a farmer about 20 percent of the rye which he had distilled into whiskey. Steele also asserted that the tax bore oppressively "upon that class of farmers whose estates are situated in the interior country and whose interests have thus far passed unnoticed in the policy of the general government," "while manufactures in other parts are not only rewarded by high protecting duties, but in some instances even by specific bounties." "And here," Steele continued, "let me ask, what is the nature of these manufactures which entitles them to such priorities and preferences?" Comparing them with agriculture, he contended that "they are nearer to perfection, that they are aided by more capital, [and] that they are therefore better able to bear taxation." "It is most sincerely to be wished," he concluded, "that the manufacturing States would fix some bounds to their expectations."[84]

[80] Eugene Tenbroeck Mudge, *The Social Philosophy of John Taylor of Caroline* (New York: Columbia University Press, 1939), pp. 174–176.

[81] *Writings of Madison* (1867), I, 583.

[82] Beard, *Economic Origins of Jeffersonian Democracy*, p. 207.

[83] *Debates of Congress*, 1 Cong., 3 Sess., II, 1891.

[84] Beard, *Economic Origins of Jeffersonian Democracy*, pp. 252–253.

CHAPTER VII

The People and the Land

REPLENISHING THE LAND

THE ways and means by which the American people made their living did not change drastically between 1775 and 1815. Year after year farmers used the same sort of tools, power, and methods. It is true that by 1815 the cotton gin, the river steamboat, and machines of the factory system had caused, or were on the verge of causing, some important changes. But the methods of producing food remained much as they had been in colonial times. Agriculture, maritime pursuits, and industries yielding raw materials continued to employ a very large majority of the people. In 1770, cities of the thirteen colonies having populations of 8,000 inhabitants or more numbered only five and domiciled, altogether, only 84,000 persons, or 3.8 percent of the total population. The comparable figure for 1790 was 3.3 percent. Twenty years later, the United States had eleven such cities, containing 356,000 people in all, in a total population of 7,239,000—or 4.9 percent of the whole.[1]

Since the great majority of the people supported themselves by farming, the methods of agriculture determined the number of people who could live on a given amount of land. For this reason the growth of the settlements resulted from the combined increase and density of population in the older communities and the quantity and accessibility of unoccupied lands along the frontiers. By 1790, the areas on or near the seacoast were peopled almost to the limit of the supporting capacity of a simple economy. The relation of mature communities to emigration to vacant lands is illustrated by population trends in the six states of Connecticut, Massachusetts, Rhode Island, New Jersey, Delaware, and Mary-

---

[1] Adna Ferrin Weber, *The Growth of Cities in the Nineteenth Century* (Columbia University *Studies in History, Economics and Public Law*, Vol. XI; New York: The Macmillan Company, 1899), pp. 21–22.

land. In 1790, their total population was 1,248,000. If these six states had grown in population as did the Union as a whole, they would have had 1,684,000 inhabitants in 1800. However, their total then was only 1,359,000.[2] Since the birth rate in these states was as high as that of the country at large, it appears that they sent out as many as 325,000 pioneering emigrants during the decade of the 1790's. Most of the emigrants went to frontier areas. Such emigration took off as many people as made up one fourth of the total population of the six states in 1790. Undoubtedly, the coastal areas of the other states sent pioneers to new lands to a similar extent.

During the years 1775–1815 the population of the United States increased by approximately 6,000,000 persons. Reliable estimates of the totals are as follows: [3]

1775	2,507,000
1780	2,781,000
1790	3,929,000
1800	5,308,000
1810	7,239,000
1815	8,500,000

The prolific increase of the species *Americanus* then owed far more to native parents than to immigration. Early marriages and large families account in the main for the fact that the population more than doubled every twenty-five years. In 1790, 62.9 percent of the families of the free population of ten states contained three or more children.[4]

The forty years after 1775 were fairly uniform with respect to the size of families, the rate of population growth, the ratio of children to adults, and the proportions of townspeople and farmers. This stability reflects the fact that the fundamental conditions of life did not change materially.[5] Early marriages and large families were the outgrowth of two such conditions, among others. In the first place, the training of youth was such as to equip boys and girls to support themselves and to begin to raise families by the time they were eighteen. Life on the farm familiarized children, from an early age, with all the work that was necessary to support a family. The federal census classified a person of sixteen as self-

[2] Bureau of the Census, *A Century of Population Growth . . . 1790–1900* (Washington: Government Printing Office, 1909), p. 96; Bureau of the Census, *Statistical Abstract of the United States, 1941* (Washington: Government Printing Office, 1942), p. 4; Henry Pratt Fairchild, *Immigration* (New York: The Macmillan Company, 1913), p. 55.

[3] Stella H. Sutherland, *Population Distribution in Colonial America* (New York: Columbia University Press, 1936), p. 271; *Statistical Abstract, 1941*, p. 4; *A Century of Population Growth*, p. 58.

[4] *A Century of Population Growth*, pp. 96, 98.

[5] *Ibid.*, pp. 14, 58, 104.

supporting. Boys were often apprenticed to a trade in their early teens and became skilled artisans at the age of twenty. Militia duty commonly began for boys at sixteen. Early marriages meant that the population contained an unusually high percentage of young children. Records for the United States as a whole show in 1790 an average of 490 white persons under sixteen to every thousand white inhabitants.[6]

The survival of a society based on the large rural family depended upon an abundance of virgin soil. In 1775, the coastal settlements were surrounded by a belt of unoccupied land, in the form of a quarter circle, that reached far into the interior, from the eastern coast of Maine to the northern border of Florida. Every part of the Union had a back country close at hand.

In the New England of 1775 nearly the whole of Maine was uninhabited by the white man—all save a narrow strip along the southern shore and two arms of settled land extending forty miles or so up the valleys of the Kennebec and the Penobscot rivers. The northern half of New Hampshire awaited the coming of the pioneer. Nearly all Vermont was a wilderness; its only settled areas were thin strips along the west bank of the Connecticut River and along the eastern shore of Lake Champlain. New Englanders could readily reach New York. There the primeval forest held undisputed sway over all the land north of the Mohawk River and embraced a great southern tract west of the seventy-fifth meridian.

To both New Englanders and the people of the middle states, Pennsylvania beckoned with a vast unsettled domain comprising the upper three fifths of the state—the area north of a line running east and west through Bethlehem. Farther west, the wooded lands of the present states of Ohio and Indiana were accessible to emigrants from both the Northeast and the upper South. Virginia offered a virtual paradise to pioneers—a forest dominion that embraced the western reaches of the state of today and the whole of modern West Virginia and Kentucky. Most of the western fifth of North Carolina remained to be occupied, although pioneers had made clearings in the Watauga River Valley. Nearly all Tennessee reposed in a state of nature. The unsettled back country of Georgia, 300 miles wide, stretched westward to the Mississippi, more than 400 miles in length at the north and nearly 600 miles at the south.[7]

The lands beyond the settlements of 1775 were destined to be peopled, in the main, by native Americans who were inured to the hard conditions of frontier life. Immigrants from Europe continued to add to the population, but the years 1775–1815 stand out as a time when their contribu-

[6] *Ibid.*, p. 103.
[7] Channing, *History of the United States*, III, 528 (map); Sutherland, *Population Distribution in Colonial America*, pp. 68, 158, 222 (maps); Herman R. Friis, "A Series of Population Maps of the Colonies and the United States, 1625–1790," *Geographical Review*, XXX, No. 3 (July, 1940), 465 (map).

tions were exceptionally light. Trustworthy estimates indicate that between 1790 and 1820 such newcomers numbered, all told, only 250,000—
an average of 8,333 a year. During the first year after 1790, the increase of
population arising from births amounted to at least 102,000—more than
twelve times the accretion from immigration.[8]

The European countries that helped to swell the population of the
young republic were those that had done the most to people the thirteen
colonies. A large majority of the Americans-to-be came from Germany,
Ireland, England, France, Scotland, and Wales. A few royalist *émigrés*
escaped to Philadelphia from the persecutions of the Revolution in France.
Some of the emigrants fled from Britain and Ireland to avoid the repres-
sions of a conservative British government that dreaded the spread of the
doctrines of the rights of man. Germans sought shelter from Europe's
incessant wars and relief from forced military service. Old World taxes,
unemployment, or meager food supplies periodically made America seem
a land where the lot of European peasants and workers could not be
worse.[9]

After 1783, many Americans, imbued with faith in mankind or intent
upon obtaining laborers or buyers of land, held out a welcoming hand to
the immigrant. "It is our business," said John Adams, "to render our
country an asylum, worthy to receive all who may wish to fly to it." In
Virginia, William Grayson, with an eye to land sales, spoke of "the want
of immigrants" as "perhaps our only calamity." [10] Promoters of manufacturing of the early Federalist era hoped to recruit skilled artisans in Europe. Hamilton's co-worker, Tench Coxe, listed the attractions of Pennsylvania in 1794 as cheap land, religious freedom, civil rights, and unshackled
industry and trade.[11] The first federal naturalization law, enacted by the
Federalists in 1790, offered citizenship to aliens after a sojourn of two
years in the country. Several land speculators and promoters sought prospective settlers in England, Germany, and France. Foremost among the
glorifiers of the New World was Hector St. John de Crèvecœur, whose
Letters from an American Farmer were widely circulated in book form
in England, Ireland, and France between 1782 and 1785. He portrayed an

[8] Edward Young, *Special Report on Immigration* . . . (Washington: Government Printing Office, 1871), p. xi; George M. Stephenson, *A History of American
Immigration, 1820–1924* (Boston: Ginn and Company, 1926), p. 99, gives the total
immigration, 1790–1800, as 50,000.

[9] Marcus Lee Hansen, *The Atlantic Migration, 1607–1860* (A. M. Schlesinger, ed.;
Cambridge, Mass.: Harvard University Press, 1940), pp. 57–63, 65–69; John Allen
Krout and Dixon Ryan Fox, *The Completion of American Independence, 1790–1830*
(Vol. V of *A History of American Life*, A. M. Schlesinger and D. R. Fox, eds.; New
York: The Macmillan Company, 1944), pp. 1–4.

[10] Greene, *The Revolutionary Generation*, p. 309.

[11] *Ibid.*, p. 54; Carl Wittke, *We Who Built America* (New York: Prentice-Hall,
Inc., 1940), pp. 95–96.

idyllic America where the poor immigrant quickly became a landowner and thereby acquired a comfortable living, a feeling of solid self-respect, and an honored place in the community as a free citizen.[12] Franklin pointed out in 1783 that the "country affords to strangers nothing but a good climate, fertile soil, wholesome air, free governments, wise laws, liberty, a good people to live among, and a hearty welcome." [13] To the hungry of Europe the plenitude of food in America made an enticing appeal. An observer wrote in 1818 of the vicinity near Wheeling: "I believe I saw more peaches and apples rotting on the ground than would sink the British fleet. I was at many plantations in Ohio where they no more knew the number of their hogs than myself . . . . And they have such flocks of turkies, geese, ducks, and hens, as would surprise you: they live principally upon fowls and eggs; and in summer upon apple and peach pies. The poorest family has a cow or two and some sheep . . . and adorns the table three times a day like a wedding dinner—tea, coffee, beef, fowls, pigs, eggs, pickles, good bread; and their favorite beverage is whiskey or peach brandy. Say, is it so in England?" [14]

Obstacles in the path of the immigrant frequently counteracted the lure of America. During the Revolution, the destruction, disturbances, and dislocations of war on land and sea deterred strangers from casting their lots with a land in the throes of strife and upheaval. Soon after the dawn of peace, Congress in 1785 adopted an ordinance for the West which threw cold water on the hopes of the immigrant, requiring as it did that he pay $640 in order to buy a farm from the national domain. For nearly ten years thereafter troubles with the British and the Spaniards on the frontiers, coupled with harrowing Indian warfare north of the Ohio River, dimmed the appeal of the West to outsiders. The long severe winters of northern New England had a discouraging effect. For such reasons, the area of Pennsylvania–New York offered the most inviting attractions to immigrants between 1783 and 1800.[15]

The European wars that began in 1792 and lasted until 1815 restrained emigration from the Old World more than they stimulated it. As Britain and France each seized neutral ships and vessels of its enemy, the emigrant en route to America traveled in constant danger of being set upon in mid-passage and taken to a port remote from his destination. In Europe, the warring powers enlisted or impressed millions of able-bodied men into their armies and navies, and an enormous demand for war goods kept the people employed at home. The British government,

---

[12] Hector St. John de Crèvecœur, *Letters from an American Farmer* (Everyman Edition; London: J. M. Dent & Sons, Ltd., n. d.), p. 42.

[13] *Writings of Franklin* (Smyth), IX, 150.

[14] Edith Abbott, *Historical Aspects of the Immigration Problem: Select Documents* (Chicago: The University of Chicago Press, 1926), p. 40.

[15] *Ibid.*, pp. 28–30; Hansen, *The Atlantic Migration*, pp. 54, 71.

in dire need of soldiers, sailors, and workers, and fearful that emigration might weaken the British Isles, acted in many ways to stop the outflow of the king's subjects who were most useful to the state. In wartime, any British emigrant on shipboard might be impressed into the service of the Royal Navy. Parliament in 1785 prohibited persons from selling their future services for a passage to America, and another statute, of 1803, required that British ships transporting emigrants should provide each with a space four feet square—a much-needed reform to stop the horrible overcrowding that had inflicted terrible sufferings on passengers.[16] The European wars also drove the United States to adopt some policies that hampered immigration. The militant revolutionists of France and their ardent partisans in American frightened the Federalists in 1798 into enacting a new naturalization law (which specified fourteen years as the residence requirement for citizenship) and two alien acts which authorized the President to deport aliens at his mere will and pleasure.[17] Nine years later, the Embargo Act of December 22, 1807, which remained in force until March 1, 1809, closed the ports of the Union to outgoing ships and restricted the organized immigrant traffic. The War of 1812 shut the gates once more and for two and a half years held the inflow of aliens to a trickle.[18]

In view of the many interruptions and discouragements that beset the immigrant traffic, its history after 1775 was irregular or haphazard. During the Revolution, German mercenaries, the "Hessians," made the most striking addititon to the American population. It appears that 12,500 of them did not return to Europe and that perhaps half of that number were absorbed into American communities. Traces of them have been found in Baltimore, Virginia, the Carolina mountains, the trans-Allegheny West, and above all in the German settlements of Pennsylvania.[19] During a span of six years after the war a fairly large number of immigrants arrived from Britain, Ireland, and Germany. One observer reported that those counties sent 25,000 servants and redemptioners to Pennsylvania at this time. In the 1790's, exiles from France, radicals from England and Ireland, and victims of hard times in Wales attracted the most attention. An interval of peace in Europe released an unusually large stream of emigrants in the summer of 1801, and the traffic went on at a fairly good pace until 1807, featured by the flight of German opponents of war and assertive Irishmen whom the British government was glad to part with.

[16] Hansen, *The Atlantic Migration,* pp. 56, 69–70; Krout and Fox, *The Completion of Independence,* p. 6.

[17] James Morton Smith, *Freedom's Fetters* (Ithaca, N. Y.: Cornell University Press, 1956), pp. 33, 47, 61.

[18] Hansen, *The Atlantic Migration,* pp. 69–70.

[19] *Ibid.,* p. 54; Carl Wittke, *We Who Built America* (New York: Prentice-Hall, Inc., 1940), pp. 95–96.

After the repeal of the embargo, another wave of emigration set in, as fugitives from a depressed linen industry in northern Ireland sought a better life in America.[20]

The numerous groups among the immigrants moved one observer to describe them as a "promiscuous crowd of all the nations of Europe" and as a mixture "that will require long fermentation before it will contain the spirit, feelings, and imprint of a united people." [21] The federal government failed to adopt any general policy for either the encouragement or the control of immigration, for most people then believed, and the Constitution provided, that newcomers should ordinarily be admitted as "any of the States . . . shall think proper . . . ." Since the states needed workers or land buyers, they left the doors wide open. And the two states best situated to receive immigrants—Pennsylvania and New York—were the ones, of the seaboard area, most in need of settlers. Both the ports of New York and Philadelphia offered employment to aliens who preferred town life, or jobs on nearby farms where others could school themselves in rural ways, or easy access to inland domains of unsettled land. New York City and Philadelphia grew at a rapid pace—a reflection of the impact of the immigrants. The populations of the two cities combined rose from 75,000 in 1790 to 187,000 in 1810.[22] Meanwhile, efforts of land speculators or idealists to utilize immigrants as pioneers generally failed or faltered. A community of 600 French colonists at Gallipolis on the Ohio River suffered hardships that vetoed a repetition of the venture and blasted plans for a later migration from France on a grandiose scale. Another failure occurred at a settlement of English idealists on the Susquehanna River, as did two efforts to plant colonies, one French and one German, on the New York frontier. French royalist *émigrés* opened an "Asylum" on the Susquehanna, only to neglect farming and to withdraw after a few years. None of these projects was sustained by religious zeal—often a potent force in the conquest of the wilderness.[23]

In 1776, Negro slaves made up between a fifth and a sixth of the population of the Union. Their relative importance declined during the Revolution, when importations ceased and the British carried thousands of them away and enabled others to escape. South Carolina lost 25,000 during the war. The foreign traffic soon revived and brought in thousands from Africa and the West Indies between 1783 and 1787. However, a

---

[20] Greene, *The Revolutionary Generation*, p. 309; Hansen, *The Atlantic Migration*, pp. 58–61, 65–66, 67–69.

[21] Greene, *The Revolutionary Generation*, p. 310.

[22] Ralph H. Brown, *Mirror for Americans* (New York: American Geographical Society, 1943), p. 36; Robert G. Albion, "New York Port and Its Disappointed Rivals, 1815–1860," *Journal of Economic and Business History*, III, No. 4 (August, 1931), 618.

[23] Hansen, *The Atlantic Migration*, pp. 57–58, 60, 62, 63; Abbott, *Historical Aspects of the Immigration Problem*, pp. 32–33.

strong prejudice against the trade moved the states to prohibit it. By 1787 slaves ceased to be imported from abroad into New England, the middle states, and Maryland. South Carolina, Georgia, and North Carolina outlawed the traffic in 1787, 1793, and 1794. The number of slaves rose from about 500,000 in 1775 to 607,000 in 1790—a gain of 21 percent, in contrast with an increase of 34 percent in the white population.[24]

The invention of the cotton gin and the rapid spread of cotton growing after 1794 created a new and vigorous demand for labor, with the result that importers ignored hostile laws and smuggled slaves into the lower South on a large scale. In December, 1803, South Carolina legalized the traffic anew. Extremely large importations followed, in anticipation of a federal prohibition which the Constitution authorized Congress to put into effect in 1808. More than 39,000 slaves entered Charleston from foreign countries in the period 1803–1806. On March 2, 1807, Jefferson signed a federal act which prohibited, after January 1, 1808, the importation of slaves "into any port or place within the jurisdiction of the United States." The act, however, did not provide for effective enforcement and failed to stop the traffic in the lower South.[25] Madison noted in December, 1810, that "American citizens are instrumental in carrying on a traffic in violation of the laws of humanity and in defiance of those of their country."[26] Vessels flying the Spanish flag transported Negroes from Africa to Florida. The traffic was described in 1812 in this way:

After resting a few days at St. Augustine, . . . I agreed to accompany Diego on a land trip through the United States, where a *kaffle* of Negroes was to precede us, for whose disposal a shrewd Portuguese had already made arrangements . . . . I soon learned how readily, and at what profits, the Florida Negroes were sold into the neighboring American States. The *kaffle*, under charge of Negro drivers, was to strike up the Escambia River, and thence cross the boundary into Georgia, where some of our wild Africans were mixed with various squads of native blacks, and driven inland, till sold off, singly or by couples, on the road . . . . The Spanish possessions were thriving on this inland exchange of Negroes and mulattoes; Florida was a sort of nursery for slave-breeders, and many American citizens grew rich by trafficking in Guinea Negroes, and smuggling them continually, in small parties, through the southern United States.[27]

By 1810, the southern slave population had grown to more than a million, at a rate of increase after 1790 that was twice that for the fifteen

[24] Greene, *The Revolutionary Generation*, p. 67; Frederic Bancroft, *Slave-Trading in the Old South* (Baltimore: J. H. Furst Company, 1931), pp. 4, 5; Du Bois, *Suppression of the African Slave-Trade*, p. 50; Kenneth M. Stampp, *The Peculiar Institution* (New York: Alfred A. Knopf, Inc., 1956), p. 25.

[25] Du Bois, *Suppression of the African Slave-Trade*, pp. 86, 90–91, 108.

[26] Richardson, *Messages of the Presidents*, I, 485.

[27] Du Bois, *Suppression of the African Slave-Trade*, p. 111, quoting Richard Drake, *Revelations of a Slave Smuggler* . . . (New York: 1860), p. 51.

years after 1775. This trend confirms the conclusion that, in regard to importations of slaves into the Cotton South, the federal prohibitory law was a dead letter during the period immediately after 1808.[28]

Few interests of the people exceeded the urge to acquire land. In the area of the United States as of 1783, the wilderness that bordered the settlements in 1775, and into which pioneers had penetrated by 1815, contained perhaps 300 million acres—enough to provide each white family of 1775 with a tract of 750 acres. Although such an estimate is very rough, and although numerous areas beyond the frontier line were not suited to cultivation, the fact remains that Americans in 1775 had a very extensive back yard. The attractions of new settlements, the price of land, legal titles, surveys, terms of sale, and forms of tenure were absorbing subjects in an age when the fever of speculation rarely abated. Basic to all such features of land disposal was initial ownership, for the original grantor determined the conditions on which titles could be obtained and the tenure on which land would be held.

The Revolution transformed land tenure in most of the states and wrought far-reaching changes in the ownership of vacant land. Today, all titles to landed and other property within the Union derive their legality from the governments to which the Revolution gave birth.

Late in the colonial era a half-dozen men had title to the vacant land beyond the settlements and held it under a form of tenure that was monarchical and feudal in principle. Of these landed magnates, the king of Great Britain ranked first. His holdings included the ungranted lands of New Hampshire, Vermont, New York, Virginia, Georgia, South Carolina, and the southern half of North Carolina. The royal claim also covered all the present states of Ohio, Indiana, Illinois, Michigan, Wisconsin, Kentucky, Alabama, and Mississippi, nearly the whole of West Virginia, and almost a third of Tennessee. With reference to the present area of the United States, the unsettled lands of the king in 1775 may have amounted to 380 million acres. In Pennsylvania, the unoccupied lands—perhaps 18 million acres in extent—belonged to Richard Penn and Thomas Penn, heirs of William Penn. In Virginia, Thomas, sixth Lord Fairfax, owned a princely estate between the Potomac and Rappahannock rivers. In 1775, perhaps a million acres of the Fairfax domain—known as the Northern Neck—remained to be settled in the northwestern part of modern Virginia and in the northeastern part of West Virginia. Farther south, Lord

[28] Stampp, *The Peculiar Institution*, p. 25; Du Bois, *Suppression of the African Slave-Trade*, pp. 108–109; Gray, *History of Agriculture in the Southern United States*, II, 649.

Granville had a title to the Granville District, which comprised the northern half of North Carolina above the line of 35° 34′ and extended westward to include more than two thirds of Tennessee. Granville's personal empire may have contained 22 million acres of vacant land in 1775. For the sixth magnate, Frederick, sixth Baron Baltimore, the ungranted lands of Maryland were held in trust. However, they did not figure prominently in the westward advance after the Revolution.[29]

The form of land tenure in force in all these lordly domains was a survival of feudalism. Each of the magnates possessed the right to exact yearly quitrents, or money payments, from settlers who bought or otherwise acquired land. In 1775, the quitrents payable under previous grants amounted to nearly $100,000 a year. By the Quebec Act of 1774, Britain added to its province of Quebec the territory north of the Ohio River between western Pennsylvania and the Mississippi and thereby extended to it the French-Canadian system of feudal landholding. In 1771 the British crown directed the governor of Quebec to grant lands there "in fief or seigneurie." This instruction was renewed in 1775 after the land north of the Ohio had been added to Quebec. Under the old French practice, the king bestowed estates on seigniors or nobles who became his vassals, and they in turn exacted various payments and duties from the settlers or *habitants* to whom they granted farms. After Britain conquered Canada, the British sovereign replaced the king of France as the overlord to whom the seigniors made their payments, rendered homage, and swore an oath of fidelity. Had the British land system of 1775 survived in the area of the United States, feudal tenure would have blanketed all future land grants there, except in Maine.[30]

Massachusetts, Connecticut, and Rhode Island evolved a type of land tenure that exempted the landowner from quitrents and personal obligations to an overlord. The independent farmer of southern New England, a virtual lord of the soil, recognized no superior except the law, which he shared in making. The land tenure of southern New England, although preferred by the colonists, did not appear in 1775 to be destined to spread over most of the new settlements. Practically all the land in present-day Massachusetts, Connecticut, and Rhode Island had then

[29] Leonard Woods Labaree, *Royal Instructions to British Governors, 1670–1776* (2 vols.; New York: D. Appleton-Century Company, 1935), II, 533–537, 607, 608; Charles Henry Ambler, *A History of West Virginia* (New York: Prentice-Hall, Inc., 1933), pp. 56–57, 172; E[llis] Merton Coulter, "The Granville District," *James Sprunt Historical Publications*, XIII, No. 1 (1913), 35–38.

[30] Beverley W. Bond, Jr., "The Quit-Rent System in the American Colonies," *American Historical Review*, XVII, No. 3 (April, 1912), 496; Jameson, *The American Revolution As a Social Movement*, p. 33; Labaree, *Royal Instructions to British Governors*, II, 587–588; Francis Parkman, *The Old Régime in Canada* (8th ed.; Boston: Little, Brown and Company, 1880), pp. 244–247, 249–250.

been granted. Massachusetts, however, owned Maine, and made grants there on the basis of free tenure. Meanwhile, the Quebec Act threatened to prevent the extension into the interior of the land system of southern New England. Connecticut and Massachusetts, under their royal charters, claimed the land westward of Pennsylvania and New York to the Mississippi River between the extensions of their northern and southern boundaries—a zone about 200 miles wide across the northern parts of Ohio, Indiana, and Illinois, and the southern parts of Michigan and Wisconsin. The Quebec Act of 1774 severed this area from Massachusetts and Connecticut, seemingly deprived them of their claims to it, and dedicated it to feudal tenure.[31]

Should feudal land law or a system of freeholds prevail in the area of the eastern United States? That was one of the paramount questions of the Revolution, and the verdict doomed the feudal principle. The victory of free tenure came in part as a result of the confiscation or forced purchase of the great feudal domains. Some of the states, as the acquiring agencies, became temporary owners of immense tracts of land.

The men of the Revolution acted on a dual theory. First, they asserted that independence automatically deprived the king of his ungranted land and vested the title to it in the new state governments. Second, the patriots recognized the validity of old royal grants, to the extent of claiming for the states the territories which the king had conferred upon the colonies by royal charters. The king's ownership of ungranted lands vanished, but the authority he had once exercised provided a basis for the territorial claims of the states. The acquisition by the states of the ungranted lands of the king was of enormous importance, in view of their vast extent.

Pennsylvania took over the ungranted lands of the Penns and gave them £130,000, though the lands were reputed to be worth £1 million. Delaware did not compensate the Penns for the ungranted proprietary lands which it acquired. The tracts involved were small in extent and poor in quality. The state acted on the assumption that the Revolution had "prostrated equally the kingly and the proprietary powers" and had transferred proprietary titles to the state "to the same extent as if the conquest had been made by France or any other nation." In Maryland, the heir of Lord Baltimore, Henry Harford, lost his proprietary rights and received only £10,000 from the state. In 1782, North Carolina confiscated the holdings of Lord Granville, and the Virginia legislature in-

[31] Viola F. Barnes, "Land Tenure in the English Colonial Charters of the Seventeenth Century," *Essays in Colonial History Presented to Charles M. Andrews* (New Haven, Conn.: Yale University Press, 1921), p. 15; Frederick S. Allis, Jr., ed., *William Bingham's Maine Lands, 1790–1820* (Colonial Society of Massachusetts, *Publications*, Vols. XXXVI, XXXVII; Boston: The Society, 1954), XXXVI, 9, 24–25.

validated the English title to the ungranted lands of the Fairfax tract and declared the state to be their owner.[32]

The confiscation of the ungranted lands of Granville, Fairfax, and the king raised a perplexing question. If the titles of such former claimants were invalid, were not grants made by them before 1776 also void? In the case of the crown's lands, Britain recognized the legality of the transfer of title from the king to the states by the Independence Treaty of 1783. Attempts of Granville's heirs to uphold his title came to nought. The Fairfax lands embroiled Virginia in a long and bitter strife. Lord Fairfax died in 1781 and left a claim to his estate to his nephew, Denny Martin Fairfax. Later a group of associates bought 160,000 acres of the Fairfax claim and thereby involved themselves in a conflict with settlers who had purchased land there from the state of Virginia. One such purchaser, David Hunter, acquired a patent to 788 acres of the Fairfax tract. Eventually the Supreme Court of the United States in 1813, and again in 1816 in the case of *Martin v. Hunter's Lessee*, upheld the validity of titles acquired by the associates from the heir of Lord Fairfax.[33]

The states added to their real-estate holdings by confiscating lands that had once belonged to loyalists. Before 1775 many British officials in the colonies had obtained large estates from the crown. The governor of New Hampshire, Sir John Wentworth, had extensive lands there. In New York, Sir John Johnson in 1775 inherited 200,000 acres from his father, Sir William Johnson. John Tabor Kempe, the king's attorney general in New York after 1759, amassed holdings in Vermont, New York, and New Jersey which he valued at £64,924. Twelve plantations, totaling more than 19,000 acres and worth $160,000, made up the estate of Sir James Wright, royal governor of Georgia in 1775.[34]

[32] Richard S. Rodney, "The End of the Penns' Claim to Delaware, 1789–1814," *Pennsylvania Magazine of History and Biography*, LXI, No. 2 (April, 1937), 196, 202–203; Jameson, *The American Revolution As a Social Movement*, pp. 34–35; Gray, *History of Agriculture in the Southern United States*, II, 618–619; William E. Dodd, "Chief Justice Marshall and Virginia," *American Historical Review*, XII, No. 4 (July, 1907), 777.

[33] Coulter, "The Granville District," p. 55; Gray, *History of Agriculture in the Southern United States*, II, 619; Albert J. Beveridge, *The Life of John Marshall* (4 vols.; Boston: Houghton Mifflin Company, 1916), IV, 147–149, 156–157, 161.

[34] Marshall Harris, *Origin of the Land Tenure System in the United States* (Ames: The Iowa State College Press, 1953), pp. 368–369; Jameson, *The American Revolution As a Social Movement*, pp. 34–35; Mabel G. Walker, "Sir John Johnson, Loyalist," *Mississippi Valley Historical Review*, III, No. 3 (December, 1916), 321; Catherine Snell Crary, "The American Dream: John Tabor Kempe's Rise from Poverty to Riches," *William and Mary Quarterly*, Third Series, XIV, No. 2 (April, 1957), 176, 186; E[llis] Merton Coulter, *Georgia: A Short History* (Chapel Hill: The University of North Carolina Press, 1947), p. 103; Lorenzo Sabine, *Biographical Sketches of Loyalists in the American Revolution* (2 vols.; Boston: Little, Brown and Company, 1864), I, 580, 599; II, 411, 458.

Confiscation of land was an extreme penalty which the states in-flicted on loyalists for such unpardonable offenses as serving in Britain's armed forces or leaving a state under the protection of British troops. An act of New York of October 22, 1779, authorized the sale at public auction of confiscated loyalist lands, in tracts not exceeding 500 acres; and a Georgia statute of March 1, 1778, listed 117 persons as guilty of treason, decreed the confiscation of their property, and set up county boards to execute the law. Under such acts many confiscations took place. New Hampshire acquired 28 estates, including that of Sir John Went-worth. The principal loyalist victim in Massachusetts was Sir William Pepperrell, whose lands extended thirty miles along the coast of Maine, from Saco to Kittery Point. New York realized about $3,100,000 specie from sales of 2,500,000 acres confiscated from 59 loyalists, among whom were Sir John Johnson, John T. Kempe, Roger Morris, James De Lancey, Beverly Robinson, and the Philipse family, whose estate comprised about 300 square miles. Loyalists in Pennsylvania forfeited 490 holdings to the state, and Maryland reaped £450,000 from the sale of confiscated prop-erty, the city of Baltimore alone receiving £36,673. Large loyalists' hold-ings were not numerous in Virginia, North Carolina, and South Carolina. Georgia took possession of thousands of loyalist acres, including those of Thomas Waters and Sir James Wright. After the war, 2,560 loyalists asked compensation from the British government for property losses of about £10,000,000 and received awards amounting to £3,292,000.[35]

STATE LAND POLICIES

The Revolution established the principle that the supreme authority over the land was vested in the people of the states. In consequence, all land titles in the United States derive their validity from the state and federal governments. The states generally recognized and confirmed old English titles that were held by persons loyal to the American cause. Deeds to lands which the states acquired after 1775 drew their legal force from the states. The people assumed the sovereign authority of eminent domain—the right to repossess privately owned lands when they were needed for public uses.

In fashioning land policies during the Revolution the states under-

[35] Claude Halstead Van Tyne, *The Loyalists of the American Revolution* (New York: The Macmillan Company, 1902), pp. 333–341; James H. Stark, *The Loyalists of Massachusetts* . . . (Boston: W. B. Clarke Co., 1907), p. 208; Cochran, *New York in the Confederation*, pp. 60, 64; Coulter, *Georgia: A Short History*, pp. 161–162; Jameson, *The American Revolution As a Social Movement*, p. 34; Alexander Clarence Flick, *Loyalism in New York During the Revolution* (New York: 1901), p. 212, appendix; Crowl, *Maryland During and After the Revolution*, p. 49; Isaac Samuel Harrell, *Loyalism in Virginia* (Durham, N. C.: Duke University Press, 1926), pp. 62–63.

took to achieve five main purposes. First, they swept away the survivals of feudalism such as the quitrents, refused to create new feudal or proprietary domains, and sold or granted lands on the basis of freehold tenure. The immunity of the United States from feudalism after 1776 quickened the democratic strivings of a pioneering, agrarian society. Second, the states stimulated private enterprise by rapidly placing lands in the hands of individuals, instead of holding them as the basis for state-owned and -operated businesses. Third, the legislatures sought to build up communities of small landowners by selling small farms on easy terms to impecunious settlers. Fourth, those states that acquired large holdings used them as a source of revenue for paying debts incurred during the war. Finally, land grants served as an inducement to citizens to enlist in the military forces and as a means of paying veterans for their services. In this respect, bounty lands foreshadowed the GI benefits of World War II.

In its land policy for Maine, between the Penobscot and St. Croix rivers, Massachusetts in 1784 authorized surveys of townships and provided that half of those located on the rivers should be sold in 500-acre lots at 6s. or more an acre, and that the other half should be sold in 150-acre tracts for what they would bring. In each of the nonriver townships the state gave thirty lots of 100 acres each to settlers. New York made only a small percentage of its vast holdings available directly to small purchasers. An act of 1786 arranged for surveys of lots, each a mile square, to be located within a township ten miles square. The lots in every fourth township were to be sold at public auction at a minimum rate of 1s. an acre, the buyer being allowed sixty days in which to pay three fourths of the purchase price. Pennsylvania opened a state land office in 1784 and sold tracts at 2s. an acre, with a limit of 400 acres to one application. Lands confiscated in Maryland varied greatly in value; hence the state did not sell them at a uniform rate. The largest part consisted of the rented estates and ungranted lands of the proprietor. The sale records of one manor show that fourteen tenants bought 2,478 acres, or 72 percent of the tract. In the state as a whole the lots which were sold varied in size from 104 to 230 acres. Most purchasers bought on credit, with the result that in November, 1787, they owed the state £303,000.[36]

The immensity of Virginia's holdings within the state as of today, and in Kentucky, West Virginia, and southern Ohio, moved the legislature to dispose of its lands liberally. The cornerstone of Virginia's policy was an act of May, 1779, which offered lands at 8s. an acre, or £40 per 100 acres, without limitation on the quantity a purchaser could buy. Since such lands could be paid for with paper money, the extreme wartime

---

[36] Allis, *Bingham's Maine Lands*, I, 26; Cochran, *New York in the Confederation*, p. 110; Solon J. Buck and Elizabeth Hawthorn Buck, *The Planting of Civilization in Western Pennsylvania* (Pittsburgh: University of Pittsburgh Press, 1939), p. 146; Crowl, *Maryland During and After the Revolution*, pp. 57–60.

inflation speeded up land sales, as knowing citizens converted their acutely depreciated paper into a durable kind of property. An increase of price to 32s. an acre in 1780 did not match the decline in the buying power of the money. Currency depreciation therefore resulted in land speculation on a large scale.[37]

North Carolina, with the lands of Tennessee at its disposal, enacted its basic land statute in November, 1777. It enabled a settler to buy 640 acres for himself, 100 acres for his wife, and 100 acres for each of his children, paying at the rate of 4.8d. an acre, with a time extension until January, 1779, for completing the payment. In 1783 the state increased the price to 2s. an acre and limited each warrant to a maximum of 5,000 acres. As the owner of an imperial domain, Georgia, by an act of 1777, made land available on extremely easy terms. A free white person could obtain 200 acres for himself, 50 acres for each member of his family, and 50 acres for each of his slaves up to ten, at the price of 2s. a 100 acres or about ¾d. an acre. To obtain such favored treatment the purchaser must settle the land within six months after he acquired it. Georgia's policy was not far from one of free land.[38]

In August, 1776, the Continental Congress originated the scheme of land bounties when it promised tracts of 50 acres to Hessians and other foreigners who would forsake the service of Britain. Next, on September 16, Congress offered 100-acre bounties to soldiers in the Continental Army and called upon the states to provide the land in proportion to their contributions for the support of the war.[39] Most of the states supplemented the Congress bounties for continental service with state grants. Late in the war, both Congress and the states that owned extensive lands permitted veterans to buy land with certificates which represented unpaid military service.

Massachusetts delayed until 1801 in providing land for most of its veterans. It then offered 200 acres on the upper Schoodic River to every volunteer among soldiers and noncoms who had served three years. Earlier, the state had granted to John Allan and a party of veterans a township on the Passamaquoddy. For the benefit of its veterans, New York in 1782 designated a Military Tract of 1,680,000 acres, extending about fifty miles eastward from the seventy-seventh meridian, between Lakes Ontario and Oneida on the north and the Pennsylvania–New York border

[37] C. H. Laub, "Revolutionary Virginia and the Crown Lands, 1775–1783," *William and Mary Quarterly*, Second Series, XI, No. 4 (October, 1931), 308; Gray, *History of Agriculture in the Southern United States*, II, 622.

[38] Amelia Clewley Ford, *Colonial Precedents of Our National Land System As It Existed in 1800* (University of Wisconsin *History Series, Bulletin*, Vol. II, No. 2; Madison: 1910), p. 134; Gray, *History of Agriculture in the Southern United States*, II, 626; L. D. Smith, "Land Laws of Tennessee," *Tennessee Law Review*, I, No. 1 (November, 1922), 34–36; Coulter, *Georgia: A Short History*, p. 163.

[39] *Journals of the Continental Congress*, V, 653–655, 763.

on the south. Grants as authorized in 1783 varied from 5,500 acres for a major general to 500 for a private. The state did not survey the tract until 1788, and soldiers did not move into it until 1789. Pennsylvania promised bounty lands in March, 1780, and in March, 1785, provided for grants ranging from 200 acres for a private to 2,000 acres for a major general. By 1810, nearly 3,000 soldiers had obtained patents to lands located in the northeastern part of the state. The small size of Maryland dictated a frugal bounty policy. Under an act of 1777, which offered 50 acres to privates and 200 acres to officers, 2,457 veterans obtained 50-acre lots located in Washington County adjacent to the upper Potomac.[40]

Virginia in October, 1776, promised 100 acres to Virginians who enlisted in the Continental Army, increased the allotments to 200 acres in 1779, and in 1782 adopted a plan that awarded 5,000 acres to a colonel, 3,000 to a captain, 400 to a noncom, and 200 to a private. North Carolina started its bounty program with a promise of 200 acres for three years' service, and in 1784 boosted the amount to 640 acres for privates and applied a scale that rose to 7,200 acres for a colonel. Georgia's initial offer of 1776—100 acres to a volunteer who served three years or for the duration—was raised to 250 acres in 1781, with a ten years' exemption from taxes.[41]

Several states gave to squatters a pre-emptive right to buy ungranted lands on which they had settled. Massachusetts, however, did not coddle the squatter. One of its acts, of March 26, 1788, which applied to only two counties in southern Maine, allowed squatters, by paying five Spanish milled dollars, to obtain deeds to 100-acre tracts they had occupied before January 1, 1784. An act of New York, of May, 1786, limited a pre-emption claim to 200 acres and required the settler to pay the minimum price of 1s. an acre. Pennsylvania, long a haven of the squatter, allowed him to buy a tract of 100 acres if he had occupied it before 1780, and charged him 2s. an acre, plus interest from the beginning of his settlement. As early as 1776 Virginia recognized pre-emptive rights of squatters on its ungranted lands, and an act of May, 1779, provided that if a settler had occupied land before 1778, had lived on it one year, and had raised a crop of corn, he might buy 400 acres at 2¼ cents an acre. If he had built a cabin he could obtain 1,000 acres. Squatters who had occupied land after January 1, 1778, might pre-empt 400 acres and pay the regular price. Claims had to be legalized by May, 1780, to be recognized. However, an act of October, 1779, gave the squatter a year in which to pay for his

[40] Allis, *Bingham's Maine Lands*, I, 32; Cochran, *New York in the Confederation*, pp. 108–109; Buck, *The Planting of Civilization in Western Pennsylvania*, pp. 205–206.

[41] Crowl, *Maryland During and After the Revolution*, pp. 56–58; Laub, "Virginia and the Crown Lands," p. 305; Ford, *Precedents of Our National Land System*, p. 108; Thomas Perkins Abernethy, *From Frontier to Plantation in Tennessee* (Chapel Hill: The University of North Carolina Press, 1932), pp. 40, 42; Coulter, *Georgia: A Short History*, pp. 163, 164.

warrant. In its land laws for Tennessee, North Carolina in November, 1777, tendered 640 acres to a squatter, plus 100 acres for his wife and 100 acres for each child, payment to be made before January, 1779, at the rate of 4.8d. an acre.[42]

Pre-emptive rights were by-products of the colonial era and the Revolution, when settlers found it difficult or impossible to secure legal titles to vacant lands. In consequence, the states with large holdings offered legal titles to squatters who had occupied land before 1778, 1780, or 1784. At the same time the states gave much land to veterans and sold tracts freely at low prices. After the states had adopted definite and liberal policies for the sale and granting of lands, pre-emptive rights lost their justification, and the states generally withheld them from lands settled after the Revolution.

Sales of land at low prices, bounties for veterans, and the legalizing of squatters' claims enlarged the body of small landowners. In New York, the growth of the class of freeholders fostered political democracy. Maryland sold 268,000 acres in lots averaging about 200 acres. In Georgia, 4,381 veterans received grants. The states with the most land to distribute —Virginia, North Carolina, Georgia, and New York—and such beneficiaries of cheap land as Kentucky and Tennessee became strongholds of the faith of Thomas Jefferson, the foremost apostle of freehold tenure, small farms, and the democratic ideals of yeomen and pioneers.[43]

THE NATIONAL DOMAIN

The United States acquired a national public domain on March 1, 1784, when Congress accepted the cession by Virginia of its claim to most of the land north of the Ohio River. This cession gave the Union a clear title to lands between western Pennsylvania and the Mississippi, north of the Ohio and south of the forty-first parallel, for Virginia alone among the states then claimed that area. The cession itself was a victory for free tenure over semifeudal tendencies. After 1763, American promoters had formed several large land companies and had endeavored to secure princely domains in the trans-Allegheny West. Prominent among them was the Illinois-Wabash Company, a vehicle of promoters in Pennsyl-

[42] Allis, *Bingham's Maine Lands*, I, 31; Cochran, *New York in the Confederation*, p. 110; Buck, *The Planting of Civilization in Western Pennsylvania*, p. 146; Laub, "Virginia and the Crown Lands," pp. 307–308; Ford, *Precedents of Our National Land System*, pp. 127–128, 131–132, 134.

[43] Cochran, *New York in the Confederation*, p. 64; Crowl, *Maryland During and After the Revolution*, p. 56; Coulter, *Georgia: A Short History*, p. 164; Robert O. De Mond, *The Loyalists of North Carolina during the Revolution* (Durham, N. C.: Duke University Press, 1940), p. 180; Anthony Marc Lewis, "Jefferson and Virginia's Pioneers, 1774–1781," *Mississippi Valley Historical Review*, XXXIV, No. 4 (March, 1948), 551–552.

vania and Maryland who had obtained Indian grants of land north of the Ohio. This company had encouraged Maryland to refuse to ratify the Articles of Confederation until Virginia agreed to surrender its claim to most of the Northwest. Opponents of land monopoly in Virginia attached to its act of cession a proviso which made its validity contingent upon the cancellation of claims which private parties had obtained from Indians in the area to be ceded. The United States therefore received the land free from prior private claims.[44]

Drawing upon the experience and practices of the states, Congress in 1785 adopted a plan for a national land system. An ordinance of May 20 provided for the sale of the federal lands to private persons, in minimum lots or sections of 640 acres, at a price of not less than $1 an acre. The ordinance also outlined a plan of surveys that has been extended to all parts of the Union except Texas, Tennessee, Kentucky, West Virginia, Maine, Vermont, Hawaii, and the original thirteen states. A township six miles square, divided into thirty-six sections—each containing a square mile or 640 acres—formed the basis of the survey plan. The ordinance reserved five sections in each township; four to the United States and one for the support of public schools in the township. The first survey was to begin at the point where a line running due north from the end of the northern boundary of Pennsylvania touches the Ohio River. From that point a base line, or geographer's line, was to be drawn due west. The townships were grouped into ranges running north and south, each six miles wide and varying in length according to the area surveyed.[45]

The first survey, begun by Thomas Hutchins in 1785, mapped out seven ranges in southeastern Ohio, extending 42 miles westward beyond Pennsylvania and 90 miles from north to south along the western side. The land Ordinance of 1785 did not immediately speed the growth of settlement north of the Ohio. A pioneer needed $640 to buy a federal tract—a sum beyond the reach of most. At that time settlers could obtain land on better terms from the states. Hence the surge of migration before 1795 carried pioneers into northern New England, inland New York, western Pennsylvania, and the back country of Virginia, North Carolina, and Georgia.[46]

Congress did not change the essentials of the land policy of 1785

[44] Clarence E. Carter, ed., *The Territorial Papers of the United States* (24 vols.; Washington: Government Printing Office, 1934–1959), II, 10–11; see articles by Merrill Jensen in *The Mississippi Valley Historical Review:* "The Cession of the Old Northwest," XXIII, No. 1 (June, 1936), 29, 37, 47–48, and "The Creation of the National Domain, 1781–1784," XXVI, No. 3 (December, 1939), 325–326, 341; George E. Lewis, *The Indiana Company* (Glendale, Calif.: The Arthur H. Clark Company, 1941), pp. 243, 253, 264.

[45] *Journals of the Continental Congress*, XXVIII, 375, 376, 378.

[46] Beverley W. Bond, *The Civilization of the Old Northwest* (New York: The Macmillan Company, 1934), pp. 18–19.

until 1796. It then made provision for selling the lands in present-day Ohio and Indiana that several Indian tribes had ceded to the United States in 1795 by the Treaty of Greenville. The Land Act of May 18, 1796, re-affirmed the township and range plan of surveys and provided for a dual system of selling sections of 640 acres. Alternate townships were to be sold in tracts equal to eight sections; in the intervening townships, the sections were to be sold singly. Congress now set the price at $2 an acre. Since $1,280 was needed to complete the smallest purchase, and $10,240 for a large one, the act did not stimulate sales. Under its terms purchasers bought only 48,566 acres. It reflected both the aversion of the Federalists to providing cheap land to Jeffersonian agrarians and the desire of the states to sell their lands without being exposed to price-cutting competition from the federal government.[47]

In 1799 the assembly of the Northwest Territory sent William Henry Harrison to Congress as its delegate. He sponsored changes in land policy which Congress soon adopted. An act of May 10, 1800, authorized the sale on credit of 320-acre tracts at $2 an acre and provided for convenient land offices at Cincinnati, Chillicothe, Marietta, and Steubenville. A buyer could pay in four installments—one fourth within forty days following the contract date and the other three quarters after two, three, and four years. A pioneer now needed to pay only $160, plus certain fees, in order to secure a claim.[48] The good things of the public domain became even more accessible to the settler by an act of 1804, which—while retaining the credit price and the credit terms of the act of 1800—enabled him to procure 160 acres with an initial payment of about $80. Coming at a time when state lands were getting scarce, the act of 1804 drew streams of settlers into the areas where the Union had lands for sale. Jeffersonian democracy rose to full tide.[49]

Five other states joined Virginia in ceding to the United States western lands they claimed under colonial charters. On April 18, 1785, Massachusetts yielded its claim to territory west of New York, and in 1786 Connecticut gave up most of its claim in the Northwest, retaining about 3,800,000 acres in the "Western Reserve," between Lake Erie and the forty-first parallel and extending 120 miles west of Pennsylvania. By the end of 1786, the Union had obtained full title to all the Northwest, except the territory not yet relinquished by the Indians, the lands included in

[47] 1 *Statutes at Large*, pp. 465–466; Payson Jackson Treat, *The National Land System, 1785–1820* (New York: E. B. Treat & Co., 1910), pp. 85–86, 100; Roy M. Robbins, *Our Landed Heritage* (Princeton, N. J.: Princeton University Press, 1942), pp. 16–17.

[48] 2 *Statutes at Large*, p. 73; Treat, *The National Land System*, pp. 94–98; Robbins, *Our Landed Heritage*, pp. 18–19.

[49] 2 *Statutes at Large*, pp. 277, 281; Treat, *The National Land System*, pp. 120–121; Robbins, *Our Landed Heritage*, p. 25; Benjamin Horace Hibbard, *A History of Public Land Policies* (New York: Peter Smith, 1939), pp. 74–75.

old French grants, the Western Reserve, and two tracts which Virginia reserved for its veterans: the Virginia Military District between the Little Miami and the Scioto rivers, and Clark's Grant of 150,000 acres opposite modern Louisville. Although the United States did not secure title to present-day West Virginia and Kentucky, it did acquire much land in Tennessee, Alabama and Mississippi. In 1787, South Carolina gave up an invalid claim to a strip 12 miles wide south of the thirty-fifth parallel, between the Chattooga and Mississippi rivers. North Carolina in 1790 ceded to the Union the ungranted lands of Tennessee, reserving the right to make additional grants to its veterans. After Georgia had surrendered, in 1802, its claim to ungranted land south of Tennessee, Congress in 1804 enlarged Mississippi Territory—organized in 1798—so as to include in it most of present-day Alabama and Mississippi. After the Louisiana Purchase of 1803, the Union soon had lands for sale in the area of the states of Louisiana and Missouri. The Land Act of 1804 thus came at a time when the federal government had immense holdings accessible to pioneers in Mississippi, Alabama, Louisiana, Missouri, Indiana, and Ohio.[50]

Several principles guided the disposal of the national domain between 1787 and 1815. Congress insisted that federal lands should not be sold to private parties until the Indians had ceded their title to the United States. Squatters received no preferences, and land could not be legally occupied or sold before it had been surveyed. The Northwest Ordinance of 1787 laid down general rules to restrain territories or states from actions injurious to the Union. Article 4 states: "The legislatures of those districts or new States shall never interfere with the primary disposal of the soil by the United States in Congress assembled, nor with any regulations Congress may find necessary for securing the title in such soil to bona fide purchasers. No tax shall be imposed on lands the property of the United States; and in no case shall non-resident proprietors be taxed higher than residents." [51]

ENTERPRISE AND SPECULATION IN LAND

Needing revenue, the states dumped onto the market far more land than pioneers could occupy within a short time. The resulting surplus invited promoters to acquire claims and titles, with the purpose either of selling them quickly at a profit, or of holding them for an increase in value. The excitements of the war, an upsurge of enthusiasm arising from independence, and the continental scope of the new nation bred an eager

[50] *Journals of the Continental Congress*, XXVIII, 271–273; Bond, *The Old Northwest*, p. 6; R. S. Cotterill, "The South Carolina Land Cession," *Mississippi Valley Historical Review*, XII, No. 3 (December, 1925), 376, 380–381; Abernethy, *From Frontier to Plantation in Tennessee*, pp. 112–113.

[51] *Journals of the Continental Congress*, XXXII, 341.

spirit of enterprise, speculation, and daring. To seek riches from rising land values was an old American custom. Washington had written in 1767: "The greatest estates we have in the colony" were made "by taking up . . . at very low rates the rich back lands which were thought nothing of in those days but are now the most valuable lands we possess." [52] "Were I to characterize the United States," said an observer in 1796, "it would be by the appellation of the land of speculations." [53] A rural population that doubled every twenty-five years was bound to force up the price of land.

To a large extent speculators did not buy and sell deeds to land that had been surveyed. Highly important in the business were land-office warrants and shares of stock in private land companies. A warrant vested its holder with the right to acquire in the future a stated number of acres that had not been surveyed when the warrant was issued. Promoters used several methods of acquiring claims. They bought up bounty warrants from veterans who had no taste for pioneering, and in some instances they sent out settlers to acquire pre-emption rights. Speculators also purchased warrants directly from the states, paying with public certificates of debt; and both the federal government and the states sold large tracts to individuals or companies for such paper, which had often been procured at a heavy discount. Dealers sold warrants either to settlers or to other speculators who counted on a profitable resale. Some of the operators worked through partnerships; others formed stock companies which assigned to trustees the land they acquired, to be sold for the benefit of the stockholders. The shares of such companies then became articles of speculation. Woe to the plunger who strained his credit to buy claims and then found that he could not sell them for enough to pay his debts.

In the Northeast, the wild lands of Maine brought forth a grand speculative venture. In July, 1791, William Duer, Hamilton's friend, and Henry Knox, then Secretary of War, contracted with Massachusetts to purchase 2 million acres in inland Maine, east of the Penobscot River. The partners agreed to pay 10 cents an acre in installments extending to 1799, and to settle 2,500 people on the land within twelve years. The state granted a ten years' exemption from taxes. Duer failed in 1792, and early in 1793 he and Knox sold their rights to William Bingham, a wealthy Philadelphia capitalist. Bingham sought buyers abroad and in 1796 conveyed 593,000 acres to Alexander Baring of London for $263,000. The speculation as a whole did not yield profits before 1820, for the unproductive region was not suited to farming. Bingham noted in 1800 that "new settlers are not to be obtained without very extraordinary encouragements, far beyond what is usually given in new countries." [54]

[52] *Writings of Washington* (Fitzpatrick), II, 459.
[53] A. M. Sakolski, *The Great American Land Bubble* (New York: Harper & Brothers, 1932), p. 30.
[54] Allis, *Bingham's Maine Lands*, I, 47–51, 62, 66, 102–103, 676; II, 1034, 1254.

New York harbored many large projects. One was the Phelps-Gorham Purchase of 1788, which grew out of the claim of Massachusetts, under its royal charter, to a zone extending east to west across New York State. In 1786 the two states agreed that Massachusetts should have pre-emptive title to practically all the western part of New York State beyond a "Pre-emption Line" that ran north and south close to the western shore of Lake Seneca. Massachusetts contracted in April, 1788, to sell its claim to this area to two of its citizens—Oliver Phelps and Nathaniel Gorham. They agreed to pay £300,000 in the debt certificates of Massachusetts, then worth about one fifth of their face value. In July, Phelps and Gorham purchased from Iroquois tribes their title to a tract of 2,600,000 acres in the area between the Pre-emption Line and the Genesee River. For this region, known as the Phelps-Gorham Tract, the partners obtained a patent from Massachusetts in November. In 1790, financial troubles forced them to give up their claim to the land west of the Phelps-Gorham Tract; whereupon Massachusetts resold it to Robert Morris. He also purchased at that time the unsold and ungranted land within the Phelps-Gorham Tract, and reaped a handsome profit by selling it in 1791 to English speculators led by Sir William Pulteney. Next, in 1792, Morris conveyed most of the western end of the state—1,500,000 acres in all—to Dutch capitalists who, in 1795, formed the Holland Land Company and proceeded to sell tracts to settlers. For a time Morris retained a third part of the Phelps-Gorham Tract—a strip, the Morris Reserve, about fifteen miles wide between the Pulteney Purchase and the Holland Purchase. This he soon sold to a Dutch banking house, W. and J. Willink. In this manner, Morris conveyed to English and Dutch capitalists the title to most of New York State west of Lake Seneca.[55]

The wild lands of northern New York also attracted speculators, the foremost of whom was Alexander Macomb. In July, 1787, his agent, Samuel Ogden, paid the state £3,200 for two ranges of townships on the south side of the St. Lawrence River—an area that became known as the Ogden Purchase. Among Macomb's associates were Henry Knox, who took 44,000 acres of the tract, and Robert Morris and Gouverneur Morris, who each took 60,000 acres, while Macomb and Ogden together got 90,000 acres. Macomb next turned to a larger venture and in 1791 bought from the state a claim to 3,635,000 acres in the Adirondack country—a domain that was styled Macomb's Great Purchase. For this principality he offered to pay in installments at the rate of 8d. an acre. Macomb later became insolvent, whereupon he sold his share of the Ogden Purchase to another

[55] O[rasmus] Turner, *History of the Pioneer Settlement of Phelps and Gorham's Purchase and Morris' Reserve* (Rochester, N. Y.: William Alling, 1851), pp. 136, 140; Shaw Livermore, *Early American Land Companies* (New York: Oxford University Press), pp. 203, 207; Sakolski, *The Great American Land Bubble*, pp. 54–55, 58–59, 61–62; Paul Demund Evans, *The Holland Land Company* (Buffalo Historical Society, *Collections*, Vol. XXVIII; Buffalo: The Society, 1924), 25–26, 34.

lordly speculator, William Constable. Macomb next conveyed his claim to Macomb's Great Purchase to Constable and his partner, Daniel McCormick, who obtained a patent to it by completing the installment payments and then tried to sell the lands abroad, particularly in France.[56]

In Pennsylvania, speculators did not acquire a few immense tracts directly from the state; instead, they obtained smaller claims and combined them into large holdings. After the Revolution, such acquisitive activity centered in one John Nicholson, who became comptroller-general of Pennsylvania in 1785, with the duties of enforcing tax collections and of supervising sales of state lands. Inside work enabled Nicholson to get titles to 4 million acres and to make himself the largest landowner in the state. Needing help to carry his enormous holdings, he turned to Robert Morris, whose zeal for speculation had been whetted by the small fortune he had reaped in 1791, when he sold most of the Phelps-Gorham Tract to the Pulteney associates. Another speculator, Boston-born John Greenleaf, joined Nicholson and Morris to form the Big Three of Pennsylvania speculation. Greenleaf was a successful merchant and dealer in United States securities in Holland, where he had made profitable contacts. The three partners in 1795 formed the North American Land Company. They proposed to pool 6 million acres of land, to assign to it a nominal value of fifty cents an acre, and to issue 30,000 shares of stock at a par value of $100 each. The company vested the titles to such lands in three trustees, who were authorized to sell them and to convey deeds to purchasers. Proceeds from sales were to provide dividends to the stockholders. The Big Three reserved a large amount of the stock for themselves and sold the rest to outside investors, pledging guaranteed yearly dividends of 6 percent. The stock actually issued amounted to 22,265 shares, representing 4,479,317 acres, which went into the pool. In 1796, Greenleaf sold his third interest, 6,119 shares, to Morris and Nicholson. Although the partners limited the lifetime of the company to fifteen years, it continued to figure in legal actions in Pennsylvania until 1869. Both Morris and Nicholson became insolvent and were confined in a Philadelphia debtors' prison, "the hotel with grated doors." [57]

Soon after Congress accepted the Virginia cession in 1784 it began to grant lands north of the Ohio River. Two New Englanders, the Reverend Manasseh Cutler and General Rufus Putnam, sponsored the initial project for a settlement there. In March, 1786, they took the leading parts in forming the Ohio Company of Associates, planning to obtain 1,000,000 acres from Congress at $1 an acre. The company sold 817 shares of stock, about a third of them to pioneers. With a down payment of $500,000 in depreciated federal debt certificates the company purchased from Con-

---

[56] Sakolski, *The Great American Land Bubble*, pp. 63–68.

[57] Livermore, *Early Land Companies*, pp. 164–168; Sakolski, *The Great American Land Bubble*, pp. 36–38.

gress on October 27, 1787, a claim to a large tract adjacent to the Muskingum River. Among the Associates were both pioneers and investors who
did not migrate. Each shareholder received land within the grant, and
the company made gifts of "donation lands" to settlers who were not shareholders. The enterprise was primarily a settlement project rather than
a speculation, despite some speculative buying of the shares. The company advertised the region, surveyed the land, provided for its initial defense, helped settlers to migrate, and conveyed claims and titles to lots.
Finding itself unable to complete the purchase in 1792, the company
secured from the federal government a lenient concession which enabled
it to acquire title to 1,064,000 acres in return for the initial $500,000 pay-
ment, plus a quantity of soldiers' warrants. Shareholders received their
returns in Ohio lands—not in cash dividends. The company disposed of
most of its remaining assets in 1796, at which time its settlements around
Marietta were a success.[58]

The Ohio country also appealed to promoters in New Jersey, among
whom were Judge John Cleves Symmes, Elias Boudinot, and Jonathan
Dayton. In October, 1788, Symmes secured from Congress a claim to 1
million acres north of the Ohio between the Miami and Little Miami
rivers, paying $70,455 in public-debt certificates and $11,743 in soldiers'
warrants, and agreeing to complete the purchase in seven later installments. Afterward he did not make additional payments in cash, and
eventually received title to only 248,540 acres. His settlers founded Cincinnati in 1788.[59]

Neither Virginia nor North Carolina gave immense tracts to speculators or companies, although each state granted 200,000 acres to the
proprietors of the Transylvania Company of 1775, in compensation for
the cancellation of a claim to 20 million acres which it had secured from
the Cherokees. In the upper South, speculators trafficked mainly in warrants to lands in Kentucky and Tennessee. Virginia issued such warrants
with lavish profusion. In North Carolina, an act of 1783 required that a
claimant must visit the tract he sought and mark its bounds before he
could obtain a warrant. The act also limited entries by an individual to
5,000 acres each. However, enterprising men, especially surveyors in the
Tennessee country, managed to acquire many small claims and to build
up large holdings. Thus one surveyor, Stockley Donelson, obtained 20,-
000 acres near present-day Chattanooga. Denouncing the warrant traffic,
Madison wrote in September, 1783: "Why did not the Assembly stop

[58] Archer Butler Hulbert, ed., *The Records of the Original Proceedings of the Ohio
Company* (Marietta College, *Historical Collections*, Vols. I–II; Marietta, Ohio: Marietta Historical Commission, 1917), I, ciii, cxx; Lois Kimball Mathews, *The Expansion
of New England* (Boston: Houghton Mifflin Comapny, 1909), pp. 175–177; Sakolski,
The Great American Land Bubble, pp. 101–106; Livermore, *Early Land Companies*,
pp. 134–135, 143, 145, 309.

[59] Treat, *The National Land System*, pp. 54, 60–63.

the sale of land warrants? They bring no profit to the public treasury, are a source of constant speculation on the ignorant, and will finally arm numbers of citizens of other States and even foreigners with claims and clamors against the faith of Virginia. Immense quantities have from time to time been vended in this place [Philadelphia] at immense profit . . . . The credulity here being exhausted I am told the land jobbers are going on with their commodity to Boston and other places." [60]

Georgia mothered the weirdest specimen of speculation. In 1789, the state offered more than 25 million acres to four Yazoo companies, which agreed to pay $200,000—less than a cent an acre. This bargain, however, fell through in 1790, when the legislature required payment in specie, although the granting act had specified public certificates of debt. In 1795, the legislature made a second set of grants, totaling about 35 million acres, to four new companies: the Upper Mississippi Company, the Tennessee Company, the Georgia Mississippi Company, and the Georgia Company. They agreed to pay $500,000. Among the participants were leading speculators in several states. In February, 1796, a new legislature voided the 1795 grants, alleging that they had been procured by large-scale bribery of the preceding legislature. Since the companies sold shares to outsiders, the business gave birth to numerous claims, the holders of which asserted the validity of the 1795 grants. The United States Supreme Court, in a decision of 1810 in the case of *Fletcher v. Peck,* ruled that the voiding act of 1795 violated the clause in the federal Constitution which forbids a state to enact a law impairing the obligations of contract. Georgia having ceded its western land claims to the Union in 1802, the federal government in 1814 made a settlement which awarded the claimants about $4,750,000. [61]

Viewed as a whole, land speculation did not meet the expectations of its devotees. The most regal operators—William Duer, Alexander Macomb, Robert Morris, John Nicholson, and Henry Knox—ended their careers in bankruptcy. Washington in 1799 estimated his holdings at 60,-200 acres, and although he made some profitable sales and avoided debt, he died land-poor, for his lands did not yield either himself or his heir the returns he anticipated. The flaw in the business was the poverty of the settlers. As pioneers, they lacked the cash needed for buying even moderately priced lands, and for many years their rude clearings pro-

[60] Archibald Henderson, "Richard Henderson and the Occupation of Kentucky, 1775," *Mississippi Valley Historical Review,* I, No. 3 (December, 1914), 352, 361; William Stewart Lester, *The Transylvania Colony* (Spencer, Ind.: Samuel R. Guard & Co., 1935), pp. 272, 275; Abernethy, *From Frontier to Plantation in Tennessee,* pp. 51, 59; Gaillard Hunt, ed., *The Writings of James Madison* (9 vols.; New York: G. P. Putnam's Sons, 1900–1910), II, 17.

[61] Charles Homer Haskins, *The Yazoo Land Companies* (New York: The Knickerbocker Press, 1891), pp. 8, 16, 24, 27–28; Livermore, *Early Land Companies,* pp. 147–152, 157–159; Beveridge, *Life of Marshall,* III, 586–587.

duced only meager surpluses. The most ambitious of the operators could not afford to tie up large sums in long-range investments, and when lands became accessible to settlers, taxes levied a toll on profits. Much land and few monied settlers meant cheap land. To most speculators it was largely a matter of trying to get blood out of a turnip.[62]

[62] Roy Bird Cook, *Washington's Western Lands* (Strasburg, Va.: Shenandoah Publishing House, Inc., 1930), p. 139; *Writings of Washington* (Fitzpatrick), XXXVII, 295–301; Allis, *Bingham's Maine Lands*, II, 1252; Paul D. Evans, "The Pulteney Purchase," *Quarterly Journal of the New York State Historical Association*, III, No. 2 (April, 1922), 102–103; Bond, *The Old Northwest*, pp. 29–30; Evans, *The Holland Land Company*, pp. 48, 51–53, 59–60, 67–70, 79.

CHAPTER VIII

The Ways of the Pioneers

BETWEEN 1775 and 1800 the American pioneers, from Georgia to Maine, shared a common experience. Alike they had to traverse mountains, grapple with the ancient forest, and contend with the Indians. They used similar modes of travel, engaged in the same kind of farming, and lived more or less the same kind of lives. It is true that in northern New England most pioneers halted in uplands or mountains, whereas in the middle states and in the South most of them crossed mountain barriers to reach level stretches of fertile land. However, the essential unity of pioneering was not broken until slavery spread over the Southwest after 1800.

SEEKING NEW LANDS

On the fringes of the frontiers dwelt settlers who lived off the forest. Pioneering was their occupation. Woodsmen and hunters rather than farmers, they made small clearings, built log cabins, and broke the soil. Relying on gun, ax, knife, spade, and hoe, and finding food in game, corn, and pork, they endured a hard, crude life suggestive of that of the Indians. As neighbors moved in, they sold their improvements and plunged anew into the dense forest. Most pioneers, however, were primarily farmers. Before 1775, all Americans had lived close to the frontier, and the older communities had repeatedly sent families into the wilderness. Near the edge of the settled area dwelt farmers whose forebears had moved inland and whose sons and daughters were trained for building new homes on adjacent lands.

The people of the oldest settlements who went to the frontier were usually neither wealthy nor extremely poor. Emigration from the seacoast required some property—supplies, a wagon, horses, or oxen. A poor man in Virginia was one who did not own land, a cow, or a horse. Ordinarily the poor of the seacoast—laborers and tenants—had remained poor because they lacked initiative and the urge to seek better opportunities inland. After 1775, they preferred a dependent lot in a secure community to the hazards of the frontier. For the most part, the pioneers of the era 1775–1815 were descendants of middling farmers who had moved inland in the past.[1]

Emigration dwindled during the Revolution. When peace came a pent-up surplus of potential pioneers broke through barriers all along the frontier line. Military service often bred a restlessness conducive to pioneering. In the settled areas the best lands had been acquired by 1783. Ambitious farmers struggling on poor soil or small holdings saw in the wilderness both a refuge from a crowded, stationary society and an opportunity to acquire larger estates for themselves and good lands for their numerous children, thereby preserving personal independence and the honored status of freeholder. In Connecticut in 1807–1809 one might sell a little farm for $20, $30, or $40 an acre and finance a migration to a New Canaan where a lordly estate could be had for $2 or $3 an acre. Agents of land companies or speculators agreed to exchange large new tracts for small, established farms, allowed seven years' credit to purchasers, offered special advantages to induce prominent men to emigrate, and sold plots as small as fifty acres to poorer farmers. Soldiers' bounties advertised the frontier far and wide among a people already acutely conscious of land.[2]

The colonists had generally advanced inland slowly, adding new farms on the outskirts of the old settlements, although pioneers from Connecticut had formed a detached outpost in the Wyoming Valley of Pennsylvania in the 1760's. After 1775, emigrants ventured far afield from their old communities. During the war many men took part in wilderness campaigns—in Vermont and northern New York, along the Mohawk River, up the Susquehanna Valley to southern New York, and down the Ohio

[1] Mathews, The Expansion of New England, pp. 139–144; Richard J. Purcell, Connecticut in Transition, 1775–1818 (Washington: American Historical Association, 1918), p. 150; Ulysses Prentice Hedrick, A History of Agriculture in the State of New York (Albany: New York State Agricultural Society, 1933), pp. 92–93, 97–99; Buck, The Planting of Civilization in Western Pennsylvania, pp. 262–263; Lowell H. Harrison, "A Virginian Moves to Kentucky, 1793," William and Mary Quarterly, Third Series, XV, No. 2 (April, 1958), 201; Jackson Turner Main, "The Distribution of Property in Post-Revolutionary Virginia," Mississippi Valley Historical Review, XLI, No. 2 (September, 1954), 243, 244, 258; Abernethy, From Frontier to Plantation in Tennessee, pp. 146, 148, 159, 161–162; Huger D. Bacot, "The South Carolina Up Country and the End of the Eighteenth Century," American Historical Review, XXVIII, No. 4 (July, 1923), 685, 693; Thomas D. Clark, A History of Kentucky (New York: Prentice-Hall, Inc., 1937), pp. 91, 107.

[2] Bond, The Old Northwest, pp. 18, 24–26, 48–49, 53–54; Main, "Property in Post-Revolutionary Virginia," p. 243; Purcell, Connecticut in Transition, p. 150; Buck, The Planting of Civilization in Western Pennsylvania, pp. 147, 204; Coulter, Georgia: A Short History, pp. 191, 196.

River to the Illinois country. En route the rural warriors observed land that was well suited to settlement. Some returned later to such scenes; others spread enticing reports of new lands of promise.[3] Certain areas gained special notoriety and served as magnets to attract pioneers. Such was Vermont, "the best west of New England." The lower Genesee Valley in New York made a powerful appeal, as did both the Muskingum River lands of the Ohio Company and the Connecticut Reserve on Lake Erie. The fine lands of the Symmes Purchase were a loadstone to pioneers from New Jersey. Virginians and Carolinians looked longingly to the Bluegrass region near central Kentucky. The area around Knoxville in the Tennessee Valley and the Cumberland Valley around Nashville both beckoned to southern pioneers. In the Southwest two areas stood out: the fabulously rich lands of the Mississippi Valley south of Memphis and the Black Belt of south-central Alabama and northern Mississippi.

By word of mouth and by letters, newspaper articles, and books the people learned about the glories of frontier Edens. Wondrous tales came from travelers, land speculators, and friends and relatives who had gone a-pioneering. In 1786 a traveler found the Muskingum country "superior to anything one can conceive of," where corn stalks, springing from "the deepest and richest garden mould," rose to a height of fourteen feet. On a trip to Marietta in 1788 Colonel John May noted that a seven-acre farm produced 700 bushels of corn. From the Oneida country in New York Judge Hugh White sent to his neighbors in Middletown, Connecticut, some choice specimens of corn, oats, wheat, potatoes, and onions as proofs of the fertility of the western soil. Messrs. Root and Holmes, Hartford dealers in land, advertised widely "the pleasing prospects" of the Connecticut Reserve. The handbills and circulars of Judge Symmes paid tribute to the mild climate, varied products, excellent soil, and accessible location of the Miami Purchase. To one booster, heaven was "a Kentucky of a place." William Breckinridge assured his brother in Virginia of the "deep satisfaction" of living on one's own land in "the rich and extensive" Bluegrass country. Another Kentucky enthusiast wrote that "female Animals of every sort are very prolifeck, its frequent for Ewes to bear 3 Lambs at a Time, and women and cows to have Twins at a time." Prominent among travelers was John Melish, whose accounts of his journeys in the Northwest between 1806 and 1811 gave a wealth of practical information to emigrants. Very commonly late-comers went where they could be near friends or relatives. One observer, Isaac Weld, Jr., explained why pioneers chose particular sites. The Americans, he said, "seldom or ever consider whether the part of the country to which they are going is healthy or otherwise . . . . If the lands in one part . . . are superior to

[3] Lois Kimball Mathews Rosenberry, *Migration from Connecticut Prior to 1800* Tercentenary Commission of the State of Connecticut, *Publications*, No. XXVIII; .Jew Haven, Conn.: Yale University Press, 1934), p. 25.

those in another in fertility; if they are in the neighborhood of a navigable river, or situated conveniently to a good market; if they are cheap and rising in value, thither the American will gladly emigrate, let the climate be ever so unfriendly to the human system." [4]

The first pioneers went to Maine by sea and settled on the coast. Thence they advanced up the river valleys. So poor were the roads that later pioneers, coming also by sea, had to walk inland or ride horseback. In 1796 a visitor described the country in this way:

> The principal settlements are on the rivers, where they always commence, and from thence they extend backwards. From this circumstance and the easy communication along the coast, the roads are neglected and bad . . . . The post road . . . is so bad that you can not find it without a guide in the woods. What is understood by making a road in a new country is merely cutting down and removing the large trees, leaving the stumps and small wood. The breadth varies from three to four and twenty feet.[5]

In contrast with the emigrants to Maine, most pioneers began their journeys by land. Their minimum supplies consisted of corn meal, seeds, blankets, additional clothing, kettles, pans, an ax, a knife, a gun, powder, shot, and the iron parts of tools. The poorest families walked, each member carrying some indispensable article. Other poor pioneers pushed their goods in carts. The middling farmers went by horseback or in wagons drawn by horses or oxen. A few miles made a good day's journey for pedestrians or for slow-moving vehicles escorted by unhurried cattle. The slow pace of the advance bred the virtues of patience, persistence, and endurance. Forest travel was almost a way of making a living, since the pioneers slept in improvised shelters and helped themselves to fuel, water, and game.[6]

The travelers crossed the rivers and creeks by fords or ferries. They ordinarily began their journeys by ascending hills or mountains. For those who did not settle in the mountain valleys, the second part of the route led down the western slopes of the Appalachian chain. Then the travelers usually went by way of a river valley to the sites of their intended settlements. Most of the time they traveled by land. As a rule they could not row or pole up the streams; and the upper rivers flowing down the western slopes of the mountains were usually too shallow, swift, or rocky to

[4] Bond, *The Old Northwest*, pp. 19, 20, 22–23, 25, 27; Harrison, "A Virginian Moves to Kentucky," pp. 203, 206–207; John Melish, *Travels through the United States of America in the Years 1806 & 1807, and 1809, 1810, & 1811* (2 vols.; Philadelphia: John Melish, 1815); Isaac Weld, Jr., *Travels through the States of North America During the Years 1795, 1796, and 1797* (2 vols.; London: John Stockdale, 1799), II, 93.

[5] Allis, *Bingham's Maine Lands*, II, 782.

[6] Seymour Dunbar, *A History of Travel in America* (4 vols.; Indianapolis: The Bobbs-Merrill Company, 1915), I, 114, 126–128, 158–159, 164.

be navigated. A few of the western rivers, suited to flatboats, served as arteries of travel where they flowed toward some land of promise. Early pioneers toiling in the mountains walked or rode horseback, taking their goods by pack horse, for beyond the last settlements the roads were only forest trails.[7]

The pioneer on the move constantly battled against hills, mud, and streams. Early trails, worn by animals and the Indians, marked out routes which reduced such obstacles to a minimum. In mountainous country, the roads often ran along the upper ridges, where the streams to be forded were narrow and shallow and the land was relatively dry. Elsewhere, as along the Connecticut, Mohawk, Susquehanna, and Shenandoah rivers, the pioneers found valley roads the least exacting.[8]

A chain of inland towns linked the highways from the seaboard with routes to the interior. In Massachusetts, Northampton and Pittsfield were outposts on two routes to Vermont. One road thither skirted the Connecticut River into the eastern part of the state; another went by way of Bennington, Otter Creek, and Rutland to Lake Champlain, where Burlington was a central point. Pioneers going north from Burlington followed blazed trails. The Old Brookfield Road ran northward above Rutland to Montpelier. Travelers crossed the north central area on the Coos Road from the Connecticut River to Burlington. Connecting with the Coos Road, the Hazen Road guided pioneers to Westfield in the central section along the northern border.[9]

Many New England emigrants crossed the Hudson near Albany and moved westward along the Mohawk River, taking a road that touched the present sites of Utica, Auburn, Geneva, and Buffalo. After 1800, boats on Lake Erie went to Cleveland with settlers bound for the Connecticut Reserve. About fifty miles south of Albany a ferry across the Hudson linked southern New England with a road, the Catskill Pike, that was extended across southern New York to Erie, Pennsylvania. Emigrants from the middle states reached southwestern New York by a road northward from Harrisburg that joined the Susquehanna Valley with the Genesee River. Pittsburgh, a thriving center of western travel and point of departure for pioneers bound down the Ohio, was also a terminal of the Franklin Road across northwestern Pennsylvania to Erie.[10]

[7] Caroline E. MacGill and others, *History of Transportation in the United States before 1860* (Balthasar Henry Meyer, ed.; Washington: Carnegie Institution of Washington, 1917), p. 41; Dunbar, *History of Travel in America*, I, 2, 19–21, 158–159, 194–195.

[8] Archer Butler Hulbert, *Historic Highways of America* (16 vols.; Cleveland: The Arthur H. Clark Company, 1902–1905), XI, 16–21.

[9] Mathews, *The Expansion of New England*, pp. 142–143.

[10] Hedrick, *New York Agriculture*, p. 176; Buck, *The Planting of Civilization in Western Pennsylvania*, pp. 235, 258, 560; Everett Dick, *The Dixie Frontier* (New

About thirty miles south of Pittsburgh, on the Monongahela, the town of Redstone or Brownsville received emigrants from northern and central Virginia. There some built or bought rafts or flatboats and then floated down the Monongahela and the Ohio to Limestone (Maysville)— a gateway to the Bluegrass region—or to Louisville, an entrance to north-central Kentucky. This route, heavily traveled by would-be Kentuckians, also gave access to present-day West Virginia, by way of the Great Kana-wha River. Through Redstone passed an important road that united the Potomac and Shenandoah valleys with Wheeling—a route destined to serve for the great National Road from Cumberland, Maryland to Zanes-ville, Ohio.[11]

Perhaps the principal road in the South was a Virginia highway, connecting with Philadelphia and Baltimore, that ran along the great valley between the Blue Ridge and the Allegheny Mountains. From this highway a spur from Staunton crossed the Alleghenies to Clarksburg in western Virginia and continued to Parkersburg on the Ohio. Another branch, starting due west of Lynchburg, led to Charleston in the valley of the Great Kanawha. The main highway went on to southwestern Virginia, where, at Fort Chiswell, travelers from the Shenandoah Valley met Virginians arriving on a road from Richmond. North Carolinians jour-neyed to Fort Chiswell from the country around the Yadkin River. The main Virginia highway continued from Fort Chiswell westward to the Watauga River in the northwestern corner of North Carolina. One extension—Boone's Wilderness Trail or Road—went westward to the Cumberland Gap and there turned north near the Warriors' Path into eastern Kentucky. On this route one could take a road leading to Lex-ington or to Louisville. At a point near the Cumberland Gap, some travel-ers turned west from Boone's road and followed the Cumberland River to Nashville. The second extension of the Virginia highway served settlers on the Holston River and led to Knoxville in eastern Tennessee.[12]

In the South Carolina up country, Spartanburg was a center from which pioneers could travel by way of the Saluda Gap to Knoxville. Georgians could reach Nashville by the Unicoy Road running northwest from Savannah.

Many roads led into the southwestern area consisting of the western

York: Alfred A. Knopf, Inc., 1948), pp. 56–57; Hulbert, *Historic Highways*, XII, 99, 145, 149.

[11] Charles H. Ambler, *A History of Transportation in the Ohio Valley* (Glendale, Calif.: The Arthur H. Clark Company, 1932), pp. 65–66; Hulbert, *Historic High-ways*, X, 35, 55.

[12] MacGill, *Transportation in the United States*, pp. 7–10; Dunbar, *History of Travel in America*, I, 136–140; Hulbert, *Historic Highways*, VI, 93–94; H. Addington Bruce, *Daniel Boone and the Wilderness Road* (New York: The Macmillan Company, 1926), pp. 103–104, 110–111, 341.

half of Georgia, the present states of Alabama and Mississippi, and southern Tennessee. Nashville became a hub of several roads. One went due west to the Tennessee River and there turned southwest to Memphis; a second, connecting with the Tennessee River near northeastern Mississippi, traversed that state diagonally to Natchez; a third pushed southward to Huntsville and bisected Alabama, running close to the middle course of the Coosa River and going by Tuscaloosa to Mobile; a fourth was the Unicoy Road that crossed the headwaters of the Coosa and Chattahoochee rivers on its way to Savannah. From Knoxville, pioneers floated or paddled down the Tennessee River to make settlements along its banks or to reach roads running south from Nashville.[13]

Carolinians and Georgians traveled to the lower Southwest by two main roads toward Montgomery: one from Spartanburg across northwestern Georgia; the other from Columbia, South Carolina, by way of Augusta, Georgia. Both these roads led to settlement sites in Georgia or eastern Alabama in the valleys of the Oconee, Flint, and Chattahoochee rivers.[14]

All along the far-extending frontiers the main highways and streams touched innumerable paths, trails, roads, creeks, rivers, and lakes that took the pioneers to their destinations.

NEW LANDS

Pioneers crossing the mountains during the summer could look down upon an immense forest that extended in all directions, like an ocean of green, often as far as the eye could see. Here and there the vast covering of foliage was broken by large rivers, lakes, sand barrens, savannas, beaver meadows, burned tracts, or gaps where the trees had been felled by violent storms. Interlocking branches of giant trees that bordered small streams formed canopies that enclosed sylvan tunnels through which canoes could travel. Commonly, the leafage of the forest was so dense that no ray of sunshine reached the ground. There, in the dusky light and the cool, damp air, a tangle of vines, saplings, shrubs, creepers, dead branches, and fallen tree trunks imposed a forbidding barrier, compelling travelers to resort to narrow trails that animals had worn through all but impenetrable thickets.[15]

Since the pioneers settled on wooded land, the forest shaped their occupations and ways of living. The lands that were occupied between

[13] MacGill, *Transportation in the United States,* pp. 31, 33; Dunbar, *History of Travel in America,* I, 152.

[14] Ulrich Bonnell Phillips, *A History of Transportation in the Eastern Cotton Belt to 1860* (New York: Columbia University Press, 1908), pp. 68–69; Randle Bond Truett, *Trade and Travel Around the Southern Appalachians Before 1830* (Chapel Hill: The University of North Carolina Press, 1935), pp. 47–48, 64–65, 81, 84–85, 94.

[15] Richard G. Lillard, *The Great Forest* (New York: Alfred A. Knopf, Inc., 1947), pp. 3–6.

1775 and 1815 formed several distinct vegetation zones. Coniferous or evergreen trees distinguished one type of woodland. A coniferous area spread over the northern half of Maine; another existed in far northern New York; a third extended along the southern shore of Lake Ontario; and a fourth ran along the Atlantic and Gulf coasts, reaching inland to embrace the southern third of Mississippi and the southern halves of South Carolina, Georgia, and Alabama. Far more important to the pioneers of 1775–1815 was the forest of deciduous or leaf-shedding trees. One deciduous area covered the western parts of Pennsylvania and Virginia, most of the present state of West Virginia, the southern tier of Michigan, all the states of Ohio, Indiana, Kentucky, and Tennessee, and the northern fringes of Alabama and Mississippi. A third type of forested area was marked by a mixture of conifers and deciduous trees. Such an area extended across southern Maine and New Hampshire and covered most of Vermont. Broken at the Hudson River, the mixed forest again appeared in interior New York, whence it extended southward across Pennsylvania into West Virginia. A similar belt in the back country of the South linked the coniferous forests of the seaboard with the deciduous area of the interior.[16]

The forest first served the pioneers by providing them with food. Deer in profusion yielded an abundance of venison. Wild turkeys were plentiful and so large that one would make a meal for a dozen men. The pioneers also feasted on the meat of ducks, pigeons, partridges, squirrels, grouse, rabbits, bears, raccoons, bullfrogs, and buffaloes. Some of the trees, such as the wild plum, the black walnut, the butternut, the hickory, and the crabapple afforded food in season. Strawberries and huckleberries graced sunlit woods, and in clearings one found blackberries and red and black raspberries. From sugar maples the pioneer obtained his ordinary sweetening. Grapevines scaled the trees, adorning them with clusters of blue and purple.[17]

The whole forest labored to overwhelm the pioneer with a superabundance of firewood for cooking and warmth. From favored trees— oak, ash, hickory, chestnut, walnut, cedar, locust, poplar—he got logs, beams, planks, and floor boards or puncheons for cabins and forts, tree trunks for troughs, slabs for trenchers, plates, and cart wheels, and posts and rails for pens and fences. Hickory made good handles for tools. With boards or pieces of pine, cedar, fir, hickory, maple, poplar, and birch, the pioneer fashioned his rude tables, boxes, bedsteads, stools, and chairs.

The men who broke the forest were hunters *par excellence* to whom the skins and peltries of wild animals were indispensable. As the deer served the pioneer by marking forest trails and by yielding venison, so

---

[16] Clifford L. Lord and Elizabeth H. Lord, *Historical Atlas of the United States* (Rev. ed.; New York: Henry Holt and Company, 1953), p. 10.

[17] Hedrick, *New York Agriculture*, pp. 7–10.

also they provided him with skins that, when dressed, were soft, tough, and pliable—well suited for the moccasins, leggings, and hunting shirts that protected him from the brambles of the forest and the bites of insects and snakes. To the most accessible trading post the pioneer could carry a bundle of skins and peltries—of beaver, fox, deer, squirrel, raccoon, otter, mink, elk, lynx, wild cat, bear—there to exchange them for powder, shot, salt, grain, ironware, or cloth.[18]

The earth did not contain a finer habitation for man than the lands which were occupied by the American pioneers between 1775 and 1815. Nearly the whole area had a healthful elevation of 500 feet or more above sea level. The only exceptions to this rule were the state of Mississippi, the southern half of Alabama, the valley of the Mississippi south of the Ohio, and the Ohio Valley west of Louisville. The domain as a whole enjoyed the priceless asset of adequate moisture, having, for the most part, an annual precipitation of thirty to sixty inches, with even more plentiful rainfall in the lower reaches of the Blue Ridge Mountains and along the coast of the Gulf of Mexico.[19]

Except in the farther North, the climate favored agriculture. The area was divided roughly into four temperature zones. The first comprised the states of South Carolina and Louisiana, plus the southern parts of Georgia, Alabama, and Mississippi. There the last killing frost of the season occurred in March and the first killing frost of autumn came in November or later, making a growing season of eight months or more, with an average summer temperature between 80 and 90 degrees. The second zone embraced the northern parts of Georgia, Alabama, and Mississippi, the states of North Carolina, Virginia, Tennessee, Kentucky, and Illinois, and the southern halves of Indiana and Ohio. In most of this area the average summer temperature ranged from 70 to 80 degrees and the growing season lasted six or seven months, from the last killing frost in April till the first killing frost in October. The third temperature zone included the northern halves of Ohio and Indiana, most of the states of West Virginia, Pennsylvania, and New York, and nearly all New England. This region had an average summer temperature of between 70 and 80 degrees and a growing season of nearly five months, extending from the last killing frost in May until the first killing frost in September or early October. In the far northern parts of New England and New York, where the average summer temperature varied from 60 to 70 de-

---

[18] J. E. Wright and Doris S. Corbett, *Pioneer Life in Western Pennsylvania* (Pittsburgh: University of Pittsburgh Press, 1940), pp. 54–55; Abernethy, *From Frontier to Plantation in Tennessee*, p. 148; Henry Howe, *Historical Collection of the Great West* (Cincinnati: Henry Howe, 1873), pp. 131–133, 215.

[19] O[liver] E. Baker, comp., *Atlas of American Agriculture* (Washington: Government Printing Office, 1936), Land Relief, pp. 6–7; Climate: Precipitation, pp. 22–23; Isaiah Bowman, *Forest Physiography* (New York: John Wiley & Sons, Inc., 1914), p. 730.

grees, the growing season, between the last killing frost in June and the first killing frost in September, was less than four months.[20]

The quality of the soil accessible to the pioneers varied greatly, but in the years 1775–1815 they had the blessing of rich land, by reason of its virgin fertility and its immense extent in relation to the small number of farmers. During uncounted centuries nature had transformed rock into earth, leisurely adding, every 500 to 1,000 years, an inch or so of topsoil to favored spots. Incessant interactions of sun, water, and plant life had produced soils of differing character and fertility. Moisture had been a particularly important factor. Streams had deposited sand and silt to form topsoil; and plants—which are three fourths water—had extracted, from air and moisture, organic matter that had later enriched the earth. So also the roots of plants had enabled water easily to penetrate and permeate the soil.[21]

Since the pioneers used primitive tools and farmed without benefit of fertilizers and crop rotation, they could rapidly overspread the land and prosper because they skimmed off the surface richness of the soil— an untouched legacy of the ages. As they moved westward they first encountered the Appalachian mountain chain, which—with the Allegheny range on the west—enclosed a great valley running toward the southwest and extending 40 miles in width and 600 miles in length—a zone of more than 20,000 square miles. Extending from New Jersey to Georgia, this valley was one of the world's most fertile tracts. The depth of the topsoil of the uplands of the United States averages about seven inches. Such a soil is usually capable of producing good crops.[22]

From the standpoint of soil, the lands to which the pioneers went after 1775 formed several areas. One, characterized by a soil now called podzol (salty soil), extended over the northern parts of Maine and New Hampshire, most of Vermont, and the Adirondack region of New York, with pockets in western Pennsylvania and West Virginia. Podzols are gray topsoils found chiefly in coniferous forests. Since conifers did not enrich the soil with heavy annual deposits of leaves, podzols were somewhat barren and ill suited to food crops.[23]

The finest area for general farming lay between the thirty-fifth and forty-fourth parallels, from the Apalachian chain to the Mississippi River. This was a realm of deciduous trees where the soil—now called gray-brown podzol—produced varied and abundant crops. Southern New

[20] Baker, *Atlas of American Agriculture,* Climate: Temperature, pp. 30–31, 34–35.

[21] Charles E. Kellogg, *The Soils That Support Us* (New York: The Macmillan Company, 1951), pp. 10–11, 15–16, 25.

[22] Nathaniel S. Shaler, "Physiography of North America," in Justin Winsor, ed., *Narrative and Critical History of America* (8 vols.; Boston: Houghton Mifflin and Company, 1884–1889), IV, iv–viii.

[23] Baker, *Atlas of American Agriculture,* Pt. III, p. 13; Kellogg, *The Soils That Support Us,* pp. 94–95, 138–139.

England, all Ohio, and most of New York, Pennsylvania, Virginia, West Virginia, Kentucky, and Indiana were favored with this fertile soil.[24]

South of the thirty-fifth parallel the land was characterized by "red soils" and "yellow soils." The names of such soils come from iron deposits. Wholly oxidized iron produced a "red soil"; partly oxidized iron gave a "yellow soil." Adjacent to several rivers—the Altamaha, the Alabama, the Tombigbee, the Pearl, the Mississippi, the Yazoo, the Tennessee, the Ohio, the Illinois, the Wabash—pioneers found alluvial deposits that formed a topsoil many feet deep.[25]

THE PIONEER FARMER

Intent upon keeping in touch with older communities, pioneers usually chose a home site near a stream or close to a road or trail. In the early days of a settlement they commonly brought in and sent out goods and livestock by land. They preferred plots on high ground, free from swamp and flood. A nearby spring and a stream with a mill site were most valuable assets. If a farm lay on a slope, the pioneer commonly located his house and barn near the lower side so that crops and timber would move downhill and the toil of carrying to and from a stream would be kept at a minimum. Experience had taught settlers to shun the light sandy soils of pine woods and to seek out the dark gray or gray-brown soils of the deciduous and mixed forests.[26]

In 1780 the French traveler Chastellux described the process of pioneering as he had observed it many times. He estimated the average pioneer's capital as about $125, a part of which he used to make a down payment on a tract of 150 to 200 acres, priced usually at not more than a dollar an acre. Arriving with a cow, a few pigs, a couple of "indifferent horses," and a stock of flour and cider, he first cleared away some of the underbrush and felled small trees and the lower branches of large ones, using the timber to make a fence enclosing a plot he intended to clear. Within the enclosure he girdled the giant trees—stripping them of their bark and cutting rings around them to keep the sap from rising. In the following spring they were dead, leafless skeletons.[27] In small patches

---

[24] Kellogg, *The Soils That Support Us*, pp. 151–152; Baker, *Atlas of American Agriculture*, Pt. III, plate 2.

[25] Kellogg, *The Soils That Support Us*, pp. 99, 171, 182; C[urtis] F. Marbut, *Soils* (Soil Science Society of America [Madison, Wis.], 1951), p. 51.

[26] Stevenson Whitcomb Fletcher, *Pennsylvania Agriculture and Country Life, 1640–1840* (Harrisburg: Pennsylvania Historical and Museum Commission, 1950), p. 63; Neil Adams McNall, *An Agricultural History of the Genesee Valley, 1790–1860* (Philadelphia: University of Pennsylvania Press, 1952), pp. 81–83; Abernethy, *From Frontier to Plantation in Tennessee*, pp. 153–154.

[27] [François Jean] Marquis de Chastellux, *Travels in North America in the Years 1780, 1781, and 1782* (2 vols.; London: G. G. J. and J. Robinson, 1787), I, 44–46.

exposed to the sun the pioneer planted his first crop—often Indian corn and pumpkins. He continually enlarged his clearing, cutting down the small and medium-sized trees and felling larger ones by encircling them with fire. With his broadax he smoothed straight logs into square timbers, which he notched at the ends and used for the sides of his cabin. In the rich humus of the forest, grass grew copiously, providing pasturage for his cattle. His first crop often yielded so plentiful an increase as to supply him with food during the winter and seeds for the next spring's planting. By autumn he had finished his cabin, adding a roof of planks and a fireplace of clay or stone, and cementing the walls with stiff clay mixed with moss or straw.[28]

After the pioneer had gained a foothold, he improved his cleared field by grubbing out roots and stumps, and by burning trees that had been girdled. From the start he felled more timber than he needed for fences, cabin, and firewood. In New England, New York, and Pennsylvania, farmers burned wood they could not use and extracted potash from the ashes by pouring water over them and then boiling the lye. Potash often yielded the pioneer a small cash crop at the end of his first season in the forest.[29]

Frontier agriculture served mainly to provide the farmer and his family with products they consumed. For many years a new farm produced only slight surpluses for sale in commercial markets. Apart from the living which the family wrung from the soil, the earnings of the farmer took the form—not of cash accumulations—but of an increase in the value of his fields, buildings, fences, orchards, and livestock.[30] The subsistence aspect of the pioneer farm appears clearly when one considers its principal products, such as game, Indian corn, pork, pumpkins, and apples.

Indian corn was an indispensable product on the frontier farm. It contributed to a variety of foods: corn on the cob, bread, mush, puddings, fritters, hominy. Corn whiskey fortified the spirits. The stalks of the plant made excellent fodder—much better than the straw of wheat or other grains—while horses relished the hard, shelled kernels. The cobs were

[28] Bidwell and Falconer, *History of Agriculture in the Northern United States,* pp. 77–78; Dick, *The Dixie Frontier,* p. 27.

[29] Buck, *The Planting of Civilization in Western Pennsylvania,* p. 265; Lillard, *The Great Forest,* pp. 88–89; Bidwell and Falconer, *History of Agriculture in the Northern United States,* p. 80.

[30] Percy W. Bidwell, "Rural Economy in New England at the Beginning of the Nineteenth Century" (Connecticut Academy of Arts and Sciences, *Transactions,* Vol. XX; New Haven, Conn.: The Academy, 1916), pp. 352–353, 371; Harold Fisher Wilson, *The Hill Country of Northern New England* (New York: Columbia University Press, 1936), p. 8; David Maldwyn Ellis, *Landlords and Farmers in the Hudson-Mohawk Region, 1790–1850* (Ithaca, N. Y.: Cornell University Press, 1946), p. 67. For estimates of the profits of pioneering, see Harry J. Carman, ed., *American Husbandry* (New York: Columbia University Press, 1939), pp. 138–139, 148–149.

useful as fireplace fuel. In a new settlement, the seeds could be planted by hoe among tree stumps in partially cleared, unplowed land. All along the frontier from Maine to Georgia the growing season was favorable, for the stalks provided edible corn three months after planting, and the crop was ready to be harvested after four months. To strip the ripened ears from the stalks was an easy kind of harvesting, and the farmer could gather them a this convenience during a period of several weeks. In his spare time he could do the shelling, free from dictates of the weather.[31]

For meat other than game the pioneers relied mainly on bacon, hams, and other kinds of salt pork. The hogs of the time were much like wild animals. They fed during most of the year on the acorns, beechnuts, chestnuts, roots, and fruit of the forest. There they often fell prey to wolves, panthers, or bears. An observer described the species in 1798: "The real American hog is called a woodhog; they are long in the leg, narrow in the back, short in the body, flat on the sides, with a long snout, very rough in their hair . . . ." Although a farmer often branded his hogs, they so roamed the forest that he sometimes hunted and shot them as if they were wild beasts. Often he kept them within range of his cabin by calling them regularly to come in and get a handout of corn. After harvest, they were commonly penned up during the winter and fed on potatoes, peas, beans, peaches, and apples. They required little care, multiplied rapidly, and put on about 200 pounds during the eighteen months or so they lived before they were slaughtered. New settlements soon competed successfully in supplying hogs to the seaboard. The costs of production were lower on the frontier than on older farms, and the hogs, good travelers, could be driven long distances to market. By 1810, the country west of Pittsburgh sent most of the 40,000 hogs that went to the Baltimore to Philadelphia area.[32]

The cows and oxen of the frontier were, for the most part, an inferior lot—lean, bony, and poorly cared for. The pioneers did not fence in pastures; instead, they let the cattle roam about, feeding on the grasses of natural meadows and on plants of the forest. Such grazing practices enabled wolves and bears to prey upon the cattle and cost the farmer much time and trouble in locating them. In Pennsylvania, farmers raised turnips and cabbage and turned the stock into the fields. In the South, pumpkins well-nigh sustained the stock during autumn weeks. There also the farmers made use of "browse"—the bark and small branches of elms, beeches, pignuts, and white hickories. In addition, Southerners fed the cattle with cabbage leaves, potato parings, and other scraps. Generally,

[31] Lillard, *The Great Forest*, p. 17; Dick, *The Dixie Frontier*, p. 99; Bidwell, "Rural Economy in New England," pp. 322–323; Bacot, "South Carolina Up Country," pp. 685, 691.

[32] Fletcher, *Pennsylvania Agriculture*, pp. 186–191; Clark, *History of Kentucky*, pp. 230–231; Abernethy, *From Frontier to Plantation in Tennessee*, p. 150.

the pioneer farm lacked an adequate supply of hay during the winter—a time when the cattle fared poorly and sometimes even starved to death. The crude shelters provided for them—pens and sheds—served to protect them against wolves and bears but failed to keep them warm in winter. By reason of crude, unscientific methods of animal husbandry, haphazard feeding, and exposure to the elements, cows yielded only small quantities of milk. Often they were dry during the winter and failed to deliver calves in the spring. Sometimes a milkmaid got a cow to come to be milked by keeping its calf near the cabin and by offering a bait of corn.[33]

In the Bluegrass country of Kentucky, deer, elk, and buffaloes had found an ideal grazing land which became a magnet attracting pioneers who, as Thomas D. Clark says, hoped to support themselves by listening to the music of cowbells. The Kentucky frontier cattleman, usually lazy and shiftless, neglected farming and, like the pioneer hunter, hearkened to the call of a farther West when dirt farmers encroached on his grazing lands.[34]

Horses served the pioneer, not only in the fields, but also as mounts and as pack animals. He depended mainly on the ox for plowing and heavy hauling about his clearing. "The advantages of employing oxen," wrote Timothy Dwight, "are, that they will endure more fatigue, draw more steadily, and surely; are purchased for a smaller price; are kept with less expense; are freer from disease; suffer less from laboring on rough grounds; and perform the labor better; and when, by age or accident they become unfit for labor, they are converted into beef. The only advantage of employing horses instead of oxen, is derived from their speed." [35]

In the Genesee Valley, oxen outnumbered horses four to one. The increase of such animals and their importance to the pioneer are indicated by conditions in western Pennsylvania, where, about 1790, the average farmer had two horses and two or three head of neat cattle. In 1810, the farmers there possessed such stock at the rate of 40 horses and 85 head of neat cattle to every 100 inhabitants—a better showing than that of the eastern part of the state.[36]

Only rarely, as in Vermont and the Mohawk Valley, did pioneers plant wheat as an initial crop. In most places they had to wait until a field had been sufficiently cleared of roots and stumps to permit plowing. A

[33] McNall, The Genesee Valley, p. 80; Buck, The Planting of Civilization in Western Pennsylvania, p. 267; Dick, The Dixie Frontier, pp. 98, 101, 104, 105; Bidwell and Falconer, History of Agriculture in the Northern United States, p. 79; Bidwell, "Rural Economy in New England," p. 337; Main, "Property in Post-Revolutionary Virginia," pp. 251, 257; Abernethy, From Frontier to Plantation in Tennessee, p. 150.
[34] Clark, History of Kentucky, pp. 224, 228–229.
[35] Quoted in Bidwell, "Rural Economy in New England," pp. 338–339.
[36] Buck, The Planting of Civilization in Western Pennsylvania, p. 271; Main, "Property in Post-Revolutionary Virginia," pp. 251, 257.

nearby gristmill was also essential. The milling of wheat was more difficult than the milling of corn, which could be ground in a homemade "sweep mill" consisting of a long, limber pole that was fastened at one end to the ground, with a long pounder or pestle at the other end. The farmer thrust the pestle into a mortar containing kernels and then let the spring of the pole pull the pestle out. For raising wheat the simplest plow was a forked sapling, one fork serving as a digging prong, the other as a beam to which handles were attached. The most common type of plow had an iron share and a wooden moldboard. Clumsy and inefficient, its cutting edge was so blunt that four oxen were required to pull it. Sometimes it would hit a root and stop abruptly; whereupon the plowman would be thrust against the handle. After the plowed ground had been harrowed, the farmer sowed the seed by hand and covered it by raking the soil with a piece of brush. At harvest time he sickled the stalks close to tree stumps; in the open field he used a cradle or a scythe. The cradle—a new device— was a scythe with a frame of thin sticks which laid the stalks in regular rows, headed in one direction. The farmer prepared for threshing by pounding the dirt of a small area—often the barn floor—to make a hard, cementlike surface. Sometimes he beat out the grain with a hand flail— a pliable tool made of two tough sticks joined by a leather thong. Using another method, he arranged the stalks in circles on the floor; whereupon the thread of horses did the threshing work. He then disposed of the straw and made ingenious use of wind to winnow the grain from the chaff.[37]

All a pioneer's cleared land was devoted to grain, with the exception of a small vegetable patch and an orchard. Among fruits, apples were the favorites, with peaches in second place. Cherries were fairly common, but other fruits, such as pears, apricots, nectarines, and quinces, were rare. The forest continued to supply berries, grapes, plums, and nuts. The character of a pioneer was indicated by his garden. If he was shiftless he neglected it; if prudent and industrious, he supplemented pumpkins with sweet potatoes—common in the South—Irish potatoes, peas, squashes, turnips, cabbages, string beans, peppers, and melons. As early as 1795 a pioneer in Ohio planted sweet marjoram, parsley, sage, cauliflower, beets, and asparagus. All the vegetables and fruits raised on a frontier farm that were not purloined by birds or wild animals were consumed by the family or fed to the livestock.[38]

[37] Bidwell and Falconer, *History of Agriculture in the Northern United States,* p. 78; Clark, *History of Kentucky,* p. 224; Dick, *The Dixie Frontier,* pp. 99, 101–103; Buck, *The Planting of Civilization in Western Pennsylvania,* pp. 269–270; Carman, *American Husbandry,* p. 133; Bidwell, "Rural Economy in New England," pp. 331– 332; Bacot, "South Carolina Up Country"; Abernethy, *From Frontier to Plantation in Tennessee,* p. 151.

[38] Carman, *American Husbandry,* p. 133; Dick, *The Dixie Frontier,* pp. 255, 289, 291; Abernethy, *From Frontier to Plantation in Tennessee,* p. 151; Bond, *The Old Northwest,* p. 322.

As the pioneer improved his holding he raised small crops of rye, oats, and barley. Flax was widely grown (though in small quantities) since tow and linen were the materials most commonly used in making clothing, especially for women and children. Flax became relatively important in New York, Kentucky, Indiana, and Ohio. In the Kentucky Bluegrass country, which in its virgin state was unsuited to grain crops, pioneers as early as 1775 fallowed the land by raising hemp, a plant that reduced the nitrogenous content of the soil. Hemp then became an important Kentucky raw material for the manufacture of rope and sailcloth needed in river transportation.[39]

After a frontier farm was secure from wolves, pioneers usually brought in sheep. As early as 1790 southwestern Pennsylvania had fewer cattle than sheep, although perhaps a third of the farmers did not own them. The land north of the Ohio River proved to be a good sheep country. In 1807 one Seth Adams took 25 Merinos to Muskingum County, Ohio, and in 1810 he drove 176 sheep into Kentucky and Tennessee. To New Harmony in Pusey County, Indiana, George Rapp in 1814 brought from Economy, Pennsylvania, a superior flock that soon helped to spread the sheep industry in Kentucky, southwestern Indiana, and southeastern Illinois. By 1813 a farmer at St. Clairsville, Ohio, had a flock of 500 sheep.[40]

Since the rivers of a new country swarmed with large fish—shad, herring, pike, bass, catfish, trout—the pioneer made good use of his skill with net and hook to add to his food supply. An observer wrote of frontier Pennsylvania: "And the rivers are most of them very full of fish, especially in the back country, to which parties are made in boats with nets; in which excursions shooting is joined: the fish they take are brought home in well-boats . . . every planter has a pond . . . ; in these stores, as they call them, are kept the products of their river-fishing, ready at all times for the table." [41]

The pioneer family supplied itself with many articles that later were to be made in factories or shops. The processes, materials, and tools used in household manufacturing between 1775 and 1815 were essentially the same as in colonial times. Every farmer operated a small packing plant, slaughtering animals, and smoking and salting meats. His cows yielded

---

[39] Bidwell, "Rural Economy in New England," p. 327; Buck, *The Planting of Civilization in Western Pennsylvania*, p. 275; Bidwell and Falconer, *History of Agriculture in the Northern United States*, p. 359; Clark, *History of Kentucky*, pp. 225, 237, 240; Dick, *The Dixie Frontier*, p. 289.

[40] Bidwell, "Rural Economy in New England," p. 340; Buck, *The Planting of Civilization in Western Pennsylvania*, p. 271; L. G. Connor, "A Brief History of the Sheep Industry in the United States" (American Historical Association, *Annual Report . . . 1918*, 2 vols.; Washington: Government Printing Office, 1921), I, 104; Bond, *The Old Northwest*, p. 324.

[41] Bidwell, "Rural Economy in New England," pp. 320–321, 326, 329; Carman, *American Husbandry*, p. 133.

milk for homemade butter and cheese. In a maple grove he obtained maple sugar. His wife dried fruits, made bread, and prepared apple butter. In his still he turned corn into whiskey, which he supplemented with apple cider, peach brandy, and homemade wines. He raised the wool, flax, or cotton that went into homespun, the family doing the work at every stage —preparing the fibers, spinning, weaving, fulling, bleaching, dyeing, cutting, sewing, knitting. He tanned hides and made leather thongs, straps, harness, moccasins, shoes, leggings, breeches, and hunting shirts. Almost as much a carpenter as a farmer, he built cabins, barns, sheds, fences, and carts, and fashioned stools, chairs, tables, trenchers, bedsteads, boxes, brooms, baskets, and the wooden parts of tools and implements. He manufactured potash, and his wife made soap and candles. As to food, fuel, beverages, lighting, furniture, laundering, medical care, and transportation, the frontier farm was well-nigh self-sufficient.[42]

Steadily the pioneer labored to extend his tillable fields. On the average, he managed to clear from one to three acres a year. In the South he commonly sought to clear an acre during the winter. After ten years of hard, incessant toil, the average family had about fifteen acres under cultivation. The pioneering stage drew to a close when the settler's orchard was bearing fruit; when his fields yielded hay, wheat, and other small grains; when he had access to a gristmill and a sawmill; when his arable land, garden, and orchard were fence-enclosed; when pens and sheds housed his livestock and poultry; when barns held his hay and grain; when his log cabin had been enlarged or replaced by a frame house; and when a road led to a trading post or a store to which his wagon could haul his surplus products for sale or barter. Most of the land of his holding was still uncleared, but the growth of settlement enhanced its value, so that he could sell at a profit such tracts as he did not intend to improve. According to one estimate, these were the capital outlays for a frontier farm for the first year: for land, 42 percent of the total; for livestock, 20 percent; for house and barn, 19 percent; for tools, 12 percent; for clothing and expenses of one year, 5 percent; for arms and ammunition, 2 percent.[43]

Although here and there in new settlements a few progressive farmers sought to introduce improvements from Europe or from the seaboard area, the great majority of pioneers continued to rely on crude methods and

[42] Tryon, *Household Manufactures*, pp. 188–241; Bidwell, "Rural Economy in New England," pp. 354–366; Bidwell and Falconer, *History of Agriculture in the Northern United States*, pp. 126–131; Fletcher, *Pennsylvania Agriculture*, pp. 416–418; Wright and Corbett, *Pioneer Life in Pennsylvania*, pp. 74–83; Buck, *The Planting of Civilization in Western Pennsylvania*, pp. 273–279; Solon Justus Buck, *Illinois in 1818* (Springfield: The Illinois Centennial Commission, 1917), pp. 131–134; Clark, *History of Kentucky*, pp. 236–238; Dick, *The Dixie Frontier*, pp. 247–255.

[43] McNall, *The Genesee Valley*, p. 85; Bidwell and Falconer, *History of Agriculture in the Northern United States*, pp. 81, 165–166; Dick, *The Dixie Frontier*, p. 99; Carman, *American Husbandry*, pp. 136–137.

George Washington's mill on Dogue Creek, Fairfax County, Virginia (Greville and Dorothy Bathe, *Oliver Evans*. Courtesy of the authors and of The Historical Society of Pennsylvania)

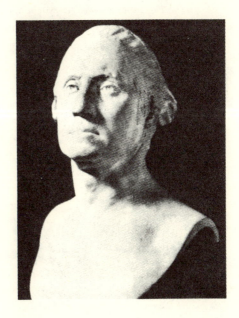

George Washington in 1785. From the Houdon Bust, modeled from life at Mount Vernon (Courtesy of the Mount Vernon Ladies' Association of the Union)

Gold half-eagle of the United States, 1795, obverse and reverse sides, in the collection of the American Numismatic Society, New York (Reproduced from *The Pageant of America*. Copyright Yale University Press)

Silver dollar of the United States, 1795, obverse and reverse sides, in the collection of the American Numismatic Society, New York (Reproduced from *The Pageant of America*. Copyright Yale University Press)

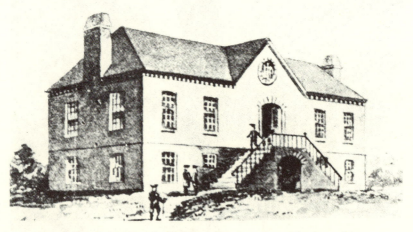

First home of the Massachusetts Bank (N. S. B. Gras, *The Massachusetts First National Bank of Boston*. Courtesy of the Harvard University Press)

Elkanah Watson, father of the country fair (Ralph H. Brown, *Mirror for Americans.* Courtesy of the American Geographical Society)

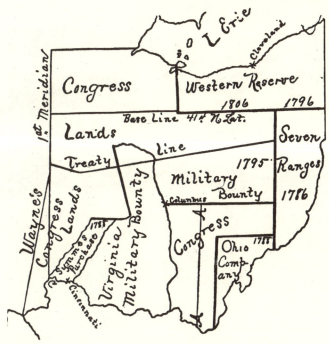

Cessions, holdings, grants, and surveys of land in Ohio before 1800 (Justin Winsor, *The Westward Movement.* Courtesy of Houghton Mifflin Company)

Agricultural implements: harrow, plow, single yokes, ox yoke (Solon J. Buck and H. Elizabeth Buck, *The Planting of Civilization in Western Pennsylvania*. Courtesy of the University of Pittsburgh Press)

View five miles from York, Pennsylvania on the Baltimore Road, 1788 (Ralph H. Brown *Mirror for Americans*. Courtesy of the American Geographical Society)

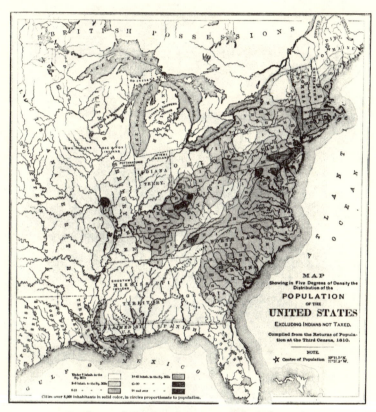

Population of the United States in 1810 (John Bach Mc-
Master, *A History of the People of the United States.* Courtesy of Appleton-Century-Crofts, Inc.)

Plantation tobacco houses and public warehouses, about 1800
(Joseph C. Robert, *The Tobacco Kingdom*. Courtesy of the
Duke University Press)

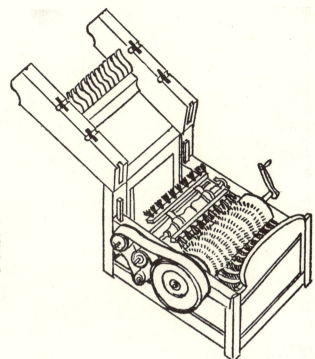

A model of the cotton gin (Jeannette Mirsky and Allan Nevins, *The World of Eli Whitney*. Courtesy of the authors and of the Macmillan Company)

Sweep mill for grinding corn (Solon J. Buck and Elizabeth H. Buck, *The Planting of Civilization in Western Pennsylvania*. Courtesy of the University of Pittsburgh Press)

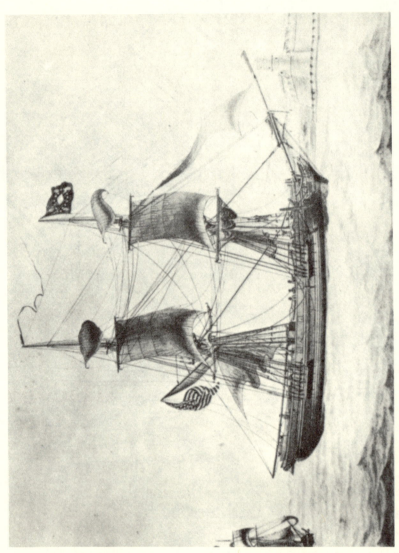

The brig *Iuliana* of Gloucester, Massachusetts (From a water-color by Nicolay Cammillieri, Peabody Museum, Salem)

tools such as had been used in ancient times. In tilling his fields, the farmer, with his cumbersome plow, could do little more than scrape the surface of the soil. Crop rotation and the planting of clover were rarely practiced, or ignored altogether. Nor did the farmer fertilize his fields. The method of caring for livestock did not provide much manure. When a field became exhausted, the pioneer let it lie fallow and planted newly cleared land—a practice that did not restore the fertility of depleted soils. Inadequate fodder and nonselective breeding manifested themselves in poor, inferior stock. A plague of gnats, mosquitoes, and flies harassed both man and beast. Without means of combating insects, except by fire and smoke, the pioneer had to wait until fields were cleared before that nuisance abated.[44]

THE GROWTH OF SETTLEMENT

The lands occupied by pioneers after 1775 may be grouped into four areas. The present states of Maine, New Hampshire, and Vermont formed a fairly distinct unit. The new settlements in New York, in western Pennsylvania, and adjacent to the Ohio River in Ohio, West Virginia, Indiana, and Illinois had an essential similarity. The mountainous parts of Virginia, North Carolina, and eastern Tennessee were a reasonably unified domain. The fourth area, consisting of western South Carolina, southern and western Georgia, Alabama, southern Mississippi, western Kentucky, western Tennessee, and Louisiana, came under the sway of staple crops produced by slave labor.

Maine, New Hampshire, and Vermont contain, all together, 52,954 square miles—for the most part mountainous or hilly. The three states have three principal types of land. The soil of the sides of the hills and mountains is thin, rocky, and ill suited to farming except on a small subsistence scale. In the upland river valleys are narrow hollows and fairly extensive stretches of level or undulating land where a fine soil is easily cultivated. Most favorable to agriculture are the lands—generally not more than 500 feet above sea level—in the lower river valleys and along Lake Champlain. The population of the three states rose from 323,850 in 1790 to 778,477 in 1820. The most rapid increase during one decade occurred in Vermont, between 1790 and 1800. Maine held to a steady rate of growth, becoming the most populous of the three states by 1810. New Hampshire, with the lowest rate of population growth, fell from first place in 1790 to second place in 1810. A marked slowing down of the rate of increase in New Hampshire and Vermont after 1810 denoted that emi-

[44] Buck, *The Planting of Civilization in Western Pennsylvania*, pp. 267–268; Bidwell and Falconer, *History of Agriculture in the Northern United States*, pp. 123–126, 167; Gray, *History of Agriculture in the Southern United States*, II, 792, 795, 799, 806, 810; McNall, *The Genesee Valley*, p. 80; Ellis, *Landlords and Farmers*, p. 116; Bidwell, "Rural Economy in New England," pp. 320–321, 326, 329.

grants from southern New England were seeking new homes in Maine or in lands west of the Hudson. The growth of population in the three states was as follows: [45]

	Maine	New Hampshire	Vermont
1775		80,547	
1786		95,801	
1790	96,540	141,885	85,425
1800	151,719	183,858	154,465
1810	228,705	214,400	217,895
1820	298,335	244,161	235,981

Apart from the lumbering industry along the Atlantic Coast, the economy of northern New England, before 1815, was that of a simple, almost self-sufficing rural community, close to the pioneer stage. Nearly all the settlers had come from lower New England. They held land in fee simple tenure by virtue of grants from friendly New England governments. By 1778, the inhabitants of Vermont, after a long, acrimonious conflict with New York, had made good their claim to the ownership of the lands they occupied. For a dozen years thereafter they formed a *de facto* independent community until Vermont was admitted as the fourteenth state in 1791. The average New England farm in 1800 varied from 100 to 200 acres, a third in woodland including wasteland, a third in pasturage, and a third in mowing lands and cultivated fields, with only ten or twelve acres in tillage. Such specialized products as maple sugar and wool were consumed locally. The area newly settled, destitute of commercial or manufacturing cities, had only rural villages. A gristmill, a sawmill, a tannery, or a fulling mill was usually owned by one man, who also engaged in farming. Farmers with specialized skills served their neighbors, during slack times on the farm, as carpenters, blacksmiths, shoemakers, and coopers. A main link with the outside was the Connecticut River, which, by 1810, was navigable as far upstream as the village of Barnet in northern Vermont. Flat-bottomed boats of ten to twelve tons' burden made nine annual round trips to Hartford, carrying thither potash, staves, shingles, grain, beef, flaxseed, and linseed oil, and bringing back rum, salt, molasses, iron, dry goods, and tea. All such shipments of one year did not exceed the capacity of a medium-sized river steamboat. In the whole area in 1790 there were only 157 slaves—all in New Hampshire, and slavery soon died out there. Most of the settlers in the three northern states lived in the southern parts of the area.[46]

[45] Wilson, *The Hill Country of Northern New England*, pp. 5–6; Sutherland, *Population Distribution in Colonial America*, p. 49; *A Century of Population Growth*, p. 156.

[46] Dixon Ryan Fox, *Yankees and Yorkers* (New York: New York University Press, 1940), pp. 172–174; Bidwell, "Rural Economy in New England," pp. 260, 261, 265–266, 309, 321, 340; *A Century of Population Growth*, pp. 61, 132, 188–191; Adams, *New England in the Republic*, p. 326.

A striking feature of the Union in 1783 was the vast extent of wild and unsettled land in New York State. As late as 1790 fully nine tenths of the state did not contain six inhabitants to the square mile. Three factors account for the early failure of pioneers to move inland. In colonial times, a few great magnates acquired immense tracts of the most accessible lands along the Hudson, upon which they imposed a semifeudal type of land tenure. Since most farmers desired to own land outright, the system of tenancy in eastern New York did not attract pioneers, who could then acquire land of their own in other colonies. Moreover, in the east-central and south-central parts of New York dwelt the Iroquois. It was long the policy of Britain to seek their aid against France—an aim that caused the crown to discourage encroachments on their lands. Since New York was the main battleground of the Revolution, the fighting of the war stunted the growth of settlement, as indicated by the flight of settlers eastward after the Cherry Valley massacre in 1778. The ending of the war removed such obstacles, just at the time when thousands of New Englanders, sorely pressed at home, were ready to move westward beyond the Hudson.[47]

In 1790, more than four fifths of the area of New York State had only 31,500 inhabitants—fewer than 10 percent of the state's total of 340,000. That the total had risen to 1,372,812 in 1820 is accounted for largely by the settlement of the interior during the thirty preceding years. The main stream of pioneers moved westward along a line between Schenectady and Buffalo, forming a triangular wedge, the point of which advanced steadily inland, while the sides gradually extended toward the north and south. The population of the southwestern part of the state—below the southern shore of Lake Ontario—increased from 1,074 in 1790 to 265,325 in 1820, registering a growth of 344 percent during the decade 1800–1810.[48]

The pioneer economy of inland New York resembled that of New England in many respects. The settlers of both areas grappled with the forest; depended upon Indian corn, hogs, and cattle; raised the same fruits and vegetables; cultivated small patches of oats, barley, flax, and rye, produced potash, maple sugar, and wool; plied the usual frontier household crafts; operated gristmills, sawmills, tanneries, and fulling mills; and worked farms that varied from 100 to 200 acres in size.[49] However, some special features differentiated the northern New England frontier from that of New York.

[47] Charles O. Paullin, *Atlas of the Historical Geography of the United States* (Carnegie Institution of Washington and the American Geographical Society of New York, 1932), plate 76; Ellis, *Landlords and Farmers*, pp. 5–10, 16; McNall, *The Genesee Valley*, pp. 6, 17.

[48] Bidwell and Falconer, *History of Agriculture in the Northern United States*, p. 152; Paullin, *Atlas*, plate 76.

[49] Ellis, *Landlords and Farmers*, pp. 67–69, 72–76, 90–92, 107–118; McNall, *The Genesee Valley*, pp. 79–81, 83–94; Hedrick, *New York Agriculture*, pp. 66–76.

For one thing, New York had its special mode of disposing of land. The state, which after 1776 owned much unoccupied land, did not operate local land offices for selling small farms to pioneers. Instead, the state government sold vast tracts to large operators, who then undertook to sell land to farmers or to put tenants on their holdings. William Cooper of Otsego County, father of the novelist, at one time held more than 750,000 acres. "I have settled more acres," he asserted, "than any other man in America. There are forty thousand souls holding direc'ly or indirectly under me." The large holders, when selling to pioneers, commonly allowed several years' credit, with payments deferred until after the first lean year or so. Rising land values continually drove newcomers into the forest. Thus in Oneida County, wilderness land sold at $1 an acre in 1788–1791, whereas an acre in a settled area was priced at $10 in 1806. The mode of selling land in New York introduced tenancy into newly settled areas, since the poorest pioneers, including squatters, were allowed to occupy tracts as renters. James Wadsworth, onetime Connecticut Yankee, acquired large holdings in the Genesee Valley, where he gave life leases, the rent payable in wheat. The tenant paid the taxes and made the improvements.[50]

By 1815, the most thickly settled part of interior New York was the central section westward to the Genesee River. This area had the benefit of much fertile land and a fairly level terrain. The limestone soils of the Genesee Valley were well suited to wheat. However, before 1815, dependence on slow wagon transportation checked severely the raising of wheat as a commercial crop. In 1804, wagons carried fourteen barrels of flour from the Genesee River to Albany and brought back assorted merchandise, the trip taking fourteen days. The freight charge was more than $50 a ton. Inadequate outlets for the farm surpluses of the interior provided a potent stimulus to the building of the Erie Canal.[51]

In 1790, more than two thirds of Pennsylvania were unsettled or in the pioneer stage. The unoccupied or undeveloped parts included the northern half of the state, the central section, and the western third. Except for the eastern and south-central border areas, only a small district in the southwestern corner had more than six inhabitants to the square mile. Seven counties, covering two thirds of the state, had only 108,934 inhabitants in a state total of 434,373. New settlements spread northward and southward from a line between Philadelphia and Pittsburgh, until by 1800 the southern half of the state had been peopled. In this advance, transportation played a decisive part. In the south-central section, the Susquehanna River provided an outlet for farm products, via Baltimore; in the southwest, Pittsburgh was a receiving point for goods that were

[50] Ellis, *Landlords and Farmers*, pp. 23–26, 55–56; McNall, *The Genesee Valley*, pp. 57–61.
[51] Paullin, *Atlas*, plate 76; McNall, *The Genesee Valley*, pp. 92, 101, 109–111.

floated down the Ohio and Mississippi to western settlements and to New Orleans. In 1820 the lands least developed were those on the upper Allegheny River, those on the Susquehanna most distant from Baltimore, and those in the south, midway between the Susquehanna and the Monongahela. The growth of the western or Allegheny District—an area about fifty miles wide south of Lake Erie—was retarded by its inaccessibility to the main line of travel from Philadelphia to Pittsburgh and by its extreme remoteness from New Orleans.[52]

By 1820, the seven counties of Pennsylvania that were unoccupied or slightly peopled in 1790 had 390,593 inhabitants. The population of the state increased as follows:

	Total	Newly Settled or Unsettled Areas
1790	434,373	108,934
1800	602,365	197,417
1810	810,091	290,115
1820	1,049,458	390,593

Compared with New York, Ohio, Tennessee, and Kentucky, Pennsylvania did not enjoy a high rate of population growth. In 1790, those four states had all together about 65,000 more inhabitants than Pennsylvania; in 1820 the comparable figure was 1,892,000.[53]

In most respects the frontier economy of Pennsylvania resembled that of New York. One difference was the greater variety of peoples in western Pennsylvania—settlers of English, German, Scottish, Irish, or Scotch-Irish stock from older settlements and immigrants from Britain, Ireland, or Germany—as contrasted with the predominance of New Englanders on the New York frontier. The Whiskey Rebellion of 1794 in southwestern Pennsylvania bespoke the early importance of whiskey there: before 1800 it was the only farm product of consequence that could bear the cost of transportation over the Alleghenies to Philadelphia. A pack horse could carry only four bushels of rye as grain as against twenty-four in the form of whiskey. On the New York frontier, whiskey served mainly to fortify the pioneers. Another distinguishing feature of frontier Pennsylvania was the rapid growth of the city of Pittsburgh, the population of which rose from 376 in 1790 to 1,565 in 1800, to 4,768 in 1810, and to 7,248 in 1820. As an entrepôt, Pittsburgh linked the main routes of river and overland travel. It also became a manufacturing center where goods needed by pioneers were produced that undersold high-priced imports carried over the mountains. When the sites of such New York cities

---

[52] Bidwell and Falconer, *History of Agriculture in the Northern United States*, p. 152; Buck, *The Planting of Civilization in Western Pennsylvania*, pp. 212, 216.

[53] Bidwell and Falconer, *History of Agriculture in the Northern United States*, p. 152.

as Buffalo, Rochester, and Syracuse were little more than wilderness, Pittsburgh was the leading frontier city of the West.[54]

North of the Ohio River, the area that was settled between 1790 and 1820 included nearly all the present state of Ohio and the southern parts of Indiana and Illinois. Michigan, with a population of only 8,896 in 1820, contributed but slightly to this frontier advance. Wisconsin remained an Indian country. In the whole Northwest in 1790 there was only one short, thin line of settlements where the inhabitants numbered six or more to the square mile. This line ran along the Ohio River opposite the western border of Pennsylvania. An extension of the Pennsylvania frontier, these settlements had their center at Steubenville, founded as Fort Steuben in 1787. Although New Englanders had founded Marietta in 1788 and associates of John Cleves Symmes had settled at Cincinnati, also in 1788, the growth of Ohio was retarded by Indian hostilities until 1794, when General Anthony Wayne defeated allied tribes of the Northwest in the Battle of Fallen Timbers at the site of present-day Toledo. By the Treaty of Greenville of 1795 the Indians surrendered to the United States their claims to approximately the lower two thirds of Ohio, plus a strip about fifty-five miles wide in the northwestern part of the state south of Lake Erie.[55]

In 1800 there were four important settlements in the Northwest. In addition to Steubenville, Marietta, and Cincinnati, the town of Chillicothe, founded in 1796, had become a center for pioneers along the Scioto River in the Virginia Military District. In 1815, Cleveland in the Western Reserve —founded in 1796—was still a frontier village. In Indiana, the principal settlements in 1820 extended along the Ohio and Wabash rivers, reaching nearly halfway up the state on the western side. About a fourth of Illinois —a U-shaped area between the Wabash, the Ohio, and the Mississippi— was then passing through the frontier stage. By 1820 the Northwest had a population larger than that of New York and Pennsylvania in 1790. The increase was as follows: [56]

	Ohio	Indiana	Illinois	Michigan
1790	—	—	—	—
1800	45,365	5,641	—	—
1810	230,760	24,520	12,282	4,762
1820	581,434	147,178	55,211	8,896

The settlements of the Old Northwest were mainly an extension of the Pennsylvania frontier. Pittsburgh served as their chief link with

[54] Buck, The Planting of Civilization in Western Pennsylvania, pp. 204, 217–218, 223–227; Fletcher, Pennsylvania Agriculture, p. 290; McNall, The Genesee Valley, p. 120; Richard C. Wade, "Urban Life in Western America, 1790–1830," American Historical Review, LXIV, No. 1 (October, 1958), 14.

[55] Paullin, Atlas, plate 76; Bond, The Old Northwest, pp. 11, 12, 15.

[56] Bond, The Old Northwest, pp. 13, 111, 284.

the East, while the upper Ohio and its tributaries provided the principal bonds of union. The products of the area, the cabins, the clearings, the livestock, the tools, the methods of work, and the hard conditions of pioneer life—all vividly portrayed by Conrad Richter in *The Trees* and *The Fields*—duplicated those of the New York–Pennsylvania frontier. The settlers were of many origins: New Englanders, emigrants from the older parts of the middle states, backwoodsmen from Pennsylvania and western Virginia, and Southerners in Indiana, Illinois, and the Virginia Military District. Only a few immigrants from Europe—French and German—mingled with the native Americans. One special feature of the Northwest was its early dependence on the Ohio-Mississippi outlet for surplus farm products. Cincinnati, with 6,500 residents in 1815, became the queen city of the Northwest. Its specialty, meat packing, gave it the nickname "Porkopolis." Most of the pioneers lived on isolated farms rather than in village communities. The growth of the area was stimulated by the pacifying of the Indians in 1794, by Spain's agreement, in the Treaty of San Lorenzo of 1795, to open the lower Mississippi to American trade, and by the Federal Land Act of 1800, which allowed a pioneer four years to pay for a 320-acre farm, priced at $2 an acre.[57]

On the whole, the pioneer settlements of the present state of West Virginia were akin to those in Ohio and Pennsylvania. Several rivers that traverse most parts of the state have their sources close together in the west-central area near the present Virginia border. The Tygart and Buchanan rivers, tributaries of the Monongahela, give access to Pittsburgh. The Little Kanawha flows northwestward to Parkersburg on the Ohio. The Elk, an upper stream of the Kanawha, leads westward to Charleston; the Greenbrier flows southwestward to the New River, another branch of the Kanawha. As early as 1769–1772 many pioneers settled in the Tygart and Buchanan valleys. Others descended the Buchanan to the Monongahela and followed that stream toward Pittsburgh. About the same time settlements were made at Lewisburg in the Greenbrier Valley and at Peterstown on the New—each a few miles from the present Virginia border—and in 1773 a pioneer built a cabin on the Kanawha. Other settlers came down the Ohio. By 1775, the country between the Kanawha, the Ohio, and the Alleghenies was being settled. In 1784, Washington visited the area south of Pittsburgh, viewed rivers and portages, and proposed a network of canals and roads to link east and west. According to Jefferson, trans-Allegheny Virginia in 1782 had 4,459 "fighting men," or 9 percent of Virginia's total. There were 41,219 pioneers in the area in 1790. At that time in only two small districts did the inhabit-

---

[57] *Ibid.*, pp. 15–16, 150–151, 183, 284, 389–391; R. Carlyle Buley, *The Old Northwest* (2 vols.; Indianapolis: Indiana Historical Society, 1950), I, 21–22, 26–28, 30–35; Clarence Walworth Alvord, *The Illinois Country, 1763–1818* (Springfield: Illinois Centennial Commission, 1920), pp. 453–458.

ants number six or more to the square mile: one in the northeastern section south of the Potomac below Cumberland; the other in the Wheeling district west of Pennsylvania.[58]

West Virginia stood out among frontier areas by reason of its slow growth. In 1810 the population had risen to but 114,195, and in 1820 only the two small districts bordering Maryland and Pennsylvania contained as many as eighteen inhabitants to the square mile. The West Virginians were typical pioneers—farmers from Pennsylvania and the upper South who cultivated small farms without the help of slaves. Hostility to slavery, dependence on the Ohio River as an outlet for their pork, flour, potatoes, and apples, cattle raising in the Allegheny Highlands, and a thriving salt-producing industry on the Kanawha—all such factors made the settlers feel independent of Virginia and linked them with the Ohio-Pennsylvania frontier.[59]

Among frontier districts Kentucky was unique in that its settlements expanded from a single center that was remote and isolated from older communities. That center was the Bluegrass region—the Eden of the West—8,000 square miles of extremely fertile and level or gently sloping land, blessed with a mild climate and numerous springs. Located south of Cincinnati, the Bluegrass was a fine cattle country that also yielded abundant crops of hemp, grain, and tobacco, the best horses of the West, and an amplitude of whiskey. Bourbon County was organized in 1784. With Lexington as the center, settlements expanded in all directions to form a closely knit community of contiguous farms. The pioneers—Americans of many ethnic strains—came chiefly from Pennsylvania, Maryland, Virginia, and North Carolina. From the South they reached the promised land by way of the Cumberland Gap and Boone's Wilderness Road; from upper Virginia and the middle states they descended the Ohio to Limestone (Maysville). Lexington, the leading city of the state before 1815 and the hub of roads and trails, was the only important frontier center not located on a navigable stream. Cattle walked to eastern markets, and horses and wagons moved freight westward to Frankfort on the Kentucky River—an outlet to the Ohio—or eastward to the Licking River, a stream that joined the Ohio opposite Cincinnati. Only with the growth of river steamboat traffic after 1815 did Louisville surpass Lexington as a commercial town.[60]

    [58] Gray, *History of Southern Agriculture in the United States*, I, 125; Ray Allen Billington, *Westward Expansion* (New York: The Macmillan Company, 1949), p. 157; *Writings of Washington* (Fitzpatrick), XXVII, 471, 477–479; Cook, *Washington's Western Lands*, p. 69; Charles Henry Ambler, *Sectionalism in Virginia from 1776 to 1861* (Chicago: The University of Chicago Press, 1910), pp. 36, 84.
    [59] Paullin, *Atlas*, plate 76; Ambler, *Sectionalism in Virginia*, pp. 82–85.
    [60] Clark, *History of Kentucky*, pp. 2–4, 94, 107, 227–228, 231, 242–243, 263; Gray, *History of Agriculture in the Southern United States*, I, 124; II, 755; Ulrich Bonnell Phillips, *American Negro Slavery* (New York: D. Appleton and Company,

In 1790 the settlements in the Bluegrass formed an oval-shaped area about 35 miles wide and 85 miles long. The pioneers of Kentucky then numbered 73,677, as against 12,000 in 1783. During the next decade the settled area, still centering at Lexington, expanded on all sides, and the population rose to 220,955, with the greatest increase in the zone south of the Ohio and east of Louisville. In 1810, when the population was 406,511, more than half the state contained six or more inhabitants to the square mile. Only the mountainous district in the east and the southwestern tip of the state were unoccupied or thinly settled in 1820, when the inhabitants numbered 564,317.

The Bluegrass was the first Eden beyond the Alleghenies to beckon to slaveowners of Virginia who were afflicted with worn-out soil. Kentucky's slave population grew from 12,430 in 1790 to 40,343 in 1800, to 80,561 in 1810, to 126,732 in 1820, while the percentage of slaves in the total population rose from 17 percent in 1790 to 22 percent in 1820. However, the large number of cattle raisers and hemp growers who clung to the Bluegrass prevented the monopolizing of that paradise by a few large slaveowners, and the large plantation did not dominate the Kentucky countryside. In the western area, slaves raised tobacco on large farms and worked at varied tasks on smaller holdings.[61]

In contrast to those in Kentucky, the settlements of Tennessee expanded from two centers—one in the extreme eastern part of the present state; the other in the western and northern area around Nashville. As early as 1768 pioneers made clearings in the Watauga River Valley. Then followed an advance by that stream to and down the Holston River, while other frontiersmen from North Carolina settled in the valley of the French Broad. Both these rivers flowed southward and westward toward Knoxville, founded in 1791—a town which served as the capital and chief trading center of the district and state until 1812. In 1790, most of the pioneers of Tennessee, numbering 35,691, lived in the river valleys east of Knoxville—a quasi-circular area about sixty miles in diameter. Toiling in a rugged country, in the face of hostile Indians, the Tennessee pioneers were backwoodsmen of the hardiest sort. By 1800, the settled area centering in Knoxville covered the eastern fourth of the state. Afterward it declined in relative importance.[62]

1918), p. 169; Clement Eaton, A History of the Old South (New York: The Macmillan Company, 1949), pp. 125–128; Mary Verhoeff, The Kentucky River Navigation (Filson Club Publications, No. 28; Louisville: John P. Morton & Company), pp. 86–94.

[61] Avery Odell Craven, Soil Exhaustion As a Factor in the Agricultural History of Virginia and Maryland, 1606–1860 (University of Illinois Studies in the Social Sciences, Vol. XIII, No. 1; Urbana: 1925), pp. 82–119; Bernard Mayo, "Lexington: Frontier Metropolis," in Eric F. Goldman, ed., Historiography and Urbanization (Baltimore: The Johns Hopkins Press, 1941), pp. 22–23; Gray, History of Agriculture in the Southern United States, II, 872–873.

[62] Abernethy, From Frontier to Plantation in Tennessee, pp. 3, 16, 53, 120, 159, 181.

Founded in 1779, Nashville grew slowly until 1795, when its hinterland entered an era of rapid progress that lasted until 1812. In 1800, the settlements there extended about 75 miles, as the crow flies, along the Cumberland River, and about 60 miles north and south. The total population of the state, which was 105,602 in 1800, rose to 261,727 in 1810 and to 422,823 in 1820.

In East Tennessee the small farmer predominated. All the slaves of the Tennessee country numbered only 3,417 in 1790—fewer than 10 percent of the total population. After 1800, the growth of the Nashville district gave a strong impetus to slavery, for cotton became the principal cash crop, with tobacco in second place. In 1820, slaves in Tennessee numbered 80,100, or 16 percent of the state's population. The emergence of the Cotton Kingdom linked the Nashville district with the frontier of the lower South.[63]

[63] *Ibid.*, pp. 27–28, 198–199, 201.

CHAPTER IX

Southern Staples and Slavery

THE BIRTH OF THE COTTON KINGDOM

IN 1790, cotton figured but slightly in the economy of the Union; in 1860, it was the leading cash crop of American agriculture, contributing two thirds to the value of the country's exports. Within the span of seventy years the phenomenal progress of the Cotton Kingdom wrought a transformation so profound as to rank with the effects of the Industrial Revolution. The cotton industry spread widely and became strongly rooted: in 1821 each one of eight states—Virginia, North Carolina, South Carolina, Georgia, Alabama, Tennessee, Mississippi, and Louisiana—produced at least five times as much cotton as did the whole Union in 1791.[1]

Conditions in Georgia and South Carolina gave birth to the new industry and nursed it during a robust infancy. By 1795, two of the old staples of those states were in a precarious plight. After the war, Britain so stimulated the production of indigo in the East Indies as to bring about a price decline that cut into the profits of American planters. A merchant near Charleston wrote about 1795: "There being no sale for indigo for some time past, money comes in vastly slow, . . . There never was perhaps so great a quantity of indigo made in my neighborhood before." South Carolina's exports of indigo fell from 839,000 pounds in 1792 to 96,000 pounds in 1797 and to 3,400[2] pounds by 1800. Within about eight years a once profitable crop had nearly expired.

The rice industry of the lower South did not fare so badly as indigo, but it also had its troubles. Rice growers had increased production until in the 1790's it reached a peak near the pre-1775 total. Distress afflicted them in 1797–1799, when the price of rice was only about half as high

[1] Frederick Jackson Turner, *The Rise of the New West, 1819–1829* (Vol. XIV of *The American Nation*, A. B. Hart, ed.; New York: Harper & Brothers, 1906), p. 47.

[2] Ulrich Bonnell Phillips, *Life and Labor in the Old South* (Boston: Little, Brown and Company, 1929), p. 119; Gray, *History of Agriculture in the Southern United States*, II, 610–611; Phillips, *American Negro Slavery*, p. 93.

as in 1795–1796. Although the total population of Georgia and South Carolina increased from 518,000 in 1800 to 843,000 in 1820, the production of rice in the two states did not expand at that time. The staple did not serve the small slaveholder or the ordinary farmer. Rice growing was so laborious and disagreeable that it could be carried on only by planters who owned several slaves. Moreover, land that could be cultivated by the usual process of controlled flooding was scarce and expensive to prepare.[3]

Before the coming of the Cotton Kingdom, southern farmers produced two kinds of cotton, each on a small scale. One type, green-seed or short-staple, had been raised since early times and could be grown widely in the South. But it had a serious drawback. Before the invention of the cotton gin, the seeds had to be cut or torn from the lint by hand, for they stuck to it as if glued. Such work was so tedious that it took a person a day to clean one pound. This defect restricted cultivation to small patches for family use.

The other type of cotton, sea-island, contained smooth seeds that could be removed easily by running the lint through a pair of rollers. This type was also called "long-staple" because the fibers attained a length of two inches—about twice that of the green-seed variety. The production of long-staple cotton began before the Revolutionary War and soon spread over the islands and lands along the coasts of South Carolina and Georgia—lands which, lacking fresh-water streams, were not suited to rice. The principal defect of long-staple cotton lay in the fact that it could be grown profitably only on the islands off the shore and on the coastal plain about forty or fifty miles inland.[4]

The South in the 1790's urgently needed a new crop. The limitations of rice, indigo, and sea-island cotton were matched by troubles that beset the tobacco planters of the upper South. Between 1791 and 1796, Virginians suffered from the low price of tobacco; between 1786 and 1789 they were the victims of short or poor crops caused by drought, storm, or frost.[5]

Both soil and climate promised that green-seed cotton might be grown profitably over vast areas of the South, and as early as 1791 farmers raised considerable crops in the hope that some machine would soon be devised to separate the seeds from the lint. In 1793, while visiting at "Mulberry Grove," the Georgia plantation of Mrs. Nathanael Greene, Eli Whitney invented the cotton gin. Its most important part was a cylin-

[3] Phillips, *Life and Labor in the Old South*, pp. 115–118; Gray, *History of Agriculture in the Southern United States*, II, 610.

[4] M. B. Hammond, *The Cotton Industry* (American Economic Association, *Publications*, New Series, No. 1; New York: The Macmillan Company, 1897), pp. 5, 17–20, 23; Gray, *History of Agriculture in the Southern United States*, II, 674; Phillips, *Life and Labor in the Old South*, pp. 91–95.

[5] Gray, *History of Agriculture in the Southern United States*, II, 604–605.

der set in a frame and turned by a hand crank. Affixed to the cylinder were rows of spikes set close together. The operator placed unseeded cotton in an adjoining box having on one of its sides narrow openings between slats. When he turned the crank, the spikes of the revolving cylinder reached into the box through the openings, speared some of the cotton, and yanked it out with such force as to tear the lint from the seeds, leaving them inside the box. Because the spikes quickly became clogged with lint, Whitney then devised a revolving brush that cleaned them as soon as they came out of the box.[6]

It is estimated that South Carolina and Georgia produced from 2 million to 3 million pounds of green-seed cotton in 1793. In 1811, the total output of the whole South was 80 million pounds and in 1810 the cotton exports of the Union amounted to 93 million pounds. This prodigious expansion transformed southern life and affected profoundly all other parts of the country.[7]

Three special features marked the extension of the short-staple cotton industry. Its initial centers of greatest importance were the piedmont districts of South Carolina and Georgia. In 1811, they produced 60 million pounds, or three fourths of all the cotton grown in the country. The industry also reached into southeastern Virginia and the central part of North Carolina. In 1811 those two states produced about 15 million pounds, or approximately 19 percent of the total. As early as 1780 a pioneer raised cotton near Nashville in middle Tennessee, and by 1811 that district, together with the areas of the present states of Alabama, Mississippi, and Louisiana, produced probably more than 10,000,000 pounds.[8]

Rarely has an infant industry been blessed with such favoring conditions as cotton enjoyed after 1792. The Revolutionary War had stimulated the growing of cotton for domestic use, so that most farmers in the South were familiar with the art of cultivating it. The cotton gin reduced to a fraction the work of cleaning the fibers. The first model enabled one worker to clean fifty pounds in a day. Almost overnight a product once limited to household use became salable at a profit. All this happened when the demand for cotton in England was growing by leaps and bounds. Of the inventions that revolutionized the English cloth industry, John Kay's flying shuttle (1733) and Edmund Cartwright's power loom (1785) had greatly facilitated weaving, and James Hargreaves' spinning

[6] Jeannette Mirsky and Allan Nevins, *The World of Eli Whitney* (New York: The Macmillan Company, 1952), pp. 73–74; Constance McL. Green, *Eli Whitney and the Birth of American Technology* (Boston: Little, Brown and Company, 1956), pp. 45–48; M. B. Hammond, ed., "Correspondence of Eli Whitney relative to the Invention of the Cotton Gin," *American Historical Review*, III, No. 1 (October, 1897), 100.

[7] Gray, *History of Agriculture in the Southern United States*, II, 680, 683; Hammond, *The Cotton Industry*, p. 240.

[8] Gray, *History of Agriculture in the Southern United States*, II, 686–687.

jenny (1764) and Samuel Crompton's mule (1779) had wrought a tremendous saving of labor in spinning. Although such inventions had been developed for the manufacture of woolens, they were soon adapted to cotton—a material that may be spun into threads of almost incredible length, of varying degrees of fineness and coarseness, and of a strength greater than that of iron wire of the same thickness. The new machines so stimulated the production of cotton goods in England that its imports of cotton rose from about 1 million pounds annually between 1701 and 1750 to 12 million pounds in 1784, to an average of 26 million pounds between 1791 and 1795, and to 56 million pounds in 1800. Drastically reduced costs gave to English manufacturers world supremacy in producing fabrics for many uses, coarse or fine, suitable to most climates, in universal demand, durable, cheaply transported, and inexpensive to store.[9]

It was the good fortune of southern farmers that England's expanding purchases of cotton were made when prices were high. In 1790, cotton in American ports sold, on the average, for 35 cents a pound. The figure in 1798 and 1800 was 44 cents. Although such quotations overstate the price of green-seed cotton, it is clear that it netted the farmer a handsome return. In 1796, green-seed cotton brought 13*d*. a pound at Savannah, whereas tobacco then sold for about 2.1*d*. a pound in Charleston. About 1800 a farmer could raise cotton profitably if he received 12 cents a pound. An estimate of 1806 indicates that a Tennessee farmer, selling at 18 cents a pound, made a net profit of $212 on four acres of cotton, not counting his labor.[10]

The principal habitat of green-seed cotton before 1815 was the up country of South Carolina and Georgia. This is a zone of fertile land, originally covered with hardwoods and cane, 75 to 100 miles wide, between the vicinity of the falls of the rivers and the mountains, and separated from the coastal plain by a belt of pine barrens or sand hills that reach 10 to 30 miles inland beyond the fall line. Until 1820 the up country of the two states was the heartland of the emerging Cotton Kingdom. The upsurge of cotton there is suggestive of the oil boom in western Pennsylvania after 1859.[11]

Cotton enabled many pioneers and poor farmers to rise into a prosper-

[9] Arnold Toynbee, *The Industrial Revolution* (Boston: The Beacon Press, 1956), pp. 23–24; J. L. Hammond and Barbara Hammond, *The Rise of Modern Industry* (New York: Harcourt, Brace and Company, 1926), pp. 181–183; Gray, *History of Agriculture in the Southern United States*, II, 678; Mirsky and Nevins, *Eli Whitney*, pp. 82–87.

[10] Gray, *History of Agriculture in the Southern United States*, II, 681; Cole, *Wholesale Commodity Prices; Statistical Supplement*, p. 111.

[11] Rupert B. Vance, *Human Factors in Cotton Culture* (Chapel Hill: The University of North Carolina Press, 1929), pp. 15–16; Ulrich Bonnell Phillips, "Georgia and State Rights" (American Historical Association, *Annual Report . . . 1901*, 2 vols.; Washington: Government Printing Office, 1902), II, 140 (map).

ing middle class. Household manufacturing declined and town industries languished as cotton yielded money for buying imported goods at stores. However, the up country continued to be one of diversified farming, producing the horses, cattle, hay, and grain for its needs, and even exporting flour. A marked increase in the use of slave labor occurred. In 1790, slaves accounted for 18.4 percent of the total population of the South Carolina and Georgia up country; in 1820, they constituted 39.5 percent. The number of slaves in the two states rose from 136,000 in 1790 to 368,000 in 1820. Because rice and indigo did not employ additional slaves after 1800, it appears that cotton was the main cause of the expansion of slavery. In South Carolina—the area of the heaviest concentration of the cotton industry before 1820—slavery grew more rapidly than in Georgia. Between 1790 and 1820 the white population of South Carolina increased by 102,000, as contrasted with an addition of 151,000 slaves. In Georgia, the white population increased during these years by 177,000; the slaves by 80,000. By 1820, slaves made up 51 percent of the population of South Carolina and only 32 percent of Georgia's. The number of slaves added to South Carolina's population between 1800 and 1820 (112,324) was larger than the state's total slave population of 107,000 in 1790.[12]

A rising province of the nascent Cotton Kingdom embraced the middle part of Tennessee and favored areas of the present states of Alabama, Mississippi, and Louisiana. This new Southwest was settled mainly by emigrants from the piedmont of Georgia and the Carolinas who moved westward after cotton had become firmly rooted there. The distinguishing feature of the frontier of the lower Southwest was the exceptional importance of slavery at the very outset. The percentage of slaves in the population of Alabama-Mississippi ranged from 39 in 1800 to 42 in 1810 to 37 in 1820. In Louisiana, 49 percent of the inhabitants were slaves in 1810 and 45 percent in 1820. Nonslaveowning frontiersmen settled in the Southwest, but, thanks to cotton, they were less important there than in any other sector of the frontier zone. The process by which slavery and the plantations were engrafted upon the Southwest was varied and complex. Frequently, a planter who intended to move to the area made an advance trip to survey the country and to select a site. Sometimes a slaveowner secured a nucleus for a plantation by purchasing a clearing and cabin from a backwoods pioneer. In other instances, planters took or sent their slaves into the forest and they did all the work of pioneering, *de novo*. Often a planter left his family in the old home until a plantation had been started. In the pioneering stage, slaveowners occasionally hired their slaves part time to other planters. In some cases a household moved

[12] Gray, *History of Agriculture in the Southern United States*, II, 685–686; William A. Schaper, "Sectionalism and Representation in South Carolina" (American Historical Association, *Annual Report . . . 1900*, 2 vols.; Washington: Government Printing Office, 1901), I, 395.

westward in a "cavalcade"—armed men on horseback, ladies in carriages, children in holiday mood, slaves on foot, livestock trudging along, and the planter's possessions trundling forward in wagons and carts drawn by horses and oxen. Now and then nonslaveholding families went west in company with a slaveowner and his entourage. In Louisiana and western Mississippi, planters purchased slaves at New Orleans. In any case, slaves did all types of work that belonged to pioneering. Once a foothold had been secured, the plantation evolved in various ways. The large slaveowner added to his lands and labor force. The most successful small slaveowners did likewise and climbed into the planter class. Among the nonslaveholders, some acquired a few slaves, with whom they toiled in the fields.[13]

By 1815, the western domain of cotton contained four principal centers. Farthest to the north was the district south of Nashville. Its production of cotton increased from an estimated 1 million pounds in 1801 to 3 million pounds in 1811. The number of slaves in Tennessee rose from 13,584 in 1800 to 44,535 in 1810. To the southwest, the country around Natchez, according to one estimate, yielded 750,000 pounds of cotton as early as 1796. In 1810, cotton production in present-day Mississippi was negligible outside the Natchez district, which then contained most of the area's 14,523 slaves. A third center was Baton Rouge. From that point planters after 1803 extended their plantations up the Mississippi and behind the river, then preferring higher sites to delta lands. By 1809 cotton was the principal staple of the lower Red River Valley. The slaves of Louisiana numbered 34,660 in 1810. New Orleans served the Baton Rouge, Natchez, and Nashville centers as a marketing outlet. Its exports of cotton were estimated as 34,000 bales in 1802. The fourth center—the lower valleys of the Tombigbee and Alabama rivers in present-day Alabama—was of minor importance before 1815. In 1810, the slaves of this district numbered 2,565 and its cotton production was estimated as 2,000 bales.[14]

COTTON AND SLAVERY

In 1793, slavery in the upper South was in a weakened, declining state. Then the invention of the cotton gin and the resulting widespread cultivation of green-seed cotton gave fresh employment to slaves. Cotton and slavery were so complementary as to seem to be made for each other.

[13] Eaton, The Old South, p. 211; Dick, The Dixie Frontier, pp. 55–58, 79–82, 84–85, 87–92; Phillips, American Negro Slavery, pp. 171–174; Phillips, Life and Labor in the Old South, pp. 290–295; Gray, History of Agriculture in the Southern United States, II, 872–873.

[14] Dick, The Dixie Frontier, pp. 54, 79; Hammond, The Cotton Industry, p. 50; Gray, History of Agriculture in the Southern United States, II, 687–689; John Hebron Moore, Agriculture in Ante-Bellum Mississippi (New York: Bookman Associates, 1958), pp. 24–26, 30–33.

Nature assisted by providing favoring conditions. Cotton could be raised on most of the tillable land south of the James and Cumberland rivers, where long summers brought crops to maturity before the autumn frosts. The climate of this vast area suited the Negro. From the point of view of the planter, slavery offered many advantages. He received most of the proceeds from the surplus produced on his land and he had the benefit of a labor force that was reasonably steady, constant, and subject to his control.[15]

The work on a cotton farm consisted of a series of simple tasks, easily learned, that continued throughout the year, employing not only the adult males but also the women and children. In the spring, crude plows scratched the soil to a depth of about two and one half inches. The slaves planted the seeds in rows three to five feet apart. Cultivating was done by plow and hoe. When the plants were small the weaker ones were cut out, leaving one plant to every twelve to eighteen inches along the row. During the picking season all hands worked from dawn till dark. The slaves transported the lint to the ginning mill and did the packing or baling. In the early days, the lint was dumped into canvas bags or gunny sacks and tramped down by foot. In the winter months, the men cleared new land. Other tasks included planting, cultivating, and harvesting corn, raising and slaughtering hogs, building and mending fences, and chopping wood.[16]

Since slaves, like other people, had an intense aversion to poorly rewarded toil in the hot sun, the cotton regime depended upon some scheme of continuing supervision. The cotton plant enabled the owner to concentrate his hands within a relatively small area and to work them together at uniform tasks. One slave could cultivate from 3 to 10 acres, so that between five and seventeen persons could be employed on a 50-acre tract, thereby enabling the owner to supervise the work. On small plantations employing a few hands the owner served as overseer or labored with them in the fields. On large plantations, a gang was commonly put in charge of a "driver"—a large, vigorous slave who set the tasks for the other hands, kept them at their work, and acted under the supervision of the owner or his overseer.[17]

Thanks to the climate and the resources of the cotton belt, the slaves could be kept in good working order at a minimum cost. Long summers and mild winters, coupled with a low standard of living, reduced to a trifle the expense of clothing. The forest and the labor of the slaves provided huts and firewood. Before 1815, most cotton farms produced enough corn

---

[15] Hammond, *The Cotton Industry*, pp. 44–45.

[16] Phillips, *American Negro Slavery*, pp. 207–209; Hammond, *The Cotton Industry*, pp. 46, 82, 92, 112; Stampp, *The Peculiar Institution*, pp. 44–46; Moore, *Agriculture in Ante-Bellum Mississippi*, p. 43.

[17] Hammond, *The Cotton Industry*, pp. 92–93.

and hogs to supply the corn bread and salt pork that sustained the slaves. Wherever cotton was grown one usually found a cornfield. Many planters permitted their slaves to raise vegetables in "truck patches" and to keep chickens and even pigs.[18]

The bonds between cotton and slavery were strengthened by the supply of slaves available after 1793. The rapid decline of indigo released one group of slaves for service in the cotton fields. Some northern states were outlawing slavery at this time; owners then took advantage of the cotton boom to sell slaves to cotton planters. The number of slaves in Delaware, Pennsylvania, New York, Connecticut, Rhode Island, and New Jersey fell from 37,500 in 1790 to 20,400 in 1810. The exhaustion of tobacco lands in Maryland impelled owners there to sell surplus slaves to the cotton country. Maryland's slave population grew but slightly—from 103,036 in 1790 to 111,917 in 1820. In Virginia and North Carolina cotton gave employment to a force of slaves large enough to produce most of the 15 million pounds which those states produced in 1811. The lower South imported many slaves from Africa between 1790 and 1808. One observer estimated such arrivals in the 1790's as 26,197. According to W. H. Collins, 39,075 slaves were brought into Charleston from Africa during four years after December, 1803. Another report states that during twelve months before February, 1804, 20,000 African Negroes entered South Carolina and Georgia.[19]

Viewing slavery from the standpoint of industrial efficiency, many observers noted certain defects in the system. Among slaves the will to work was feeble. Since the fruits of their toil went mainly to the owner, they felt little or no incentive to exceptional exertion. They received only a meager livelihood—and that was assured, whether they strained or lagged. Because the women and children belonged to the owner and were cared for by the plantation, the adult male slaves were not spurred by the urgent necessity of supporting a family, nor were they animated by the ambition that springs from the opportunity to acquire wealth, to raise one's standard of living, or to improve the status of one's children. Plantation efficiency depended primarily upon force. Whether the whip was used freely or sparingly, its menace was ever-present. The treatment of the slaves varied widely, depending as it did upon the dispositions of owners; and differences among them on that score was legion. Suffice it to say that normal individuals do not choose to be subjected to the will of an alien in a regime which awards most of the fruits of their labor to

[18] *Ibid.*, pp. 46–47; John Hope Franklin, *From Slavery to Freedom* (2d ed.; New York: Alfred A. Knopf, Inc., 1956), pp. 193–195.

[19] Hammond, *The Cotton Industry*, pp. 47–48; Schaper, "Sectionalism in South Carolina," p. 388; Phillips, *American Negro Slavery*, pp. 137–138; Winfield H. Collins, *The Domestic Slave Trade of the Southern States* (New York: Broadway Publishing Company, 1904), pp. 11–12.

him. Commonly the planters sought to obtain work by offering special inducements. To each slave was assigned a daily task—such as hoeing an acre of cotton. The completion of the task freed the slave from work in the fields during the rest of the day. Otherwise, he worked until sundown. Often the hands finished their tasks by midafternoon. The reward was rest and leisure—not money or goods. The truck patches of the slaves also spurred them to do extra work. If they raised some surplus produce they were permitted to sell it and buy such luxuries as whiskey, tobacco, and "Sunday finery." [20]

Cotton farming before 1815 was a crude type of agriculture that mined the soil of its fertility and withheld from the Negro workers most of the product of their labor. The planters adapted to cotton the primitive practices of colonial times. They regarded land as something to be exploited a few years and then abandoned. They did little or nothing to check or prevent erosion—an evil of particular potency when most of the lands devoted to cotton were hilly or rolling. Generally, the planters did not bother to enrich the land by using fertilizers or by rotating crops. Jefferson expressed the prevailing attitude when he said that "we can buy an acre of new land cheaper than we can manure an old one." Capital figured but slightly in the early cotton industry. The slave's defective sense of property restrained owners from entrusting him with expensive tools. Little care was taken of wagons, plows, and hoes; they were given hard use until they wore out and then they were thrown away. The cotton regime contributed nothing in the way of laborsaving devices for use in the fields. The slaves lacked the knowledge essential to invention, and the owners did not have the necessary incentive, since their wealth was largely invested in workers whose bodies took the place of machines.[21]

Profits of individual cotton farms cannot be determined with precision. Most planters did not keep detailed records of expenses and income. Differences in the fertility of land, in the skill of planters, and in the efficiency of slaves resulted in great variations of earnings from plantation to plantation. Estimates for the South Carolina upcountry in 1812 give a maximum yield of 300 pounds of cotton an acre, average yields of 100 to 300 pounds an acre, and yields of 60 to 100 pounds an acre on inferior land. If one laborer could cultivate 3 to 10 acres a year, it appears that in the most favorable conditions a slave produced about 3,000 pounds of cotton annually, whereas the yield under the least favorable conditions was only 180 pounds. Such estimates must include the work of women and children as cotton pickers. Expenses varied in a similar way. On a large plantation the cost of keeping a slave for one year was estimated as $15;

[20] Hammond, *The Cotton Industry*, pp. 43, 90, 92; Franklin, *From Slavery to Freedom*, pp. 191–192, 204–205.

[21] Hammond, *The Cotton Industry*, pp. 39, 79–81, 83; Moore, *Agriculture in Ante-Bellum Mississippi*, p. 41.

on small plantations, the cost ranged from $30 to $40. In 1799, Wade Hampton of South Carolina had a crop of 600 bales valued at $90,000. Such a return suggested a fabulous profit.[22]

On the whole, the period 1794–1815 was one of extraordinary profitability for cotton growers. The total output of green-seed cotton rose from 2 million–3 million pounds in 1793 to 80 million in 1811. During these years the price of cotton was favorable. Sales of slaves bespoke profitable operations. In 1790, the best slaves sold at $200 each. The average price of prime field hands at Charleston rose from $300 in 1795 to $400 in 1797 to $500 in 1800 and to $600 in 1804. Between 1805 and 1812 such Charleston prices were stable at about $550. Most prosperous were the years 1794–1798. The export price of cotton then rose from 26 cents to 44 cents a pound. The period 1799–1810 was one of good or fair profits, when export prices ranged from 19 to 15 cents a pound, with the exception of the year 1800, when the price shot up to 44 cents. During the period 1794–1815, only two years—1811 and 1812—were lean ones. Export prices then were 11 cents and 12 cents a pound.[23]

The southern staples produced by slave labor had the effect of enlarging favored farms into plantations and of forcing poor farmers to migrate or to work inferior lands. In the plantation or seacoast area of South Carolina in 1790 the average holding contained 725 acres, as contrasted with average farms of 225 acres in the then nonplantation up country, and the colored inhabitants of the coast outnumbered the resident whites by nearly 3 to 1, whereas in the up country, the whites outnumbered the colored people by more than 3½ to 1. Between 1790 and 1800 the white population of South Carolina increased by 40 percent; the slaves by 36.4 percent. During the next twenty years a marked change occurred. Between 1800 and 1810 the whites increased at the rate of only 9.4 percent; the slaves at the rate of 34.3 percent. The comparable figures for 1810–1820 were 10.8 percent and 31.6 percent. By 1810, in the east-central part of the up country the slaves outnumbered the whites. The high price of slaves after 1800 and differentials in the productivity of farms permitted only the most successful planters to buy additional slaves and to acquire more land.[24]

Many observers have regarded slavery as inefficient because it entailed the use of primitive methods and tools and because it failed to animate the slave with a strong will to work. It forced the planter to invest much of his wealth in the purchase of his working force. An em-

[22] Phillips, *Life and Labor in the Old South*, p. 98; Hammond, *The Cotton Industry*, pp. 46–47, 90–91; Gray, *History of Agriculture in the Southern United States*, II, 708.

[23] Phillips, *American Negro Slavery*, p. 370 (map); Gray, *History of Agriculture in the Southern United States*, II, 682; Hammond, *The Cotton Industry*, p. 42.

[24] Schaper, "Sectionalism in South Carolina," pp. 391, 395.

ployer who hired workers could invest such wealth in machines, thereby earning a return on both capital and labor. Two conditions account in good measure for the survival of the cotton regime. One was an abundance of good, cheap land. Rich soil overcame the inherent defects of slave labor. The other condition was the absence of a large wage-earning class. The South did not attract free laborers from the North or from foreign lands. At the same time, slavery caused a large emigration of poor farmers to frontier zones, and it instilled in the southern white people a fierce prejudice against doing, as wage earners, the kind of field work that was performed by slaves. The progress of the cotton regime therefore depended upon an abundance of good, virgin land and a continuing shortage of cheap, free labor. Both conditions were destined to exist long after 1815.[25]

OTHER STAPLES

The rise of cotton accompanied a relative decline of tobacco, long the foremost staple of the South. In the period before 1860, tobacco reached its peak in 1790, when exports totaled about 118,000 hogsheads. In that year green-seed cotton was in its infancy and exports of sea-island cotton from South Carolina were only 9,840 pounds. In 1811, cotton produced in the South amounted to 80 million pounds; tobacco to about 56 million pounds. The export value of the cotton crop of 1811 was about $7,200,000; that of tobacco, about $4,450,000. In 1820, the production of raw cotton was double that of 1811, whereas tobacco production in 1820 was less than in 1790.[26]

Many factors besides the competition of cotton contributed to the decline of the Tobacco Coast. Before 1815, tobacco growers continued to use, in the main, the old one-crop, soil-exhausting methods that had worn out their once rich tidewater lands. After 1775 a few progressive planters, like Washington, sought to rid the Tobacco Coast of the ills that beset it. Their experiments generally pointed toward an abandonment of the one-crop routine, a lessened emphasis on tobacco, deep plowing, the cultivation of grasses and grains, an increase of livestock, and a greater use of manure. However, the influence of such reformers was slight, for the great majority of farmers clung to old methods. Not until 1810 did the first farm journal of the South, the *Agricultural Museum* of Georgetown, make its appearance. In its first issue its editor, the Reverend David Wiley, deplored that most farmers remained wedded to old practices and that new improvements were "circumscribed within narrow

[25] *Ibid.*, p. 393; Eaton, *The Old South*, pp. 229–230.
[26] Joseph Clarke Robert, *The Tobacco Kingdom* (Durham, N. C.: Duke University Press, 1938), p. 120; Gray, *History of Agriculture in the Southern United States*, II, 679, 682, 683, 765, 1026, 1027, 1035.

limits." [27] Between 1795 and 1820 observers of the Tobacco Coast spoke of agriculture as "in the lowest state of degradation," of "poor and ill favored cattle," of farms that were so "worn out, washed and gullied that scarcely an acre could be found . . . fit for cultivation," of "butchered" land, "poor and barren," "drained by long growth of tobacco," "exhausted, worn-out, rusty, and hung up to . . . bake in the sun," and of "dreary and uncultivated wastes, a barren and exhausted soil, half clothed negroes, lean and hungry stock, a puny race of horses, a scarcity of provender, houses falling to decay, and fences wind shaken and dilapidating." [28]

Tobacco maintained itself largely by the old practice of abandoning worn-out fields in favor of newly cleared land. The industry therefore took part in the westward movement. Its principal domain between 1790 and 1815 was the piedmont of central and southern Virginia and northern North Carolina. There the farmers engaged in a more diversified agriculture than that of the colonial tidewater. The Virginians sent their tobacco down the rivers to Lynchburg, Richmond, and Petersburg, receiving points for shipments en route to Norfolk, the main entrepôt of the export trade. In 1805, Lynchburg had six warehouses for tobacco, much of which was rolled thither in hogsheads. Beyond the mountains, tobacco took root in two centers in Kentucky. One was located along the Ohio River in Breckinridge and Hardin counties, southwest of Louisville. The other, in the southwest, extended from Hopkinsville southward to Clarksville, a center of tobacco growing in Tennessee. That state produced 10,000 hogsheads in 1816. Louisville, the main gathering point for the tobacco of north-central Kentucky preparatory to shipment to New Orleans, received 2,400 hogsheads in 1801. Its shipments rose from 6,210 hogsheads in 1814 to 28,000 hogsheads during the twelve months before September 30, 1817. [29]

During the period 1793–1814 the tobacco industry suffered a severe decline. Exports of leaf tobacco, 1790–1792, averaged 110,000 hogsheads. The comparable average for the fifteen years 1793–1807 was 75,000 hogsheads, with variations ranging from a minimum of 58,000 hogsheads in 1797 to a maximum of 103,000 hogsheads in 1801. After 1807 occurred a contraction that brought exports to their lowest ebb. During the years 1808–1814 they averaged only 31,000 hogsheads. They shrank to 9,500 hogsheads in the embargo year of 1808; they averaged only 7,500 hogsheads during the period 1811–1814; and they fell to 3,125 hogsheads in 1814. Jefferson said in May, 1812: "Tobacco (excepted for favorite quali-

[27] Craven, *Soil Exhaustion*, pp. 81, 85–103, 105, 109.

[28] *Ibid.*, pp. 82–84; William Faux, *Memorable Days in America* . . . (London: W. Simkin and R. Marshall, 1823, p. 99; Vol. XI of *Early Western Travels*, Reuben Gold Thwaites, ed.; Cleveland: The Arthur H. Clark Company, 1904), p. 112.

[29] Robert, *The Tobacco Kingdom*, pp. 55, 57; Gray, *History of Agriculture in the Southern United States*, II, 754–755, 772–773; Craven, *Soil Exhaustion*, 76–78, 80.

ties) is nothing. Its culture is very much abandoned." To add to the distress of the planters, the shrinkage of exports was accompanied by a drop in prices. In the period 1802–1809 export prices had ranged from 7 to 9 cents a pound; during the four years 1810–1813 they averaged only 6 cents a pound.[30]

Soil exhaustion in the tidewater, diversified farming in the piedmont, and interruptions of foreign trade incident to the Napoleonic Wars contributed to the distress of the tobacco industry. In 1792, France imported nearly 30,000 hogsheads of American tobacco; in the period 1800–1816, the maximum of such imports in one year was 16,000 hogsheads, and only a few hundred hogsheads came into France during each of eight of these years. Britain subjected American tobacco to heavy import duties that rose from about 30 cents a pound in 1784, to 1s. 7d. a pound in 1795, and to 3s. 2d. a pound in 1815. The attacks of belligerents on the export trade of the United States stimulated the production of tobacco in Europe, and the expanded industry there did not contract after the war.[31]

With the coming of peace the tobacco planters again prospered for a time, as exports of leaf tobacco rose to 85,000 hogsheads in 1815 and prices went up to 10 cents a pound. During the disastrous decline of tobacco after 1807, slavery proved to be a heavy burden to the planters. Virginia's slave population grew from 287,000 in 1790 to 383,000 in 1810. Some relief came with the growth of the domestic market for tobacco. Americans consumed between 10,000 and 12,000 hogsheads in 1809 and 15,000 hogsheads in 1817. Tench Coxe estimated Virginia's output of snuff and manufactured tobacco in 1810 as 2,726,000 pounds. Not until 1823 did the American tobacco industry attain the strength it had had in 1790. By that time cotton was so far ahead that it yielded the southern planters an income about twice the proceeds from tobacco.[32]

The Louisiana Purchase of 1803 put sugar into the economy of the United States. While yet a French colony, Louisiana had produced some cane sugar for the domestic use of resident planters. Then in 1795 one Étienne Boré, a French soldier, utilizing the labor of thirty slaves, succeeded in producing sugar from cane on a scale that netted a profit of $12,000. Soon afterward émigrés from French Santo Domingo—fugitives from slave insurrections there—arrived in Louisiana. Familiar with the art of cultivating sugar cane, and inspired by Boré's example, they imported slaves from the West Indies and established additional plantations. The first locale of the new industry was the area south of the junction of the Red River with the Mississippi. By 1801–1802, 75 plantations were yielding sugar estimated at 4,000,000 to 8,500,000 pounds. In these early days

[30] Robert, *The Tobacco Kingdom*, pp. 136–137; Gray, *History of Agriculture in the Southern United States*, II, 752, 765, 766, 1035.

[31] *Ibid.*, II, 760, 762.

[32] *Ibid.*, II, 753, 765, 1035.

French planters dominated the enterprise. The Louisiana Purchase, giving them free access to the markets of the Union, stimulated the growth of the industry.[33] In 1817, Estwick Evans described the sugar area that then extended along the Mississippi, 100 miles above and 20 miles below New Orleans:

> The plantations within these limits are superb beyond description . . . . The dwelling houses of the planters are not inferior to any in the United States, either with respect to size, architecture, or the manner in which they are furnished. The gardens and yards contiguous to them are decorated with much taste. The cotton, sugar, and ware houses are very large, and the buildings for the slaves are well finished. The latter buildings are, in some cases, forty or fifty in number, and each of them will accommodate ten or twelve persons . . . . The planters here derive immense profits from the cultivation of their estates. The yearly income from them is from 20,000 to 30,000 dollars.[34]

In starting a sugar plantation the slaves plowed the fields into furrows and planted the cane by laying stalks in the ground. From the joints of the stalks sprang shoots, "rattoons," which matured to the point that the cane could be cut before the first frost of the season. Wielding sharp cane knives, sturdy field hands stripped the plants of leaves, cut off the green tops— which were used as forage or fertilizer—and felled the stalks. Other slaves gathered and bound the stalks and carted them to the cane mill, where they were twice run through a set of rollers that squeezed out most of the juice. The refuse stalks were used as fuel. The juice was then boiled successively in four caldrons in order to remove moisture and impurities. After the last boiling a heavy sirup was poured into a hogshead placed above a vat. Some of the sirup, in the form of molasses, trickled into the vat; most of it remained in the hogshead as brown or muscovado sugar. Water and yeast mixed with molasses and other by-products caused a fermentation preparatory to the distilling of rum. The brown sugar usually went to a city refinery, which converted it into white sugar.[35]

Sugar plantations differed in many respects from the typical cotton farm. In Louisiana, a planting of one bed of cane stalks usually yielded three crops; hence the planting work was less than that for cotton. A sugar planter employed relatively more capital and more field hands and fewer women and children than did a cotton planter. On the whole, the sugar plantation produced less food than did a comparable cotton farm and in

[33] J[oseph] Carlyle Sitterson, *Sugar Country* (Lexington: The University of Kentucky Press, 1953), pp. 9–12, 23–24; Phillips, *American Negro Slavery*, pp. 163–165; Gray, *History of Agriculture in the Southern United States*, II, 739.

[34] Estwick Evans, *A Pedestrious Tour . . . through the Western States and Territories* (Concord, N. H.: Joseph C. Spear, 1819; Vol. VIII of Thwaites, ed., *Early Western Travels*), pp. 325–326.

[35] Phillips, *American Negro Slavery*, pp. 54–57; Gray, *History of Agriculture in the Southern United States*, II, 750.

consequence found it necessary to buy pork, beef, rice, cowpeas, and corn from the outside. American cane sugar never gained the strong competitive position in world trade which was held by southern cotton. The sugar area was limited to the rich lands of the lower Mississippi. Only the extreme fertility of the soil made the industry profitable. Even then the American planters soon sought tariff protection from Congress to enable them to compete with West Indian plantations, which had the benefit of a climate without frosts, a long growing season, and a soil that produced twelve crops from one planting and yielded cane of a saccharine content higher than that of the Louisiana product. In the delta area the plantations lay close to swamp, bog, and bayou; and the danger of flooding entailed the expense of building levees which were liable to breaks that let in the far-spreading waters of the Mississippi. Unhealthful sites, excessive moisture, swarms of mosquitoes, and loneliness incident to life on spots isolated by sloughs, freshets, lagoons, and forests contrasted with the generally pleasant scenes of cotton farms.[36]

In addition to raising the sugar crop, the slaves cleared land; chopped and hauled cordwood; sawed lumber; repaired buildings; made bricks, staves, hoops, and hogsheads; mended levees; dug ditches; worked on roads; mowed hay; cared for the livestock; and planted and harvested sweet potatoes, peas, pumpkins, and corn. The plowman used mules, the planter preferring them to the ox because they were faster and stronger. The most critical time was the harvest. All hands then worked at top speed, for the cane had to be cut and milled or covered before the frosts either damaged or ruined it.[37]

In 1805, Thomas Spalding of Sapelo produced sugar on his plantation in Georgia. Other planters followed his example and, by 1828, 200 plantations near the coast of Georgia and South Carolina were yielding sirup crops for domestic use, supplementary to sea-island cotton. Louisiana continued to dominate the industry, accounting for about 95 percent of the nation's total output.[38]

Slavery needed a salable crop to enable the planter to purchase workers and to obtain a cash return on his investment. Such a product was hemp. It derived its commercial importance largely from cotton, for most of it that was produced in the states before 1815 went into the manufacture of cotton bagging and cotton-bale rope. In colonial times, farmers in the South and in Pennsylvania, particularly in frontier districts, had raised considerable quantities of hemp, using it to make coarse cloth. However,

---

[36] Eaton, *The Old South*, pp. 185, 242–244, 246; Gray, *History of Agriculture in the Southern United States*, II, 743, 744, 747.

[37] Phillips, *American Negro Slavery*, pp. 242–243; Gray, *History of Agriculture in the Southern United States*, II, 749.

[38] E[llis] Merton Coulter, *Thomas Spalding of Sapelo* (University: Louisiana State University Press, 1940), pp. 111–116.

it did not become an export staple, largely because it could not be produced as cheaply as Russian hemp of superior quality. Exports from Maryland, Virginia, and North Carolina in 1768 amounted to only 406 tons. After 1790, pioneers from the South and from Pennsylvania raised hemp in Kentucky, under the dual impetus of the fertile soil of the Bluegrass country and the growing demand for cotton bagging and rope.[39]

Well suited to slave labor, hemp could be grown readily on virgin soil. Slaves plowed the ground and sowed the seeds broadcast by hand. During a growing season of four months the stalks rose to heights of eight, ten, or more feet and grew to the thickness of a lead pencil. In the early days the slaves harvested the crop by pulling the stalks by hand—hard work that only the strongest men could do. Later, the planters utilized an especially designed hemp hook or knife. On the average a slave harvested from a quarter to a third of an acre a day. The next task was to separate the fibers from the woody substance inside. Kentucky planters used the "dew" method of rotting. The stalks were left on the ground three or four weeks, exposed to dew and rain. Then wielding a hinged hand tool, the slaves "broke" the fibers from the rotted inner substance. Ordinarily a man broke from 75 to 100 pounds a day, but under the spur of special rewards the best worker could break 300 pounds. The fibers were sold to manufacturers of rope, bagging, and sailcloth. In 1800, Kentucky had four ropewalks, long covered buildings in which rope was manufactured; and thirty-eight in 1810. Henry Clay, the political mentor of Lincoln, reflected the social importance of hemp. In 1799 he married the daughter of Thomas Hart, a wealthy hemp manufacturer, and soon afterward acquired Ashland, a 600-acre plantation near Lexington.[40]

Farmers in the uplands of South Carolina and Georgia made rather fruitless efforts to produce salable hemp, but Virginians succeeded to the point that in 1817 it was one of their staple exports to the North. The principal scenes of hemp production in Kentucky before 1815 were the southern border of the Bluegrass district in and near Garrard County, and farms in the vicinity of Maysville and Louisville. Most of Kentucky's hemp was manufactured within the state. In 1801, Louisville shipped out only 2,587 pounds of the raw material. On the average, one acre yielded 600 pounds, and one field hand could cultivate three acres a year. If the planter received 5 cents a pound—about $90 per slave—he could produce at a profit. Like tobacco, hemp did not require large-scale operations; hence the great plantation with its host of slaves did not develop in Kentucky. The tasks of raising hemp and Indian corn dovetailed rather nicely. After

[39] Eaton, The Old South, p. 436; Gray, History of Agriculture in the Southern United States, I, 25, 46, 104, 123, 181, 182, 339.

[40] Eaton, The Old South, p. 234, 306, 436; Gray, History of Agriculture in the Southern United States, I, 552; II, 821–822.

1800, visitors in the Bluegrass district noted the unusual neatness and prosperity of the plantations there.[41]

TRADE AND TRAFFIC

The property feature of slavery required that the owner should have the legal right to sell slaves at will. They were often disposed of at auction in settling estates. Owners sometimes found it imperative to part with surplus hands or to sell those who were particularly refractory. Law and public opinion in the slave states always sanctioned local sales, from neighbor to neighbor. The privilege of taking slaves from a state to slave territory was also essential to the system. Travelers desired to be accompanied by their personal servants; emigrants needed their laborers to work on new plantations; persons who inherited nonresident slaves often wished to import them. Frequent neighborhood sales and the widespread and indispensable practice of moving slaves from state to state, when a sale was not involved, made it impossible to prevent an owner from taking them outside a state with the intention of selling them as articles of traffic.[42]

Between 1783 and 1795 the aversion to slavery in the North and the distress of the tobacco planters tended to restrict the domestic slave trade to importations into South Carolina and Georgia. U. B. Phillips found only one specific evidence of interstate traffic at that time—a sale made in New London, Connecticut, and registered in Savannah, Georgia. The sudden rise of cotton seems to have invigorated the domestic traffic. In 1795, a ship brought three slaves into Norfolk from Boston, and at Knoxville a dealer reported that he intended to engage extensively in the business. Two years later, a traveler in South Carolina met a company of about one hundred slaves who were bound for Charleston, apparently for sale. Late in the 1790's a Georgian engaged an agent to buy slaves in Virginia. A would-be purchaser at Charleston offered in 1800 to buy two Negroes "whose characters will not be required," and in 1802 a South Carolinian went to Virginia to obtain hands for a plantation in Georgia. At that time citizens of Alexandria deplored "the practice of persons coming from distant parts of the United States into this district for the purpose of purchasing slaves." Somewhat cryptically a Virginian wrote, also in 1802: "With respect to the negro business we perfectly concur, 'tis cruel and dangerous, and I am fearful subject to many accidents." Early in the century many slaves were sent south from New Jersey and New York. At Natchez a newcomer advertised

[41] Phillips, *American Negro Slavery*, pp. 155, 169; Gray, *History of Agriculture in the Southern United States*, II, 612, 830, 870; Phillips, *Life and Labor in the Old South*, pp. 80–81.

[42] John R. Commons and others, *A Documentary History of American Industrial Society* (11 vols.; Cleveland: The Arthur H. Clark Company, 1910–1911), II, 50–52; Phillips, *American Negro Slavery*, pp. 190–192.

in 1810: "I have upwards of twenty likely Virginia born slaves now in a flat bottomed boat lying in the river . . . , for sale cheaper than has been sold here in years. Part of said negroes I wish to barter for a small farm. My boat may be known by a large cane standing on deck." Slaves transported in ships for interstate sale may have numbered about 2,200 in 1815. A news item published at New Orleans in 1818 reported that a seizure by pirates of 72 slaves from Chesapeake Bay had cost two insurance firms the sum of $40,000, and another item noted that "Jersey negroes appear to be peculiarly adapted to this market . . . . We have the right to calculate on large importations in future, from the success which hitherto attended the sale." [43]

The domestic slave trade revived at a time when most Americans, finding slavery to be unprofitable, subjected it to severe criticism and favored its abolition. Repugnance to the mercenary aspects of slavery impelled southern legislatures to enact a series of laws that aimed to outlaw the business of trafficking in slaves. Between 1778 and 1815, Virginia, Maryland, North Carolina, South Carolina, Georgia, Kentucky, and Tennessee adopted statutes that had the common aim of prohibiting the importation of slaves for the purpose of selling them as merchandise. In nearly all instances, such statutes permitted immigrants who intended to settle in a state to import their slaves. In most cases, travelers sojourning in or passing through a state were allowed to bring in slaves, and legatees were authorized to import nonresident slaves they had inherited.[44]

Legislation proved to be futile as a means of preventing the interstate traffic. In every southern state, slave traders always had the legal right to enter, travel within, and leave the state, and its residents had the legal right to buy and sell slaves. To a large extent the success of the effort to prevent an interstate traffic hinged upon proof of the trader's intent. Thus a Virginia act of 1778 specified the following oath: "I, A. B., do swear that my removal to the State of Virginia was with no intention to evade the act for preventing the further importations of slaves within this commonwealth . . . ." A slave trader might declare, when arriving with slaves, that he intended to use them in his own service and then declare, soon afterward, that circumstances had forced him to change his mind and to sell them. Men who engaged in the traffic were not too squeamish to make such declarations. In addition, most of the laws imposed either slight penalties for violations or none at all. U. B. Phillips attributes the failure of such laws in part to the "passiveness of the public." [45]

[43] Phillips, *American Negro Slavery*, pp. 187–190, 193, 195, 197; Gray, *History of Agriculture in the Southern United States*, II, 592, 658; Phillips, *Life and Labor in the Old South*, p. 159.

[44] Collins, *The Domestic Slave Trade*, pp. 109–124, 133–136; Gray, *History of Agriculture in the Southern United States*, II, 659–660; Phillips, *American Negro Slavery*, pp. 202–203.

[45] Collins, *The Domestic Slave Trade*, pp. 109, 131, 133, 135.

In most states the laws aimed at the domestic slave trade were not repealed or seriously relaxed until after 1815, and it is probable that they helped to determine the nature of the traffic as it was carried on before that year, when it was conducted largely on an individual basis, in a loosely organized fashion, and somewhat in the dark. It appears that the repeal or the watering down of laws against the interstate trade after 1818 soon transformed it into an organized business, characterized by recognized firms which employed agents, maintained branch offices, and owned visible facilities for housing and transporting slaves in large groups. But the stigma that clung to the traffic, together with surviving legal restraints, gave to the professional dealer a social status somewhat akin to that of a bootlegger under Prohibition.[46]

The southern planter produced export staples in order to purchase capital goods and consumer goods that were conducive to a rising standard of living. The principal sources of such goods were Europe, Britain, and the eastern seacoast of the United States. The variety of products sent to the planting districts is indicated by exports from Baltimore to New Orleans in 1801. Consumer articles included dry goods, clothing, soap, candles, wine, brandy, gin, raisins, crackers, frying pans, glassware, and tableware. Among producers' goods were bricks, oil, paint, steel, lead, iron, bagging, rope, casks, hoops, spades, hardware, and anchors.[47]

The general trade in southern staples is best illustrated by cotton. To a large extent that traffic was governed by sales to England. Exports of southern cotton to England rose from nearly 500,000 pounds in 1793 to 15,680,000 pounds in 1800, and to perhaps 48,000,000 pounds in 1807. In the embargo year 1808, three fourths of southern cotton exports found their way to England. Between 1805 and 1811 England obtained about 53 percent of its cotton imports from the United States.[48]

On the whole, British imports of American cotton were paid for with British exports. In 1807, exports of English cotton goods to the United States had an estimated value of $11 million. Such sales placed funds in the hands of British exporters which they used to buy cotton and other American products. British merchants also extended credit to American correspondents, enabling them to obtain English goods in advance of sales. Thus the House of Baring, about 1800, granted credits of £40,000 and £10,000, respectively, to two Baltimore firms. Occasionally an English

[46] T. D. Clark, "The Slave Trade between Kentucky and the Cotton Kingdom," *Mississippi Valley Historical Review,* XXI, No. 3 (December, 1934), 332; Du Bois, *Suppression of the African Slave-Trade,* p. 154; Phillips, *American Negro Slavery,* pp. 189, 192; Collins, *The Domestic Slave Trade,* pp. 112, 115, 118, 119, 127, 129.

[47] Lewis E. Atherton, "John McDonogh—New Orleans Mercantile Capitalist," *Journal of Southern History,* VII, No. 4 (November, 1941), 459, 468.

[48] Norman Sydney Buck, *The Development of the Organisation of Anglo-American Trade, 1800–1850* (New Haven, Conn.: Yale University Press, 1925), p. 36 note; Hammond, *The Cotton Industry,* pp. 237–240.

spinner bought cotton directly through American agents whom he engaged for that purpose. However, it appears that the cotton trade was carried on mainly by American merchants of New York, Philadelphia, Baltimore, Charleston, Savannah, and New Orleans, who bought cotton from planters and sold it to English spinners through the agency of a Liverpool dealer or broker who received a commission, commonly of 2½ percent on such sales. The broker also bought goods in England and sent them to his correspondents in the United States.[49]

American merchants of the eastern cities usually consigned manufactured and imported goods to their agents or correspondents at interior points where cotton was assembled: the towns of Cheraw, Camden, Columbia, and Augusta in the up country of South Carolina and Georgia; Nashville, Natchez, New Orleans, and Mobile in the Southwest. The correspondent or factor sold the goods to other traders or directly to planters and invested the proceeds in cotton for exportation, either to an eastern city or directly to Europe. In this commission business, the products exchanged were the property of the eastern merchant and he assumed the risks and paid the transportation, insurance, and storage costs. The inland agent received a commission on both the goods he sold and the cotton he purchased. Such commissions often enabled an agent to acquire a trading capital and to go into business on his own account. When trade was dull, agents sold goods at auction, the auctioneer receiving—in one instance—2½ percent of the proceeds of the sale.[50]

At the interior towns independent traders or agents of eastern merchants sold to and bought from the large planters of the vicinity. In the expanding cotton industry both merchants and planters employed all their capital and stretched their credit to the limit. Because the planter's assets went largely into the purchase of land and slaves he commonly bought imported goods on credit, arranging to pay for them from his next crop. In the Southwest the large planters usually consigned their cotton to a merchant or factor at New Orleans. He sold the cotton for them and used the proceeds to buy goods which they ordered. In such transactions the planter owned the products, bore the risk of shipping the cotton by flatboat

[49] G. W. Daniels, "American Cotton Trade with Liverpool under the Embargo and Non-Intercourse Acts," *American Historical Review*, XXI, No. 2 (January, 1916), 276–277; Leland Hamilton Jenks, *The Migration of British Capital to 1875* (New York: Alfred A. Knopf, Inc., 1927), p. 67; Buck, *Anglo-American Trade*, pp. 6–8, 67, 85–86; Hammond, *The Cotton Industry*, p. 241; Ralph W. Hidy, *The House of Baring in American Trade and Finance: English Merchant Bankers at Work, 1763–1861* (Cambridge, Mass.: Harvard University Press, 1949), pp. 29–30, 33; Hedges, *The Browns of Providence*, pp. 298, 300, 304.

[50] "Despatches from the United States Consulate in New Orleans, 1801–1803," *American Historical Review*, XXXII, No. 4 (July, 1927), 810, 814; Atherton, "John McDonogh," pp. 455, 456–461, 465, 468; Buck, *Anglo-American Trade*, p. 69; Gray, *History of Agriculture in the Southern United States*, II, 870; Hammond, *The Cotton Industry*, pp. 114–115; Phillips, *Life and Labor in the Old South*, p. 142.

to New Orleans, and paid the costs of insurance, commission, and storage that were incurred before, or in the course of, a sale. In 1810 it cost a Tennessee planter from 3 to 5 percent of the proceeds received at New Orleans from the sale of his cotton to buy drafts for remitting money to the East, where he then commonly bought manufactured goods.[51]

Small farmers in the Southwest usually sold their cotton to local traders, and at a price much lower than that at New Orleans. In 1810, farmers in the Nashville area received only 8 cents a pound for cotton when it was selling at 14 to 15 cents in New Orleans. Agents of eastern merchants bought the cotton which local buyers obtained from the small farmers. Local buyers also imported merchandise from the East and supplied the small farmers. During the years of the cotton boom before 1808, the exceptional demand for cotton, competition among local buyers, and the urgent needs of farmers for manufactured goods caused traders, in order to obtain cotton in the future, to sell goods on credits secured by the next crop.[52]

Before 1811, planters in the Southwest, remote from New Orleans, obtained imported goods from Baltimore and Philadelphia that reached the West by a wagon route to the Ohio and thence by river boats to Nashville and interior points. Cotton en route to market was carried by wagon to a river port and then sent downstream to New Orleans. In the up country of Georgia and South Carolina many of the rivers—such as the Catawba, the Ocmulgee, and the Oconee—were not navigable far above the falls. However, in South Carolina, a flat-bottomed boat could carry 50 bales of cotton 84 miles down the Saluda River to Columbia, and the Broad River was navigable 28 miles above that town. The farmer who did not live on a navigable stream sent his cotton to a river town. A wagon so employed in 1805, drawn by six horses, carried 5 or 6 bales.[53]

During the years of the embargo and the War of 1812 the cotton planters fared better than the tobacco grower, for their domestic market expanded to a greater extent than did his. The falling off of imports from England in 1808 and in 1812–1814 stimulated the production of cotton goods in the states. In 1805, American cotton mills operated 4,500 spindles and used 333,000 pounds of cotton; in 1815, 213 or more mills had 130,000 spindles, 119,300 of them in New England. The total consumption of raw

[51] Alfred Holt Stone, "The Cotton Factorage System in the Southern States," *American Historical Review*, XX, No. 3 (April, 1915), 560–561; Buck, *Anglo-American Trade*, pp. 67–68; Atherton, "John McDonogh," p. 464 note; Gray, *History of Agriculture in the Southern United States*, II, 870; Phillips, *Life and Labor in the Old South*, p. 142; Phillips, *American Negro Slavery*, p. 340.

[52] Gray, *History of Agriculture in the Southern United States*, II, 870; Abernethy, *From Frontier to Plantation in Tennessee*, p. 201; Moore, *Agriculture in Ante-Bellum Mississippi*, pp. 54–56; Atherton, "John McDonogh," p. 459.

[53] Gray, *History of Agriculture in the Southern United States*, II, 683–685, 870; Abernethy, *From Frontier to Plantation in Tennessee*, p. 200.

cotton by American producers, in both mills and household manufactures, rose from 8,000,000 pounds in 1800 to 31,500,000 in 1815. This growth enabled the cotton planters to escape the catastrophic losses which the tobacco industry suffered during the War of 1812. The domestic cotton trade resembled the export trade, as American spinners joined English manufacturers as buyers from merchants of the eastern cities.[54]

The rise of cotton, supplemented by the introduction of sugar into the American economy, affected the country in many ways. Immediately before 1792 slavery in the South was profitable only in the rice industry, and its scope there was extremely limited. If cotton had not spread over the lower South it is probable that slavery in the United States would have expired quickly or have declined to the point that its eventual abolition might have been effected without a disastrous national upheaval. Sugar added only slightly to the strength of slavery; the impetus it gave was largely offset by the demise of indigo. Cotton invigorated the domestic slave trade and revitalized slavery in the upper South by enabling tobacco planters to profit by selling unneeded hands. At the same time the plantations of the lower Mississippi created a demand for such products of western farms as corn, flour, pork, and beef. The western farmers thus obtained purchasing power in the Southwest which they used to buy manufactured goods in the East. Hence the domain of cotton stimulated the growth of settlement in the West. Purchases of finished goods by planters in the South and the West expanded internal trade and fostered domestic manufacturing, while southern cotton nourished the pioneer promoters of the factory system in New England. The benefit to the cotton grower of an expanding domestic market when trade with Europe faltered after 1807 —in contrast with the acute losses then suffered by tobacco planters, who were rigidly bound to foreign markets—provided a potent argument for a protective tariff designed to foster national self-sufficiency and to lessen the country's dependence on foreign trade.[55]

[54] Hammond, *The Cotton Industry*, pp. 238–239, 241–242; Taussig, *Tariff History of the United States*, p. 28 note.

[55] Hammond, *The Cotton Industry*, pp. 41, 42, 54; Atherton, "John McDonogh," p. 465; Moore, *Agriculture in Ante-Bellum Mississippi*, pp. 56–57; Louis Martin Sears, "Philadelphia and the Embargo: 1808" (American Historical Association, *Annual Report . . . 1920*; Washington: Government Printing Office, 1925), pp. 258–259; Taussig, *Tariff History of the United States*, pp. 28–29.

CHAPTER X

Reaching Outward

TO DISTANT LANDS

AMERICANS, when British colonists, had not been permitted to trade eastward of the Cape of Good Hope, nor could they import the products of Asia and the East Indies except from Britain. The Revolution swept away such restraints and opened the sea lanes to China. There existed in the United States a market for tea, silks, spices, and chinaware. If Americans could reach Asia they might carry its products to many lands. Although the Union had few native commodities that the Chinese wanted, they esteemed an American forest plant, ginseng, as an invigorating medicine. After the war, a spirit of daring, fostered by privateering and other maritime exploits, animated many merchants who owned swift vessels that needed new seas to conquer. The thoughts of such adventurers turned to the once-forbidden markets of China and India.

Near the end of the war a young New Englander, John Ledyard—a Connecticut Marco Polo—returned from Asia, where he had taken part in the last Pacific expedition of Captain James Cook. In China, Ledyard had seen pelts sold for $100 apiece that had been bought for 6d. on the Pacific Coast of North America. With a crusader's zeal he urged American merchants to engage in such a fabulous business. For some time Robert Morris had been interested in opening a trade with China. In 1783 he helped to plan a voyage thither, with the intent of reaching Asia by the route around the Cape of Good Hope rather than by way of the American west coast. He and his partners fitted out the *Empress of China*, of 360 tons, which sailed from New York on February 22, 1784, laden with 40 tons of ginseng and other goods. The vessel went to Canton, stayed there four months, and returned to New York on May 11, 1785 with a cargo of teas, silks, nankeens, chinaware, and cassia, which netted a profit of $37,000 on an outlay of $120,000.[1] Private merchants had done this alone, except that Congress had

[1] Tyler Dennett, *Americans in Eastern Asia* (New York: Barnes & Noble, Inc., 1941), pp. 4–7; Foster Rhea Dulles, *The Old China Trade* (Boston: Houghton Mifflin Company, 1930), pp. 4–12.

furnished their captain with a letter of introduction to the "Most Serene, Serene, Most Puissant, Puissant, High, Illustrious, Noble, Honorable, Venerable, Wise, and Prudent Emperors, Kings, Republics, Princes, Dukes, Earls, Barons, Lords, Burgomasters, Councillors, as also Judges, Officers, Justiciars, and Regents of all the Good Cities and Places, whether Ecclesiastical or Secular, who shall see these Patents or hear them read." [2]

The second ship from China, the *Pallas*, which had been chartered at Canton, came into New York soon after the arrival of the *Empress of China*. Robert Morris took its $50,000 cargo of tea. These successful ventures excited the interest of other merchants and moved Congress to send a consul to Canton. The promoters justified the voyages as a means of stopping the drain of specie from the states in payment for Asian goods previously imported from Britain. France encouraged the Americans by permitting them to use its islands in the Indian Ocean, especially Île de France (Mauritius), as ports of call. Among the vessels in the trade in the 1780's were the *Experiment* of New York, the *Astrea* and the *Grand Turk* of Salem, the *Alliance* of Philadelphia, and the *Chesapeake* of Baltimore.[3] The United States soon needed exports other than ginseng, a wild forest plant that did not respond to man's efforts to cultivate it.[4] Commonly, the outbound vessels carried meat, fish, tobacco, naval stores and similar American products to European ports and exchanged them there for European goods, Spanish coin, and other things suitable for Asian markets. In India, the Americans called at Calcutta and Bombay, where they received friendly treatment from British traders. On return voyages the captains sold Asian products at the ports they visited, purchased whatever was salable in Europe or American markets, and brought home a variety of goods, many of which were re-exported. Thus the vessels were something like traveling department stores. In the 1780's the trade had significance as a symbol of enterprise and as a source of large profit to a few merchants. As yet it contributed but slightly to American commerce as a whole. Jefferson did not mention it in an official report of 1793 on American commerce. In 1809, it took about 2 percent of the exports of the United States. The trade remained entirely an enterprise of individuals; the government merely endorsed and reinforced their activities and policies.[5]

The demand in China for furs and the dearth of exports thither from the Atlantic seaboard caused American merchants to seek furs in the Pacific Northwest. Foremost among such pioneers were several Bostonians

---

[2] *Journals of the Continental Congress*, XXVI, 58–59.

[3] Dennett, *Americans in Eastern Asia*, pp. 8, 9, 26; East, *Business Enterprise*, pp. 254–256.

[4] Hedrick, *New York Agriculture*, p. 136.

[5] Dennett, *Americans in Eastern Asia*, pp. 18–19, 26–27; East, *Business Enterprise*, p. 254; *American State Papers* (Wait), I, 425.

who in 1787 initiated a joint-stock venture that attracted $49,000 to finance the westward voyages of two vessels, the *Columbia* and the *Lady Washington*. They left Boston in September, rounded Cape Horn, and reached Nootka Sound in August, 1788, carrying an assortment of iron tools, beads, buttons, jew's-harps, earrings, snuffboxes, and other interesting articles. After obtaining a cargo of otter skins, Captain Robert Gray took them in the *Columbia* to Canton, where he exchanged them for tea. He came home via the Cape of Good Hope, thereby distinguishing himself as the first American captain to circumnavigate the globe.[6]

In 1792, while on his second voyage, Captain Gray discovered the Columbia River, which he named for his ship, the first vessel to anchor in that stream. Other Boston merchants sent four vessels to the Pacific Northwest in 1790. In this wise, Bostonians pre-empted a lucrative trade, glamorous but relatively of minor importance. In 1801 fifteen American ships put in at Canton with 18,000 skins valued at more than $500,000. Washington Irving has described the ways of the American traders:

They generally remained on the coast and about the adjacent seas, for two years, carrying on as wandering and adventurous a commerce on the water as did the traders and trappers on land. Their trade extended along the whole coast from California to the high northern latitudes. They would run in near shore, anchor, and wait for the natives to come off in their canoes with peltries. The trade exhausted at one place, they would up anchor and off to another. In this way they would consume the summer, and when autumn came on, would run down to the Sandwich Islands and winter in some friendly and plentiful harbor. In the following year they would resume their summer trade, commencing at California and proceeding north: and, having in the course of two seasons collected a sufficient cargo of peltries, would make the best of their way to China. Here they would sell their furs, take in teas, nankeens, and other merchandise, and return to Boston, after an absence of two or three years.[7]

A gentle and inoffensive animal, the sea otter, linked Americans, Indians, Russians, Spaniards, and Chinese together in a prolonged search for riches. Valued for their long, thick, soft fur, brown or black with a silvery tinge, sea otters before 1775 abounded in the waters off the Pacific Coast, from the Alaskan Peninsula to Lower California. The pelts varied from 70 to 90 inches in length and from 30 to 36 inches in width. Chinese nobles eagerly sought the fur for robes, capes, caps, belts, and trimmings of gowns. The Indians who hunted the animals used light, narrow, sharply pointed, skin-covered canoes or kayaks in which two or three hunters were encased as in a water-tight compartment. The hunter hurled a bone-tipped

[6] Dulles, *The Old China Trade*, pp. 50, 52–55.
[7] Washington Irving, *Astoria* (Philadelphia: J. B. Lippincott and Company, 1871), pp. 24–25.

dart or arrow from a small wooden holder. When the sea otter scented danger it fled by diving; hence the Indians hunted in parties made up of several kayaks so that they could surround the prey and spear it when it came up for air. Only the Indians living along the northern coasts became skilled hunters. Because of its warm climate the natives of California did not need furs; consequently they did not build kayaks or master the hunter's art.[8]

About 1750 Russian pioneers, advancing from Siberia via the Aleutian Islands, first obtained sea otter furs from native hunters. In 1783 the Russians established a permanent post on Kodiak Island, south of the Alaskan Peninsula, and in 1799 they founded Sitka. At the start they sent furs to China by way of Siberia. Southward, the Spaniards in California obtained a few otter pelts from resident Indians unskilled in the hunt. Ships from New England entered the trade in the late 1780's, concentrating on the northwest coast. There they so stimulated the hunters that soon the area was depleted of the coveted furs. By 1797 Yankee ships were trading along the California coast. The lack of an American base in the Northwest, the dependence of visiting traders on Indian hunters, and the close ties between the Russians and the natives induced Yankee sea captains to join with the Russians in a "contract system" which functioned between 1803 and 1811. At Kodiak Island an American ship supplied the Russians with products which they used to employ 50 to 150 Indian hunters (Aleuts) who, with their kayaks, were put on the ship. It then sailed to the coastal waters off California, where the hunters secured as many as a thousand pelts. Thereupon the ship went back to Kodiak Island, discharged the hunters, took the furs to China, and returned to its home port. The Russians and the Americans each got half of the furs. At Kodiak Island the Russian governor, Alexander Baranov, an ambitious expansionist, endorsed and participated in the enterprise. About 1810, however, the Russians, intent upon operating independently off the California coast, withdrew from the partnership. Unable to obtain native hunters, American ships were then obliged to act as carriers for the Russians, transporting their furs to China. Such was the state of the sea otter trade in 1815.[9]

A companion industry—an American seal fishery—came into being soon after the Revolution. The Boston ship *States* then voyaged to the Falkland Islands to obtain seal skins, which found their way to Canton,

[8] Adele Ogden, *The California Sea Otter Trade, 1784–1848* (University of California *Publications in History*, Vol. XXVI; Berkeley and Los Angeles: University of California Press, 1941), pp. 3–6, 11–14; George Brown Goode and others, *The Fisheries and Fishery Industries of the United States* (7 vols.; Washington: Government Printing Office, 1884–1887), Sec. 5, Vol. II, p. 490.

[9] Ogden, *The Sea Otter Trade*, pp. 1, 3, 32–41, 45–47, 53, 57–60, 65; Goode, *The Fisheries of the United States*, Sec. 5, Vol. II, pp. 321, 485; Oscar Osborn Winther, *The Old Oregon Country* (Stanford, Calif.: Stanford University Press, 1950), pp. 20–23.

where they sold for a dollar or two dollars apiece. Because as many as 100,000 skins could be procured by one vessel, simply by clubbing the defenseless creatures, the trade gave rise to many voyages that carried Yankee sealers far and wide. The industry centered in the Juan Fernández Islands off the coast of Chile and extended northward to other islands—Santa Catalina and the Farallons—off California. Some vessels hunted in the Indian Ocean. The seal fishery mothered the first traffic of the United States with the western coast of South America, as sealers smuggled merchandise into Concepción, Valparaíso, and Coquimbo in Chile and Callao and Pisco in Peru. Such trade, never more than a trifle, manifested the eagerness of Yankee sailors to ransack the globe and to barter goods wherever they could find an opening.[10]

THE INLAND FUR TRADE

Commercial ties with China stimulated the fur trade within the United States, as well as on the Pacific Coast. After 1775, American trappers, frontiersmen, and traders sought skins and furs throughout vast areas of the country—north, south, and west—in territory occupied by the Indians and in lands in the pioneer stage of settlement. Before 1803, when the United States had only a few professional fur traders, the traffic was conducted in a somewhat haphazard manner. Pioneer hunters and farmers, along with the Indians, took peltries to outlying trading posts for shipment to the eastern ports, there to be used by domestic furriers and hatmakers or to be exported to Europe. Most coveted was the beautiful fur of the innocent beaver. The otter, the muskrat, the raccoon, the fox, the mink, and the marten also yielded valuable pelts, while the hides of deer, bear, and buffalo were useful mainly as skins. In return, the Indians and the pioneers received many things: gunpowder, shot, lead, and flints; kettles and pans; rum and tobacco; buttons, rings, beads, buckles, looking glasses, and bracelets; axes, awls, beaver traps, files, bridles, spurs, horseshoes, nails, and wire; blankets, calicoes, cottons, flannel, thread, ribbons, and handkerchiefs.[11]

The Revolutionary War and its aftermath sharply curtailed the activities of citizens of the United States as fur traders. During the war the northern Indians were hostile toward the pioneers. Raids and reprisals on the frontier all but ended trade with the tribes. For many years after 1783 the people of the Union busied themselves with politics, land speculation, and the building of new settlements, to the neglect of the fur trade. For about twenty years after 1775 foreign traders dominated the traffic with

[10] Morison, *Maritime History of Massachusetts,* pp. 61–62; Goode, *The Fisheries of the United States,* Sec. 5, II, 365–366, 401–402.
[11] Hiram Martin Chittenden, *The American Fur Trade of the Far West* (2 vols.; Stanford, Calif.: Academic Reprints, 1954), I, 4–5 note.

the Indians who occupied the most sparsely peopled parts of the Union and the lands adjacent to its borders. The Spaniards, with headquarters at Pensacola and New Orleans, acted aggressively in the lower South, east of the Mississippi. St. Louis was the entrepôt from which French traders ruled the fur trade of the lower Missouri River Valley. Northward, the British, firmly entrenched at Montreal virtually monopolized the Indian trade of the Great Lakes country, from New York to present-day Minnesota. The United States, before 1803, did not control either of the two great rivers—the St. Lawrence and the Mississippi—that determined the course of the fur trade. The presence of foreign traders on the inland frontiers of the Union largely shaped its diplomacy and Indian policy between 1783 and 1815.[12]

In their conflict with the United States the Spaniards in the Floridas and Louisiana turned to the Indians of the Southwest for aid. Those provinces in 1783 did not contain more than 25,000 inhabitants of European stocks, whereas the pioneers of Tennessee, Kentucky, and Georgia numbered 120,000. The Spaniards therefore sought reinforcements from the four Indian tribes of the Southwest—the Creeks, the Cherokees, the Chickasaws, and the Choctaws. Together they had 14,000 warriors. The success of Spain in wooing them depended largely on its ability to supply them with goods, including firearms, in exchange for furs. The Indian chief who best served the Spaniards was Alexander McGillivray, whose mother was a Creek Indian and whose father was a loyalist émigré from Georgia. Strongly hostile to the United States and resentful of the encroachments of Georgians on the lands of the Indians between the Oconee and Savannah rivers, McGillivray in 1784 helped to form an alliance among the Spaniards, the Creeks, the Chickasaws, and the Choctaws by which the tribes agreed to accept Spain's protection, to ban the fur traders of the United States from their territory, and to trade, on a preferential basis, with a loyalist firm, Panton, Leslie and Company, which had trading posts in East Florida. As the Indians were supplied with firearms in the ensuing trade they became formidable foes of the frontiersmen of Georgia and Tennessee. A series of border wars, beginning in the summer of 1785, and rising to ferocious intensity in 1787–1788, revealed that the neglect of the Indian trade by the United States and the dependence of the tribes upon pro-Spanish traders served to align them with Spain and to make them effective fighters.[13]

Before 1800, present-day Missouri was a hunter's paradise, abounding with game—a land where Indians hunted the buffalo on the prairies or

[12] Harlow Lindley, "Western Travel, 1800–1820," *Mississippi Valley Historical Review*, VI, No. 2 (September, 1919), p. 173; Chittenden, *The Fur Trade of the Far West*, I, 163.

[13] Kinnaird, *Spain in the Mississippi Valley*, III, 31–32, 112–113, 295; Billington, *Westward Expansion*, pp. 227–230, 239–240; John Walton Caughey, *McGillivray of the Creeks* (Norman: University of Oklahoma Press, 1938), pp. 23–24.

along the rivers. Daniel Boone had entered the country as early as 1795. Other Americans followed him, but the growth of settlement was so slow that the district had only 20,000 non-Indian residents in 1810. On the Mississippi, below St. Louis, stood a few towns: New Madrid, Cape Girardeau, and Ste. Genevieve. As late as 1807 a fifty-mile stretch of the western side of the Mississippi south of St. Louis was virtually unoccupied by settlers, though pioneers had built cabins in the Missouri Valley between St. Louis and the mouth of the Osage River.[14]

After the cession of Louisiana by France to Spain in 1763 St. Louis remained predominantly French—a frontier village favorably situated for receiving trading goods from Montreal and New Orleans, for trafficking with the Indians of the lower Missouri and of the central Mississippi valleys, and for shipping furs to New Orleans or to the St. Lawrence. John Jacob Astor estimated that in the Missouri Valley fur trade a trader spent one fourth of his outlay for trading goods and the other three fourths for wages, transportation, and provisions. Foremost among the St. Louis fur merchants were Francis M. Benoit, the Chouteau brothers, Auguste and Pierre, and their brother-in-law, Charles Gratiot—all French—and Manuel Lisa, most eminent among the Spaniards. In the late 1790's the St. Louis traders—in competition with the British of the Northwest—sent trading parties up the Missouri River as far as the Mandan villages, near the site of present-day Bismarck, North Dakota. The fur trade as carried on from St. Louis did not menace the United States because the French and Spaniards there did not seriously encroach upon its territory or incite the Indians against the western settlers.[15]

Quite different was the effect of British fur traders in the Northwest. After the British had acquired Canada and a clear title to the Illinois country in 1763 they valued the Northwest for its fur trade and fashioned an imperial policy that discouraged settlement there. Expansionists of the thirteen colonies, regarding the West as a land to be occupied by pioneers, manifested but a feeble interest in fur trade. The resulting clash of interests, imperial and colonial, was an important cause of the Revolution. After 1783 the prewar objectives of the two antagonists reasserted themselves, with the British intent upon the fur trade and the Americans intent upon settlement. During the Revolution the British had greatly strengthened their grip on the traffic, at the expense not only of the United States but also of the French Canadians. In 1777 the northwestern trade exceeded that of any previous year. It increased again in 1778.[16]

Strongly entrenched throughout the whole Northwest in 1783, British

---

[14] Lindley, "Western Travel," pp. 172, 174–175.

[15] Kenneth Wiggins Porter, *John Jacob Astor* (Vol. I of *Harvard Studies in Business History*, 2 vols.; Cambridge, Mass.: Harvard University Press, 1931), I, 165; Kellogg, *The British Régime in Wisconsin*, pp. 97, 229–230, 242.

[16] Nettels, *George Washington and American Independence*, pp. 72–76; Kellogg, *The British Régime in Wisconsin*, p. 146.

fur traders did not intend to relinquish the prize they had won. They then held seven posts which the Treaty of 1783 placed within the United States —Dutchman's Point and Pointe-au-Fer at the head of Lake Champlain, Oswegatchie on the St. Lawrence, Oswego on Lake Ontario, Niagara on the American side of the Niagara River below the Falls, Detroit, and Michilimackinac. Montreal served as the headquarters of a group of strong British firms which had crowded out most of the small traders or had reduced them to the status of subordinates. Such firms sent agents to inland posts whence trading goods were carried directly to the Indians in their villages and where the furs were brought for reshipment to Montreal. In 1779 eight British firms joined together to form a company to trade with the Indians who inhabited the lands south and west of Lake Superior. Reorganized in 1783, and known as the North West Company, this group made its headquarters at the Grand Portage on the western side of Lake Superior, gained a monopoly of the fur trade of northern Wisconsin and Minnesota, and sent traders across North Dakota to the Missouri River. Other traders, operating from Montreal and sending goods by way of Mackinac and the Fox-Wisconsin rivers to Prairie du Chien, held for the British a tight monopoly of the trade of the land between Lake Michigan and the Mississippi, south of the domain of the North West Company. The Illinois country was not important in the fur trade.[17]

By 1795 the neglect of the fur trade by the United States and its prevailing interest in western settlement had reduced its influence among the Indians to the vanishing point. Both Spain and Britain, wooing the tribes and concentrating on the fur trade, had gained a decisive influence over them, for the Indians allied themselves with the whites from whom they obtained trading goods. Britain and Spain supplied them with firearms and powder, and encouraged them to resist the settlers. The merciless wars of the late 1780's on the southwestern frontier were soon followed by raids and incursions in the Northwest. In the spring of 1793 pioneers in Kentucky, Ohio, and southwestern Pennsylvania had either been attacked or were in imminent danger. Congress and the President concluded that, in order to gain the good will of the tribes, the United States must supply them with trading goods. And because American traders were few and inadequate, the Federalist leaders decided that the federal government must engage directly in the traffic.[18]

[17] W. Stewart Wallace, ed., *Documents Relating to the North West Company* (Toronto: The Champlain Society, 1934), pp. 6, 8, 11; Porter, *John Jacob Astor*, I, 164; Chittenden, *The Fur Trade of the Far West*, I, 93; Kellogg, *The British Régime in Wisconsin*, pp. 197–199, 202, 237–238, 241; Frederick Jackson Turner, "The Character and Influence of the Indian Trade in Wisconsin," in *The Early Writings of Frederick Jackson Turner* (Fulmer Mood, ed.; Madison: The University of Wisconsin Press, 1938), p. 145; Alvord, *The Illinois Country*, p. 279.

[18] Royal B. Way, "The United States Factory System for Trading with the Indians, 1796–1822," *Mississippi Valley Historical Review*, VI, No. 2 (September, 1919), 221–223.

In 1795 and 1796 Congress enacted laws which appropriated $200,000 and authorized the President to use the money for the purchase of goods for the Indian trade and to establish government posts where federal agents would sell the goods to the Indians. The posts which were established before 1816 formed a long line in the North, West, and South, from Sandusky through Mackinac, Prairie du Chien, Fort Osage on the Missouri, Natchitoches in Louisiana, and Fort Stephens in southwestern Alabama to Coleraine in southeastern Georgia. Other posts, at one time or another, existed at Detroit; Green Bay, Wisconsin; Fort Madison, Iowa; Arkansas Post at the mouth of the Arkansas River; Chickasaw Bluffs near Memphis; Tellico and Hiwassee in eastern Tennessee; and Fort Wilkinson and Fort Hawkins in Georgia.[19]

The capital fund which Congress had provided—increased to $300,000 in 1811—was maintained from the sale of the furs received at the posts. Congress also provided each year a few thousand dollars for operating expenses. An act of 1806 created the office of superintendent of Indian trade. The superintendent purchased the trading goods at Philadelphia or Georgetown and sent them to distributing centers at Detroit, St. Louis, and New Orleans, whence they were forwarded to the posts or factories, which were located at United States forts. The law required that the goods purchased must be American-made. They included blankets, guns, powder, lead, axes, knives, kettles, wampum, trinkets, tin cups, cowbells, hoes, frying pans, arm bands, shirts, socks, tinsel, hatbands, jew's-harps, and saddles. The factors sold to chiefs on credit, adding (in 1808) 68 percent to the purchase price of the goods. Articles obtained from the Indians consisted of furs, skins, beeswax, tallow, bear oil, and feathers. Such returns were sent to the distributing centers and then to the superintendent, who sold them at auction to private merchants. In emergencies the posts sold to settlers, soldiers, private traders, and travelers. Between 1805 and 1815 the value of goods sent to the posts ranged from $100,000 in 1806 to $28,000 in 1812, with a yearly average of $51,000. The system never supplied more than a fraction of the goods needed by the Indians. However, its operations were extensive enough to antagonize private traders. Their business expanded after 1808 and their determined opposition killed the experiment in 1822.[20]

John Jacob Astor of New York became the most influential fur merchant of the United States. Born at Waldorf in Germany in 1763, he arrived at New York, via London and Baltimore, in 1784, bringing some musical instruments which he sold. He invested the proceeds in furs and took them to London, where he became familiar with the international fur market. Returning to New York he continued to buy furs brought in by

[19] Edgar B. Wesley, "The Government Factory System among the Indians, 1795–1822," *Journal of Economic and Business History*, IV, No. 3 (May, 1932), 490–492, 494–496.

[20] *Ibid.*, pp. 493–494, 497–501, 504–505, 508.

nearby Indians, settlers, or traders. He then traveled through frontier districts of the state and learned all the arts of buying and shipping furs. Going farther afield, he gained mastery of the Canadian trade, visiting remote posts and making annual buying trips to Montreal. Britain's withdrawal in 1796 from the posts of the United States increased his business in the Northwest. His unresting labors and his shrewd bargaining augmented his wealth to the point that by 1800 his fortune amounted to $250,000. About 1800 he began to export furs to China.[21]

The addition to the Union of the vast territory of the Louisiana Purchase stimulated the interest of many Americans in the fur trade of the trans-Mississippi West, at the very time when the growth of the China trade was increasing the demand for furs. The return and reports of the Lewis and Clark Expedition in 1806 called attention to the abundance of furs between St. Louis and the Pacific Coast. These events inspired Astor to form a grand project designed to break the hold of the British on the interior trade between the Mississippi and Missouri valleys. Before 1808 the United States had to import from Montreal about three fourths of the furs it consumed, often paying more than comparable furs sold for in London. Astor estimated that annual imports by the United States of Canadian furs obtained on the Mississippi and the Missouri amounted to $400,000. Seeking to tap this lucrative trade, he planned to build a chain of posts from St. Louis via the Missouri to the coast. He anticipated that goods could be sent inland over such a route more cheaply than from Montreal and that American traders would benefit by their right to export directly to all countries, whereas Britain restricted the exportation of Canadian furs to Britain or the United States. Astor also proposed to build a post on the Columbia River, to be supplied by vessels from New York and to serve as a receiving point for furs to be collected in the Far West for exportation to China. In this plan he hoped to overreach British fur traders, who were prohibited by British law from exporting directly to Asia, such export trade being a monopoly of the British East India Company.[22]

In April, 1808, the New York legislature issued a charter to the American Fur Company, authorizing it to raise a capital fund of $1,000,000, and to operate during a term of twenty-five years. Astor provided the capital, named the directors, and managed the new company, which was merely himself in a corporate form. Before 1815 it acted on two fronts in the West: in the Missouri Valley and on the Columbia River.[23]

Meanwhile, the Lewis and Clark Expedition had aroused the interest of the traders of St. Louis in the area westward to the Rockies. In the spring

[21] Porter, *John Jacob Astor*, I, 12, 19, 21–23, 48–49, 52–53, 57, 62–64; Chittenden, *The Fur Trade of the Far West*, I, 165, 168.

[22] Porter, *John Jacob Astor*, I, 164–165; Chittenden, *The Fur Trade of the Far West*, I, 166, 168; Turner, "The Indian Trade of Wisconsin," p. 151.

[23] Porter, *John Jacob Astor*, I, 167–169.

of 1807 a party of fifty-two trappers, led by Manuel Lisa, ascended the Missouri and the Yellowstone rivers to the mouth of the Big Horn River, where they erected Fort Manuel. During the winter of 1807–1808 they ranged widely in search of furs among the Indians of the northern Rockies. Returning to St. Louis in 1808, they proceeded to organize, early in 1809, the Missouri Fur Company. Among its members were Lisa, the Chouteau brothers, and other leading traders. Their resources made up a capital of $40,000, with which they sought to secure a monopoly of the fur trade westward from St. Louis. The company sent out a large, well-equipped expedition in the spring of 1809 which erected Fort Mandan for trade with Indians of the Plains. The main party went on to Fort Manuel and traded with the Crow Indians during the winter of 1809–1810. One band invaded the country of the Blackfeet near Three Forks and was driven back with severe losses. Another group moved southward along the Madison River and crossed to the Snake River, returning to St. Louis in 1811. These dramatic excursions proved to be so unprofitable that the company abandoned Forts Manuel and Mandan in 1811–1812, withdrew from the Rocky Mountain trade, and concentrated on the lower Missouri Valley.[24]

The early activities of the Missouri Fur Company were paralleled by those of Astor's American Fur Company. In October, 1810, Astor's lieutenant, Wilson Hunt, led an expedition from St. Louis with the objectives of selecting sites for trading posts along the Missouri, of winning the good will of the Indians, of obtaining furs, and of reaching the site of a post that Astor planned to establish on the Columbia. The expedition eventually divided into four groups, which suffered many hardships before they reached Astor's Columbia post early in 1812.[25]

When forming plans for the Far West, Astor had decided to make his principal effort on the Pacific Coast. In June, 1810, he joined with several partners to set up the Pacific Fur Company—a concern which he financed and operated. His partners were essentially profit-sharing employees. In September, 1810, the company sent from New York the ship *Tonquin* on a trading voyage, with the additional mission of establishing a settlement on the Pacific Coast. The expedition reached the mouth of the Columbia River in the spring of 1812 and soon began the construction of a trading post, Astoria. A small party then journeyed overland, via the South Pass and the Platte River, to St. Louis, bringing reports of the success of Astoria in obtaining furs. The infant settlement was reinforced in 1812 by a supply ship, the *Beaver*, sent by Astor from New York, and by the arrival of the overland expedition led by Wilson Hunt. Unhappily, soon after the outbreak of the War of 1812, a report that a British frigate was en route to seize Astoria impelled Astor's partners there to sell its effects in 1813 to the

[24] Chittenden, *The Fur Trade of the Far West*, I, 120, 126, 138–143, 145–147; Billington, *Westward Expansion*, pp. 453–455.
[25] Porter, *John Jacob Astor*, I, 202–203.

British North West Company for $58,000. Astor then withdrew from the Pacific Coast, leaving it to the North West Company. Thereafter he concentrated on the northern trade within the United States eastward of the Rocky Mountains.[26]

THE FISHERIES

After 1789, New England fishermen ranged the seas, obtaining products that enlarged the country's foreign trade. One of the two main branches of their industry was the whale fishery; in the other "the sacred codfish" predominated, although the fishermen also brought in small quantities of mackerel, herring, hake, haddock, and pollock. The codfishery flourished in two areas: the Grand Banks of the North Atlantic, southeast of Newfoundland; and the Bay of Chaleur, adjacent to the Gulf of St. Lawrence, together with the waters off the coast of Labrador. Vessels fishing off Newfoundland were called "bankers." The cod was a large, bold, greedy fish that multiplied at an incredible rate. Inexhaustible seemed a fishery stocked by a species of which one female was capable of producing 9,000,000 eggs a season. Off Newfoundland the fish, averaging 10 to 12 pounds, were larger than those farther south or nearer the coast.[27]

The fishing industry, all but ruined during the Revolution, revived slowly after the war. During the years 1786–1790 Massachusetts, the king fishing state, employed about 3,300 hands in 539 vessels that averaged 35 tons. Annual sales of the fish abroad amounted to 250,000 quintals, worth nearly $610,000. A third of the state's fishermen were then unemployed and wages were only $93 a year. New Englanders attributed the depression of the industry to efforts of Britain and France to foster their fisheries by favoring them with bounties, by recruiting American fishermen, and by excluding American fish from their markets. In 1789, defenders of the fishery defeated in Congress a proposal to lay a high duty on molasses from the West Indies, contending that such a tax would reduce American imports of that commodity and deprive the islanders of the means of buying fish.[28]

The decision in Congress to levy a tax on imported salt gave birth to federal bounties for the benefit of the codfishery. The salt duty varied from

[26] Frederick Merk, "The Genesis of the Oregon Question," *Mississippi Valley Historical Review*, XXXVI, No. 4 (March, 1950), 588; Oscar Osburn Winther, *The Great Northwest* (New York: Alfred A. Knopf, Inc., 1947), pp. 96–97; Porter, *John Jacob Astor*, I, 168, 171, 185–187, 188–203, 226–229.

[27] McFarland, *The New England Fisheries*, pp. 148–149, 153; Harold A. Innis, *The Cod Fisheries* (New Haven, Conn.: Yale University Press, 1940), pp. 3–5, 221.

[28] Lorenzo Sabine, *Report on the Principal Fisheries of the American Seas* (Washington: Robert Armstrong, 1853), pp. 155–160, 174; McFarland, *The New England Fisheries*, pp. 131–134; *Debates of Congress*, 1 Cong., 1 Sess., I, 231–233.

12 cents a bushel in 1790, to 20 cents a bushel in 1797, to 40 cents a bushel in 1812. The first bounty for the codfishery, authorized in 1789, allowed 5 cents a quintal on exports of dried fish and 5 cents a barrel of pickled fish—a subsidy of perhaps $12,000 a year, or less than $3.00 for each fisherman. Congress changed the bounty in 1790 to 10 cents a barrel on pickled fish and 10 cents a quintal on dried fish, and authorized payments based on the size of fishing vessels—$1.20 a ton for vessels under 20 tons, $1.80 a ton for vessels of 20 to 30 tons, and $3 a ton for vessels over 30 tons, with a maximum of $175 to one ship. Three eighths of such payments went to the owners; five eighths to the crew. In 1797, Congress raised the allowances to $1.60, $2.40, and $4 respectively. The removal of the salt duty in 1807 put an end to bounties granted for vessels, but an act of July 29, 1813, which imposed a new salt duty, restored the bounty plan for vessels, with a maximum of $4 a ton for vessels over 30 tons. Federal bounties to the fisheries, 1789–1818, amounted to $2,653,000; receipts from the salt duty were $12,928,000.[29]

Undoubtedly the federal bounties contributed to a steady expansion of the fisheries that began in the early 1790's and continued until 1800, when the industry entered the era of its greatest activity prior to 1815, reaching the peak in 1807. The embargo idled the fishermen in 1808 but after its repeal they enjoyed four good years until the conflict with England again halted their operations. Another revival ensued after the ending of the war.[30]

Massachusetts and Maine carried on between 90 and 92 percent of the nation's fishery. Outside New England, New York led the other states, but its contribution was negligible. Before 1818 its fishing vessels did not exceed 900 tons—and at a time when New England's vessels totaled 78,000 tons. Marblehead in Massachusetts was the principal center. Other fishing towns were Newburyport, Gloucester, Salem, Plymouth, Provincetown, Wellfleet, Duxbury, Yarmouth, and Chatham. Bred to the sea, the Yankee fisherman did not respond to the lure of cheap lands and move west.

Long before a lad could . . . read half the precepts his primer contained, he knew the name of every brace and stay, every sail and part of a Grand Banker and a Chebacco boat, all the nautical terms . . . . By . . . his tenth birthday he was old enough not to be seasick, not to cry during a storm at sea, and to be of some use about a ship, and he went on his first trip to the Banks. The skipper and the crew called him "cut-tail," for he received no money from the fish he caught, and each one he caught was marked by snipping a piece of the tail. After an apprenticeship of three or four years the "cut-tail" became a "header," . . . and learned all the duties which a "splitter," and a "salter," must perform.

[29] McFarland, *The New England Fisheries*, pp. 135–138, 140; Innis, *The Cod Fisheries*, pp. 220–221.
[30] McFarland, *The New England Fisheries*, pp. 141, 150, 154.

When twenty, the seafaring Yankee was a full-fledged member of the crew, with the prospect of becoming an owner or skipper of a schooner. Life on the sea made the fisherfolk conservative, stolid, and taciturn. The men worked together almost in silence; gestures and perceptions of others' movements served in place of words.[31]

In 1791, Jefferson summarized the competitive advantages of the New England fishery. The nearness of home villages to the fishing grounds enabled the fishermen to use small, inexpensive vessels, to find ports in storms, thereby reducing risks and insurance, to supply themselves cheaply with provisions, and to employ wives and children in the task of salting fish. The excellence of vessels and the skill, energy, and steadiness of the men minimized hazards and magnified returns. The cheapness of casks afforded an "extra profit" of 15 percent.[32]

New England's fishery at Newfoundland had flourished before the Revolution. After the war it continued in its old channels. The fishermen commonly made two or three "fares" (catches) a year, the first voyage ending late in May, when the boats returned to the settlements, where most of the fish was dried and salted, although a part was often cured on the coast of Nova Scotia. Apparently the vessels that went to the Grand Banks were not improved before 1815—an evidence of a strongly conservative habit. A "banker" was a round-bottomed schooner, under 70 tons, called a "heel-tapper" by reason of its high rear deck and low middle section.[33]

Soon after the war New Englanders developed a thriving fishery at the Bay of Chaleur and off the coast of Labrador. Newburyport sent its first ship to Labrador in 1794; in 1807, 65 of its vessels were fishing there. Gradually the fishermen extended their range, combing the bays of the Gulf of St. Lawrence, passing through the Strait of Belle Isle, and sailing northward to the entrance to Hudson Bay. An observer in 1807 or 1808 counted 938 New England vessels at the Strait of Canso. At that time fishing towns from New London, Connecticut, to the Schoodic in Maine sent out swarms of vessels, perhaps 2,000 in all, employing from 15,000 to 20,000 men. Large ships called at Labrador to load fish from smaller vessels, preparatory to direct voyages to Europe. The fish obtained from the Bay-Labrador area made up three fourths of the dried fish exported from New England, though they were smaller than their Newfoundland cousins and worth less by the quintal in European markets. A Boston merchant estimated in 1815 that operating costs and gross proceeds of "bankers" exceeded those of vessels engaged in the Bay-Labrador fishery.[34]

In addition to voyaging far asea, New Englanders also fished during

---

[31] Morison, *Maritime History of Massachusetts,* pp. 137–138; McFarland, *The New England Fisheries,* pp. 136, 146–152.

[32] McFarland, *The New England Fisheries,* pp. 135–136.

[33] Morison, *Maritime History of Massachusetts,* p. 135.

[34] McFarland, *The New England Fisheries,* pp. 151, 153–154; Innis, *The Cod Fisheries,* pp. 222–223, 246–247; Sabine, *The Fisheries of the American Seas,* p. 170.

the winter months in their home waters, finding a market for their catches in the nearby settlements.[35]

During the winter months fishing vessels carried dried and pickled fish to foreign ports, returning in time for the next season's operations. The West Indies took between 56 and 62 percent of New England's fish, mainly the cheaper grades, including pickled fish and mackerel. The value of all dried fish exported was normally four times that of exports of pickled fish. In Europe the chief receiving ports were Marseilles, Bilbao, Alicante, Leghorn, and Naples. Europeans favored the small fish from Labrador. France and Spain together absorbed between 75 and 88 percent of the exports to Europe. Ordinarily American traders did not take on goods in Spain; rather, they obtained coin and then went to the Cape Verde Islands to load cargoes of salt for the homeward voyage. Returns from France included wines, silks, olive oil, and other French products. The fishery fluctuated drastically in keeping with the hazards of the sea. Vessels employed in 1789 totaled 19,000 tons; in 1793, 50,000 tons; in 1794, 28,000 tons; in 1798, 42,000 tons; in 1807, 69,000 tons; in 1809, 34,000 tons; in 1814, 17,000 tons. Prices ranged from an average of $2.50 a quintal in 1789–1790 to $3.25 to $4.80 in 1807–1816. Both the Bank and the Bay-Labrador fisheries yielded oil, estimated as 37,500 barrels yearly before 1810, worth about $375,000. One estimate gives $2,850,000 a year as the average value of all fish exported during twenty years after 1788.[36]

Whaling, one of the oldest industries of America, reached its pre-1815 zenith in the years immediately before the Revolution. Sperm whales, found mainly in tropical or temperate zones, yielded sperm oil and spermaceti, the raw material of fine candles; the right or baleen whale gave up whale oil—an illuminant—and whalebone, used in making corset stays. The whalemen of the era before 1815 were New Englanders, American Indians, and Negroes who operated from a few ports in Massachusetts. Nantucket and New Bedford together sent out about 85 percent of the whaling vessels leaving the Union during the years 1788–1815, Nantucket alone accounting for 58 percent. By 1775 sperm whalers had overspread the Atlantic from the coast of Georgia to Brazil. After 1783 they pushed into the South Atlantic; then in 1791 six vessels left Nantucket and New Bedford for the Pacific Ocean, via Cape Horn. The range soon expanded to include the waters off Chile, Peru, the Galápagos Islands, California, Hawaii, the Fiji Islands, New Zealand, Tasmania, Java, the China Sea, and the Indian Ocean from the Red Sea to Madagascar. In the North Atlantic, hunters pursued the right whale from Newfoundland to the Bahamas and also to Greenland, Baffin's Bay, and Hudson Bay; in the Pacific they reached the northwest coast of America, penetrated Bering Sea to the Arctic

---

[35] Morison, *Maritime History of Massachusetts*, p. 147; Innis, *The Cod Fisheries*, pp. 9, 222.

[36] McFarland, *The New England Fisheries*, pp. 135, 140–142; Innis, *The Cod Fisheries*, pp. 10 note, 239.

Ocean, and visited Okhotsk Sea. An Atlantic sphere extended southward from Brazil to Patagonia and eastward to Africa; a Pacific sphere reached from the coast of Chile to New Zealand and Australia.[37]

A whaling voyage commonly lasted two or three years. The vessels increased in size from an average of 83 tons in 1788 to an average of 312 tons in 1806—a change caused by the lengthening of the voyages and marked by a growing importance of capital relative to labor. In addition to the captain, a whaler carried a mate, steward, carpenter, cooper, cook, blacksmith, and cabin boy, plus a steersman and four or five seamen for each small whaleboat on board. A ship that carried four boats had a crew of 32 men who received their pay, not as a rule in wages, but in shares of the catch—$3/5$ths going to the owners, $1/18$th to the master, $1/75$th to each seaman, and $1/120$th to the cabin boy. The men hunted in boats from which they speared the whales with harpoons attached to lines that served to fasten the whales to the boats. Lances or spears were then used for killing the prey. Harpoon guns, available after 1730, were sometimes employed, but most American whalemen seem to have clung to the hand method of hurling the harpoon. Earnings of a common seaman did not ordinarily exceed $250 a year; hence whaling appealed to men who were willing to accept an assured though meager living on shipboard, letting others give orders and provide supplies. Since a cargo worth $100,000 netted $60,000 to the owners, success yielded large returns on invested capital and fostered the growth of private fortunes.[38]

During the Revolution the whaling fleets of Nantucket and New Bedford shrank from 190 or more to about 5 vessels. However, the lull in the industry increased the number of whales afloat. Revival came slowly: only about 20 whalers sailed from New England ports each year in 1784, 1785, and 1786. During the first good postwar year, 1789, 57 vessels began voyages. Several prosperous years followed and the maximum exportation of whale products before 1815 was attained in 1796. Except for two bad years, 1798 and 1799, the whalemen kept up a good pace until another high point was reached in 1804, when 91 vessels sailed. A downward trend then set in, as shipowners reaped great profits in the carrying trade. The industry all but dried up in 1812–1814, when sailings averaged only 3 a year. Another upsurge occurred in 1815. After 1796, exports of sperm oil and whalebone declined sharply, whereas exports of whale oil increased to a great extent and became the mainstay of the business. Between 1804 and 1814 the prices of sperm oil ranged from 60 cents to $1.40 a gallon; of

[37] Walter S. Tower, *A History of the American Whale Fishery* (University of Pennsylvania *Publications in Political Economy and Public Law*, No. 20; Philadelphia: 1907), pp. 81, 92–94, 96, 122; Morison, *Maritime History of Massachusetts*, p. 158; Goode, *The Fisheries of the United States*, Sec. 5, II, 69–70.

[38] Tower, *The American Whale Fishery*, pp. 81, 87, 89, 91; Morison, *Maritime History of Massachusetts*, pp. 158, 376; Alexander Starbuck, *The History of Nantucket* (Boston: C. E. Goodspeed & Co., 1924), pp. 403–425.

whale oil, from 40 cents to $1.40 a gallon; of whalebone from 7 cents to
10 cents a pound—fluctuations that denote the precarious instability of
the industry.[39]

A WORLD-WIDE FOREIGN TRADE

Before 1775 Britain had not permitted vessels of the thirteen colonies
to transport any goods directly to points on the European continent north
of Cape Finisterre. British law also prohibited the exportation of certain
"enumerated articles," including tobacco, rice, indigo, furs, and naval
stores, from a colonial port to any place except Britain or another British
colony. The monopoly of the British East India Company excluded Americans from trading with the vast area eastward of the Cape of Good Hope
to Asia. Goods produced in Europe or in Asia or India could lawfully enter
the colonies only from Britain. Foreign ships were not allowed to serve
American producers and consumers. The Revolution effaced all such restraints and enabled American merchants to trade with nearly all parts of
the world. Moreover, in time of war in Europe, the United States possessed
the legal right to trade with Britain's enemies—a benefit that had been
denied to the thirteen colonies. After 1783, American vessels scoured the
seas and visited every quarter of the globe. The Declaration of Independence was an Emancipation Proclamation for American commerce.[40]

In 1793 Jefferson described the character of the country's foreign
trade: "The commodities we offer," he said, "are either necessaries of life,
or materials for manufacture . . . ; and we take in exchange, either manufactures, when they have received the last finish of art and industry, or
mere luxuries." An indication of the relative importance of various kinds
of exports appears in the following survey: [41]

ANNUAL EXPORTS. 1791

General Farm Products	Value
Breadstuffs: grains, meals, bread	$7,649,887
Horses and mules	339,753
Flaxseed	236,072
Live provisions	137,743
Salted meats	599,130
	$8,962,585

[39] John R. Spears, *The Story of the New England Whalers* (New York: The
Macmillan Company, 1908), pp. 109–116; Tower, *The American Whale Fishery*,
pp. 4, 42–43, 127–128; Morison, *Maritime History of Massachusetts*, p. 159.
[40] Spears, *New England Whalers*, pp. 106–107.
[41] "Report of the Secretary of State on the . . . Commerce of the United States
in Foreign Countries, December 16, 1793," *State Papers* (Wait), I, 433, 424.

ANNUAL EXPORTS, 1791 (*continued*)

	Value
Southern Staples	
Tobacco	$4,349,567
Rice	1,753,796
Indigo	537,379
	$6,640,742
Products of Fisheries	
Whale oil	$252,591
Salted fish	941,696
	$1,194,287
Forest Products	
Wood	$1,263,534
Pot- and pear ash	839,093
Tar, pitch, turpentine	217,177
	$2,319,804
Foreign goods	$620,274
Total Value of Exports	$19,737,687

The record of foreign trade after 1791 shows enormous gains, as follows: [42]

EXPORTS OF THE UNITED STATES

	Domestic Products	Foreign Products	Total
1790	$19,666,000	$539,000	$20,205,000
1791	18,500,000	512,000	19,012,000
1792	19,000,000	1,753,000	20,753,000
1795	39,500,000	8,490,000	47,990,000
1800	31,841,000	39,130,000	70,971,000
1805	42,387,000	53,179,000	95,566,000
1806	41,253,000	60,283,000	101,536,000
1807	48,700,000	59,643,000	108,343,000
1810	42,366,000	24,391,000	66,757,000

In Northern Europe, direct trade with Sweden, which began as early as 1780, provided a market for American tobacco after the war. In 1784, E. H. Derby and the Cabots dispatched ships to Russia. Other merchants followed, seeking such products as duck and tallow, but the ensuing trade was small because it required more capital than most Americans could supply. The Netherlands received the common export products of the United States except salt pork, salted beef, flour, and bread. Holland consumed only a small part of the American goods it imported; most of these

[42] Johnson, *History of Commerce*, II, 20.

went to the interior of Europe or were re-exported by sea. Shipping from the United States to the Netherlands increased nearly fivefold between 1785 and 1788. Dutch imports of American products in 1788—principally tobacco and rice—nearly equaled in value the exports of the United States to Britain. In 1791–1792, the Netherlands, Denmark, and Sweden took about 11 percent of the exports of the United States, the Dutch alone absorbing 10 percent.[43]

In the Mediterranean, the Barbary pirates continued to prey upon American shipping and, indeed, increased their depredations after 1793. Severe attacks in 1801 moved Congress in February, 1803 to appropriate $146,000 for building or buying four small warships and as many as fifteen gunboats. An American fleet soon went into action against Tripoli. In April, 1805, American forces conquered the Tripolitan port of Derna, and in May the pasha agreed to a treaty by which Tripoli pledged not to molest American vessels in the Mediterranean. In 1806, Mediterranean countries were providing a good market for New England fish.[44]

France, the main customer of the United States on the Continent, consumed the American products it imported: grain, flour, rice, potash, and naval stores. Early efforts to exclude New England fish by means of a prohibitory duty had to be abandoned, and France became a principal buyer of that product. In 1791, France and its colonies took 24 percent of all the exports of the United States, such purchases by France alone increasing more than threefold between 1789 and 1792. At that time large quantities of American tobacco, grain, and rice reached France by way of Britain. French importing houses were insignificant in the American trade; ship captains exchanged their cargoes for such French products as brandy, wine, linen, silks, and salt. Of minor importance were hats, hosiery, lace, gloves, parasols, ribbons, soaps, oils, glassware, liqueurs, and perfume. France was sorely disappointed in its ambition to supply the states with European goods; American imports from France, 1784–1790, did not equal 5 percent of the comparable imports from Britain. After 1800, American merchants vastly expanded their trade with France. Both Britain and France warred against each other's shipping, thereby opening to American vessels important trades that had previously been served by French and British ships. Thus American vessels replaced French vessels as carriers

[43] East, *Business Enterprise*, pp. 253–254; *State Papers* (Wait), I, 429; Albert Ludwig Kohlmeier, "The Commerce between the United States and the Netherlands, 1783–1789" (*Studies in American History Dedicated to James Albert Woodburn*, Indiana University *Studies*, Vol. XII, Nos. 66–68; Bloomington: 1925), pp. 17–19, 25–26.

[44] Johnson, *History of Commerce*, II, 17; Wright and McLeod, *The First Americans in North Africa*, pp. 132, 174, 183, 192; Thomas Pemberton, "A Topographical and Historical Description of Boston, 1794" (Massachusetts Historical Society, *Collections*, Vol. III; Boston: The Society, 1810), p. 286.

of products from the French colonies to France and superseded British vessels as carriers of goods from Britain to France.[45]

Portugal and Spain, together with their Atlantic islands—the Azores, the Madeiras, the Cape Verde Islands, and the Canaries—formed a unified area of American trade. Thither the United States sent salted fish, grain, bread, timber, lumber, and naval stores, together with smaller quantities of flaxseed, potash, rice, and whale oil. Like France, both Portugal and Spain consumed the American produce they imported; neither was an important entrepôt for a re-export trade. The two countries and their colonies provided a market for about 16 percent of all the exports of the United States in 1791. Later, a striking increase in shipments of American flour to the Iberian Peninsula took place, rising from 7,883 barrels in 1800 to 144,900 barrels in 1803, and finally to an average of 459,000 barrels during the years 1811–1813, when British armies created an unprecedented demand at abnormally high prices.[46]

As early as 1786, American ships ventured into the Indian Ocean. There they found lucrative bases in two French islands, Mauritius (Île de France) and Réunion (Bourbon), from which they could sail eastward to Java and Sumatra, northeastward to Calcutta and Bombay, and northward to Mocha and Aden at the entrance to the Red Sea and Muscat on the Persian Gulf. A fine harbor in Mauritius could accommodate fifty warships. American exports thither, and to Réunion, consisted of beef, flour, naval stores, lumber, and timber, as well as specie, which reputedly made up three fourths of the cargoes. One observer reported that, before 1806, Americans had shipped between $50,000,000 and $60,000,000 of specie eastward around the Cape of Good Hope, of which four fifths to five sixths had been obtained outside the United States, principally in Europe. Products of the Indian Ocean lands included the coffee, cloves, indigo, and sugar of Mauritius and Réunion; the highly prized coffee of Mocha; the gums and medicines of Mocha, Aden, and Muscat; the cotton of Bombay; the sugar, indigo, cotton goods, and silks of Calcutta; and the sugar, coffee, and pepper of Java and Sumatra. Some American ships leaving Mauritius returned directly to the United States; some went to Arabia, India, or the East Indies; others put in at European ports to exchange their India goods

[45] State Papers (Wait), I, 426–427; B. Barrere, "Report upon the Navigation Act, made in the name of the Committee on Publick Safety," ibid., p. 470; Henri Sée, "Commerce between France and the United States, 1783–1784," American Historical Review, XXXI, No. 4 (July, 1926), 735–737; John F. Stover, "French-American Trade during the Confederation, 1781–1789," North Carolina Historical Review, XXXV, No. 4 (October, 1958), 411, 413; John D. Forbes, "European Wars and Boston Trade, 1783–1815," New England Quarterly, XI, No. 4 (December, 1938), 712, 719.

[46] State Papers (Wait), I, 425–426; McFarland, The New England Fisheries, p. 141; W. Freeman Galpin, "The American Grain Trade to the Spanish Peninsula, 1810–1814," American Historical Review, XXVIII, No. 1 (October, 1922), 25–26.

for European wares for the home market. Much of the Indian Ocean traffic was carried on from port to port, as by a "tramp" ship, effecting sales of all sorts of European, American, or India goods wherever demand was favorable. Memorable in the annals of this trade was the "youngsters' voyage" to Mauritius in 1792–1794 of the Salem ship *Benjamin,* Nathaniel Silsbee, captain, age nineteen, which netted a profit of 500 percent. Prize ships taken by the French from the British and sold in American ports were sometimes sailed to Mauritius, there to be resold to the French.[47]

An informed observer stated that fifty American ships visited Java in 1805 and that more than twenty then traded with Sumatra. Beyond those islands Yankee sailors traversed the vast expanse of the China Sea and the Southwest Pacific, touching at the Philippines, Canton, Japan, Hawaii, and the Fiji Islands. They came from both the Indian Ocean and the western coast of America. During several years before 1806 between three and five American vessels traded coin and European goods at Manila for sugar and indigo. By 1806 a year's trade at Canton employed fifty American ships that brought in dollars, India products, ginseng, and furs, together with otter and seal skins worth from $400,000 to $600,000 a year. Returns were chinaware, teas, nankeens, sugar, and silks. The first known American ship to trade with Japan went to Nagasaki from Batavia in 1797 in the service of the Dutch. Six or seven similar voyages followed before the traffic was stopped by orders from Holland. On the last voyage in 1803 Captain Stewart failed in his efforts to open an independent American trade with Japan.[48]

In the Western Hemisphere, Britain's North American colonies—Newfoundland, Canada, and Nova Scotia—contributed in a minor vein to New England's trade. After the Revolutionary War Britain attempted to make that area a supplier of fish, lumber, and provisions for the British West Indies, thereby freeing those island colonies from dependence on the United States. To this end the British government excluded the vessels and products of the United States from its North American ports. However, the northern colonies produced little for export except the furs of Canada and the fish of Newfoundland and Nova Scotia. The European wars exposed British vessels in the North Atlantic to French cruisers, with the result that New England vessels took over the business of carrying much

[47] Stuart Weems Bruchey, *Robert Oliver, Merchant of Baltimore, 1783–1819* (Johns Hopkins University *Studies in Historical and Political Science,* Series LXXIV, No. 1; Baltimore: The Johns Hopkins Press, 1956), pp. 178–180, 182–183; Morison, *Maritime History of Massachusetts,* pp. 73–74; John H. Reinoehl, ed., "Some Remarks on the American Trade: Jacob Crowninshield to James Madison, 1806," *William and Mary Quarterly,* Third Series, XVI, No. 1 (January, 1959), pp. 89, 107–113.

[48] Reinoehl, "Remarks," pp. 103–104, 106; Inazo Nitobé, "American-Japanese Intercourse Prior to the Advent of Perry" (American Historical Association, *Annual Report . . . 1911,* 2 vols.; Washington: Government Printing Office, 1913), I, 131–132.

of the fish of Nova Scotia to foreign ports. In 1806, Nova Scotia produced about 50,000 quintals of fish, of which one half was carried in British ships to Boston and then re-exported by New Englanders to the Mediterranean and the West Indies. In the Caribbean trade, New England vessels paid 7 to 10 percent insurance "out and home," whereas British vessels paid 25 to 30 percent in wartime. The fish of Nova Scotia re-exported by New Englanders in 1806 amounted to perhaps one thirteenth of their total exports of fish. Among the products reaching Nova Scotia from the United States were lumber, salt, molasses, rum, flour, corn, livestock, and India goods—shipments often smuggled in to evade British duties and restrictions. Describing Canada in 1806, an observer remarked that it "has no shipping and can not spare any considerable supplies. It is brought in debt every year for English manufactures etc., and its fur trade alone supports it . . . . Half a million dollars must be annually acquired by British merchants in profit from this single branch of commerce. Canada may furnish masts and timber but the people are not commercial. They export very little provisions." Furs to a reported value of $400,000 made up the principal Canadian exports to the United States in 1806.[49]

The West Indian possessions of Spain, France, and Britain, together with the American mainland colonies of Spain, formed a large branch of the commerce of the United States. Exports included fish, fish oil, salt pork, flour, corn, peas, beans, potatoes, butter, lard, rice, tobacco, timber, boards, planks, staves, shingles, horses, cattle, pitch, tar, turpentine, and such European goods as Russian linens and German hardware. All the states engaged in this traffic. In 1805 it took off products to an estimated value of $21,000,000 or about 22 percent of the total exports of the Union.[50]

Normally Spain required that all foreign goods imported into its American colonies must be carried thither directly from Spain and in Spanish ships. Direct exports from the United States therefore had to be smuggled into the colonial ports or landed with the connivance of Spanish officials. However, during six years, 1795–1799 and 1804–1806, Spanish-American ports freely received the vessels of the United States; whereupon the goods they supplied reached an estimated value of $7,700,000 in 1805. Exports to Cuba increased to the point that, during four months of 1805, 175 United States ships entered Havana, as against 25 Spanish ships and 1 British vessel. American ships returned from Havana or Vera Cruz with silver and other colonial products, especially sugar, which was re-exported to Cadiz, Hamburg, or Amsterdam. A British critic of this trade complained that the Spanish colonies were "quietly reaping the fruit of . . . the suspension of their prohibitory laws." "The neutral flag," he explained, "gives

[49] *State Papers* (Wait), I, 431; Reinoehl, "Remarks," pp. 92, 94–95; Innis, *The Cod Fisheries*, pp. 231–232; Charles H. Ambler, "The Oregon Country, 1810–1830," *Mississippi Valley Historical Review*, XXX, No. 1 (June, 1943), 10.

[50] Reinoehl, "Remarks," p. 99.

to them not only protection but advantages before unknown. The gigantic infancy of agriculture in Cuba . . . is greatly aided in its portentous growth during the war, by the boundless liberty of trade . . . . To the Spanish continental colonies also, war has changed its nature; it has become the handmaid of commerce, the parent of plenty." [51]

By an act of August 30, 1784, France opened seven of its West Indian ports to foreign ships and approved the importation into its Caribbean colonies of salted fish and salted meats from the United States. In 1792 a similar permission applied to vegetables, horses, lumber, naval stores, rice, and corn, although wheat and flour were prohibited unless admitted by the colonial legislatures in times of distress. When the British Navy drove French Merchantmen from the ocean in 1793, France opened its colonies to neutral shipping, and the United States rapidly took over the business of carrying products from the French West Indies to France—a trade that Britain permitted until 1805, if the French products were reshipped from ports of the United States. The French islands in 1805 imported American commodities to an estimated value of $7,300,000. In 1807, British West Indian planters complained that the trade of the United States was ruining them by flooding their markets with French sugar.[52]

After 1789, the trade of the United States with the British West Indies shrank in importance in comparison with that with the French and Spanish islands. Before 1794 Britain continued to exclude the vessels and the salted fish and salted meats of the United States from its Caribbean colonies. A clause in Jay's Treaty of 1794 proposed to admit American vessels of not more than 70 tons to the British West Indies on the condition that American ships should not export sugar, coffee, molasses, cocoa, or cotton from the United States. The rejection of this clause by the Senate left intact the British ban excluding American vessels from the British islands. However, Britain intermittently opened its West Indian ports to American ships. Exports from the United States to the British islands varied, between 1795 and 1807, from $2,147,000 to $9,699,000; imports from the islands ranged from $2,925,000 to $6,968,000. In 1805, the British islands took about 28 percent of all exports from the United States to the Caribbean.[53] Two

[51] *State Papers* (Wait), I, 430; Dorothy Burne Goebel, "British Trade to the Spanish Colonies, 1796–1823," *American Historical Review*, XLIII, No. 2 (January, 1938), 297; Roy F. Nichols, "Trade and the Establishment of the United States Consulates in Spanish America, 1779–1809," *Hispanic American Historical Review*, XIII, No. 3 (August, 1933), 296, note 25; 303, note 44.

[52] Sée, "France and the United States," pp. 736–737; *State Papers* (Wait), I, 430; Henry Adams, *History of the United States* . . . (4 vols.; New York: Albert and Charles Boni, 1930), Vol. I, Bk. 2, p. 321; Forbes, "Boston Trade," pp. 713, 722; Reinoehl, "Remarks," p. 99.

[53] Lowell Joseph Ragatz, *The Fall of the Planter Class in the British Caribbean, 1763–1833* (New York: The Century Company, 1928), pp. 180, 231, 235–236; Samuel Flagg Bemis, *Jay's Treaty* (New York: The Macmillan Company, 1923),

persistent handicaps in the British West Indian trade were described by an American merchant in 1806. Britain allowed American ships to export only rum and molasses from its islands—a rule that enabled the British planters to charge an excessive price for their rum. The Americans had to "take it or leave it," with the result that their loss on rum frequently ran "as high as 20 or 25 per cent." In addition, the British West Indian trade was generally in a precarious state—"languid," "palsied," "half shut, half open, never free." "Our merchants know not what articles will be admitted into the English islands from day to day . . . . Occasionally they are shut. One island admits fish; another excludes it at the same time. Beef and pork are occasionally excluded. Rice is not always admitted. It is the same with lard and butter. Large live cattle are often refused at the same time that small live stock is received. By proclamation, boards, planks, and certain kinds of timber will be admitted when other woods will not be." [54]

The activities of Stephen Girard illustrate the trend of the West Indian trade. In 1789–1793 he did twice as much business with the islands as with Europe; in 1794–1807 his European ventures were three times greater than those with the Caribbean. He withdrew from the West Indies in 1812, when superior opportunities beckoned in Europe, Asia, Africa, and South America. [55]

The Caribbean continued to serve as a receiving point for slaves from Africa. State laws enacted between 1783 and 1795 which prohibited the slave trade, together with the stigma attached to it, gave it an unsavory and clandestine character and tended to obliterate the records of its motions. It appears that a slaver went out from Salem in 1785 and that eight ship captains of that port operated in the traffic between 1788 and 1802. Certainly, Salem regularly sent fish and rum to Africa to be exchanged for palm oil, gold dust, and ivory. Vessels importing slaves into Charleston between 1804 and 1808 numbered 191—61 belonging to Charleston, 59 to Rhode Island, and 1 to Boston. In 1803, seven leading Boston merchants insured for $33,000 the vessel *Hope* on a slaving voyage from Africa to Havana under the Danish flag, each slave being valued at $200. In 1807, imports of the United States from Africa which paid ad valorem duties were valued at $108,000; all other imports so taxed were valued at $58,665,000. [56]

The European wars enabled American merchants to push into the trade of South and Central America. They first gained footholds in British and French Guiana, whither they sent flour to be exchanged for sugar,

---

pp. 258, 301; 8 *Statutes at Large*, 122; Johnson, *History of Commerce*, II, 24; *State Papers* (Wait), I, 430.

[54] Reinoehl, "Remarks," pp. 92–93, 95.

[55] Albert J. Gares, "Stephen Girard's West Indian Trade, 1789–1812," *Pennsylvania Magazine of History and Biography*, LXXII, No. 4 (October, 1948), 341–342.

[56] Morison, *Maritime History of Massachusetts*, pp. 33–34; Pitkin, *Statistical View of the Commerce of the United States*, p. 151.

coffee, and molasses. Such products come mainly from Venezuela and Brazil, so that the Guiana trade declined after Americans established direct contacts with those areas. During the years 1798–1810 at least 125 vessels of the United States traded at Buenos Aires and Montevideo, exchanging dry goods, spirits, lumber, shoes, and crockery for cotton, rice, hides, copper, and chocolate. In 1806–1807, Baltimore sent 47 vessels to Vera Cruz with cargoes of European goods, East Indian products, pork, and beef. Returns consisted mainly of silver. During eighteen months this business netted the Oliver Brothers a profit of $775,000. By 1810, ships from Baltimore were trading with Colombia, Venezuela, Guiana, Brazil, Uruguay, and Argentina. The value of Baltimore's exports—of which 70 percent were foreign goods—was three times greater than the value of the South American returns. The War of 1812 stopped this trade, as Baltimore's ships turned to privateering at the expense of Britain.[57]

[57] See two articles by Charles Lyon Chandler in *The Hispanic American Historical Review:* "United States Merchant Ships in the Rio de la Plata (1801–1808), As Shown by Early Newspapers," II, No. 1 (February, 1919), 49, and "United States Shipping in the La Plata," III, No. 2 (May, 1920), 160–162; Frank R. Rutter, *South American Trade of Baltimore* (Johns Hopkins University *Studies in Political and Historical Science,* Series XV, No. 9; Baltimore: The Johns Hopkins Press, 1897), pp. 10–12; Bruchey, *Robert Oliver,* pp. 262, 267, 294.

CHAPTER XI

A Balance Sheet of Foreign Trade

THE BRITISH CONNECTION

DESPITE the broadening of American commerce, Britain remained its principal center abroad. However, Anglo-American trade after 1783 differed from its colonial parent: not so large a percentage of American exports went to Britain as formerly. Britain no longer purchased American-built ships as she had done on a large scale in colonial times. After 1783, exports of Chesapeake tobacco went directly to foreign ports to a much greater extent than before. This change is accounted for, not by a decline of British consumption of American tobacco, but by Britain's loss of most of the business of carrying tobacco from the United States to foreign markets. In 1771–1775 Britain re-exported nine tenths of the tobacco she imported from North America; in 1802–1804, less than one half. In 1792, the British were still the best customers of the Union, taking goods twice the value of the purchases of France, which ranked second among the markets for American exports. Britain favored imports from the United States of potash, bar iron, lumber, indigo, flaxseed, pitch, and tar; prohibited or discouraged imports of rice, fish, whale oil, and salted meats except bacon; and discouraged the importation of grain and flour unless the price of wheat in Britain was abnormally high. Jefferson observed in 1793 that the "greater part of what they receive from us is re-exported to other countries, under the useless charge of intermediate deposit and double voyage." However, after 1793, the pressure of a wartime demand for food, enhanced by the progress of the Industrial Revolution, expanded Britain's purchases of foreign grain and flour. In 1807, the exports of wheat from the United States to Britain amounted to 1,997,000 bushels—more than three times the total for 1806.[1]

[1] Gray, *History of Agriculture in the Southern United States*, II, 752, 760; *State Papers* (Wait), I, 425, 427–429; Galpin, "American Grain Trade under the Embargo," pp. 85–86.

Britain kept its grip on American commerce by supplying most of the imports of the states. Thus in 1792 such imports from the British Empire amounted to $15,285,000 in a total of $19,823,000 from European countries and their possessions. The British then took only 47 percent of American exports to Europe and its colonies while providing 77 percent of the Union's imports from those sources. This happened because American merchants used proceeds from their sales in Europe to buy goods in Britain. In 1791–1792 Spain, Portugal, France, the Netherlands, and Denmark and their dominions imported American goods to the value of $5,685,000 in excess of their exports to the United States, whereas Britain's exports to the United States exceeded its American purchases (of $9,363,000) by $5,922,000. Thus it appears that a large share of the earnings of the European trade of the states found their way to Britain for the purchase of goods to be sent home. Why did this happen? For one thing, many articles—hardware, woolens, cottons, leather goods—could be obtained at low cost in Britain. In 1799 the states imported British woolens to a value of £2,800,000—40 percent of all Britain's woolen exports. London was a vast emporium with great warehouses that suggested an enormous department store where buyers could conveniently make up varied cargoes of all sorts of goods. American merchants felt at home in London, knew its commercial habits, and understood the language and money of account. Above all, British merchants, having abundant capitals, advanced goods on credits running from twelve to eighteen months.[2]

Anglo-American trade revolved around British merchants who imported foreign wares and bought goods from British manufacturers. In some instances British merchants sent goods to America to be sold at random, consigning them to agents or correspondents, the merchant assuming the risk and the seller receiving a commission. A few Americans, whether residents or visitors in Britain, bought goods for cash from British merchants. It was fairly common for American merchants to consign produce to a British merchant, who would sell it and use the proceeds to buy in Britain such goods as the Americans ordered. British merchants also advanced goods on credit to American merchants who had placed specific orders. The methods of paying for British exports varied. Cash purchases were the exception. Sometimes American merchants consigned produce to a British merchant in order to pay existing debts. British agents in America who sold goods there purchased bills of exchange drawn by an American exporter on a British merchant or firm. American exporters used a large part of the proceeds of their sales in Europe to buy bills of exchange pay-

[2] Edmund C. Burnett, ed., "Observations of London Merchants on American Trade, 1783," *American Historical Review*, XVIII, No. 4 (July, 1913), 774–776, 779; *State Papers* (Wait), I, 425; Callender, *Selections*, p. 213; Herbert Heaton, "Benjamin Gott and the Anglo-American Cloth Trade," *Journal of Economic and Business History*, II, No. 1 (November, 1929), 147.

able in Britain. The bill of exchange, similar to a bank check, was drawn on funds which accrued from the sale of products received from a foreign country. The promptness of American merchants in paying debts after 1790 fortified the British credit system in Anglo-American trade. British exports to the United States usually went out during two intervals: between January 15 and April 15, and in July and August.[3]

THE BALANCE OF TRADE

In 1790, goods produced in the states and exported were valued at $19,666,000. A regular increase then brought the total to $26,500,000 in 1794. In 1795, it shot up to $39,500,000. During the years 1801–1807 the lowest total was $36,708,000; the highest, $48,700,000. In large measure the swell in values after 1792 resulted from price inflation. Wholesale commodity prices at New York rose from an average of about 90 points in 1790 to 120 points in 1794, reached 132 points in 1795, and varied from 110 to 140 points during 1801–1807. However, price inflation alone did not account for the increases of values of American products exported; it was supplemented by a substantial increase in the quantities of such exports, particularly cotton. High prices, coupled with expanding production, made the years 1793–1807 exceptionally prosperous. A prime factor in the price inflation was the expansion of currency and credit in Europe to finance the wars. Between 1793 and 1815 Britain alone issued public certificates of debt totaling £911,000,000, thereby swelling the currency available in the British market. Since the total value of American goods exported, 1790–1815, was less than $850,000,000, the inflationary impact of British credit expansion on American prices is apparent.[4]

During twenty-six years, 1790–1815, exports produced in the states had a combined value of $847,000,000. Foreign goods imported and not reexported came to $1,231,000,000. Thus the total balance of trade against the states amounted, on paper, to $384,000,000.[5] This figure, however, does not mean that the country had imported to that extent in excess of its earnings abroad. Such trade statistics state the prices of American products before exportation. When American shipowners exported goods, foreigners paid the freights to them. Such earnings, which do not appear in the statistics of trade, were akin to an export.

Freight earnings cannot be ascertained with precision because American merchants owned the ships in which they traded and did not make freight charges against themselves for the goods they carried. Their earn-

[3] Buck, *Anglo-American Trade*, pp. 102–120.

[4] Johnson, *History of Commerce*, II, 20; Cole, *Wholesale Commodity Prices*, p. 106, chart; Hidy, *The House of Baring in American Trade*, p. 27; Galpin, "Grain Trade to Spanish Peninsula," pp. 25–26.

[5] Johnson, *History of Commerce*, II, 20.

ings blended profits and freights in such a way that the two cannot be separated. How could one compute the freight earnings on a voyage such as that of the ship *Confederacy*, which left New York in 1795, visited London, Madeira, Mauritius, Réunion, Bombay, Calcutta, Canton, and Hamburg, handled en route a great variety of products, and trafficked at any port of call? However, despite the inadequacy of evidence concerning individual voyages, the records of American shipping as a whole signify that the earnings of American shipowners, on the joint account of profits and freights, increased phenomenally between 1793 and 1808.[6]

In 1790, American shipping amounted to 355,000 tons and made up 58.6 percent of all shipping engaged in the foreign trade of the Union. The principal countries which gave favorable treatment to American vessels were France, Spain, Portugal, the Netherlands, and Denmark. Measured by tonnage, 84 percent of American-owned vessels engaged in importing into the states in 1790–1791 from Europe and its empires entered from those five countries and their possessions. However, the value of the imports into the Union from those five nations and their colonies was only 24 percent of the total value of American imports from the European powers. In the trade with only one country—Britain—were conditions unfavorable to American shippers. Although 77 percent of the imports of the Union from Europe and its colonies came from the British Empire in 1792, the tonnage of American vessels arriving from British ports was only 16 percent of all American shipping engaged in such import trade. Manifestly, British vessels carried the bulk of the goods that entered the states from British ports. Jefferson complained in 1793 that only Britain singled out the shipping of the United States for discriminatory treatment. Not only did Britain normally exclude American vessels from the British West Indies, British North America, and Newfoundland; American ships sailing to Britain operated under a provisional permission that might be revoked by the crown at any time, without prior notice. "Our navigation," Jefferson noted, "is excluded from the security of fixed laws, while that security is given to the navigation of others." In his foreign policy Jefferson aimed first of all to force Britain to cease its discrimination against American vessels and to accord to them the same legal rights she conceded to the vessels of all other nations.[7]

A golden age of American shipping was the period 1793–1807. Of Boston it was said in 1794 that "not less than four hundred and fifty sail of ships, brigs, schooners, sloops, and small craft are now in this port. The prospect is pleasing, as it affords the expectation of employment for the industrious mechanic and laborer, who may not, we think, be idle unless they choose." During seventeen years before 1808, American shipowners acquired more than twice as much shipping as they had owned in 1790—

---

[6] Porter, *The Jacksons and the Lees*, I, 85.

[7] Johnson, *History of Commerce*, II, 28; *State Papers* (Wait), I, 425–431.

an increase from 355,000 tons to 1,089,000 tons, or a gain of 734,000 tons. In 1790, American ships carried only 40.5 percent of the value of all the goods in transit in the Union's foreign trade; the corresponding figures were 79.5 percent in 1793, 90 percent in 1795, 91 percent in 1805, and 92 percent in 1807. And this percentagewise increase occurred in company with an enormous increase in the volume of foreign trade—from combined imports and exports of $43,000,000 in 1790 to $246,000,000 in 1807. Measured by the value of goods transported, the American shipping business increased thirteenfold during these years.[8] More specifically, the following increases occurred: [9]

TONNAGE OF SHIPPING OWNED IN

	New York City	Boston	Massachusetts
Dec. 31, 1798	155,435	80,741	215,177
Dec. 31, 1800	146,442	96,312	231,258
Dec. 31, 1807	217,381	119,510	321,035
Dec. 31, 1810	268,548	149,121	354,153

Several factors contributed to the shipping boom. The United States engrossed most of the carrying trade between Europe and the French and Spanish territories in the Western Hemisphere; American shipowners increased their share of the shipping plying between Britain and the states from less than 50 percent in 1790 to 95 percent in 1800; a large part of the exports of Britain to Europe went in American ships; and trade with China and Indian Ocean ports rose to new heights.[10]

American shippers profited from war in Europe because they enjoyed certain assets at the start. For one thing, the shipyards of the Union provided vessels at low cost. In 1791, Tench Coxe estimated that French shipbuilders produced at a rate of $55 to $60 a ton; Americans at $33 to $35 a ton.[11] Abundant timber resources and skilled shipwrights had long enabled New Englanders to build vessels more cheaply than could their British competitors. Federal legislation after 1790 stimulated shipowning in the states by barring foreigners from holding shares in American vessels.[12] In addition, American carriers operated at a high pitch of efficiency. Of the West Indian trade, Jacob Crowninshield said in 1806:

We sail our vessels cheaper than most other nations; we make shorter voyages; we are more economical in our expenses. Our vessels stay but little time in port. The captains transact their own business, seldom going consigned.

[8] Pemberton, "Description of Boston," p. 287; Johnson, History of Commerce, II, 20, 28.

[9] Morison, Maritime History of Massachusetts, p. 378.

[10] Forbes, "Boston Trade," p. 712.

[11] Coxe, A View of the United States, p. 184.

[12] Robert G. Albion, "Early Nineteenth-Century Shipowning," Journal of Economic History, I, No. 1 (May, 1941), 9; Robert G. Albion, Square-Riggers on Schedule (Princeton, N. J.: Princeton University Press, 1938), p. 20.

Here two commissions are saved, one on the sales and another on the purchase. English vessels from Europe go out half loaded and frequently with ballast. They frequently make but one voyage in a year and seldom more than two. Our northern vessels make three or four, southern vessels more and go full loaded and do not depend on freights out or home.[13]

An official British report of 1805 estimated the operating expenses of an American vessel of 250 tons on a round trip, Britain to the United States, as £513; for a similar British vessel, £1,083.[14] The shipping boom inflated sailors' wages from $8 to $30 a month and drew many foreigners into the service of American owners, who engrossed most of Europe's sea-borne trade as the merchantmen of Britain's enemies vanished from the sea.[15]

The shipping business was complex and many-sided. Only a few merchants appear to have operated vessels on regular routes, serving other shippers at fixed charges. Most frequently merchants shipped their own goods in their vessels and depended upon the captain or supercargo to make sales and to buy returns. It was also a usual practice for such vessels to earn freights by carrying additional goods which had been consigned by other traders. Many vessels, including the largest, were owned by one merchant, although joint ownership was common. In one case, seventeen persons representing nine occupations owned a New England brig of 197 tons. Among the master shipowners were William Gray, reputed to have owned 115 vessels before 1815, Elias Hasket Derby, and Joseph Peabody, all of Salem; John Jacob Astor and Archibald Gracie of New York; and Stephen Girard of Philadelphia.[16]

After 1791, American merchants increasingly re-exported goods they had imported, thereby adding to their freights and profits earned abroad, for their ships carried by far the larger part of the products. During the years 1790–1793 the value of re-exports rose steadily—from $539,000 to $2,110,000. In 1794, the total stood at $6,526,000; in 1796, at $26,300,000. The peak was reached in 1806 at $60,283,000. During fifteen years, 1793–1807, the combined value of all re-exports was $493,000,000—an average of $32,800,000 a year.[17]

The re-export trade followed several channels. Great quantities of British and European goods were reshipped to the West Indies, with Cuba as a principal recipient. Boston merchants usually brought home teas, nankeens, and chinaware from Canton by way of Cape Horn, preparatory to re-exportation to Europe. Salem merchants dominated the trade with

[13] Reinoehl, "Remarks," pp. 92–93.
[14] Ernest Ludlow Bogart and Charles Manfred Thompson, eds., *Reedings in the Economic History of the United States* (New York: Longmans, Green and Company, 1929), p. 206.
[15] John Bach McMaster, *A History of the People of the United States* . . . (8 vols.; New York: D. Appleton and Company, 1885–1913), III, 225.
[16] Albion, "Early Nineteenth-Century Shipowning," pp. 4–6, 9.
[17] Johnson, *History of Commerce*, II, 20.

the Indian Ocean. As a rule, their vessels carried sugar, coffee, spices, silks, cottons, indigo, and China goods directly to Salem, whence they went to Europe and the West Indies. American re-exports of West Indian products pushed into the markets of Europe. In 1807, the Netherlands ranked first among such outlets on the Continent, followed by France, Italy, and Spain. American merchants in 1805 re-exported more than twice as much sugar as was consumed in the states and more than eight times as much coffee. Of all re-exports in 1807 that had paid ad valorem duties upon importation, about 74 percent came from the British Empire, 11 percent from Asia, and 6 percent from France and its possessions. The yearly average of certain re-exports, 1805–1807, was as follows: wines and spirits, 5,023,000 gallons; teas, 2,151,000 pounds; cocoa, 5,937,000 pounds; pepper, 5,292,000 pounds.[18]

So great was the re-export trade that during each of six years, 1798–1800 and 1805–1807, the value of goods re-exported exceeded the value of domestic products sent abroad. The gains to American merchants arising from re-exports undoubtedly so added to the foreign assets of the Union as to give it a favorable balance of trade. Bogart states that during 1803–1807 the freights earned by American shipping averaged $32,000,000 a year. At this time the average annual balance of trade against the states amounted, on paper, to about $20,000,000. Whatever the exact figures, it seems certain that freights and profits, added to the value of American products exported, gave the Union a profitable status in world commerce.[19]

Other facts support this conclusion. For one thing, American merchants did not contract long-term debts abroad to a noticeable extent. In all countries except Britain they customarily bought goods for cash. It appears that foreign holdings of the securities of the United States government varied from about $20,000,000 in 1795 to about $23,000,000 in 1809. Estimates of British investments in United States securities ranged from £4,182,000 in 1801 to £4,000,000 to £5,000,000 in 1808–1810. Jacob Crowninshield put the combined debts, public and private, which the United States owed to British creditors in 1806 as $40,000,000. During ten years, 1801–1810, when the paper balance of trade against the United States showed a total of $180,725,000, the indebtedness of Americans to foreigners did not increase by an appreciable amount. From all this it follows that the earnings of American exporters, on account of freights and profits, went far to pay for the imports of the Union and to give it, in reality, a favorable balance of trade.[20]

[18] Albion and Pope, *Sea Lanes in Wartime*, p. 93; Reinoehl, "Remarks," pp. 99, 104; Porter, *The Jacksons and the Lees*, I, 38; Pitkin, *Statistical View of the Commerce of the United States*, p. 151.

[19] Ernest Ludlow Bogart, *Economic History of the American People* (2d ed.; New York: Longmans, Green and Company, 1939), pp. 233–234.

[20] Reinoehl, "Remarks," p. 90; Hidy, *The House of Baring in American Trade*, pp. 34–35.

The movement of coin in foreign exchanges throws light on the commerce of the states. American merchants obtained coin and bullion chiefly from Mexico and Peru, via the West Indies, and in Europe, principally from Spain. Such acquisitions signify that in the trades with the West Indies and Europe the balance of payments favored the United States. Although the Spanish milled dollar outweighed the American silver dollar by 2 percent, the two coins circulated at par. Before 1806, American exporters made a profit by exchanging American dollars in the West Indies for Spanish dollars, which they had reminted into American dollars to be sent out to repeat the cycle. China and the Indian Ocean area were the magnets that attracted most of the coin which American merchants obtained. Jacob Crowninshield estimated that before 1806 they had shipped $50,000,000 to $60,000,000 in coin around the Cape of Good Hope, of which not more than $10,000,000 "was in the United States at any one time." He also asserted that a third of such specie shipments in 1804–1805 had been made directly from Europe. At that time they amounted to $3,000,000 a year.[21]

In colonial times most of the specie exported from the thirteen colonies had gone directly to England in order to pay for imports of English goods (or to redress an unfavorable balance of trade); after 1790, specie exports enabled Americans to buy goods in the East Indies that yielded profits in the re-export trade. This altered use of coin—from the purchase of goods for the home market to the purchase of goods to be re-exported—suggests that foreign trade had taken a profitable turn. In the meantime, the supply of coin within the states was more plentiful after 1793 than before. One estimate gives the amount in 1800 as $16,525,000. Despite the exportation in 1811 of $7,000,000 to foreign owners of stocks of the Bank of the United States, the banks of the country had $17,000,000 in specie in their vaults in 1815. However, the profits from the re-exportation of coin to the East Indies kept the money supply of the Union at a low ebb—insufficient to back up the note issues of commercial banks.[22]

The favorable state of foreign commerce is revealed by the profits of American merchants and the fortunes they acquired. Excessively high profits accompanied severe losses. The earnings on a three years' voyage to the Indian Ocean that ended in 1790 came to $100,000—a feat repeated by E. H. Derby, Jr., in the *Mount Vernon* on a venture to the Mediterranean in 1799–1800. A sloop worth $1,500 earned as much as $2,500 in the 1790's on a voyage between Boston and Surinam. On a trip to the East Indies after 1795 Joseph Lee reaped a profit of 100 percent. In 1805 the *Ambition* gained nearly 60 percent on a four months' voyage from New York to Havana and back. In the East Indian trade a successful venture probably yielded about 20 percent. Joseph Lee, Jr., informed Rufus King in 1806

---

[21] Porter, *The Jacksons and the Lees*, I, 26, 33; Reinoehl, "Remarks," pp. 112–113; Clark, *History of Manufactures in the United States*, p. 238.

[22] Dewey, *Financial History of the United States*, pp. 145, 149, 154.

that trade to Calcutta offered "a *moral certainty* of 6 per cent per annum, with a *reasonable expectation* of 10 per cent . . . & *a chance* for 12 per cent . . . with very little hazard." Lee added: ". . . if Calcutta goods are as high next year as this an adventure will give a profit of 15 to 20 per cent per annum after paying all charges, including insurance." [23]

The profits of foreign trade produced many fortunes. At New York Archibald Gracie's gains from shipping enabled him to build an imposing country house in 1799. When E. H. Derby died in 1799 he left one of the largest American estates of his day. John Jacob Astor owned property in 1800 estimated at $250,000; in 1815 he owned nine vessels and had $800,000 invested in trade. In 1804, George Crowninshield and his five sons possessed a family estate worth $469,000, and by 1809 William Gray had amassed a reputed fortune of $3,000,000. The shipping ventures of Stephen Girard rewarded him so handsomely that in 1812 he could found the "Bank of Stephen Girard," with a capital of $1,200,000. By 1815, commercial towns from Boston to Portsmouth were graced with stately mansions built with profits from foreign trade.[24]

BUILDERS OF SHIPS

The American shipowner was indebted in large measure to American shipbuilders for his success in world commerce, for they supplied him with superior vessels at relatively low cost. They in turn profited from his earnings, which financed the construction of new ships. The 1,089,000 tons of American shipping engaged in foreign trade in 1807 certainly represented a minimum investment of $40 million—an indicator both of the profits garnered from foreign trade and of the capital invested in the shipbuilding industry. In addition, American shipwrights contributed to the exports of the Union through the sale abroad of American-built vessels. Merchants occasionally sold ships which they sent out on trading voyages. Thus in 1788–1789 the Derbys disposed of the *Grand Turk* at Mauritius, and the *Atlanta* and the *Three Sisters* at Canton. It is estimated that between 1798

[23] Albion and Pope, *Sea Lanes in Wartime*, pp. 69, 89; Porter, *The Jacksons and the Lees*, I, 26, 30, 72–73; John R. Spears, *The Story of the American Merchant Marine* (New York: The Macmillan Company, 1910), p. 118.
[24] Albion and Pope, *Sea Lanes in Wartime*, p. 69; Reinoehl, "Remarks," p. 85; Allen Johnson, Dumas Malone, and others, eds., *Dictionary of American Biography* (22 vols.; New York: Charles Scribner's Sons, 1928–1958), V, 250; VII, 321, 523; N. S. B. Gras and Henrietta Larson, eds., *Casebook in American Business History* (New York: F. S. Crofts & Co., 1939), pp. 87–88; Raymond Walters, Jr., *Albert Gallatin* (New York: The Macmillan Company, 1957), p. 294; Hammond *Banks and Politics in America*, p. 226; Margaret L. Brown, "Mr. and Mrs. William Bingham of Philadelphia: Rulers of the Republican Court," *Pennsylvania Magazine of History and Biography*, LXI, No. 3 (July, 1937), 296–298.

and 1812 American owners sold American-built ships totaling more than 200,000 tons—an export value probably in excess of $7 million.[25]

In 1791 Hamilton observed that American-built vessels were unsurpassed. One natural advantage favored American builders—an abundance of excellent timber in forests accessible to all the centers of construction. New England's forests furnished the ships with white oak for bottoms, lower sides, knees, and flooring, and pine for upper sides, superstructures, and masts. Spruce, cedar, and maple were also used. Most valuable was the decay-resistant live oak of South Carolina and Georgia—so coveted that Congress appropriated $200,000 to enable President John Adams to purchase groves of the precious trees, already in danger of extinction. Thus the Union took its first step toward the conservation of its timber resources. Shipbuilders often found it more economical to move their yards to the edge of a virgin forest than to bring timber from remote points. For this reason the industry after 1790 advanced northward along the wilderness coast of Maine. Boston and New York contended with dwindling timber supplies by building canals to tap unexploited forest lands.[26]

In 1775 the shipbuilding industry of the Union, with more than 140 years of successful experience to its credit, extended all along the coast and employed a host of superior craftsmen. Low costs of construction had enabled colonial builders to sell ships regularly to British merchants. About 50 vessels were thus delivered annually before the Revolution, when the general trade of Britain made use of an estimated 398,000 tons of American-built shipping. In 1769, the thirteen colonies produced 389 ships aggregating nearly 24,000 tons, with New England accounting for about 61 percent, New York 15 percent, the Delaware River 7 percent, Chesapeake Bay 12 percent, and the lower South 4 percent. Despite the decline suffered during the Revolution, the building of warships and privateers kept the industry alive. In 1789 it received encouragement from Congress through the Tonnage Act of July 31, which imposed a duty of 50 cents a ton on foreign-built, foreign-owned vessels entering the Union, as against a duty of only 6 cents a ton on vessels that were American-built and American-owned. Tench Coxe described the prospects of the industry in 1794 in glowing terms:

Shipbuilding is an art for which the United States are peculiarly qualified by their skill in the construction and by the materials with which this country abounds: and they are strongly tempted to pursue it by their commercial spirit,

[25] John G. B. Hutchins, *The American Maritime Industries and Public Policy, 1789–1914* (Vol. LXXI of *Harvard Economic Studies;* Cambridge, Mass.: Harvard University Press, 1941), p. 171; Porter, *The Jacksons and the Lees*, I, 30, 31.
[26] Cole, *Hamilton's Industrial Correspondence*, p. 305; Hutchins, *The American Maritime Industries*, pp. 172, 177; Lillard, *The Great Forest*, p. 161; Clark, *History of Manufactures in the United States*, p. 486.

by the capital fisheries in their bays and on their coasts, and by the productions of a great and rapidly increasing agriculture. They build their oak vessels on lower terms than the cheapest European vessels of fir, pine, and larch. The cost of an oak ship in New England is about 24 Mexican dollars per ton fitted for sea: a fir vessel costs in the ports of the Baltic, 35 Mexican dollars: and the American ship will be much the most durable. The cost of a vessel of the American live oak and cedar, which will last (if salted in her timbers) thirty years is only 36 to 38 dollars in our different ports; an oak ship in the cheapest port of England, Holland, or France fitted in the same manner will cost 55 to 60 dollars.[27]

Immigration and the training of apprentices steadily enlarged the class of master shipbuilders, many of whom owned large shipyards, turned out two or three vessels a year, and enjoyed the status of solid citizen. Ship carpenters, mechanics, and apprentices worked together under a contract system in which a prospective owner engaged a master builder to meet detailed specifications, from the laying of the keel to the launching of the ship. The most successful builders employed subcontractors. After 1790, buyers made cash advances to the builders, enabling them to pay their hands in coin. The apprenticeship system recruited and trained novices to the extent that the industry was able to keep pace with the demands created by the boom times after 1790. The yards produced all sorts of craft—small boats, coasting and fishing vessels, and large ships for foreign trade—ranging from fewer than 20 to 700 tons. Long, heavy timbers featured the structures of American ships. New Englanders, prejudiced against large vessels as not seaworthy in storms, deemed 500 tons to be the maximum for safety, and preferred ships that were broad at the water line, both fore and aft, "to support them from being plunged into the sea." Experience was the school of shipbuilding, as fathers instructed sons in the secrets of the art. Although master builders did not get rich, many of them prospered: at New York two had property in 1815 assessed for personal taxes at $15,000, one at $7,000, and one at $30,000. Another in 1810 bought real estate worth $17,370.[28]

Americans made some striking improvements in the building of ships. During the Revolution, designers defied prevailing practice and prejudice by constructing enlarged brigs and schooners—long and narrow—that sailed with unwonted speed. John Peck of Boston modeled ships on scientific principles, in a manner that achieved both swiftness and a carrying capacity beyond that of comparable vessels. Baltimore builders were

[27] Bishop, *History of American Manufactures*, I, 90–91; Hutchins, *The American Maritime Industries*, p. 192; *Debates of Congress*, 1 Cong., 1 Sess., II, 2186; Coxe, *A View of the United States*, pp. 99–100.

[28] John H. Morrison, *History of New York Ship Yards* (New York: William F. Sametz & Co., 1909), pp. 17–24, 31, 36–44, 48–49; Morison, *Maritime History of Massachusetts*, pp. 80, 97, 99, 102; Hutchins, *The American Maritime Industries*, pp. 178, 182; Coxe, *A View of the United States*, p. 221.

among the first to cover the bottom of a ship with copper sheeting. At Salem, E. H. Derby's experiments bore fruit in four large ships distinguished for both speed and strength. His *Astrea* ran from Salem to Ireland in eleven days and made a round trip to France in five weeks. New York turned out the longest vessel built before 1807—the frigate *President,* with a gun deck of 174 feet. Although not a quantity producer, Philadelphia before 1800 designed and built the finest ships. It was once a truism that an ideal vessel would combine "a Boston bottom and Philadelphia sides." [29]

After the Revolution, shipbuilding remained of minor importance in the South, where Charleston and Norfolk were the main centers. Baltimore distinguished itself with the 360-ton *Empress of China,* completed in 1784; later progress appeared in the building there of the frigates *Constellation* and *Chesapeake* and the continuing construction of fast brigs and schooners. Philadelphia specialized in superior vessels of live oak; the largest builder among American ports in 1793, its industry declined to second rank in 1815. Several able shipwrights sought New York after the Revolution and enlivened its waterfront along the East River near Corlaer's Hook. Records of 36 vessels built there, 1788–1812, give a total of 12,571 tons—an average of 347 tons. The most productive years were 1807 and 1809; the largest vessel was of 666 tons. Nearby, on the Connecticut River at Haddam, Essex, and Middletown, new yards arose under the impact of a growing demand for sturdy and durable whalers. Three districts served the industry in Massachusetts: the Merrimac River from Plum Island to Haverhill; the North River upstream to Hanover, with 25 yards; and the small port towns of the Boston area, which completed 26 ships, brigs, and schooners in 1815. Salem's rise before 1800 was then followed by a decline. On the coast of Maine, builders after 1783 established yards at Kennebunkport, Portland, Yarmouth, Bath, and Camden which specialized in cheaper vessels of small or medium size.[30] S. E. Morison portrays a scene on the tidal North River in Massachusetts:

> Looking downstream from the Hanover bridge, eleven shipyards were in view, filled with vessels in various stages of construction. Every morning at daybreak the shipwrights might be seen crossing the pastures or walking along the sedgy riverbank to their work, for a dollar a day from dawn to dark. When the sun rose above the Marshfield hills, like a great red ball through the river mist, there began the cheery clatter of wooden shipbuilding—clean, musical sounds of steel on wood, iron on anvil, creak of tackle and rattle of sheave; with much geeing and hawing as ox-teams brought in loads of fragrant oak,

[29] Bishop, *History of American Manufactures,* I, 47, 92; Morrison, *New York Ship Yards,* pp. 18, 26, 38; Spears, *The American Merchant Marine,* p. 99.

[30] Hutchins, *The American Maritime Industries,* pp. 178–179, 181–183; Morrison, *New York Ship Yards,* pp. 18, 46–47; Bishop, *History of American Manufactures,* I, 73; Clark, *History of Manufactures in the United States,* p. 470; Forbes, "Boston Trade," p. 714; William Hutchinson Rowe, *The Maritime History of Maine* (New York: W. W. Norton & Company, 1948), pp. 120–127.

pine, and hackmatack, and a snatch of chanty as a large timber is hoisted into place.[31]

Although American merchants owned but relatively few vessels in 1783, these greatly excelled the ships of colonial days and were indeed the best in the world. Construction was slow until 1789, when a revival occurred. American-built shipping owned by Americans increased from 123,000 tons in 1789 to 364,000 tons in 1790. Vigorous activity marked the year 1793; total construction in 1795 probably reached 100,000 tons. The quasi war with France depressed the industry as a whole, although some builders profited from contracts for warships, such as the *Constitution* and the *Boston*. Americans owned 669,000 tons of American-built shipping in 1800. Average yearly construction during the good times, 1801–1807, was 110,000 tons. Three prosperous years followed the lifting of the embargo of 1808 and culminated in a peak of 146,000 tons in 1811. The War of 1812 disrupted the industry as buyers defaulted on contracts, speculative concerns stopped work, many builders failed, and construction sank to 29,000 tons in 1814. However, a rapid recovery set a new record of 154,000 tons in 1815.[32]

American shipowners profited from practices of several European countries that discriminated against American-built vessels. Britain, France, Spain, and the Netherlands each gave special protection and privileges to vessels built by its inhabitants. In general, restrictive navigation laws excluded foreign-built vessels from most of the colonial trades of the European powers; consequently, European merchants were prevented from buying ships built in the United States. As a result, American shipyards built in the main for American purchasers, who were shielded from the competition of foreign buyers. However, this condition did not injure the American shipbuilding industry. American merchants provided a steady, familiar, convenient market that taxed the resources of American shipyards to the limit as the employment of American vessels increased by leaps and bounds when the warring powers of Europe preyed upon each other's ships. In this wise the builder served the merchant—a result foreseen by Tench Coxe in 1794 when he wrote: "And should the French, British, and other foreign nations continue to decline the purchase of American-built ships, there can be no doubt that we shall take a greater portion of the carrying trade for ourselves and other countries, from that cause." [33]

[31] Morison, *Maritime History of Massachusetts*, p. 103.

[32] Spears, *The American Merchant Marine*, p. 99; Hutchins, *The American Maritime Industries*, pp. 185–186; Bishop, *History of American Manufactures*, I, 92, 147, 216; Forbes, "Boston Trade," p. 718.

[33] Hutchins, *The American Maritime Industries*, pp. 175–176; Coxe, *A View of the United States*, p. 185.

CHAPTER XII

The Spirit of Improvement

INNOVATIONS IN AGRICULTURE

HAVING separated from Britain, Americans strove to justify independence by demonstrating that it would elevate life in the states in such a manner as to glorify the new republic. After 1783 a vigorous spirit of progress animated the country, expressing itself first of all in projects for the improvement of agriculture.[1] That industry, having marked time during the war, exhibited at its end the crude, wasteful methods and primitive conditions of colonial times. Successive crops of wheat, corn, or tobacco, followed by grazing of the land, quickly robbed it of its fertility. Inefficient plows turned up only two or three inches of soil; farmers cut grain with scythes or sickles and threshed with hand flails; cattle and horses, ill fed in winter, were weak and scrawny; pests and parasites ravaged fields and orchards; the loose, lightly sodded soils of the South were eroded by heavy rains.

> No smiling pastures spread inviting here,
> But hot dry fields on ev'ry side appear.[2]

Many gentlemen farmers, with large estates in the East, became increasingly conscious of the menace of soil exhaustion. They also suffered from a scarcity of free farm workers—occasioned by the westward movement—or from the inefficiency of laggard slaves. Such landowners looked to science to provide a magic stimulus that might compensate for the inadequacy of farm labor. Never before or since has so influential a group of Americans stood forth as patrons of agricultural reform.[3] They drew their

[1] Brooke Hindle, *The Pursuit of Science in Revolutionary America, 1735–1789* (Chapel Hill: The University of North Carolina Press, 1956), p. 355.

[2] N. F. Cabell, "Some Fragments of an Intended Report on the Post-Revolutionary Agriculture of Virginia," E. G. Swem, ed., *William and Mary College Historical Quarterly*, First Series, XXVI, No. 1 (January, 1918), 147; Craven, *Soil Exhaustion*, pp. 97, 100, 112–113, 304.

[3] Olive Moore Gambrill, "John Beale Bordley and the Early Years of the Philadelphia Agricultural Society," *Pennsylvania Magazine of History and Biography*,

inspiration from England, where numerous experiments had greatly increased the productivity of farms.[4] Washington described the situation when he wrote in 1791:

> The aim of the farmers in this country (if they can be called farmers) is not to make the most they can from the land, which is, or has been cheap, but the most of labor, which is dear; the consequence of which has been, much ground has been *scratched* over and none cultivated or improved as it ought to have been; whereas a farmer in England, where land is dear, and labor cheap, finds it his interest to improve and cultivate highly, that he may reap large crops from a small quantity of ground.[5]

The reformers of the era before 1815 sought to realize four main objectives. First, they labored to restore depleted soils, chiefly by means of fertilizers. "No profit," said John Taylor of Caroline, "can be made by tilling poor land . . . . To make it rich, therefore, ought to be the first object of our efforts." Second, the reformers strove to preserve the fertility of good lands. To this end they experimented with crop rotations and with new methods of plowing that were designed to prevent rains from forming gullies and washing away the precious topsoil. Third, they endeavored to make the most effective use of soil by means of deep plowing. Fourth, they gave attention to the improvement of horses and cattle. This they did by importing superior breeds and by cultivating hay crops, such as alfalfa, to increase the winter's supply of fodder.[6]

The reformers made use of several agencies. First in importance were learned societies. The American Philosophical Society, organized at Philadelphia in 1743 and revived in 1767, concerned itself partly with agriculture and published many papers on rural themes. Massachusetts followed in 1780, when the legislature incorporated the American Academy of Arts and Sciences. Its interest in farming moved it to set up a special committee on agriculture in 1786. Early in 1785 a group of prominent Pennsylvanians,

---

LXVI, No. 4 (October, 1942), 416–418, 433; Carl Raymond Woodward, *The Development of Agriculture in New Jersey, 1640–1880* (New Brunswick: New Jersey Agricultural Experiment Station, 1927), p. 11; Hedrick, *New York Agriculture*, pp. 113–114.

[4] Leading English innovators and writers were Robert Bakewell, Thomas Coke of Holkham, Arthur Young, Charles Varo, Sir John Sinclair, "Turnip" Townshend, and Jethro Tull, whose *Horse-hoeing Husbandry* . . . (1733) was probably the most widely read book on farm problems during this period. Rodney C. Loehr, "The Influence of English Agriculture on American Agriculture, 1775–1825," *Agricultural History*, XI, No. 1 (January, 1937), 5–11; Hindle, *The Pursuit of Science*, pp. 358, 359, 366.

[5] *Writings of Washington* (Fitzpatrick), XXXI, 440.

[6] Avery O. Craven, "The Agricultural Reformers of the Ante-Bellum South," *American Historical Review*, XXXIII, No. 2 (January, 1928), 305–306; Rodney H. True, "The Early Development of Agricultural Societies in the United States" (American Historical Association, *Annual Report . . . 1920;* Washington: Government Printing Office, 1925), p. 297.

along with a progressive Maryland planter, John Beale Bordley, organized the Philadelphia Society for Promoting Agriculture. In the same year appeared the South Carolina Society for Promoting and Improving Agriculture and Other Rural Concerns. The first successful organization in New Jersey was the Burlington Society for the Promotion of Agriculture and Domestic Manufactures, of 1790. New Yorkers joined the movement in 1791 by forming the New York Society for Agriculture, Arts, and Manufactures; the Massachusetts Society for Promoting Agriculture entered the field in 1792; and the Society of Virginia for Promoting Agriculture came into being in 1811. After 1790, smaller county societies devoted to farming sprang up throughout the states.[7]

The patrons of such organizations were southern planters, gentlemen farmers in the North, wealthy merchants, and professional men. A limited membership—the result of punctilious election of members and fairly high annual dues—gave the societies a high-toned, exclusive cast. Jefferson once spoke of the members of the Philadelphia Society as the "elect." The societies chose honorary associates, helped to start new groups, and encouraged members to make and keep records of experiments and to report the results. Income from dues was used to provide prizes—cash or medals —for new methods, choice products, or superior animals which were exhibited at gatherings of country folk. The leading societies published volumes of scientific papers and printed pamphlets or sent approved articles to rural newspapers or periodicals such as the *American Museum,* the *Columbian Magazine,* and the *Worcester Magazine.* In their efforts to enlighten dirt farmers the societies sounded a somewhat democratic note.[8]

The improvements of the era were the fruit of experiments of individuals who made up a fairly large company. One pioneer, John Beale Bordley, of Wye Island in Chesapeake Bay, used his large farm as an experimental station to test and modify English methods of tillage and crop rotation as advocated by Arthur Young. Bordley's books mark him as the most prolific American writer on the agriculture of his day.[9] At Princeton, New Jersey, George Morgan's 300-acre farm, "Prospect," was the scene of new methods of keeping bees, of raising corn, and of exterminating pests, particularly the Hessian fly. There, in 1787, Morgan's garden displayed

[7] Hindle, *The Pursuit of Science,* pp. 127–129, 264, 357, 359, 362–363; True, "Agricultural Societies," pp. 296, 299; Gambrill, "John Beale Bordley," p. 418; Woodward, *New Jersey Agriculture,* pp. 51–54; Cabell, "Report," p. 169.

[8] True, "Agricultural Societies," pp. 297–300, 304–305; Hindle, *The Pursuit of Science,* pp. 357, 360–363; Woodward, *New Jersey Agriculture,* p. 25; Gambrill, "John Beale Bordley," pp. 423–428.

[9] Hindle, *The Pursuit of Science,* pp. 358–359; Gambrill, "John Beale Bordley," pp. 413–414. Bordley's books are *A Summary View of the Course of Corps in the Husbandry of England and Maryland* (Philadelphia: 1784); *Sketches on Rotations of Crops* (Philadelphia: 1797); and *Essays and Notes on Husbandry and Rural Affairs* (Philadelphia: 1799).

rows of Indian corn grown "from different kinds of seed, collected from the different latitudes . . . , as far north as . . . Canada, and south as far as the West Indies." Among products Morgan advertised for sale were seeds of alfalfa, clover, timothy, rye, and grass. In 1796 he moved to Washington County, Pennsylvania, where he set out a nursery of small fruits.[10] Southward, many planters carried on unending experiments. At Mount Vernon, Washington tested many new plants, introduced selective stock breeding, and tried out various fertilizers and plans of crop rotation. He divided his estate into farms and the farms into fields, in order to check results of crops grown on a small scale, under careful supervision.[11] The foremost reformer of the South was John Taylor of Caroline, who worked out a complete system of tillage that called for enriching the soil with animal manures and with plants plowed under and enclosing arable fields to keep out the stock. He extolled Indian corn as a sovereign crop, prizing its stalks, shucks, and cobs as vegetable manure.[12] Thick hedges, deep plowing, imported fertilizers, selected seeds, and improved machines figured in his system, which he expounded in his book *Arator*, published in 1813.[13]

"The importance of the giving the best shelter to cattle and in such a way as to procure the greatest quantities of manure" prompted the Philadelphia Society for the Promotion of Agriculture to offer in 1791 a gold medal "for the best design of a farmyard and method of managing it." Earlier the Society had awarded its first prize to George Morgan for an essay on his farmyard system. Progressive farmers generally urged the use of fertilizers on depleted soil and took pains to enlarge and conserve a farm's supply of animal manures. Washington's method was to house cattle in specially built pens. However, since most farms yielded insufficient quantities of manure, the improvers were forced to turn to other agents. By 1790, informed men, such as Noah Webster, knew that plants extracted

[10] Woodward, *New Jersey Agriculture*, pp. 20–21, 26; Max Savelle, *George Morgan: Colony Builder* (New York: Columbia University Press, 1932), pp. 184–187.

[11] Paul Leland Haworth, *George Washington: Country Gentleman* (Indianapolis: The Bobbs-Merrill Company, 1915), pp. 116–124, 136–140; Craven, *Soil Exhaustion*, pp. 87–89.

[12] Henry R. Simms, *Life of John Taylor* (Richmond: The William Byrd Press, Inc., 1932), pp. 149–150; Kathleen Bruce, "Virginian Agricultural Decline to 1860: A Fallacy," *Agricultural History*, VI, No. 1 (January, 1932), 5–6. See also Craven, "Agricultural Reformers," pp. 305–306.

[13] Other American writings of the period are Metcalf Bowler, *A Treatise on Agriculture and Practical Husbandry* (Providence: 1786); Samuel Deane, *The New England Farmer* (Worcester, Mass.: 1790); George Logan, *Fourteen Agricultural Experiments to Ascertain the Best Rotation of Crops* (Philadelphia: 1797); John A. Binns, *A Treatis on Practical Farming* (Fredericktown: 1803); George Redd, *A Late Discovery . . . Relative to Fertilizing Poor and Exhausted Lands* (Winchester, Va.: 1809).

nitrogen from the air and that soil was enriched if certain green crops were plowed under. For this purpose a few efficient farmers devoted a field every sixth or seventh year to a crop of buckwheat or cowpeas. This method, however, did not serve the small farmer who sought a yearly return from a limited acreage. The spur given by the European wars to wheat growing popularized a special fertilizer, gypsum, which added calcium, sulfur, and nitrogen to the soil and invigorated clover, corn, and wheat. First among experimenters with gypsum was John Alexander Binns of Virginia, whose tests—beginning in 1784—seemed to prove it to be a rapid restorer of his land. It absorbed moisture readily, resisted extreme heat, and produced wheat and grass on otherwise sterile soil. In his *Treatis on Practical Farming* (1803) Binns recommended gypsum for red clover and wheat. From his farm in Loudoun County its use spread throughout the wheat-growing districts of Virginia, Maryland, the middle states, and New England. Much of it came from Nova Scotia and New Brunswick. Annual imports rose within a few years after 1800 from 30,000 to 100,000 tons and the price went up from $4 to $36 a ton. After 1815 some onetime votaries of gypsum feared that it was a stimulant that quickly drained depleted land of its remaining fertility. Among other fertilizers used on a small scale were marl, lime, marsh mud, ashes, fish, leaves, and pine cones. Washington tried, without success, to dredge up muck from the bed of the Potomac.[14]

The emphasis on wheat to a large extent guided other experiments. It was assumed that the rotating of different crops on a designated field would give it an occasional rest, increase or conserve its fertility, and assure a maximum yield of wheat when it was sown. Various grasses were thought to be capable of conferring such benefits, in addition to providing hay for the stock in winter. The forested land of the East produced inferior native grasses that did not afford good winter fodder. Gentlemen farmers made experiments with timothy, alfalfa—then called lucerne—chicory or succory, and various kinds of clover, red and white. An observer in New Jersey saw in 1806 a patch of alfalfa six inches high that had been cut four times during the season. Root crops, such as turnips and rutabagas, were not well suited to American farms: freezing reduced their value as winter feed. Clover proved to be the most valuable "grass," both as a fertilizer and as a hay crop. Experimenters evolved innumerable rotation systems; each farmer worked out his own in response to the peculiar needs of his land. At one time Washington had seven fields in cultivation under a seven-year plan. Each year two of the fields were sown in wheat, one in corn and

[14] True, "Agricultural Societies," p. 297; Craven, *Soil Exhaustion,* pp. 88, 92–96, 111–112; Simms, *John Taylor,* p. 150; Charles S. Graham, "The Gypsum Trade of the Maritime Provinces," *Agricultural History,* XII, No. 3 (July, 1938), 209–210; Haworth, *George Washington,* pp. 102–103.

potatoes, one in buckwheat to be plowed under, and three in clover or grass; hence each field yielded only three crops of wheat and corn every seven years.[15]

Such a system required additional plowing each year, relative to the production of wheat, and therefore emphasized the need for better plows. An absorbing interest in such improvements inspired farmers, plowrights, and blacksmiths to work out new models. An iron plow patented by Charles Newbold in 1797, which combined moldboard and share in one piece, did not succeed, partly because a broken part could not be replaced, and partly because farmers found it too expensive and feared that it encouraged weeds. However, Newbold helped Robert Smith of Bucks County, Pennsylvania, to make an improved moldboard that was widely used in the middle states. A Virginian said in 1818 that the improvement of the plow "was the first step we took to improve our lands . . . . We have constructed our plows much larger and stronger; the moldboards are all of cast iron. We seldom break our land with less than three horses to a plow." Deep plowing became the fashion; presumably it was better than shallow plowing because it turned up unused subsoil, admitted more moisture and air, and enabled roots to grow more vigorously.

> Plow deep while sluggards sleep
> And you shall have corn to sell and keep.

Another reform widely adopted was that of plowing sloping land in horizontal ridges to keep water from running off and washing away the topsoil.[16]

The need for better oxen and horses intensified the progressive farmer's desire to improve his livestock. Before 1815 the best native cows and oxen grazed on farms in Rhode Island and the Connecticut Valley. The middle states, devoted to wheat, were content with rather scrawny cattle. On the whole, progress in cattle raising after 1775 came from improving native strains. England, however, made one contribution. By 1780 English breeders had developed Shorthorn cattle to the extent that they could be exported. In 1783, Messrs. Miller of Virginia and Gough of Baltimore imported improved English cattle, descendants of which found their way to the farm of Matthew Patton on the South Branch of the Potomac. About 1790 John and James Patton, sons of Matthew, took some of these superior animals to Kentucky, where they flourished on the excellent pas-

---

[15] Carleton R. Ball, "The History of American Wheat Development," *Agricultural History*, IV, No. 2 (April, 1930), 56–57; Craven, *Soil Exhaustion*, pp. 97–98; Hedrick, *New York Agriculture*, p. 119; Woodward, *New Jersey Agriculture*, p. 61; Loehr, "Influence of English Agriculture," p. 7; Haworth, *George Washington*, pp. 120–121.

[16] True, "Agricultural Societies," p. 302; Craven, *Soil Exhaustion*, pp. 87, 90–92; Woodward, *New Jersey Agriculture*, p. 65; John W. Oliver, *History of American Technology* (New York: The Ronald Press Company, 1956), pp. 129–130.

ture land of the Bluegrass country. Others soon followed, including a prize bull named Mars. Between 1799 and 1807 several of the Miller-Patton cattle—now aristocrats of the West—were taken to the Scioto and Miami valleys in Ohio. This South Branch–Bluegrass–Ohio cattle triangle represented England's chief contribution to American agriculture during our period. Unhappily, interest in improving livestock did not extend to those parts of the South under the sway of slavery and staple crops.[17]

Zeal for progress gave birth to a new American institution—the county fair—an outgrowth of efforts to improve the quality of sheep. As early as 1793 one William Foster brought three highly prized Merinos from Spain; in 1802 Robert R. Livingston sent four of them from France to his Hudson River estate, and David Humphreys sent a flock of 100 from Spain to Connecticut. About this time pioneer sheep raisers began to hold sheep-shearing exhibits on their farms. In 1807 Elkanah Watson caused a stir in western Massachusetts by displaying two Merinos on a public square in Pittsfield. His success inspired him to organize a Berkshire County general fair, which —held at Pittsfield in 1811—attracted a large and enthusiastic crowd. It featured pens "handsomely occupied by some excellent animals" and a line of 69 oxen "connected by chains, drawing a plow held by the oldest man in the county." Watson acclaimed his fair as "splendid, noble, and inspiring, beyond anything of its kind ever exhibited in America." Other counties adopted his plan so rapidly that farmers all over the country were soon gathering after harvest to view the superior animals, farm products, and household manufactures with which they and their neighbors competed for prizes.[18]

Despite the stirrings of reform, most farmers adhered to old ways. For a time the European wars gave them unprecedented resources and a potent incentive for improvements. Yet the fluctuations of foreign trade did not provide a solid footing for an uninterrupted advance. The wars clearly increased the use of gypsum, but in the end it appeared to have been a food for wheat and clover rather than a restorer of the soil. The reform movement did not establish experimental farms supported by government or cause agriculture to be studied in the schools. The first journal devoted to farming, the *Agricultural Museum*, did not appear until 1810.[19]

[17] Charles T. Leavitt, "Attempts to Improve Cattle Breeds in the United States, 1790–1860," *Agricultural History*, VII, No. 2 (April, 1933), 52–55, 58; Paul C. Henlein, *Cattle Kingdom in the Ohio Valley, 1783–1860* (Lexington: University of Kentucky Press, 1959), pp. 25, 27.

[18] True, "Agricultural Societies," pp. 300–302; Connor, "The Sheep Industry in the United States," p. 101; Hedrick, *New York Agriculture*, pp. 123–125.

[19] W. Freeman Galpin, *The Grain Supply of England during the Napoleonic Period* (New York: The Macmillan Company, 1925), pp. 135–149, 249; True, "Agricultural Societies," p. 299; John G. Gagliardo, "Germans and Agriculture in Colonial Pennsylvania," *Pennsylvania Magazine of History and Biography*, LXXXIII, No. 2 (April, 1959), 207.

The pervasive foe of improved methods was the abundance of land, along with the steady migration of farmers westward. Some observers thought that the emigrants were mainly energetic, ambitious young people —the very ones most likely to attempt something new and better. But pioneering committed them to the crude practices of cropping virgin lands. When farmers in the East decided to go west they often neglected their farms in the interval before they left. The sale of used lands by emigrants tended to keep down land prices in the East, enabled farmers who did not migrate to add to their holdings, and confirmed them in the wasteful methods of extensive farming.[20]

Consider the small farmer. He worked on a slender margin that did not encourage the taking of risks. Familiar methods would at least feed his family; failure of an ambitious experiment might threaten starvation. So why tempt fate? He could not afford to buy imported livestock; he had to be content to improve what he had—a slow process. He had neither the labor nor the arable land needed for extensive systems of crop rotation.[21]

The southern planters' mode of living resisted the proposed reforms. Since they required capital they demanded that he sacrifice some of his luxuries. That was too high a price. Moreover, the new ways called upon him to stay home and supervise his estate. But life in isolation among slaves was not always attractive. Strong was the temptation to leave one's fields to the care of an overseer and to seek diversion at a county seat or a nearby plantation. There was no place like home—to be away from. In other cases, long public service prevented owners from becoming effective progressive farmers.[22]

But the reform movement was not a failure. Societies, publications, experiments, exhibits, and fairs created a climate that favored improvements, although most farmers had to move slowly and act on a modest scale. Better plows and seed drills, improved livestock, and an increased use of clover and fertilizers were important gains. Perhaps the most general advance came from a host of practical suggestions that were limited in scope and inexpensive to apply. The numerous almanacs of the time repeatedly told the farmer how to perform his customary tasks in more efficient ways—how to make corn sirup, to kill peach-tree borers, to use turnips and beets as feed for horses and cows, to clear a room or a chimney of smoke, to destroy caterpillars, to preserve butter, to raise turkeys, to kill bugs, to make better cider, and to use ashes as manure. The stolidity

[20] Craven, *Soil Exhaustion*, pp. 118–119; L. C. Gray, "Economic Efficiency and Competitive Advantages of Slavery under the Plantation System," *Agricultural History*, IV, No. 2 (April, 1930), 37.

[21] Hindle, *The Pursuit of Science*, p. 362.

[22] Craven, *Soil Exhaustion*, pp. 114–115; Loehr, "Influence of English Agriculture," p. 9.

of the farmer resisted innovation but that trait was doubtless essential to his regimen of hard and tedious labor.[23]

TRANSPORTATION ON LAND

Transportation before 1815 served mainly to supply farmers with needed goods, to get their produce to market, and to take pioneers to new homes. In most shipments goods had to move by both land and water. The chief obstacles to land travel were mud, hills, and streams to be crossed; the great deterrent to river travel was the current on trips upstream. Roads enabled travelers to use horses and oxen to surmount obstacles; before the advent of the steamboat, human labor had to be used to overcome the river currents. Migrating pioneers could use pack horses, carts, or wagons on all stages of a journey but they could not propel large boats upstream or usually afford to buy them simply for travel downstream. Nor could most pioneers afford to ship their goods and livestock by river freighters.[24]

The primacy of roads accounts for the emphasis given to them in early plans for improving the means of transportation. The Revolutionary War had greatly increased travel but had done little to improve the highways. Since neither Congress nor the states had effected improvements during the 1780's, the condition of the roads in 1790 was deplorable. A widespread campaign for improving them coincided with the launching of the new federal government. The interest was especially strong in Pennsylvania, the state that introduced one of the principal innovations of the period—the private turnpike company.[25]

In American practice, local agencies of town or county had supervised the building and maintenance of roads. In 1790 the highways most urgently in need of improvement were those over which large quantities of freight moved to and from the principal towns. The extension of settlement and the streams of pioneers going west meant that a much traveled road served many people besides the residents of the localities through which it ran. Consequently, local taxpayers were unwilling to pay all the cost of improving a highway that benefited many outsiders. None of the states had resources sufficient for providing a complete system of hard-surfaced roads, and the legislatures generally refused to favor only a few localities at the expense of all the others. Since the users of an improved road were the ones who benefited from it, it followed that they should help to pay for improv-

[23] Hindle, *The Pursuit of Science*, pp. 366–367; Woodward, *New Jersey Agriculture*, pp. 67–70, 77–78; Joseph Schafer, *The Social History of American Agriculture* (New York: The Macmillan Company, 1936), pp. 50, 52, 55–56, 66–67.

[24] William F. Gephart, *Transportation and Industrial Development in the Middle West* (New York: 1909), pp. 57–58, 67.

[25] Frederic J. Wood, *The Turnpikes of New England* (Boston: Marshall Jones Company, 1919), pp. 28–29.

ing it. Such needs and conditions explain why legislatures were willing to allow private companies to improve and control important highways. Land speculators and merchants of large towns had the most direct interest in improving roads; hence they took the lead in organizing road companies that would not only earn a return on the capital invested but also increase land values and enlarge the area from which merchants derived the profits of trade.[26]

The turnpike movement was strongest in New England and the middle states, where the main highways accommodated much long-distance traffic. The legislatures chartered many small companies, authorizing each to construct or improve and to maintain a relatively short road within the state and to raise the money therefor by selling stock to the public. Such a company obtained the right to erect tollhouses and to collect tolls from all users of the road. State laws outlined the character of the improvements to be made and prescribed in detail the charges for a horse and rider, for different vehicles, and for animals on the hoof. The companies were commonly empowered to purchase, by forced sales if necessary, such land as they required and such needed building materials as were located on privately owned tracts adjacent to the road. Some charters ran for an indefinite period; others for a specified number of years. Failure to perform the assigned tasks entailed the forfeiture of a company's rights. Opponents of turnpikes objected to turning over public highways to private toll collectors and occasionally damaged the properties or evaded the tolls, but the legislatures stood firm and imposed fines on such miscreants.[27]

In 1792 a group of Pennsylvania promoters organized a company to establish a turnpike from Philadelphia to Lancaster. On April 8 the legislature granted them an act of incorporation, whereupon they soon raised $300,000 by sales of stock at $300 a share. Within about two years the company completed an excellent stone roadbed covered with gravel. The success of the Lancaster Pike encouraged promoters to organize similar companies. Before 1804 other turnpikes were established east of the Susquehanna; afterward, in the other parts of the state. The legislature aided in 1806 by appropriating $825,000 for the purchase of stock in the companies. A state-wide network contained 1,807 miles of turnpikes in 1821.[28]

Rhode Island chartered its first turnpike company in 1794. Other states soon followed: Connecticut in 1795; Maryland, Massachusetts, New Hampshire, and Vermont in 1796; New York in 1797; and New Jersey in 1801. Although Virginia in 1785 authorized the first American turnpikes—

[26] Joseph Austin Durrenberger, *Turnpikes* (Valdosta, Ga.: Southern Stationery and Printing Company, 1931), pp. 46–48.
[27] Wood, *New England Turnpikes*, pp. 31–34; Davis, *Earlier History of American Corporations*, II, 216, 227–228.
[28] Durrenberger, *Turnpikes*, pp. 51–55; Davis, *Earlier History of American Corporations*, II, 218–220.

to be located on roads leading to Alexandria from the Blue Ridge Mountains—the state did not resort to private companies. Instead, state commissioners directed the building of tollhouses and the money was used to keep up the roads on which it was collected. Gallatin's comprehensive report of 1808 on internal improvements indicated that states south of Virginia had not yet established turnpike companies. Most of the projects of the time aimed to shorten roads between familiar points and to reduce hills and slopes. Careful studies computed the rates of speed at which a horse could pull a given load up different grades. The turnpike companies most commonly built or improved dirt roads by giving them a convex form and by digging drainage ditches along the sides. Stone and gravel roads were rare. Massachusetts built only three of that type before 1815—about 105 miles in all. Travelers on the Lancaster Pike preferred, in dry weather, to use a dirt road that adjoined the graveled highway.[29]

Before 1815 most of the turnpikes of Massachusetts and Rhode Island radiated from Boston or Providence. Those of Connecticut made a statewide network, giving a checkerboard effect. The New York pikes ran north and west from points on the Hudson and featured one of the masterworks of the era—a line from Albany via Schenectady, Utica, and Canandaigua to Lake Erie near Buffalo. The rage for turnpikes in New York had brought forth, by 1811, acts authorizing 135 companies empowered to raise $7,558,000 and to erect tollgates on 4,500 miles of roads. Work on about 1,500 miles had then been completed. New Jersey's turnpikes—built partly with New York capital—served mainly to link the countryside with Philadelphia and New York City. Maryland's system connected Baltimore with southern Pennsylvania and with Harpers Ferry. The building of short roads remained the rule, although the planners joined roads with one another, so that many long continuous highways were formed. Turnpikes did not make large profits. The best road in Massachusetts earned an average of 3.1 percent. Some companies provoked complaints that they forced the public to pay tolls without giving real service. Legislatures commonly authorized special commissioners or local officials to inspect the roads and to report malpractices—a method of supervision that proved to be feeble and ineffectual.[30]

On a busy turnpike one saw riders on horseback, carts drawn by horses and oxen or pushed by pedestrians, wagons of various kinds, carriages, pack animals, stagecoaches, and farmers or drovers herding sheep, cattle,

[29] Wood, *New England Turnpikes*, pp. 7, 17, 35–36, 63, 215, 250, 287, 331; Durrenberger, *Turnpikes*, pp. 59, 65, 71; Davis, *Earlier History of American Corporations*, II, 221–222, 224–226.

[30] Wood, *New England Turnpikes*, pp. 35, 57, 287, 331; Durrenberger, *Turnpikes*, pp. 58–61, 66, 70–71, 93–95; Davis, *Earlier History of American Corporations*, II, 223; Wheaton J. Lane, *From Indian Trail to Iron Horse* (Princeton, N. J.: Princeton University Press, 1939), p. 146.

and hogs. The most common freight carrier was the Conestoga wagon, an American invention of about 1783 that probably originated near Lancaster. Broad-wheeled, its wagon bed low in the center to keep freight in place, its under wooden parts painted blue and its upper parts red, the Conestoga wagon after 1790 ruled the central highways to the West, as its four or six hefty horses galloped, trotted, or toiled onward, the driver astride a wheel horse. Americans also devised new types of stagecoaches. The one most in use between 1790 and 1806 contained three or four benches, without backs, each holding three persons. The driver sat on the front bench, with a passenger on either side. Eight slender pillars supported a light top. The only window coverings were side and rear leather curtains that might be rolled down. Passengers, entering at the front, had to climb over the front seats to get to the rear. Mail was stored under the driver's seat; baggage went under the other seats or was tied on behind. A curved spring, invented by Obadiah Elliot in 1804, permitted the use of smaller wheels and reduced the height of the vehicle. The Concord coach, celebrated in western lore, was not in use before 1828.[31]

Wagon builders endeavored to make the wagon box watertight to protect the freight when streams were forded. Ferryboats, propelled by oars, poles, or sails, still provided a common mode of crossing large bodies of water, as in colonial times. Bridges had many advantages over ferries, but the American art of bridge building, still in its infancy, did not afford the means of spanning the great rivers with permanent structures. Much progress in bridge building, however, was made before 1815 and several methods were employed to encourage the erection of bridges of various types. Most commonly the states chartered special toll-bridge companies and empowered them to erect bridges in conjunction with the turnpikes, although occasionally a turnpike company built a bridge for its road and collected a separate toll. A new era began in 1786 with the construction of a toll bridge, 1,503 feet long, over the Charles River at Boston. New Yorkers in 1800 completed a mile-long structure across Lake Cayuga for the turnpike between Auburn and Geneva, and then claimed that they had the longest bridge in the world. By 1807 the New York legislature had authorized the formation of 21 toll-bridge companies with a combined capital stock of $415,000; by 1811, 36 companies had been empowered to raise $509,000. A novel floating bridge at Lynn, Massachusetts, 511 feet long, constructed in 1804, consisted of several layers of logs and timbers, with a plank floor. In Pennsylvania, one Abraham Witmer built a bridge of nine arches across the Conestoga River near Lancaster. When it failed to pay, the county took it over and reimbursed him for his outlay. At Dowingtown on the Brandywine a stone bridge was the most expensive one built by the Lancaster Turnpike Company. The high point was reached in 1805 when a toll-bridge company spanned the Schuylkill at Philadelphia with

[31] Ambler, *Transportation in the Ohio Valley*, pp. 36–37; Wood, *New England Turnpikes*, pp. 47–49, 114.

a bridge costing $250,000 that was featured by two heavy stone piers and a timbered superstructure. A traveler in 1807 noted that the whole bridge was "covered by a roof and the sides closed in, to preserve the timber from the decay occasioned by exposure to the weather." Thus originated the American covered bridge. Widely copied, it was a picturesque contribution of this period to transportation in the states.[32]

In his report of 1808 Gallatin observed that in "the Eastern States, and particularly in Massachusetts, wooden bridges, uniting boldness and elegance, and having no defect except want of durability, have been erected over the broadest and deepest rivers." Two leading builders were Timothy Palmer of Newburyport and Theodore Burr. Palmer, a self-taught engineer, achieved his greatest success in the Permanent Bridge over the Schuylkill. One of its piers was "sunk in a depth of water unexampled in hydraulic architecture, in any part of the world." Burr constructed the "most unusual timber bridge in America" over the Mohawk at Schenectady in 1808. Another of his structures, which spanned the Hudson at Waterford, New York, lasted more than 100 years. The foremost builder was James Finley of Fayette County, Pennsylvania, who originated the modern suspension bridge, featured by a nearly level roadway that was supported by vertical rods suspended from chains which—bolted to rocks on shore—rested on masonry towers set in the stream. His first bridge, over Jacob's Creek in western Pennsylvania, was soon followed by many others: over the Monongahela at Brownsville, the Brandywine at Wilmington, the Potomac at Washington, the Cumberland in Maryland, the Merrimac near Newburyport, and the Lehigh at Allentown. Finley's method, patented June 17, 1808, served to shift the weight from the bridge floor to the chains and their supporting rocks. Gallatin was particularly impressed by Finley's bridge at Washington, which, "without any supporting piers," was "wholly suspended to iron chains from bank to bank"—an innovation which he thought to be "applicable to all rapid streams of a moderate breadth." [33]

Despite the vogue for bridges and turnpikes, most travelers in the South, in the West, and in isolated districts in the East continued to use poor roads supervised by public officials, and to struggle against mud, bogs, hills, sand, tree stumps, rocks, and unbridged streams.

TRANSPORTATION BY WATER

Most farm produce en route to market went by road to a seaport or to a river town, whence it moved by ship or boat to its final destination. A

[32] Davis, *Earlier History of American Corporations*, II, 188; Hedrick, *New York Agriculture*, p. 178; Durrenberger, *Turnpikes*, pp. 91–92; Wood, *New England Turnpikes*, 85, 366; Lane, *From Indian Trail to Iron Horse*, pp. 126–127.

[33] Henry Grattan Tyrrell, *History of Bridge Engineering* (Chicago: The author, 1911), pp. 131–133, 204–206; Richard Shelton Kirby and Philip Gustave Laurson, *The Early Years of Modern Civil Engineering* (New Haven, Conn.: Yale University Press, 1932), pp. 141–143, 151–152.

vast inland river traffic was epitomized in the shipping that animated the Ohio, the Mississippi, and their tributaries. The inhabitants of the West displayed no little ingenuity in building and manning a bewildering variety of river craft that journeyed downstream from countless villages, landings, and ports.

The simplest carriers were rafts that took lumber to New Orleans. Somewhat less primitive was the flatboat—a low, boxlike structure that rose a few feet above water. Most of its space was given over to boarded-in sections that provided crude living quarters, sheltered livestock, and housed freight. On some boats one entered the enclosed parts from a deck at the rear. Forty to fifty tons made a good load. Since a flatboat had neither sails nor oars it depended on the power of the current, and the boatmen did little more than steer it—one with a rear rudder and one with a sweep or "broadhorn" at each side. Such boats could not go upstream; hence they were abandoned or reduced to lumber at the end of a trip. Pioneers of means often bought them before starting down the Ohio and put the boards into the first buildings on their farms.[34]

More advanced than the flatboat was the canoe-shaped keelboat—a vessel built to ascend the western rivers. Its features included a cabin, seats at the bow for oarsmen, a mast, a rudder, and cleated footways on which the boatmen walked when poling upstream. Forty to eighty feet long, the keelboat carried about thirty tons of freight on two or three yearly round trips on the Ohio-Mississippi. Somewhat akin to keelboats was the barge. It differed from them in that it was wider, required a larger crew—fifteen to fifty men—and made greater use of sails and oars. The trip down the river was like a pleasure cruise compared with the laborious return upstream. The keelboat, propelled mainly by poles, was best suited to the firm bed of the Ohio; the barge was better suited to the muddy Mississippi.[35]

Canoes, pirogues, and bateaux of the French regime continued to move on the western waters, although their relative importance declined sharply after 1790. The bateau was a strong, broad, flat-bottomed craft, somewhat like a rowboat in form, supplemented by poles and sails, well suited to navigating shallow, rocky streams and to shooting over rapids. Keelboats and bateaux ascended the smaller rivers, bringing articles of light weight in relation to value: sugar, coffee, dry goods, notions, edged tools, gunpowder, and salt.[36]

[34] Leland D. Baldwin, *The Keelboat Age on Western Waters* (Pittsburgh: University of Pittsburgh Press, 1941), pp. 41–42, 47–49; Gephart, *Transportation in the Middle West*, pp. 61–62.

[35] Baldwin, *The Keelboat Age*, pp. 44–46; Gephart, *Transportation in the Middle West*, p. 63; Mildred L. Hartsough, *From Canoe to Steel Barge on the Upper Mississippi* (Minneapolis: The University of Minnesota Press, 1934), pp. 29–30.

[36] Baldwin, *The Keelboat Age*, p. 42; Ambler, *Transportation in the Ohio Valley*, p. 44.

The forests of the Ohio Valley supplied excellent oak, pine, and walnut timbers for the building of ships. At Elizabeth and Brownsville on the Monongahela, and later at Marietta and Pittsburgh, shipwrights constructed ocean-going vessels ranging from 120 to 400 tons. Loaded with western produce, such ships descended to New Orleans, where they were sold or whence they proceeded to the West Indies, to an eastern port, or even to Europe. The first of such vessels appears to have been built on the Monongahela in 1792; the first at Marietta in 1798 or 1799, and at Pittsburgh in 1803. Difficulties of navigating the island-studded Ohio soon cooled the ardor of the western shipbuilders, and although they built, before 1820, as many as 67 ocean vessels, of perhaps 10,050 tons, worth more than $500,000, nearly all the products of the West bound for New Orleans went on barges, flatboats, keelboats, and rafts.[37]

The bête noire of shippers was the trip upstream. More crude than poling were the methods by which men either pulled boats up a river from a towpath along the bank, or tied a rope to a tree ahead and then drew the boat forward, constantly repeating the process. A trip from New Orleans to Pittsburgh by keelboat took four times longer and eight times more labor than the passage downstream. More efficient power was the pressing need of the time. Boatmen were not paragons of virtue, nor did their labors on the lawless river have a refining effect. "Half horse, half alligator," they continually bedeviled the inhabitants of towns and farms.

> When the boatman goes on shore,
> Look, old man, your sheep is gone,
> He steals your sheep and steals your shote,
> He puts 'em in a bag and totes 'em to the boat.

The chance that improvements in river travel might displace the boatmen was not a deterrent to progress.[38]

American ingenuity overcame the river current through the invention of the steamboat—an achievement made possible by developments in England, where Thomas Savery and Thomas Newcomen had devised, before 1715, a simple steam engine of cylinder and piston that pumped water from mines. In 1769 James Watt patented a greatly improved engine which condensed steam in a separate chamber; in 1781 he devised a mechanism that enabled the engine to turn a wheel; in 1782 he perfected his engine by injecting steam at both ends of the cylinder and condenser, so that the piston was driven by steam in both directions, whereas in the Newcomen

---

[37] Baldwin, The Keelboat Age, pp. 161–163, 173–174; Archer W. Hulbert, "Western Ship-Building," American Historical Review, XXI, No. 4 (July, 1916), 722–724, 732; Gephart, Transportation in the Middle West, pp. 59–60, 65.

[38] Baldwin, The Keelboat Age, pp. 46, 92, 100–102; Gephart, Transportation in the Middle West, pp. 63–64; Hartsough, From Canoe to Steel Barge, p. 37; W. Wallace Carson, "Transportation and Traffic on the Ohio and Mississippi Before the Steamboat," Mississippi Valley Historical Review, VII, No. 1 (June, 1920), 37.

engine the piston was moved upward by steam and downward by atmospheric pressure. Watt appears to have had little if any interest in a steamboat. The first builder of a steam vessel was a Frenchman, Marquis de Jouffroy d'Abbans. In 1783 his boat moved a short distance on the Saône River. There the experiment ended. Inventors in England, though partly successful, did not develop a practical model. In both France and England, improved roads, numerous canals, and short, gentle rivers did not create an urgent demand for a steamboat.[39]

The first American to arouse interest in a self-propelled boat was James Rumsey, a man of many gifts, described by Jefferson as the greatest mechanical genius he had ever seen. Born in Maryland in 1743, Rumsey engaged in various practical pursuits before he built a model of a boat that "walked" upstream. He attached to it a water wheel that moved a set of poles which dug into the ground and pushed the boat forward against the current. After Washington saw the model at Bath, Virginia, he became Rumsey's active patron, acclaiming his invention as of "vast importance to our inland navigation." When Rumsey exhibited an actual boat in September, 1786, the poles failed to dig firmly into the river bed and the mechanism caused excessive vibration and unsteadiness. Rumsey then took up another plan. In 1785 Franklin gave publicity to an idea of a Swiss, Daniel Bernoulli, that a boat might be moved by ejecting a stream of water at the stern, below the water line. This scheme of jet propulsion, which called for a steam engine on board to pump water from the river, won widespread support among men interested in a steamboat. Rumsey experimented with the idea in 1785, and later secured the backing of a group of promoters who sent him to England to buy a Watt-Boulton engine and to complete his experiments. Before he died in December, 1792, he had built a boat on the jet principle that moved at the rate of four knots.[40]

The credit for inventing the first operating steamboat belongs to John Fitch—an eccentric genius who was born at Windsor, Connecticut, in 1743. With little formal schooling he gained technical skill by working as a button molder, brass founder, silversmith, clockmaker, surveyor, and cartographer. His speculations in western lands induced him to go to the Ohio country in 1782. There he encountered at firsthand the hardships of river travel. He claimed that, unaided, he worked out a plan for a steamboat. The first one he built, in 1786, was propelled by twelve long-handled paddles, connected with the engine by horizontal rods. The paddles worked alternately in such a way that when six of them—three on each side—were making a work stroke, the others were returning, out of the

[39] James T. Flexner, *Steamboats Come True* (New York: The Viking Press, 1944), pp. 17–18, 39, 45.

[40] H. A. Gosnell, "The First American Steamboat: James Rumsey Its Inventor, Not John Fitch," *Virginia Magazine of History and Biography*, XL, No. 2 (April, 1932), 125; Flexner, *Steamboats Come True*, pp. 67–69, 71, 91–92, 98, 140, 212.

water, to a forward position. Although the boat moved, the engine did not generate enough power to make it practical. Fitch then made a second type which was featured by a single paddle wheel driven by steam. Completed in 1790, this boat went eight miles an hour. It made several scheduled trips on the Delaware River from Philadelphia to Trenton but soon ceased operations because its combined freight and passenger business did not pay expenses. It did not go as fast as a stagecoach. Fitch had had to use a rather crude American-made engine. Lacking capital and wealthy backers, he had failed in his efforts to secure financial aid from Congress or Pennsylvania. He invented anew a condenser similar to Watt's and built the first steamboat to use a paddle wheel. Poverty, opposition, a difficult personality, and the popularity of his rival, Rumsey, overcame Fitch's genius, forcing him to quit the steamboat venture on the eve of success. He died tragically in Kentucky in 1798, unrewarded for his invention of "the first great American contribution to technology"—the steamboat.[41]

When seeking aid from New Jersey in 1786, Fitch became known to John Stevens, a wealthy landowner, born in New York in 1749, who had bought an estate at Hoboken and who later acquired a ferry thence to New York City. This business stimulated his interest in the steamboat and led him to make experiments to reduce the weight of the engine's boiler, which he thought to be the principal obstacle to steam navigation. Highly gifted in mechanics, Stevens in 1802 built the first steamboat to be driven by a screw propeller—an invention that did not take hold because the boiler he used did not produce sufficient steam, although the boat made several trips across the Hudson. Stevens later built the *Phoenix*—a successful boat that was powered by two side wheels driven by an improved engine which Stevens had designed. The *Phoenix*, however, encountered a monopoly of Hudson River traffic which Stevens's rivals had secured. In 1809 he sponsored the first ocean steamboat voyage by sending the *Phoenix* from the Hudson to Philadelphia. Stevens also became a votary of steam railroads. In 1812 he championed them as superior to canals, and in 1815 he secured from New Jersey the first American railway charter—for a line between the Delaware and Raritan rivers.[42]

In New York, Stevens's brother-in-law, Robert R. Livingston, had acquired a conditional monopoly of steamboat traffic in New York State before he went to France in 1802. There he met a versatile Pennsylvanian, Robert Fulton, whose work as jeweler, portrait painter, and engineer had put him in touch with leading artists and mechanics of Philadelphia, England, and France. In October, 1802, Fulton contracted with Livingston for

[41] Thompson Westcott, *The Life of John Fitch* (Philadelphia: J. B. Lippincott Company, 1857), pp. 28–29, 45, 57, 71, 74, 160–161, 178, 281–288, 300.

[42] Archibald Douglas Turnbull, *John Stevens* (New York: The American Society of Mechanical Engineers, 1928), pp. 3–4, 82, 100, 177, 185–186, 260–262, 275–279, 363–365, 368–370, 383.

the building of a steam vessel, and in August, 1803, he demonstrated, on the Seine River, a boat that made three or four miles an hour. He returned to New York late in 1806 and supervised the construction of a long, narrow ship, later known as the *Clermont*, which in August, 1807, completed a round trip from New York City to Albany—about 300 miles—in 62 hours' running time. This trip inaugurated steamboat traffic as a profitable business. Fulton had not originated any important feature of the steamboat. He succeeded because he used a superior Watt-Boulton engine, employed a skilled shipwright, Charles Brownne, to build the vessel, improved Fitch's paddle-wheel device, and had adequate political and financial backing. Fulton's main achievement was his calculating with precision such factors as water resistance, the strength and capacity of the ship, the power of the engine, and the pressures on the different parts of the mechanism.[43]

Before Fulton died in 1815, he had designed twenty-one successful steamboats. He enlarged his later vessels, striving for greater capacity rather than speed. The Livingston-Fulton monopoly in New York was strengthened in 1811 when the state legislature authorized the partners to seize competing vessels. In that year they also secured from the legislature of Orleans Territory a monopoly on the lower Mississippi. Later, the Fulton boats concentrated on traffic between New Orleans and Natchez. At Pittsburgh the Fulton party built several steamboats, the first of which made the pioneer voyage to New Orleans in 1811. Fulton also planned a steamboat and stagecoach service from Lake Champlain to Savannah, and proposed to operate his ships in Russia and India. He built the first steam warship, *Demogolos*, a floating fortress designed to protect New York Harbor during the War of 1812. His efforts to secure a national monopoly failed and his legal battles to save his New York monopoly sapped his energy and raised up a host of enemies. In a steamboat war with New Jersey he lost the right to navigate the Delaware River.[44]

Fulton's success fired so many rivals that by 1815 steamboats were plying the principal rivers of the country and the public had accepted them as a godsend. A competing group in the West, led by Daniel French, a skilled engine designer, built several boats at Brownsville on the Monongahela. Their third vessel, the *Enterprise*, made, in 1815, the first trip from New Orleans to Louisville. The Fulton party's preference for New York left the western traffic to builders who specialized in simple, high-pressure engines ideally suited to the Mississippi. Profits of steamboating at the outset were sometimes as high as 50 percent. In 1823, the New York mo-

[43] H. W. Dickinson, *Robert Fulton* (London: John Lane, Ltd., 1913), pp. 135–136, 149–150, 157–158, 206, 215, 217–221, 241.

[44] Louis C. Hunter, *Steamboats on the Western Rivers* (Cambridge, Mass.: Harvard University Press, 1949), pp. 10–12; Dickinson, *Robert Fulton*, pp. 230, 240, 242–246, 252, 258–259, 264–265, 326–327.

nopoly and five Fulton ships were valued at $660,000 and yielded a return of 8 percent.[45]

The first American canals were built at the time the steamboat was being developed. Some transportation needs could not be met by improving roads and river craft. Canals promised to do several things: to enable boats to by-pass the falls of rivers, to shorten lines of travel along the coast, as between Chesapeake Bay and Delaware Bay, to link together inland waters, such as the Hudson and Lake Erie or upper streams that were connected by portages, and to open cheaper routes from eastern seaports to nearby rivers.[46]

A movement for canals got started immediately after 1783. However, with respect to achievements, it moved at a snail's pace before 1816, when all the canals in operation totaled about 100 miles. Eventually, the bellwether was the Middlesex Canal, 27 miles long, that connected Boston with the Merrimac River, with the object of diverting the trade of western New Hampshire and eastern Vermont to the metropolis. Serving this canal was a series of six short canals around falls in the Merrimac that made the river navigable to Concord. Southern projects included the Santee and Cooper Canal that linked Charleston with the Santee River, and the Dismal Swamp Canal from Norfolk to Albemarle Sound. Washington served as the first president of two canal companies: the Potomac Company, chartered in 1784, which built five short canals on the Potomac between Georgetown and the vicinity of Harpers Ferry; and the James River and Kanawha Company, chartered in 1785, which completed two canals around the falls of the James at Richmond. Pennsylvania's first important venture was the Schuylkill and Susquehanna Canal, promoted by Robert Morris, which was designed to draw the trade of north-central Pennsylvania to Philadelphia. This project was not completed until after 1815.[47]

The promoters of canals used business methods similar to those of the builders of turnpikes and toll bridges. From state legislatures they secured acts incorporating companies of proprietors who were authorized to

[45] Louis C. Hunter, "The Invention of the Western Steamboat," *Journal of Economic History*, III, No. 2 (November, 1943), 201–204, 209, 214–215; Flexner, *Steamboats Come True*, pp. 348, 354.

[46] George Washington Ward, *The Early Development of the Chesapeake and Ohio Canal Propect* (Johns Hopkins University *Studies in Historical and Political Science*, Series XVII, Nos. 9–11; Baltimore: The Johns Hopkins Press, 1899), pp. 26–28; Alvin F. Harlow, *Old Towpaths* (New York: D. Appleton and Company, 1926), pp. 11–15, 17, 19.

[47] Christopher Roberts, *The Middlesex Canal, 1793–1860* (Vol. LXI of *Harvard Economic Studies*; Cambridge, Mass.: Harvard University Press, 1943), pp. 26, 134; Phillips, *Transportation in the Eastern Cotton Belt*, pp. 38–43; Ward, *The Chesapeake and Ohio Canal Project*, pp. 13–14; Wayland Fuller Dunaway, *History of the James River and Kanawha Company* (New York: 1922), p. 28; Davis, *Earlier History of American Corporations*, II, 148–157.

sell stock, buy land, construct canals, and collect designated tolls. Merchants seeking to enlarge the trade of their towns and land speculators usually instigated the projects, stimulated by the success of contemporary canals in England. Many obstacles retarded the work: the use of hand tools, such as picks and shovels; inefficient blasting of rock with gunpowder; scarcity of workmen; lack of trained canal engineers; shortage of capital; opposition of wagon freighters and boatmen; high costs of construction, often in excess of estimates by reason of encountering unforeseen obstacles; and the failure of the projects in their initial stages to yield profits to the proprietors. The objective of the promoters was not to secure a quick return on an investment; rather, they expected to share in indirect benefits of the future. Few were the men who had the capital, tenacity, prudence, and business acumen necessary for completing a large project which had to be sustained during many years of uncompensated expense, on the assumption that public benefits and private profits would eventually be forthcoming.[48]

[48] Roberts, *The Middlesex Canal*, pp. 4, 25, 29–30, 43, 45, 49–53, 66–67, 72, 74, 89, 179, 182; Dunaway, *James River and Kanawha Company*, pp. 24–26, 34–38; Noble E. Whitford, *History of the Canal System of New York* (2 vols.; Albany: 1960), I, 42–43.

CHAPTER XIII

Labor and Industry

BY quickening internal trade, improvements in transportation stimulated the growth of manufacturing. Artisans, inventors, and entrepreneurs labored to simplify methods of work and to produce better goods. Diversified activities increasingly characterized American society. By 1815 at least 150 vocations, trades, and professions were served by specialists. Since farming remained the principal occupation it exerted a potent influence on industry, particularly with respect to attitudes toward work, employers, property rights, and bargaining. The rural family gave training in the arts of household manufacturing; the farm supplied raw materials to industry; wage earners were recruited mainly from farm-bred folk; artisans and workshops specialized in goods needed by farmers. Agriculture largely determined wages in industry, in that employers had to offer as much to husky workers as farmers could afford to pay to hired hands.

PEOPLE AT WORK

An outstanding feature of labor during this period was self-employment. Skilled artisans, shopkeepers, professional men, planters, proprietors of small businesses, merchants, traders, pioneers, and landowning farmers made up a majority of the free population. The wage-earning group included farm hands, sailors, dock workers, fishermen, boatmen, miners, lumbermen, clerks, journeymen, domestic servants, laborers on roads, bridges, and canals, and helpers in factories, forges, foundries, and mills. Minors and apprentices formed a large part of the working force. Common laborers were often farmers who hired their services during slack times at home. Slavery gained in importance in the South. "Labor" as defined today —employees organized in unions—was in its infancy.

Prosperous farmers in the East commonly employed hired laborers. Some hands were engaged by the year; others by the day; in some instances wages consisted of money; sometimes they also included board and lodg-

ing. Rates of pay indicate how tasks differed with respect to the laborious-
ness of farm work and the urgency of getting it done. Farm hands in Pennsylvania in 1792 received the following wages in addition to board and
lodging: 27 cents a day during the three winter months; from 66 to 80
cents a day for harvesting grain; and about 33 cents a day at other times.
A marked increase in farm wages occurred during this period. Thus in
Massachusetts the average wage, without board, rose from 48 cents a day
during the years 1791–1800 to 78 cents during the period 1801–1815.
Changes in wages adhered closely to changes in the prices of farm products. Yearly wages, with board, varied from $60 in Pennsylvania in 1792,
to $120 in Virginia and New York in 1795, and to a minimum of $156 in
Illinois in 1818. Hired hands were so scarce in frontier districts that women
and girls helped with planting, hoeing, and raking hay and grain. That
frontier farmers readily helped neighbors indicates that the practice also
prevailed in the East. In new settlements a laborer could save enough in
two or three years to buy a small farm.[1]

Most industrial producers operated in small groups that served limited
local markets—a condition accounted for by primitive means of transportation and the absence of large cities. However, improvements in roads,
bridges, and river boats, together with an increasing use of power-driven
machinery, were slowly reducing transportation costs, widening markets
of favored localities, and preparing the way for businesses conducted on a
large scale. Although local markets, self-employment, and small production
units continued to dominate the scene, the foundations of a new order
were being laid.

In a general way, industry exhibited two kinds of establishments. One
type required power-driven machinery or other expensive equipment. In
this category were various kinds of mills—fulling, lumber, flour, sugar,
paper, flax, cotton, woolen, iron, and gunpowder—along with iron furnaces
and forges, iron and brass foundries, distilleries, breweries, shipyards, ropewalks, tanneries, brick kilns, glass factories, and works devoted to the
production of anchors, engines, steamboats, sailcloth, mill saws, and printing presses. Mines and quarries may also be included in this category. Although some of such establishments were small, they tended to grow in
size and to come under the sway of companies or proprietors who engaged
experts to manage them. A large enterprise in 1815 represented an investment of about $200,000, with a force of 150 employees.

In other branches of industry, handicraftsmen worked in small shops
or on construction jobs, without the aid of power-driven machinery or
other expensive fixed equipment. Among such artisans were blacksmiths,
shoemakers, hatters, tailors, bakers, coopers, carpenters, cabinetmakers,

[1] Bidwell and Falconer, *History of Agriculture in the Northern United States,*
pp. 118, 163–164, 206–207; Clark, *History of Manufactures in the United States,*
p. 392.

clockmakers, button makers, tinsmiths, potters, weavers, printers, masons, chandlers and soapmakers, saddlers, barbers, silversmiths, jewelers, wheelwrights, coppersmiths, and manufacturers of brooms, brushes, combs, locks, farm implements, and tobacco products. Where work was done in such shops a master artisan commonly owned the tools, procured the raw material, employed journeymen wage earners, trained apprentices, and sold the products. It was in such trades that antecedents of the modern labor movement are found.[2]

The master craftsman was both a worker and an employer, for he commonly labored at the side of his journeymen and apprentices. Most masters had only a few helpers on the job or in the shop; a force of fifteen was exceptional. In each of the main towns, masters of the principal trades —such as the shoemakers or the carpenters—formed societies somewhat similar to medieval guilds. In forming such societies the masters acted as producing workmen rather than as employers; their original purpose was to uphold the prices of their goods or labor and to provide loans, and accident, sickness, and death benefits to the members. Only when confronted by organized activity of journeymen did the masters use their trade societies for opposing employees. The societies enabled the members to improve themselves in various ways. Thus one purpose of a fund established by the Philadelphia master carpenters was to enable them to obtain instruction in the "sciences of architecture." As early as 1786 the masters of New York formed a "General Society of Mechanics and Tradesmen" to which each individual trade organization sent a delegate. Many other towns—Providence, Albany, Baltimore, Norfolk, Savannah—set up similar general societies.[3]

The journeyman was a skilled employee who lived on his wages. No doubt most journeymen hoped to become masters and accepted the existing order. Conflicts between masters and journeymen—almost invariably over wages—were not only disputes between employer and employee but also contests between masters and would-be masters, since higher wages would hasten the rise of journeymen into the master class.[4]

Organizations of journeymen were usually temporary, formed to secure a wage increase and discontinued after a dispute had been settled. At least twelve strikes occurred between 1786 and 1816. Masters who produced for individual customers and who were not tied down by contracts

[2] John R. Commons and associates, *History of Labour in the United States* (4 vols.; New York: The Macmillan Company, 1918–1935), I, 70, 72–73, 104, 127–128; Blanche E. Hazard, "The Organization of the Boot and Shoe Industry in Massachusetts Before 1875," *Quarterly Journal of Economics*, XXVII, No. 2 (February, 1913), 239–242.

[3] Commons, *History of Labour*, I, 72–73, 76–77, 84, 100, 121–122, 124; Selig Perlman, *A History of Trade Unionism in the United States* (New York: The Macmillan Company, 1922), p. 6.

[4] Commons, *History of Labour*, I, 108–111, 125.

with dealers were prone to grant wage demands and to pass on the increased cost to the consumer. Among the journeymen only the printers and shoemakers kept up continuing organizations after 1800. The shoemakers were the more militant. They insisted that all journeymen of their trade should join their society and refused to work with nonmembers. During a strike at Philadelphia in 1805 they assaulted "scabs" and broke shopwindows. With the growth of inland trade, employers made contracts for future deliveries at prices based on existing wages; hence they opposed wage increases that would make such contracts unprofitable. Wage demands and coercive actions of the journeymen drove the masters to seek protection in the courts, charging that their employees had entered into a criminal conspiracy to raise their wages and to inflict injury on others. All together, six suits were brought against the journeymen shoemakers before 1816. All were prosecuted on the theory that certain acts of the men were contrary to the English common law, which was presumed to be in force in the United States. Four of the cases were decided against the men. However, only the decision in the Philadelphia case of 1806 held that the simple act of organizing for the purpose of raising wages was illegal. In that instance the journeymen were fined eight dollars each. In three later cases the courts found the journeymen guilty because they had violated the rights of other persons.[5]

From time out of mind the skilled trades had been maintained by an apprenticeship system. Parents approved of indentures by which a master craftsman, in return for the labor of boys, undertook to instruct, clothe, board, and lodge them during a period of from three to seven years until they became twenty-one. Although such indentures were legally binding, their terms were prescribed by custom rather than by statutes, and their enforcement usually depended more on the parties concerned than on the courts. The practice survived in part because it provided masters with cheap labor. Journeymen sought to restrict the number of apprentices and to prevent masters from employing men who had not served the full term. The masters in turn strove to hold apprentices during the specified time. Few trades required six years of training to equip a person to do the common types of work. After 1800 the system seemed to be faltering. Apprentices often ran away as soon as they acquired enough training to support themselves. Journeymen printers charged that masters hired partly trained men and even took adults as apprentices. On the whole the enforcement of the system depended more on the journeymen than on the masters.[6]

[5] *Ibid.*, I, 7, 62, 71, 109–110, 126–127, 139–141, 145–146; Foster Rhea Dulles, *Labor in America* (New York: Thomas Y. Crowell Company, 1949), pp. 24–25, 29–30; *Documentary History of American Industrial Society* (Commons), III, 62–63, 236; Edwin E. Witte, "Early American Labor Cases," *Yale Law Review*, XXXV, No. 7 (May, 1926), 825–826.

[6] Paul H. Douglas, *American Apprenticeship and Industrial Education* (New York: 1921), pp. 51, 55–56; James M. Motley, *Apprenticeship in American Trade*

Wartime prosperity, the westward movement, the building of turn-pikes, bridges, and canals, and limited immigration worked together to improve slightly the condition of unskilled workers after 1793. This trend is illustrated by the building of the Middlesex Canal. The proprietors usu-ally engaged laborers to work by the month, from the end of March until late in November. The men came mainly from inland villages of New Hampshire and Massachusetts. The company provided food and lodged the men in barracks, where they slept in bunks on straw covered with tow cloth. The workday began at sunrise and lasted until sunset, with time out for meals and two pauses for grog. Wages rose from $8 a month in 1794 to $11 to $17 in 1803. The monthly cost to the company for the food and lodg-ing of a laborer was about equal to his wage.[7]

Sailors formed the largest specialized group of wage earners. Their numbers increased greatly during the period. American vessels engaged in all branches of shipping—foreign commerce, the coastwise trade, and the fisheries—rose from 201,000 tons in 1789 to 1,368,000 tons in 1815. This extraordinary growth did not cause a comparable increase in the number of American seamen. Although natives of New England manned the vessels belonging to that area, a considerable number of foreign seamen served on the ships of the middle and southern states. According to one authority, one seventh of the seamen employed by American shipping in 1807 were foreigners; another report for the year 1813 gives the proportion as one fifth. In view of both the vigorous demand for labor during the boom period after 1792 and the extraordinary growth of the merchant marine, such a resort to foreign labor was inevitable. In New England the captains re-cruited their hands largely from boys and young men of the farms and seaports—adventure seekers who spent a few years before the mast and then settled down to more prosaic work on land. Thus seafaring did not provide a lifelong occupation. Among New Englanders, seamen over forty were virtually unknown; men in their thirties were very few. Common sailors received about the same rate of pay as a common laborer. Their wages rose from $4.50 a month in 1790 to $16 in 1811. Able seamen earned more: $7 a month in 1790; $20 to $21 in 1811. American shipowners could afford to pay relatively high wages because their crews were smaller than those of similar British vessels. Wage increases were also a result, in part, of the assertiveness of the men. One of the most sensational labor struggles of the era occurred at New York in 1800, when a band of striking sailors on shore attacked a ship which had a party of nonstrikers on board. Citizens rallied to the defense of the vessel and repelled the strikers, who advanced "with drums and fife, and colors flying." "As they attempted to get on

Unions (Johns Hopkins University *Studies in Historical and Political Science*, Series XXV, Nos. 11–12; Baltimore: The Johns Hopkins Press, 1907), pp. 12–16; Edward Raymond Turner, *The Negro in Pennsylvania* (Washington: The American Historical Association, 1911), pp. 103–106.
    [7] Roberts, *The Middlesex Canal*, pp. 74–78.

board they were opposed, when a severe conflict ensued, and notwithstanding the vessel lay close along side the wharf, they were three times repulsed with broken heads and bloody noses . . . and several . . . who were on board . . . were very considerably wounded." [8]

One group of workers, prominent in colonial times, dwindled in importance after 1775. Thousands of immigrants had bound themselves, or had been bound by others, to serve employers as indentured servants, without compensation other than a livelihood, during terms of from four to seven years. The Revolutionary War stopped the traffic in such immigrants and although it revived after 1782, it did not attain its former volume. By 1785 slavery had supplanted white servitude in the area south of Maryland. Independence freed the states from Britain's practice of shipping convicts to America from British prisons. After 1783 the British government and British publicists worked together to discourage emigration from Britain and Ireland and to suppress the outward traffic in bonded servants. So effective were efforts to stigmatize indentured servants in America as convicts, outcasts, and consorts of slaves that British and Irish workers preferred to stay home if they could not go as free emigrants. New England had never attracted many indentured servants. The middle states, particularly Pennsylvania, continued to receive redemptioners from Germany and Switzerland, but the number was small compared with arrivals before 1775. The traffic expired soon after 1815.[9]

The Revolution and its aftermath brought into being a new group of domestic workers in the North. Americans of that day disliked to be called servants and objected to being subject to another person's will and command. In the free states the women of the young republic who did the work of domestic servants were called "help" or "helps" and worked *with*, rather than *for*, an employer. They did not form a fixed class; often their employment was only temporary. Commonly they were natives of the community in which they worked and did not move from place to place in search of better positions. Nor did they have specialized training; they usually performed all the tasks of a housewife of the time. Often they were neighbors or friends who were almost like members of the family: "they had the same religious belief, attended the same church, sat at the same fireside, ate at the same table, had the same associates." No stigma was attached to a capable neighbor who helped some busy mother of a large family. The stipend consisted of board and room, plus a few dollars a month. In-

[8] Pitkin, *Statistical View of the Commerce of the United States*, p. 361; Morison, *Maritime History of Massachusetts*, pp. 106–110; Commons, *History of Labour*, I, 110–111.

[9] James Curtis Ballagh, *White Servitude in the Colony of Virginia* (Johns Hopkins University *Studies in Historical and Political Science*, Series XIII, Nos. 6–7; Baltimore: The Johns Hopkins Press, 1895), pp. 65–67; Eugene Irving McCormac, *White Servitude in Maryland, 1634–1820* (Johns Hopkins University *Studies in Historical and Political Science*, Series XXII, Nos. 3–4; Baltimore: The Johns Hopkins Press, 1904), pp. 107–110.

Pack horse train, showing methods of packing burdens (Solon J. Buck and Elizabeth H. Buck, *The Planting of Civilization in Western Pennsylvania*. Courtesy of the University of Pittsburgh Press)

Conestoga wagon on "Long Bridge" across Lake Cayuga, New York (Jared Van Wagenen, Jr., *The Golden Age of Homespun*. Courtesy of the Cornell University Press)

River scene showing flatboat and two keelboats (Solon J. Buck and Elizabeth H. Buck, *The Planting of Civilization in Western Pennsylvania.* Courtesy of the University of Pittsburgh Press)

Stagecoach of the late 1790's (Isaac Weld, Jr., *Travels through the States of North America*, London, 1799. Courtesy of the Cornell University Library)

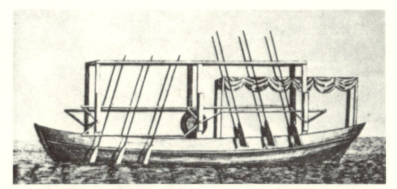

The first steamboat of John Fitch (Brooke Hindle, *The Pursuit of Science in Revolutionary America*. Courtesy of the author and of The University of North Carolina Press)

John Fitch (woodcut from *Lloyd's Steamboat Directory*, 1856)

John Fitch's steamboat of 1790 (Engraving from Thompson Westcott, *The Life of John Fitch*. 1857)

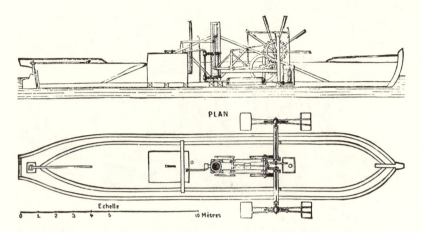

PLAN

Echelle

0 1 2 3 4 5   10 Mètres

Design of Robert Fulton's first steamboat, 1803

James Rumsey (Courtesy of the West Virginia State Department of Archives and History)

Canal boat of 1796 (Robert Fulton, *A Treatise on the Improvement of Canal Navigation*, London, 1796. Courtesy of the Cornell University Library)

Blacksmith's tools: headers for shaping nails and bolts, hardies for shaping chains, swadges for cutting and driving holes, tongs, sledges and shapers, wrench

Coopering: pulling the staves together; driving on a hoop, using a croze to make a groove for a barrel head. (Both illustrations from Solon J. Buck and Elizabeth H. Buck, *The Planting of Civilization in Western Pennsylvania*. Courtesy of the University of Pittsburgh Press)

Model of Oliver Evans' 100 H. P. Columbian engine at Fairmount Waterworks, Philadelphia

Oliver Evans
(Both illustrations from Greville and Dorothy Bathe, *Oliver Evans*. Courtesy of the authors and of The Historical Society of Pennsylvania)

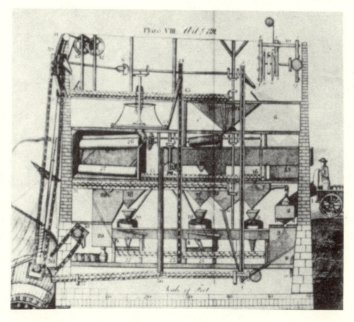

The Oliver Evans mill machinery, 1791 (Greville and Dorothy Bathe, *Oliver Evans*. Courtesy of the authors and of The Historical Society of Pennsylvania)

1—The wagoner emptying grain into scale pan
2—Scale pan, to weigh the grain
3—Small garner and wind chest for cleaning wheat
4–5—Elevator to top floor of mill
6—Main store for wheat
7—Garner, feeding the shelling or rubbing stones
8—The rubbing stones
9—Grain is again elevated and deposited in garners 10–11
12—Rolling screen
13—Fan for cleaning the grain
15–16—The conveyor to garners 7–17 and 18
8–19–20—Millstones
20–21—The conveyor, collecting meal after it is ground

23–24—Elevator to hopper-boy 25
25—Hopper-boy, which spreads and cools the meal and supplies the bolting chest
26–27—Bolting reels
28—The chest containing the superfine flour
29—Spout for filling barrels
35–39—Elevator for unloading ships. This rises and falls in the curved slots and is driven by the universal coupling at G
40—One view of the mechanism 42–43 for hoisting the elevator clear of the ship
38—A temporary elevator for short lifts

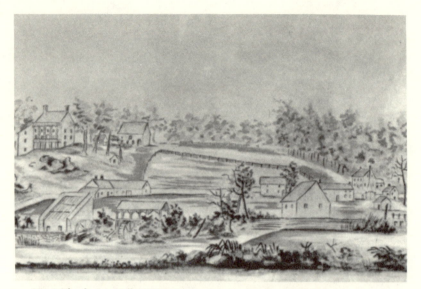

No. 1 Eleutherian Mills, 1806. From a drawing by Charles Dalmas
(Both illustrations by the courtesy of E. I. du Pont de Nemours and Company)

E. I. du Pont de Nemours

dentured servitude had degraded the name and status of servants during the colonial era. In the South, domestic service was performed by slaves; hence it was an occupation beneath the whites, however humble. The equalitarian ideals of the Revolution decreed that a free citizen should not be the personal dependent of another. Even trained servants who came to America from Europe soon felt a sense of personal independence, importance, and equality. Domestic service was one of the occupations open to free Negroes, of whom there were 59,500 in 1790 and 186,000 in 1810.[10]

The twenty years after 1775 are notable for the beginning of the employment of women and children in factories or mills. As women from time immemorial had spun wool, flax, and cotton into yarn and thread, it is not strange that after 1795 they were called upon to tend new spinning machines, housed in mills and driven by water power, that replaced the old-fashioned spinning wheel of the fireside. The labor force of such a mill consisted of women and children, male overseers, machinists, and men to prepare and move the raw material. Cotton mills were the pioneer employers of women as wage earners. The percentage of women and children employees varied from 65 to 90 of all workers in such mills. Owners in New England used two labor plans. In Rhode Island the mills commonly employed several members of a family. Thus the workers lived at home, close to the mill site. In Massachusetts, on the other hand, owners preferred to employ unmarried girls and young women from surrounding farms and to domicile them in strictly regulated boardinghouses. As to food and lodging, the employees fared as well as most farm people. The work—from dawn till dark—was not strenuous, though it was monotonous, confining, and probably less healthful than farm life. According to a report of 1810, a mill averaged 20 spindles to each worker. Women spinners appear to have received less than common laborers; wages of children were extremely low. No labor unions were formed by the cotton operatives before 1816. Gallatin estimated the number of employees in cotton mills in 1809 as 4,000—500 men and 3,500 women and children. The later growth of the industry was so rapid that a congressional committee reported in 1816 that the mills then employed 100,000 hands—90 percent being women, girls, and boys under seventeen. However, it seems likely that this figure is excessive. One estimate gives only 6,000 employees in 1815. Whatever the exact total, it is clear that a new, distinctive group of industrial workers had come into being.[11]

[10] Lucy Maynard Salmon, *Domestic Service* (New York: The Macmillan Company, 1897), pp. 54–55, 59, 61, 65–66, 69–70; Arnett G. Lindsay, "The Economic Condition of Negroes of New York Prior to 1861," *Journal of Negro History*, VI, No. 2 (April, 1921), 190–191.

[11] Edith Abbott, *Women in Industry* (New York: D. Appleton and Company, 1910), pp. 39–40, 44–45, 88–89, 102; Commons, *History of Labour*, I, 105, 111; Oscar Handlin, *Boston's Immigrants* (Rev. ed.; Cambridge, Mass.: Harvard University Press, 1959), p. 11; William R. Bagnall, *Samuel Slater* . . . (Middletown, Conn.: J. S. Stewart, 1890), pp. 44–45.

METAL INDUSTRIES AND MINING

Before 1815 the locations of mills and plants in industries of primary importance—iron, flour, lumber, textiles—were determined by nearness to either raw materials or water power, or both. Most of the products were consumed locally or exported. If they were heavy they were usually floated down streams and then transported by ships; if light, they were carried by boat or wagon to inland consumers. American farmers or foreign countries provided the principal markets—not American cities. Industries especially suited to urban locations were meat packing, printing, sugar refining, rum distilling, and the manufacturing of rope, furniture, and engines. Such industries generally did not require water power. Some of them processed nearby raw materials; some utilized imported raw materials; some depended upon highly skilled craftsmen who fared best in a city environment.[12]

The task of the iron industry was to supply the country with numerous articles: nails, spikes, brads, tacks, and wire; shovels, spades, hammers, and hoes; horseshoes, bits, and stirrups; edged tools (axes, chisels, handsaws, knives, scythes, mill saws); anvils, anchors, and cannon; stoves, skillets, kettles, and other hollow ware; and the iron parts of mill machinery, engines, firearms, wagons, harrows, and plows. The primary operations of the iron industry—mining, smelting, and forge work—were usually performed by men who worked for owners of furnaces, forges, and large tracts of land that provided iron ore, timber for charcoal, limestone, and water power. The iron deposits of the East were abundant, widespread, and diversified as to quality. By 1800, numerous furnaces and forges dotted an iron belt that extended from Rutland County, Vermont, through the Berkshires of Massachusetts to Orange County, New York, and Morris County, New Jersey. Ores near Lake Champlain were worked after 1801. In Pennsylvania, mines in the valleys of the Schuylkill, Susquehanna, Lehigh, and Juniata rivers, as well as in the district south of Pittsburgh, supported many iron works. The industry was well established in Maryland by 1783; thereafter it spread into the western part of the state. In the piedmont country and on the slopes of the Appalachian chain in Virginia and the Carolinas one found many forges and a few furnaces that were built between 1783 and 1812. At that time the pioneer works were also erected in eastern and middle Kentucky and Tennessee.[13]

The furnaces in operation before 1815 used only charcoal for smelting.

[12] Clark, *History of Manufactures in the United States,* p. 465.

[13] James M. Swank, *History of the Manufacture of Iron in All the Ages* (2d ed.; Philadelphia: The American Iron and Steel Association, 1892), pp. 122, 128, 141–142, 161, 195, 204–208, 216–219, 255, 267, 273, 277, 285, 288; Lester J. Cappon, "Trend of the Southern Iron Industry under the Plantation System," *Journal of Economic and Business History,* II, No. 2 (February, 1930), 354–360.

A large furnace of the time produced 2,400 tons of pig iron a year. Forges removed impurities from pig iron by a hammering process that yielded bar iron—a malleable product used in making strain-resisting articles. Water power operated the bellows of the furnaces and the trip hammers of the forges. Some forges adjoined furnaces; others were separate works. The ironmasters of the period failed to improve their methods or their products. Commonly they lived in isolation among dependent workers, whom they ruled in lordly fashion. Miners in Pennsylvania in 1783 received between $5 to $6 a month, plus provisions. Although much American bar iron was of good quality, the quantity produced did not meet the domestic demand, with the result that manufacturers imported, in 1810, about 9,000 tons from Russia, Sweden, and England.[14]

Much of the crude iron went to the shops of village blacksmiths, there to be shaped into numerous articles needed by neighboring farmers. Other users of crude iron were foundries in which molten metal was poured into molds or cavities formed in moistened, heat-resistant sand. Cast iron products included shovels, plow irons, cooking utensils, hammer heads, anvils, and stove plates. After 1783 many foundries were erected, largely to meet specialized needs of the larger cities. Pittsburgh acquired its first one in 1804. The building of steam engines gave a new impetus to foundry work, as did Eli Whitney's method of making firearms in identical parts, as described by an observer in 1807: "For every part of a musket he has a mold; and there is said to be such exactitude in the finishing that every one part of any one musket may be adapted to all the parts of any other." In 1810, national arsenals at Springfield, Massachusetts, and at Harpers Ferry, several privately owned factories, and a state works at Richmond produced 39,000 muskets a year, in addition to those made by gunsmiths. Many of the iron foundries of the period evolved from brass foundries. Several cast bells, shells, and cannon. Each having machinery for boring and finishing, a foundry in Maryland and one at Richmond cast large cannon in solid form. In 1810 a foundry at Philadelphia manufactured steam engines. By that time foundries produced all the kettles and other cooking utensils required by the domestic market.[15]

[14] Clark, *History of Manufactures in the United States*, pp. 393, 412, 417, 445; Arthur Cecil Bining, "The Rise of Iron Manufacture in Western Pennsylvania," *Western Pennsylvania Historical Magazine*, XVI, No. 4 (November, 1933), 237–238; Charles S. Boyer, *Early Forges & Furnaces in New Jersey* (Philadelphia: University of Pennsylvania Press, 1931), pp. 4–7, 123.

[15] Clark, *History of Manufactures in the United States*, pp. 171, 416, 420, 502–503; Bishop, *History of American Manufactures*, II, 35, 105, 154–155; Louis C. Hunter, "Influence of the Market upon Technique in the Iron Industry in Western Pennsylvania up to 1860," *Journal of Economic and Business History*, I, No. 2 (February, 1929), 245–246; George W. Hughes, "The Pioneer Iron Industry in Western Pennsylvania," *Western Pennsylvania Historical Magazine*, XIV, No. 3 (July, 1931), 209–215.

In 1810 about 7,000 tons of crude iron went to fifty rolling and slitting mills, which turned it into nail rods, hoops, wagon tires, and sheet iron. The machinery of such a mill included a pair of rollers and a pair of cutters, each usually operated by a water wheel. A workman cut cold bars of iron into pieces that were brought to a white heat in an air furnace, then rolled into thin plates varying from three to five feet in length, and finally run through cutters which slit them into strips or rods. Massachusetts, with twelve such mills at Dover, Plymouth, Beverly, Amesbury, Norton, Newton, Taunton, and Bridgewater, produced half of the rolled iron of the country in 1810.[16]

Nail factories took about 50 percent of the rods that came from the rolling and slitting mills. A nail-making machine, which produced a hundred nails a minute and which had been developed at a reputed cost of $1,000,000, was an American innovation of this period. By 1810, cut nails were made at one third of the cost of producing wrought forged nails. In 1810, the value of the country's output of cut nails was estimated as $1,200,000. Exports then amounted to 280 tons. Lexington, Kentucky, had a nail factory in 1793; Pittsburgh had four naileries in 1807. Specialization in iron manufactures was accelerated after 1806 to the point that in 1812 each of several small plants was devoted to making products of one type: shovels and spades, wire, scythes, and mill saws.[17]

All the products of American iron works were valued in 1810 at between $12,000,000 and $15,000,000. The industry supplied the domestic market with the crude, inexpensive articles which were most needed by the primitive agriculture of the time. Superior bar iron and the best edged tools and wrought-iron products came from Europe. Total imports of iron and ironware amounted to nearly $4,000,000. American producers made some important advances during the period: machine production of nails, the building of the first steam engines, and improvements in foundry work that attained greater precision in casting. A rapid expansion of the industry during the War of 1812 proved to be premature, for many new high-cost concerns failed during the contraction that occurred after 1817.[18]

On the whole, American ironmasters resisted innovations, clung to old practices, and looked to government for protection against foreign competitors. The continued use of water power in furnaces and forges retarded technological progress, for the clumsy machines driven by water wheels were inefficient. The limitations of the water wheel in generating power confined expansion to the building of additional small works, pre-

[16] Clark, *History of Manufactures in the United States*, pp. 172, 510; Bishop, *History of American Manufactures*, I, 153, 154, 163.

[17] Clark, *History of Manufactures in the United States*, pp. 222, 339, 340, 341; Bishop, *History of American Manufactures*, II, 34–35, 154, 177, 205; Swank, *Iron in All the Ages*, p. 144.

[18] Bining, "The Rise of Iron Manufacture in Western Pennsylvania," p. 242; Bishop, *History of American Manufactures*, II, 154–155.

vented the enlargement of existing ones, and delayed the introduction of more efficient machines. So also the prevailing use of charcoal in smelting tied producers to old methods. A limited use of coal in forges and urban shops supported a small trade in soft coal that was mined in Virginia near Richmond and sent to cities of the Northeast. In 1804, bituminous coal was regarded by residents near Lancaster as a curiosity. As late as 1814 a Pennsylvania senator representing a district rich in anthracite coal described the black diamonds as stones that wouldn't burn. A company was formed in 1793 to mine anthracite coal in the Lehigh Valley; the first arkload reached Philadelphia from Mauch Chunk in 1805. It proved to be so unmanageable that another load did not arrive until 1814. Its worth having been proved in blacksmiths' shops in the Lehigh Valley, promoters persuaded several families and smiths in Philadelphia to give it a trial. The relative backwardness of the iron industry is indicated by the failure of steel manufacturers to make noteworthy progress between 1783 and 1815, and by annual imports, around 1810, of 11,000 tons of foreign steel, as contrasted with a domestic output of 918 tons.[19]

A striking feature of the years after 1803 was an expanding production of lead and lead products. In the East, two principal mines were worked: one in southwestern Virginia and one near Southampton, Massachusetts. They provided raw material for bullets, pewter, printing type, colors, white and red lead for paints, and litharge or powdered lead, used in making glass. American mines, however, did not suffice for domestic needs; yearly imports of lead and lead products, not including colors, averaged 2½ million pounds in 1809–1810. The Louisiana Purchase brought to the Union the immensely valuable lead mines of eastern Missouri near St. Louis. Production there had been carried on since 1719. In the late 1790's a Virginia pioneer, securing a grant from Spain, erected the first reverbatory furnace in the district, operated a shot tower, and supplied Spanish arsenals at New Orleans and Havana. By 1810, the Missouri mines met the needs of the West and sent 200 tons of lead to the Atlantic states; by 1819, 41 mines employed 1,100 miners who produced 3,000,000 pounds a year. Mine à Burton and the Potosi Diggings together yielded an average of 500,000 pounds annually between 1798 and 1816. Centers at which shot, white lead, and litharge were produced in 1815 included Richmond, Philadelphia, Cincinnati, and Lexington. On the eve of the War of 1812, one Joseph Herzog established in St. Louis a factory to supply Philadelphia and Pittsburgh glassworks with red lead. He also manufactured white lead and operated a shot tower. The value of the output of the Missouri

[19] Louis C. Hunter, "Factors in the Early Pittsburgh Iron Industry," in *Facts and Factors in Economic History: Articles by former students of Edwin Francis Gay* (Cambridge, Mass.: Harvard University Press, 1932), p. 431; Bishop, *History of American Manufactures*, II, 46, 105, 117, 154, 185, 203; Clark, *History of Manufactures in the United States*, pp. 406, 412, 417, 516.

mines between 1804 and 1819 amounted to one fifth of the price paid by the United States in making the Louisiana Purchase.[20]

Some other metals were worked on a small scale. Copper mining, though not extensive, was carried on in 1810 in Vermont, New Jersey, Virginia, and Tennessee, supplementing annual imports of 400 tons of crude copper from Mexico, Caracas, Buenos Aires, and the western coast of South America. Shipbuilding, which used copper bolts and sheathing, provided the most important demand. Small copper refineries were located near eastern shipyards and ports of entry for foreign copper. By 1813, entrepreneurs had established three rolling mills at or near Boston, Baltimore, and New York which produced copper sheets, bolts, rods, spikes, and nails. The pioneer mill—that of Paul Revere and J. W. Revere at Boston—represented an investment of $25,000. The Reveres also cast bells. Numerous coppersmiths, principally in Philadelphia and New York, manufactured kettles, stills, machine parts, and other copper wares. Throughout the period, foreign copper sheets entered the United States duty-free, largely as an encouragement to shipbuilding. In 1808 and again in 1813, American producers of copper sheets and bolts asked Congress to impose a heavy duty on imports of foreign copper in such forms, asserting that their works could supply all the country's needs. In reply the coppersmiths of New York and Philadelphia, supported by local merchants, pointed out that duty-free copper enabled them to supply the domestic market and to export copper wares to the West Indies. In this case the coppersmiths and shipowners triumphed, for Congress refused to grant the protection desired by the producers of sheet copper.[21]

The copper industry, in conjunction with small imports of zinc, supported a number of brass founders in Pennsylvania and Connecticut whose business gained in importance after 1800, when the manufacture of bells, cannon, andirons, pistols, buttons, and engine parts increased the demand for brass castings.[22]

MILL INDUSTRIES

Of all American industries, cotton manufacturing went through the most radical changes during this period—from spinning wheel and hand

[20] Bishop, *History of American Manufactures*, II, 134, 155, 208, 254; Clark, *History of Manufactures in the United States*, pp. 329, 341, 344, 346; Henry R. Schoolcraft, *A View of the Lead Mines of Missouri* (New York: Charles Wiley & Co., 1819), pp. 19, 65–67, 120–121, 138.

[21] Clark, *History of Manufactures in the United States*, pp. 295, 525; Bishop, *History of American Manufactures*, II, 35, 126, 155, 156, 190; *American State Papers, Finance*, II, 257, 268.

[22] William G. Lathrop, *The Brass Industry in Connecticut* (New Haven, Conn.: Price, Lee & Adkins Company, 1909), pp. 38, 44; Bishop, *History of American Manufactures*, II, 155, 240.

loom in 1775 to machine production in 1815. The impetus came from a series of English inventions. The spinning jenny (1764) enabled one person to operate 30 spindles simultaneously; Richard Arkwright's water frame (1769) accelerated the spinning of coarse thread by running fibers through pairs of rollers revolving at different speeds; Samuel Crompton's mule (1779) made the fine thread of the jenny with the speed of Arkwright's machine.

The spinning jenny was the first of the new machines to be used in the states. During the Revolution a shop of the United Company of Philadelphia housed a jenny with 24 spindles. A pioneer cotton factory at Beverly, Massachusetts began operations in 1787 and survived until 1807. In 1789 it utilized 10 jennies and 636 spindles. Several other jenny mills appeared before 1794 but soon expired, victims of the superior Arkwright machine. In 1790 a young English immigrant, Samuel Slater, working under the auspices of Moses Brown of Providence, constructed from memory an Arkwright machine. Installed in a factory at Pawtucket, and operated by water power and child labor, it was producing in the winter of 1790–1791 the first cotton warps that were spun in an American mill. Before 1807 about 15 other cotton factories with Arkwright machines were erected, principally in southern New England. The embargo and the War of 1812 reduced imports of English yarn and diverted much American capital from shipping to cotton mills. At this time, also, improvements of American machinery enabled factories to spin the upland cotton of the South. A cotton craze after 1807 gave birth to numerous mills. In 1815 the spinning industry was heavily concentrated in southern New England, with sizable branches in New York, New Jersey, and Baltimore, plus a few mills in the South and the West. Clark cites 213 mills operating in 1815, when the total number of spindles was 130,000, as contrasted with 87,000 in 1810, 8,000 in 1807, and 4,500 in 1805.[23]

The spinning mill did not cause unemployment: no housewife lost her job because the family spinning wheel ceased to whirl. The principal advance in weaving came in 1814, when Francis Cabot Lowell of Boston, after studying English machines, devised a power loom which was built by Paul Moody, a mechanical genius of Amesbury. In 1813 Lowell and other Massachusetts capitalists formed the Boston Manufacturing Com-

[23] Clark, History of Manufactures in the United States, pp. 190–192, 261, 357, 534–539; Broadus Mitchell, The Rise of Cotton Mills in the South (Johns Hopkins University Studies in Historical and Political Science, Series XXXIX, No. 2; Baltimore: The Johns Hopkins Press, 1921), pp. 13–17; William R. Bagnall, The Textile Industries of the United States (Cambridge, Mass.: H. O. Houghton & Company, 1893), pp. 69, 89, 96; Clive Day, "The Early Development of the American Cotton Manufacture," Quarterly Journal of Economics, XXXIX, No. 3 (May, 1925), 452, 463–466; Caroline F. Ware, "The Effect of the American Embargo, 1807–1809, on the New England Cotton Industry," Quarterly Journal of Economics, XL, No. 4 (August, 1926), 674–677.

pany, with an authorized capital of $400,000, which erected a large spinning mill at Waltham. There, in 1814, they installed the new power loom. Thus for the first time spinning and weaving were done by machinery in one factory. By 1815 the company was earning a profit of 25 percent. Heavy imports of English cotton goods after 1815 closed many of the small mills that had mushroomed during the recent past. When American manufacturers later reconstructed the cotton industry, they utilized the Waltham plan, so that the typical factory after 1820 combined spinning and weaving.[24]

For several reasons the manufacturing of cotton goods forged ahead of machine production of woolens. The country's supply of raw wool did not increase as rapidly as did the domestic supply of cotton after 1794; woolen manufactures demanded special skills in finishing and dyeing cloth; woolen fabrics—then used chiefly for clothing—required better workmanship than the first factory-made cotton cloth, which served in the main for bedticks and sheets. Woolen mills also differed from the cotton mill in that they were located close to the raw material; consequently they were concentrated in the wool-growing districts of New England and the middle states and were uncommon in the South and the West. Throughout this period the central feature of the woolen industry was the fulling mill, which cleaned, shrank, smoothed, sheared, and dyed cloth that had been woven by nearby farmfolk in their homes. The Census of 1810 reported 1,682 fulling mills in the country, of which 6.6 percent were in the South, 3.3 percent in the West, and 90.1 percent in the Northeast, Vermont alone having more than the West and South combined. After 1793, when the carding machine was introduced from England into Massachusetts, numerous carding mills were erected which served farmers by combing their raw wool preparatory to spinning. Woolen factories which spun yarn and wove cloth commonly developed from fulling or carding mills when their proprietors added jennies or looms to their equipment. Such a factory manufactured yarn and cloth for general sale and did custom work, whether carding, spinning, weaving, fulling, or dyeing, for farmers, utilizing local labor and occupying a site close to its rural patrons. The water wheel provided power for spinning jennies and for carding and fulling machines, but before 1815 all factory weaving was done on hand looms. A few small woolen factories established in the 1790's struggled and faltered; all had expired, apparently, by 1801. More substantial progress then followed; in 1809, woolen factories numbered 17, as compared with 87 cotton factories. Gallatin reported in 1810 that 14 woolen factories each produced an average of 10,000 yards of cloth a year, and that nearly all domestic woolens were then woven in private families. Many factories were built during the

[24] Bishop, *History of American Manufactures*, II, 188, 196, 213; Dirk J. Struik, *Yankee Science in the Making* (Boston: Little, Brown and Company, 1948), pp. 144–145.

War of 1812. Connecticut became the principal center of the woolen manufacture, with 25 mills that employed 1,200 operatives in 1815. Several factories were then at work in the middle states; a few had been erected in the South and West, where family production was still the rule. Interest in woolen manufactures produced the "Merino mania" after 1809; a leading importer of Merinos, David Humphreys, operated in 1811 an ultramodern factory that employed 150 hands. In 1815, one factory with 50 employees and a capital of $50,000 produced 22 yards of broadcloth a day—an output worth between $65,000 and $85,000. In New England, a fabric called satinette—a mixture of cotton and wool—took hold after 1808. Factory cloth soon began to alter old distinctions in men's apparel—to induce gentlemen to abandon elegant knee breeches in favor of pantaloons somewhat similar to the linen and denim trousers of sailors and laborers. Thus the Industrial Revolution reinforced the democratic tendencies of the times.[25]

Judged by the value of exports of the United States, forest industries ranked second to agriculture and outdistanced all other manufacturing industries and the fisheries combined. During thirteen years, 1803–1815, products of agriculture amounted to nearly 80 percent of all exports, forest products to 11 percent, manufactures to 4½ percent, and products of the sea to 5 percent. Total exports of forest products for these thirteen years were valued at $49,612,000—an average of $3,816,000 a year.[26]

The forests of the country were still so bountiful and accessible that every community supplied itself with lumber from nearby sources. In good measure, lumbering was a branch of farming in that the supply of timber came largely from the clearing of land. The farmer was a woodman who hauled logs to a sawmill and brought home boards and timbers. Throughout all the interior of the country there was neither a central lumber market nor a centralized lumber traffic. Furniture, improved farmhouses, better farm buildings, manufacturing equipment, and town construction provided the chief demand. With the growth of settlement, production for domestic use increased in importance relative to the export trade. The typical sawmill, owned and operated by an individual, driven by water power, and built at a cost of about $1,000, consisted of a shed that housed a single saw which cut about 1,000 feet of lumber of day: clapboards, staves, heading, and planks. Improvement of saws was negligible during this period. Mill operators failed to utilize an effective device, patented in 1802, which returned logs to the saw after they had been cut. Oliver Evans, perhaps the foremost engineer and inventor of the time, did not concern himself with improving the sawmill. The steam sawmill, intro-

[25] Cole, The American Wool Manufacture, I, 64, 70, 88, 111, 123, 179, 180, 220–223; Albert Gallatin, "Report on Manufactures, 1810," American State Papers, Finance, II, 427; Clark, History of Manufactures in the United States, pp. 534, 554, 560–564; Bishop, History of American Manufactures, II, 150 note, 161.
[26] Pitkin, Statistical View of the Commerce of the United States, p. 117.

duced in 1798, tended to keep the industry decentralized in that it made possible the building of a small mill anywhere, without reference to water power. A widespread and continuous demand sustained manufacturers of mill saws in Philadelphia and New England, who supplied the country's needs. New York and Pennsylvania became the leading lumber states. The Census of 1810 reported 2,526 sawmills and an output of 94,000,000 feet of lumber.[27]

In some heavily timbered areas with good outlets to the sea a commercial lumber industry was carried on. Sawmills in Maine—which ranked in 1815 as a leading exporter of lumber and ship timber—gave winter employment to farmers, who hauled boards by sled to the seaports. In New England, New York, and Pennsylvania the upland country supported large mills that sent lumber down the rivers to the seaboard cities, either for local use or for exportation. As early as 1769, 14 saws were operated as a unit in the Mohawk Valley. Beginning in 1795, the Allegheny River Valley sent lumber to Pittsburgh and later for export by New Orleans. In the South the coastal streams harbored many mills—particularly at the falls of the Carolinas. Other large mills were erected near Savannah, Mobile, and New Orleans. Such mills eventually contributed most to the technological progress of the industry. In a steam mill at Cincinnati in 1815, four saws cut boards at the rate of 800 feet an hour.[28]

After 1790, the manufacture of flour made notable progress—a trend indicated by a marked increase in the exportation of flour and a drastic decline in exports of wheat. Flour exports rose from 620,000 barrels in 1790 to a yearly average of 1,500,000 barrels during 1810–1817; exports of wheat fell from 1,000,000 bushels to an average of 100,000. The Census of 1810 reported 2,917 flour mills in the country. In 1811, flour exported amounted to 1,445,000 barrels, valued at $14,662,000—more than double the exports of 1810. The flour manufacturers of the period developed large mills and introduced many improvements in machinery. Wheat and flour required the protection of better buildings than the sawmill sheds that sufficed for logs and boards.[29]

The principal wheatlands of the era extended from the Hudson-Mohawk valleys across New Jersey and Pennsylvania to Ohio and reached southward through Maryland and the Shenandoah Valley and the piedmont of Virginia into North Carolina. Somewhat akin to local sawmills

[27] Clark, *History of Manufactures in the United States*, pp. 176–177, 316–317, 467; Bishop, *History of American Manufactures*, II, 80, 97; Greville Bathe and Dorothy Bathe, *Oliver Evans* (Philadelphia: The Historical Society of Pennsylvania, 1938), pp. 138–139.

[28] Clark, *History of Manufactures in the United States*, pp. 176, 316, 467; Bishop, *History of American Manufactures*, II, 63, 99, 217, 403.

[29] Clark, *History of Manufactures in the United States*, p. 237; Bishop, *History of American Manufactures*, II, 161, 171; Pitkin, *Statistical View of the Commerce of the United States*, pp. 119–120.

were the small gristmills that did custom work for neighboring farmers. Exporters of flour depended upon large merchant mills that stood on sites which were accessible to wheat growers and to vessels engaged in external trade. The vicinity of Catskill, New York, the Delaware Valley, Pittsburgh, Cincinnati, Baltimore, Richmond, and Petersburg became important milling centers. A merchant mill ordinarily consisted of a stone building, two or three stories high, that housed two or three pairs of stones which were turned, raised, and lowered by a water wheel enclosed within the building. Idled when the mill race was low during dry spells or frozen in winter, such a mill ordinarily ground 100 bushels of wheat a day. A larger mill with twelve pairs of stones attained a maximum of 75,000 bushels a year. Other facilities included a storehouse, screens for cleaning wheat, a bolting house, and occasionally a bake shop. Owners, whether individuals or partnerships, made large purchases of wheat from the surrounding country, held flour when prices were low, and rushed shipments to favorable markets.[30]

In 1775 the flour mills of the Delaware and Chesapeake districts ranked among the best in the world. Such success inspired Oliver Evans of Philadelphia to design an improved mill which probably originated automation in manufacturing. By 1803 he had built and linked together machines that weighed, cleaned, ground, and bolted wheat, returned middlings to be reground, and packed superfine flour in barrels. Hand labor was used only to pour wheat into an entrance chute and to head the barrels. In the early 1790's Evans's brother traveled widely, explaining the invention to millers. It proved to be so effective that Evans had difficulty in protecting his patent rights. In the ensuing struggle the United States Circuit Court of Pennsylvania declared his original patent of 1791 to be invalid, whereupon he obtained a new patent by a special act of Congress of January 22, 1808. He then raised his fees: for a mill with one pair of stones, from $30 to $300; for a mill with five pairs of large stones, from $200 to $3,675. Mills operated by water wheels had generally been restricted to two or three pairs of stones. To free his mill from water power and to increase the number of stones, Evans devoted much of his energy to the improvement and manufacture of steam engines. Descriptions of large mills erected after 1800 indicate that his invention had gained general favor. Most probably it contributed to the striking increase in the milling of flour and the decline in the exports of wheat that occurred during this period.[31]

The manufacture of sugar remained a small industry and made only slight progress before 1815. The first sugarhouse for extracting raw sugar

[30] Clark, *History of Manufactures in the United States,* pp. 77, 175, 178–180, 317, 337.

[31] Bathe, *Oliver Evans,* pp. 42–44, 84, 128–132; Bishop, *History of American Manufactures,* II, 98, 131–133, 217.

and molasses from cane was built on a plantation near New Orleans in 1795. Three horizontal rollers, turned by horses, squeezed the juice from the cane; then the water in the juice was evaporated in open pans during a crystallizing process. Such crude mills, each costing about $1,000, with a capacity of 2 tons of sugar a day, were erected on individual plantations. In the East, imported raw sugar was refined at Philadelphia and New York. The small refinery of the time, manned by a head boiler and a few helpers, produced loaves of white sugar. The total output of the country's refineries in 1800 amounted to 3,350,000 pounds; in 1816, to 5,000,000 pounds valued at $1,000,000. Gallatin estimated the capital invested in the industry in 1810 as $3,500,000. Progress in machines and methods was negligible; an increase in the number of plants reduced the business of some producers. By 1818 refineries had been built at New Orleans, Cincinnati, and Louisville. Since refined sugar was then scarce and expensive—20 cents or more a pound—storekeepers did not stock large quantities; hence it was produced in loaves of 5 pounds.[32]

The spirit of independence evoked by the Revolution inspired a demand for American-made books and newspapers that stimulated the manufacture of paper. In 1810, American printers supplied readers with 22,000,000 copies of newspapers. At that time 185 paper mills, located in all sections except the Northwest, produced paper, cardboard, and cards valued at $1,939,000. Pennsylvania, the leading manufacturing center, with 60 mills, surpassed Massachusetts, with 38 mills, partly by reason of a larger supply of linen cloth. At the typical mill, workmen cut rags and ran the pieces through rollers, moved by water power, that revolved over knives or ridges on an iron plate. The cuttings then went into vats, where they were reduced to pulp that was molded into small sheets which were pressed, glazed, and finished by hand. The industry benefited from promotional work of paper users. In 1804 the American Company of Booksellers offered prizes for wrapping and printing papers made of material other than rags. At Pittsburgh, an ultramodern mill, completed in 1816—the first to use steam power—employed 40 hands to convert 120,000 pounds of rags annually into paper worth $30,000. In 1816, also, a leading Philadelphia papermaker, Thomas Gilpin, secured a patent for the first American cylinder pressing machine—an improvement capable of producing sheets of paper 27 inches wide and 1,000 feet long.[33]

[32] Clark, *History of Manufactures in the United States*, pp. 218, 231, 394, 490–491; Bishop, *History of American Manufactures*, I, 25–26, 41, 64–65, 83, 148, 220, 247; *American State Papers, Finance*, II, 426.

[33] David Hunter, *Papermaking in Pioneer America* (Philadelphia: University of Pennsylvania Press, 1952), p. 86; Lyman Horace Weeks, *A History of Paper-Manufacturing in the United States, 1690–1916* (New York: The Lockwood Trade Journal Company, 1916), p. 93; Clark, *History of Manufactures in the United States*, p. 168; Bishop, *History of American Manufactures*, II, 63, 107, 162, 164, 231–232, 234–235.

CONTINUITY AND CHANGE

With respect to the progress of manufacturing, the period under scrutiny was a time of stirrings and beginnings rather than one of pervasive changes. A Rip Van Winkle awakening in 1815 after a forty years' sleep would have found many things unaltered. The rural family still made most of the manufactured goods it used. Weaving remained an important household occupation. The defective Census of 1810 estimated that families then produced 47,320,000 yards of linen, cotton, and woolen cloth a year—at least 63 percent of the total. The needles of wives and daughters knitted and sewed nearly all articles of clothing, with the exceptions mainly of hats and shoes. So also the rural family supplied itself with candles, practically all its food products, many articles of wood, and soap for laundering, which was done at home by hand. Bakers, butchers, barbers, and tailors, few and relatively unimportant, plied their trades chiefly in the towns. No marked improvements elevated the standard of living of the people as a whole. One study of the nation's wealth estimates that the per capita income of the people did not increase between 1799 and 1819. The continuing lack of refrigeration in kitchens and storage houses, coupled with slow and expensive means of transportation, denied to consumers the benefit of fresh foods out of season and condemned them to a generally monotonous and none too healthful diet. Copious quantities of spirits served to combat fatigue, pain, and cold. In the summer months the absence of screens exposed the occupants of houses to the flies that proliferated near horses and other livestock. Plumbing and other modern sanitary facilities were unknown. Wood fires in open fireplaces still heated houses; most rooms in midwinter were bitterly cold. Many commercial industries continued to rely on tools and methods that were in use in 1775.[34]

From the standpoint of the value of products, the tanning of hides and the making of leather goods ranked among the four leading American industries, according to the Census of 1810, when 4,316 ordinary tanneries were supplemented by 9 morocco factories that dressed goatskins and sheepskins. The common tannery consisted of vats in which the hides were impregnated with tannin from the bark of oak or hemlock to make them pliable, durable, and waterproof; other vats or pools in which the hides were soaked in lime to remove the hair; a circular trough in which bark was crushed by wheels; a house in which bark was stored; and a shop or shops where the hides were scraped, beaten, scoured, and smoothed. By

[34] Tench Coxe, ed., *A Statement of the Arts and Manufactures of the United States for . . . 1810* (Philadelphia: A. Cornman, Jr., 1814), pp. 2–3; Jared Van Wagenen, Jr., *The Golden Age of Homespun* (Ithaca, N. Y.: Cornell University Press, 1953), pp. 3, 255, 256; Bishop, *History of American Manufactures,* II, 147, 160; Robert F. Martin, *National Income in the United States, 1799–1938* (New York: National Conference Board, Inc., 1939), pp. 3–4, 6, 8.

1775, the tanners of the northern colonies were importing hides and exporting leather to other colonies and Spanish America. Hamilton found the industry so firmly rooted in 1791, thanks to an abundance of bark, as to withstand foreign competition. An incipient trade in oak bark moved the tanners of the middle states to appeal to Congress in 1792 to prevent its exportation. The common tannery was a small works that served a local market. In 1809, 22 Baltimore tanneries processed 19,000 hides and 25,000 calfskins. Farmers also carried on tanning as a family industry. New England tanners, who used hemlock bark, were the most ingenious. Their improvements set in motion a trend toward large-scale operations. In 1809, Boston merchants formed the Hampshire Leather Company, with an authorized capital of $100,000, which bought tanneries at Northampton and other towns from William Edwards and his partners. Edwards had introduced some important innovations—particularly a rolling machine, patented in 1812, that imparted a smoothness and firmness like that of hammered leather.[35]

Dressed hides and skins went mainly to saddlers, harness makers, and manufacturers of boots and shoes. In 1810 Gallatin estimated the annual value of all leather products as $20,000,000. Master shoemakers, employing journeymen and apprentices, made boots and shoes for general sale in their shops, on order from local customers ("bespoke work," usually the best), for an export trade, and for dealers who supplied the markets of the South. Exports in 1809 amounted to 8,500 pairs of boots and 127,000 pairs of shoes. Master shoemakers also furnished materials to artisans who, aided by their families, made complete shoes in their homes. Lynn, Massachusetts, the foremost shoe town, specialized in women's shoes, producing 100,000 pairs in 1809. At Philadelphia the shoe trade in 1813 revolved around arrivals from New England—particularly from Lynn. Large shipments of cheap New England shoes to inland markets menaced the journeymen shoemakers of Baltimore, Philadelphia, and New York. In the years 1806–1815, Philadelphia journeymen received $9 a week, as contrasted with shoemakers' wages of $4 to $4.50 in Massachusetts. Such wage differences handicapped manufacturers in Philadelphia and forced them to resist wage increases demanded by their employees.[36]

The Census of 1810 noted 8 drug factories and 14,191 distilleries that produced 25,804,000 gallons of spirits—about a quart a week for every man. Spirits distilled from grain and fruit amounted to 22,977,000 gallons; rum to 2,827,000 gallons. Massachusetts, with 60 distilleries in 1783, specialized

[35] Blanche Evans Hazard, *The Organization of the Boot and Shoe Industry in Massachusetts before 1875* (Vol. XXIII of *Harvard Economic Studies;* Cambridge, Mass.: Harvard University Press, 1921), pp. 6–7; Clark, *History of Manufactures in the United States*, pp. 167–168, 317; Bishop, *History of American Manufactures*, II, 36, 44, 145, 189, 217.

[36] Hazard, *The Massachusetts Shoe Industry*, pp. 12, 19, 22–23, 33–35, 40, 44–45; *American State Papers, Finance*, II, 426.

in rum, producing more than all the other states combined. In 1796 its output was 1,475,000 gallons—of which about 27 percent was exported—and only 11,490 gallons of other spirits. Baltimore, Philadelphia, and New York were the chief producers of beer. Breweries in 1810, numbering 132, produced 5,750,000 gallons. The distilling of gin became moderately important during this period, although American producers needed tariff protection to meet the competition of Holland gin.[37]

Common materials of the earth supported many industries. In 1810, limestone quarries supplied at least 489 kilns in Pennsylvania and Rhode Island that produced lime for tanning, masonry, and glassmaking. From sandstone in Pennsylvania and western Virginia and from deposits in New Jersey, glass manufacturers obtained white sand, which they mixed with cullet or broken glass and heated in clay pits that surrounded a central furnace. Glass blowers then shaped the molten glass into hollow ware or pressed it into flat pieces. A typical glassworks, employing about 14 men, was operated by a company. At Pittsburgh, Messrs. Bakewell and Page began in 1808 the manufacture of flint or crystal glass, used for making tumblers, decanters, and other wares. The Census of 1810 reported 22 glassworks that produced 4,967,000 square feet of window glass and 14,600 bottles. A Boston firm then made crown or plate glass of the best quality. The steady growth of the industry after 1800 reduced imports of glass to less than half of the country's purchases. An abundance of clay enabled kilns in three states in 1810 to produce more than 94,000,000 bricks a year and sustained thriving potteries in all sections that met the domestic demand for coarse articles. In 1810, also, a Philadelphia firm manufactured earthenware deemed equal to that of Staffordshire, England, and three other potteries made queen's ware—glazed products of a cream color.

Among the principal sources of salt in 1810 were springs in central New York, the Wabash Saline, and newly discovered deposits along the Kanawha River. Sixty-two works then produced salt at the rate of 1,238,000 bushels a year—nearly half the quantity imported. Deposits of saltpeter in caves in Virginia, Kentucky, and West Tennessee contributed to the output of 208 gunpowder mills, amounting in 1810 to 1,397,000 pounds of powder. On the Brandywine, four miles west of Wilmington, E. I. du Pont de Nemours established in 1802–1803 a powder works noted for a detached mill constructed with thick stone walls on three sides, with light framework for the roof and the wall adjacent to the stream, so that the force of an accidental explosion would shoot upward and toward the water, sparing the other buildings.[38]

[37] Bishop, *History of American Manufactures*, II, 30, 37, 65, 83, 153, 161–162; Coxe, *Arts and Manufactures of the United States*, pp. 22, 29; Isaac Lippincott, *A History of Manufactures in the Ohio Valley to the Year 1860* (New York: The Knickerbocker Press, 1914), pp. 88–89.

[38] Harry S. Hower, "Some Scientific and Technological Contributions to the Glass Industry in the Pittsburgh District," *Western Pennsylvania Historical Magazine*,

By reason of the cultivation of flax throughout the country, linen woven in homes was the cloth most widely produced during this period. A slight trend toward factory production after 1790 was soon arrested by the rise of cotton mills, with the result that only a very few linen factories existed in 1815. Exports of flaxseed after 1790 varied from 200,000 to 400,000 bushels a year. In 1810, 383 flaxseed mills produced 770,000 gallons of linseed oil, processing about that many bushels of flaxseed. Such mills supplied neighboring painters who mixed the paints they used. At Philadelphia, a leading center of paint manufactures, Samuel Wetherill, onetime proprietor of a drug and paint store, founded a successful factory which specialized in white and red lead. In 1810, hemp growers supplied 173 ropewalks that made 10,843 tons of cables and cordage.[39]

The preparation of meat products was a widely diffused occupation. Meats cured on farms supplied fully 80 percent of the consumers. Country storekeepers packed pork for shipment to town merchants; at the principal cities butchers prepared beef and pork for exportation and for urban markets, receiving hogs and cattle that had been fattened on nearby farms or driven in from interior districts. During twenty-five years, 1791–1815, annual exports of beef averaged 73,300 barrels; of pork, 47,000 barrels. Soap and tallow candles, like meats, were mainly products of individual farms, although sizable factories made them in all the large cities. In 1810, Gallatin estimated the total value of such products as $8,000,000 and total exports as 1,775,000 pounds of candles and 2,220,000 pounds of soap. He also reported that the output of one factory, which earned 15 percent on a capital of $100,000, equaled 20 percent of all exports of soap and candles of domestic production.[40]

XVIII, No. 1 (March, 1935), 35–37; Bishop, *History of American Manufactures*, II, 155–157, 161, 184–185, 216; Harrold E. Gillingham, "Pottery, China, and Glass Making in Philadelphia," *Pennsylvania Magazine of History and Biography*, LIV, No. 2 (April, 1930), 111–119, 126–129; William S. Dutton, *Du Pont: One Hundred and Forty Years* (New York: Charles Scribner's Sons, 1942), pp. 35–38; Brown, *Mirror for Americans*, pp. 96, 169, 172; Coxe, *Arts and Manufactures of the United States*, pp. 28, 34; William Bining, "The Glass Industry of Western Pennsylvania, 1797–1857," *Western Pennsylvania Historical Magazine*, XIX, No. 4 (December, 1936), 257–260.

[39] Clark, *History of Manufactures in the United States*, pp. 325, 531; Bishop, *History of American Manufactures*, II, 161; Miriam Hussey, *From Merchants to "Colour Men"* (Philadelphia: University of Pennsylvania Press, 1956), pp. 4–8, 42, 116.

[40] Charles B. Kuhlmann, "Processing Agricultural Products in the Pre-Railway Age," in *The Growth of the American Economy*, Harold F. Williamson, ed. (New York: Prentice-Hall, Inc., 1955), pp. 156–159; Rudolph Alexander Clemen, *The American Livestock and Meat Industry* (New York: The Ronald Press Company, 1923), pp. 36–43; Bidwell and Falconer, *History of Agriculture in the Northern United States*, pp. 174, 177–178, 222–225; Bishop, *History of American Manufactures*, II, 147–148; Pitkin, *Statistical View of the Commerce of the United States*, p. 105.

A trend toward enlarged shops appeared in the well-established hat industry. The Census of 1810 noted 842 hatteries, and Gallatin then stated that their annual output, estimated as $10 million, nearly sufficed for domestic buyers and provided exports worth $100,000. The shops were concentrated in New England, New York, and Pennsylvania. Those of Massachusetts, with a capital of $3 million, accounted for about half of the domestic production. Sales of one factory on the Charles River came to $175,000; at Danbury, Connecticut, the country's largest shop employed 200 hands; a small hattery at Albany made a profit of 15 to 20 percent on an investment of $8,000 and sales of $19,000. Using wool and the fur of beaver, raccoon, and muskrat, the shops made hats of four grades: from the best beavers at $7—deemed superior to their English counterparts—to wool hats at $1 for the country trade. No striking improvements transformed the processes of hatmaking during this period.[41]

Handicraftsmen in small shops continued to make many articles requiring special skills: silverware, jewelry, cooperage stock, carriages, clocks, and cabinetwork. The manufacture of cheap gold jewelry began about 1805. Silversmiths and jewelers were equipped in 1812 to supply the domestic market. Cooper shops in Philadelphia in 1811—124 in all—were outnumbered only by blacksmith shops. According to the Census of 1810, 89 carriage makers annually assembled 2,413 carriages, and clockmakers fabricated 14,569 wooden clocks. At that time the value of all manufactures of wood was $5,554,000. Cabinetmakers fashioned tables, chairs, bedsteads, desks, chests, bookcases, sofas, settees, couches, stands, stools, fire screens, dumb-waiters, clothespresses, cupboards, clock cases, and trays of the finest quality. The price sheet of one cabinetmaker listed 240 different pieces to be made on order, most of them in either walnut or mahogany, including 73 varieties of tables, and chairs of 32 designs. Mahogany, the only wood imported in quantity, employed 21 sawmills in Pennsylvania in 1810.[42]

The manufacture of several articles either was introduced or attained some importance during these years: spinning jennies for family use, stove grates, gaslights, pianos, carriages, straw hats, gingham, cotton duck, haircloth, oilcloth, wallpaper, artificial globes, porcelain, ivory combs, pins, lead pencils, metal pens, liquid blacking, isinglass, cigars, castor oil, copperas, and emery.

A bird's-eye view of the United States in 1815 would have revealed a vast, busy land inhabited by 8,500,000 people. A great majority of them were farm folk who used simple tools and processes to manufacture large quantities of the goods they needed. In villages and towns and at mill sites

[41] Bishop, *History of American Manufactures*, II, 39, 57, 151, 161–162.

[42] *Ibid.*, II, 112, 161, 173, 183; Harrold E. Gillingham, "Benjamin Lehman, a Germantown Cabinet-Maker," *Pennsylvania Magazine of History and Biography*, LIV, No. 4 (October, 1930), 290–304.

one could have found many small shops and mills in which the proprietors, each working alone or with a few hands, made specialized products for surrounding farms, urban markets, and the export trade. In every important industry fairly large works or factories had come into being, owned and managed by partners or companies, employing from 20 to 200 workers, and utilizing capitals up to $300,000 in the form of the latest equipment and machines. Every stage of industrial evolution was represented in the national economy, from Indian village and primitive farm to factory. Perhaps the sharpest contrast appeared in the new cities of the West, where entrepreneurs, encircled by a frontier society, were introducing up-to-date machinery and establishing fairly large plants in the principal industries. In Cincinnati in 1815 there were 6 tanneries, several distilleries, 4 cotton factories, 2 ropewalks, 2 breweries, and 2 printing offices equipped to print books. Steam engines generated power for a woolen factory, a large sawmill, and a large flour mill. There were factories, 1 in each line, for textile machinery, white lead, mustard, and mineral waters. A sugar refinery and 2 glasshouses were planned or under construction. Other products included boots, shoes, gloves, saddles, dressed deerskins, tobacco, snuff, soap, candles, pottery, silverware, swords, clocks, furniture, carriages, meats, potash, pearlash, and stone and marble work.[43]

Industrial technology advanced at an accelerating pace. Since the expanding use of machinery was the keynote of such progress, improvements in metalworking were of primary importance. By 1792, Massachusetts mechanics had developed a machine that cut boards into convex and concave forms and a lathe which turned out oval and round pieces, thereby facilitating the making of wooden patterns used in casting and preparing the way for Eli Whitney's method, evolved in 1798–1801, of producing firearms of standard, identical parts. Another pioneer, Simeon North, applied the Whitney principle to the manufacture of pistols, under a government contract of 1813. Improved castings enabled Oliver Evans to develop the high-pressure steam engine, patented in 1804, and featured by "strong boilers to retain and confine the steam, thereby increasing the heat in the water, which increases the elastic power of the steam to a great degree." The Evans engine, powerful and simple in action, inexpensive to build, and easy to maintain, proved to be ideally suited to the western steamboat. Other capital improvements were the Evans automatic milling machinery, the Lowell power loom which made possible weaving and spinning by water power in one factory, and the slide lathe or screw-cutting machine, patented by David Wilkinson of Pawtucket in 1798. Before 1815, machine parts were built mainly by wheelwrights, blacksmiths, and founders in their shops or at the factories in which the machines were to be installed. Inventions multiplied to the extent that the 166 patents

[43] Daniel Drake, *Natural and Statistical View, or Picture of Cincinnati and the Miami Country* (Cincinnati: Looker and Wallace, 1815), pp. 143–147.

issued in 1815 were more than six times the yearly average of 27 between 1790 and 1800 and twice as many as in 1804. In 1814 Archibald Binney of Philadelphia patented molds for casting type which increased a founder's efficiency by 50 percent and gained recognition as the foremost improvement in the printer's art since its inception. Other notable inventions were a grate by Oliver Evans (1800) that made possible the burning of anthracite coal in stoves, the first planing machine (1805), a ventilator for holds of ships (1795), a pioneer mowing machine (1803), a tobacco-cutting machine patented by Pierre Lorillard of New York (1800), a carding machine and other textile machines invented by Amos Whittemore of Massachusetts for which a New York company paid $120,000 in 1812, and a machine for granulating gunpowder, patented by E. I. du Pont in 1804.[44]

The affinity of businessman and inventor was evident in the team work of Moses Brown and Samuel Slater, of F. C. Lowell and Paul Moody, of R. R. Livingston and Robert Fulton, and of Phineas Miller and Eli Whitney, as well as in the careers of David Humphreys, John Stevens, Samuel Wetherill, Pierre Lorillard, Oliver Evans, E. I. du Pont, and Thomas Gilpin.

The workings of a successful industrial firm are revealed in the records of E. I. du Pont de Nemours and Company for the years 1804–1809. The capital stock consisted of 18 shares of $2,000 each—a total of $36,000. Receipts from powder sales and other sources amounted to $243,554.79 during the six years; profits to $43,613.68, or approximately 20.1 percent a year on the capital stock. Workmen in 1809 numbered 36, and the net assets of the company at the end of that year were $81,613.68, denoting both an appreciation of the value of buildings and real estate in a time of rising prices, and a substantial reinvestment of profits in the business.[45]

During the years under review there occurred a sizable increase in the number of wage earners, particularly of those employed in fairly large plants. Laborers and mill hands commonly moved from one kind of work to another. The organization of workers in unions was confined to a few artisans in a few skilled trades. The low income of farmers and the meager wages paid to farm hands favored the manufacturer, since agriculture was

[44] Clark, *History of Manufactures in the United States*, pp. 421, 518; Green, *Eli Whitney*, pp. 119, 124–125; S. N. D. North, *Simeon North* (Concord, N. H.: The Rumford Press, 1913), pp. 13, 80–82; Bathe, *Oliver Evans*, p. 207; Hunter, *Western Steamboats*, pp. 124–125; Constance McLaughlin Green, "Light Manufactures and the Beginnings of Precision Manufacture," in Williamson, *Growth of the American Economy*, pp. 193–194; Jonathan Thayer Lincoln, "The Beginnings of the Machine Age in New England: David Wilkinson of Pawtucket," *New England Quarterly*, VI, No. 4 (December, 1933), 722–728, 731; Bishop, *History of American Manufactures*, II, 63, 85, 103, 107, 108, 112, 151, 175, 187, 209, 218; United States Commissioner of Patents, *List of Patents Granted by the United States from April 10, 1790 to December 31, 1836* (Washington: 1872), pp. 4–21, 40, 88, 102, 149–157.

[45] B[essie] G. du Pont, *E. I. du Pont de Nemours and Company* (Boston: Houghton Mifflin Company, 1920), pp. 31–34; John K. Winkler, *The Du Pont Dynasty* (New York: Reynal & Hitchcock, 1935), pp. 67–70.

his main competitor for labor. Because most employees were either journeymen who aspired to become masters or men who, bred on farms, might
hope to become freeholders, practically all workers took the wage system
for granted—an attitude that was reinforced by the prosperity and high
employment of the era, the slight volume of immigration, and the migration
of pioneers to cheap lands on the frontiers. Neither labor philosophies nor
programs for reforming industrial society had yet taken shape. The prevailing attitude was doubtless expressed by the master carpenters of Philadelphia in 1791, when they said:

> The wages of all artificers must be regulated by the number of persons
> wanting employment: high wages induce masters to increase the number of
> apprentices, and journeymen to come from other places: low wages produce
> the contrary effect. It is not, therefore, in the power of any set of them in a
> free country to keep the price of labor much below, or raise it far above, a cer-
> tain medium, for any great length of time together.[46]

[46] Roberts, *The Middlesex Canal*, p. 87; Commons, *History of Labour*, I, 111, 125,
128; Anne Bezanson, "Some Historical Aspects of Labor Turnover," in *Facts and
Factors in Economic History*, pp. 693–694.

CHAPTER XIV

The Evolution of Business

BUSINESS ORGANIZATION

THE world of American business of 1815 differed in many respects from its progenitor of 1775. In 1780, 76,000 persons lived in five cities of 8,000 or more residents; in 1810, eleven such cities had 356,000 inhabitants. No commercial banks served the Union in 1775; in 1815 they numbered 208. Only seven business corporations that had been chartered before 1775 continued to function afterward, and not until 1781 was another company incorporated. By 1815 several hundred companies had been chartered for the construction of turnpikes, bridges, aqueducts, and canals; for insuring property; for providing banking facilities; and for operating factories. Whereas in 1775 nothing akin to a stock market existed, in 1815 brokers in Philadelphia and New York were operating rudimentary stock exchanges which dealt mainly in United States government securities—a form of wealth that was nonexistent in 1775.[1]

In spite of such developments, many features of business activity had not changed materially since colonial times. The farmers, planters, store keepers, craftsmen, and small traders who made up a very large majority of producers and businessmen were individual proprietors: managers and owners of the property they used—men who bore the risks of their businesses and were liable for the debts they incurred. Next in importance to individual proprietors were unincorporated partnerships of two or a few persons who pooled their capital, performed the tasks of management, assumed individual liability for all debts of the firm, and shared the profits. The partnership was widely used by shipowners, merchants engaged in foreign trade, and, to a lesser extent, by owners of fairly large works, such as furnaces, forges, mines, and mills. A third feature of the business community was the unincorporated company of shareholders—a strictly pri-

---

[1] Dewey, *Financial History of the United States*, p. 154; Davis, *Earlier History of American Corporations*, II, 294, 331.

vate organization which rested upon written articles of agreement. Such a company resembled a partnership in that all the members were individually liable for all debts. However, the unincorporated company was more permanent, for a member could withdraw by selling his shares and without dissolving the firm. Moreover, owners commonly employed managers or directors to operate the business. Often a partnership was changed to an unincorporated company after shares of members had been divided and inherited by widows or minors who were not qualified to conduct the business. The unincorporated company differed from corporations in that the latter derived their legal status directly from charters issued by a government.[2]

American practice prior to 1775 had a marked effect on the development of chartered companies during the following forty years. In colonial times public authorities had chartered corporations to perform services in such fields as local government, education, religion, and public and private charity. The purpose of benefiting the community, without any consideration of private profit, provided a justification for the granting of a public charter which exempted the members of the corporation from liability for any indebtedness it incurred, beyond the sums they subscribed to its capital stock. When promoters sought to secure a charter for a private business company they commonly justified it on the ground that it would contribute to the welfare of the public. Of the seven corporations chartered before 1775 which continued to operate afterward, three supplied water to towns and two maintained wharves. The first corporation chartered after 1775— the Bank of North America—was designed to support the American cause during the war. The first important charters issued by individual states were granted to banks and canal companies on the theory that they performed a useful public service. Then followed the incorporations of numerous companies for turnpikes, bridges, insurance, public water supply, and manufacturing—all on the same theory of public benefit. Such charters gave to the companies a public sanction that aided them in obtaining relatively large sums of money for enterprises that were either too large or too uncertain of profit to be undertaken by an individual or a few partners. The chief advantage of a corporation over unincorporated companies was the limited liability of its members.[3]

---

[2] Shaw Livermore, "Unlimited Liability in Early American Corporations," *Journal of Political Economy*, XLIII, No. 5 (October, 1935), 674–676; Oscar Handlin and Mary Flug Handlin, "Origins of the American Business Corporation," *Journal of Economic History*, V, No. 1 (May, 1945), 6; H. A. Shannon, "The Coming of General Limited Liability," *Economic History*, II, No. 6 (January, 1931), 271.

[3] Davis, *Earlier History of American Corporations*, II, 329, 331; G. S. Callender, "The Early Transportation and Banking Enterprises of the States in Relation to the Growth of Corporations," *Quarterly Journal of Economics*, XVII, No. 1 (November, 1902), 132, 147, 148; Joseph G. Blandi, *Maryland Business Corporations, 1783–1852* (Johns Hopkins University *Studies in Historical and Political Science*, Series LII,

Once a corporation had been chartered, its shareholders elected a board of directors who made its bylaws and conducted the business. The shareholders also commonly elected the president and treasurer of the company and empowered the president to appoint minor officers. In most cases a company did not sell stock to the public at a fixed price; instead, a few men pledged to contribute a specified amount, whereupon the directors assessed them for small sums as money was needed for the project. The early company was more akin to a circle of relatives, friends, and acquaintances than to an impersonal organization of investors who were unknown to one another. Of the largest companies chartered before 1792 —excluding the Bank of the United States—none had more than 150 original stockholders. As a rule, members either retained their shares or disposed of them privately; before 1800 they were not bought and sold widely in the embryonic stock exchanges of the leading cities.[4]

Between 1775 and 1801 the states issued 326 charters to corporations. This period was distinguished by a predominant interest in companies organized to build bridges, turnpikes, and canals. Of the charters granted, 207 or 63 percent were designed for such projects. Banks were favored with 34 charters; insurance companies with 33. Manufacturing did not then inspire many promoters to use the corporate form: only 8 charters designated that purpose. New England led the movement. Its legislatures authorized 194 charters, or 59 percent of the total number. Massachusetts and Connecticut together issued 102, as contrasted with 63 granted by New York–New Jersey–Pennsylvania, and 69 by all the other states. South Carolina issued 10; Georgia and Kentucky 1 each.[5]

During the years 1800–1817 the states issued at least 1,794 corporate charters, of which the New England governments authorized 849. New York, New Jersey, Maryland, Pennsylvania, and Ohio combined granted 845. New York forged ahead of Massachusetts as the leading incorporator; its charters, 1800–1817, outnumbered those of Massachusetts by 546 to 318. Turnpike companies continued to be favored: Pennsylvania chartered 86 between 1802 and 1816. Manufacturing corporations proliferated after 1806 and reached a peak in 1814. In that year New York authorized 46 of the 161 manufacturing companies to which it granted charters during the period 1809–1815.[6]

No. 3; Baltimore: The Johns Hopkins Press, 1934), pp. 10–11; Shaw Livermore, "Advent of Corporations in New York," *New York History*, XVI, No. 3 (July, 1935), 289.

[4] Davis, *Earlier History of American Corporations*, II, 299, 300, 322–323.

[5] Callender, "Early Transportation and Banking Enterprises," p. 131; Davis, *Earlier History of American Corporations*, II, 26–27; Blandi, *Maryland Business Corporations*, p. 14.

[6] George Hebertson Evans, Jr., *Business Incorporations in the United States, 1800–1943* (New York: National Bureau of Economic Research, Inc., 1948), pp. 12, 17, 21, 24; W. C. Kessler, "Incorporation in New England: A Statistical Study, 1800–

Two factors stimulated the early growth of corporations. The Federalist program, centering in the Funding Act of 1790 and the chartering of the Bank of the United States in 1791, created an abundance of wealth that was used in part to finance new enterprises. Then, after 1792, the expansion of foreign trade provided additional funds for investment. Before 1809 most corporations—for banking, insurance, canals, turnpikes, and bridges—served to promote foreign commerce, either by enlarging credit facilities, by lessening business risks, or by facilitating the transportation of goods from the interior to the seaports. The principal investors in banks and insurance companies were city merchants. Other investors included retired farmers, widows, minors, landowners, and town dwellers with small savings. Turnpike companies, with shares of an average par value of $25, made the strongest appeal to such investors. The Bank of the United States, holding private investments of $8,000,000, towered above all other corporations. By 1807 the six leading canal companies had raised $2,570,000. Before 1800, only banks possessed paid-in capitals of $1,000,000 or more; a few companies—insurance and banking—had capitals of between $1,000,000 and $500,000; banks, insurance companies, a few bridge and turnpike companies, the Boston Aqueduct Corporation, and one manufacturing company made up a group with capitals ranging from $50,000 to $100,000; most of the companies raised less than $50,000 each.[7]

Except for the Bank of North America and the Bank of the United States, all corporations of the era were essentially local enterprises. The longest canal was only 27.25 miles; only three canals extended more than 2 miles. The capital for such canals had been obtained only with great difficulty, and the most ambitious canal projects of the era did not receive any support whatsoever. Before 1815, eastern investors did not contribute to the settlement of the West. Foreign commerce, shipping, and agriculture continued to absorb most of the capital available for investment. The absence of savings banks and life insurance companies prevented corporation promoters from drawing widely upon the savings of small investors. In the new states, banks with solid capital assets did not exist. The difficulty of securing capital for corporate projects induced the state legislatures to assist many companies. Virginia subscribed $77,500 to two canal companies; New York paid $92,000 to its Western Canal Company. Most of the states invested in banks they chartered: in 1812, such investments of Massachusetts amounted to $1,000,000; of Pennsylvania, to $2,108,000; of Maryland, to $54,000. The profits of the war years do not alone account for the rise of the corporation, for it lagged in the South, which prospered greatly

1875," *Journal of Economic History*, VIII, No. 1 (May, 1948), 46; William Miller, "A Note on the History of Business Corporations in Pennsylvania, 1800–1860," *Quarterly Journal of Economics*, LV, No. 1 (November, 1940), 156–157.

[7] Davis, *Earlier History of American Corporations*, II, 291, 296, 298, 330; Callender, "Early Transportation and Banking Enterprises," pp. 137–138.

at the time. Other important factors were the influence of merchants, accustomed as they were to the share plan of partnerships, and the habit of group action that had grown strong in the compact, incorporated towns of the New England states.[8]

Petitions for corporate charters and ensuing actions of legislatures gave expression to current ideas with respect to the proper relations between government and business. Before 1800, lawmakers made a distinction between corporations that undertook to provide essential services to the general public (public-service companies) and those which were designed to produce articles, for private profit, for a limited group of purchasers. Among public-service companies were those devoted to banking, turnpikes, and canals, and, to a lesser extent, insurance. Legislatures generally dealt liberally with such companies, with respect to their powers of acquiring real estate, extensions of time limits for the completion of projects, and the amount of capital they were authorized to acquire. Pennsylvania usually approved of requests to raise additional capital when needed; Massachusetts did not limit such companies to specified amounts. Before 1785 it appears that legislatures did not regard peacetime manufacturing projects as vested with a public interest. In consequence, promoters of manufactures expounded a theory of justification, asserting that home industries would make the country self-sufficient, particularly in wartime, reduce debts to and dependence upon foreign creditors, check the exportation of specie in payment for imports, and assure an adequate domestic supply of coin that would increase the value of land. Under the impetus of such arguments legislatures freely chartered manufacturing companies during the era of interrupted foreign trade between 1807 and 1815.[9]

Early experience of legislatures with corporations soon led many of them to modify the English common-law rule which limited the financial liability of a shareholder to the amount of a company's capital stock which he owned. The 1791 charter of the Bank of New York forbade it to incur debts in excess of three times the value of its capital stock and made the directors liable for such excess indebtedness if they had concurred in contracting it. Later, in 1797, the New York legislature, in chartering the Hamilton Manufacturing Society, first asserted the requirement that every member of a corporation should be individually liable for the payment of any debt due from the corporation to any person. Charters granted by New York to insurance companies after 1798 usually required shareholders, in case a company failed, to contribute toward its debts a sum equal to the

[8] Davis, *Earlier History of American Corporations*, II, 229, 338; Callender, "Early Transportation and Banking Enterprises," pp. 112, 113, 116, 132, 133, 138; Blandi, *Maryland Business Corporations*, p. 91; Louis Hartz, "Laisser-Faire Thought in Pennsylvania, 1776–1860," *Tasks of Economic History* (1943), p. 69.

[9] Livermore, "Unlimited Liability," pp. 674–676, 684; Davis, *Earlier History of American Corporations*, II, 326, 329; Oscar Handlin and Mary Flug Handlin, *Commonwealth* (New York: New York University Press, 1947), p. 135.

value of the stock they owned. Between 1792 and 1805 Massachusetts issued five corporate charters which subjected members individually to full responsibility for debts incurred, and in 1809 a general law of Massachusetts made shareholders of an insolvent manufacturing company individually liable for all debts in excess of the company's assets. By charters issued in 1813–1815, Massachusetts shareholders were exposed to full liability if a company became insolvent or if its property could not be found. Such obligations of members of manufacturing companies help to explain why manufacturers after 1815 preferred the unincorporated association to the corporation.[10]

Unlimited, or even double, liability of shareholders magnified the personal element in new corporations, as in partnerships, for it was of paramount importance for members to know and trust the persons who were contracting debts and managing the business.

Since the incorporation of a company originally required a special law, the task of granting charters soon became oppressive to the legislatures of states in which promoters were most numerous. New York granted fifty-three charters in 1805–1806. This situation prompted the New York legislature to enact, in 1811, a general incorporation law which permitted the issuing of a charter to a manufacturing company without the enactment of a special statute. The law limited the capital of such a company to $50,000 and its existence to five years, designated the directors as "trustees," defined the shares as personal property, permitted them to be transferred as directed by the company's bylaws, and decreed that, when a company expired, its shareholders were to be liable for its debts "to the extent of their respective shares in the said company, and no further." An act of Massachusetts of 1809 laid down general rules to which manufacturing companies must conform, thereby extricating the legislature from a maze of detailed charter bills.[11]

Although many promoters who received charters did not establish companies, and although many groups did not secure all the capital they were authorized to raise, the continuing popularity of corporations indicates that they were generally profitable. Few of the early companies, however, made exceptionally large profits. The most successful were those

[10] Livermore, "Unlimited Liability," pp. 677–680, 683–684; Blandi, *Maryland Business Corporations*, p. 39; E. Merrick Dodd, "The Evolution of Limited Liability in Massachusetts" (Massachusetts Historical Society, *Proceedings*, Vol. LXVIII; Boston: The Society, 1952), p. 234.

[11] Livermore, "Unlimited Liability," pp. 684–685; W. C. Kessler, "A Statistical Study of the New York General Incorporation Act," *Journal of Political Economy*, XLVIII, No. 6 (December, 1940), 878–879; Charles M. Haar, "Legislative Regulations of New York Industrial Corporations, 1800–1850," *New York History*, XXII, No. 2 (April, 1941), 193, 195; Edwin Merrick Dodd, Jr., "The First Half Century of Statutory Regulation of Business Corporations in Massachusetts," in *Harvard Legal Essays* (Cambridge, Mass.: Harvard University Press, 1934), p. 89.

devoted to banking, insurance, and bridges. Canal companies, the least profitable, had to contend with the most difficult problems of labor and management. No bankruptcies of banks or insurance companies occurred before 1800. In the era of most active incorporation, 1808–1815, successful companies made profits of 10, 12, 15, and even 20 percent. Opponents of the corporation objected that it enabled a few rich men to gain an unfair advantage by pooling their wealth, that they obtained rights that properly belonged to the public, and that their privileges tended to create a monopoly. Legislatures heeded such protests by defining the duties of corporations, by fixing the charges they could make, by subjecting them to restrictions to prevent monopoly or other abuses, and by providing for forfeiture of privileges if they failed to abide by their charters. During this period the states did not set up special central agencies to supervise corporations; enforcement depended mainly upon aggrieved persons who appealed to the courts.[12]

TWENTY YEARS OF BANKING

Before 1815, American corporations derived their primary importance from the business of banking, for chartered banks supplied the country with most of its currency. During the thirty-five years after 1780 the history of banking discloses two fairly distinct phases. Until 1799, most banks were dominated by conservative men of the kind who adhered to the Federalist party. In addition to the first Bank of the United States, twenty-two banks affiliated with individual states were established during the years 1781–1798. Their authorized capital amounted to at least $15,250,000, and in the main they served the merchant class by providing credit for the financing of foreign trade. In 1798, Boston, Philadelphia, and Baltimore each had two state banks; Charleston, Alexandria, Wilmington in Delaware, New York, New Haven, New London, Providence, Newport, Nantucket, Newburyport, Salem, and Portsmouth each had one, as did each of four inland ports: Hudson and Albany in New York and Hartford and Norwich in Connecticut. Massachusetts led with five banks; Connecticut followed with four; the New England states together had twelve of the twenty-two, as contrasted with only two south of Maryland. Early promoters had hoped to limit a state to a single local bank and strove to maintain a monopoly where and when only one bank had been established. None of the banks of this early period became insolvent or even failed to redeem its notes in specie on demand. Generally, the managers kept adequate specie reserves

---

[12] Louis Hartz, *Economic Policy and Democratic Thought: Pennsylvania, 1776–1860* (Cambridge, Mass.: Harvard University Press, 1948), p. 69; Davis, *Earlier History of American Corporations*, II, 293–294, 303–309; Handlin, *Commonwealth*, pp. 113, 114, 119, 121; John W. Cadman, Jr., *The Corporation in New Jersey* (Cambridge, Mass.: Harvard University Press, 1949), pp. 72–74.

against liabilities. The strongest impetus for establishing banks evidently came from the creation of new federal securities by the Funding Act of 1790. Thirteen banks with authorized capitals amounting to $8,890,000 were established in 1791–1793. With few exceptions the early banks served a small clientele of capitalists who were affiliated with them or their directors. Of practices in New York before 1799 an observer wrote in 1804: "It is well known that . . . the Branch [of the] Bank [of the United States] and the New York Bank, governed by *federal* gentlemen, were ᵉ ᵐ₋ₚloyed in a great measure as *political engines*. A close system of seclusion against those who differed from them on political subjects was adopted and pursued. There were but few active and useful Republicans that could obtain from those banks discount accommodations . . . ." A similar situation evidently existed in other centers, with the exception of Philadelphia, where the Bank of Pennsylvania had been established under Republican auspices in 1793.[13]

After 1798 the banking world experienced a vigorous growth and expansion of interests and activities. The banks of 1800 numbered 29; in 1811 there were 89, with authorized capitals of $52,600,000 and notes in circulation amounting to $28,110,000. Many conditions contributed to this advance. The growth of population—from 5,308,000 in 1800 to 7,239,000 in 1810—caused an increase of production and business that called for additional currency and credit. Wartime trade yielded profits that provided capital for the formation of new banks and enlarged the country's fund of the precious metals, as evidenced by state bank reserves of specie amounting to $15,400,000 in 1811. The internal development of the country created a demand for bank credit for the financing of agriculture, manufactures, transportation, insurance, and public works. The growing political influence of the Republicans soon swept away the near monopoly of the Federalists in the field of banking. Despite Jefferson's continued criticism of banks that created credit in excess of their specie holdings, his partisans established many banks. Since the great expansion of banking occurred during the rule of the Republicans, it appears that in the past many of them had objected mainly to Federalist banks and that they welcomed new banks that provided credit for enterprises in which they were interested.[14]

In Pennsylvania the Federalist Bank of North America was the only

[13] Hammond, *Banks and Politics in America*, pp. 135, 144–145, 149, 158; Joseph Edward Hedges, *Commercial Banking and the Stock Market Before 1860* (Johns Hopkins University *Studies in Historical and Political Science*, Series LVI, No. 1; Baltimore: The Johns Hopkins Press, 1938), pp. 16–18; Alfred Cookman Bryan, *History of State Banking in Maryland* (Johns Hopkins University *Studies in Historical and Political Science*, Series XVII, Nos. 1–3; Baltimore: The Johns Hopkins Press, 1899), pp. 19–21.

[14] Hammond, *Bank and Politics in America*, pp. 145–148, 165–167, 190; Bryan, *State Banking in Maryland*, pp. 22, 40–41.

state bank until 1793, when the legislature chartered the Bank of Pennsylvania, with a capital of $3 million, one third of which was owned by the state. Although sponsored by Albert Gallatin and designed to serve the rural southwestern section, the Bank of Pennsylvania soon fell under the control of a few men who were accused of refusing loans to Republican applicants. In consequence, a group of merchants outside the mercantile aristocracy of the state organized the Bank of Philadelphia, capitalized at $1 million, for which they obtained a charter in 1804. Five years later the Pennsylvania legislature incorporated the Farmers and Mechanics Bank under a charter that required that a majority of its directors should be bona fide farmers, mechanics, and manufacturers. Perhaps the foremost breach in Federalist domination was made in 1799 when Aaron Burr, by skillful political maneuvering, obtained a charter for the Manhattan Company which authorized it to amass a capital of $2 million and empowered it to supply New York City with "pure and wholesome water" and to engage in all lawful "monied transactions or operations." In Boston, Republican businessmen scored their first victory in 1811 when they secured a charter for the state bank and acquired the quarters of the branch of the then expiring Bank of the United States.[15]

A democratic urge in banking manifested itself in the establishment of public state banks, which were designed to serve the citizens by issuing notes and making loans. In 1806 Vermont established such a bank. Evidently without specie capital, it was owned wholly by the state, managed by directors elected by the legislature, and made the sole depository and fiscal agent of the state. Losses which it incurred forced it to close in 1812, when it owed $200,000—claims that the state apparently paid in full. Kentucky erected a similar bank in 1806, although the state owned only half its capital. Its monopoly of banking in Kentucky lasted until 1818. The Bank of South Carolina, chartered in 1812, owned wholly by the state, sustained by a pledge of the state to make good its debts, and favored with a monopoly of the banking business of the state government, supplemented two private state banks in Charleston and earned profits which were used to pay interest on the state's debts. Prudently managed, this bank was a distinct success.[16]

The pre-1815 bank served to enlarge a community's currency and credit, to make loans available to eligible borrowers, and to provide profits to owners of bank stock by increasing the earning capacity of specie through the issuance of notes and the granting of loans in excess of the value of such specie. Originally, specie made up the capital stock of a

[15] Nicholas B. Wainwright, *History of the Philadelphia Bank* (Philadelphia: William F. Fell Company, 1953), pp. 5–6; Hammond, *Banks and Politics in America*, pp. 149–158, 164–166; Gras, *The Massachusetts First National Bank*, p. 68; Bryan, *State Banking in Maryland*, p. 25.

[16] Hammond, *Banks and Politics in America*, pp. 166, 168, 170.

bank. However, the early banks usually began to operate before all the authorized capital had been paid in, in the form of specie. Subscribers commonly contributed to the capital fund by means of installment payments. Also, successful banks increased their capitals by selling additional stock. Thus the capital of the Massachusetts Bank grew from $255,000 in 1784 to $400,000 in 1792, to $800,000 in 1808, and to $1,600,000 in 1810. The capitalization of all banks exceeded their specie holdings in 1811 by $52,600,-000 to $15,400,000. A report of 1810 affirms that "none of the banks ʻ..ʼided less than 8 percent and some of them much more." [17]

In 1812 the currency of the country consisted mainly of bank notes which were not legally money but merely a bank's promise to pay. Most people thought that such notes would depreciate if the issuing bank failed to redeem them in specie on demand. The earliest banks received deposits in specie for safekeeping, much as a modern bank provides safe-deposit boxes. In the main, deposits were created when a bank gave a borrower a credit on its books and allowed him to draw on it by check. Such deposits probably equaled in amount the total value of the notes issued by the banks. Together, the two classes of claims made up a bank's principal liabilities. Increasingly bankers lengthened the terms of loans—from three to four to six months. Many thirty- or sixty-day notes of solvent customers were automatically renewed.[18]

In 1792, Massachusetts restricted the notes and loans of the Massachusetts Bank to twice its specie capital. A Massachusetts charter to the Gloucester Bank in 1800 limited loans and discounts to double its capital and imposed a similar restraint on its note issues. In 1809, the Massachusetts legislature inflicted a penalty of 2 percent a month on notes which a bank failed to redeem in specie on demand. This law was evoked by the failure in 1809 of the Farmers Exchange Bank of Glocester, Rhode Island, which had been manipulated by a Boston financier, Andrew Dexter, Jr., to the point that it reputedly had issued $800,000 in notes on a specie capital of $45—the only instance of flagrant mismanagement before 1812.[19]

Even so, the pioneer banker did not escape criticism. His enemies complained that banks prevented other kinds of lending, increased usury,

[17] Gras, *The Massachusetts First National Bank,* p. 25; Hammond, *Banks and Politics in America,* pp. 134–135, 190; Bryan, *State Banking in Maryland,* pp. 20, 32.

[18] Lloyd W. Mints, *A History of Banking Theory in Great Britain and the United States* (Chicago: The University of Chicago Press, 1945), p. 67; Margaret Hadley Foulds, "The Massachusetts Bank, 1784–1865," *Journal of Economic and Business History,* II, No. 2 (February, 1930), 258–259; Bray Hammond, "Long and Short Term Credit in Early American Banking," *Quarterly Journal of Economics,* XLIX, No. 1 (November, 1934), 84–87; Hammond, *Banks and Politics in America,* pp. 137–140, 146, 178–180, 192; Davis R. Dewey, *State Banking Before the Civil War* (National Monetary Commission, *Senate Document,* No. 581, 61 Cong., 2 Sess., Vol. IV, No. 2; Washington: Government Printing Office, 1910), pp. 182–186.

[19] Gras, *The Massachusetts First National Bank,* p. 62; Hammond, *Banks and Politics in America,* pp. 140–141, 172–176, 178.

caused the exportation of coin, usurped the power of government over the currency, and aided adventurers and insolvent traders, thereby enabling them to deceive others and to unsettle business. It was charged that bank notes were an imitation of wealth that devoured the coin of a community. Jefferson asserted in 1813 that, by reason of bank currency, money invested in loans had lost half its real value during the preceding twenty years. He spoke of bankers as a set of people who had incurred debts of about $200 million, who were exempted by law from paying more than a third of such debts, and who collected interest on them from the public through the channels of trade.[20] John Adams observed in 1809:

> Our medium is depreciated by the multitude of swindling banks, which have emitted bills to an immense amount beyond the deposits of gold and silver in their vaults, by which means the price of labor and land and merchandise and produce is doubled, tripled, and quadrupled in many instances. Every dollar of a bank bill that is issued beyond the quantity of gold and silver in the vaults, represents nothing, and is therefore a cheat upon somebody.[21]

The hostility to private banks prompted many promoters to seek public approval for their projects by linking them with other useful enterprises. Thus corporations which were chartered in part for such purposes as insuring lives and property, providing annuities, building canals, supplying water to cities, erecting factories, and operating salt works were granted the power to issue notes and to engage in a banking business. Bank currency provoked conflicts between men who feared that large note issues would debase the currency and those who wished to obtain credit for production and business. The years of prosperity after 1792 favored expansion and speculation, with the result that the interests of promoters, debtors, and rising men prevailed, and banks multiplied to feed the swelling stream of credit available for enterprise.[22]

Apart from banks that issued notes and conducted a general local loan and deposit business, others specialized in foreign trade. Such was the private, unincorporated bank—a creation of merchants of the principal seaports—which differed from ordinary banks in that it was owned and managed by a few men who shrank from the public interference incident to a legislative charter. Ordinarily, the unincorporated bank did not issue notes, and it served only a small coterie of merchants with whom it had intimate connections. It commonly owned ships, imported goods—both on its own account and for its associates—sold such imports, and held the

---

[20] Paul Leicester Ford, ed., *The Writings of Thomas Jefferson* (10 vols.; New York: G. P. Putnam's Sons, 1892–1899), IX, 394, 411 note; M. St. Clair Clarke and D. A. Hall, *Legislative and Documentary History of the Bank of the United States* . . . (Washington: Gales and Seaton, 1832), pp. 18–21.

[21] Charles Francis Adams, ed., *The Works of John Adams* (10 vols.; Boston: Little, Brown and Company, 1856), IX, 610.

[22] Hammond, *Banks and Politics in America*, pp. 154, 171, 180.

proceeds temporarily as deposits. It made sales and collections for foreign correspondents and remitted funds to them by means of bills of exchange payable in Europe. It also advanced credit to American importers and purchased American products for exportation, both on its own account and for others. Prominent among such houses were the firm of Alexander Brown and Sons of Baltimore and the Bank of Stephen Girard of Philadelphia. After 1800, state legislatures commonly prohibited unincorporated banks from issuing notes.[23]

State banks acted in conjunction with the federal Treasury and with the First Bank of the United States, which flourished during the twenty years allotted to it by its charter of 1791. As intended by its authors, the dealings of the bank permeated the fiscal operations of the federal government. The notes of the bank, when redeemable in specie on demand, were usable in all payments to the Union. By increasing the country's supply of paper currency and bank credit, the bank facilitated the collection of federal taxes. As the principal depository of federal monies, it transferred such deposits from place to place without charge, as directed by Treasury officials. It made loans to the government and marketed its securities; it effected payments alike of federal salaries and of interest on the national debt; it advanced cash to merchants to enable them to pay import duties; and it sent foreign coins and bullion to the mint to be recast into United States coins.[24]

Guided until August, 1807, by its able and prudent president, Thomas Willing, the First Bank of the United States avoided pitfalls, redeemed its notes in specie on demand, remained solvent, and steadily enhanced its reputation among conservative businessmen. In all probability its notes never exceeded $6 million of the $10 million it was authorized to issue. It not only served as fiscal agent of the Treasury and as a central bank; it also made loans to private borrowers. A statement of its condition in 1809 revealed that its specie reserves amounted to $5 million, its notes in circulation to $4.5 million, and its deposits to $8.5 million, thereby denoting specie holdings of 38 percent of its note and deposit liabilities. It was the good fortune of the bank to function during an era of high or rising prices which expedited the payment of loans.[25]

Perhaps the First Bank of the United States derived its primary importance from its relations with the state banks, for it served as a regulator of and a check upon them, with respect to the issuance of notes. When such notes were redeemable in specie on demand, the Treasury accepted them in payment of federal taxes and then deposited them in the bank. Thus it

[23] Kenneth L. Brown, "Stephen Girard's Bank," *Pennsylvania Magazine of History and Biography*, LXVI, No. 1 (January, 1942), 29–35; Hammond, *Banks and Politics in America*, pp. 184, 193–194.

[24] James O. Wettereau, "New Light on the First Bank of the United States," *Pennsylvania Magazine of History and Biography*, LXI, No. 3 (July, 1937), 270–272.

[25] Hammond, *Banks and Politics in America*, pp. 190, 208; Wettereau, "New Light on the First Bank," pp. 263, 268.

became the creditor of the state banks. In 1802 the Bank of Pennsylvania reported that it regularly became indebted to the First Bank of the United States to the amount of $100,000 a week. On one day in 1809, claims of the bank on state banks came to $800,000; in 1811 the figure was once $1,287,-500. The bank had the unpleasant duty of presenting notes of state banks for payment in specie—a practice which forced them to curtail loans and note issues in order to maintain adequate specie reserves. In thus acting as a brake on credit expansion, the First Bank of the United States antagonized sanguine entrepreneurs who sought loans for their speculative ventures.[26]

The financial genius of the Republicans, Albert Gallatin, highly esteemed the bank for its services to the government. During his secretaryship of the Treasury his banking policies deviated from the ideas which most Republicans had previously avowed. In 1802 the government sold its remaining shares in the bank—2,220 in all—in a sale effected through the British House of Baring. Despite the reluctance of both President Jefferson and the bank, Gallatin persuaded Congress to authorize, in 1804, the establishment of branch offices in the territories. In 1810–1811, when the question of rechartering the bank was agitated, the Republicans were split into factions. The smaller—led by Gallatin, Madison, and William H. Crawford, and supported by nearly all the Federalists—defended the bank for its services to the government and for its restraining influence on state banks. A larger group, led by William B. Giles, Henry Clay, Richard M. Johnson, and George Clinton, included agrarian opponents of a powerful central bank, partisans of state banks which hoped to secure the government's deposits, and rising businessmen who wished to remove the restraints which the First Bank of the United States had imposed on the expansion of bank credit. A central bank, said R. M. Johnson, "would contract very much the circulation of state bank notes." So evenly were the forces divided that the bill to recharter the bank failed in the House by a vote of 65 to 64. In the Senate, Vice-President Clinton cast an opposing vote which broke a 17 to 17 tie. After the demise of the bank, newly formed state banks bought its various branches. Stephen Girard acquired the Philadelphia office and business and operated them as the unincorporated Bank of Stephen Girard.[27]

INTERNAL TRADE

The principal function of banking was to finance trade, both foreign and domestic. Bank loans enabled merchants to pay for imports and to advance goods on credit to inland buyers. The relatively slow progress of

---

[26] Hammond, *Banks and Politics in America*, pp. 198–199, 201.

[27] Konkle, *Thomas Willing*, pp. 180–181; Spaulding, *George Clinton*, pp. 297–300; Hammond, *Banks and Politics in America*, pp. 207, 212–213, 215–216, 222–223, 226.

banking before 1800 reflected the restricted character of internal trade, which consisted, in the main, of the exchange of the surplus products of farms, plantations, sawmills, and the fisheries for local manufactures and imported goods. Outside the plantation area, most farms yielded only small surpluses. Inland trade was restricted because many kinds of goods were made on the farm and because bulky articles were produced in places close to the consumer.[28]

Since imports largely shaped internal commerce, the seaports served as the animating centers. Philadelphia, New York, Boston, Baltimore, and Charleston surpassed all other cities as entrepôts. Of these five, Baltimore ranked last in 1790, with a population of 13,500; New York led in 1810 with 96,000. Between 1775 and 1800, Philadelphia held first place and was only slightly behind New York in 1810. Baltimore rose from fifth place in 1790 to third in 1810, as Boston dropped from third to fourth and Charleston from fourth to fifth.[29]

Each port largely depended on a hinterland, which it supplied with imports. Boston dominated eastern New England, deriving its importance largely from the maritime industries along the coast. Its relative decline after 1790 is explained by its small hinterland, the lessening importance of its West Indian trade, the restricted resources of the fisheries, the uncertain and variable nature of the China trade, and the loss to New York of much of the business of the Connecticut River Valley. New York, offering a market for the flour, salted meats, flaxseed, potash, and pearlash of western New England, Long Island, the Hudson-Mohawk valleys, and eastern New Jersey, grew in response to the increase of the state's population from 340,000 in 1790 to 959,000 in 1810. Philadelphia drew grain, meats, lumber, and flour from western New Jersey, southern New York, Pennsylvania, Delaware, and the back country of the South. The city also sent manufactures to the Ohio Valley. The large hinterland of Philadelphia stimulated its manufacturing industries to the point that in 1810 their products were valued at $16 million. The trading area of Baltimore embraced Maryland, Delaware, western Virginia, the basin of the Susquehanna, and the Ohio Valley. Favorably situated for the West Indian trade, blessed with fast clipper ships, and well suited to serve as outlet and milling center for farms producing wheat, Baltimore became the leading flour city of the country. As the entrepôt of the lower South, Charleston made only slight gains during the period 1790–1810, when its population increased from 16,000 to 21,000.[30]

[28] Johnson, *History of Commerce*, I, 202.

[29] *A Century of Population Growth*, p. 11; Brown, *Mirror for Americans*, p. 36; Albion, "New York Port and Its Rivals," p. 618.

[30] Handlin, *Commonwealth*, pp. 59–60; Martin, *Trade of the Connecticut Valley*, pp. 14, 58–59, 135, 137; Albion, *Rise of the Port of New York*, pp. 78–81; Johnson, *History of Commerce*, I, 203; Bishop, *History of American Manufactures*, II, 172–173;

The ships of the merchants of the leading ports brought in the varied products of an expanding world of trade. The principal importers commonly owned the wharves, warehouses, and offices which served their businesses. They reshipped European, West Indian, East Indian, and American wares to dealers and correspondents throughout the country, reaching inland distributing points by wagons and other seaports by small coasting vessels. The advances made by the city merchants on the prices of goods supplied to inland dealers averaged between 20 and 25 percent.

In addition to the five principal entrepôts, many lesser ports participated directly in foreign ventures. Such towns, with populations ranging from 1,500 to 12,000, included Portland, Portsmouth, Salem, Newburyport, Nantucket, New Bedford, New London, New Haven, Wilmington in Delaware, Alexandria, Norfolk, New Bern, Wilmington in North Carolina, and Savannah. Some of these towns engaged in specialized trades: Salem, in East Indian goods; and Newburyport, Nantucket, and New Bedford, in the fisheries. Otherwise the lesser port resembled the principal cities, save that it served a smaller hinterland. On the whole, its chief function was to collect interior products and to ship them in small coasting vessels to the larger ports in payment for the imports it received from them. The shipping engaged in the coastal trade increased from 103,000 tons in 1790 to 272,000 tons in 1800.[31]

Inland, the larger towns distributed the goods they received from the seaports and collected products for return shipments. With very few exceptions, such towns—ranging in population from about 1,000 to 10,000—were located at convenient points on navigable streams. Their merchants were both retailers in local trade and suppliers of country storekeepers in distant villages and settlements. Worcester, Springfield, and Hartford ranked high among the secondary towns of New England. In New York, Albany was pre-eminent—a focal point for furs from Canada, lumber from the mountains, and grain from the Mohawk Valley. Newark and Trenton served the farmers of northern and central New Jersey; in Pennsylvania, Lancaster—the largest eastern town not located on an important waterway—was supplemented by Reading and Harrisburg. Pittsburgh, Brownsville, and Wheeling combined the functions of rural entrepôt with the business of outfitting emigrants en route by river to the West. In northern Virginia, Winchester, a milling center, shipped flour to Alexandria; farther south, Richmond and Petersburg linked the rich Virginia piedmont with Norfolk, while produce moving by the Roanoke River went to Halifax in North Carolina above Albemarle Sound. The cotton farms of the piedmont of South Carolina and Georgia found outlets at Columbia and Augusta

James Weston Livingood, *The Philadelphia-Baltimore Trade Rivalry, 1780–1860* (Harrisburg: The Pennsylvania Historical and Museum Commission, 1947), p. 15.

[31] Brown, *Mirror for Americans*, p. 36; Crittenden, *Commerce of North Carolina*, pp. 165–166; Johnson, *History of Commerce*, I, 208.

above Charleston and Savannah. In the Ohio Valley, the pioneer towns of Steubenville and Marietta soon fell behind Cincinnati, which—favored by its access to the Licking Valley in Kentucky and the Miami country in Ohio—specialized in flour milling and meat packing. So also did Louisville, in addition to its manufactures of hemp and tobacco. St. Louis, mainly a commercial town, exported furs and lead; Natchez served the cotton planters of its hinterland. In the Bluegrass region, Lexington in 1815 was the most flourishing city of the West, the metropolis of the trade of most of interior Kentucky. In middle Tennessee, Nashville obtained imports from the East via the Ohio and Cumberland rivers and shipped the products of its vicinity to New Orleans. Knoxville became a receiving point for the cattle of eastern Tennessee, which were driven to the plantation areas of Alabama, western Georgia, and the Southeast.[32]

The staple imports of the inland trade consisted of wines, rum, sugar, molasses, salt, tea, pepper, ginger, chocolate, cotton goods, silk, lace, china-ware, gunpowder, tobacco, ironware, and notions. The merchants of a secondary town obtained the produce of its hinterland from country store-keepers who had taken it in payment for store goods, from nearby farmers, or from traveling agents who bought for cash. Since in most communities the individual farm yielded only a small surplus, the merchants obtained supplies in driblets from a large number of producers. The farmers, planters, and pioneers of the time aspired to an improved standard of living that depended upon the acquisition of land, capital, and consumer goods. Since the cash resources of most farmers were slight they were prone to strain their credit to the limit. Hence they became involved in a network of credit relations. The chain of debt began in England. A report of about 1811 estimated that American importers were constantly indebted to British merchants and manufacturers, "upwards of £2,000,000 sterling, for which they had a credit of eighteen months." The American importer in turn extended credits to inland dealers and country storekeepers, thereby enabling them to advance goods to farmers. Such coined money as found its way into rural districts soon flowed to the principal cities in payment for imports, there to be exported or to go into the specie reserves of banks. Rare was the pioneer who had any cash after he had bought a farm and had paid the costs of migrating westward.[33]

[32] Martin, *Trade of the Connecticut Valley*, pp. 7, 16; Johnson, *History of Commerce*, I, 204; Randolph C. Downes, "Trade in Frontier Ohio," *Mississippi Valley Historical Review*, XVI, No. 4 (March, 1930), 481; Theodore G. Gronert, "Trade in the Blue-Grass Region, 1810–1812," *Mississippi Valley Historical Review*, V, No. 3 (December, 1918), 318; Lippincott, *Manufactures in the Ohio Valley*, p. 64; Richard C. Wade, *The Urban Frontier* (Vol. XLI of *Harvard Historical Monographs*; Cambridge, Mass.: Harvard University Press, 1959), pp. 43, 49, 53, 59, 64.

[33] Martin, *Trade of the Connecticut Valley*, pp. 5–6, 14–15, 141–143; Hammond, *Banks and Politics in America*, p. 218; Gronert, "Trade in the Blue-Grass Region,"

Farmers on the frontiers and in areas remote from navigable streams were unable to transport grain to distant consumers—a handicap that encouraged them to raise cattle and hogs, which could walk to urban markets. On the other hand, farmers living near large cities found it profitable to devote their pasture lands to dairy cows and horses, thereby leaving to remoter settlements the business of raising cattle and hogs to be turned into beef and pork. An extensive grazing area that bordered the older settlements included the hilly district east of the Connecticut River, the Genesee Valley, the frontier settlements south of Pittsburgh, the Shenandoah Valley, the piedmont of North Carolina, the Appalachian Mountains, the Kentucky Bluegrass, and the valleys of the Hocking, Scioto, and Miami rivers in southern Ohio. Drovers visited these areas during the winter months and bought hogs and cattle to be driven cityward during the following spring and early summer. The steers thus purchased, commonly weighing from 900 to 1,000 pounds, could be expected to lose 100 to 150 pounds on a long drive; hogs, averaging about 150 pounds at the start, usually gained en route—in one instance as much as a half pound a day. The loss of weight suffered by cattle on long drives led drovers to sell them to eastern farmers, who fattened them for city butchers. The overland cattle business served mainly to provide fresh meats to urban dwellers, salted provisions to sailors, and beef for the export trade. After a drover had sold his stock for cash, either to butchers or to eastern farmers, he returned to the grazing country to make new purchases during the following winter.[34]

The hilly district of central New England sent cattle eastward to Boston and westward to the river towns of the Connecticut Valley. In the Genesee country, farmers found outlets at Fort Niagara, New York City, Philadelphia, and Baltimore. Western Pennsylvania supplied Pittsburgh and Philadelphia; the Shenandoah Valley depended mainly on Baltimore and Richmond and to a lesser extent on Charleston. The cattle of the Appalachian Mountains went to farmers of the Valley of Virginia, eastern Tennessee, and the southern piedmont, who fattened them for town markets. The Carolina piedmont supplied Charleston, the southern plantations, and Philadelphia. As early as 1790 the Kentucky Bluegrass sent hogs and cattle eastward via the Wilderness Trail—"the Kaintuck Hawg Road"; by 1815 the markets included Nashville, Charleston, Louisville, Cincinnati, and Pittsburgh. Southern Ohio was linked with Baltimore by the National Road by way of Wheeling, Brownsville, Cumberland, and Frederick, and

pp. 315–316; Downes, "Trade in Frontier Ohio," p. 483; Crittenden, *Commerce of North Carolina*, pp. 163–164.

[34] Martin, *Trade of the Connecticut Valley*, p. 6; Downes, "Trade in Frontier Ohio," pp. 493–494; Thomas Senior Berry, *Western Prices Before 1861* (Vol. LXXIV of *Harvard Economic Studies*; Cambridge, Mass.: Harvard University Press, 1943), p. 216; Henlein, *Cattle Kingdom in the Ohio Valley*, pp. 4, 7, 109–112, 114.

with Philadelphia by a trail from Steubenville to Pittsburgh and thence by two routes: a northern through Harrisburg and Reading, and a southern through Bedford, York, and Lancaster. A report for 1810–1811 estimated that 40,000 to 70,000 hogs crossed the mountains in one year.[35]

The cattle trade, in its developed state, is thus described by L. C. Gray:

> The driving of hogs and cattle came to be a specialized employment, with more or less standardized practices. The usual drove of cattle was described as 120 head, attended by a manager on horseback and two footmen. One of the latter went ahead leading a steer. There were stations along the entire route where the drovers found taverns and where farmers supplied feed and grass lots. The road expenses for a drove of cattle from Kentucky were somewhat less when the stock were fed on grass alone, but the loss in weight was as much as 15 per cent and quality was also considerably impaired. . . . Hogs were driven about 8 miles daily. It was estimated that about 24 bushels of corn daily, purchased along the route, was required to feed a thousand head.[36]

Inland farmers also sold cattle and hogs, singly or a few at a time, to country storekeepers, who slaughtered them and packed salted meats in barrels for outside sale. Such products figured particularly in the trade down the Ohio and the Mississippi to Natchez and New Orleans. The population of the settlements of the Ohio-Mississippi valleys westward of Pennsylvania and Virginia grew from 109,000 in 1790 to 386,000 in 1800, and to 1,078,000 in 1810. The first settlers had only a few products—furs, gingseng, and whiskey—that could bear carrying charges to the East. Western purchases of gunpowder, ironware, cloth, hats, boots, and other leather products steadily enlarged the wagon trade from Baltimore and Philadelphia to Brownsville, Wheeling, and Pittsburgh, whence the goods moved downstream to the settlements. So few were the native products of the Ohio Valley shipped directly to the East that wagons returned empty from Pittsburgh to Philadelphia. The Westerners found means of paying for imports by floating whiskey, grain, lumber, pork, and flour down the rivers to New Orleans, where boats and goods were sold for Spanish dollars and drafts on eastern merchants. Natchez also took such products for plantations nearby. Most of the downstream traders sailed for Baltimore or Philadelphia or brought cash home by land. In either case the money went to Baltimore or Philadelphia merchants to pay for goods sent West. Before the coming of the steamboat, the tonnage of goods carried upstream from New Orleans was only 10 percent of the shipments downstream. In

---

[35] Johnson, *History of Commerce*, I, 206, 211; Gray, *History of Agriculture in the Southern United States*, II, 840, 877; Henlein, *Cattle Kingdom in the Ohio Valley*, pp. 105–108; Charles T. Leavitt, "Transportation and the Livestock Industry of the Middle West to 1860," *Agricultural History*, VIII, No. 1 (January, 1934), 20.

[36] Gray, *History of Agriculture in the Southern United States*, II, 841.

1798, Kentucky alone sent products to New Orleans valued at $1,182,000.
Later receipts at New Orleans of western produce were as follows:

1801	$3,649,000
1802	4,475,000
1803	4,720,000
1804	4,275,000
1805	4,371,000
1806	4,937,000
1807	5,370,000

A minor port in 1790, New Orleans in 1815 ranked in commercial importance with the five leading cities of the East.[37]

In the Old South, tobacco gave a special character to inland trade.
The principal domain of the tobacco kingdom was the piedmont of Virginia, south of Fredericksburg, and the northern tier of upland counties of
North Carolina—a land featured by small and middle-sized farms worked
by owners and slaves where tobacco was supplemented by wheat, corn,
and livestock. After tobacco had been cured it was packed into stout,
round hogsheads, each containing 1,400 pounds. Some farmers attached
shafts to the hogsheads and used horses to roll them to market towns.
Other hogsheads went in wagons—two to a load. Most commonly the
tobacco was loaded onto bateaux—five to eight hogsheads to a load—and
floated down the upland streams. Lynchburg on the James was an important collecting point above the tidewater for tobacco bound for Richmond,
the chief storage, manufacturing, and export center of the trade. To the
southward many shipments went by bateaux down the Roanoke to the falls
at Weldon and thence by wagon to Petersburg, second only to Richmond
as an entrepôt.[38]

For most communities poor roads and a localized economy kept trade
at a minimum. Farmers rarely traveled, except on short trips. A wagon with
two horses could haul a load of one ton about 18 or 19 miles a day. Grain
and flour could not profitably be transported by land more than 150 miles.
During the winter months internal trade and travel came to a virtual standstill. The rural family produced most of its food, fuel, clothing, and articles
of wood. At the country store the farmer bartered livestock and small
quantities of produce, homespun, feathers, beeswax, furs, and skins for tea,
coffee, sugar, hardware, earthenware, tableware, and imported dry goods;
to a local distillery he brought grain to be made into whiskey; at a nearby
mill he had his corn ground, paying the miller in kind. Town dwellers

[37] Johnson, *History of Commerce*, I, 205–210; Gronert, "Trade in the Blue-Grass
Region," p. 315; Carson, "Transportation on the Ohio," p. 34; Lippincott, *Manufac-
tures in the Ohio Valley*, p. 65; Downes, "Trade in Frontier Ohio," pp. 470–471, 479;
Wade, *The Urban Frontier*, pp. 20, 26, 40–42, 48, 55–56.

[38] Robert, *The Tobacco Kingdom*, pp. 16–19, 21, 47, 53–63.

provided themselves with much of their food and firewood, which they supplemented with supplies from the surrounding countryside. The shops, mills, and distilleries of the towns met the local needs for wagons, furniture, leather goods, lumber, whiskey, and ironware, and also afforded such products to nearby farmers who came in to market produce. At taverns on main traveled roads enterprising farmers sold provisions to pioneers at prices two or three times higher than those paid by traders. Contractors who supplied army posts were thrice welcome on the frontier because they purchased produce with bills on Philadelphia that were as good as coin.[39]

AUXILIARIES OF TRADE

Various agencies of commerce aided it by quickening inland communications, by affording security to owners of buildings and ships, and by facilitating buying and selling. Of central importance was the federal postal service. On July 26, 1775, the Continental Congress authorized the establishment of a line of posts from Falmouth, Maine, to Savannah, with Benjamin Franklin as postmaster general. The initial service of 1775–1776, designed to keep Congress in touch with the army, was provided by riders who carried public papers thrice weekly each way between Philadelphia and Cambridge. By 1789, Congress had repeatedly asserted several principles: the postal service should be a self-supporting monopoly of the general government; postage should be paid in specie; the system should combine a main route along or near the coast with cross lines to inland towns. During the Revolution the service had failed to pay its way and had labored fitfully, harassed by currency depreciation, by enemy troop movements, and by a dearth of good riders. In 1777, Congress designated two districts—a northern and a southern, divided at Philadelphia; in 1782 it authorized the carrying of newspapers at rates to be set by the postmaster general. Foremost among the founders of the service was Ebenezer Hazard, postmaster general between 1782 and 1789, who operated it on a paying basis. By 1788 stagecoaches made triweekly trips on the main route between Portsmouth, New Hampshire, and Savannah, and postriders carried the mail on roads that linked Springfield and Albany, New York and Hartford, Philadelphia and Pittsburgh, Baltimore and Annapolis, Wilmington in North Carolina and Fayetteville, and Camden and Augusta. The country had 75 post offices and 2,400 miles of post roads in 1789.[40]

[39] McMaster, History of the United States, III, 463–464; Crittenden, Commerce of North Carolina, pp. 32–33; Lippincott, Manufactures in the Ohio Valley, pp. 50–51, 56, 63; Martin, Trade of the Connecticut Valley, p. 5; Downes, "Trade in Frontier Ohio," pp. 478, 493.

[40] Journals of the Continental Congress, II, 208–209; XXIII, 677; Wesley Everett Rich, The History of the United States Post Office to the Year 1829 (Vol. XXVII of Harvard Economic Studies; Cambridge, Mass.: Harvard University Press, 1924), pp. 49–50, 53–56, 59–64, 67.

As a rule, postriders first carried the mail on newly established routes. As the volume increased, pack horses were added, to be superseded by carts, and finally by stagecoaches. "In the selection of riders," wrote Postmaster General Granger to an agent, "you must always take persons of integrity, sound health, firmness, perseverance, and high ambition . . . . Among these a preference is due to young men, the less their size the better." Riders and stages divided the business in 1807 at the ratio of 45 to 41, according to distance traveled. Between 1790 and 1800 the service was expanded throughout the seaboard states and extended to the towns on and near the Ohio River. The mails of 1799 moved over 16,000 miles of roads. "Crossroads," said a report of 1801, "are now established so extensively that there is scarcely a village, court house or public place of any importance but is accommodated with the mail." By 1815 the outposts were New Orleans, St. Louis, Detroit, Fort Wayne, Cleveland, Erie, and Buffalo, and the western states and territories were served by 364 offices and 12,174 miles of roads. The busy routes subsidized the weak ones, subject to the rule that a route must pay at least half its expenses. "The mail," wrote the Postmaster General, "is not to stop except five minutes once in ten miles to breathe the horse and twenty minutes for breakfast and supper and thirty minutes for dinner." On the frontier, riders averaged 35 to 40 miles a day. The lower South endured the slowest service, by reason of poor roads and dispersed settlements.[41]

The mails befriended the stagecoach, as illustrated by its progress in New England. In 1783, only a few stages were operating there, the longest routes linking Boston with Portsmouth and with Providence. The leading New England organizer of stage lines was Levi Pease, onetime blacksmith, postrider, and tavern keeper. In 1783 he initiated a weekly service from Boston to New York that soon connected with southbound stages that led to Richmond. When Congress in 1785 authorized that stagecoaches carry mail, Postmaster General Hazard contracted with Pease for the New York to Boston route. The stages proved to be safer and more secure for the mails, though slower, than postriders. A postal contract added to a stage proprietor's income, without additional expense. With such support Pease reduced the Boston to New York run from 6 or 8 days in 1783 to 3½ days in 1793. He also expanded his business so that, by 1795, stage lines connected New York and Albany, Boston and Albany, and Springfield with Hanover, New Hampshire. Pease made contracts with the Postmaster General for fairly long routes and then engaged other proprietors to provide service between local points. By 1800 he headed a group of fourteen or fifteen proprietors who acted together to coordinate the business as a whole. Drivers served customers by transmitting money and by conveying

[41] Daniel C. Roper, *The United States Post Office* (New York: Funk & Wagnalls Company, 1917), pp. 44–49; Rich, *History of the United States Post Office*, pp. 70, 72, 74–75, 78–79, 83, 85–87, 89, 92, 96.

requests for special services. To execute such commissions the proprietors employed agents at the principal towns. Printed tickets were in use by 1804. Travelers—usually four or six to a coach—commented on the dangers of many of the roads, the dexterity and daring of the drivers, and the varying accommodations of the taverns, which the coach approached with a flourish of its horn. One specification for coaches called for red wheels, green body, red rails, yellow moldings, and "lettered on the doors in Roman Capitals with patent yellow *United States Mail Stage* and over those words a Spread Eagle of a size and colour to match." Troubles with contractors moved Postmaster General Habersham in 1799 to establish a line of government-owned and -operated coaches on the Philadelphia to Baltimore route. Although the experiment succeeded, the department abandoned it in 1809 in favor of private contractors, having found that the growth of the business was involving the government in a maze of petty details. In 1807, stages were making weekly trips to a total of 41,528 miles.[42]

In the work of multiplying and quickening business contacts, the postrider and the stagecoach were aided by the peddler. Farmers in thinly peopled areas found it cheaper to buy small articles from travelers than to make trips to town. In the Connecticut Valley, traders and manufacturers supplied peddlers with tinware, pins, needles, scissors, buttons, combs, small articles of hardware, cheap shoes, trinkets, ribbons, children's books, and cotton stuffs, which they loaded onto carts or wagons and distributed throughout the countryside. From Maine to Georgia and from Cape Cod to the Mississippi, thousands of peddlers plied their trades. Journeying from six to twenty-five miles a day, the itinerant salesman visited farms, villages, and taverns, and sold his wares for cash or bartered them for lodging, meals, and feed. Returning home when his stock was exhausted, he paid his debts to his suppliers and prepared for another trip. Working with a capital of about $400, he probably made little more than a living while on the road, but some of his clan became successful merchants. On the Ohio, store boats floated downstream bringing to river towns not only the light wares of the peddler but also heavier manufactures from Pittsburgh, in addition to corn, pork, bacon, flour, whiskey, and cattle.[43]

The chief rivals of the peddler were the country stores that overspread the land—dealers in farm products of the locality, in articles made by village craftsmen, and in European, East Indian, and West Indian goods obtained from a port merchant on a twelve months' credit, with an interest charge of 6 percent after six months. A traveler noted in 1806 that the stock of a store in western Pennsylvania included "both a needle and an

[42] Holmes, "Levi Pease," pp. 241–243, 245–246, 253–262.

[43] Lewis E. Atherton, *The Pioneer Merchant in Mid-America* (University of Missouri *Studies*, Vol. XIV, No. 2; Columbia: 1939), pp. 35–37; Johnson, *History of Commerce*, I, 203; Harvey A. Wooster, "A Forgotten Factor in American Industrial History," *American Economic Review*, XVI, No. 1 (March, 1926), 17–18.

anchor, a tin pot and a large copper boiler, a child's whistle and a piano-forte, a ring dial and clock, a skein of thread and trimmings of lace, a check frock and a muslin gown, a frieze coast and a superfine cloth, a glass of whiskey and barrel of brandy, a gill of vinegar and a hogshead of Madeira wine." Most trading at country stores was by barter. The exportable products the storekeepers received went to merchant creditors; perishable produce and local manufactures were taken by villagers and farmers. Often a store was kept by an owner of another property, such as a gristmill, a forge, a distillery, a potash works, or a cotton gin. The investment in one primitive store—a log house and stock of goods—amounted to less than $500. The store rivaled the tavern as a dispenser of liquor. As a town grew, the storekeeper visited large distributing centers to buy goods, gave orders to drummers, sold at wholesale to nearby dealers, and tended to supplant the peddler, since the store offered a larger stock of goods, made sales on a twelve months' credit, and provided a market for perishable produce. Accounts with customers were commonly settled once a year.[44]

In the Tobacco Kingdom country stores were supplemented by public warehouses. In colonial times Virginia had established a network of rural warehouses to which farmers brought their tobacco. There it was examined by a public inspector, who gave the farmer a note or a warehouse receipt that specified the quantity and quality of the tobacco he had delivered. He then sold or assigned such notes or receipts to traders who shipped the tobacco to market towns for sale to exporters or to American manufacturers. The inspection system—often defective because lax inspectors over-rated inferior parcels—tended to establish a single, average price for warehouse tobacco that covered variations in quality. About 1800, manufacturers who objected to receiving the poorer grades along with the good began to send buyers to the country warehouses at inspection time in order to purchase directly from the farmers. This practice served to price the different grades according to quality. Farmers then found it prudent to accept the prices offered by the buyers. After 1810 such sales gave birth to the custom of auctioning tobacco when buyers assembled at the warehouses.[45]

In colonial days, sales at auction—used mainly to dispose of goods under a court order, at secondhand, or in bankruptcy proceedings—were somewhat lacking in prestige. An auctioneer was confined by law to selling for a commission at a vendue. After 1780 the occupation gained in repute

[44] Fred Mitchell Jones, *Middlemen in the Domestic Trade of the United States* (University of Illinois *Studies in the Social Sciences,* Vol. XXI, No. 3; Urbana: University of Illinois, 1937), pp. 44–46; Lewis E. Atherton, *The Southern Country Store, 1800–1860* (Baton Rouge: Louisiana State University Press, 1949), pp. 14–15, 34, 51–52, 63–64, 71, 118, 123; Wooster, "A Forgotten Factor," pp. 18–22; Atherton, *The Pioneer Merchant,* p. 37.

[45] Joseph Clarke Robert, "Rise of the Tobacco Warehouse Auction System in Virginia, 1800–1860," *Agricultural History,* VII, No. 4 (October, 1933), 170–174.

as it was increasingly employed at the leading cities in the sale of imported goods to local retailers and to visiting country merchants. By one plan, an auctioneer sold a whole cargo in large lots, in the original packages; by another, he exhibited individual articles for the buyer's inspection and sold each separately. New York City's auctioneers, whose number increased from 24 in 1801 to 36 in 1813, and whose sales rose from $6,100,000 in 1810 to $13,200,000 in 1815, had headquarters as early as 1780 at the "Merchants' Promenade or Auctioneers' Row" on present-day Water Street. In selling for British exporters, the auctioneer accepted promissory notes from buyers, discounted them at a bank, deducted auction sales taxes, took his commission, and remitted the balance to Britain. In 1813–1815, state taxes netted $436,000 from auction sales in New York City, as compared with $5,700 in Albany. A few men, headed by Charles Town, dominated the business in New York City. A federal tax on auction sales—ranging from $\frac{1}{4}$ to 1 percent—was in force between 1794 and 1802. The tax was revived in 1813 and the rates were doubled in 1814 to $\frac{1}{2}$ and 2 percent. Federal collections denote that auction sales in 1815 were more than twice as large as in 1795. New York's liberal auction policy—low state taxes on sales and a rule that goods offered must be sold if bid for—proved to be an important factor in New York City's rise to commercial supremacy after 1817. In inland towns, such as Hartford, auctioneers accommodated merchants with weekly or semiweekly sales of surplus or damaged goods.[46]

The first agency in the United States for the sale of American manufactures appears to have originated in 1805, when Elijah Waring, agent of Almy and Brown of Providence, established a Philadelphia depot for consignments of cotton yarns and threads. An agent of Samuel Slater started a similar business in Philadelphia in 1812.[47]

Like auctioneering, pawnbroking combined selling and credit dealings. In Boston, Philadelphia, and New York, proprietors of secondhand clothing stores often made loans to neighbors on the security of their possessions. The pawnbroker—who did not receive promissory notes from borrowers—derived his claim to compensation from the common-law rule that allowed him to make a storage charge. The business did not become a recognized one until about 1800. In 1809, a grand inquest in New York reported that "the great number of pawnbrokers and the unrestrained manner in which they conduct themselves had become a source of serious and alarming mischief." High interest charges and short terms allowed for redeeming property—abuses practiced particularly on immigrants—led the New York Common Council in 1812 to limit interest to 25 percent on loans of $25 or less and to 7 percent on loans over $25, and to require the pawn-

[46] Ray Bert Westerfield, "Early History of American Auctions" (Connecticut Academy of Arts and Sciences, *Transactions*, Vol. XXIII; New Haven: Yale University Press, 1920), pp. 164–165, 171–172, 174–176, 178, 183–184, 200, 202–203.

[47] Bishop, *History of American Manufactures*, II, 111.

broker to hold articles a year before selling them at a public auction. This ordinance encouraged the making of several loans of $25 instead of a single larger one.[48]

Auctioneers gave an impetus to the initial organization of stockbrokers in New York. The business of selling securities gained momentum from the issuance of new federal stocks under the Funding Act of 1790. The first dealers in such paper were merchants and auctioneers. So extensive were early sales that brokers were soon specializing in the business. Their offices were the first stock exchanges. The *Columbian Centinel* noted in 1791 that in "all countries it is in the power of *Bulls* and *Bears* to lower or raise the public paper several per cent." When menaced by auctioneers in 1792, the brokers made an agreement whereby they pledged to patronize each other, to shun the auctioneers, and to insist on minimum commissions of ¼ percent. Speculation in stocks was rare, but much trading appears to have been financed with borrowed money. The usage of the time was to sell, for cash, only such securities as were owned by the brokers or their clients. That dealings in futures and sales on credit may have taken place is suggested by a New York law of 1812 which invalidated a contract for the sale of securities if the seller was not either the owner or the agent of the owner at the time of the sale. A lull occurred in the security business after the speculative flurry of the early 1790's died down. Owners of government stocks became reluctant to part with them. In consequence, brokers found it necessary to engage also in ordinary trade and in other ventures. Large government issues during the War of 1812 revived the brokerage business, now reinforced by dealings in the stocks of banks and insurance companies and the securities of the states. In 1817, seven New York firms and eleven individuals, adopting a plan of their Philadelphia brethren, formed a stock exchange where members who paid an initiation fee of $25 traded every day in a well-regulated and decorous manner.[49]

While specialists were facilitating business, insurance was reducing its risks. Shippers had long guarded against maritime hazards through an arrangement whereby several individuals and partnerships each pledged to pay a part of the value of a vessel and its cargo in case of loss at sea, the owner contracting to compensate the underwriters at a definite rate for such protection. The underwriter did not pay any cash until a claim was settled; hence the method did not require large initial capital outlays. Marine insurance policies gave protection against losses from any source:

[48] Foulke, *Sinews of American Commerce*, pp. 115–116.

[49] Walter Buckingham Smith and Arthur Harrison Cole, *Fluctuations in American Business, 1790–1860* (Vol. L of *Harvard Economic Studies*; Cambridge, Mass.: Harvard University Press, 1935), pp. 7, 23; Margaret G. Myers, *Origins and Development* (Vol. I of *The New York Money Market*, 4 vols.; New York: Columbia University Press, 1931), pp. 14–17; Arthur G. Peterson, "Futures Trading with Particular Reference to Agricultural Commodities," *Agricultural History*, VII, No. 2 (April, 1933), 68.

wrecks, pirates, war, fires, collisions, or mutinies. Before 1790, when American shipowners had purchased most of their insurance in England, they suffered from certain handicaps. The number of underwriters in the United States was inadequate, and in case of loss the owner was forced to collect the indemnity money from several persons. The corporation promised to overcome such handicaps, but it was not suited to the insurance business before 1790 because the country lacked safe, long-term securities in which capital funds could be invested. Soon after the creation of new federal securities by the Funding Act of 1790, a group of Philadelphians organized the Insurance Company of North America, for which they obtained in 1794 a state charter authorizing them to acquire a capital fund of $600,000 to be invested only in the paper of the United States, the stocks of the Bank of the United States, and the stocks of companies incorporated by Pennsylvania. During its first ten years the company did a thriving business; its receipts from premiums amounted to $6,037,000, rising from $298,000 in 1793 to $1,304,000 in 1798. The company accepted notes of shippers in payment of premiums under a schedule which assumed that voyages would be completed before the notes fell due. The company also made general commercial loans, as well as loans to shippers that were secured by vessels and that were to be paid when cargoes were sold. Other loans included an insurance feature: when a shipper agreed to an especially high rate—24 percent—he was not required to pay either principal or interest if the vessel and cargo were lost.[50]

Insurance companies multiplied rapidly. The Massachusetts Fire and Marine Company was organized in 1795, followed by the Insurance Company of New York in 1796. Companies active in 1800 numbered 33—15 in New England, 7 in Pennsylvania, and 11 in Maryland, Virginia, and South Carolina. Philadelphia alone had 11 companies in 1811. The era 1802–1815 was a time of stress and uncertainty, as competition became intense, rates fluctuated, and the volume of business rose and fell sharply in response to attacks of belligerents, the embargo, and the War of 1812. Seizures of American vessels by European raiders, 1803 to 1812, were estimated as nearly 1600.[51]

Fire insurance, as a successful business, originated in 1752, when a party of Philadelphia businessmen formed The Philadelphia Contributorship for the Insurance of Houses from Loss by Fire. Its assets consisted of its paid-in capital and the monies it received from premiums. Such funds,

---

[50] Solomon Huebner, "History of Marine Insurance," in Lester W. Zartman and William H. Price, eds., *Property Insurance: Marine and Fire* (Rev. ed.; New Haven, Conn.: Yale University Press, 1926), pp. 1–3, 16–18; Foulke, *Sinews of American Commerce*, pp. 124–129.

[51] Huebner, "History of Marine Insurance," pp. 17–19; Foulke, *Sinews of American Commerce*, pp. 129–130; Marquis James, *Biography of a Business, 1792–1942: Insurance Company of North America* (Indianapolis: The Bobbs-Merrill Company, 1942), pp. 84–96.

which in 1793 amounted to £16,640, were invested in mortgages. In 1784 Philadelphia hatched a second firm, The Mutual Assurance Company—an outgrowth of the decision of the Contributorship not to insure houses with trees nearby, on the theory that they hampered firemen. Since the Mutual Assurance Company insured such houses, it became known as "The Green Tree." Before 1815 it was common for a company to insure against either loss by fire or hazards at sea. In 1801 the Mutual issued a policy by which a single premium purchased protection during the life of a building; previously, policies had run for seven years. Rate makers classified buildings and applied the lowest rates to structures wholly of stone, brick, or slate and the highest rates to those wholly of wood. Thus one company set a yearly rate for fireproof buildings of 30 cents for $100; for wooden buildings containing inflammable materials the rate was 75 cents for $100. Two important companies organized in Connecticut were the Hartford Insurance Company, chartered in 1803, and the Hartford Fire, chartered in 1810. Most of the paid-in capital of the fire companies consisted of personal notes of the members that required them to provide cash when it was needed to pay claims. On the whole, the fire insurance business was much less important than the marine. However, when foreign trade languished, a company's fire business helped to sustain it in the face of losses on the marine side.[52]

[52] F. C. Oviatt, "History of Fire Insurance in the United States," in Zartman and Price, *Property Insurance*, pp. 72–77; Foulke, *Sinews of American Commerce*, pp. 122–124; Edward F. Hardy, *The Making of the Fire Insurance Rate* (Chicago: The Spectator Company, 1926), pp. 31–35.

CHAPTER XV

Economic Aspects of Jeffersonian Democracy

NATIONAL FINANCE

THE movements of American business were continually influenced by the fiscal measures of the federal government. "Public and private credit," said Alexander Hamilton, "are closely allied, if not inseparable." It will be recalled that the Federalist financial system, as established between 1789 and 1793, centered in the national debt and the Bank of the United States. The new securities of the government and the bank could be used to buy shares of a business corporation, thereby making up a part of its working capital. Such paper also provided a durable form of wealth in which cash could be invested. Hamilton observed that "in countries in which the national debt is properly funded, and an object of confidence, it answers most of the purposes of money. Transfers of stock or public debt are there equivalent to payments in specie . . . ." So important to national finance was the public debt that interest payments on its account consumed more than half the government's income until 1797. The idea that public securities should serve as a substitute for money and as a fund for investment presupposed that they would long continue to exist. Hamilton's critics charged that he wished to give permanence to the national debt. As a matter of fact, he advised in 1795 that it be extinguished "in a period not exceeding thirty years." In 1825, presumably, private banks and corporations would provide a sufficiency of currency substitutes and outlets for investment.[1]

In its essentials, the Federalist financial system was completed by the

[1] Samuel McKee, ed., *Alexander Hamilton's Papers on Public Credit, Commerce, and Finance* (New York: The Liberal Arts Press, 1957), pp. 7, 154, 171; Lewis H. Kimmel, *Federal Budget and Fiscal Policy, 1789–1958* (Washington: The Brookings Institution, 1959), pp. 8–11.

end of Washington's first term. During the years 1793–1801 the Federalists operated the system with success, on principles advocated by John Adams, who said in 1797 that the "consequences arising from the continual accumulation of public debts in other countries ought to admonish us to be careful to prevent their growth in our own. The national defense must be provided for as well as the support of Government; but both should be accomplished as much as possible by immediate taxes, and as little as possible by loans." Two factors shaped the course of later Federalist finance: the rapid growth of foreign trade, which greatly enlarged the Treasury's income from tariff duties, and a substantial increase in expenditures for the army and navy during the quasi war with France of 1799–1800. The total revenues of the government rose from $4,652,000 in 1793 to $12,936,000 in 1801, of which latter sum the tariff receipts accounted for $10,751,000. Total expenditures —which in 1793 amounted to $3,846,000—averaged $10,054,000 in 1799 and 1800. During three of the four years of the administration of John Adams the Treasury enjoyed a surplus. The national debt increased but slightly—from $80,300,000 in 1793 to $83,000,000 in 1801—a result attained in part by new tax levies. By acts of June 5 and 9, 1794, Congress imposed taxes on refined sugar, snuff, carriages, retailers of wines and foreign liquors, and auction sales. An act of July 6, 1796, levied a stamp tax on legal documents, and on July 14, 1798, Congress, seeking to raise a special fund of $2,000,000, authorized a direct tax on dwelling houses, land, and slaves. Happily for the Jeffersonians, Federalist management provided a surplus of $3,600,000 for the year 1801.[2]

On May 23, 1792, Jefferson wrote a memorable letter to Washington which summarized current criticisms of the Federalist financial program and by inference set forth principles to which the Republicans adhered. Jefferson reported the complaint that a public debt had been "artificially created" and burdened with an excessively high interest rate, that the administration had been obliged "to strain the impost till it produces clamor," that the excise act was "of odious character with the people," and that the Bank of the United States had the power to create $10,000,000 of paper money and to exact a profit of 10 or 12 percent by lending it. But Jefferson did not propose any acts of repudiation. "The only hope of safety," he said, "hangs now on the numerous representation which is to come forward the ensuing year . . . . It is expected that the great mass will form an accession to the republican party. They will not be able to undo all which the two preceding legislatures . . . have done. Public faith and right will oppose this. But some parts of the system may be rightfully reformed; a liberation from the rest unremittingly pursued as fast as right

<hr />

[2] Richardson, *Messages of the Presidents*, I, 253–254; Leonard D. White, *The Federalists* (New York: The Macmillan Company, 1948), p. 335; Dewey, *Financial History of the United States*, pp. 108–113; 1 *Statutes at Large*, pp. 373–374, 376–377, 384–386, 397, 527–529, 597–599.

will permit, and the door shut in future against similar commitments of the nation." [3]

Among Republicans skilled in finance, Albert Gallatin of Pennsylvania so excelled his colleagues as to be the only qualified candidate for the post of Secretary of the Treasury. As financial leader of the Republicans in the House, 1795–1801, he had been active in creating its standing committee on taxes and revenues, or ways and means. His political philosophy and his ideas on finance harmonized with those of Jefferson. Both men favored a simple, frugal government, fortified at all points against inefficiency, corruption, and waste. Both thought that the Federalists had established a needlessly large bureaucracy and hoped to deflate it. They shared a common aversion to large military and naval forces and undertook to halt the campaign for preparedness that the Federalists had instigated. Jefferson spoke of the national debt as a "canker"—as "the greatest of dangers to be feared." To eliminate it was the primary goal of Gallatin, who believed that heavy commitments to the payment of interest cramped the Treasury in all its operations. Both leaders strongly objected to internal taxes, especially of the kind that caused federal assessors and collectors to invade the homes of citizens. Both men preferred to obtain most of the government's revenue from duties on imports—"the most productive, cheapest to collect, least vexatious, and in general the least offensive" of all taxes. Such levies, Gallatin thought, least burdened productive workers and fell mainly on wealthy consumers of luxuries.[4]

In seeking to attain their common objectives, Jefferson left to Gallatin the shaping of detailed policies. Both men agreed that the income of the government must be adequate to legitimate demands. It was Gallatin's duty to assure that tax revenues were sufficient; hence his recommendations carried great weight, even when they called for a postponement of specific reforms sought by Jefferson. The Republicans found their hands tied by certain long-term features of the Federalist program—the twenty-year charter of the Bank of the United States, the national debt, and taxes necessary to support it. In his first Inaugural Address Jefferson proclaimed "the honest payment of our debts and sacred preservation of the public faith," to be one of "the essential principles of our Government." For the most part, economic conditions aided the Republicans. They inherited a large surplus and benefited from a trade boom that filled the Treasury during Jefferson's terms, as revenues increased from $12,935,000 in 1801 to $17,060,000 in 1808.[5]

In the main, the Republicans applied financial policies that realized

[3] *Writings of Jefferson* (Ford), VI, 2–4.

[4] Walters, *Albert Gallatin*, pp. 88–89, 151; *Writings of Jefferson* (Ford), VII, 327; Richardson, *Messages of the Presidents*, I, 344–345; Chien Tseng Mai, *The Fiscal Policies of Albert Gallatin* (New York: 1930), pp. 39, 45, 58–64.

[5] Alexander Balinky, *Albert Gallatin: Fiscal Theories and Policies* (New Brunswick, N. J.: Rutgers University Press, 1958), pp. 61–63; Richardson, *Messages of the Presidents*, I, 323; Dewey, *Financial History of the United States*, p. 123.

their underlying aims. At the outset they reduced outlays for military purposes, restoring the army to its modest status of 1796 and stopping the construction of several warships which the Federalists had undertaken. Expenditures for the War Department and the Navy dropped from $3,784,000 in 1801 to an average of $2,111,000 during the years 1802–1805. In April, 1802, Congress repealed the internal taxes on stills, domestic spirits, refined sugar, auction sales, carriages, and legal documents. Another unpopular tax—on imported salt—was abolished in March, 1807. These two reforms eventually saved the taxpayers $1,100,000 a year. The Republicans left the tariff substantially intact and used the surplus which it yielded to reduce the national debt, scaling it down from the $83,000,000 figure of 1801 to $45,200,000 in 1813.[6]

At the same time, neither Jefferson nor Gallatin permitted fiscal theories to stand in the way of actions which they deemed to be necessary. They agreed to finance the Louisiana Purchase largely by loans, at the cost of a temporary increase of the national debt. Of the $15,000,000 needed for that purpose, $11,250,000 was obtained by borrowing, and the Treasury's surplus was drawn on to provide the remaining $3,750,000. The war with Tripoli, which broke out in the spring of 1801, forced Jefferson to ask Congress in 1804 to increase the naval appropriations by $750,000 a year. Gallatin then proposed and Congress authorized, March 26, 1804, a 10 percent tax on goods imported in foreign vessels and additions of 2½ percent to existing ad valorem tariff rates which boosted their average level from 13½ to 16 percent. However, such additions to the tax burden were to be removed soon after the end of the war. That occurred in May, 1805. Thus Gallatin prevented an emergency from causing a permanent tax increase.[7]

The good fortune of the Republicans ended in 1809, when the embargo reduced the income of the government to $7,773,000, as compared with $17,060,000 in 1808. In the meantime, expenditures for needs other than the national debt had grown from $4,900,000 in 1807 to $7,500,000 in 1809. However, during the years 1801–1807, Gallatin's management had amassed a surplus of $17,000,000, which enabled the Treasury to meet all ordinary expenditures during the stringency of the embargo and even to effect an additional reduction of the national debt—all without resort to new loans or taxes. Perhaps the most striking evidence of the determination of Gallatin and Jefferson to restrain the federal bureaucracy was their success in accumulating a large surplus during the years of plenty.[8]

One critic of Gallatin's fiscal policy condemns its almost exclusive de-

[6] 2 *Statutes at Large*, p. 148, 436; Dewey, *Financial History of the United States*, p. 124.

[7] J. E. Winston and R. W. Colomb, "How the Louisiana Purchase Was Financed," *Louisiana Historical Quarterly*, XXI, No. 2 (April, 1929), 196–197, 200; 2 *Statutes at Large*, pp. 291–292.

[8] Sidney Ratner, *American Taxation* (New York: W. W. Norton & Company, 1942), pp. 32–33.

pendence on import duties. It succeeded when foreign trade flourished, but when serious contraction occurred, the finances of the government were beset with uncertainties. A program that drew revenue also from internal taxes would presumably have given greater stability to the Treasury's income. Gallatin's preference for tariff duties harmonized with his intention to pay the national debt within the relatively short span of sixteen years. Since the debt was not popular, it was necessary to pay it from taxes that were the least rasping. Such undoubtedly were duties on imports. Gallatin's point of view was that of a moralist who thought that debt tended to breed debt, that the habit of borrowing fostered waste, profligacy, and corruption, and that in the end the process exploited the productive workers for the benefit of idlers. His ideas suited an age of scarcity when many people were prone to make virtues of work, self-denial, and economy.[9]

BACKGROUND OF THE WAR OF 1812: THE WEST

The War of 1812 exerted a considerable influence on the economic development of the United States. Economic factors relating to maritime trade and inland settlement combined to bring on the conflict. Both the Northwest and the Southwest were goaded by interests that evoked hostility toward Britain.

On the northern frontiers several conditions were productive of strife. The expansion of settlements near Canada threatened the Indians with expulsion or extinction, kindled their resentment, and incited them to resist. By 1810 the settled area of the Union extended, in the North, along the Canadian border from the Connecticut River to Cleveland. The policy of the government was stated by the American peace commissioners in September, 1814, when they avowed that "the United States . . . are fully determined, . . . progressively, and in proportion as their growing population may require, to reclaim from the state of nature, and to bring into cultivation every portion of the territory contained within their acknowledged boundaries . . . ." Confronted by the advance of settlers, the Indians of the Northwest looked to Canada for assistance. There the British, commanding the fur trade of the Great Lakes region and intent upon guarding their territory from attack by the United States, were disposed to encourage the tribes to cling to hunting lands which yielded furs and formed a protecting barrier to Canada. By Article 3 of Jay's Treaty, British subjects and Indians living in Canada enjoyed the right to enter and to travel and trade within the United States.[10]

[9] Balinky, *Albert Gallatin*, pp. 138–139, 144–147; Henry Carter Adams, *Taxation in the United States, 1789–1816* (Johns Hopkins University *Studies in Historical and Political Science*, Series II, Nos. 5–6; Baltimore: 1884), pp. 68–70.

[10] *American State Papers, Foreign Relations*, III, 719; Reginald Horsman, "British Indian Policy in the Northwest, 1807–1812," *Mississippi Valley Historical Review*, XLV, No. 1 (June, 1958), 52; 8 *Statutes at Large*, p. 117.

At the beginning of the War of 1812 the most articulate spokesmen of the northern frontier clamored for the conquest of Canada. Why? One explanation emphasizes a frontier urge to acquire additional land. Prominent among the "war hawks" was Peter B. Porter of the Genesee-Buffalo district in New York. In December, 1811, he pointed out that Canada was "immensely valuable" and predicted that by means of a war with Britain "we should be able in a short time to remunerate ourselves tenfold for all the spoliations she has committed on our commerce." Another interpretation attributes the belligerency of western farmers to Britain's war on American trade which restricted their markets, reduced the prices of their products, and inflicted hardships on the settlements. After nonmilitary measures had failed to stop Britain's depredations, the Westerners demanded war and the conquest of Canada.[11]

A third analysis, perhaps the most widely accepted, explains the attitude of the northern frontiersmen by Britain's aid to and incitement of the Indians of the Ohio Valley in their armed resistance to the United States. Between 1795 and 1806 the British in Canada had neglected the tribes. But after the *Chesapeake* incident of May, 1807, British agents again became active in the Northwest. The encouragement they gave to Tecumseh infuriated the settlers after his brother, the Prophet, attacked the American force under William Henry Harrison at Tippecanoe Creek in November, 1811. The ensuing border warfare evoked widespread demands for the expulsion of the British from Canada in order to end their incitements of the Indians and to gain security for the settlements. President Madison did not proclaim the conquest of Canada as a war aim, but he was prepared to use American victories to effect the expulsion of the British from the territory of the Union and to eliminate their influence among the Indians of the Old Northwest. By recognizing the full authority of the United States over its territory, the Treaty of Ghent of December 24, 1814, brought about a *de facto* cancellation of Article 3 of Jay's Treaty. Thus the official acts of Madison asserted that the objective of the war, in regard to Canada, was the ending of raids by Britain's Indian allies within the United States.[12]

Florida was also a source of the conflict that exploded in the War of 1812. Under Spanish rule, that strategic area consisted of two provinces—

[11] Louis M. Hacker, "Western Land Hunger and the War of 1812," *Mississippi Valley Historical Review*, X, No. 4 (March, 1924), 367, 379, 387; George Rogers Taylor, "Agrarian Discontent in the Mississippi Valley Preceding the War of 1812," *Journal of Political Economy*, XXXIX, No. 4 (August, 1931), 497–501; Julius W. Pratt, *Expansionists of 1812* (New York: The Macmillan Company, 1925), p. 51.

[12] Christopher B. Coleman, "The Ohio Valley in the Preliminaries of the War of 1812," *Mississippi Valley Historical Review*, VII, No. 1 (June, 1920), 48; Warren H. Goodman, "The Origins of the War of 1812," *Mississippi Valley Historical Review*, XXVIII, No. 2 (September, 1941), 179; Julius W. Pratt, "Western Aims in the War of 1812," *Mississippi Valley Historical Review*, XII, No. 1 (June, 1925), 45; Charles M. Gates, "The West in American Diplomacy, 1812–1815," *Mississippi Valley Historical Review*, XXVI, No. 4 (March, 1940), p. 510.

East Florida and West Florida, separated by the Apalachicola River. The claim of the United States—as asserted by Congress when it organized Mississippi Territory in 1798—extended southward to the thirty-first parallel, from the Chattahoochee River to the Mississippi. For various reasons the Jeffersonians desired to acquire the Floridas. Frontiersmen in southern Tennessee and in Mississippi Territory depended upon the Tombigbee, Alabama, and Mobile rivers as an outlet for their produce en route to Mobile, and objected to Spain's ownership of that port and her control of Mobile Bay. By 1810 settlers had reached the northern border of West Florida, in the district west of the Tombigbee. Although Spanish rule in the Floridas was weak after 1803, a possibility existed that the provinces might be used to the detriment of the lower South and the Southwest—as retreats for fugitive slaves and as bases for Indian raids on the settlements. Furthermore, many Republican leaders believed that the acquisition of all Florida and American control of the northern coast of the Gulf of Mexico were necessary to the defense of New Orleans, the Mississippi Valley, and the lower South.[13]

After 1803, Jefferson's first aim in diplomacy was the acquisition of the Floridas. He claimed, without good cause, that Louisiana, as purchased from France, extended eastward to Mobile Bay. To a large extent his Florida policy involved France. In October, 1803, Spain allied itself with France, soon fell under the sway of Napoleon, and became an enemy of Britain. Napoleon occupied Spain in 1808 and placed his brother Joseph on the throne at Madrid. Since Napoleon upheld Spain's claim to Florida, the Jeffersonians could not conquer the two provinces without opposing him and allying themselves with Britain. When Jefferson considered hostile measures against France in 1805 he was restrained by his adherents in the North. A partnership with Britain would have strengthened its grip on the Northwest. As long as France dominated Spain and Florida, Jefferson could not strike in the Southwest lest he alienate the northern wing of his party and fail to enlist its support in a war against France. Eventually the situation in Europe changed decisively. In 1808, Britain began to subsidize the Spanish opponents of Napoleon. A general popular uprising, assisted by British troops under Wellesley, soon weakened Napoleon's hold on Spain, while his mounting troubles in Europe induced him to court the United States by acceding to its wishes concerning Florida. An alliance between Britain and the Spanish patriots, made in January, 1809, simplified the situation in the American West. A war of the United States with Britain would also be a war with Spain and thus offer an opportunity to satisfy both the southern and northern expansionists by means of simultaneous conquests of Florida and Canada. There is evidence that southern Republicans

[13] Julius W. Pratt, "Footnote to the War of 1812," *American Mercury*, XII, No. 46 (October, 1927), 232; Pratt, *Expansionists of 1812*, p. 66.

urged the conquest of Canada in order to gain northern support for the acquisition of Florida.[14]

In 1810–1811, American residents in West Florida staged an armed revolt, cast off the authority of Spanish officials, declared the province to be an independent state, and accepted a proclamation of President Madison of October 27, 1811, which in effect annexed it to the United States. In 1812, Congress added to Mississippi Territory the land between the Pearl and the Perdido rivers, south of the thirty-first parallel. Less decisive events occurred in East Florida. Early in 1812 an agent of Madison, George Mathews, collected a band of Georgia frontiersmen, and—with the aid of United States gunboats and riflemen and with the knowledge and implied approval of Secretary of State Monroe—invaded the province, seized the town of Fernandina and invested St. Augustine. Other happenings forced Madison to dismiss Mathews, but without withdrawing American troops. Intervention in both West Florida and East Florida was justified on the ground that Britain intended to assume control.[15]

When Congress adopted the declaration of war in June, 1812, it was supported by practically all the representatives of the West and the lower South, whereas the states east of the mountains and north of the Potomac cast four fifths of the votes in opposition. However, western interests alone did not cause the war, for Britain's attacks on the commerce of the United States had long been a source of irritation. In the House, Massachusetts, New Hampshire, Vermont, Pennsylvania, and Maryland cast 34 votes in favor of war. The coastal areas of North Carolina and Virginia also upheld the administration. Thus a fusion of western interests and maritime issues overcame the desire for peace. Given the political victory of the "war hawks," military considerations dictated an attack on Canada. The Americans of 1812 thought that a war should be waged offensively and be crowned with shining victories. It was impossible for the feeble navy of the Union to vanguish the British on the high seas. Only Canada offered the opportunity to strike at Britain in a decisive manner. In a proclamation of May 2, 1812, to Tennessee volunteers, Andrew Jackson said: "Should the occupation of the Canadas be resolved upon by the general government how pleasing the prospect that would open to the young volunteer while performing a military promenade into a distant country. A succession of new and interesting objects would perpetually fill and delight the imagination, the effect of which would be heightened by the war-like appearances, the martial music, and the grand evolutions of an army of fifty thousand

[14] Adams, *History of the United States*, Vol. II, Bk. 3, pp. 39, 61–67; J. Holland Rose, "Canning and the Spanish Patriots in 1808," *American Historical Review*, XII, No. 1 (October, 1906), 39–41.

[15] Adams, *History of the United States*, Vol. III, Bk. 5, pp. 305–311; Vol. III, Bk. 6, pp. 237–241; Isaac Joslin Cox, "The American Intervention in West Florida," *American Historical Review*, XVII, No. 2 (January, 1912), 304–307.

men." Once the United States had occupied Canada it might retained—a vast addition to the wealth of the Union. Or an offer to return it might be used to induce Britain to agree to respect the maritime rights of the United States, to recognize American interests in the Floridas, and to cease its fur-trading activities and Indian intrigues in the American Northwest. When General Hull invaded Canada in July, 1812, he assured the Canadians that he came as one tendering "the invaluable blessings of civil, political, and religious liberty." "You will be emancipated," he said, "from tyranny and oppression, and restored to the dignified station of freemen." [16]

TRADE IN WAR AND WAR ON TRADE

During most of the period between April, 1793, and June, 1815, American commerce was beset by hazards of war. The political and diplomatic quarrels of the time may give the impression that losses to American ship-pers all but ruined their business and drove their vessels from the sea. Actually, they prospered as never before. Ships that completed voyages greatly outnumbered those that fell prey to belligerents. The combined imports and exports of the Union rose from $52 million in 1792 to $246 million in 1807. American vessels supplied France with foodstuffs, particu-larly flour, and carried sugar, coffee, and chocolate from the French West Indies to France. The British utilized American vessels to ship their manu-factures to the United States—their principal market; to import American cotton, wheat, and flour; and to export British goods to European ports. Between 1803 and 1812 the United States held first place among neutral carriers. Wartime business put the country in the position of a man who wished to trade with two valued customers, each of whom sought his services while trying to prevent his dealings with the other. During the years 1803–1811, the British seized 917 American vessels; French seizures numbered 764. Each belligerent sought to deprive the United States of its neutral role and to reduce it to the status of a commercial satellite. Most Americans wished to do business with each belligerent and resented the efforts of the one to prevent neutrals from trading with the other.[17]

In their contests with European powers after 1800 the Jeffersonians acted in the light of experiences of the Federalist era. Soon after war between Britain and France broke out in February, 1793, France arranged for large importations of flour from the United States. Regarding certain foodstuffs as essential to France's war effort, Britain in June, 1793, desig-nated corn, flour, and meal as contraband and proceeded to seize American

---

[16] Pratt, "Footnote to the War of 1812," p. 234; Goodman, "Origins of the War of 1812," pp. 176–177; Hacker, "Western Land Hunger," pp. 379, 394–395.

[17] Thomas A. Bailey, A Diplomatic History of the American People (2d ed.; New York: F. S. Crofts & Co., 1944), pp. 108, 115, 136; Albion and Pope, Sea Lanes in Wartime, pp. 44–45, 68, 92–93; Johnson, History of Commerce, II, 20.

ships that were carrying them to French ports. At the same time France opened to neutrals the trade of its West Indian islands and American shippers hastened to grasp it. Britain countered with an Order in Council of November 6, 1793, which authorized the detention of all neutral ships that supplied the French islands or exported their products. In seizing American vessels in the Caribbean or en route to France, Britain violated the neutral rights of the United States. By 1805, American claims arising from British seizures in the French West Indian trade amounted to $12 million. The seizures of 1793–1794 were rendered doubly obnoxious by aid then given by the British to Indians who were warring on the Ohio Valley settlements. So intense became the indignation of the country that the Republicans in 1794 were on the point of leading it into a war against Britain. To prevent such a calamity Washington sent John Jay on a peace mission to London. Jay's Treay of 1794 did not gain from Britain a recognition of all the rights claimed by the United States in its trade with France and the French West Indies. However, the treaty promised some benefits: permission for American vessels under 70 tons to trade with the British West Indies, provision for a commission to act on American claims arising from British seizures, and a promise that Britain would soon withdraw from all posts within the United States. Acquiescence in the treaty dispelled the war fever and ended the first crisis that emanated from wartime trade.[18]

By securing benefits from Britain while failing to assert American rights in French-American trade, Jay's Treaty provoked the French government to charge that the United States had abandoned neutrality and had become a partisan of Britain. Soon after the treaty became effective, French privateers swarmed out in quest of American ships. Between June, 1796, and June, 1797, they took 316 prizes; by 1800, losses arising from such seizures amounted to an estimated $20 million. The effort of John Adams to end the quasi war with France succeeded in 1800 when the two countries signed a convention which had the effect of canceling the French-American Alliance Treaty of 1778 in return for the abandonment by the United States of its spoliation claims against France. The settlement also stopped the raids of French privateers. In March, 1802, the European powers made peace by signing the Treaty of Amiens. Although the war was renewed in May, 1803, the era of relatively free trade that began in 1801 blessed Jefferson's administration until 1804.[19]

During the years of quasi war with France, Britain had refrained from molesting seriously the shipping of the United States. In 1800, a British court ruled in the case of the American ship *Polly* that goods imported from the French West Indies into the United States might be re-exported to France if the shipper had unloaded them and had paid duties on them in

[18] Forbes, "Boston Trade," pp. 712, 719; Bemis, *Jay's Treaty*, pp. 186–188, 193–197, 260–261; 8 *Statutes at Large*, pp. 117, 121, 122.

[19] Forbes, "Boston Trade," pp. 717–719; 8 *Statutes at Large*, p. 178.

an American port. Under this lenient policy the value of American exports of foreign goods averaged $35,600,000 a year during the period 1796–1805. Soon after the renewal of the European war a British judge modified the *Polly* decision and set forth a new doctrine in the case of the *Essex*, in 1805, to the effect that the landing of French goods in an American port and the payment of duties on them there did not entitle the shipper to carry them to a French port until he had proved that his original intention was not to re-export them. Since British courts presumed to determine such intention, and since Americans in 1805 were carrying on a systematic re-export trade in French goods, it was easy to conclude that a shipper who re-exported goods had intended to do so. The *Essex* decision gave rise to scores of British seizures of American vessels which set in motion another wave of anti-British feeling in the United States.[20]

After 1804, the war in Europe became a remorseless struggle featured by an intensified use of commercial weapons. Napoleon strove to close the Continent to British manufactures in order to shut down British factories, to cause widespread unemployment and distress, and to bring about the overthrow of the government and the making of peace on his terms. Britain sought to undermine Napoleon's power by cutting off the countries he controlled from outside sources of food and war material. In this grim struggle the rights of neutrals counted for little. After the British had crushed the French at Trafalgar, October 21, 1805, their superiority on the sea was uncontested. On May 16, 1806, they declared a blockade of the European coast from Brest to the River Elbe. By the Berlin Decree of November 21, 1806, Napoleon set forth the principles of his Continental System. It prohibited vessels coming from England or its colonies from entering France, Spain, Holland, and parts of Italy. It also declared the British Isles to be in a state of blockade and forbade all trade with them. Britain retaliated on November 11, 1807, by issuing Orders in Council which claimed for Britain the right to stop neutral ships, imposed a blockade on all ports under Napoleon's control, denied to neutrals the right to trade independently with such ports, and required neutral vessels going thither to enter a British harbor, to pay duties there, and to secure permission to complete their voyages. Napoleon then struck again by issuing the Milan Decree of December 17, 1807, which declared his blockade of Britain to be enforceable on the seas and asserted that any neutral vessel that submitted to British search or that was bound to or from Britain thereby forfeited its neutrality and became "good prize." [21]

Britain's attacks on American trade during the 1790's had been made

[20] Herbert Whittaker Briggs, *The Doctrine of Continuous Voyage* (Johns Hopkins University *Studies in Historical and Political Science,* Series XLIV, No. 2; Baltimore: The Johns Hopkins Press, 1926), pp. 17–18, 21–22.

[21] Adams, *History of the United States,* Vol. II, Bk. 3, p. 398; Frank Edgar Melvin, *Napoleon's Navigation System* (New York: D. Appleton and Company, 1919), pp. 7, 44–45; *American State Papers: Foreign Relations,* III, 269–270, 289–290.

mainly by privateers; after 1800, the Royal Navy played the decisive part in stopping, searching, and seizing neutral vessels. Its expanded task called for an enlarged force of seamen at a time when profits of neutral trade lured sailors from its service—a servitude so repelling that men had to be forced into it by press gangs and ruled by the lash. Frequent desertions from British cruisers seriously threatened their efficiency. Whether stationed off the coasts of the United States or ranging the seas, such cruisers had a golden opportunity to take from neutral vessels any seamen who were claimed by British officers to be deserters from the king's ships. Heedless of the nationality of the men they challenged, the British arbitrarily impressed about 10,000 American citizens during the period 1805 to 1812. In 1806, Jefferson attempted to make a peaceful settlement of differences with Britain. The effort failed because they refused to accept his demand that they cease their impressment practices. On June 22, 1807, they inflicted an intolerable insult when their frigate, the *Leopard*, fired on the *Chesapeake*, a new American warship not fully fitted out for action. The attack, which occurred off the coast of Virginia, killed three American seamen and enabled the British to remove four alleged deserters. The storm of protest that swept over the country raised the war spirit to its highest pitch since 1775. Such was the tension existing when Britain, by issuing its Orders in Council of November 11, 1807, prohibited American vessels from trading directly with European ports under Napoleon's control.[22]

Since both belligerents were violating American rights, Jefferson faced a hard problem. To declare war against only one of the powers would have condoned the attacks of the other and would have strengthened the favored one in America—whether France in Florida or Britain in Canada. To go to war with both simultaneously would have been extreme folly. Jefferson sought a peaceful solution in economic coercion, to be applied equally to both offenders. He thought that the closing of the United States to British goods would inflict severe hardships on British traders, manufacturers, and workers and would force Britain to agree to respect American rights in order to regain access to the American market. Similarly, if American food was denied to Napoleon he would be compelled to cease his attacks as the price for obtaining it. Acting on such assumptions, Jefferson proposed to Congress the measure which became the Embargo Act of December 22, 1807. It prohibited nearly all ships in the United States from leaving for foreign ports and required special bonds for vessels engaged in the coastwise trade.[23]

The embargo endured until March 1, 1809. It seriously disrupted the

[22] Adams, *History of the United States*, Vol. I, Bk, 2, pp. 335–337, 423; Vol. II, Bk. 3, pp. 409, 439; Vol. II, Bk. 4, pp. 8–9, 16–20, 27.

[23] 2 *Statutes at Large*, pp. 451–453; Louis Martin Sears, *Jefferson and the Embargo* (Durham, N. C.: Duke University Press, 1927), pp. 55, 59–60; Walter Wilson Jennings, *The American Embargo, 1807–1809* (University of Iowa Studies in the Social Sciences, Vol. VIII, No. 1; Iowa City: 1921), pp. 41, 66.

American economy but did not ruin it. The mercantile interests suffered most acutely. The exports of the country fell from $108,343,000 in 1807 to $22,430,000 in 1808, while imports declined from $138,500,000 to $56,990,000. British exports sent directly to the United States dropped by £6,604,000. Legitimate business of the embargo year was less than one fourth of the volume for 1807. The course of trade is illustrated by leading commodities. The price of wheat at Philadelphia went down from $1.33 a bushel in December, 1807, to an average of $1 during 1808. Wheat exports to Britain in 1808 were 5 percent of the 1807 quantity and 7 percent of those of 1809. Whereas in 1807 Britain obtained 61 percent of its wheat from the United States, the amount in 1808 was only 13 percent. The embargo effectively excluded American flour and grain from the British West Indies. More drastic was the effect on the cotton trade. At Charleston the price of upland cotton sank from 21 cents a pound in December, 1807, to 13 cents in February, 1808, and did not rise to about 15 cents until November. In Britain, American cotton went up from 14d. a pound in December, 1807, to 32d. in December, 1808, as cotton imports from the United States shrank from 143,000 to 25,000 bags. The price of tobacco declined so sharply that farmers refused to sell their crops and sympathetic judges protected debtors by withholding judgments sought by importunate creditors. Warehouses filled to overflowing. At Charleston the price of tobacco dropped from $6.75 a hundredweight in December, 1807, to $3.25 in March, 1808.[24]

With the exception of Philadelphia, the chief sufferers from the embargo were the leading seaports. Contemporary accounts told of stagnant business, deserted wharves, and harbors filled with idle ships. Boston and seaboard New England bore the heaviest losses. The fisheries languished as exports of dried and smoked fish fell from 473,000 quintals in 1807 to 155,000 in 1808. Draymen, dock laborers, and workers in ropewalks, shipyards, and sailcloth factories lost their jobs; 30,000 sailors were idled; unemployed hands were estimated as 100,000. At New York 120 business failures occurred and 1,200 debtors went to jail. Philadelphia saved itself from the worst evils of the depression by developing manufacturing industries to tap the growing markets of the interior.[25]

Loopholes in the embargo act and outright violations of its provisions lessened its depressive force. The act authorized foreign ships in American ports to leave in ballast or with products that had been put on board before

---

[24] Johnson, *History of Commerce*, II, 20; Sears, *Jefferson and the Embargo*, pp. 284, 287; Cole, *Wholesale Commodity Prices, Statistical Supplement*, pp. 145–150; Galpin, "American Grain Trade under the Embargo," pp. 87, 94; Daniels, "American Cotton Trade under the Embargo," pp. 278, 287; Robert, *The Tobacco Kingdom*, pp. 136–137; Jennings, *The American Embargo*, pp. 211, 213.

[25] Otto C. Lightner, *The History of Business Depressions* (New York: The Northeastern Press, 1922), pp. 102–103; Sears, *Jefferson and the Embargo*, p. 176; Jennings *The American Embargo*, pp. 97, 100; Sears, "Philadelphia and the Embargo: 1808," p. 126.

the embargo became effective. All told, 590 permits were granted for departures of such ships. With regard to the coastwise trade, the act allowed vessels that encountered "dangers of the seas" to take refuge in foreign ports. A host of vessels met that fate and found it necessary to sell their cargoes abroad in order to make repairs or replenish their stores. Furthermore, the act permitted whalers to engage in their usual business. Some of them came back with cargoes of general merchandise. Off the northern coast of Florida, Amelia Island became a rendezvous sought by ships that traded cotton for foreign goods needed by the lower South. On the northeast coast a thriving trade sprang up at Passamaquoddy Bay, where New Englanders and Canadians exchanged flour and other American products for European and West Indian goods. Halifax, the entrepôt of this trade, prospered greatly. The farmers of northern New Hampshire, Vermont, and New York sent large quantities of produce by way of Lake Champlain to Montreal in payment for customary imports. Intense opposition to the embargo in northern New England thwarted Jefferson's rather halfhearted efforts to enforce it there.[26]

The country survived the embargo without disaster largely because it had acquired ample reserves during the preceding years. The Treasury's surplus in 1807 amounted to $17 million. Merchants had recently made large profits, and although the embargo cost most of them a year's business, it did not seriously impair their capital accumulations. The losses that they suffered by reason of the fall in the prices of export products they held were offset by increases in the prices of imports they had in stock. Imports continued to arrive in large quantities. Traders who violated the embargo fared well, since prices of American exports were low at home and high abroad. Thanks to adequate specie reserves, the banks withstood the shock. None suspended specie payments and only one indulged in practices so loose as to cause it to fail. Farmers had enjoyed several good years and were able to protect themselves from price declines by withholding crops from sale. Bank currency, more plentiful than ever, helped to sustain domestic prices. Commodity prices as a whole did not decline so sharply as did the prices of export staples. At Charleston, Philadelphia, and New York the general level of wholesale prices fell about 15½ percent from its average in December, 1807, to its low point in 1808. The depression did not create widespread distress among rural debtors. Workers dependent upon maritime industries suffered the most galling hardships. Since much of the fat of the good years was consumed during the months of the embargo, a severe crisis might have developed if it had been continued. It

[26] Albion and Pope, *Sea Lanes in Wartime*, pp. 100–101; Sears, *Jefferson and the Embargo*, pp. 167–168; Daniels, "American Cotton Trade under the Embargo," p. 281; Virginia D. Harrington, "New York and the Embargo of 1807," *Quarterly Journal of the New York State Historical Association*, VIII, No. 2 (April, 1927), 147–148; Jennings, *The American Embargo*, pp. 113–116.

had not brought the British to their knees, partly because they economized in the use of wheat and partly because in 1808 they greatly increased their exports to Spanish America.[27]

The policy of an inclusive embargo was abandoned by the enactment of the Non-Intercourse Act of March 1, 1809, which reopened the foreign trade of the United States with all countries except Britain and France and their dependencies. In effect, the act continued the embargo against the two belligerents, prohibiting the vessels of either from entering United States ports and decreeing the forfeiture of such vessels as should arrive after May 20, 1809. The act also forbade importations of British and French goods and of all products exported from Britain or France or their dependencies. The President received authority to reopen trade with Britain or France if either power should revoke or modify its edicts in such a manner as to put an end to violations of neutral rights.[28]

The Non-Intercourse Act did not force either Britain or France to cease its attacks on American shipping. The foreign trade of the United States of 1809 showed a 40 percent gain over 1808 but it was less than half the volume of 1807 and smaller than that of any year since 1794. The act did not restore prosperity or silence the demand for the removal of all restrictions on foreign trade. In consequence, Congress yielded again when it adopted Macon Bill No. 2 of May 1, 1810. This act reopened trade with Britain and France and provided that if either belligerent should repeal its orders against neutral shipping, the United States would cease to trade with the other power if it did not withdraw its hostile decrees. In response to Macon Bill No. 2, Napoleon on August 5, 1810, through the medium of the Cadore Letter, informed the United States that he would repeal his decrees if the British would withdraw their orders, or if, failing that, the United States would cease to trade with them. On the strength of this elusive promise, Madison declared, November 2, 1810, that nonintercourse would again be put into effect against the British unless they repealed their orders within three months. Again Britain refused to yield; whereupon Congress on March 2, 1811, enacted a law which applied the nonintercourse ban to Britain. Since the pressure of the United States was now directed solely against Britain, a continuation of the commercial conflict threatened to end in an Anglo-American war. Madison's actions so favored the French as to give color to the charge that he was their puppet. But his favoritism to Napoleon also supports the view that the desire to acquire

[27] John H. Reinoehl, "Post-Embargo Trade and Merchant Prosperity: Experiences of the Crowninshield Family, 1809–1812," *Mississippi Valley Historical Review*, XLII, No. 2 (September, 1955), 231; Cole, *Wholesale Commodity Prices*, p. 106 (chart); Taylor, "Prices in the Mississippi Valley," p. 162; Hammond, *Banks and Politics*, pp. 172, 190, 208–209; Galpin, "American Grain Trade under the Embargo," pp. 88–89; Jennings, *The American Embargo*, p. 82.

[28] 2 *Statutes at Large*, pp. 528–530.

Canada and Florida was the strongest force behind the Republican moves that led to war.[29]

WARTIME FINANCE

From an economic standpoint, the most lasting effects of the War of 1812 were felt in the spheres of manufacturing, banking, and national finance. Inflated currency and swelling government expenditures sent prices soaring to the highest point they reached between 1781 and 1860. In 1814, the payments of the federal government amounted to $34,720,000, as contrasted with $8,178,000 in 1811. During the period 1812–1815, the federal outlays averaged $29,900,000 a year. All told, the war caused the Treasury to spend at least $87,000,000 for goods, interest, and services.[30]

The determining factor of federal finance was the inability of Madison's administration to obtain an adequate income from taxes. Throughout the war, Congress never enacted effective revenue laws. Many Jeffersonians, true to the principles of pristine Republicanism, opposed the levying of internal taxes such as the Federalists had resorted to in the 1790's. In this attitude the old-school Republicans were joined by New England opponents of the war, who were reluctant to vote for any war taxes. Congress made only one provision for additional taxes in 1812: on July 1 it enacted a law that doubled the existing tariff rates.[31] This expedient failed to fill the war chest by reason of the shrinkage of imports which occurred during the war. Customs duties, which had yielded $13,-300,000 in 1811, netted but $6,000,000 in 1814 and only a yearly average of $9,400,000 in 1812, 1813, and 1814. In mid-1813 the administration was attempting to finance a year's expenditure of $39,000,000 with revenues of less than $15,000,000. In this extremity Madison secured from Congress revenue acts of July and August, 1813, which imposed duties on carriages, refined sugar, the distillation of spiritous liquors, imported salt, auction sales, bank notes, and retail sales of wines and spirits.[32] Calculated to yield $2,000,000 a year, these acts reinstated the Federalist tax program of the 1790's, which Congress had adopted for financing the quasi war with France. The revenue legislation of 1813 also imitated the earlier Federalist policy by levying a direct tax of $3,000,000 on lands, dwellings, and slaves, to be assessed in 1813.[33] The receipts from the new

[29] Johnson, *History of Commerce*, II, 20; 2 *Statutes at Large*, pp. 605–606, 651; Richardson, *Messages of the Presidents*, I, 481–482.

[30] Dewey, *Financial History of the United States*, pp. 125, 141.

[31] Balinky, *Albert Gallatin*, p. 186; Adams, *History of the United States*, Vol. III, Bk, 6, p. 207; 2 *Statutes at Large*, pp. 768–769.

[32] Dewey, *Financial History of the United States*, pp. 125, 142; 3 *Statutes at Large*, pp. 35, 40, 42–43, 44, 49, 72, 77; Ratner, *American Taxation*, p. 34.

[33] 3 *Statutes at Large*, pp. 26, 53.

taxes were so meager during the following months that Congress in December, 1814, and January, 1815, enacted another series of revenue laws which added a tax on distilled spirits; increased the duties on carriages, auction sales, and retail sales of wines and spirits; levied new duties on certain domestic manufactures such as furniture and watches; raised the direct tax to $6,000,000; and made it permanent. During the years 1812–1815 the expenditures of the Treasury exceeded its revenues from sources other than loans by $68,600,000.[34]

In 1810 Gallatin presented a plan which proposed that a war should be financed mainly with borrowed money. The method so appealed to Congress that between March 14, 1812, and March 3, 1815, it enacted six laws which, all together, authorized the Treasury to obtain $80,952,000 by selling government stocks (or bonds).[35] Banks and wealthy citizens were the principal purchasers, and the proceeds received by the government took the form of bank notes and bank deposits. This method of war finance encouraged cooperating banks to enlarge their note issues. The South and the West were deficient in banking capital; most New Englanders refused to lend to the government; hence the burden of financing the war fell mainly on the middle states. Of $41,000,000 obtained by the Treasury before 1815 through loans, New York, Philadelphia, Baltimore, and the District of Columbia provided 87 percent; New England, 7 percent, and the South and the West, less than 6 percent.[36] The securities of the first issue were disposed of at par; thereafter the loans were negotiated at a discount. An act of August 2, 1813, authorized the Treasury to sell a security of $100 for $88; under an act of March 24, 1814, the government received only 80 cents on the dollar and was paid in bank notes that were worth in specie only 65 percent of their face values. The price of United States stocks fell from an index figure of 65 in March, 1812, to 44 in July, 1815. A study made in 1830 estimated that the war caused the government to incur obligations amounting to $80,000,000, for which it received a value of $34,000,000 in specie.[37]

Congress also authorized the issuance and sale of short-term Treasury notes. Five statutes for that purpose were enacted between June 30, 1812,

[34] Dewey, *Financial History of the United States*, pp. 141–142; 3 *Statutes at Large*, pp. 148, 152–153, 159, 164, 180, 186.

[35] Act of March 14, 1812—$11,000,000; of February 8, 1813—$16,000,000; of August 2, 1813—$7,500,000; of March 24, 1814—$25,000,000; of November 15, 1814—$3,000,000; of March 3, 1815—$18,452,800. 2 *Statutes at Large*, pp. 694, 798; 3 *Statutes at Large*, pp. 76–77, 111, 144, 227.

[36] Henry Adams, ed., *The Writings of Albert Gallatin* (3 vols.; Philadelphia: J. B. Lippincott and Company, 1879), III, 284.

[37] Dewey, *Financial History of the United States*, pp. 132–134, 138; Smith and Cole, *Fluctuations in American Business*, p. 22; Hammond, *Banks and Politics in America*, p. 229.

and February 24, 1815. Such notes enabled the Treasury to obtain cash in advance of tax collections and in anticipation of receipts from long-term loans. Late in the war, new emissions of the notes were used to redeem those previously issued. All the notes had some things in common. The government did not pledge to redeem them in specie on demand. Although they were not legal tender, the Treasury accepted them in all payments due the United States. Most of the notes bore interest at 5.4 percent, were payable after one year, and were issued in denominations of $20 or more. The last act, of February 24, 1815, provided for the issuance of a limited quantity of noninterest-bearing notes in small denominations. Such small notes—the minimum was $3—resembled government paper currency; had they been legal tender they would have anticipated the greenbacks of the Civil War. Although Congress authorized issues of Treasury notes to a total of $55,500,000, the maximum amount outstanding at any time was less than $18,000,000. The notes passed at par in specie until August, 1814. Those outstanding after the end of the war were soon funded into government bonds.[38]

State banks, acting in concert with the Treasury, shaped the course of wartime finance and exerted a predominant influence on credit, currency, and prices. The demise of the Bank of the United States in 1811 and the failure of Congress to provide a national paper currency created an opportunity which promoters seized with avidity. Gallatin once reported that between January 1, 1811, and January 1, 1816, at least 158 new banks came into being—a number he thought to be greatly in excess of the country's needs and its capital resources. The notes of state banks formed the common currency which the government received from tax collections and loans. Not subject to effective control, the banks rapidly expanded their note issues and deposits, partly in response to the Treasury's need for cash and partly by reason of "expectations of great profits." Notes in circulation grew from an estimated $22,700,000 on January 1, 1811, to $45,500,000 on January 1, 1815—a gain of 100 percent—whereas specie holdings increased by 67 percent: from $9,600,000 to $17,000,000. During 1815, new notes amounted to $22,500,000; additional specie reserves came to only $2,000,000. By virtue of the expansion of note issues and swollen government expenditures sustained largely by newly created bank credits, prices of commodities soared. Between June, 1812, and December, 1814, wholesale prices at Philadelphia rose by 54 percent; at New York, by 57 percent; at Charleston, by 90 percent. Since the exports of the country in

[38] Act of June 30, 1812—$5,000,000; of February 25, 1813—$5,000,000; of March 4, 1814—$10,000,000; of December 26, 1814—$10,500,000; of February 24, 1815—$25,000,000. 2 *Statutes at Large*, pp. 767, 801; 3 *Statutes at Large*, pp. 100, 161–162, 213–214; John Jay Knox, *United States Notes* (New York: Charles Scribner's Sons, 1894), pp. 38–39.

1814 were only 11 percent of the exports of 1811, it is evident that the price inflation arose from increased government spending and its stimulator—expanded bank currency and deposits.[39]

Late in August and early in September of 1814 the banks outside New England suspended specie payments. An underlying reason for this step was the failure of reserves to keep pace with expanding note issues and deposits. The government's purchases of war supplies also put a strain on the reserves of the banks of the middle states. New Englanders sold goods to the armed forces and received notes of and drafts on Philadelphia, New York, and Baltimore banks that had extended credit to the Treasury. New England banks then presented such paper for payment in specie. The banks of Massachusetts increased their specie holdings from $1,709,000 in June, 1811, to $7,326,000 in June, 1814. Foreign trade also contributed to the pressure on specie reserves. During the years 1812–1814, the imports of the country exceeded its exports by $38,691,000. Merchants therefore needed specie as a remittance abroad when commodity exports were deficient. Reports in 1814 told of large shipments of silver dollars from New England to Canada for the purchase of drafts on the British government, which were then sold widely in the eastern ports of the United States. By June 1, 1815, the specie holdings of Massachusetts banks had dropped to $3,915,000.[40]

Banks that suspended specie payments continued to do business as usual. Of the effect of suspensions on bank notes Gallatin wrote: "In New England, where those payments were not discontinued, the currency was equal in value to specie; it was at the same time at a discount of seven per cent in New York and Charleston, of fifteen per cent in Philadelphia, of twenty and twenty-five per cent in Baltimore and Washington, with every possible variation in other places and States." The depreciation forced the Treasury to keep special accounts with banks in order to differentiate note deposits from other assets. During 1815, the banks, freed from their principal obligations, made reputed profits ranging from 12 to 20 percent.[41]

By reason of their virtual monopoly of the power to issue paper currency, the banks acquired great political influence. "You might as well attack Gibraltar with a pistol," said John Randolph, "as to attempt to punish them." "Every man you meet . . . , with some rare exceptions, was either a stockholder, president, cashier, clerk, doorkeeper, runner, engraver, paper maker or mechanic, in some way or other, to a bank." How-

[39] Gallatin's Writings (Adams), III, 285–286; Cole, Wholesale Commodity Prices, pp. 22, 44, 60.

[40] Smith and Cole, Fluctuations in American Business, pp. 27–29; Gallatin's Writings (Adams), III, 283; Johnson, History of Commerce, II, 20.

[41] Hammond, Banks and Politics in America, pp. 228, 242; Gallatin's Writings (Adams), III, 331–332.

ever, the evils of a depreciated currency that differed in value from place to place and the losses suffered by the government from its dependence on unchecked state banks evoked an insistent demand for reform. In 1814 some leading investors in public loans, including John Jacob Astor and Stephen Girard, calculated that government bonds would rise in value if they were made exchangeable for stock of a new bank of the United States. When Congress approved of a bill for such a bank in January, 1815, Madison vetoed it because its plan did not meet all the fiscal needs of the Treasury. Congress did not act on the subject again until 1816.[42]

A WARTIME ECONOMY

Thanks to thirty years of progress, the country was much better equipped to sustain a large war effort in 1812 than it had been in 1776. The iron industry was equal to the demand for firearms and ordnance. Numerous factories met the need for gunpowder, while workers in homes and nascent mills produced an adequate amount of cloth and articles of clothing. A crudely self-sufficient economy freed the Union from the uncertainties of foreign aid. The reduction of imports deprived consumers mainly of luxuries; government purchases of food and domestic manufactures made good some of the losses from the shrinkage of exports. Transportation facilities in the older settlements had been substantially improved and numerous steamboats plied the eastern rivers. The expanding cotton manufacture of New England provided an additional market for the cotton of the South.

During the years 1809–1816, foreign trade did not again reach its peak of 1807, when combined imports and exports amounted to $246 million. The average for 1810 and 1811 was $133 million. A decline to 115 million occurred in 1812. The war reduced the volume to $50 million in 1813 and to $20 million in 1814. A revival in 1815 raised the total to $165 million.[43]

Many obstructions hampered foreign commerce. On April 4, 1812, Congress, anticipating war, placed a ninety-day embargo on vessels in American ports in order to prevent seizures by the enemy. Britain again undertook to blockade the United States but did not succeed in 1812. However, by November, 1813, the Royal Navy had established an effective blockade from Chesapeake Bay to New London, Connecticut; by June, 1814, it had been extended along the New England coast to New Brunswick. In order to prevent trade with the enemy, Congress on December 17, 1813, imposed an embargo on both foreign and coastwise trade. Strong

---

[42] Kenneth L. Brown, "Stephen Girard, Promoter of the Second Bank of the United States," *Journal of Economic History*, II, No. 2 (November, 1942), 129–131; Philip G. Walters and Raymond Walters, Jr., "The American Career of David Parish," *Journal of Economic History*, IV, No. 2 (November, 1944), 159–160, 163–164.

[43] Johnson, *History of Commerce*, II, 20.

opposition brought about its repeal on April 14, 1814. British privateers and warships seized many American vessels; 450 were taken to Halifax, Nova Scotia, during the war.[44]

The actions of Britain most affected the wartime commerce of the Union. In 1813 Parliament stimulated British trade with the East Indies and in so doing eliminated many American merchants and reduced the business of others to a trifle. A once-valuable pepper trade of Salem with Sumatra was lost. Acting with Spain, and prizing its new opportunities in Spanish America, Britain ruled the Caribbean and drove most American vessels from that sea. Exports from the United States to Britain shrank drastically. Early in the war, cotton piled up in southern ports. Later, licensed neutrals were permitted to carry it to Britain. Shipments amounting to 83 million pounds arrived there in 1814, when American export prices rose to 21 cents a pound, from 15 cents in 1813. Wheat and flour exports to Britain all but ceased. For a time the British bought large quantities of American flour for the use of their troops in the Peninsular Campaign; 165 American vessels arrived at Lisbon during the first half of 1813. This trade vanished in 1814. The need of servicing United States securities owned in Britain forced up the price of bills payable there and occasioned a large exportation of specie to provide cash for paying them. In London the House of Baring acted as a fiscal agent of the United States in making payments to holders of American securities.[45]

Merchants, sailors, and workers about the wharves suffered most from the wartime reduction of foreign trade. Large ships stayed at home; most voyages were made by small, fast blockade-runners. American shipping entering from abroad shrank from 667,000 tons in 1812 to 59,000 tons in 1814. Only 34 vessels cleared from Boston in 1813; in September, 247 were idle. Exports from Chesapeake Bay, Philadelphia, and New York dropped from $18,756,000 in 1813 to $477,000 in 1814. Salem's merchant fleet in 1815 was only 23 percent of its prewar strength.[46]

Minor exceptions to the general stagnation of foreign trade alleviated the distress of the merchants. Neutral vessels—of Sweden, Portugal, and Spain—became relatively more important as carriers for the Union. Their share of its import trade—as judged by tonnage of vessels—rose from 6 percent of the whole in 1812 to 32 percent in 1813 and to 44 percent in 1814. Some American shippers took out foreign papers. Imports on hand in June,

[44] 2 *Statutes at Large*, pp. 700–701; 3 *Statutes at Large*, pp. 88, 123; Morison, *Maritime History of Massachusetts*, pp. 206–207.

[45] Porter, *The Jacksons and the Lees*, I, 39; James Duncan Phillips, *Pepper and Pirates* (Boston: Houghton Mifflin Company, 1949), p. 53; Goebel, "British Trade to the Spanish Colonies," pp. 300–301; Gray, *History of Agriculture in the Southern United States*, II, 682–683; Galpin, *The Grain Supply of England*, pp. 149–150; Hidy, *The House of Baring in American Trade*, p. 52.

[46] Albion and Pope, *Sea Lanes in Wartime*, pp. 115, 121; Morison, *Maritime History of Massachusetts*, pp. 205, 206; James Duncan Phillips, *Salem and the Indies* (Boston: Houghton Mifflin Company, 1947), p. 406.

1812, and goods entering during the war sold at abnormally high prices. One merchant reaped $100,000 in 1812 from a "corner" on molasses. At Amelia Island and at Passamaquoddy Bay traders with the enemy re-enacted evasions of the law such as had occurred during the embargo era.[47]

Once again privateering offered an escape to merchants shackled by war. The infant navy of the United States could not protect all American shipping; only a few unarmed ships dared to go to sea in defiance of Britain's overwhelming naval power. Of armed craft there were two types: ordinary privateers and letter-of-marque vessels which, although devoted to regular trade, were equipped to resist an enemy cruiser and even to capture a tempting prize.[48] The number of such American ships at sea during the war has been estimated as 526, of which perhaps 250 were privateers. Chesapeake Bay was a principal base. Its "clipper schooners, with their sharp ends, shoal draft, and cloud of canvas" were the most popular performers. Baltimore sent out the largest number of raiders, with 58 to its credit; New York followed with 55; Salem dispatched 41; Boston fitted out 31; Philadelphia, Portsmouth, New Hampshire, and Charleston together supplied 35. The 45 in the fleet of Casco Bay varied in size from 367 to 4 tons. Maine's shipyards built many new privateers, small and designed for speed. The business side of privateering is illustrated by the *Grand Turk* of Salem. Its owners paid half the expenses of a cruise and received half of the prize money. The other half went in shares to the mariners: 10 to the captain; 7½ to the first lieutenant; 6 each to the second lieutenant, sailing master, and surgeon; 3 each to the secretary, paymaster, and pilot; 2 or 2½ to each gunner and petty officer; and 1 to each of 95 seamen.[49] The raiders skirted the coasts of the states, haunted the sea lanes linking Britain, North America, and the West Indies, invaded the English Channel, and frequented French ports.[50] "The American cruisers," lamented the London *Times*, "daily enter in among our convoys, seize prizes in sight of those that should afford protection, and if pursued, 'put on their sea-wings' and laugh at their clumsy English pursuers." The *America*, king of the New England privateers, took 26 vessels that netted more than $1,000,000; three other raiders averaged 22 victims apiece; Maine harvested 89 prizes during the war.[51] In all,

---

[47] Albion and Pope, *Sea Lanes in Wartime*, pp. 117, 120; Morison, *Maritime History of Massachusetts*, p. 205; Smith and Cole, *Fluctuations in American Business*, p. 19.

[48] Rowe, *Maritime History of Maine*, pp. 88–89; Henry Wyckoff Belknap, "A Check List of Salem Privateers in the War of 1812," *Essex Institute Historical Collections*, LXXVIII, No. 3 (July, 1942), p. 241.

[49] Phillips, *Salem and the Indies*, pp. 405–406; Rowe, *Maritime History of Maine*, p. 89; Morison, *Maritime History of Massachusetts*, pp. 199–202.

[50] Edgar Stanton Maclay, *A History of American Privateers* (New York: D. Appleton and Company, 1899), pp. 401–403.

[51] Rowe, *Maritime History of Maine*, pp. 88, 90–91; Morison, *Maritime History of Massachusetts*, p. 202.

about 2,000 British ships were captured or destroyed.[52] After 1813, coun-terattacks of an aroused Britain sharply reduced the profits of the busi-ness. In the end, Salem probably lost two thirds of its privateering fleet.[53]

The reductions of foreign trade hastened the growth of manufacturing within the country. The embargo and the war induced merchants to invest profits of the preceding prosperous years in domestic industries, thereby providing the initial resources for enterprises conducted on a large scale. The ground had been prepared by earlier technological improvements: the spinning jenny, the carding machine, the steam engine, automatic milling machinery, the slide lathe, better casting methods, and the process of making articles of standard parts. The shrinkage of imports favored manufacturers by causing prices of finished goods to rise faster than prices of domestic produce; the decline of exports provided large supplies of tobacco, cotton, and wheat for factories and mills. War expenditures created a demand for both farm products and manufactures, while new banks, by expanding currency and credit, facilitated production, inflated prices, and bolstered the income of farmers. The banking system in 1815 contained 208 banks with a capitalization of $82 million, as contrasted with 89 banks in 1811 having combined capitals of $52 million. The busi-ness of transporting goods by land and river reached a new peak, as wagons hauled most of the freight that had formerly gone in coasting vessels. Cotton moved overland to northern cities; great quantities of New England goods were distributed throughout the South; keelboat traffic on the Ohio and Mississippi increased rapidly.[54] For a time it seemed that the early Federalist ideal of a self-sufficing nation might be realized. The factory system in the cotton manufacture became firmly rooted. During the years 1807–1815 the number of spindles in cotton mills increased at least sixteenfold. The value of factory-made woolens rose from an estimated $4 million in 1810 to $19 million in 1815. Between 1805 and 1815 the number of post offices increased by 92 percent; the mileage of post roads, by 42 percent. The growth of transportation by horse and wagon enlarged the demand for farm products. In the West, the emerging cities owed their rapid progress in manufacturing to short-ages of foreign goods during the war.[55]

[52] George Coggeshall, *History of the American Privateers and Letters-of-Marque, during Our War with England in the Years 1812, '13 and '14* (New York: The au-thor, 1856), p. 394.

[53] William Dinsmore Chapple, "Salem and the War of 1812," *Historical Collec-tions of the Essex Institute*, LX, No. 1 (January, 1924), 71.

[54] Clark, *History of Manufactures in the United States*, p. 239; Porter, *The Jack-sons and the Lees*, I, 115; Gray, *History of Agriculture in the Southern United States*, II, 683, 765; Martin, *Trade of the Connecticut Valley*, p. 203; Wade, *The Urban Frontier*, p. 203.

[55] Taussig, *Tariff History of the United States*, pp. 28–29, 39–40; Philip S. Foner, *History of the Labor Movement in the United States* (New York: International Pub-lishers, 1947), pp. 50, 93–95; Wade, *The Urban Frontier*, p. 161.

Besides losses in maritime trade and a depressed tobacco industry, the wartime prosperity revealed other defects. The failure of Congress to levy adequate taxes forced the Treasury to borrow excessively large sums from banks, thereby causing an expansion of notes and deposits that afflicted the country with a depreciating currency. Abnormal conditions gave birth to many inefficient mills which were soon unable to compete with foreign merchandise, once the revival of trade with Britain had deprived them of the artificial protection they had received from embargo, nonintercourse, and blockade. Overland transportation was far more expensive than coastwise traffic.[56]

By the end of the war the leading Jeffersonians had moved far from the ground they had occupied before 1800. Then they had cherished a simple agrarian society—an Arcadia in which the virtuous husbandman, owner of the land he tilled, dwelt in peace and contentment, under his own vine and fig tree—a rural paradise unmarred by great cities, factories, machines, excise taxes, protective tariffs, banks, and government bonds.

> Happy the man whose wish and care
> A few paternal acres bound,
> Content to breathe his native air,
> On his own ground.
>
> Whose herds with milk, whose fields with bread,
> Whose flocks supply him with attire,
> Whose trees in summer yield him shade,
> In winter fire.

The stern demands of political power and the trend of the times soon forced the Jeffersonian leaders into actions at variance with their pristine ideal. When he was Secretary of State, Jefferson inaugurated the patent system—an accomplishment in which he later took a justifiable pride. In 1807–1808 he assisted Oliver Evans to make good his claim to a patent for his automatic milling machinery.[57] So also Jefferson encouraged a promoter, then obscure, who was destined to overshadow, in retrospect, all his business contemporaries. With Jefferson's approval, E. I. du Pont de Nemours established his first powder mill on the Brandywine in 1802–1803. When it succeeded its founder notified Jefferson of the fact. On July 29, 1803, Jefferson suggested to the Secretary of War that public patronage of Du Pont's improvements would encourage progress in "one of the most essential manufactures." [58] Du Pont powder help to chastise the Barbary pirates. Its superiority secured a promise from the Secretary

---

[56] Johnson, *History of Commerce*, I, 212.

[57] Bathe, *Oliver Evans*, pp. 127, 131, 142.

[58] Gilbert Chinard, ed., *The Correspondence of Jefferson and Du Pont de Nemours* (Johns Hopkins University *Studies in International Thought*; Baltimore: The Johns Hopkins Press, 1931), pp. 46, 58, 78, 83, 90, 107, 164–165, 171.

of War "that in the future we shall have all the Government work." The company's sales rose from $10,000 in 1804 to $148,000 in 1812; its profits in 1811 exceeded $40,000; during the years 1811–1813 it supplied the army with 750,000 pounds of powder.[59] Jefferson wrote in August, 1807: "No one wishes success, more than I do, to domestic manufacture . . . ." Soon afterward he added: "I am much pleased to find our progress in manufactures to be so great. That of cotton is peculiarly interesting, because we raise the raw material in such abundance, and because it may to a great degree supply our deficiencies both in wool and linen." [60] The embargo and the War of 1812 did more than Hamilton's *Report on Manufactures* to popularize factories and machines. A high protective tariff survived the war and was to agitate the country for many years.

While the embargo was in effect Jefferson in 1808 permitted John Jacob Astor's *Beaver* to sail for Canton on a voyage that returned goods worth $200,000 more than its outward cargo.[61] In the world of banking, the Republicans pressed forward with a speed that shamed their Federalist predecessors. When Jefferson took office the country had 29 banks; in 1816 there were 246, with a total capitalization of $89,822,000. Ten Republican senators voted in 1811 to continue the first Bank of the United States; the second Bank of the United States was chartered in 1816 with the approval of Gallatin and Madison.[62] In 1806, when the Treasury had a large surplus, Jefferson did not propose a drastic reduction of taxes; instead, he suggested that the normal tariff duties remain in force and that surpluses be used for "the great purposes of the public education, roads, rivers, canals, and such other objects of public improvement as it may be thought proper to add to the constitutional enumeration of Federal powers. By these operations new channels of communication will be opened between the States, the lines of separation will disappear, their interests will be identified, and their union cemented by new and indissoluble ties." [63] During the War of 1812 the Republicans resurrected the internal tax laws which the Federalists had enacted to finance the quasi war with France. In 1815 the national debt far exceeded that which the Republicans had inherited in 1801. Surely the advance guard of the Jeffersonians was leaving the outskirts of Arcadia and moving toward a land of banks and bonds, of factories and cities, of excise taxes and protective tariffs, of engines and machines.

[59] Dutton, *Du Pont*, pp. 30–31, 39, 42, 45, 49; Du Pont, *E. I. du Pont and Company*, p. 29; Winkler, *The Du Pont Dynasty*, p. 79.
[60] Quoted in Sears, *Jefferson and the Embargo*, pp. 61, 62.
[61] Albion and Pope, *Sea Lanes in Wartime*, pp. 101–102.
[62] Raymond Walters, Jr., "The Origins of the Second Bank of the United States," *Journal of Political Economy*, LIII, No. 2 (June, 1945), 130.
[63] Richardson, *Messages of the Presidents*, I, 409.

Bibliography

AIDS AND INTRODUCTORY WORKS

OSCAR HANDLIN and others, *Harvard Guide to American History* (Cambridge, Mass.: Harvard University Press, 1954) provides the best approach to the study of American history. Of special value for their subjects are Henrietta Larson, *Guide to Business History: Materials for the Study of American History and Suggestions for Their Use* (Vol. XII of *Harvard Studies in Business History;* Cambridge, Mass.: Harvard University Press, 1948); Everett E. Edwards, *A Bibliography of the History of Agriculture in the United States* (U. S. Department of Agriculture, *Miscellaneous Publications,* No. 84; Washington: Government Printing Office, 1930); and Samuel Flagg Bemis and Grace Gardner Griffin, *Guide to the Diplomatic History of the United States* (Washington: Government Printing Office, 1935). The literature of pioneering to 1800 is covered in R. W. G. Vail, *The Voice of the Old Frontier* (New York: Thomas Yoseloff, Inc., 1949). A similar work is Thomas D. Clark, ed., *Travels in the Old South: A Bibliography* (3 vols.; Norman: University of Oklahoma Press, 1956, 1959). The series *Writings on American History,* commonly known as the Griffin Guide, is described in Handlin and others, *Harvard Guide to American History,* p. 106. See also American Historical Association, *Index to the Writings on American History* (Washington: The Association, 1956). Early periodicals are described at length in Lyon N. Richardson, *A History of Early American Magazines, 1741–1789* (New York: Thomas Nelson and Sons, 1931). For newspapers see Sidney Kobre, *The Development of the Colonial Newspaper* (Pittsburgh: Colonial Press, Inc., 1944), and Clarence S. Brigham, *History and Bibliography of American Newspapers, 1690–1820* (2 vols.; Worcester, Mass.: American Antiquarian Society, 1947).

A model of the mapmakers' art is Charles O. Paullin, *Atlas of the Historical Geography of the United States* (Carnegie Institution of Washington and the American Geographical Society of New York: 1932). Of similar importance is O[liver] E. Baker, comp., *Atlas of American Agriculture* (Washington: Government Printing Office, 1936): "Land Relief," by F. J. Marschner (1936); "Climate: Temperature, Sunshine and Wind," by Joseph B. Kincer (1928); "Climate: Frost and the Growing Season," by William Gardner Reed (1918);

"Climate: Precipitation and Humidity," by J. B. Kincer (1922); Part III: "Soils of the United States," by C. F. Marbut (1935); "Natural Vegetation," by H. L. Schantz and Raphael Zon (1924). For the early history of all areas of the United States an admirable work is James Truslow Adams and R. V. Coleman, eds., *Atlas of American History* (New York: Charles Scribner's Sons, 1943). A comprehensive, useful collection is Clifford Lord and Elizabeth H. Lord, *Historical Atlas of the United States* (New York: Henry Holt and Company, rev. ed., 1953).

The Bureau of the Census, in cooperation with the Social Science Research Council, has issued a convenient volume: *Historical Statistics of the United States, Colonial Times to 1957* (Washington: Government Printing Office, 1960). Other works emphasizing statistical data are Timothy Pitkin, *A Statistical View of the Commerce of the United States* (New Haven, Conn.: Durrie and Peck, 1835); Adam Seybert, *Statistical Annals* (Philadelphia: Thomas Dobson and Son, 1818); George Tucker, *Progress of the United States in Population and Wealth* (New York: Hunt's Merchants' Magazine, 1843); D. B. Warden, *A Statistical, Political, and Historical Account of the United States of North America, from the Period of Their First Colonization to the Present Day* (3 vols.; Edinburgh: Archibald Constable and Co., 1819); Charles H. Evans, "Exports . . . from the American Colonies from 1697 . . . [and] Exports, Domestic, from the United States to All Countries from 1789 to 1883, Inclusive" (*House Miscellaneous Document*, No. 49, Pt. 2, 48 Cong., 1 Sess.); and "Statistical Tables Exhibiting the Commerce of the United States with European Countries from 1790 to 1890" (*House Miscellaneous Document*, No. 117, 52 Cong., 2 Sess.).

Three useful collections of documents of primary importance are Ernest Ludlow Bogart and Charles Manfred Thompson, eds., *Readings in the Economic History of the United States* (New York: Longmans, Green and Company, 1929); Guy Stevens Callender, ed., *Selections from the Economic History of the United States, 1765–1860* (Boston: Ginn and Company, 1909); and N[orman] S. B. Gras and Henrietta M. Larson, *Casebook in American Business History* (New York: F. S. Crofts & Company, 1939).

The most valuable single work on American history is Allen Johnson, Dumas Malone, and others, eds., *Dictionary of American Biography* (22 vols.; New York: Charles Scribner's Sons, 1928–1958). The best collection of illustrations is Ralph H. Gabriel, ed., *The Pageant of America* (15 vols.; New Haven, Conn.: Yale University Press, 1925–1929).

PUBLIC DOCUMENTS AND SEMIPUBLIC RECORDS

Standard collections of essential documents are Leonard Woods Labaree, ed., *Royal Instructions to British Governors, 1670–1776* (2 vols.; New York: D. Appleton–Century Company, 1935); Peter Force, ed., *American Archives: Fourth Series* (6 vols.; Washington: M. St. Clair Clarke and Peter Force, 1837–1846); Worthington C. Ford and others, eds., *Journals of the Continental Congress, 1774–1789* (34 vols.; Washington: Government Printing Office, 1904–1937); Edmund C. Burnett, ed., *Letters of Members of the Continental Congress* (8 vols.; Washington: Carnegie Institution of Washington, 1921–1936)— valuable as a supplement to the *Journals;* S[amuel] E. Morison, ed., *Sources and Documents illustrating the American Revolution, 1764–1788, and the formation of the Federal Constitution* (2d ed.; Oxford: The Clarendon Press, 1929); Charles H. Lincoln, ed., *Naval Records of the American Revolution, 1775–1788* (Washington: Government Printing Office, 1906); Francis Wharton, ed., *The Revolutionary Diplomatic Correspondence of the United States* (6 vols.; Washington: Government Printing Office, 1889); *The Diplomatic Correspondence of the United States of America from . . . 10th September, 1783 to . . . March 4, 1789* (7 vols.; Washington: Francis Preston Blair, 1833–1834); E. H. Scott, ed., James Madison, *Journal of the Constitutional Convention* (Chicago: Albert, Scott and Company, 1895); Max Farrand, ed., *The Records of the Federal Convention of 1787* (4 vols.; New Haven, Conn.: Yale University Press, 1911–1937); Paul Leicester Ford, ed., *Pamphlets on the Constitution of the United States, . . . 1787–1788* (Brooklyn: Historical Printing Club, 1892); Henry Cabot Lodge, ed., *The Federalist: A Commentary on the Constitution of the United States* (New York: G. P. Putnam's Sons, 1888); *The Debates and Proceedings in the Congress of the United States* (42 vols.; Washington: Gales and Seaton, 1834–1856); Richard Peters, ed., *The Public Statutes at Large of the United States from . . . 1789 to March 3, 1845* (8 vols.; Boston: Charles C. Little and James Brown, 1848–1850); James D. Richardson, ed., *A Compilation of the Messages and Papers of the Presidents, 1789–1897* (10 vols.; Washington: Government Printing Office, 1896–1899); and Clarence E. Carter, ed., *The Territorial Papers of the United States* (24 vols.; Washington: Government Printing Office, 1934–1959). The United States Census reports before 1820 are valuable mainly for population data. The extant returns for 1790 have been published by the Bureau of the Census under the title *Heads of Families at the First Census of the United States Taken in the Year 1790* (12 vols.; Washington: Government Printing Office, 1907–1908). These volumes do not give the returns, which have been destroyed, for Delaware, Georgia, Kentucky, New Jersey, Tennessee, and Virginia. One of the volumes presents comparable but incomplete data for Virginia, drawn from Virginia records of the 1780's. For 1800 there is a printed summary: *Return of the Whole Number of Persons within the Several Districts of the United States* (Washington: William Duane, 1802). The Census of 1810 contained much information, though incomplete, which was digested and arranged by Tench Coxe and printed as *A Statement of the Arts and Manufactures of the United States for . . . 1810* (Philadelphia: A. Cornman, Jr., 1814). Volumes in *American State Papers: Documents, Legislative and Executive of the Congress of the United States* (38 vols.; Washington: Gales and Seaton, 1832–1834) which pertain to economic affairs before 1816 are Class 1, *Foreign Affairs*, I–III; Class 2, *Indian Affairs*, I; Class 3, *Finance*, I–II; Class 4, *Commerce and Navigation*, I; Class 7, *Post Office*, only 1 vol.; Class 8, *Public Lands*, I–II; Class 10, *Miscellaneous*, I–II. Another useful collection pertaining to foreign relations is: *State Papers of the United States* (10 vols.; Boston: T. B. Wait and Sons, 1817).

CONTEMPORARY WRITINGS

Leading public men were so concerned with the economic scene that their writings are essential sources of information pertaining to it. The principal collections are Charles Francis Adams, ed., *The Works of John Adams* (10 vols.;

Boston: Little, Brown and Company, 1856); Albert Henry Smyth, ed., *The Writings of Benjamin Franklin* (10 vols.; New York: The Macmillan Company, 1905–1907); Henry Adams, ed., *The Writings of Albert Gallatin* (3 vols.; Philadelphia: J. B. Lippincott and Company, 1879); Henry Cabot Lodge, ed., *The Works of Alexander Hamilton* (9 vols.; New York: G. P. Putnam's Sons, 1885–1886); Samuel McKee, ed., *Alexander Hamilton's Papers on Public Credit, Commerce, and Finance* (New York: The Liberal Arts Press, 1957); Arthur Harrison Cole, ed., *Industrial and Commercial Correspondence of Alexander Hamilton* (Chicago: A. W. Shaw Company, 1928); Henry P. Johnston, ed., *The Correspondence and Public Papers of John Jay* (4 vols.; New York: G. P. Putnam's Sons, 1890–1893); Julian P. Boyd and others, eds., *The Papers of Thomas Jefferson* (15 vols., in progress; Princeton, N. J.: Princeton University Press, 1950–1958); Paul Leicester Ford, ed., *The Writings of Thomas Jefferson* (10 vols.; New York: G. P. Putnam's Sons, 1892–1899); Andrew A. Lipscomb and Albert Ellery Bergh, eds., *The Writings of Thomas Jefferson* (20 vols.; Washington: The Thomas Jefferson Memorial Association of the United States, 1903); Gilbert Chinard, ed., *The Correspondence of Jefferson and Du Pont de Nemours* (Johns Hopkins University *Studies in International Thought;* Baltimore: The Johns Hopkins Press, 1931); Gaillard Hunt, ed., *The Writings of James Madison* (9 vols.; New York: G. P. Putnam's Sons, 1900–1910); *Letters and Other Writings of James Madison* (4 vols.; Philadelphia: J. B. Lippincott and Company, 1867); John C. Fitzpatrick, ed., *The Writings of George Washington from the Original Sources, 1745–1799* (39 vols.; Washington: Government Printing Office, 1931–1944).

Important letters and essays are *Warren-Adams Letters* (Massachusetts Historical Society, *Collections,* Vols. LXXII, LXXIII; Boston: The Society, 1917, 1925); J[ohn] Franklin Jameson, ed., "Letters of Phineas Bond, British Consul at Philadelphia to the Foreign Office of Great Britain, 1787, 1788, 1789" (American Historical Association, *Annual Report . . . 1896,* 2 vols.; Washington: Government Printing Office, 1897), Vol. I; *The Deane Papers: Correspondence between Silas Deane and His Brothers . . . , 1771–1795* (Connecticut Historical Society, *Collections,* Vol. XXIII; Hartford: The Society, 1930); J[ohn] Franklin Jameson, ed., "Letters of Stephen Higginson, 1783–1804" (American Historical Association, *Annual Report . . . 1896,* 2 vols.; Washington: Government Printing Office, 1897), Vol. I; Samuel Eliot Morison, ed., "William Manning's, *The Key of Libberty,*" *William and Mary Quarterly,* Third Series, Vol. XIII, No. 2 (April, 1956); Harry H. Clark, ed., *Six New Letters of Thomas Paine* (Madison: The University of Wisconsin Press, 1939); Pelatiah Webster, *Political Essays on the Nature and Operation of Money, Public Finance, and Other Subjects* (Philadelphia: 1791); Harry R. Warfel, ed., *Letters of Noah Webster* (New York: Library Publishers, 1953); M. B. Hammond, ed., "Correspondence of Eli Whitney relative to the Invention of the Cotton Gin," *American Historical Review,* Vol. III, No. 1 (October, 1897).

SPECIAL SOURCE MATERIALS

The following records of commerce are readily accessible: Kenneth Wiggins Porter, ed., *The Jacksons and the Lees: Two Generations of Massachusetts Mer-*

chants 1765–1844 (Vol. III of *Harvard Studies in Business History,* 2 vols.; Cambridge, Mass.: Harvard University Press, 1937); *Commerce of Rhode Island, 1726–1800* (Massachusetts Historical Society, *Collections,* Vols. LXIX, LXX; Boston: The Society, 1914–1915); Sir Francis Piggott and G. W. T. Omond, eds., *Documentary History of the Armed Neutralities, 1780 and 1800* (London: University of London Press, Ltd., 1919); Edmund C. Burnett, ed., "Observations of London Merchants on American Trade, 1783," *American Historical Review,* Vol. XVIII, No. 4 (July, 1913); Henry Sée, ed., "Commerce between France and the United States, 1783–1784," *American Historical Review,* Vol. XXXI, No. 4 (July, 1926); Herbert Van Houtte, ed., "American Commercial Conditions and Negotiations with Austria, 1783–1786," *American Historical Review,* Vol. XVI, No. 3 (April, 1911); Frederick W. Howay, ed., *Voyages of the "Columbia" to the Northwest Coast, 1787–1790* (Massachusetts Historical Society, *Collections,* Vol. LXXIX; Boston: The Society, 1941); F. W. Howay, ed., "Letters Relating to the Second Voyage of the 'Columbia,' " *Quarterly Journal of the Oregon Historical Society,* Vol. XXIV, No. 2 (June, 1923); Alexander Ross, *The Fur Hunters of the Far West: A Narrative of Adventures in the Oregon and Rocky Mountains* (The Lakeside Classics, Milo M. Quaife, ed.; Chicago: R. R. Donnelley & Sons Company, 1924); W. Stewart Wallace, ed., *Documents Relating to the North West Company* (Toronto: The Champlain Society, 1934); "Despatches from the United States Consulate in New Orleans, 1801–1803," *American Historical Review,* Vols. XXXII, No. 4 (July, 1927), and XXXIII, No. 2 (January, 1928); John H. Reinoehl, ed., "Some Remarks on the American Trade: Jacob Crowninshield to James Madison, 1806," *William and Mary Quarterly,* Third Series, Vol. XVI, No. 1 (January, 1959); *Autobiography of Charles Biddle,* . . . *1745–1821* (Philadelphia: E. Claxton and Company, 1883); Martha Nichols, ed., *A Salem Shipmaster and Merchant: The Autobiography of George Nichols* (Boston: The Four Seas Company, 1921).

On agriculture, land, and settlement see Harry J. Carman, ed., *American Husbandry* (New York: Columbia University Press, 1939); Harry J. Carman and Rexford G. Tugwell, eds., *Essays upon Field Husbandry in New England and Other Papers, 1748–1762, by Jared Eliot* (New York: Columbia University Press, 1934); Frederick S. Allis, Jr., ed., *William Bingham's Maine Lands, 1790–1820* (Colonial Society of Massachusetts, *Publications,* Vols. XXXVI, XXXVII; Boston: The Society, 1954); Archer Butler Hulbert, ed., *The Records of the Original Proceedings of the Ohio Company* (Marietta College *Historical Collections,* Vols. I–II; Marietta, Ohio: Marietta Historical Commission, 1917); "Certificate Book of the Virginia Land Commission, 1779–80," *Register of the Kentucky State Historical Society,* Vol. XXI, Nos. 61–63 (January, May, September, Supplement, 1923); Lawrence W. Kinnaird, ed., *Spain in the Mississippi Valley, 1765–1794* (American Historical Association, *Annual Report* . . . *1945,* Vols. II–IV; Washington: Government Printing Office, 1946–1949); Arthur P. Whitaker, ed., "The South Carolina Yazoo Company," *Mississippi Valley Historical Review,* XVI, No. 3 (December, 1929).

On labor and industry two useful collections are John R. Commons and others, eds., *A Documentary History of American Industrial Society* (11 vols.; Cleveland: The Arthur H. Clark Company, 1910–1911); and Rita Susswein

Gottesman, *The Arts and Crafts in New York, 1726–1779* (The New York State Historical Society, *Collections*, Vols. LXIX, LXXI; New York: The Society, 1938, 1954).

TRAVELS AND DESCRIPTIVE ACCOUNTS

Comments by contemporary observers on American conditions appear in the following: Rayner Wickersham Kelsey, ed., *Cazenove Journal, 1794: A Record of the Journey of Theophile Casenove through New Jersey and Pennsylvania* (Haverford, Penn.: The Pennsylvania History Press, 1922); [François Jean] Marquis de Chastellux, *Travels in North America in the Years 1780, 1781, and 1782* (2 vols.; London: G. G. J. and J. Robinson, 1787); Tench Coxe, *A View of the United States of America* (Philadelphia: William Hall and Wrigley & Berriman, 1794); *The Journal of Nicholas Cresswell, 1774–1777* (New York: The Dial Press, 1924); Hector St. John de Crèvecœur, *Letters from an American Farmer* (London: J. M. Dent & Sons, Ltd., n. d.); Daniel Drake, *Natural and Statistical View, or Picture of Cincinnati and the Miami Country* (Cincinnati: Looker and Wallace, 1815); John Melish, *Travels through the United States of America in the Years 1806 & 1807, and 1809, 1810, & 1811 . . .* (2 vols.; Philadelphia: John Melish, 1815); Thomas Pemberton, "A Topographical and Historical Description of Boston, 1794" (Massachusetts Historical Society, *Collections*, Vol. III; Boston: The Society, 1810); Hans Huth and Wilma J. Pugh, eds., *Talleyrand in America As a Financial Promoter, 1794–96* (American Historical Association, *Annual Report . . . 1941*, 3 vols.; Washington: Government Printing Office, 1942), Vol. II; Isaac Weld, Jr., *Travels through the States of North America . . . during the Years 1795, 1796, and 1797* (2 vols.; London: Printed for John Stockdale, 1799); and Frederick J. Turner, ed., "Correspondence of the French Ministers to the United States, 1791–1797" (American Historical Association, *Annual Report . . . 1903*, 2 vols.; Washington: Government Printing Office, 1904), Vol. II. Reuben Gold Thwaites, ed., *Early Western Travels* (32 vols.; Cleveland: The Arthur H. Clark Company, 1904–1907) includes Estwick Evans: *A Pedestrious Tour . . . through the Western States and Territories* (1819), Vol. VIII; and William Faux, *Memorable Days in America* (1823), Vols. XI, XII.

GENERAL HISTORIES

The following works contain much information relating to economic themes: Henry Adams, *History of the United States . . .* (4 vols.; Albert and Charles Boni, 1930); Edward Channing, *A History of the United States* (6 vols.; New York: The Macmillan Company, 1905–1925); John Bach McMaster, *A History of the People of the United States from the Revolution to the Civil War* (8 vols.; New York: D. Appleton and Company, 1883–1913); Curtis P. Nettels, *The Roots of American Civilization: A History of American Colonial Life* (New York: F. S. Crofts and Company, 1938); and Justin Winsor, ed., *Narrative and Critical History of America* (8 vols.; Boston: Houghton Mifflin and Company, 1884–1889). Special studies dealing with the American economy include Ernest Ludlow Bogart, *Economic History of the American People* (2d ed.; New York: Longmans, Green and Company, 1939); Joseph Dorfman, *The Economic Mind in American Civilization, 1606–1933* (5 vols.; New York: The Viking Press, 1946–1959); Harold U. Faulkner, *American Economic History* (8th ed.; New York: Harper & Brothers, 1960); Louis M. Hacker, *The Triumph of American Capitalism* (New York: Simon and Schuster, Inc., 1940); Donald L. Kemmerer and C. Clyde Jones, *American Economic History* (New York: McGraw-Hill Book Company, 1959); Fred A. Shannon, *America's Economic Growth* (Rev. ed.; New York: The Macmillan Company, 1951); and Harold F. Williamson, ed., *The Growth of the American Economy* (New York: Prentice-Hall, Inc., 1955). Thomas A. Bailey, *A Diplomatic History of the American People* (2d ed.; New York: F. S. Crofts & Company, 1944) emphasizes economic factors.

THE PHYSIOGRAPHICAL SETTING

The fullest statement of the influence of the material environment in American history is given in Ralph H. Brown, *Historical Geography of the United States* (New York: Harcourt, Brace and Company, 1948). Other useful surveys are Wallace W. Atwood, *The Physiographic Provinces of North America* (Boston: Ginn and Company, 1940); and Rupert B. Vance, *Human Geography of the South: A Study in Regional Resources and Human Adequacy* (Chapel Hill: The University of North Carolina Press, 1935). The United States Department of Agriculture *Yearbook, 1938* (Washington: Government Printing Office, 1939 ?), *Soils and Men*, is an able exposition of soil science. A full discussion of soils also appears in Curtis F. Marbut, Hugh H. Bennett, J. E. Lapham, and M. H. Lapham, *Soils of the United States* (U. S. Department of Agriculture, Bureau of Soils, *Bulletin* No. 96; Washington: Government Printing Office, 1913). Another important study is Charles E. Kellogg, "Development and Significance of the Great Soil Groups of the United States," U. S. Department of Agriculture, *Miscellaneous Publication* No. 229 (Washington: Government Printing Office, April, 1936). Other standard works are E. W. Hilgard, *Soils: Their Formation, Properties, Composition, and Relations to Climate and Plant Growth* (New York: The Macmillan Company, 1906); Gilbert Woodring Robinson, *Soils: Their Origin, Constitution and Classification* (2d ed.; London: Thomas Murby & Co., 1936); Charles E. Kellogg, *The Soils That Support Us* (New York: The Macmillan Company, 1951); and C[urtis] F. Marbut, *Soils: Their Genesis and Classification* (Soil Science Society of America [Madison, Wis.]: 1951). For their particular subjects the following are noteworthy: U. S. Department of Agriculture, *Climate and Man: Yearbook of Agriculture, 1941* (Washington: Government Printing Office, 1941); Richard G. Lillard, *The Great Forest* (New York: Alfred A. Knopf, Inc., 1947); and Isaiah Bowman, *Forest Physiography* (New York: John Wiley & Sons, Inc., 1914). Introductory surveys of the effects of nature on American life are Albert Perry Brigham, *Geographic Influences in American History* (Boston: Ginn and Company, 1903); Livingston Farrand, *Basis of American History, 1500–1900* (Vol. II of *The American Nation*, A. B. Hart, ed.; New York: Harper & Brothers, 1904); Ellen Churchill Semple, *American History and Its Geographic Conditions*

(Boston: Houghton Mifflin Company, 1903); and N[athaniel] S. Shaler, *Nature and Man in America* (New York: Charles Scribner's Sons, 1906).

POPULATION AND IMMIGRATION

On the peopling of the United States the following analyses are of first importance: Stella H. Sutherland, *Population Distribution in Colonial America* (New York: Columbia University Press, 1936); Herbert Moller, "Sex Composition and Correlated Culture Patterns of Colonial America," *William and Mary Quarterly*, Third Series, Vol. II, No. 2 (April, 1945); Evarts B. Greene and Virginia D. Harrington, *American Population Before the Federal Census of 1790* (New York: Columbia University Press, 1932); "Report of Committee on Linguistic and National Stocks in the Population of the United States" (American Council of Learned Societies, American Historical Association, *Annual Report . . . 1931;* Washington: Government Printing Office, 1932); Warren S. Thompson and P. K. Whelpton, *Population Trends in the United States* (New York: McGraw-Hill Book Company, 1933); and Adna Ferrin Weber, *The Growth of Cities in the Nineteenth Century* (Columbia University Studies in History, Economics and Public Law, Vol. XI; New York: The Macmillan Company, 1899). The growth of settlements is shown graphically in Herman R. Friis, "A Series of Population Maps of the Colonies and the United States, 1625–1790," *Geographical Review*, Vol. XXX, No. 3 (July, 1940). Statistical reports are contained in Bureau of the Census, *A Century of Population Growth, from the First Census of the United States to the Twelfth, 1790–1900* (Washington: Government Printing Office, 1909), and Bureau of the Census, *Statistical Abstract of the United States, 1941* (Washington: Government Printing Office, 1942). Among the foremost studies of immigration to the United States are Edith Abbott, *Hisorical Aspects of the Immigration Problem: Select Documents* (Chicago: The University of Chicago Press, 1926); Oscar Handlin, *Boston's Immigrants* (Rev. ed.; Cambridge, Mass.: Harvard University Press, 1959); Marcus Lee Hansen, *The Atlantic Migration, 1607–1860: A History of the Continuing Settlement of the United States* (A. M. Schlesinger, ed.; Cambridge, Mass.: Harvard University Press, 1940); George M. Stephenson, *A History of American Immigration, 1820–1924* (Boston: Ginn and Company, 1926); Carl Wittke, *We Who Built America: The Saga of the Immigrant* (New York: Prentice-Hall, Inc., 1940); Henry Pratt Fairchild, *Immigration: A World Movement and Its American Significance* (New York: The Macmillan Company, 1913); Edward Young, *Special Report on Immigration . . .* (Washington: Government Printing Office, 1871); and F[rank] G. Franklin, "The Legislative History of Naturalization in the United States, 1776–1795" (American Historical Association, *Annual Report . . . 1901,* 2 vols.; Washington: Government Printing Office, 1902), Vol. I. Movements of peoples within the country are treated in Louis Kimball Mathews, *The Expansion of New England: The Spread of New England Settlement and Institutions to the Mississippi River, 1620–1865* (Boston: Houghton Mifflin Company, 1909); Lois Kimball Mathews Rosenberry, *Migrations from Connecticut Prior to 1800* (Tercentenary Commission of the State of Connecticut, *Publications*, No. XXVIII; New Haven, Conn.: Yale University Press, 1934); Lewis D. Stillwell, *Migration from Ver-*

mont, 1776–1860 (Vermont Historical Society, *Proceedings*, New Series, Vol. V, No. 2; Montpelier: The Society, 1937); C. Warren Thornthwaite and Helen I. Slentz, *Internal Migration in the United States* (Philadelphia: University of Pennsylvania Press, 1934); and Otis Tufton Mason, "Migration and the Food Quest: A Study in the Peopling of America" (Smithsonian Institution, *Annual Report, 1894;* Washington: Government Printing Office, 1896). Special ethnic groups are dealt with in John Hope Franklin, *From Slavery to Freedom: A History of American Negroes* (2d ed.; New York: Alfred A. Knopf, Inc., 1956); John Hope Franklin, *The Free Negro in North Carolina, 1790–1860* (Chapel Hill: The University of North Carolina Press, 1943); Arnett G. Lindsay, "The Economic Condition of the Negroes of New York Prior to 1861," *Journal of Negro History*, Vol. VI, No. 2 (April, 1921); and Edward Raymond Turner, *The Negro in Pennsylvania: Slavery-Servitude-Freedom, 1639–1861* (Washington: The American Historical Association, 1911).

LABOR

The labor movement or the history of trade unions is the principal subject of the following standard works: John R. Commons and associates, *History of Labour in the United States* (4 vols.; New York: The Macmillan Company, 1918–1935); Anthony Bimba, *The History of the American Working Class* (New York: International Publishers, 1927); Foster Rhea Dulles, *Labor in America: A History* (New York: Thomas Y. Crowell Company, 1949); Philip S. Foner, *History of the Labor Movement in the United States* (New York: International Publishers, 1947); Selig Perlman, *A History of Trade Unionism in the United States* (New York: The Macmillan Company, 1922); George A. Tracy, *History of the Typographical Union* (Indianapolis: International Typographical Union, 1913); and Edwin E. Witte, "Early American Labor Cases," *Yale Law Journal*, Vol. XXXV, No. 7 (May, 1926). Outstanding studies of indentured servitude are Abbot Emerson Smith, *Colonists in Bondage: White Servitude and Convict Labor in America, 1607–1776* (Chapel Hill: The University of North Carolina Press, 1947); James Curtis Ballagh, *White Servitude in the Colony of Virginia* (Johns Hopkins University *Studies in Historical and Political Science*, Series XIII, Nos. 6–7; Baltimore: The Johns Hopkins Press, 1895); and Eugene Irving McCormac, *White Servitude in Maryland, 1634–1820* (Johns Hopkins University *Studies in Historical and Political Science*, Series XXII, Nos. 3–4; Baltimore: The Johns Hopkins Press, 1904). Special aspects of the history of wage earners are sketched in Edith Abbott, *Women in Industry: A Study in American Economic History* (New York: D. Appleton and Company, 1910); Paul H. Douglas, *American Apprenticeship and Industrial Education* (New York: 1921)—Columbia University thesis; James M. Motley, *Apprenticeship in American Trade Unions* (Johns Hopkins University *Studies in Historical and Political Science*, Series XXV, Nos. 11–12; Baltimore: The Johns Hopkins Press, 1907); and Lucy Maynard Salmon, *Domestic Service* (New York: The Macmillan Company, 1897). The literature pertaining to slavery includes the following important studies: Ulrich Bonnell Phillips, *American Negro Slavery: A Survey of the Supply, Employment and Control of Negro Labor as Determined by the Plantation Regime* (New York: D. Appleton and Company, 1918);

Ulrich Bonnell Phillips, *Life and Labor in the Old South* (Boston: Little, Brown and Company, 1929); Kenneth M. Stampp, *The Peculiar Institution: Slavery in the Ante-Bellum South* (New York: Alfred A. Knopf, Inc., 1956); John Spencer Bassett, *Slavery in the State of North Carolina* (Johns Hopkins University *Studies in Historical and Political Science*, Series XVII, Nos. 7–8; Baltimore: The Johns Hopkins Press, 1899); Ralph Betts Flanders, *Plantation Slavery in Georgia* (Chapel Hill: The University of North Carolina Press, 1933); James Benson Sellers, *Slavery in Alabama* (University: University of Alabama Press, 1950); and L. C. Gray, "Economic Efficiency and Competitive Advantages of Slavery under the Plantation System," *Agricultural History*, Vol. IV, No. 2 (April, 1930). Varied aspects of the life of working people are presented in Richard B. Morris, *Government and Labor in Early America* (New York: Columbia University Press, 1946); Anne Bezanson, "Some Historical Aspects of Labor Turnover," in *Facts and Factors in Economic History: Articles by former students of Edwin Francis Gay* (Cambridge, Mass.: Harvard University Press, 1932); and *History of Wages in the United States from Colonial Times to 1928* (U. S. Department of Labor, Bureau of Labor Statistics, *Bulletin No. 499*; Washington: Government Printing Office, 1929).

LAND

Features of land tenure are the main subjects of the following scholarly accounts: Marshall Harris, *Origin of the Land Tenure System in the United States* (Ames: The Iowa State College Press, 1953); Viola F. Barnes, "Land Tenure in the English Colonial Charters of the Seventeenth Century," *Essays in Colonial History Presented to Charles M. Andrews* (New Haven, Conn.: Yale University Press, 1921); Beverley W. Bond, Jr., *The Quit-Rent System in the American Colonies* (New Haven, Conn.: Yale University Press, 1919); Beverley W. Bond, Jr., "The Quit-Rent System in the American Colonies," *American Historical Review*, XVII, No. 3 (April, 1912); E[llis] Merton Coulter, "The Granville District" (The University of North Carolina, *The James Sprunt Historical Collections*, Vol. XIII, No. 1; Durham, N. C.: 1913); William E. Dodd, "Chief Justice Marshall and Virginia, 1813–1821," *American Historical Review*, Vol. XII, No. 4 (July, 1907); Richard S. Rodney, "The End of the Penns' Claim to Delaware, 1789–1814," *Pennsylvania Magazine of History and Biography*, Vol. LXI, No. 2 (April, 1937); and St. George L. Sioussat, "The Breakdown of the Royal Management of Lands in the Southern Provinces," *Agricultural History*, Vol. III, No. 2 (April, 1929). The most significant writings on the public lands of the United States are Thomas Donaldson, *The Public Domain* (Washington: Government Printing Office, 1884); Amelia Clewley Ford, *Colonial Precedents of Our National Land System As It Existed in 1800* (University of Wisconsin *History Series, Bulletin*, Vol. II, No. 2; Madison: 1910); Benjamin Horace Hibbard, *A History of Public Land Policies* (New York: Peter Smith, 1939); Roy M. Robbins, *Our Landed Heritage: The Public Domain, 1776–1936* (Princeton, N. J.: Princeton University Press, 1942); Payson Jackson Treat, *The National Land System, 1785–1820* (New York: E. B. Treat & Company, 1910); R. S. Cotterill, "The National Land System in the South: 1803–1812," *Mississippi Valley Historical Review*, XVI, No. 4 (March,

1930); R. S. Cotterill, "The South Carolina Land Cession," *Mississippi Valley Historical Review*, Vol. XII, No. 3 (December, 1925); Merrill Jensen, "The Cession of the Old Northwest," *Mississippi Valley Historical Review*, Vol. XXIII, No. 1 (June, 1936); Merrill Jensen, "The Creation of the National Domain, 1781–1784," *Mississippi Valley Historical Review*, Vol. XXVI, No. 3 (December, 1939); and Henry Tatter, "State and Federal Laws Policy During the Confederation Period," *Agricultural History*, Vol. IX, No. 4 (October, 1935). The literature concerning investment and speculation in land is extensive. The most valuable studies are Shaw Livermore, *Early American Land Companies: Their Influence on Corporate Development* (Columbia University School of Law Publications of the Foundation for Research in Legal History; New York: Oxford University Press, 1939); A. M. Sakolski, *The Great American Land Bubble: The Amazing Story of Land-Grabbing, Speculations, and Booms from Colonial Days to the Present Time* (New York: Harper & Brothers, 1932); Thomas Perkins Abernethy, *Western Lands and the American Revolution* (New York: D. Appleton–Century Company, 1937); Kenneth P. Bailey, *The Ohio Company and the Westward Movement: 1748–1792: A Chapter in the History of the Colonial Frontier* (Glendale, Calif.: The Arthur H. Clark Company, 1939); J. P. Boyd, "Connecticut's Experiment in Expansion: The Susquehanna Company, 1753–1803," *Journal of Economic and Business History*, Vol. IV, No. 1 (November, 1931); Roy Bird Cook, *Washington's Western Lands* (Strasburg, Va.: Shenandoah Publishing House, Inc., 1930); Paul Demund Evans, *The Holland Land Company* (Buffalo Historical Society, *Collections*, Vol. XXVIII; Buffalo: The Society, 1924); Paul D. Evans, "The Pulteney Purchase," *Quarterly Journal of the New York State Historical Association*, Vol. III, No. 2 (April, 1922); Charles Homer Haskins, *The Yazoo Land Companies* (New York: The Knickerbocker Press, 1891); Archibald Henderson, "Dr. Thomas Walker and the Loyal Company of Virginia" (American Antiquarian Society, *Proceedings*, New Series, Vol. XLI; Worcester, Mass.: The Society, 1931); Archibald Henderson, "Richard Henderson and the Occupation of Kentucky, 1775," *Mississippi Valley Historical Review*, Vol. I, No. 3 (December, 1914); William Stewart Lester, *The Transylvania Colony* (Spencer, Ind.: Samuel R. Guard & Co., 1935); George E. Lewis, *The Indiana Company, 1763–1798: A Study in Eighteenth Century Frontier Land Speculation and Business Venture* (Glendale, Calif.: The Arthur H. Clark Company, 1941); Neil Adams McNall, *The First Half-Century of Wadsworth Tenancy* (Cornell University Studies in American History, Literature, and Folklore, Vol. II; Ithaca, N. Y.: Cornell University Press, 1945); Max Savelle, *George Morgan: Colony Builder* (New York: Columbia University Press, 1932); O[rasmus] Turner, *History of the Pioneer Settlement of Phelps and Gorham's Purchase and Morris' Reserve* (Rochester, N. Y.: William Alling, 1851); Albert T. Volwiler, *George Croghan and the Westward Movement, 1741–1782* (Cleveland: The Arthur H. Clark Company, 1926); and A. P. Whitaker, "The Muscle Shoals Speculation, 1783–1789," *Mississippi Valley Historical Review*, Vol. XIII, No. 3 (December, 1926). Three useful surveys of state land policies are C. H. Laub, "Revolutionary Virginia and the Crown Lands, 1775–1783," *William and Mary Quarterly*, Second Series, Vol. XI, No. 4 (October, 1931); Elizabeth K. Henderson, "The Northwestern Lands of Pennsylvania, 1790–1812," *Pennsylvania Magazine of History and*

Biography, Vol. LX, No. 2 (April, 1936); and L. D. Smith, "Land Laws of Tennessee," *Tennessee Law Review,* Vol. I, No. 1 (November, 1922). Works relating to the Loyalists and the confiscation of their lands include Lorenzo Sabine, *Biographical Sketches of Loyalists in the American Revolution* (2 vols.; Boston: Little, Brown and Company, 1864); Claude Halstead Van Tyne, *The Loyalists of the American Revolution* (New York: The Macmillan Company, 1902); Robert O. De Mond, *The Loyalists of North Carolina During the Revolution* (Durham, N. C.: Duke University Press, 1940); Alexander Clarence Flick, *Loyalism in New York During the Revolution* (New York: 1901)— Columbia University thesis; Isaac Samuel Harrell, *Loyalism in Virginia: Chapters in the History of the Revolution* (Durham, N. C.: Duke University Press, 1926); James H. Stark, *The Loyalists of Massachusetts . . .* (Boston: W. B. Clarke Co., 1907); Catherine Snell Crary, "The American Dream: John Tabor Kempe's Rise from Poverty to Riches," *William and Mary Quarterly,* Third Series, Vol. XIV, No. 2 (April, 1957); and Mabel G. Walker, "Sir John Johnson, Loyalist," *Mississippi Valley Historical Review,* Vol. III, No. 3 (December, 1916).

AGRICULTURE

Indispensable to the study of American agriculture are Percy Wells Bidwell and John I. Falconer, *History of Agriculture in the Northern United States* (Washington: Carnegie Institution of Washington, 1925); and Lewis Cecil Gray, *History of Agriculture in the Southern United States to 1860* (2 vols.; Washington: Carnegie Institution of Washington, 1933)—one of the greatest works of American scholarship.

Good surveys are Lyman Carrier, *The Beginnings of Agriculture in America* (New York: McGraw-Hill Book Company, 1923); Edward E. Edwards, "American Agriculture—The First 300 Years," (U. S. Department of Agriculture, *Yearbook, 1940;* Washington: Government Printing Office, 1941 ?); Albert Hart Sanford, *The Story of Agriculture in the United States* (Boston: D. C. Heath & Company, 1916); Joseph Schafer, *The Social History of American Agriculture* (New York: The Macmillan Company, 1936); and Louis Bernard Schmidt and Earle Dudley Ross, *Readings in the Economic History of Agriculture* (New York: The Macmillan Company, 1925). The United States Department of Agriculture *Yearbook* for 1899 (Washington: Government Printing Office, 1900) contains twenty-six articles pertaining to the history of American Agriculture. There are several excellent regional and state studies, as follows: Percy W. Bidwell, "Rural Economy in New England at the Beginning of the Nineteenth Century" (Connecticut Academy of Arts and Sciences, *Transactions,* Vol. XX; New Haven, Conn.: The Academy, 1916); Clarence Albert Day, *A History of Maine Agriculture, 1604–1860* (University of Maine *Studies,* Second Series, No. 68; Orono: 1954); Ulysses Prentice Hedrick, *A History of Agriculture in the State of New York* (Albany: New York State Agricultural Society, 1933); David Maldwyn Ellis, *Landlords and Farmers in the Hudson-Mohawk Region, 1790–1850* (Ithaca, N. Y.: Cornell University Press, 1946); Neil Adams McNall, *An Agricultural History of the Genesee Valley, 1790–1860* (Philadelphia: University of Pennsylvania Press, 1952); Carl Raymond Woodward, *The Development of Agriculture in New Jersey, 1640–1880* (New Brunswick: New Jersey Agricultural Experiment Station, 1927); Stevenson Whitcomb Fletcher, *Pennsylvania Agriculture and Country Life* (Harrisburg: Pennsylvania Historical and Museum Commission, 1950); Avery Odell Craven, *Soil Exhaustion As a Factor in the Agricultural History of Virginia and Maryland, 1606–1860* (University of Illinois *Studies in the Social Sciences,* Vol. XIII, No. 1; Urbana: 1925); Cornelius Oliver Cathey, *Agricultural Developments in North Carolina, 1783–1860* (Fletcher M. Green and others, eds., *The James Sprunt Studies in History and Political Science,* Vol. XXXVIII; Chapel Hill: The University of North Carolina Press, 1956); and John Hebron Moore, *Agriculture in Ante-Bellum Mississippi* (New York: Bookman Associates, 1958). Important works dealing with individual farm industries and branches of agriculture are Arthur Pierce Middleton, *Tobacco Coast: A Maritime History of Chesapeake Bay in the Colonial Era* (Newport News, Va.: The Mariners' Museum, 1953); Meyer Jacobstein, *The Tobacco Industry in the United States* (Columbia University *Studies in History, Political Science and Public Law,* Vol. XXVI; New York: 1907); Joseph Clarke Robert, *The Tobacco Kingdom: Plantation, Market, and Factory in Virginia and North Carolina, 1800–1860* (Durham, N. C.: Duke University Press, 1938); L. G. Connor, "A Brief History of the Sheep Industry in the United States" (American Historical Association, *Annual Report . . . 1918,* 2 vols.; Washington: Government Printing Office, 1921), Vol. I; Paul C. Henlein, *Cattle Kingdom in the Ohio Valley, 1783–1860* (Lexington: University of Kentucky Press, 1959); J[oseph] Carlyle Sitterson, *Sugar Country: The Cane Sugar Industry in the South, 1753–1950* (Lexington: University of Kentucky Press, 1953); James F. Hopkins, *History of Hemp in Kentucky* (Lexington: University of Kentucky Press, 1951); M. B. Hammond, *The Cotton Industry: An Essay in American Economic History* (American Economic Association, *Publications,* New Series, No. 1; New York: The Macmillan Company, 1897); James L. Watkins, *King Cotton: A Historical and Statistical Review, 1790–1908* (New York: James L. Watkins & Sons, 1908); Rupert B. Vance, *Human Factors in Cotton Culture* (Chapel Hill: The University of North Carolina Press, 1929); and Charles Shepard Davis, *The Cotton Kingdom in Alabama* (Montgomery: State Department of Archives and History, 1939). For briefer treatments of special topics see Albert Laverne Olson, *Agricultural Economy and Population in Eighteenth-Century Connecticut* (Tercentenary Commission of the State of Connecticut, *Publications,* No. XL; New Haven, Conn.: Yale University Press, 1935); Richard H. Shryock, "British Versus German Traditions in Colonial Agriculture," *Mississippi Valley Historical Review,* Vol. XXVI, No. 1 (June, 1939); John G. Gagliardo, "Germans and Agriculture in Colonial Pennsylvania," *Pennsylvania Magazine of History and Biography,* Vol. LXXXIII, No. 2 (April, 1959); W. J. Hayward, "Early Western Pennsylvania Agriculture," *Western Pennsylvania Historical Magazine,* Vol. VI, No. 3 (July, 1923); Kathleen Bruce, "Virginian Agricultural Decline to 1860: A Fallacy," *Agricultural History,* Vol. VI, No. 1 (January, 1932); N. F. Cabell, "Some Fragments of an Intended Report on the Post-Revolutionary History of Agriculture in Virginia," E. G. Swen, ed., *William and Mary College Historical Quarterly,* First Series, Vol. XXVI, No. 1 (January, 1918); Jackson Turner Main, "The Distribution of Property in Post-Revolutionary Virginia," *Mississippi Valley Historical Review,* Vol. XLI, No. 2 (September, 1954); Edmund C. Burnett, "The Continental Congress and Agricultural Supplies," *Agricultural History,* Vol. II, No. 3 (July, 1928); Rodney C. Loehr, "The Influence of English Agriculture on American Agriculture, 1775–1825," *Agricultural History*, Vol. XI, No. 1 (January, 1937); Charles S. Graham, "The Gypsum Trade of the Maritime Provinces: Its Relation to American Diplomacy and Agriculture in the Early Nineteenth Century," *Agricultural History*, Vol. XII, No. 3 (July, 1938); Charles T. Leavitt, "Transportation and the Livestock Industry of the Middle West to 1860," *Agricultural History*, Vol. VIII, No. 1 (January, 1934); Charles T. Leavitt, "Attempts to Improve Cattle Breeds in the United States, 1790–1860," *Agricultural History*, Vol. VII, No. 2 (April, 1933); and Carleton R. Ball, "The History of American Wheat Improvement," *Agricultural History*, Vol. IV, No. 2 (April, 1930). The progressive spirit in the farmer's world is reflected in the following: Rodney H. True, "The Early Development of Agricultural Societies in the United States" (American Historical Association, *Annual Report . . . 1920;* Washington: Government Printing Office, 1925); Avery O. Craven, "The Agricultural Reformers of the Ante-Bellum South," *American Historical Review*, Vol. XXXIII, No. 2 (January, 1928); E[llis] Merton Coulter, *Thomas Spalding of Sapelo* (University: Louisiana State University Press, 1940); Olive Moore Gambrill, "John Beale Bordley and the Early Years of the Philadelphia Agricultural Society," *Pennsylvania Magazine of History and Biography*, Vol. LXVI, No. 4 (October, 1942); Paul Leland Haworth, *George Washington: Country Gentleman* (Indianapolis: The Bobbs-Merrill Company, 1915); Earle D. Ross, "Benjamin Franklin As an Eighteenth-Century Agricultural Leader," *Journal of Political Economy*, Vol. XXXVII, No. 1 (February, 1929); and Henry R. Simms, *Life of John Taylor* (Richmond: The William Byrd Press, 1932).

TRANSPORTATION

The best introduction to its subject is Caroline E. MacGill and others, *History of Transportation in the United States before 1860* (Balthasar Henry Meyer, ed.; Washington: Carnegie Institution of Washington, 1917). Still useful, is J. L. Ringwalt, *Development of Transportation Systems in the United States* (Philadelphia: J. R. Ringwalt, 1888). Good general surveys of transportation in particular areas are Wheaton J. Lane, *From Indian Trail to Iron Horse: Travel and Transportation in New Jersey, 1620–1680* (Princeton, N. J.: Princeton University Press, 1939); Ulrich Bonnell Phillips, *A History of Transportation in the Eastern Cotton Belt to 1860* (New York: Columbia University Press, 1908); Randle Bond Truett, *Trade and Travel Around the Southern Appalachians Before 1830* (Chapel Hill: The University of North Carolina Press, 1935); William F. Gephart, *Transportation and Industrial Development in the Middle West* (New York: Columbia University, 1909); and Charles H. Ambler, *A History of Transportation in the Ohio Valley* (Glendale, Calif.: The Arthur H. Clark Company, 1932). Among specialized studies of transportation on land are Joseph Austin Durrenberger, *Turnpikes: A Study of the Toll Road Movement in the Middle Atlantic States and Maryland* (Valdosta, Ga.: Southern Stationery and Printing Company, 1931); Archer Butler Hulbert, *Historic Highways of America* (16 vols.; Cleveland: The Arthur H. Clark Company, 1902–1905); Frederic J. Wood, *The Turnpikes of New England* (Boston: Marshall Jones Company, 1919); H. Addington Bruce, *Daniel Boone and the*

Wilderness Road (New York: The Macmillan Company, 1926); and Adelbert M. Jakeman, *Old Covered Bridges* (Brattleboro, Vt.: Stephen Daye Press, 1935). The beginnings of American canals are described in Wayland Fuller Dunaway, *History of the James River and Kanawha Company* (New York: 1922)—Columbia University thesis; Alvin F. Harlow, *Old Towpaths: The Story of the American Canal Era* (New York: D. Appleton and Company, 1926); Christopher Roberts, *The Middlesex Canal, 1793–1860* (Vol. LXI of *Harvard Economic Studies;* Cambridge, Mass.: Harvard University Press, 1943); George Washington Ward, *The Early Development of the Chesapeake and Ohio Canal Project* (Johns Hopkins University *Studies in Historical and Political Science,* Series XVII, Nos. 9–11; Baltimore: The Johns Hopkins Press, 1899); and Noble E. Whitford, *History of the Canal System of the State of New York, Supplement to the Annual Report of the State Engineer and Surveyor of New York, 1905* (2 vols.; Albany: 1906). The history of transportation by water is the theme of Leland D. Baldwin, *The Keelboat Age on Western Waters* (Pittsburgh: University of Pittsburgh Press, 1941); Mildred L. Hartsough, *From Canoe to Steel Barge on the Upper Mississippi* (Minneapolis: The University of Minnesota Press, 1934); Mary Verhoeff, *The Kentucky River Navigation* (Filson Club, *Publications,* No. 28; Louisville: John P. Morton & Company, 1917); and James Cooke Mills, *Our Inland Seas: Their Shipping & Commerce for Three Centuries* (Chicago: A. C. McClurg & Co., 1910). Popular and informative accounts of conditions affecting travelers are Seymour Dunbar, *A History of Travel in America* (4 vols.; Indianapolis: The Bobbs-Merrill Company, 1915); Alice M. Earle, *Stage-Coach and Tavern Days* (New York: The Macmillan Company, 1901); and Archer B. Hulbert, *The Paths of Inland Commerce: A Chronicle of Trail, Road, and Waterway* (Vol. XXI of *The Chronicles of America,* Allen Johnson, ed; New Haven, Conn.: Yale University Press, 1920). Detailed studies limited to states or regions include Oliver W. Holmes, "The Turnpike Era," in *Conquering the Wilderness* (Vol. V of *History of the State of New York,* A. C. Flick, ed.; New York: Columbia University Press, 1934); Harry F. Jackson, "The Utica Turnpike Road Company," *New York History,* Vol. XL, No. 1 (January, 1959); Dorothy Kendall Cleaveland, "The Trade and Trade Routes of Northern New York from the Beginning of Settlement to the Coming of the Railroad," *Quarterly Journal of the New York State Historical Association,* Vol. IV, No. 4 (October, 1923); and W. Wallace Carson, "Transportation and Traffic on the Ohio and the Mississippi Before the Steamboat," *Mississippi Valley Historical Review,* Vol. VII, No. 1 (June, 1920). Three articles by Charles Christopher Crittenden in *The North Carolina Historical Review* are "Inland Navigation in North Carolina, 1763–1789," Vol. VIII, No. 2 (April, 1931); "Overland Travel and Transportation in North Carolina, 1763–1789," Vol. VIII, No. 3 (July, 1931); and "Means of Communication in North Carolina, 1763–1789," Vol. VIII, No. 4 (October, 1931).

EXTRACTIVE INDUSTRIES, MANUFACTURING, AND PROCESSING

The most important studies of American industrial society are Victor S. Clark, *History of Manufactures in the United States, 1607–1860* (Washington:

Carnegie Institution of Washington, 1916), and J[ohn] Leander Bishop, *A History of American Manufactures from 1608 to 1860* (2 vols.; Philadelphia: Edward Young and Company, 1864).

Other introductory general accounts are Albert S. Bolles, *Industrial History of the United States* (Norwich, Conn.: The Henry Bill Publishing Company, 1879); and [Robert] Malcolm Keir, *Manufacturing* (New York: The Ronald Press Company, 1928). For English backgrounds see J. L. Hammond and Barbara Hammond, *The Rise of Modern Industry* (New York: Harcourt, Brace and Company, 1926); Arnold Toynbee, *The Industrial Revolution* (Boston: The Beacon Press, 1956); and Earl J. Hamilton, "Profit Inflation and the Industrial Revolution, 1751–1800," *Quarterly Journal of Economics*, Vol. LVI, No. 2 (February, 1942). Emphasizing the practice of industrial arts in the home are Rolla M. Tryon, *Household Manufactures in the United States, 1640–1860* (Chicago: The University of Chicago Press, 1917); Jared Van Wagenen, Jr., *The Golden Age of Homespun* (Ithaca, N. Y.: Cornell University Press, 1953); and Isaac Lippincott, *A History of Manufactures in the Ohio Valley to the Year 1860* (New York: The Knickerbocker Press, 1914). Two valuable studies in Williamson, ed., *Growth of the American Economy* are Louis C. Hunter, "The Heavy Industries Before 1860," and Constance McLaughlin Green, "Light Manufactures and the Beginnings of Precision Manufacture." Another excellent article is Samuel Rezneck, "The Rise and Early Development of Industrial Consciousness in the United States, 1760–1830," *Journal of Economic and Business History*, Vol. IV, No. 4 (August, 1932, Supplement).

The writings of Arthur Cecil Bining provide the best introduction to the study of the iron manufacture. They include *British Regulation of the Colonial Iron Industry* (Philadelphia: University of Pennsylvania Press, 1933); *Pennsylvania Iron Manufacture in the Eighteenth Century* (Pennsylvania Historical Commission, *Publications*, Vol. IV; Harrisburg: The Commission, 1938); and "The Rise of Iron Manufacture in Western Pennsylvania," *Western Pennsylvania Historical Magazine*, Vol. XVI, No. 4 (November, 1933). An older work that has stood the test of time is James M. Swank, *History of the Manufacture of Iron in All Ages* (2d ed.; Philadelphia: The American Iron and Steel Association, 1892). Among scholarly studies of the iron industry the following are especially useful: Charles S. Boyer, *Early Forges & Furnaces in New Jersey* (Philadelphia: University of Pennsylvania Press, 1931); Kathleen Bruce, *Virginia Iron Manufacture in the Slave Era* (New York: The Century Company, 1931); Lester J. Cappon, "Trend of the Southern Iron Industry under the Plantation System," *Journal of Economic and Business History*, Vol. II, No. 2 (February, 1930); George W. Hughes, "The Pioneer Iron Industry in Western Pennsylvania," *Western Pennsylvania Historical Magazine*, Vol. XIV, No. 3 (July, 1931); Louis C. Hunter, "Factors in the Early Pittsburgh Iron Industry," in *Facts and Factors in Economic History: Articles by former students of Edwin Francis Gay* (Cambridge, Mass.: Harvard University Press, 1932); and Louis C. Hunter, "Influence of the Market upon Technique in the Iron Industry in Western Pennsylvania up to 1860," *Journal of Economic and Business History*, Vol. I, No. 2 (February, 1929).

Eminent among writings on the textile industry before 1815 are Arthur Harrison Cole, *The American Wool Manufacture* (2 vols.; Cambridge, Mass.:

Harvard University Press, 1926); Caroline Ware, *The Early New England Cotton Manufacture* (Boston: Houghton Mifflin Company, 1924); and Caroline F. Ware, "The Effect of the American Embargo, 1807–1809, on the New England Cotton Industry," *Quarterly Journal of Economics,* Vol. XL, No. 4 (August, 1926). The beginnings of factory production of cotton goods are sketched in the following: Melvin Thomas Copeland, *The Cotton Manufacturing Industry of the United States* (Vol. VIII of *Harvard Economic Studies;* Cambridge, Mass.: Harvard University Press, 1912); Clive Day, "The Early Development of the American Cotton Manufacture," *Quarterly Journal of Economics,* Vol. XXXIX, No. 3 (May, 1925); Broadus Mitchell, *The Rise of Cotton Mills in the South* (Johns Hopkins University *Studies in Historical and Political Science,* Series XXXIX, No. 2; Baltimore: The Johns Hopkins Press, 1921); and Thomas Russell Smith, *The Cotton Textile Industry of Fall River, Massachusetts* (New York: King's Crown Press, 1944). Older works valuable for detailed information are William R. Bagnall, *The Textile Industries of the United States* (Cambridge, Mass.: H. O. Houghton & Company, 1893); William R. Bagnall, *Samuel Slater and the Development of the Cotton Manufacture in the United States* (Middletown, Conn.: J. S. Stewart, 1890); Samuel Batchelder, *Introduction and Early Progress of the Cotton Manufacture in the United States* (Boston: Little, Brown and Company, 1863); and George S. White, *Memoir of Samuel Slater* (Philadelphia: 1836).

For extractive industries and processing the foremost studies available are the following: Rudolph Alexander Clemen, *The American Livestock and Meat Industry* (New York: The Ronald Press Company, 1923); W. F. Fox, *A History of the Lumber Industry in the State of New York* (Department of Agriculture, Bureau of Forestry, *Bulletin* No. 34: 1902); Theodore J. Kreps, "Vicissitudes of the American Potash Industry," *Journal of Economic and Business History,* Vol. III, No. 4 (August, 1931); Charles B. Kuhlmann, *Development of Flour Milling in the United States* (Boston: Houghton Mifflin Company, 1929); Charles B. Kuhlmann, "Processing Agricultural Products in the Pre-Railway Age," in Williamson, ed., *Growth of the American Economy;* Henry R. Schoolcraft, *A View of the Lead Mines of Missouri* (New York: Charles Wiley & Co., 1819); and Justin Williams "English Mercantilism and Carolina Naval Stores, 1705–1776," *Journal of Southern History,* Vol. I, No. 2 (May, 1935).

The most useful works on the fisheries are Harold A. Innis, *The Cod Fisheries: The History of an International Economy* (New Haven, Conn.: Yale University Press, 1940); Elmo Paul Hohman, *The American Whaleman: A Study of Life and Labor in the Whaling Industry* (New York: Longmans, Green and Company, 1928); Raymond McFarland, *A History of the New England Fisheries* (University of Pennsylvania *Publications, Series in Political Economy and Public Law;* New York: D. Appleton and Company, 1911); and Walter S. Tower, *A History of the American Whale Fishery* (University of Pennsylvania *Publications in Political Economy and Public Law,* No. 20; Philadelphia: 1907). Of special interest and merit is Adele Ogden, *The California Sea Otter Trade, 1784–1848* (University of California *Publications in History,* Vol. XXVI; Berkeley and Los Angeles: University of California Press, 1941). Older surveys valuable for their wealth of data are George Brown Goode and others, eds., *The Fisheries and Fishery Industries of the United States* (7 vols.; Washington: Government Printing Office, 1884–1887); Lorenzo Sabine, *Report on the Principal Fisheries of the American Seas* (Washington: Robert Armstrong, 1853); and Alexander Starbuck, *The History of Nantucket: County, Island and Town* (Boston: C. E. Goodspeed & Co., 1924). In the popular vein is John R. Spears, *The Story of the New England Whalers* (New York: The Macmillan Company, 1908). The early history of the Newfoundland fishery is given in Ralph Greenlee Lounsbury, *The British Fishery at Newfoundland, 1634–1763* (Vol. XXVII of *Yale Historical Publications;* New Haven, Conn.: Yale University Press, 1934).

The best book on shipbuilding is John H. Morrison, *History of New York Ship Yards* (New York: William F. Sametz and Company, 1909). See also Leland D. Baldwin, "Shipbuilding on the Western Waters, 1793–1817," *Mississippi Valley Historical Review,* Vol. XX, No. 1 (June, 1933); Charles Lyon Chandler, *Early Shipbuilding in Pennsylvania, 1683–1812* (Philadelphia: The Colonial Press, Inc., 1932); Howard I. Chapelle, *The History of the American Sailing Navy: The Ships and Their Development* (New York: W. W. Norton and Company, 1949); James E. Hancock, "The Baltimore Clipper and the Story of an Old Baltimore Shipbuilder," *Maryland Historical Magazine,* Vol. XXX, No. 2 (June, 1935); and Archer W. Hulbert, "Western Ship-Building," *American Historical Review,* Vol. XXI, No. 4 (July, 1916).

Specialized industries are treated in the following: Blanche Evans Hazard, *The Organization of the Boot and Shoe Industry in Massachusetts Before 1875* (Vol. XXIII of *Harvard Economic Studies;* Cambridge, Mass.: Harvard University Press, 1921); Blanche E. Hazard, "The Organization of the Boot and Shoe Industry in Massachusetts Before 1875," *Quarterly Journal of Economics,* XXVII, No. 2 (February, 1913); Harrold E. Gillingham, "Benjamin Lehman, a Germantown Cabinet-Maker," *Pennsylvania Magazine of History and Biography,* Vol. LIV, No. 4 (October, 1930); William G. Lathrop, *The Brass Industry in Connecticut* (New Haven, Conn.: Price, Lee & Adkins Co., 1909); William Bining, "The Glass Industry of Western Pennsylvania, 1797–1857," *Western Pennsylvania Historical Magazine,* Vol. XIX, No. 4 (December, 1936); Harry S. Hower, "Some Scientific and Technological Contributions to the Glass Industry in the Pittsburgh District," *Western Pennsylvania Historical Magazine,* Vol. XVIII, No. 1 (March, 1935); Harrold E. Gillingham, "Pottery, China, and Glass Making in Philadelphia," *Pennsylvania Magazine of History and Biography,* Vol. LIV, No. 2 (April, 1930); Lyman Horace Weeks, *A History of Paper-Manufacturing in the United States* (New York: The Lockwood Trade Journal Company, 1916); David Hunter, *Papermaking in Pioneer America* (Philadelphia: University of Pennsylvania Press, 1952); and Miriam Hussey, *From Merchants to "Colour Men": Five Generations of Samuel Wetherill's White Lead Business* (Philadelphia: University of Pennsylvania Press, 1956).

On the manufacture of firearms and gunpowder the leading authorities are Felicia Johnson Deyrup, *Arms Makers of the Connecticut Valley . . . 1798–1870* (Smith College *Studies in History,* Vol. XXXIII; Northampton, Mass.: 1948); S. N. D. North and Ralph H. North, *Simeon North: First Official Pistol Maker of the United States* (Concord, N. H.: The Rumford Press, 1913); B[essie] G. du Pont, *E. I. du Pont de Nemours and Company: A History, 1802–1902* (Boston: Houghton Mifflin Company, 1920); William S. Dutton, *Du Pont:*

One Hundred and Forty Years (New York: Charles Scribner's Sons, 1942); and John K. Winkler, *The Du Pont Dynasty* (New York: Reynal & Hitchcock, 1935).

INVENTION AND TECHNOLOGY

General surveys of the growth of scientific inventions in America and their application to industry are as follows: Brooke Hindle, *The Pursuit of Science in Revolutionary America, 1735–1789* (Chapel Hill: The University of North Carolina Press, 1956); Waldemar Kaempffert, *A Popular History of American Invention* (2 vols.; New York: Charles Scribner's Sons, 1924); John W. Oliver, *History of American Technology* (New York: The Ronald Press Company, 1956); Dirk J. Struik, *Yankee Science in the Making* (Boston: Little, Brown and Company, 1948); Holland Thompson, *The Age of Invention: A Chronicle of Mechanical Conquest* (Vol. XXXVII of *The Chronicles of America,* Allen Johnson, ed.; New Haven, Conn.: Yale University Press, 1921); and Abbott Payson Usher, *A History of Mechanical Inventions* (New York: McGraw-Hill Book Company, 1929). See also Whitford J. Bell, "The Scientific Environment of Philadelphia, 1775–1790," American Philosophical Society, *Proceedings,* Vol. XCII (March, 1948).

Standard works on engineering, machinery, and tools are Joseph Wickham Roe, *English and American Tool Builders* (New Haven, Conn.: Yale University Press, 1916); Jonathan Thayer Lincoln, "The Beginnings of the Machine Age in New England: David Wilkinson of Pawtucket," *New England Quarterly,* Vol. VI, No. 4 (December, 1933); Richard Shelton Kirby and Philip Gustave Laurson, *The Early Years of Modern Civil Engineering* (New Haven, Conn.: Yale University Press, 1932); Henry Grattan Tyrrell, *History of Bridge Engineering* (Chicago: The author, 1911); and A. A. Jakkula, *A History of Suspension Bridges in Bibliographical Form* (Agricultural and Mechanical College of Texas, *Bulletin,* Fourth Series, Vol. XII, No. 7; Washington: Federal Works Agency, 1941). U. S. Commissioner of Patents, *List of Patents Granted by the United States from April 10, 1790 to December 31, 1836* (Washington: 1872) is a convenient compilation. See also Fritz Redlich, "The Philadelphia Water Works in Relation to the Industrial Revolution in the United States," *Pennsylvania Magazine of History and Biography,* Vol. LXIX, No. 3 (July, 1945).

The literature relating to the invention of the steamboat includes many valuable studies. The most important are H. W. Dickinson, *Robert Fulton, Engineer and Artist: His Life and Works* (London: John Lane, Ltd., 1913); Archibald Douglas Turnbull, *John Stevens: An American Record* (New York: The American Society of Mechanical Engineers, 1928); Thompson Westcott, *The Life of John Fitch, the Inventor of the Steamboat* (Philadelphia: J. B. Lippincott Company, 1857); H. A. Gosnell, "The First American Steamboat: James Rumsey Its Inventor, Not John Fitch," *Virginia Magazine of History and Biography,* Vol. XL, No. 1 (January, 1932), No. 2 (April, 1932); Louis C. Hunter, *Steamboats on the Western Rivers: An Economic and Technological History* (Cambridge, Mass.: Harvard University Press, 1949); Louis C. Hunter, "The Invention of the Western Steamboat," *Journal of Economic History,* Vol. III, No. 2 (November, 1943); James Thomas Flexner, *Steamboats Come True:*

American Inventors in Action (New York: The Viking Press, 1944); John H. Morrison, *History of American Steam Navigation* (New York: William F. Sametz and Company, 1903); and Carl D. Lane, *American Paddle Steamboats* (New York: Coward-McCann, Inc., 1943).

For individual inventions and inventors, the following accounts are very useful: Greville Bathe and Dorothy Bathe, *Oliver Evans: A Chronicle of Early American Engineering* (Philadelphia: The Historical Society of Pennsylvania, 1935); Constance McL. Green, *Eli Whitney and the Birth of American Technology* (Boston: Little, Brown and Company, 1956); Jeannette Mirsky and Allan Nevins, *The World of Eli Whitney* (New York: The Macmillan Company, 1952); and Nathan Appleton, *The Introduction of the Power Loom* (Lowell, Mass.: B. H. Penhallow, 1858).

COMMERCE: FOREIGN AND DOMESTIC

Pre-eminent among general surveys of American commerce is Emory R. Johnson, T. W. Van Metre, G. G. Huebner, and D. S. Hanchett, *History of Domestic and Foreign Commerce of the United States* (2 vols.; Washington: Carnegie Institution of Washington, 1915). See also Clive Day, *History of Commerce in the United States* (New York: Longmans, Green and Company, 1925), and Roy A. Foulke, *The Sinews of American Commerce* (New York: Dun and Bradstreet, Inc., 1941).

Foremost among studies of public policies relating to American commerce are John G. B. Hutchins, *The American Maritime Industries and Public Policy, 1789–1914: An Economic History* (Vol. LXXI of *Harvard Economic Studies;* Cambridge, Mass.: Harvard University Press, 1941); Albert Anthony Giesecke, *American Commercial Legislation Before 1789* (University of Pennsylvania *Publications;* New York: D. Appleton and Company, 1910); Vernon G. Setser, *The Commercial Reciprocity Policy of the United States, 1774–1829* (Philadelphia: University of Pennsylvania Press, 1937); Vernon G. Setser, "Did Americans Originate the Conditional Most-Favored-Nation Clause?" *Journal of Modern History,* Vol. V, No. 3 (September, 1933); and Edmund C. Burnett, "Note on American Negotiations for Commercial Treaties, 1776–1786," *American Historical Review,* Vol. XVI, No. 3 (April, 1911).

Of the surveys of the commerce of individual states, Samuel Eliot Morison, *The Maritime History of Massachusetts* (Boston: Houghton Mifflin Company, 1921) is a classic. Other useful studies of New England trade are James Duncan Phillips, *Salem in the Eighteenth Century* (Boston: Houghton Mifflin Company, 1937); George Granville Putnam, "Salem Vessels and Their Voyages," *Historical Collections of the Essex Institute,* Vol. LXV, No. 1 (January, 1929); and William Hutchinson Rowe, *The Maritime History of Maine: Three Centuries of Shipbuilding & Seafaring* (New York: W. W. Norton and Company, 1948). Margaret E. Martin, *Merchants and Trade of the Connecticut River Valley, 1750–1820* (Smith College *Studies in History,* Vol. XXIV, Nos. 1–4; Northampton, Mass.: 1938–1939) is excellent. Studies of similar value are Robert Greenhalgh Albion, *The Rise of the Port of New York [1815–1860]* (New York: Charles Scribner's Sons, 1939); Robert G. Albion, "New York Port and Its Disappointed Rivals, 1815–1860," *Journal of Economic and Business*

History, Vol. III, No. 4 (August, 1931); Paul H. Giddens, "Trade and Industry in Colonial Maryland, 1753–1769," *Journal of Economic and Business History,* Vol. IV, No. 3 (May, 1932); and Charles Christopher Crittenden, *The Commerce of North Carolina, 1763–1789* (Vol. XXIX of *Yale Historical Collections;* New Haven, Conn.: Yale University Press, 1936).

The works on the commerce of particular areas are supplemented by several able studies of shipping and the carrying trade, as follows: Robert Greenhalgh Albion, *Square-Riggers on Schedule: The New York Sailing Packets to England, France, and the Cotton Ports* (Princeton, N. J.: Princeton University Press, 1938); Winthrop L. Marvin, *The American Merchant Marine: Its History and Romance from 1620 to 1902* (New York: Charles Scribner's Sons, 1910); John R. Spears, *The Story of the American Merchant Marine* (New York: The Macmillan Company, 1910); Robert G. Albion, "Early Nineteenth-Century Shipowning—A Chapter in Business Enterprise," *Journal of Economic History,* Vol. I, No. 1 (May, 1941); Charles Christopher Crittenden, "Ships and Shipping in North Carolina, 1763–1789," *North Carolina Historical Review,* Vol. VIII, No. 1 (January, 1931).

Trade with Britain is dealt with in these scholarly works: Robert Greenhalgh Albion, *Forests and Sea Power: The Timber Problem of the Royal Navy, 1652–1862* (Vol. XXIX of *Harvard Economic Studies;* Cambridge, Mass.: Harvard University Press, 1926); Samuel Flagg Bemis, *Jay's Treaty: A Study in Commerce and Diplomacy* (New York: The Macmillan Company, 1923); Norman Sydney Buck, *The Development of the Organisation of Anglo-American Trade, 1800–1850* (New Haven, Conn.: Yale University Press, 1925); G. W. Daniels, "American Cotton Trade with Liverpool under the Embargo and Non-Intercourse Acts," *American Historical Review,* Vol. XXI, No. 2 (January, 1916); W. Freeman Galpin, *The Grain Supply of England During the Napoleonic Period* (New York: The Macmillan Company, 1925); W. Freeman Galpin, "The Source of American Corn Exports to England, 1801–1806," *Georgia Historical Quarterly,* Vol. X, No. 4 (December, 1926); Herbert Heaton, "Benjamin Gott and the Anglo-American Cloth Trade," *Journal of Economic and Business History,* Vol. II, No. 1 (November, 1929); Ralph W. Hidy, *The House of Baring in American Trade and Finance: English Merchant Bankers at Work, 1763–1861* (Vol. XIV of *Harvard Studies in Business History;* Cambridge, Mass.: Harvard University Press, 1949); and Leland Hamilton Jenks, *The Migration of British Capital to 1875* (New York: Alfred A. Knopf, Inc., 1927).

On the trade of the United States with Europe and Africa the following detailed studies are available: Claude H. Van Tyne, "French Aid Before the Alliance of 1778," *American Historical Review,* Vol. XXXI, No. 1 (October, 1925); Thomas P. Abernethy, "Commercial Activities of Silas Deane in France," *American Historical Review,* Vol. XXXIX, No. 3 (April, 1934); Paul Walden Bamford, "France and the American Market in Naval Timber and Masts, 1776–1786," *Journal of Economic History,* Vol. XII, No. 4 (Winter, 1952); Gaston Martin, "Commercial Relations between Nantes and the American Colonies During the War of Independence," *Journal of Economic and Business History,* Vol. IV, No. 4 (August, 1932, Supplement); Frederick L. Nussbaum, "American Tobacco and French Politics, 1783–1789," *Political*

Science Quarterly, Vol. XL, No. 4 (December, 1925); Frederick L. Nussbaum, "The French Colonial Arrêt of 1784," *South Atlantic Quarterly,* Vol. XXVII, No. 1 (January, 1928); John F. Stover, "French-American Trade During the Confederation, 1781–1789," *North Carolina Historical Review,* Vol. XXXV, No. 4 (October, 1958); Knute Emil Carlson, *Relations of the United States with Sweden* (Allentown, Penn.: H. Ray Haas & Co., 1921); Albert Ludwig Kohlmeier, "The Commerce between the United States and the Netherlands, 1783–1789" (*Studies in American History Dedicated to James Albert Woodburn,* Indiana University *Studies,* Vol. XII, Nos. 66–68; Bloomington: 1925); W. Freeman Galpin, "The American Grain Trade to the Spanish Peninsula, 1810–1814," *American Historical Review,* Vol. XXVIII, No. 1 (October, 1922); and Louis B. Wright and Julia H. Macleod, *The First Americans in North Africa* (Princeton, N. J.: Princeton University Press, 1945).

American commerce with the West Indies and Latin America is treated or touched upon in a number of scholarly works, as follows: Lowell Joseph Ragatz, *The Fall of the Planter Class in the British Caribbean, 1763–1833* (New York: The Century Company, 1928); Margaret L. Brown, "William Bingham, Agent of the Continental Congress in Martinique," *Pennsylvania Magazine of History and Biography,* Vol. LXI, No. 1 (January, 1937); J. Franklin Jameson, "St. Eustatius in the American Revolution," *American Historical Review,* Vol. VIII, No. 4 (July, 1903); Albert J. Gares, "Stephen Girard's West Indian Trade, 1789–1812," *Pennsylvania Magazine of History and Biography,* Vol. LXXII, No. 4 (October, 1948); Dorothy Burne Goebel, "British Trade to the Spanish Colonies, 1796–1823," *American Historical Review,* Vol. XLIII, No. 2 (January, 1938); Roy F. Nichols, "Trade Relations and the Establishment of the United States Consulates in Spanish America, 1779–1809," *Hispanic American Historical Review,* Vol. XIII, No. 3 (August, 1933); Frank R. Rutter, *South American Trade of Baltimore* (Johns Hopkins University *Studies in Political and Historical Science,* Series XV, No. 9; Baltimore: The Johns Hopkins Press, 1897); Charles Lyon Chandler, "The River Plate Voyages, 1798–1800," *American Historical Review,* Vol. XXIII, No. 4 (July, 1918); Charles Lyon Chandler, "United States Merchant Ships in the Rio de la Plata (1801–1808), As Shown by Early Newspapers," *Hispanic American Historical Review,* Vol. II, No. 1 (February, 1919); Charles Lyon Chandler, "United States Shipping in the La Plata Region, 1809–1810," *Hispanic American Historical Review,* Vol. III, No. 2 (May, 1920); and Charles Lyon Chandler, "United States Commerce with Latin America at the Promulgation of the Monroe Doctrine," *Quarterly Journal of Economics,* Vol. XXXVIII, No. 3 (May, 1924).

Trade with Asia, the East Indies, and the coast of the American Northwest is surveyed in the following: Tyler Dennett, *Americans in Eastern Asia* (New York: Barnes & Noble, Inc., 1941); Foster Rhea Dulles, *The Old China Trade* (Boston: Houghton Mifflin Company, 1930); James Duncan Phillips, *Pepper and Pirates: Adventures in the Sumatra Pepper Trade of Salem* (Boston: Houghton Mifflin Company, 1949); and James Duncan Phillips, *Salem and the Indies: The Story of the Great Commercial Era of the City* (Boston: Houghton Mifflin Company, 1947). More detailed studies are F. W. Howay, "Voyages of Kendrick and Gray in 1787–1790," *Oregon Historical Quarterly,* Vol.

XXX, No. 2 (June, 1929); F. W. Howay, "The Voyage of the *Hope*, 1790–1792," *Washington Historical Quarterly*, Vol. XI, No. 1 (January, 1920); F. W. Howay, "Voyages of the 'Jenny' to Oregon, 1792–94," *Oregon Historical Quarterly*, Vol. XXX, No. 3 (September, 1929); F. W. Howay, "A List of Trading Vessels in the Maritime Fur Trade, 1785–1794" (Royal Society of Canada, *Transactions*, Third Series, Vol. XXIV, Sec. 2; Ottawa: 1930); F. W. Howay, "Indian Attacks upon Maritime Traders of the North-West Coast, 1785–1805," *Canadian Historical Review*, Vol. VI, No. 4 (December, 1925); F. W. Howay, "A List of Trading Vessels in the Maritime Fur Trade, 1795–1804" (Royal Society of Canada, *Transactions*, Third Series, Vol. XXV, Sec. 2; Ottawa: 1931); Kenneth Scott Latourette, "Voyages of American Ships to China, 1784–1844" (Connecticut Academy of Arts and Sciences, *Transactions*, Vol. XXVIII; New Haven: April, 1927), "Vessels Trading to the Northwest Coast of America, 1804–1814," *Washington Historical Quarterly*, Vol. XIX, No. 4 (October, 1928); Samuel Eliot Morison, "Boston Traders in the Hawaiian Islands, 1789–1823" (Massachusetts Historical Society, *Proceedings*, Vol. LIV; Boston: The Society, 1922); Inazo Nitobé, "American-Japanese Intercourse Prior to the Advent of Perry" (American Historical Association, *Annual Report . . . 1911*, 2 vols.; Washington: Government Printing Office, 1913), Vol. I; Samuel Eliot Morison, "The India Ventures of Fisher Ames, 1794–1804" (American Antiquarian Society, *Proceedings*, New Series, Vol. XXXVII; Worcester, Mass.: The Society, 1928); and S. E. Morison, "Forcing the Dardanelles in 1810, with Some Account of the Early Levant Trade of Massachusetts," *New England Quarterly*, Vol. I, No. 2 (April, 1928).

Two careful, intensive studies of privateering are Gardner Weld Allen, *Massachusetts Privateers of the Revolution* (Massachusetts Historical Society, *Collections*, Vol. LXXVII; Cambridge, Mass.: Harvard University Press, 1927); and Octavius T. Howe, "Beverly Privateers in the Revolution" (Colonial Society of Massachusetts, *Publications*, Vol. XXIV; Boston: The Society, 1924). Older surveys of privateering that emphasize individual ships and voyages are George Coggeshall, *History of the American Privateers and Letters-of-Marque, During Our War with England in the Years 1812, '13 and '14* (New York: The author, 1856); and Edgar Stanton Maclay, *A History of American Privateers* (New York: D. Appleton and Company, 1899). Franklin's relation to privateering is portrayed in two attractive books: Helen Augur, *The Secret War of Independence* (New York: Duell, Sloan and Pearce, 1955); and William Bell Clark, *Ben Franklin's Privateers: A Naval Epic of the American Revolution* (Baton Rouge: Louisiana State University Press, 1956). See also Sidney G. Morse, "State or Continental Privateers?" *American Historical Review*, Vol. LII, No. 1 (October, 1946); Henry Wyckoff Belknap, "A Check List of Salem Privateers in the War of 1812," *Historical Collections of the Essex Institute*, Vol. LXXVIII, No. 3 (July, 1942), No. 4 (October, 1942); Vol. LXXIX, No. 1 (January, 1943), No. 2 (April, 1943), No. 3 (July, 1943), No. 4 (October, 1943); and Vol. LXXX, No. 1 (January, 1944), No. 2 (April, 1944); also Bernard C. Steiner, "Maryland Privateers in the American Revolution," *Maryland Historical Magazine*, Vol. III, No. 2 (June, 1908).

The influence of the European wars, 1793–1815, is revealed in many studies. A popular, scholarly résumé of commercial difficulties in periods of war is Robert Greenhalgh Albion and Jessie Barnes Pope, *Sea Lanes in Wartime: The American Experience, 1775–1942* (New York: W. W. Norton and Company, 1942). Conflicts growing out of wartime trade is a leading theme in an important survey by A. L. Burt, *The United States, Great Britain and British North America, from the Revolution to the Establishment of Peace After the War of 1812* (New Haven, Conn.: Yale University Press, 1940). Authoritative accounts of Jefferson's efforts to avoid war are Walter Wilson Jennings, *The American Embargo, 1807–1809* (University of Iowa *Studies in the Social Sciences*, Vol. VIII, No. 1; Iowa City: 1921); and Louis Martin Sears, *Jefferson and the Embargo* (Durham, N. C.: Duke University Press, 1927). Two valuable studies of wartime policies of European belligerents are Herbert Whittaker Briggs, *The Doctrine of Continuous Voyage* (Johns Hopkins University *Studies in Historical and Political Science*, Series XLIV, No. 2; Baltimore: The Johns Hopkins Press, 1926); and Frank Edgar Melvin, *Napoleon's Navigation System: A Study of Trade Control During the Continental Blockade* (New York: D. Appleton and Company, 1919). Special aspects of wartime trade are dealt with in Robert G. Albion, "Admiralty Prize Case Briefs," *American Historical Review,* Vol. XXXIII, No. 3 (April, 1928); John D. Forbes, "European Wars and Boston Trade, 1783–1815," *New England Quarterly,* Vol. XI, No. 4 (December, 1938); Virginia D. Harrington, "New York and the Embargo of 1807," *Quarterly Journal of the New York State Historical Association,* Vol. VIII, No. 2 (April, 1927); Louis Martin Sears, "Philadelphia and the Embargo: 1808" (American Historical Association, *Annual Report . . . 1920;* Washington: Government Printing Office, 1925); W. Freeman Galpin, "The American Grain Trade under the Embargo of 1808," *Journal of Economic and Business History,* Vol. II, No. 1 (November, 1929); John H. Reinochl, "Post-Embargo Trade and Merchant Prosperity: Experiences of the Crowninshield Family, 1809–1812," *Mississippi Valley Historical Review,* Vol. XLII, No. 2 (September, 1955); William Dinsmore Chapple, "Salem and the War of 1812," *Historical Collections of the Essex Institute,* Vols., LIX, No. 4 (October, 1923), and LX, No. 1 (January, 1924); and "Essex County Vessels Captured by Foreign Powers, 1793–1813," *Historical Collections of the Essex Institute,* Vol. LVIII, No. 4 (October, 1922), and Vol. LIX, No. 1 (January, 1923).

The best introduction to the trans-Mississippi fur trade is Hiram Martin Chittenden, *The American Fur Trade of the Far West* (2 vols.; Stanford, Calif.: Academic Reprints, 1954). An outstanding biography of a businessman who specialized in the fur trade is Kenneth Wiggins Porter, *John Jacob Astor: Business Man* (Vol. I of *Harvard Studies in Economic History,* 2 vols.; Cambridge, Mass.: Harvard University Press, 1931). Another important study is Wayne E. Stevens, *The Northwest Fur-Trade, 1763–1800* (University of Illinois *Studies in the Social Sciences,* Vol. XIV, No. 3; Urbana: 1928). Useful monographs that describe the fur trade of the Old Northwest and the Far West are Ida Amanda Johnson, *The Michigan Fur Trade* (Lansing: Michigan Historical Commission, 1919); Frederick Jackson Turner, "The Character and Influence of the Indian Trade in Wisconsin," *The Early Writings of Frederick Jackson Turner* (Fulmer Mood, ed.; Madison: The University of Wisconsin Press, 1938); Gordon Charles Davidson, *The North West Company* (University of California *Publications in History,* Vol. VII; Berkeley: University of California Press, 1918); Harold A. Innis, *The Fur Trade in Canada: An Introduction to Canadian Economic History* (Rev. ed.; Toronto: University of Toronto Press, 1956); and Clarence A. Vandiver, *The Fur-Trade and Early Western Exploration* (Cleveland: The Arthur H. Clark Company, 1929). For popular accounts of the fur trade of the Far West see Washington Irving, *Astoria; or, Anecdotes of an Enterprise Beyond the Rocky Mountains* (Philadelphia: J. B. Lippincott Company, 1871); and Constance L. Skinner, *Adventurers of Oregon: A Chronicle of the Fur Trade* (Vol. XXII of *The Chronicles of America*, Allen Johnson, ed.; New Haven, Conn.: Yale University Press, 1920). The experiment of the federal government in engaging in the fur trade is given adequate treatment in Royal B. Way, "The United States Factory System for Trading with the Indians, 1796–1822," *Mississippi Valley Historical Review*, Vol. VI, No. 2 (September, 1919); Edgar B. Wesley, "The Government Factory System among the Indians, 1795–1822," *Journal of Economic and Business History*, Vol. IV, No. 3 (May, 1932); George D. Harmon, "Benjamin Hawkins and the Federal Factory System," *North Carolina Historical Review*, Vol. IX, No. 2 (April, 1932); and R. S. Cotterill, "Federal Indian Management in the South, 1789–1825," *Mississippi Valley Historical Review*, Vol. XX, No. 3 (December, 1933). Useful articles of limited scope are Wayne E. Stevens, "The Organization of the British Fur Trade, 1760–1800," *Mississippi Valley Historical Review*, Vol. III, No. 2 (September, 1916); Paul Chrisler Phillips, "The Fur Trade in the Maumee-Wabash Country," in *Studies Dedicated to James Albert Woodburn*; Charles H. Ambler, "The Oregon Country, 1810–1830: A Chapter in Territorial Expansion," *Mississippi Valley Historical Review*, Vol. XXX, No. 1 (June, 1943); F. W. Howay, "Early Days of the Maritime Fur-Trade on the Northwest Coast," *Canadian Historical Review*, Vol. IV, No. 1 (March, 1923); and Frederick Merk, "The Genesis of the Oregon Question," *Mississippi Valley Historical Review*, Vol. XXXVI, No. 4 (March, 1950).

The principal works on the slave trade, both foreign and domestic, are W[illiam] E. Burghardt Du Bois, *The Suppression of the African Slave-Trade to the United States of America, 1638–1870* (New York: The Social Science Press, 1954); Frederic Bancroft, *Slave-Trading in the Old South* (Baltimore: J. H. Furst Company, 1931); and Winfield H. Collins, *The Domestic Slave Trade of the Southern States* (New York: Broadway Publishing Company, 1904). Specific aspects of the slave traffic are dealt with in the following: Elizabeth Donnan, "The Slave Trade into South Carolina Before the Revolution," *American Historical Review*, Vol. XXXIII, No. 4 (July, 1928); T. D. Clark, "The Slave Trade betwen Kentucky and the Cotton Kingdom," *Mississippi Valley Historical Review*, Vol. XXI, No. 3 (December, 1934); "Account of Sales of 106 Africans Brought into Charleston, S. C., . . . October 12, 1807," Rhode Island Historical Society, *Collections*, Vol. XII, No. 1 (January, 1919).

Standard accounts of the methods by which trade was carried on within the United States are Lewis E. Atherton, *The Pioneer Merchant in Mid-America* (University of Missouri *Studies*, Vol. XIV, No. 2; Columbia: 1939); Lewis E. Atherton, *The Southern Country Store, 1800–1860* (Baton Rouge: Louisiana State University Press, 1949); Fred Mitchell Jones, *Middlemen in the Domestic Trade of the United States* (University of Illinois *Studies in the Social Sciences*,

Vol. XXI, No. 3; Urbana: University of Illinois, 1937); and Alfred Holt Stone, "The Cotton Factorage System of the Southern States," *American Historical Review*, Vol. XX, No. 3 (April, 1915). On the ubiquitous peddler see Richardson Wright, *Hawkers & Walkers in Early America* (Philadelphia: J. B. Lippincott Company, 1927); and Harvey A. Wooster, "A Forgotten Factor in American Industrial History," *American Economic Review*, Vol. XVI, No. 1 (March, 1926). Careful studies of limited aspects of internal trade are Arthur P. Whitaker, "Reed and Forde: Merchant Adventurers of Philadelphia: Their Trade with New Orleans," *Pennsylvania Magazine of History and Biography*, Vol. LXI, No. 3 (July, 1937); James Weston Livingood, *The Philadelphia-Baltimore Trade Rivalry, 1780–1860* (Harrisburg: The Pennsylvania Historical and Museum Commission, 1947); Catherine Elizabeth Reiser, *Pittsburgh's Commercial Development, 1800–1850* (Harrisburg: Pennsylvania Historical and Museum Commission, 1951); Randolph C. Downes, "Problems of Trade in Early Western Pennsylvania," *Western Pennsylvania Historical Magazine*, Vol. XIII, No. 4 (October, 1930); W. Freeman Galpin, "The Grain Trade of Alexandria, Virginia, 1801–1805," *North Carolina Historical Review*, Vol. IV, No. 4 (October, 1927); Theodore G. Gronert, "Trade in the Blue-Grass Region, 1810–1812," *Mississippi Valley Historical Review*, Vol. V, No. 3 (December, 1918); Randolph C. Downes, "Trade in Frontier Ohio," *Mississippi Valley Historical Review*, Vol. XVI, No. 4 (March, 1930); Paul C. Henlein, "Cattle Driving from the Ohio Country, 1800–1850," *Agricultural History*, Vol. XXVIII, No. 1 (January, 1954); Lewis E. Atherton, "John McDonogh—New Orleans Mercantile Capitalist," *Journal of Southern History*, Vol. VII, No. 4 (November, 1941); and W. F. Galpin, "The Grain Trade of New Orleans, 1804–1814," *Mississippi Valley Historical Review*, Vol. XIV, No. 4 (March, 1928).

First among the institutions which facilitated internal trade was the federal postal service. Its history is recorded in Wesley Everett Rich, *The History of the United States Post Office to the Year 1829* (Vol. XXVII of *Harvard Economic Studies;* Cambridge, Mass.: Harvard University Press, 1924); Daniel C. Roper, *The United States Post Office* (New York: Funk & Wagnalls Company, 1917); and Alvin F. Harlow, *Old Post Bags* (New York: D. Appleton and Company, 1928). The most scholarly accounts of stagecoaching are Oliver W. Holmes, "Levi Pease, The Father of New England Stage-Coaching," *Journal of Economic and Business History*, Vol. III, No. 2 (February, 1931); and Oliver W. Holmes, "The Stage-Coach Business in the Hudson Valley," *Quarterly Journal of the New York State Historical Association*, Vol. XII, No. 3 (July, 1931). The most useful introductions to the history of insurance are Lester W. Zartman and William H. Price, eds., *Insurance: Marine and Fire* (Rev. ed.; New Haven, Conn.: Yale University Press, 1926), which contains the following: Solomon Huebner, "History of Marine Insurance," and F. C. Oviatt, "History of Fire Insurance in the United States"; Marquis James, *Biography of a Business, 1792–1942: Insurance Company of North America* (Indianapolis: The Bobbs-Merrill Company, 1942); and Edward F. Hardy, *The Making of the Fire Insurance Rate: A Treatise on Past and Present Methods of Calculating Premium Rates* (Chicago: The Spectator Company, 1926). On the subjects of brokerage and the antecedents of the stock market see Margaret G. Myers, *Origins and Development* (Vol. I of *The New York Money Market*, 4 vols.;

New York: Columbia University Press, 1931); Albert O. Greef, *The Commercial Paper House in the United States* (Vol. LX of *Harvard Economic Studies;* Cambridge, Mass.: Harvard University Press, 1938); Henrietta Larson, "S. & M. Allen—Lottery, Exchange, and Stock Brokerage," *Journal of Economic and Business History,* Vol. III, No. 3 (May, 1931); and Arthur G. Peterson, "Futures Trading, with Particular Reference to Agricultural Commodities," *Agricultural History,* Vol. VII, No. 2 (April, 1933). Other features of the business world are described in Ray Bert Westerfield, "Early History of American Auctions: A Chapter in Commercial History" (Connecticut Academy of Arts and Sciences, *Transactions,* Vol. XXIII; New Haven, Conn.: Yale University Press, 1920); and Joseph Clarke Robert, "Rise of the Tobacco Warehouse Auction System in Virginia, 1800–1860," *Agricultural History,* Vol. VII, No. 4 (October, 1933).

MERCHANTS, BUSINESS, PRICES, AND INCOME

An original, intensive study that has exerted a wide influence is Gustavus Meyers, *History of the Great American Fortunes* (3 vols.; Chicago: Charles H. Kerr & Company, 1911). Indispensable for its subject, Robert A. East, *Business Enterprise in the American Revolutionary Era* (New York: Columbia University Press, 1938) presents a wealth of data concerning the activities of American merchants. A well-informed interpretive essay is Robert A. East, "The Business Entrepreneur in a Changing Colonial Economy, 1763–1795," *Tasks of Economic History* (1946). Among the most thorough and illuminating studies of business leaders are James B. Hedges, *The Browns of Providence Plantations: Colonial Years* (Cambridge, Mass.: Harvard University Press, 1952); and Stuart Weems Bruchey, *Robert Oliver, Merchant of Baltimore, 1783–1819* (Johns Hopkins University *Studies in Historical and Political Science,* Series LXXIV, No. 1; Baltimore: The Johns Hopkins Press, 1956). Of lesser stature but useful in filling in the picture of business enterprise are the following: Edward Gray, *William Gray of Salem, Merchant: A Biographical Sketch* (Boston. Houghton Mifflin Company, 1914); Thomas Wentworth Higginson, *Life and Times of Stephen Higginson* (Boston: Houghton Mifflin Company, 1907); Henry Cabot Lodge, *Life and Letters of George Cabot* (Boston: Little, Brown and Company, 1878); John Bach McMaster, *The Life and Times of Stephen Girard* (2 vols.; Philadelphia: J. B. Lippincott Company, 1918); Lawrence Shaw Mayo, *John Langdon of New Hampshire* (Concord, N. H.: The Rumford Press, 1937); and Glenn Weaver, *Jonathan Trumbull: Connecticut's Merchant Magistrate, 1710–1785* (Hartford: The Connecticut Historical Society, 1956). Briefer studies of value are Susie M. Ames, "A Typical Virginia Business Man of the Revolutionary Era: Nathaniel Littleton Savage . . . ," *Journal of Economic and Business History,* Vol. III, No. 3 (May, 1931); Margaret L. Brown, "William Bingham, Eighteenth Century Magnate," *Pennsylvania Magazine of History and Biography,* Vol. XLI, No. 4 (October, 1937); Margaret L. Brown, "Mr. and Mrs. William Bingham of Philadelphia: Rulers of the Republican Court," *Pennsylvania Magazine of History and Biography,* Vol. LXI, No. 3 (July, 1937); S. E. Morison, "Elbridge Gerry, Gentleman-Democrat," *New England Quarterly,* Vol. II, No. 1 (January,

1929); and James Duncan Phillips, "The Life and Times of Richard Derby, Merchant of Salem," *Historical Collections of the Essex Institute*, Vol. LXV, No. 3 (July, 1929). Roy F. Nichols, *Advance Agents of American Destiny* (Philadelphia: University of Pennsylvania Press, 1956) sketches the career of William Shaler as sea captain and trader.

A notable feature of American scholarship since 1930 is the study of price history. The leading fruits of this work are Arthur Harrison Cole, *Wholesale Commodity Prices in the United States, 1700–1861* (with *Statistical Supplement;* Cambridge, Mass.: Harvard University Press, 1938); Anne Bezanson, Robert D. Gray, and Miriam Hussey, *Prices in Colonial Pennsylvania* (Philadelphia: University of Pennsylvania Press, 1935); Anne Bezanson, Blanch Daley, Marjorie C. Denison, and Miriam Hussey, *Prices and Inflation During the American Revolution: Pennsylvania, 1770–1790* (Philadelphia: University of Pennsylvania Press, 1951); Anne Bezanson, Robert D. Gray, and Miriam Hussey, *Wholesale Prices in Philadelphia, 1784–1861* (Philadelphia: University of Pennsylvania Press, 1936); Anne Bezanson, "Inflation and Controls in Pennsylvania, 1774–1779," *Tasks of Economic History*, Vol. VIII (1948); George Rogers Taylor, "Wholesale Commodity Prices at Charleston, South Carolina, 1732–1791," *Journal of Economic and Business History*, Vol. IV, No. 2 (February, 1932); George Rogers Taylor, "Prices in the Mississippi Valley Preceding the War of 1812," *Journal of Economic and Business History*, Vol. III, No. 1 (November, 1930); and Thomas Senior Berry, *Western Prices Before 1861: A Study of the Cincinnati Market* (Vol. LXXIV of *Harvard Economic Studies;* Cambridge, Mass.: Harvard University Press, 1943).

Variations in the course of business are sketched in the following: Walter Buckingham Smith and Arthur Harrison Cole, *Fluctuations in American Business, 1790–1860* (Vol. L of *Harvard Economic Studies;* Cambridge, Mass.: Harvard University Press, 1935); Otto C. Lightner, *The History of Business Depressions* (New York: The Northeastern Press, 1922); and Willard Long Thorp, *Business Annals* (New York: National Bureau of Economic Research, 1926).

Estimates of the income of the country are given in Robert F. Martin, *National Income in the United States, 1799–1938* (New York: National Industrial Conference Board, 1939). For a criticism of Martin's findings see Simon Kuznets, "National Income Estimates for the United States Prior to 1870," *Journal of Economic History*, Vol. XII, No. 2 (Spring, 1952).

CORPORATIONS AND PUBLIC ECONOMIC POLICY

American corporations have received the benefit of intensive study. A distinguished pioneering work is Joseph Stancliffe Davis, *Essays in the Earlier History of American Corporations* (Vol. XVI of *Harvard Economic Studies,* 2 vols.; Cambridge, Mass.: Harvard University Press, 1917). Less intensive though broader in scope is George Hebertson Evans, Jr., *Business Incorporations in the United States, 1800–1943* (New York: National Bureau of Economic Research, Inc., 1948). A luminous study is G. S. Callender, "The Early Transportation and Banking Enterprises of the States in Relation to the Growth of Corporations," *Quarterly Journal of Economics*, Vol. XVII, No. 1 (November, 1902); another incisive article is Oscar Handlin and Mary F. Handlin, "Origins of the American Business Corporation," *Journal of Economic History,* Vol. V, No. 1 (May, 1945). Three good essays review the subject of corporate liability: H. A. Shannon, "The Coming of General Limited Liability," *Economic History,* Vol. II, No. 6 (January, 1931); Shaw Livermore, "Unlimited Liability in Early American Corporations," *Journal of Political Economy,* Vol. XLIII, No. 5 (October, 1935); and E. Merrick Dodd, "The Evolution of Limited Liability in Massachusetts" (Massachusetts Historical Society, *Proceedings,* Vol. LXVIII; Boston: The Society, 1952). For regions and states there are several excellent analyses, as follows: W. C. Kessler, "Incorporation in New England: A Statistical Study, 1800–1875," *Journal of Economic History,* Vol. VIII, No. 1 (May, 1948); Edwin Merrick Dodd, Jr., "The First Half Century of Statutory Regulation of Business Corporations in Massachusetts," in *Harvard Legal Essays* (Cambridge, Mass.: Harvard University Press, 1934); Charles M. Haar, "Legislative Regulation of New York Industrial Corporations, 1800–1850," *New York History,* Vol. XXII, No. 2 (April, 1941); W. C. Kessler, "A Statistical Study of the New York General Incorporation Act of 1811," *Journal of Political Economy,* Vol. XLVIII, No. 6 (December, 1940); Shaw Livermore, "Advent of Corporations in New York," *New York History,* Vol. XVI, No. 3 (July, 1935); William Miller, "A Note on the History of Business Corporations in Pennsylvania, 1800–1860," *Quarterly Journal of Economics,* Vol. LV, No. 1 (November, 1940); John W. Cadman, Jr., *The Corporation in New Jersey: Business and Politics, 1791–1875* (Cambridge, Mass.: Harvard University Press, 1949); and Joseph G. Blandi, *Maryland Business Corporations, 1783–1852* (Johns Hopkins University *Studies in Historical and Political Science,* Series LII, No. 3; Baltimore: The Johns Hopkins Press, 1934).

Since 1940, investigation of the relations of business and government have yielded three valuable monographs: Oscar Handlin and Mary Flug Handlin, *Commonwealth: A Study of the Role of Government in the American Economy: Massachusetts, 1774–1861* (New York: New York University Press, 1947); Louis Hartz, *Economic Policy and Democratic Thought: Pennsylvania, 1776–1860* (Cambridge, Mass.: Harvard University Press, 1948); and Milton Sydney Heath, *Constructive Liberalism: The Role of the State in Economic Development in Georgia to 1860* (Cambridge, Mass.: Harvard University Press, 1954). In the *Tasks of Economic History* (December, 1943), are three articles on the relation of state governments to economic activity: Oscar Handlin, "Laissez-Faire Thought in Massachusetts, 1790–1880," Louis Hartz, "Laissez-Faire Thought in Pennsylvania, 1776–1860," and Milton S. Heath, "Laissez-Faire in Georgia, 1732–1860." See also E. James Ferguson, "Business, Government, and Congressional Investigation in the Revolution," *William and Mary Quarterly,* Third Series, Vol. XVI, No. 3 (July, 1959); and Charles Warren, *Bankruptcy in United States History* (Cambridge, Mass.: Harvard University Press, 1935).

FINANCE

An indispensable introductory survey is Davis Rich Dewey, *Financial History of the United States* (8th ed.; New York: Longmans, Green and Company, 1922). Older, yet useful, is Albert S. Bolles, *The Financial History of the United States from 1774 to . . . 1885* (3 vols.; New York: D. Appleton and Company, 1879–1886). The best analysis of the finances of the Union before 1791 is E. James Ferguson, *The Power of the Purse: A History of American Public Finance, 1776–1790* (Chapel Hill: The University of North Carolina Press, 1961).

Financial measures and problems during the Revolution are ably analyzed in Clarence L. Ver Steeg, *Robert Morris, Revolutionary Financier* (Philadelphia: University of Pennsylvania Press, 1954); Ralph Volney Harlow, "Aspects of Revolutionary Finance, 1775–1783," *American Historical Review*, Vol. XXXV, No. 1 (October, 1929); William Graham Summer, *The Financier and Finances of the American Revolution* (2 vols.; New York: Dodd, Mead and Company, 1891); and Charles J. Bullock, *The Finances of the United States from 1775 to 1789* (University of Wisconsin *Economics, Political Science and History Series, Bulletin*, Vol. I, No. 2; Madison: 1895).

Federal taxation is dealt with competently in the following works: Sidney Ratner, *American Taxation: Its History As a Social Force in Democracy* (New York: W. W. Norton and Company, 1942); Henry Carter Adams, *Taxation in the United States, 1789–1816* (Johns Hopkins University *Studies in Historical and Political Science*, Series II, Nos. 5–6; Baltimore: 1884); Orrin Leslie Elliott, *The Tariff Controversy in the United States, 1789–1833* (Leland Stanford Junior University *Monographs: History and Economics*, No. 1; Palo Alto, Calif.: 1892); F[rank] W. Taussig, *The Tariff History of the United States* (8th ed.; New York: G. P. Putnam's Sons, 1931); and Edward Stanwood, *American Tariff Controversies in the Nineteenth Century* (2 vols.; Boston: Houghton Mifflin Company, 1904).

Among studies of the national credit, the following are useful: Jonathan Elliot, *The Funding System of the United States and Great Britain* (Washington: Blair and Rives, 1845); Rafael A. Bayley, *The National Loans of the United States, from July 4, 1776 to June 30, 1880* (Washington: Government Printing Office, 1881); E. James Ferguson, "Speculation in the Revolutionary Debt: The Ownership of Public Securities in Maryland, 1790," *Journal of Economic History*, Vol. XIV, No. 1 (Winter, 1954); Paul B. Tescott, "Federal-State Financial Relations, 1790–1860," *Journal of Economic History*, Vol. XV, No. 3 (September, 1955); and J. E. Winston and R. W. Colomb, "How the Louisiana Purchase Was Financed," *Louisiana Historical Quarterly*, Vol. XII, No. 2 (April, 1929).

The Treasury of the United States, its Secretaries, and their policies are the subjects of the following valuable contributions: James O. Wettereau, "Letters from Two Business Men to Alexander Hamilton on Federal Fiscal Policy, November, 1789," *Journal of Economic and Business History*, Vol. III, No. 4 (August, 1931); Alexander Balinky, *Albert Gallatin: Fiscal Theories and Policies* (New Brunswick, N. J.: Rutgers University Press, 1958); Chien Tseng Mai, *The Fiscal Policies of Albert Gallatin* (New York: Columbia University, 1930); Esther Rogoff Taus, *Central Banking Functions of the United States Treasury, 1789–1941* (New York: Columbia University Press, 1943); and Lewis H. Kimmel, *Federal Budget and Fiscal Policy, 1789–1958* (Washington: The Brookings Institution, 1959).

Standard works on the coinage of the United States are Neil Carothers, *Fractional Money: A History of the Small Coins and Fractional Paper Currency of the United States* (New York: John Wiley & Sons, Inc., 1930); J[ames] Laurence Laughlin, *The History of Bimetallism in the United States* (New York: D. Appleton and Company, 1896); A. Barton Hepburn, *A History of Currency in the United States* (New York: The Macmillan Company, 1915); and David K. Watson, *History of American Coinage* (New York: G. P. Putnam's Sons, 1899).

For the backgrounds of paper currency see Richard A. Lester, *Monetary Experiments: Early American and Recent Scandinavian* (Princeton, N.J.: Princeton University Press, 1939); Curtis Putnam Nettels, *The Money Supply of the American Colonies Before 1720* (University of Wisconsin *Studies in the Social Sciences and History*, No. 20; Madison: 1934); and Curtis P. Nettels, "The Origins of Paper Money in the English Colonies," *Economic History*, Vol. III (January, 1934).

Among the treatments of the paper currencies of the United States the following studies are good surveys: William M. Gouge, *A Short History of Paper Money and Banking in the United States* (Philadelphia: T. W. Ustick, 1833); Henry Phillips, *Continental Paper Money: Historical Sketches of American Paper Currency* (Roxbury, Mass.: Privately printed, 1866); Kathryn L. Behrens, *Paper Money in Maryland, 1727–1789* (Johns Hopkins University *Studies in Historical and Political Science*, Series XLI, No. 1; Baltimore: The Johns Hopkins Press, 1923); William B. Norton, "Paper Currency in Massachusetts During the Revolution," *New England Quarterly*, Vol. VII, No. 1 (March, 1934); and John Jay Knox, *United States Notes: A History of the Various Issues of Paper Money by the Government of the United States* (New York: Charles Scribner's Sons, 1894).

On the subject of banking, an outstanding volume, written with distinction, is Bray Hammond, *Banks and Politics in America, from the Revolution to the Civil War* (Princeton, N. J.: Princeton University Press, 1957). Older surveys, still serviceable, are John Jay Knox, *A History of Banking in the United States* (New York: Bradford Rhodes & Company, 1900), and William G. Sumner, *A History of Banking in the United States* (Vol. I of *A History of Banking in All the Leading Nations*; New York: The Journal of Commerce and Commercial Bulletin, 1896).

The Bank of North America and the First and Second Banks of the United States are discussed in several important studies, as follows: Lawrence Lewis, *A History of the Bank of North America* (Philadelphia: J. B. Lippincott and Company, 1882); Janet Wilson, "The Bank of North America and Pennsylvania Politics: 1781–1787," *Pennsylvania Magazine of History and Biography*, Vol. LXVI, No. 1 (January, 1942); M. St. Clair Clarke and D. A. Hall, *Legislative and Documentary History of the Bank of the United States, including the Original Bank of North America* (Washington: Gales and Seaton, 1832); John Thom Holdsworth and Davis R. Dewey, *The First and Second Banks of the United States* (National Monetary Commission, Vol. IV, No. 1; Washington: Government Printing Office, 1910; also printed as *Senate Document*, No. 571, 61 Cong., 2 Sess.); James O. Wettereau, "The Branches of the First Bank of the United States," *Tasks of Economic History* (December, 1942); James O.

Wettereau, "New Light on the First Bank of the United States," *Pennsylvania Magazine of History and Biography*, Vol. LXI, No. 3 (July, 1937); Burton Alva Konkle, *Thomas Willing and the First American Financial System* (Philadelphia: University of Pennsylvania Press, 1937); Raymond Walters, Jr., "The Origins of the Second Bank of the United States," *Journal of Political Economy*, Vol. LIII, No. 2 (June, 1945); Kenneth L. Brown, "Stephen Girard, Promoter of the Second Bank of the United States," *Journal of Economic History*, Vol. II, No. 2 (November, 1942); and Philip G. Walters and Raymond Walters, Jr., "The American Career of David Parish," *Journal of Economic History*, Vol. IV, No. 2 (November, 1944).

Scholarly monographs on state banks and banking are Davis R. Dewey, *State Banking Before the Civil War* (National Monetary Commission, *Senate Document*, No. 581, 61 Cong., 2 Sess., Vol. IV, No. 2; Washington: Government Printing Office, 1910); Joseph Edward Hedges, *Commercial Banking and the Stock Market Before 1863* (Johns Hopkins University *Studies in Historical and Political Science*, Series LVI, No. 1; Baltimore: The Johns Hopkins Press, 1938); and Alfred Cookman Bryan, *History of State Banking in Maryland* (Johns Hopkins University *Studies in Historical and Political Science*, Series XVII, Nos. 1–3; Baltimore: The Johns Hopkins Press, 1899). The best studies of individual banks are N[orman] S. B. Gras, *The Massachusetts First National Bank of Boston* (Vol. IV of *Harvard Studies in Business History;* Cambridge, Mass.: Harvard University Press, 1937); Margaret Hadley Foulds, "The Massachusetts Bank, 1784–1865," *Journal of Economic and Business History*, Vol. II, No. 2 (February, 1930); Henry W. Domett, *A History of the Bank of New York, 1784–1884* (3d ed.; Cambridge, Mass.: Riverside Press [Preface, 1884]); Allan Nevins, *History of the Bank of New York and Trust Company: 1784 to 1934* (New York: Privately printed, 1934); Nicholas B. Wainwright, *History of the Philadelphia Bank: A Century and a Half of Philadelphia Banking, 1803–1953* (Philadelphia: William F. Fell Company, 1953); and Kenneth L. Brown, "Stephen Girard's Bank," *Pennsylvania Magazine of History and Biography*, Vol. LXVI, No. 1 (January, 1942).

Banking theory and practice are treated adequately in Lloyd W. Mints, *A History of Banking Theory in Great Britain and the United States* (Chicago: The University of Chicago Press, 1945); Harry E. Miller, *Banking Theories in the United States Before 1860* (Vol. XXX of *Harvard Economic Studies;* Cambridge, Mass.: Harvard University Press, 1927); and Bray Hammond, "Long and Short Term Credit in Early American Banking," *Quarterly Journal of Economics*, Vol. XLIX, No. 1 (November, 1934).

PUBLIC MEN

Many of the biographies of men active in public life throw much light on economic affairs. The following are especially important: Kenneth Weyer Rowe, *Mathew Carey: A Study in American Economic Development* (Johns Hopkins University *Studies in Historical and Political Science*, Series LI, No. 4; Baltimore: The Johns Hopkins Press, 1933); E. Wilder Spaulding, *His Excellency, George Clinton: Critic of the Constitution* (New York: The Macmillan Company, 1938); Harold Hutcheson, *Tench Coxe: A Study in American*

Economic Development (Johns Hopkins University *Studies in Historical and Political Science,* New Series, No. 26; Baltimore: The Johns Hopkins Press, 1938); George Adams Boyd, *Elias Boudinot, Patriot and Statesman, 1740–1821* (Princeton, N. J.: Princeton University Press, 1952); Carl Van Doren, *Benjamin Franklin* (New York: The Viking Press, 1938); W. A. Wetzel, *Benjamin Franklin As an Economist* (Johns Hopkins University *Studies in Historical and Political Science,* Series XIII, No. 9; Baltimore: The Johns Hopkins Press, 1895); Raymond Walters, Jr., *Albert Gallatin: Jeffersonian Financier and Diplomat* (New York: The Macmillan Company, 1957); Louis M. Hacker, *Alexander Hamilton in the American Tradition* (New York: McGraw-Hill Book Company, 1957); John C. Miller, *Alexander Hamilton: Portrait in Paradox* (New York: Harper & Brothers, 1959); Broadus Mitchell, *Alexander Hamilton: Youth to Maturity, 1755–1788* (New York: The Macmillan Company, 1957); Frank Monaghan, *John Jay* (Indianapolis: The Bobbs-Merrill Company, 1935); Marie Kimball, *Jefferson: War and Peace, 1776 to 1784* (New York: Coward-McCann, Inc., 1947); Dumas Malone, *Jefferson and His Time* (2 vols.; Boston: Little, Brown and Company, 1948–1951); North Callahan, *Henry Knox: General Washington's General* (New York: Rinehart & Company, 1958); Bernard C. Steiner, *The Life and Correspondence of James McHenry* (Cleveland: The Burrows Brothers Company, 1907); Irving Brant, *James Madison* (5 vols.; Indianapolis: The Bobbs-Merrill Company, 1941–1956); Albert J. Beveridge, *The Life of John Marshall* (4 vols.; Boston: Houghton Mifflin Company, 1916); Kenneth R. Rossman, *Thomas Mifflin and the Politics of the American Revolution* (Chapel Hill: The University of North Carolina Press, 1952); Richard Gabriel Stone, *Hezekiah Niles As an Economist* (Johns Hopkins University *Studies in Historical and Political Science,* Series LI, No. 5; Baltimore: The Johns Hopkins Press, 1933); Rose Charlotte Engelman, "Washington and Hamilton: A Study in the Development of Washington's Political Ideas" (Cornell University, Doctoral Thesis, 1948); Douglas Southall Freeman, John Alexander Carroll, and Mary Wells Ashworth, *George Washington* (7 vols.; New York: Charles Scribner's Sons, 1948–1957); Nathaniel Wright Stephenson and Waldo Hilary Dunn, *George Washington* (2 vols.; New York: Oxford University Press, 1940); and Charles Page Smith, *James Wilson: Founding Father, 1742–1798* (Chapel Hill: The University of North Carolina Press, 1956).

SECTIONS, STATES, AND LOCALITIES

The influence of geography in shaping sections, together with their effects on historical developments, is the theme of suggestive essays by Frederick Jackson Turner, *The Significance of Sections in American History* (New York: Henry Holt and Company, 1932).

The life of communities of the eastern seaboard is portrayed in two attractive, informative works: Carl Bridenbaugh, *Cities in Revolt: Urban Life in America, 1743–1776* (New York: Alfred A. Knopf, Inc., 1955); and Ralph H. Brown, *Mirror for Americans: Likeness of the Eastern Seaboard, 1810* (New York: American Geographical Society, 1943).

Two useful surveys of southern states are Clement Eaton, *A History of the Old South* (New York: The Macmillan Company, 1949)—an excellent study; and Emory Q. Hawk, *Economic History of the South* (New York: Prentice-Hall, Inc., 1934).

Good studies of New England which give much emphasis to economic factors include William B. Weeden, *Economic and Social History of New England, 1620–1789* (2 vols.; Boston: Houghton Mifflin Company, 1891); James Truslow Adams, *New England in the Republic, 1776–1850* (Boston: Little, Brown and Company, 1926); and Harold Fisher Wilson, *The Hill Country of Northern New England: Its Social and Economic History, 1790–1830* (New York: Columbia University Press, 1936).

Useful histories that throw light on economic conditions in individual states are Richard J. Purcell, *Connecticut in Transition, 1775–1818* (Washington: American Historical Association, 1918); Jeremy Belknap, *The History of New Hampshire* (3 vols.; Philadelphia: The author, 1784–1792); Alexander C. Flick, ed., *History of the State of New York* (10 vols.; New York: Columbia University Press, 1933–1937); Dixon Ryan Fox, *Yankees and Yorkers* (New York: New York University Press, 1940); Wayland Fuller Dunaway, *A History of Pennsylvania* (New York: Prentice-Hall, Inc., 1935); Charles Henry Ambler, *Sectionalism in Virginia from 1776 to 1861* (Chicago: The University of Chicago Press, 1910); E[llis] Merton Coulter, *Georgia: A Short History* (Chapel Hill: The University of North Carolina Press, 1947); Ulrich Bonnell Phillips, "Georgia and State Rights" (American Historical Association, *Annual Report . . . 1901*, 2 vols.; Washington: Government Printing Office, 1902), Vol. II; and William A. Schaper, "Sectionalism in South Carolina" (American Historical Association, *Annual Report . . . 1900*, 2 vols.; Washington: Government Printing Office, 1901), Vol. I.

The literature of the Western Movement figures prominently in this era of origins of many communities within, near, or beyond the Appalachian Mountains. The story of the advance into and the settlement of new frontiers is told in several able surveys: Ray Allen Billington, *Westward Expansion: A History of the American Frontier* (New York: The Macmillan Company, 1949); E[dward] Douglas Branch, *Westward: The Romance of the American Frontier* (New York: D. Appleton and Company, 1930); Dan Elbert Clark, *The West in American History* (New York: Thomas Y. Crowell Company, 1937); Thomas E. Clark, *Frontier America: The Story of the Westward Movement* (New York: Charles Scribner's Sons, 1959); Le Roy R. Hafen and Carl Coke Rister, *Western America* (New York: Prentice-Hall, Inc., 1941); William Christie McLeod, *The American Indian Frontier* (New York: Alfred A. Knopf, Inc., 1928); Frederic L. Paxson, *History of the American Frontier, 1763–1893* (Boston: Houghton Mifflin Company, 1924); Robert E. Riegel, *America Moves West* (New York: Henry Holt and Company, 1930); and Frederick Jackson Turner, *The Frontier in American History* (New York: Henry Holt and Company, 1921).

Studies which apply to the whole western area, and which are limited to periods or subjects, include the following standard works: John Anthony Caruso, *The Appalachian Frontier: America's First Surge Westward* (Indianapolis: The Bobbs-Merrill Company, 1959); Samuel Flagg Bemis, *Pinckney's Treaty: A Study of American Advantage from Europe's Distress* (Baltimore:

The Johns Hopkins Press, 1926); Henry Howe, *Historical Collections of the Great West* (Cincinnati: Henry Howe, 1873); Theodore Roosevelt, *The Winning of the West* (4 vols.; New York: G. P. Putnam's Sons, 1889–1896); Frederick Jackson Turner, *The Rise of the New West, 1819–1829* (Vol. XIV of *The American Nation*, A. B. Hart, ed.; New York: Harper & Brothers, 1906); Richard C. Wade, *The Urban Frontier: The Rise of Western Cities, 1790–1830* (Vol. XLI of *Harvard Historical Monographs;* Cambridge, Mass.: Harvard University Press, 1959); Richard C. Wade, "Urban Life in Western America, 1790–1830," *American Historical Review*, Vol. LXIV, No. 1 (October, 1958); and Justin Winsor, *The Westward Movement: The Colonies and the Republic West of the Alleghanies, 1763–1798* (Boston: Houghton Mifflin and Company, 1897).

On the frontiers of the South and the Southwest the principal studies are Arthur Preston Whitaker, *The Spanish-American Frontier, 1783–1795* (Boston: Houghton Mifflin Company, 1927); Everett Dick, *The Dixie Frontier: A Social History of the Southern Frontier from the First Transmontane Beginnings to the Civil War* (New York: Alfred A. Knopf, Inc., 1948); John C. Campbell, *The Southern Highlander and His Homeland* (New York: Russell Sage Foundation, 1921); and John Walton Caughey, *McGillivray of the Creeks* (Norman: University of Oklahoma Press, 1938).

The early history of the Old Northwest is treated in the following standard works: Beverley W. Bond, *The Civilization of the Old Northwest: A Study of Political, Social, and Economic Development, 1788–1812* (New York: The Macmillan Company, 1934); R. Carlyle Buley, *The Old Northwest: Pioneer Period, 1815–1840* (2 vols.; Indianapolis: Indiana Historical Society, 1950); Nelson Vance Russell, *The British Régime in Michigan and the Old Northwest, 1760–1796* (Northfield, Minn.: Carleton College, 1939); Louise Phelps Kellogg, *The British Régime in Wisconsin and the Northwest* (State Historical Society of Wisconsin, *Publications;* Madison: The Society, 1935); James M. Miller, *The Genesis of Western Culture: The Upper Ohio Valley, 1800–1825* (Columbus: The Ohio State Archaeological and Historical Society, 1938); and James Alton James, "Some Phases of the History of the Northwest, 1783–1786," *Mississippi Valley Historical Association, Proceedings*, Vol. VII (1913–1914).

For the early activities of the Far West the most useful surveys are Katherine Coman, *Economic Beginnings of the Far West* (2 vols.; New York: The Macmillan Company, 1912); Oscar Osburn Winther, *The Great Northwest: A History* (New York: Alfred A. Knopf, Inc., 1947); and Oscar Osburn Winther, *The Old Oregon Country: A History of Frontier Trade, Transportation, and Travel* (Stanford, Calif.; Stanford University Press, 1950). See also Harlow Lindley, "Western Travel, 1800–1820," *Mississippi Valley Historical Review*, Vol. VI, No. 2 (September, 1919).

For the advance of pioneers into particular areas and early conditions of frontier life, several competent studies give reliable and useful accounts: Ruth L. Higgins, *Expansion in New York, with Especial Reference to the Eighteenth Century* (Ohio State University *Contributions in History and Political Science*, No. 14; Columbus: 1931); Blake McKelvey, *Rochester, the Water-Power City, 1812–1854* (Cambridge, Mass.: Harvard University Press, 1945); Solon J. Buck and Elizabeth Hawthorn Buck, *The Planting of Civilization in*

Western Pennsylvania (Pittsburgh: University of Pittsburgh Press, 1939); Solon J. Buck, "Frontier Economy in Southwestern Pennsylvania," *Agricultural History*, Vol. X, No. 1 (January, 1936); J. E. Wright and Doris S. Corbett, *Pioneer Life in Western Pennsylvania* (Pittsburgh: University of Pittsburgh Press, 1940); Huger D. Bacot, "The South Carolina Up Country at the End of the Eighteenth Century," *American Historical Review*, Vol. XXVIII, No. 4 (July, 1923); Thomas Perkins Abernethy, *From Plantation to Frontier in Tennessee: A Study in Frontier Democracy* (Chapel Hill: The University of North Carolina Press, 1932); Thomas D. Clark, *A History of Kentucky* (New York: Prentice-Hall, Inc., 1937); Anthony Marc Lewis, "Jefferson and Virginia's Pioneers, 1774–1781," *Mississippi Valley Historical Review*, Vol. XXXIV, No. 4 (March, 1948); Lowell H. Harrison, "A Virginian Moves to Kentucky, 1793," *William and Mary Quarterly*, Third Series, Vol. XV, No. 2 (April, 1958); Bernard Mayo, "Lexington: Frontier Metropolis," in Eric F. Goldman, ed., *Historiography and Urbanization: Essays in Honor of W. Stull Holt* (Baltimore: The Johns Hopkins Press, 1941); Charles Henry Ambler, *A History of West Virginia* (New York: Prentice-Hall, Inc., 1933); Beverley W. Bond, *The Foundations of Ohio* (Vol. I of *History of the State of Ohio*, Carl Wittke, ed.; Columbus: Ohio State Archaeological and Historical Society, 1941); Logan Esarey, *History of Indiana from Its Exploration to 1922* (4 vols.; Dayton, Ohio: Dayton Historical Publishing Co., 1923–1924); F. Clever Bald, *Detroit's First American Decade, 1796 to 1805* (University of Michigan Publications: History and Political Science, Vol. XVI; Ann Arbor: University of Michigan Press, 1948); Clarence Walworth Alvord, *The Illinois Country, 1673–1818* (Vol. I of *The Centennial History of Illinois;* Springfield: Illinois Centennial Commission, 1920); Solon Justus Buck, *Illinois in 1818* (Springfield: The Illinois Centennial Commission, 1917); and Francis Parkman, *The Old Régime in Canada* (8th ed.; Boston: Little, Brown and Company, 1880).

Western interests and influence as a cause of the War of 1812 are expounded or touched upon in the following: Julius W. Pratt, *Expansionists of 1812* (New York: The Macmillan Company, 1925); Christopher B. Coleman, "The Ohio Valley in the Preliminaries of the War of 1812," *Mississippi Valley Historical Review*, Vol. VII, No. 1 (June, 1920); Isaac Joslin Cox, "The American Intervention in West Florida," *American Historical Review*, Vol. XVII, No. 2 (January, 1912); Charles M. Gates, "The West in American Diplomacy, 1812–1815," *Mississippi Valley Historical Review*, Vol. XXVI, No. 4 (March, 1940); Warren H. Goodman, "The Origins of the War of 1812: A Survey of Changing Interpretations," *Mississippi Valley Historical Review*, Vol. XXVIII, No. 2 (September, 1941); Louis Morton Hacker, "Western Land Hunger and the War of 1812," *Mississippi Valley Historical Review*, Vol. X, No. 4 (March, 1924); Reginald Horsman, "British Indian Policy of the Northwest, 1807–1812," *Mississippi Valley Historical Review*, Vol. XLV, No. 1 (June, 1958); Julius W. Pratt, "Footnote to the War of 1812," *American Mercury*, Vol. XII, No. 46 (October, 1927); Julius W. Pratt, "Western Aims in the War of 1812," *Mississippi Valley Historical Review*, Vol. XII, No. 1 (June, 1925); J. Holland Rose, "Canning and the Spanish Patriots in 1808," *American Historical Review*, Vol. XII, No. 1 (October, 1906); and George Rogers Taylor, "Agrarian Discontent in the Mississippi Valley Preceding the War of 1812," *Journal of Political Economy*, Vol. XXXIX, No. 4 (August, 1931).

GENERAL AND SPECIAL "PERIOD" STUDIES, 1775–1815

The historical literature for the years 1775–1815 is notable for a large number of writings that are confined to short periods and that contain much information concerning economic issues, conditions, and changes, although they are not limited to those subjects. The periods most commonly treated in such writings are 1775–1783, 1783–1789, and 1789–1815, with some overlapping.

Standard general works concerned mainly with the Revolution are John Richard Alden, *The American Revolution, 1775–1783* (The New American Nation Series, H. S. Commager and R. B. Morris, eds.; New York: Harper & Brothers, 1954); Evarts Boutell Greene, *The Revolutionary Generation, 1763–1790* (Vol. IV of *A History of American Life*, A. M. Schlesinger and D. R. Fox, eds.; New York: The Macmillan Company, 1943); J[ohn] Franklin Jameson, *The American Revolution Considered As a Social Movement* (Princeton, N. J.: Princeton University Press, 1940); John C. Miller, *Triumph of Freedom, 1775–1783* (Boston: Little, Brown and Company, 1948); Allan Nevins, *The American States During and After the Revolution, 1775–1789* (New York: The Macmillan Company, 1924); and Claude Halstead Van Tyne, *The American Revolution, 1776–1783* (Vol. IX of *The American Nation*, A. B. Hart, ed.; New York: Harper & Brothers, 1905).

The following contain information regarding foreign commerce during the Revolution: Samuel Flagg Bemis, *The Diplomacy of the American Revolution* (New York: D. Appleton–Century Company, 1935); and Curtis P. Nettels, *George Washington and American Independence* (Boston: Little, Brown and Company, 1951).

Valuable studies of individual states during the Revolution are Robert E. Brown, *Middle-Class Democracy and the Revolution in Massachusetts, 1690–1780* (Ithaca, N. Y.: Cornell University Press, 1955); Lee Nathaniel Newcomer, *The Embattled Farmers: A Massachusetts Countryside in the American Revolution* (New York: King's Crown Press, 1953); Oscar Handlin and Mary F. Handlin, "Revolutionary Economic Policy in Massachusetts," *William and Mary Quarterly*, Third Series, Vol. IV, No. 1 (January, 1947); Ralph V. Harlow, "Economic Conditions in Massachusetts, 1775–1783" (Colonial Society of Massachusetts, *Publications*, Vol. XX; Boston: The Society, 1920); Richard Francis Upton, *Revolutionary New Hampshire: An Account of the Social and Political Forces Underlying the Transition from Royal Province to American Commonwealth* (Dartmouth College *Publications*, Hanover, N. H.: 1936); New York State Division of Archives and History, *The American Revolution in New York:* (Albany: The University of the State of New York, 1926); and Kenneth Coleman, *The American Revolution in Georgia, 1763–1789* (Athens: University of Georgia Press, 1958).

For the bearings of military and naval affairs on economic activities the following are useful: Christopher Ward, *The War of the Revolution* (John

Richard Alden, ed., 2 vols.; New York: The Macmillan Company, 1952);
Willard M. Wallace, *Appeal to Arms: A Military History of the American Revolution* (New York: Harper & Brothers, 1951); Charles Knowles Bolton, *The Private Soldier under Washington* (New York: Charles Scribner's Sons, 1902); Louis Clinton Hatch, *The Administration of the American Army* (Vol. X of *Harvard Historical Studies;* New York: Longmans, Green and Company, 1904); Victor Leroy Johnson, *The Administration of the American Commissariat During the Revolutionary War* (Philadelphia: University of Pennsylvania, 1941); Orlando W. Stephenson, "The Supply of Gunpowder in 1776," *American Historical Review,* Vol. XXX, No. 2 (January, 1925); Robert C. Pugh, "The Revolutionary Militia in the Southern Campaign, 1780–1781," *William and Mary Quarterly,* Third Series, Vol. XIV, No. 2 (April, 1957); James G. Randall, "George Rogers Clark's Service of Supply," *Mississippi Valley Historical Review,* Vol. VIII, No. 3 (December, 1921); William M. James, *The British Navy in Adversity* (London: Longmans, Green and Company, 1926); Gerald S. Brown, "The Anglo-French Naval Crisis, 1778: A Study of Conflict in the North Ministry," *William and Mary Quarterly,* Third Series, Vol. XIII, No. 1 (January, 1956); and French E. Chadwick, "Sea Power: The Decisive Factor in Our Struggle for Independence" (American Historical Association, *Annual Report . . . 1915;* Washington: Government Printing Office, 1916).

The best general survey of the confederation period is Merrill M. Jensen, *The New Nation: A History of the United States During the Confederation, 1781–1789* (New York: Alfred A. Knopf, Inc., 1950). See also Andrew Cunningham McLaughlin, *The Confederation and the Constitution, 1783–1789* (Vol. X of *The American Nation,* A. B. Hart, ed.; New York: Harper & Brothers, 1905).

Writings on individual states, 1783–1789, include many excellent studies that describe the conditions which figured in the movement for the making of the federal Constitution. The most useful special works on Shays' Rebellion are Marion L. Starkey, *A Little Rebellion* (New York: Alfred A. Knopf, Inc., 1955); George Richards Minot, *The History of the Insurrections in Massachusetts . . .* (2d ed.; Boston: James W. Burditt and Company, 1810); Robert A. East, "The Massachusetts Conservatives in the Critical Period," in *The Era of the American Revolution: Studies Inscribed to Evarts Boutell Greene* (Richard B. Morris, ed.; New York: Columbia University Press, 1939); Andrew MacFarland Davis, "The Shays Rebellion: A Political Aftermath" (American Antiquarian Society, *Proceedings,* New Series, Vol. XXI; Worcester, Mass.: The Society, 1911); Walter A. Dyer, "Embattled Farmers," *New England Quarterly,* Vol. IV, No. 3 (July, 1931); Richard B. Morris, "Insurrection in Massachusetts," in *America in Crisis* (Daniel Aaron, ed.; New York: Alfred A. Knopf, Inc., 1952); and "The Depression of 1785 and Daniel Shays' Rebellion" (by Jonathan Smith), *William and Mary Quarterly,* Third Series, Vol. V, No. 1 (January, 1948). For other states the following are valuable accounts of the confederation era: Frank Greene Bates, *Rhode Island and the Formation of the Union* (Columbia University *Studies in History, Economics and Public Law,* Vol. X, No. 2; New York: The Macmillan Company, 1898); Thomas C. Cochran, *New York in the Confederation* (Philadelphia: University of Pennsylvania Press, 1932); E. Wilder Spaulding, *New York in the Critical Period,*

1783–1789 (New York: Columbia University Press, 1932); Robert L. Brunhouse, *The Counter-Revolution in Pennsylvania, 1776–1790* (Harrisburg: Pennsylvania Historical Commission, 1942); Richard P. McCormick, *Experiment in Independence: New Jersey in the Critical Period, 1781–1789* (New Brunswick, N. J.: Rutgers University Press, 1950); Philip A. Crowl, *Maryland During and After the Revolution* (Johns Hopkins University *Studies in Historical and Political Science,* Series LXI, No. 1; Baltimore: The Johns Hopkins Press, 1943); and William W. Abbot, "The Structure of Politics in Georgia, 1782–1789," *William and Mary Quarterly,* Third Series, Vol. XIV, No. 1 (January, 1957).

Standard histories of the making and ratification of the Constitution are George Bancroft, *History of the Formation of the Constitution of the United States of America* (New York: D. Appleton and Company, 1896); Max Farrand, *The Framing of the Constitution of the United States* (New Haven, Conn.: Yale University Press, 1913); Charles Warren, *The Making of the Constitution* (Cambridge, Mass.: Harvard University Press, 1937); and Orin Grant Libby, *The Geographical Distribution of the Vote of the Thirteen States on the Federal Constitution, 1787–8* (University of Wisconsin *Economics, Political Science, and History Series, Bulletin,* Vol. I, No. 1; Madison: 1894).

An original and provocative analysis, Charles A. Beard, *An Economic Interpretation of the Constitution of the United States* (New York: The Macmillan Company, 1913; reissue 1935) has been subjected to corrections in two critiques: Robert E. Brown, *Charles Beard and the Constitution: A Critical Analysis of "An Economic Interpretation of the Constitution"* (Princeton, N. J.: Princeton University Press, 1956), and Forrest McDonald, *We the People: The Economic Origins of the Constitution* (Chicago: The University of Chicago Press, 1958). See also Curtis P. Nettels, "The American Merchant and the Constitution" (Colonial Society of Massachusetts, *Publications,* Vol. XXXIV; Boston: The Society, 1943).

A well-informed commentary is Joseph Story, *A Familiar Exposition of the Constitution of the United States* (New York: Harper & Brothers, 1879); an elaborate and novel interpretation is William Winslow Crosskey, *Politics and the Constitution in the History of the United States* (2 vols.; Chicago: The University of Chicago Press, 1953).

A convenient survey of the forty years after 1789 is John Allen Krout and Dixon Ryan Fox, *The Completion of American Independence, 1790–1830* (Vol. V of *A History of American Life,* A. M. Schlesinger and D. R. Fox, eds.; New York: The Macmillan Company, 1944). Two important studies by Leonard D. White, *The Federalists: A Study in Administrative History* (New York: The Macmillan Company, 1948) and *The Jeffersonians: A Study in Administrative History, 1801–1829* (New York: The Macmillan Company, 1951), although concerned primarily with the management of the federal government, shed much light on its bearings on the national economy. Outstanding studies of the Federalist era, with special reference to the background of Jeffersonian democracy, are Charles A. Beard, *Economic Origins of Jeffersonian Democracy* (New York: The Macmillan Company, 1915); Charles A. Beard, "Some Economic Origins of Jeffersonian Democracy," *American Historical Review,* Vol. XIX, No. 2 (January, 1914); Eugene Tenbroeck Mudge, *The Social Philosophy of John Taylor of Caroline: A Study in Jeffersonian Democracy* (New York: Columbia University Press, 1939); Leland D. Baldwin, *Whiskey Rebels: The Story of a Frontier Uprising* (Pittsburgh: University of Pittsburgh Press, 1939); and James Morton Smith, *Freedom's Fetters: The Alien and Sedition Laws and American Civil Liberties* (Ithaca, N. Y.: Cornell University Press, 1956). Special studies of state leaders and politics are Anson Ely Morse, *The Federalist Party in Massachusetts to the Year 1800* (Princeton, N. J.: The University Library, 1909); Charles Warren, *Jacobin and Junto, or Early American Politics As Viewed in the Diary of Dr. Nathaniel Ames, 1758–1822* (Cambridge, Mass.: Harvard University Press, 1931); Bernard Drell, "John Taylor of Caroline and the Preservation of an Old Social Order," *Virginia Magazine of History and Biography*, Vol. XLVII, No. 4 (October, 1938); John A. Munroe, *Federalist Delaware, 1775–1815* (New Brunswick, N. J.: Rutgers University Press, 1954); and Delbert Harold Gilpatrick, *Jeffersonian Democracy in North Carolina, 1789–1816* (New York: Columbia University Press, 1931).

Appendix

TABLE 1
THE GROWTH OF POPULATION, 1790–1820 [a]

Area and State	1790	1800	1810	1820
New England	1,009,408	1,233,011	1,471,973	1,660,071
Massachusetts	378,787	422,845	472,040	523,287
Maine	96,540	151,719	228,705	298,335
Connecticut	237,946	251,002	261,942	275,248
New Hampshire	141,885	183,858	214,460	244,161
Vermont	85,425	154,465	217,895	235,981
Rhode Island	68,825	69,122	76,931	83,059
Middle Atlantic	958,632	1,402,565	2,014,702	2,699,845
New York	340,120	589,051	959,049	1,372,812
New Jersey	184,139	211,149	245,562	277,575
Pennsylvania	434,373	602,365	810,091	1,049,458
South Atlantic	1,851,806	2,286,494	2,674,891	3,061,063
Delaware	59,096	64,273	72,674	76,748
Maryland	319,728	341,548	380,546	407,350
District of Columbia	————	8,144	15,471	23,336
Virginia	691,737	807,557	877,683	938,261
West Virginia	55,873	78,592	105,469	136,808
North Carolina	393,751	478,103	555,500	638,829
South Carolina	249,073	345,591	415,115	502,741
Georgia	82,548	162,686	252,433	340,989
East North-Central	————	51,006	272,324	792,719
Ohio	————	45,365 [b]	230,760	581,434
Indiana	————	5,641 [c]	24,520 [c]	147,178
Illinois	————	————	12,282 [d]	55,211
Michigan	————	————	4,762 [e]	8,896 [e]
East South-Central	109,368	335,407	708,590	1,190,489
Kentucky	73,677	220,955	406,511	564,317
Tennessee	35,691	105,602	261,727	422,823
Alabama	————	1,250 [f]	9,046 [f]	127,901
Mississippi	————	7,600 [g]	31,306 [g]	75,448
West South-Central	————	————	77,618	167,680
Louisiana	————	————	76,556	153,407
Arkansas	————	————	1,062	14,273
West North-Central	————	————	19,783	66,586
Missouri	————	————	19,783	66,586

[a] *Historical Statistics of the United States, Colonial Times to 1957* (Washington: Government Printing Office, 1960), p. 13.

[b] Territory northwest of the Ohio River.

[c] 1810 includes population of area separated in 1816; 1800 includes 3,124 persons in those parts of Indiana Territory which were taken to form Michigan and Illinois territories in 1805 and 1809, and that portion which was separated in 1816.

[d] Illinois Territory.

[e] Michigan Territory as then constituted.

[f] Those parts of Mississippi Territory now in Alabama.

[g] Those parts of Mississippi Territory now in Mississippi.

TABLE 2
THE NATIONAL CREDIT OF THE UNITED STATES, 1791–1815

Year	Total Amount of the National Debt [a]	Prices of United States 3% Stock in Boston [b]			
		Jan.	April	July	Oct.
1791	$75,400,000				
1792	77,200,000				
1793	80,300,000				
1794	78,400,000				
1795	80,700,000				
1796	83,700,000	50⅝	50⅝	50⅞	51¼
1797	82,000,000	45⅝	47½	50	50⅝
1798	79,200,000	51½	50	46½	44¾
1799	78,400,000	50	49	46¼	45
1800	82,900,000	47½	50	51¼	53
1801	83,000,000	52½	52½	56¼	56¾
1802	80,700,000	60	59	65	65
1803	77,000,000	61⅝	59½	57¾	58

Year	Total Amount of the National Debt	Prices of United States 3% Stock in Boston			
		Jan.	April	July	Oct.
1804	$77,000,000	59	57¾	57¾	57½
1805	86,400,000	56⅞	56	55½	55½
1806	82,300,000	57	59¾	61½	62¾
1807	75,700,000	61¾	63¼		63¾
1808	69,200,000	64	64	64½	65
1809	65,100,000	65	65¼	65¾	65¾
1810	57,000,000	66¼	65¾	65⅝	65¼
1811	53,100,000	65¼	65⅝	65⅛	58
1812	48,000,000	61¼	61	57½	57¾
1813	45,200,000	57½	52½	53½	52¾
1814				52¼	
1815	119,635,000		50½	44½	

[a] Dewey, *Financial History of the United States*, pp. 113, 125; Elliot, *The Funding System of the United States*, p. 635.
[b] Smith and Cole, *Fluctuations in American Business*, p. 171.

TABLE 3

RECEIPTS OF THE GOVERNMENT OF THE UNITED STATES, 1791–1815 [a]

Year	Customs	Internal Revenue	Miscellaneous [b]	Total Ordinary
1791 [c]	$ 4,399,000		$ 10,000	$ 4,409,000
1792	3,443,000	$ 209,000	17,000	3,669,000
1793	4,255,000	338,000	59,000	4,652,000
1794	4,801,000	274,000	356,000	5,431,000
1795	5,588,000	338,000	188,000	6,114,000
1796	6,568,000	475,000	1,334,000	8,377,000
1797	7,550,000	575,000	563,000	8,688,000
1798	7,106,000	644,000	150,000	7,900,000
1799	6,610,000	779,000	157,000	7,546,000
1800	9,081,000	1,543,000 [d]	224,000	10,848,000
1801	10,751,000	1,582,000 [d]	602,000	12,935,000
1802	12,400,000	800,000 [d]	1,700,000	14,900,000
1803	10,400,000	200,000	300,000	11,000,000
1804	11,000,000		600,000	11,800,000
1805	12,900,000		600,000	13,500,000
1806	14,600,000		800,000	15,500,000
1807	15,800,000		500,000	16,300,000
1808	16,300,000		600,000	17,000,000
1809	7,200,000		500,000	7,700,000
1810	8,500,000		800,000	9,300,000
1811	13,300,000		1,100,000	14,400,000
1812	8,900,000		800,000	9,800,000
1813	13,200,000		1,100,000	14,300,000
1814	6,000,000	3,800,000 [e]	1,300,000	11,100,000
1815	7,300,000	6,800,000 [e]	1,500,000	15,600,000

[a] Dewey, *Financial History of the United States,* pp. 110, 126, 142.

[b] Including sales of public lands; dividends on bank stock; in 1796 and 1797, proceeds of sales of bank stock owned by the government; and, in 1801, sales of public stores.

[c] Practically two years.

[d] Including direct tax in 1800, 1801, and 1802.

[e] Including direct tax in 1814 and 1815.

TABLE 4
EXPENDITURES OF THE GOVERNMENT OF THE
UNITED STATES, 1791–1815 [a]

Year	War	Navy	Interest on Debt	Miscellaneous [b]	Total
1791	$ 633,000		$1,178,000	$1,286,000	$ 3,097,000
1792	1,101,000		2,373,000	2,795,000	6,269,000
1793	1,130,000		2,097,000	618,000	3,846,000
1794	2,639,000	$ 61,000	2,752,000	844,000	6,297,000
1795	2,481,000	410,000	2,947,000	1,471,000	7,309,000
1796	1,260,000	274,000	3,239,000	1,016,000	5,790,000
1797	1,039,000	382,000	3,172,000	1,414,000	6,008,000
1798	2,009,000	1,381,000	2,955,000	1,260,000	7,607,000
1799	2,467,000	2,858,000	2,815,000	1,155,000	9,295,000
1800	2,561,000	3,448,000	3,402,000	1,401,000	10,813,000
1801	1,673,000	2,110,000	4,412,000	1,197,000	9,393,000
1802	1,179,000	915,000	4,239,000	1,642,000	7,976,000
1803	822,000	1,215,000	3,949,000	1,965,000	7,952,000
1804	875,000	1,189,000	4,185,000	2,387,000	8,637,000
1805	713,000	1,597,000	2,657,000	4,846,000	9,014,000
1806	1,224,000	1,649,000	3,368,000	3,206,000	9,449,000
1807	1,288,000	1,722,000	3,369,000	1,973,000	8,354,000
1808	2,900,000	1,884,000	2,557,000	1,719,000	9,061,000
1809	3,345,000	2,427,000	2,886,000	1,641,000	10,280,000
1810	2,294,000	1,654,000	3,163,000	1,362,000	8,474,000
1811	2,032,000	1,905,000	2,585,000	1,594,000	8,178,000
1812	11,817,000	3,959,000	2,451,000	2,052,000	20,280,000
1813	19,652,000	6,446,000	3,599,000	1,983,000	31,681,000
1814	20,350,000	7,311,000	4,593,000	2,465,000	34,720,000
1815	14,794,000	8,660,000	5,990,000	3,499,000	32,943,000

[a] Dewey, *Financial History of the United States,* pp. 111, 124, 141.
[b] Including Indians and pensions.

TABLE 5

POPULATION, PRODUCTION, PRODUCTIVITY, AND INCOME,
1799, 1800, AND 1809, 1810 [a]

	1799, 1800	1809, 1810
Population: 10 years of age and over	3,509,000	4,800,000
Total number of persons gainfully employed	1,523,000	2,107,000
Number of persons gainfully employed in agriculture	1,109,000	1,513,000
Percent of persons gainfully employed in agriculture	72.8	71.8
Income from agriculture, current prices	$266,000,000	$307,000,000
Income from agriculture: percent of national income	39.3	33.6
Per capita income, 1926 purchasing power	$216	
Income per worker in agriculture, 1926 prices	$340	$330
Income per worker, nonagricultural industries, 1926 prices	$1,783	$1,586
Production: grain products (bushels)	160,000,000	
Production: wheat crop (bushels)	22,000,000	30,000,000
Production: tobacco products (pounds)	107,000,000	117,000,000
Production: cotton crop (bales)	73,000	178,000
Production: lumber cut, board measure (feet)	300,000,000	400,000,000

Man-hour productivity in agriculture

Wheat: yield per acre (bushels)	15
Wheat: man-hours per acre	56
Wheat: man-hours per bushel	3.73
Corn for grain: yield per acre (bushels)	25
Corn for grain: man-hours per acre	86
Corn for grain: man-hours per bushel	3.44
Cotton: yield per acre, lint (pounds)	154
Cotton: man-hours per acre	185
Cotton: man-hours per pound	1.2

[a] Simon Kuznets, "National Income Estimates for the United States Prior to 1870," *Journal of Economic History*, XII, No. 1 (Spring, 1952), pp. 115, 117, 119, 121, 124, 125.

TABLE 6

PRODUCTION OF RAW COTTON IN THE UNITED STATES, 1790–1816 [a]

Year	Production Bales	Year	Production Bales	Year	Production Bales
1790	3,135	1799	41,797	1808	156,740
1791	4,180	1800	73,145	1809	171,369
1792	6,270	1801	100,313	1810	177,638
1793	10,449	1802	114,943	1811	167,189
1794	16,719	1803	125,392	1812	156,740
1795	16,719	1804	135,841	1813	156,740
1796	20,899	1805	146,290	1814	146,290
1797	22,989	1806	167,189	1815	208,986
1798	31,348	1807	167,189	1816	259,143

[a] Gray, *History of Agriculture in the Southern United States,* II, 1026.

TABLE 7

PRICES OF FARM PRODUCTS AND GENERAL PRICES, 1801–1815 [a]

(1825 = 100)

Year	Index No. of General Prices	Index No. of Farm Products	Year	Index No. of General Prices	Index No. of Farm Products	Year	Index No. of General Prices	Index No. of Farm Products
1801	155.5	183.8	1806	141.6	155.4	1811	145.7	147.4
1802	127.7	130.7	1807	134.3	146.7	1812	148.1	136.9
1803	131.2	128.2	1808	131.0	125.2	1813	172.4	172.8
1804	140.6	139.8	1809	145.0	132.9	1814	214.8	212.4
1805	144.9	159.7	1810	150.4	153.2	1815	168.6	170.1

[a] Bidwell and Falconer, *History of Agriculture in the Northern United States,* p. 493.

TABLE 8
PRICES OF AGRICULTURAL AND OTHER PRODUCTS, 1791–1801 AND 1807–1811 [a]

Products	1791–1801 [b]	1807–1811 [b]
Farm products	100 [c]	84
Hides and leather	66	76
Building materials	52	58
Foods	158	133
Fuel and lighting	150	158
Textiles	231	279
Metals and metal products	317	334
Chemicals and drugs	462	497

[a] Kuznets, "National Income Estimates for the United States Prior to 1870," p. 127.
[b] Quinquennial averages.
[c] All price indexes to the base 1910–1914 = 100.

TABLE 9
WAGES OF FARM LABOR AND PRICES OF FARM PRODUCTS, 1801–1816 [a]

Year	Wages per Day of Farm Labor [b]	Index No. of Wages [c]	Index No. of Prices of Farm Products	Year	Wages per Day of Farm Labor	Index No. of Wages	Index No. of Prices of Farm Products
1801	0.577	77.6	183.8	1809	0.540	72.6	132.9
1802	0.622	83.6	130.7	1810	0.936	125.8	153.2
1803	0.517	69.5	128.2	1811	0.592	79.6	147.4
1804	0.806	108.3	139.8	1812	0.854	114.8	136.9
1805	0.958	128.8	159.7	1813	0.958	128.8	172.8
1806	0.932	125.3	155.4	1814	0.699	94.0	212.4
1807	0.692	93.0	146.7	1815	0.868	116.7	170.1
1808	0.865	116.3	125.2	1816	0.752	101.0	180.1

[a] Bidwell and Falconer, *History of Agriculture in the Northern United States,* p. 495.
[b] Without board.
[c] 1825 = 100.

TABLE 10

VALUES OF THE MANUFACTURES OF THE UNITED STATES, EXCLUSIVE
OF DOUBTFUL ARTICLES, ACCORDING TO THE CENSUS OF 1810 [a]

1. Goods manufactured by the loom, of cotton, wool, flax, hemp, and silk, with stockings	$ 39,497,000
2. Other goods of these five materials, spun	2,052,000
3. Instruments and machinery manufactured—value $186,650, carding, fulling, and floor cloth, stamping by machinery—value $5,957,816	6,144,466
4. Hats of wool, fur, etc., and mixtures of them	4,323,000
5. Manufactures of iron	14,364,000
6. Manufactures of gold, silver, set work, mixed metals	2,483,000
7. Manufactures of lead	325,000
8. Soap, tallow, candles, and spermaceti, spring oil, and whale oil	1,766,000
9. Manufactures of hides and skins	17,935,000
10. Manufactures from seeds	858,000
11. Grain, fruit, and case liquors, distilled and fermented	16,528,000
12. Dry manufactures from grain, exclusively of flour, meal	75,000
13. Manufactures of wood	5,554,000
14. Manufactures of essences of oils, of and from wood	179,000
15. Refined or manufactured sugars	1,415,000
16. Manufactures of paper, pasteboard, cards, etc.	1,939,000
17. Manufactures of marble, stone, and slate	462,000
18. Glass manufactures	1,047,000
19. Earthen manufactures	259,000
20. Manufactures of tobacco	1,260,000
21. Drugs, dyestuffs, paints, etc., and dyeing	500,000
22. Cables and cordage	4,243,000
23. Manufactures of hair	129,000
24. Various and miscellaneous manufactures	4,347,000
	$127,694,000

[a] Bishop, *History of American Manufactures*, II, 161–162.

TABLE 11
VALUES OF THE MANUFACTURES OF THE UNITED STATES IN 1810, ACCORDING TO INCOMPLETE CENSUS RETURNS AND AS ESTIMATED BY TENCH COXE[a]

Area	Value as Returned	Value as Estimated	Area	Value as Returned	Value as Estimated
Maine	$ 2,137,781	$ 3,741,116	North Carolina	$5,323,322	$6,653,152
Massachusetts	17,516,423	21,895,528	East Tennessee	1,156,049	} 3,611,029
New Hampshire	3,135,027	5,225,045	West Tennessee	1,552,225	
Vermont	4,325,824	5,407,280	South Carolina	2,174,157	3,623,595
Rhode Island	3,079,556	4,106,074	Georgia	2,743,863	3,658,481
Connecticut	5,900,560	7,771,928	Orleans Territory	814,905	1,222,357
New York	14,569,136	25,370,289	Mississippi Territory	314,305	419,073
New Jersey	4,703,063	7,054,594	Louisiana Territory	34,657	200,000
Pennsylvania	32,089,130	33,691,111	Indiana Territory	196,582	300,000
Delaware	990,711	1,733,744	Illinois Territory	71,703	120,000
Maryland	6,553,597	11,468,794	Michigan Territory	37,018	50,000
Virginia	11,447,605	15,263,473	District of Columbia	719,400	1,100,000
Ohio	1,987,370	2,894,290			
Kentucky	4,120,683	6,181,024			
			Total	$127,694,602	$172,762,676

[a] Bishop, *History of American Manufactures*, II, 163.

TABLE 12
DAILY WAGE RATES FOR SPECIFIED BUILDING TRADES IN MASSACHUSETTS, 1800–1815 [a]

Year	Carpenters High	Carpenters Medium	Carpenters Low	Masons High	Masons Medium	Masons Low	Painters Medium	Laborers High	Laborers Medium	Laborers Low
1800	6s.		5s.2d.				3s.9d.	4s.2d.		2s.
1801	5s.10½d.		4s.6d.					5s.8d.		3s.10d.
1802		5s.						6s.	5s.	4s.6d.
1803		$1.08			$1.66		$1.33		$0.42	
1804	5s.9d.	1.16	4s.6d.					5s.3d.	.89	4s.
1805	$1.75	1.46	$1.17					$1.02	.84	$0.25
1806		1.46						1.27	1.84	.86
1807		1.50					1.50	6s.	4s.6d.	3s.6d.
1808	1.75	1.00	0.67					$1.00	$0.85	$0.50
1809	1.33		1.06	$1.75		$1.33		1.67	1.23	.99
1810	1.11		1.00	1.33		1.00		1.10	.84	.51
1811	1.24	1.00	0.75		1.50				1.00	
1812		1.40			3.25		1.50	1.25	1.07	.67
1813	1.43	1.26	1.00	1.74		1.50		1.33	1.00	.57
1814		1.04						1.35	1.00	.78
1815			.75				1.13		.99	.50

[a] *History of Wages in the United States from Colonial Times to 1928* (United States Department of Labor, Bureau of Labor Statistics, *Bulletin*, no. 499, Washington: Government Printing Office, 1929), p. 58.

392

TABLE 13
EXPORTS OF WHEAT AND FLOUR FROM THE UNITED STATES, 1791–1815 [a]

Year	Wheat Bushels [b]	Year	Wheat Bushels	Year	Wheat Bushels
1791	3,807,000	1800	2,966,000	1809	4,202,000
1792	4,564,000	1801	5,201,000	1810	3,919,000
1793	6,286,000	1802	5,483,000	1811	6,719,000
1794	4,504,000	1803	6,590,000	1812	6,550,000
1795	3,234,000	1804	3,772,000	1813	5,963,000
1796	3,295,000	1805	3,517,000	1814	870,000
1797	2,336,000	1806	3,609,000	1815	3,900,000
1798	2,569,000	1807	6,797,000		
1799	2,347,000	1808	1,274,000		

[a] Bidwell and Falconer, *History of Agriculture in the United States,* p. 493.
[b] Including flour, equivalent: 4½ bus. = 196 lbs. flour.

TABLE 14
EXPORTS OF INDIAN CORN AND MEAL FROM THE UNITED STATES, 1791–1815 [a]

Year	Corn (Bushels)	Meal (Barrels)	Value
1791	1,713,241	351,695	
1792	1,964,973	263,405	
1793	1,233,768	189,715	
1794	1,505,977	241,570	
1795	1,935,345	512,445	
1796	1,173,552	540,286	
1797	804,922	254,789	
1798	1,218,231	211,694	
1799	1,200,492	231,226	
1800	1,694,327	338,108	
1801	1,768,162	919,355	
1802	1,633,283	266,816	
1803	2,079,608	133,606	$2,025,000
1804	1,944,873	111,327	2,500,000
1805	861,501	116,131	1,442,000
1806	1,064,263	108,342	1,286,000
1807	1,018,721	136,460	987,000
1808	249,533	30,818	298,000
1809	522,047	57,260	547,000
1810	1,054,252	86,744	1,138,000
1811	2,790,850	147,426	2,896,000
1812	2,039,999	90,810	1,939,000
1813	1,486,970	58,521	1,838,000
1814	61,284	26,438	170,000
1815	830,516	72,364	1,140,000

[a] Pitkin, *A Statistical View of the Commerce of the United States,* p. 102.

TABLE 15
EXPORTS OF ANIMAL PRODUCTS FROM THE UNITED STATES, 1791–1816 [a]

Year	Pork, Hams, Bacon, and Lard (1,000 lbs.)	Beef and Tallow (1,000 lbs.)	Butter and Cheese (1,000 lbs.)	Year	Pork, Hams, Bacon, and Lard (1,000 lbs.)	Beef and Tallow (1,000 lbs.)	Butter and Cheese (1,000 lbs.)
1791	6,145	12,791	1,054	1804	26,776	27,015	3,776
1792	8,720	15,020	785	1805	13,797	23,120	2,499
1793	8,831	15,331	661	1806	10,137	23,538	2,582
1794	12,139	20,360	2,773	1807	10,982	16,895	2,843
1795	20,908	19,235	3,933	1808	3,939	4,025	1,211
1796	17,998	18,692	4,349	1809	10,984	5,716	1,955
1797	9,841	10,388	2,512	1810	10,026	9,551	2,362
1798	8,605	17,901	2,497	1811	10,668	15,393	2,823
1799	13,317	18,284	2,497	1812	6,895	8,568	2,322
1800	13,900	15,024	2,736	1813	5,159	8,749	696
1801	18,567	15,103	4,505	1814	1,469	4,062	370
1802	19,194	12,337	3,694	1815	3,556	2,664	1,313
1803	23,059	15,646	3,681	1816	5,474	6,670	1,354

[a] Bidwell and Falconer, *History of Agriculture in the Northern United States*, p. 494.

TABLE 16
EXPORTS OF TOBACCO AND RICE FROM THE
UNITED STATES, 1790–1815 [a]

| | Tobacco | | Rice | | Tobacco | | Rice |
| | Unmanu-factured | Manu-factured | | | Unmanu-factured | Manu-factured | |
Year	Hogsheads	Pounds	Pounds	Year	Hogsheads	Pounds	Pounds
1790	118,460	15,350	74,136,000	1803	86,291	169,949	47,031,000
1791	101,272	96,811	85,057,000	1804	83,343	298,139	34,098,000
1792	112,428	127,916	80,767,000	1805	71,252	428,460	61,576,000
1793	59,947	173,343	69,892,000	1806	83,186	381,733	56,815,000
1794	72,958	56,785	83,116,000	1807	62,232	274,952	5,537,000
1795	61,050	149,699	78,623,000	1808	9,576	36,332	70,144,000
1796	69,018	296,227	36,067,000	1809	53,921	350,835	78,805,000
1797	58,167	78,508	75,146,000	1810	84,134	529,285	71,614,000
1798	68,567	256,420	66,359,000	1811	35,828	752,553	46,314,000
1799	96,070	525,758	67,234,000	1812	26,094	586,618	72,506,000
1800	78,680	499,166	56,920,000	1813	5,314	283,512	6,886,000
1801	103,758	524,579	47,893,000	1814	3,125	79,377	77,549,000
1802	77,721	276,752	49,103,000	1815	85,337	1,034,045	82,706,000

[a] Gray, *History of Agriculture in the Southern United States*, II, 1030, 1035.

TABLE 17

TOTAL FOREIGN TRADE OF THE UNITED STATES, 1790–1815 [a]

Year	Domestic Exports	Foreign Exports	Total Exports	Imports Retained For Domestic Consumption	Total Imports
1790	$19,666,000	$ 539,000	$ 20,205,000	$ 22,461,000	$ 23,000,000
1791	18,500,000	512,000	19,012,000	28,688,000	29,200,000
1792	19,000,000	1,753,000	20,753,000	29,747,000	31,500,000
1793	24,000,000	2,110,000	26,110,000	28,990,000	31,100,000
1794	26,500,000	6,526,000	33,026,000	28,074,000	34,600,000
1795	39,500,000	8,490,000	47,990,000	61,267,000	69,756,000
1796	40,764,000	26,300,000	67,064,000	55,136,000	81,436,000
1797	29,850,000	27,000,000	56,850,000	48,379,000	75,379,000
1798	28,527,000	33,000,000	61,527,000	35,552,000	68,552,000
1799	33,142,000	45,523,000	78,665,000	33,546,000	79,069,000
1800	31,841,000	39,130,000	70,971,000	52,122,000	91,253,000
1801	47,473,000	46,642,000	94,115,000	64,721,000	111,364,000
1802	36,708,000	35,775,000	72,483,000	40,558,000	76,333,000
1803	42,206,000	13,594,000	55,800,000	51,073,000	64,666,000
1804	41,467,000	36,232,000	77,699,000	48,768,000	85,000,000
1805	42,387,000	53,179,000	95,566,000	67,421,000	120,600,000
1806	41,253,000	60,283,000	101,536,000	69,127,000	129,410,000
1807	48,700,000	59,643,000	108,343,000	78,856,000	138,500,000
1808	9,433,000	12,997,000	22,430,000	43,993,000	56,990,000
1809	31,406,000	20,797,000	52,203,000	38,602,000	59,400,000
1810	42,366,000	24,391,000	66,757,000	61,009,000	85,400,000
1811	45,294,000	16,022,000	61,316,000	37,377,000	53,400,000
1812	30,032,000	8,495,000	38,527,000	68,535,000	77,030,000
1813	25,008,000	2,847,000	27,855,000	19,157,000	22,005,000
1814	6,782,000	145,000	6,927,000	12,820,000	12,965,000
1815	45,974,000	6,583,000	52,557,000	106,458,000	113,041,000

[a] Johnson, *History of Commerce*, II, 20.

TABLE 18
VALUES OF THE EXPORTS OF THE UNITED STATES, 1803–1815,
CLASSIFIED ACCORDING TO THE ORIGIN AND NATURE OF PRODUCTS [a]

Year	Of Agriculture	Of the Forest	Of the Sea	Of Manufactures
1803	$32,995,000	$4,850,000	$2,635,000	$1,355,000
1804	30,890,000	4,630,000	3,420,000	2,100,000
1805	31,562,000	5,261,000	2,884,000	2,300,000
1806	30,125,000	4,861,000	3,116,000	2,707,000
1807	37,832,000	5,476,000	2,804,000	2,120,000
1808	6,746,000	1,399,000	832,000	344,000
1809	23,234,000	4,583,000	1,710,000	1,506,000
1810	33,502,000	4,978,000	1,481,000	1,907,000
1811	35,556,000	5,286,000	1,413,000	2,376,000
1812	24,555,000	2,701,000	935,000	1,355,000
1813	23,119,000	1,107,000	304,000	399,000
1814	5,613,000	570,000	188,000	246,300
1815	38,910,000	3,910,000	912,000	1,553,000

[a] Pitkin, *A Statistical View of the Commerce of the United States*, p. 117.

TABLE 19
DESTINATIONS OF THE EXPORTS OF THE UNITED STATES, 1801–1815 [a]

Year	Europe Domestic Dollars	Foreign Dollars	Asia Domestic Dollars	Foreign Dollars
1801	27,569,699	31,380,558	371,737	1,136,517
1802	19,904,389	23,575,108	547,386	820,423
1803	25,989,111	8,561,834	292,593	149,600
1804	23,094,946	27,468,725	546,278	830,223
1805	23,640,776	36,341,320	612,683	2,156,229
1806	24,384,020	40,267,711	514,621	1,968,860
1807	31,012,947	38,882,633	497,769	1,598,445
1808	5,185,720	7,202,232	26,649	267,542
1809	17,838,502	13,072,045	703,900	1,218,228
1810	27,202,534	17,786,614	377,795	406,646
1811	29,552,442	8,727,011	581,815	812,950
1812	20,626,488	5,644,433	308,510	588,299
1815	33,728,025	4,388,719	319,667	347,394

	Africa		West Indies, American Continent, etc.	
1801	934,331	756,445	17,482,025	13,369,201
1802	747,544	411,855	14,962,854	10,967,585
1803	636,106	148,004	15,338,151	4,734,634
1804	1,264,737	681,499	16,561,516	7,251,150
1805	1,359,518	1,726,987	16,774,025	12,954,483
1806	1,371,475	901,916	14,983,611	17,144,759
1807	1,296,375	1,627,177	15,892,501	17,535,303
1808	278,544	218,950	3,939,633	5,608,690
1809	3,132,687	1,472,819	9,732,613	5,034,439
1810	2,549,744	722,777	12,236,602	5,475,258
1811	1,804,998	622,445	13,354,788	5,860,384
1812	1,235,457	197,587	7,861,655	2,064,808
1815	155,582	113,017	11,720,887	1,768,220

[a] D. B. Warden, A *Statistical, Political, and Historical Account of the United States* . . . (3 vols., Edinburgh: Archibald Constable and Co. 1819), III, 308.

TABLE 20
EXPORTS OF FOREIGN PRODUCTS FROM THE
UNITED STATES, 1800–1815 [a]

Year	Sugar (lbs.)	Coffee (lbs.)	Pepper (lbs.)	Cocoa (lbs.)	Goods Mostly Paying Duties ad valorem Dollars
1800	56,432,516	38,597,479	635,849	4,925,518	16,076,848
1801	97,565,732	45,106,494	3,135,139	7,012,155	17,159,016
1802	61,061,820	36,501,998	5,422,144	3,878,526	14,906,081
1803	23,223,849	10,294,693	2,991,430	367,177	5,351,524
1804	74,964,366	48,812,713	5,703,646	695,135	9,377,805
1805	123,031,272	46,760,294	7,559,224	2,425,680	15,201,483
1806	145,839,320	47,001,662	4,111,983	6,846,758	19,016,909
1807	143,136,905	42,122,573	4,207,166	8,540,524	18,971,539
1808	28,974,927	7,325,448	1,709,978	1,896,990	4,765,737
1809	45,248,128	24,364,099	4,722,098	2,029,336	5,889,669
1810	47,038,125	31,423,477	5,946,336	1,286,010	8,438,349
1811	18,381,673	10,261,442	3,057,456	2,221,462	8,815,291
1812	13,927,277	10,073,722	2,251,003	752,148	3,591,755
1813	7,347,038	6,568,527	99,660	108,188	368,603
1814	762	220,594	none	27,386	41,409
1815	3,193,908	7,501,384	746,349	1,065,582	3,486,178

[a] Warden, *A Statistical Account of the United States*, III, 309.

TABLE 21
STATISTICS OF SHIPPING ENGAGED IN THE CARRYING TRADE
OF THE UNITED STATES, 1789–1815 [a]

Year	Total Tonnage in Foreign Trade of the United States	Tonnage of American Vessels in Foreign Trade	Proportion American	Value of Foreign Trade—. Proportion in American Vessels Imports	Exports	Total
1789	233,983 [b]	127,329 [b]	54.4	17.5	30	23.6
1790	603,825	355,079	58.6	41.0	40	40.5
1793	611,320	447,754	73.3	82.0	77	79.5
1795	637,109	580,277	91.1	92	88	90
1800	806,753	682,871	84.6	91	87	89
1805	1,010,141	922,298	91.3	93	89	91
1807	1,176,198	1,089,876	92.7	94	90	92
1810	986,750	906,434	91.9	93	90	91
1811	981,450	948,247	96.6	90	86	88
1812	715,098	667,999	93.4	85	80	82.5
1813	351,175	237,348	52.0	71	65	68
1814	107,928	59,626	55.3	58	51	54.5
1815	917,227	700,500	76.4	77	71	74

[a] Johnson, *History of Commerce*, II, 28.
[b] For period from July 20 to end of calendar year, 1789.

TABLE 22
THE FIRST BANK OF THE UNITED STATES—STATEMENTS
OF CONDITION, 1809, 1811 [a]

Resources	January, 1809	January, 1811
Loans and discounts	$15,000,000	$14,578,294
United States 6 percent stock	2,230,000	2,750,000
Other United States indebtedness . . .	———	57,046
Due from other banks	800,000	894,145
Real estate	480,000	500,653
Notes of other banks on hand	———	393,341
Specie	5,000,000	5,009,567
	23,510,000	24,183,046

Liabilities		
Capital Stock	$10,000,000	$10,000,000
Undivided surplus	510,000	509,678
Circulating notes outstanding	4,500,000	5,037,125
Individual deposits	8,500,000	5,900,423
United States deposits	———	1,929,999
Due to other banks	———	634,348
Unpaid drafts outstanding	———	171,473
	23,510,000	24,183,046

[a] Knox, *History of Banking in the United States*, p. 39.

Index

Index

403